European social democracy is undergoing a period of transformation not seen since World War II. New patterns of international economic competition and protest movements demanding a more open, participatory society have forced social democratic parties to rethink such traditional programmatic mainstays as the expansion of the welfare state and the mixed economy. *The Transformation of European Social Democracy* examines the variety of electoral strategies that parties in the nine major European democracies have adopted to meet this challenge. Going beyond a traditional analysis of the influence of class structures and political economic institutions on social democratic parties, it emphasizes explicitly political factors for each party. These include each party's position vis-à-vis competitors, internal and external constraints on party organization, and the legacies of party ideology. The lessons drawn from successful social democratic adaptations show that despite far-reaching changes in the economies and societies of Western Europe, social democratic parties are not doomed to political decline. Their survival and political influence depend on the extent to which they overcome their entrenchment in working-class politics and bring together new electoral coalitions.

D0913703

# CAMBRIDGE STUDIES IN COMPARATIVE POLITICS

*General editor*

PETER LANGE   Duke University

*Associate editors*

ELLEN COMISSO   University of California, San Diego
PETER HALL   Harvard University
JOEL MIGDAL   University of Washington
HELEN MILNER   Columbia University
SIDNEY TARROW   Cornell University

This series publishes comparative research that seeks to explain important cross-national domestic political phenomena. Based on a broad conception of comparative politics, it hopes to promote critical dialogue among different approaches. While encouraging contributions from diverse theoretical perspectives, the series will particularly emphasize work on domestic institutions and work that examines the relative roles of historical structures and constraints, of individual or organizational choice, and of strategic interaction in explaining political actions and outcomes. This focus includes an interest in the mechanisms through which historical factors impinge on contemporary poltical choices and outcomes.

Works on all parts of the world are welcomed, and priority will be given to studies that cross traditional area boundaries and that treat the United States in comparative perspective. Many of the books in the series are expected to be comparative, drawing on material from more than one national case, but studies devoted to single countries will also be considered, especially those that pose their problem and analysis in such a way that they make a direct contribution to comparative analysis and theory.

### OTHER BOOKS IN THE SERIES

David D. Laitin, *Language Repertoires and State Construction in Africa*
Allan Kornberg and Harold D. Clarke, *Citizens and Community: Political Support in a Representative Democracy*
Sven Steinmo, Kathleen Thelen, and Frank Longstreth, eds., *Structuring Politics: Historical Institutionalism in Comparative Analysis*
Ellen M. Immergut, *Health Politics: Interests and Institutions in Western Europe*
Catherine Boone, *Merchant Capital and the Roots of State Power in Senegal, 1930—1985*

# THE TRANSFORMATION OF

# EUROPEAN SOCIAL DEMOCRACY

# THE TRANSFORMATION OF EUROPEAN SOCIAL DEMOCRACY

HERBERT KITSCHELT

*Duke University*

CAMBRIDGE
UNIVERSITY PRESS

Published by the Press Syndicate of the University of Cambridge
The Pitt Building, Trumpington Street, Cambridge CB2 1RP
40 West 20th Street, New York, NY 10011-4211, USA
10 Stamford Road, Oakleigh, Melbourne 3166, Australia

First published 1994
Reprinted 1996

Printed in the United States of America

Library of Congress Cataloging-in-Publication Data is available.

A catalogue record for this book is available from the British Library.

ISBN 0-521-45106-X hardback
ISBN 0-521-45715-7 paperback

For Elaine

# Contents

30 - 149
198 - 232
200 - 301

# Tables and figures

## TABLES

## FIGURES

# Preface

European social democracy is undergoing a transformation. Party programs are diluting the conventional tenets of the Keynesian welfare state with substantial doses of free market pragmatism, on the one hand, and ideas of participatory democracy and communitarian social life organized by the citizens themselves, on the other. At the same time, social democratic parties have also begun to reorganize themselves internally by questioning large bureaucratic mass organizations in favor of looser frameworks. These changes coincide with efforts to refashion the parties' electoral coalitions, which no longer primarily depend on a blue collar core constituency. In this book, I examine how and why social democratic parties in most West European democracies have participated in this transformation in different ways and with widely varying results. These diverse outcomes show that social democracy is not condemned to electoral decline, but that the parties' rejuvenation depends on their capacity to go beyond the parties' programmatic, organizational, and electoral legacies.

This book grew out of previous studies of European left-libertarian parties I conducted in the 1980s. Critics of those works argued that left-libertarian parties may be fleeting phenomena that will decline or disappear once established left parties are able to incorporate their new competitors' issue agenda into their own programmatic appeal. For this reason, I set out to explore the extent to which social democratic parties have embraced left-libertarian concerns and what effect such efforts have had on their new competitors. Soon I discovered that this question was too narrow to explain the trajectory of European social democracy and of related changes in European party systems more generally. The emergence of left-libertarian parties constitutes only one of several new challenges and opportunities social democrats faced in the party systems of the 1970s and 1980s. I therefore began to examine the broader parameters of party competition and the strategic choices they open up for social democracy.

At the core of this study, I develop a model of political preference change and a theory of party competition that includes the interaction between parties in the party system as well as the struggle among activists within party organizations. I explore the model with empirical evidence, but this test remains necessarily incomplete. To avoid making a long book even longer, I have resisted the temptation to overload the book with survey evidence and other empirical data. I am sure that future debates with my critics will give me ample opportunity to present more evidence backing the most controversial contentions of this book.

The completion of this project would not have been possible without the help of a number of organizations, colleagues, and students. In the summers of 1990 and 1991, I interviewed social democratic party leaders and activists in three countries for which there are few studies of social democratic party organization: Austria, Belgium, and Sweden. I would like to thank the party secretariats for their assistance in arranging these interviews. For financial support, I would like to thank Duke University's Research Council. I would also like to express my appreciation to the Trent Foundation, which funded a small exploratory workshop on the future of social democracy at Duke University in 1989.

Among my colleagues, Peter Lange, Gary Marks, and Jonas Pontusson read a draft of the entire manuscript. For their critical comments and constructive suggestions for an argument none yet fully subscribes to, I offer my gratitude. Among my graduate students at Duke, thanks are due to William Bernhard, Torben Iversen, and Brian Loynd for their comments and research assistance. I have presented bits and pieces of this book at a number of conferences, including the 1990 Council of European Studies conference and the 1990 and 1992 American Political Science Association conferences. The critical scrutiny of my arguments by the panelists, discussants, and floor participants at these meetings contributed significantly to this work.

Finally, I would like to thank Elaine Madison, who read the manuscript and whose criticisms were always important, although sometimes painful, precisely because of the common sense of her objections and the accuracy of her insights into the weaknesses of my arguments. More than anyone she has seen my work on this project develop with all its ups and downs. I dedicate this book to her.

# Glossary of political parties by country

| Abbreviation | English name | Domestic language name |
|---|---|---|
| | **1. Austria** | |
| FPÖ | Austria Free Party | Freiheitliche Partei Österreichs |
| ÖVP | Austrian People's Party | Österreichische Volkspartei |
| SPÖ | Austrian Socialist Party (since 1990: Austrian Social Democratic Party) | Sozialistische Partei Österreichs (since 1990: Sozialdemokratische Partei Österreichs) |
| VGÖ | Austrian United Greens | Vereinigte Grüne Österreichs |
| | **2. Belgium** | |
| AGALEV | Flemish Greens ("Live Differently") | Anders Gaan Leven |
| BSP | Belgian Socialist Party (Flemish) | Belgische Socialistische Partij |
| CVP | Christian People's Party (Flemish) | Christlijke Volkspartij |
| Ecolo | Ecologists (Francophone) | Ecologists |
| FDF | Francophone Democratic Front | Front Démocratique Francophone |
| PRL | Reform Liberal Party (Francophone) | Parti pour Reform et Liberté |
| PSB | Belgian Socialist Party (Francophone) | Parti Socialiste Belge |
| PSC | Social Christian Party (Francophone) | Parti Social Chrétien |
| PVV | Party of Liberty and Progress (Flemish) | Partij voor Vrijheid and Vooruitgang |
| VB | Flemish Block | Vlaams Block |
| VU | Flemish People's Party | Vlaams Volksunie |
| | **3. Denmark** | |
| CD | Center Democrats | |
| FP | Progress Party | Fremskridtspartiet |
| G | Greens | De Grønne |
| KF | Conservative People's Party | Det Konservative Folkesparti |
| KrF | Christian People's Party | Kristelig Folkeparti |
| RV | Radical Liberal Party | Det radikale Venstre |
| SD | Social Democratic Party | Socialdemokratiet |
| SPP | Socialist People's Party | Socialistisk Folkeparti |
| V | Liberal Party | Venstre |
| VS | Left Socialist Party | Venstresocialisterne |

### 4. France

| | | |
|---|---|---|
| Ecolo | Ecologists/Greens | Ecologists/Verts |
| FN | National Front | Front National |
| MRG | Left Radicals | Mouvement Radicale de Gauche |
| PCF | French Communist Party | Parti Communiste Français |
| PS | Socialist Party | Parti Socialiste |
| PSU | Unified Socialist Party | Parti Socialiste Unifié |
| RPR | Rally for the Republic | Rassemblement pour la République |
| UDF/CDS | Union for French Democracy/Center Democrats | Union pour la Démocratie Français/Centre Democratique |
| UDF/PR | UDF/Republican Party | UDF/Parti Républicain |
| UDF/RAD | UDF/Radical Party | UDF/Radicaux de Gauche |
| V | Greens | Verts |

### 5. Germany

| | | |
|---|---|---|
| CDU | Christian Democratic Union | Christlich Demokratische Union |
| CSU | Christian Social Union (Bavaria) | Christlich Soziale Union |
| FDP | Free Democratic Party | Freie Demokratische Partei |
| G | Greens | Grüne |
| NDP | National Democratic Party | Nationaldemokratische Partei |
| REP | Republicans | Republikaner |

### 6. Greece

| | | |
|---|---|---|
| KKE-ex | Greek Communist Party (exterior) | Kommunistiko Komma Ellados-Exoterikon |
| KKE-es | Greek Communist Party (interior) | Kommunistiko Komma Ellados-Esoterikon |
| ND | New Democracy | Nea Demokratia |
| PASOK | Pan-Hellenic Socialist Movement | Panellimon Sosialistikon Kinema |

### 7. Italy

| | | |
|---|---|---|
| DC | Christian Democratis | Democrazia Cristiana |
| DP | Demoproletarians | Democrazia Proletaria |
| MSI | Italian Social Movement | Movimento Sociale Italiano |
| PCI | Italian Communist Party | Partito Communista Italiano |
| PDS | Party of the Democratic Left | Partito della Sinistra Democratica |
| PLI | Italian Liberal Party | Partito Liberale Italiano |
| PR | Radical Party | Partito Radicale |
| PRI | Italian Republican Party | Partito Repubblicano Italiano |
| PSDI | Italian Social Democratic Party | Partito Socialista Democratico Italiano |
| PSI | Italian Socialist Party | Partito Socialista Italiano |
| V | Greens | Verdi |

### 8. Japan

| | | |
|---|---|---|
| CGP | Clean Government Party | Komeito |
| DSP | Democratic Socialist Party | Minshato: Minsha |
| JCP | Japan Communist Party | Nihon Kyosanto |
| JSP | Japan Socialist Party | Nihon Shakaito |
| LDP | Liberal Democratic Party | Jiyuminshuto |

## 9. Netherlands

| | | |
|---|---|---|
| CDA | Christian Democratic Appeal | Christian Democratisch Appel |
| CPN | Dutch Communist Party | Communistische Partij in Nederland |
| D '66 | Democrats '66 | Democraten '66 |
| EVP | Evangelical Political Federation | Evangelische Volkspartij |
| GVP | Reformed Political Union | Gereformeerd Politiek Verbond |
| KVP | Catholic People's Party | Katholieke Volkspartij |
| PPR | Party of Political Radicals | Politieke Partij Radikalen |
| PSP | Pacifist-Socialist Party | Pacifistisch Socialistische Partij |
| PvdA | Labor | Partij van de Arbeid |
| RPF | Reformed Political Federation | Reformatorische Politieke Federatie |
| VVD | Party for Freedom and Democracy | Volkspartij voor Vrijheid en Democratie |

## 10. Norway

| | | |
|---|---|---|
| C | Center Party | Senterpartiet |
| DNA | Norwegian Labor Party | Det Norske Arbeiderparti |
| FRP | Progress Party | Fremskridtspartiet |
| H | Conservatives | Hoyre |
| KRF | Christian People's Party | Kristelig Folkeparti |
| SF | Socialist People's Party | Socialistik Folkparti |
| V | Liberal Party | Venstre |

## 11. Spain

| | | |
|---|---|---|
| AP | Popular Alliance (now PP) | Alianza Popular |
| CDS | Democratic and Social Center | Centro Democratico y Social |
| CiU | Convergence and Unity (Catalan) | Convergencia i Unió |
| HB | Herri Batsuna (Basque) | Herri Batazuna |
| IU | United Left | Izquierda Unida |
| PCE | Spanish Communist Party | Partido Communista de España |
| PP | Popular Party | Partido Popular |
| PSOE | Spanish Socialist Workers' Party | Partido Socialista Obrero Español |

## 12. Sweden

| | | |
|---|---|---|
| C | Center Party | Centerpartiet |
| KDS | Christian Democrats | Kristdemokratiska samhällspartiet |
| M | Moderates | Moderata Samlingspartiet |
| MP | Environment Party/Greens | Miljöpartiet de Gröna |
| ND | New Democracy | Ny Demokrati |
| PP | People's Party | Folkpartiet |
| SAP | Swedish Social Democratic Party | Sveriges Socialdemokratiska Arbetarparti |
| VPK | Left Party (Communists) | Vänsterpartiet Kommunistarna |

# Introduction

More than thirty years ago, Seymour Martin Lipset (1961/1981: 17) observed a curious lopsidedness in the literature on European parties: Social scientists are more inclined to write about the Left than the Right. This observation strikes me as true today as well. Some of the best scholars of advanced capitalism, such as Gösta Esping-Andersen (1985), Adam Przeworski (1985), and Fritz Scharpf (1987a), have published comparative studies on the development of European social democracy in the last several decades. So is another book on the career of social democratic and socialist parties, two labels I will use interchangeably for the same set of parties, really warranted?

My answer is yes for two reasons. First, social democratic parties have experienced considerable change and widely diverse fortunes since the 1970s. Second, the old categories and theorems that have accounted for social democratic party dynamics no longer apply at the end of the twentieth century.

The 1970s was the decade of social democracy in Northwestern Europe.[1] Austrian socialists and West German social democrats governed throughout the decade. Belgian socialists and the Dutch Labor Party were involved in government and decisively shaped public policy in social and economic areas. In Britain, the Labour Party struggled back to power in 1974 and for a while achieved some success in moderating inflation and unemployment through incomes policies. In Sweden and other Scandinavian countries, social democrats were temporarily turned out of office, though their electoral support remained strong enough to force their opponents in government to pursue essentially social democratic policies for fear of losing control of the executive. In contrast to the European Northwest, socialist parties in Southern Europe were less successful. In France the socialists were regrouping as an opposition party after a devastating decline of their party in the first decade of the Fifth Republic. By the late 1970s, the Italian and Spanish socialists had each gone through several elections without making headway. In Greece, the socialist party was on the upswing but still fell short of attaining

---

1 "Social democracy" is employed here as a generic concept to cover a broad cohort of parties that run under socialist, labor, and social democratic labels. Because party names do not directly reveal differences and similarities in the parties' appeals and strategies, I will employ "socialist" and "social democratic" interchangeably in reference to the generic group of parties.

government power. In Portugal, where the socialist party assumed power soon after the revolution, the party's imprint on the country's emerging democracy was ephemeral and the party soon met electoral defeat.

In the 1980s, European socialist parties experienced an almost complete reversal of fortune. Early in the decade, it became apparent that the popular appeal and intellectual vision of conventional Northern European moderate left parties had been exhausted. In 1981 in Belgium and in 1982 in the Netherlands, socialist parties were displaced by liberal–Christian Democratic governments and could not rally a new winning coalition around an alternative to economic austerity policy. Similarly, Germany's social democracy, after a successful decade of economic policy between the two oil shocks, lost office in 1982, when ecologists, pacifists, union stalwarts, and free marketeers toppled the social democratic–liberal coalition government. The British Labour Party, however, suffered the most precipitous decline. In the 1979 election, Labour fell to its lowest level of electoral support since World War II and then slid even further in 1983. And although the Swedish social democrats regained power in 1982, they lost control of the policy agenda and saw their electoral support steadily erode in the years prior to their crushing defeat at the polls in September 1991.

While social democrats of Northern Europe tried to cope with electoral decline and policy drift, left parties across Southern Europe celebrated spectacular electoral success. The most notable socialist performers were the parties of France, Spain, and Greece, and, to a lesser extent, Italy. During the same time, Southern communist parties entered an era of unprecedented electoral, organizational, and intellectual decay. Southern socialists also successfully stunted the growth of left-libertarian ecology and New Left parties that were taking votes from the social democratic parties of Northern Europe.

The social democrats' and socialists' changing electoral fortunes and capacity to control government power have been closely associated with their shifting programmatic appeals. In the 1970s, all moderate left parties shared at least three basic demands. First, they generally called for economic redistribution toward lower economic strata and employed social and taxation policies for doing so. They also committed themselves to place wage earners' job security and income equality at the top of their policy agenda. They were markedly less concerned with policy initiatives to extend civil liberties or to promote communitarian values of participation and citizens' self-governance. Second, to one degree or another, all social democratic and socialist parties sought to make corporate managers more accountable to their employees. Even the most moderate social democrats sought some system of codetermination or control that would give nonowners of capital a say over investment and employment decisions in private enterprises. Third, all socialist parties fully accepted a pluralist civil society and competitive parliamentary democracy as the benchmark of an open political order. Until well into the 1970s, this set them apart from most radical-left or communist competitors. In the international arena, the moderate social democratic Left organized itself as the

Socialist International, a loose association of social democratic, socialist, and labor parties instrumental in democratizing Southern Europe as well as Latin America.

From the early 1980s to the early 1990s, socialist, social democratic, and labor ideologies underwent more change than in any decade since World War II. Parties everywhere began to withdraw from old programmatic priorities, yet the pace, extent, and direction of that strategic transformation have varied across countries. Issues as diverse as citizens' autonomy and privacy vis-à-vis state surveillance, participatory politics, the development of a more communal self-organized social order, environmental protection, and efforts to promote economic productivity through more market competition signal new priorities that have begun to complement, if not eclipse, conventional social democratic concerns with social security and income equality. In a nutshell, social democracy has moved beyond the arena of resource *distribution* to address the physical and social organization of *production* and the cultural conditions of *consumption* in advanced capitalist societies.[2] Issues of technology, the environment, urban planning, health care, and women's role in society raise questions pertaining to the form of production and consumption, although they also touch upon distributive politics.

In this book, I seek to explain the electoral fortunes of the European noncommunist Left in the last two decades by the parties' strategies and public policies in the changing arenas of electoral competition and by their organizational and intellectual resources to cope with the new situation. At the same time, the development of the Left may serve as a barometer of a more encompassing transformation of European politics and raises broader questions: Are there decisive shifts in the central divisions of political competition? Are there new socioeconomic programs around which winning electoral coalitions can be built? Has the European welfare state lost voter appeal? Are centralized, encompassing interest groups and bureaucratic mass parties likely to survive in their present form?

In order to throw light on the varying fortunes of the European socialist Left, I will compare the trajectory of parties in nine countries. Their electoral performance varies in two respects. First, they achieved different levels of average voter support in the 1980s. At one extreme, the Austrian, Spanish, and Swedish parties were supported by more than 40 percent of voters in that decade. In a middle group, the French, German, and Dutch parties averaged between 30 and 40 percent of the vote. At the other extreme, the Belgian, Italian, and British parties gathered less than 30 percent of the vote. The absolute level of electoral support in the 1980s, taken by itself, is a poor indicator of party performance. More important is the second dimension of variance among the parties, the *average loss or gain* the parties experienced in the 1980s compared to the preceding decade. Only this change rate provides a useful measure of relative success and failure. "Winners" in the 1980s improved their electoral share by an average of at least 3 percent over the 1970s (Spain, France, Italy). "Stabilizers" stayed within a range of plus or minus 3

---

2 Social democracy thus acts on a new "politicization of production." For a comparative-historical analysis, see Kitschelt (1985).

percent from one decade to the next (Belgium, the Netherlands, Sweden). "Losers" shed more than three percentage points in the same era (Austria, Germany, United Kingdom). In the nine parties I will examine, levels and change rates of electoral support do not covary (see Table I.1). The critical dependent variable of this study is the change rate of socialist electoral support from the 1970s to the 1980s. The level of electoral support serves as a control variable that captures a variety of systemic conditions, such as the pre-existing fragmentation of the party system, in each country.

Comparing the change of averages of electoral support in the 1970s and the 1980s is not an arbitrary choice of time frames, but captures in almost all instances the timing of a watershed in each party's electoral history. Changes of electoral fortune are most dramatic, of course, among the losers and the winners of the 1980s. In each of the six countries falling into those categories, the crucial crossover was indeed the time from the last election in the 1970s to the first election in the 1980s. This applies even to the British Labour Party, although the party had already lost votes in 1979. As might be expected, among social democratic "stabilizers" in the 1980s matters are less clear-cut. But even here, electoral variance within each decade tends to be smaller than across the decades. For the Swedish and Belgian parties, the first elections in the 1990s, however, brought serious losses I will include in my discussion.

I will argue that the future of social democracy to a large extent lies in the hands of party leaders and activists. External social, economic, and institutional settings within which parties operate are less important for determining a party's fortunes than its own choice of objectives and strategies in the arena of party competition. In this sense, I am arguing against accounts of social democracy that locate the sources of success or failure *outside* the arena of party competition and *outside* the strategic debates of the parties themselves. Such explanations come in two varieties. First, changes in the socioeconomic class structure are suggested as constituting the ultimate determinants of social democratic success or failure. Instead, I wish to show that, contingent upon the parties' strategic appeals, social democrats may or may not take advantage of such changes and bring together new electoral coalitions. Second, social democrats' past government involvement and public policies are presented as historical legacies that determine the parties' success or failure later. Such hypotheses focus on social democrats' government incumbency, economic performance during left administrations, and the institutional residues of past social democratic cabinets, manifested in the organization of welfare states and political-economic institutions of interest intermediation. Again, such accounts tend to underestimate the parties' freedom to forge new electoral coalitions in the competitive arena. External political-economic constraints imposed on social democratic parties are less decisive than the internal constraints and opportunities for strategic adjustment and renewal generated by changing competitive situations within party systems and the dynamic of political choice inside party organizations.

This is not to say that examining the social and economic transformation of

Table I.1. *Electoral performance of social democratic and socialist parties in the 1970s and 1980s*

| Change in electoral performance from the 1970s to the 1980s | Average level of support, 1981–90 | | |
|---|---|---|---|
| | Less than 30% | Less than 40% | More than 40% |
| Loss of more than 3% | British Labour<br>−8.9%<br>37.8% → 28.9%<br>2/74: 37.2;  1983; 27.1<br>10/74: 39.2;  1987: 30.7<br>1979: 36.9 | West German SPD<br>−6.6%<br>43.5% → 36.9%<br>1972: 44.9;  1983: 38.2<br>1976: 42.6;  1987: 37.0<br>1980: 42.9;  1990: 35.5 | Austrian SPÖ<br>−5.7%<br>50.4% → 44.7%<br>1971: 50.0;  1983: 47.6<br>1975: 50.4;  1987: 43.1<br>1979: 51.0;  1990: 43.5 |
| Gain/loss within 3% | Belgian BSP/PSB<br>+1.6%<br>26.4% → 28.0%<br>1971: 27.2;  1981: 25.1<br>1974: 26.7;  1985: 28.3<br>1977: 26.4;  1987: 30.6<br>1978: 25.4; | Dutch pvdA<br>+2.4%<br>28.6% → 31.0%<br>1971: 24.6;  181: 28.3<br>1972: 27.3;  1982: 30.3<br>1977: 33.8;  1986: 33.3<br>1989: 31.9 | Swedish SAP<br>+1.3%<br>43.2% → 44.5%<br>1973: 43.6;  1982: 45.6<br>1976: 42.7;  1985: 44.7<br>1979: 43.2;  1988: 43.2 |
| Gain of more than 3% | Italian PSI<br>+3.2%<br>9.7% → 12.9%<br>1972: 9.6;  1983; 11.4<br>1976: 9.6;  1987: 14.5<br>1979: 9.8    :   . | French PS*)<br>+9.5%<br>27.0% → 36.5%<br>1973: 25.0;  1981: 39.7<br>1978: 28.9;  1986: 31.8<br>1988: 37.9 | Spanish PSOE<br>+14.3%<br>29.9% → 44.2%<br>1977: 29.3;  1982: 48.2<br>1979: 30.5;  1986: 44.4<br>1989: 39.9 |

*Includes votes cast for the Mouvement des Radicaux de Gauche (MRG).

advanced capitalism to explain social democratic party strategy is without merit. But these changes can no longer be described in the language of class theory that has become so familiar to students of social democratic party fortunes. Instead, I will argue that we must develop a more refined analysis of citizens' market, occupational, and consumption experiences to understand the formation of popular political preferences and demands to which parties may appeal.

In contrast to "external" class theoretic and political economic approaches, my analysis of social democratic party transformation in the 1980s is preoccupied with the "internal" process of political choice in the arenas where parties and party activists are political players: the field of interparty competition and the intraparty organization of strategic choice. The ways in which parties strategically act on the competitive situation in the party system explain electoral success and failure to a large extent, but they do not provide the whole picture. Strategies can aim at different objectives, such as vote seeking, government participation, or destruction of a particular competitor. Moreover, parties sometimes fail to reach their strategic goals. In order to account for the conditions of strategic choice in political parties, I analyze the political dynamic of intraparty organization and the intellectual legacies that inform social democratic political debates.

My study challenges four premises underlying much of the existing literature on social democratic party fortunes. First, politics is conceived as a distributive game about income shares. Second, collective political actors are defined by the class divisions of capitalist market society. Third, social democracy is the political representative of the blue collar working class. And fourth, the relative electoral strength and policy-making capacity of social democracy depends on the centralized organization of the working class and its ability to forge alliances with other wage earners.

Against the first hypothesis, I argue that distributive questions of income have become intertwined with noneconomic, sociopolitical and cultural controversies that have changed the nature of the game. Politics now involves a struggle over the *salience* of distributive choices relative to other political choices. In this process, a deepening of political conflict takes place from struggles over the collectively binding distribution of scarce resources to struggles over the *democratic procedures* according to which the resources are allocated. Against the second hypothesis, I show that in advanced capitalism class divisions based on property rights and exploitation are not the most plausible sources of collective political mobilization. The work and market experiences of blue collar workers and white collar workers are often not significantly different. Instead, divisions in the work force based on education, occupation, gender, and employment sector are likely to shape citizens' political consciousness and their availability for political appeals in more powerful ways than class.

Given the changing conditions for individual and collective political preference formation in advanced capitalism, the third and fourth conventional premises about social democracy also fall by the wayside. Social democrats are no longer primarily the political agents of blue collar workers, but forge socioeconomic coalitions that include different segments of the labor market. While in the past strong working-class organization in centralized labor unions, allied with social democratic parties, was a political asset that boosted the parties' electoral fortunes and policy effectiveness, this asset has now turned into a liability as the very success of past social democratic policies has created new socioeconomic constituencies that are no longer attracted by the traditional message. As a consequence, in many electoral markets, social democratic politicians have been well advised to retreat from certain blue collar constituencies in order to build the parties' fortunes on different electoral coalitions.

The organization of this book follows the arguments described in the preceding paragraphs. I begin with an analysis of the social structure of advanced capitalist societies and the formation of political preferences that are influenced by citizens' experiences in markets, work organizations, and the sphere of consumption. This account is very different from conventional class-theoretic analyses and provides the theoretical underpinnings for my analysis of the competitive space in which social democratic and socialist parties now choose their strategies. Before fleshing out and empirically testing the argument that "internal" developments in the electoral arena of party competition, social democratic party organization, and intellectual traditions account for the parties' success and failure in the 1970s and 1980s, I will examine the empirical adequacy of "external" explanations that account for social democratic party fortunes by changes in the socioeconomic class structure (Chapter 2) and the political economy (Chapter 3). In both cases, external explanations of social democratic party fortunes are unsatisfactory, particularly arguments based on economic class structure, government incumbency, economic performance during social democratic governments, and institutions of (class) interest intermediation. Only the nature of the welfare state shows a moderately close affinity to social democratic party performance, but of a rather different sort than political economists have hypothesized. Having cleared away the underbrush of rival theories, the following three chapters then lay out and empirically substantiate the critical elements of an "internal" explanation of social democratic fortunes. Chapter 4 is devoted to the analysis of party systems and social democratic strategies. Chapter 5 deals with the interaction between strategic choice and internal party organization. Chapter 6 turns to the role of ideological legacies in party strategy. In the conclusion, I show that my core arguments can be applied to a variety of other socialist parties not included in the detailed analysis.

While political scientists aim at strictly explanatory acc⸱ ⸱, they tend to generate prescriptions as well. "Is" may not imply "ought," but "cannot" implies "ought not," because explanatory accounts delimit a range of feasible strategies. At least in this sense, theories about the fortunes of social democratic parties also have normative implications. Conventional political economy accounts of European social democracy *have assumed theoretical premises that also historically served as the political premises of social democratic parties themselves,* such as the emphasis on distributive politics and "class compromise." With the change of the economic and political environment in which social democrats exist, not only conventional party strategies, but also the scholarly theories that have explained such strategies become invalid. A change in political reality thus also leads to a new theory of social democratic success and failure and a new normative critique of party strategy. I therefore conclude that traditional social democratic policies *ought no longer* be pursued, because they *cannot* be successfully implemented in the socioeconomic and cultural environment of advanced capitalism.

# 1

## Social structure and collective preference formation: Opportunities for left party strategy in the 1970s and 1980s

People make history, but not under freely chosen conditions, and political parties are more than the passive reflection of collective demands and preferences originating in the prepolitical sphere of social relations. Politicians actively participate in shaping people's political views ("issue leadership"). Nevertheless, it is misleading to attribute the power to create political consciousness and action exclusively to the realm of politics. Both sociological determinism and political voluntarism shun a more complex reconstruction of the relationship between social structure and politics.

In this book I argue that politicians' strategies in intra- and interparty competition primarily determine their parties' electoral fortunes. Yet social and institutional settings structure the opportunities politicians may seize upon in the competitive process. Experiences in markets, work organization, and the sphere of consumption profoundly affect citizens' political aspirations and preferences. In order to promote their objectives, politicians must recognize such preferences. Is is only in the long run that public policies are likely to alter the social structure that affects citizens' everyday experiences and thus to induce a change in the process of popular preference formation itself.

In this chapter I first present a sociological theory of political preference formation in advanced capitalist democracies. My argument proceeds in three steps. I begin by delineating the range of preferences people may rank order in their most basic political choices. Next, I examine the social experiences that affect citizens' predispositions over the choice of fundamental preferences. Finally, I move from the micro-level of individual experiences to the macro-level of group formation and present hypotheses about the constitution of collective ideological currents that are centered around socioeconomic categories in contemporary society.

In the second part of this chapter, I outline a theory of strategic choice for social democratic parties. I elaborate this theory and test it empirically later in the book, particularly in Chapters 4 through 6. The intervening chapters show how my theoretical argument can account for the deficiencies of most existing run-of-the-mill theories of social democratic party performance that build on class structure and political economy.

## 1.1 SOCIAL INSTITUTIONS AND POLITICAL VALUES

The universe of possible political demands and programs in the modern age is captured in the slogan of the French Revolution, "liberty, equality, fraternity." This slogan identifies three ultimate values endorsed by most citizens, but which are difficult to combine in a single design of viable social institutions. Each value envisions societal end-states associated with different, at times complementary, but more often conflicting modes of social organization. Social institutions, in Daniel Bell's (1973) terminology, embody "axiological principles" that are related to ultimate values. In many ways, the programmatic content of political competition in contemporary democracies constitutes nothing but the perpetual struggle to cope with the trade-offs among the three ultimate values, when citizens and their political representatives try to build actual institutions to translate them into social practice.

The axiological principle of social organization that fosters liberty is the marketplace, based on free voluntary exchange among individuals as the premier mode of human interaction. The axiological principle permitting equality, in contrast, relies on formal collective organization with some kind of centralized mechanism of allocation (a dictator, majority voting, etc.) that discharges collective decisions binding all members of the organization. The complementarity or competition between liberty and equality, markets and formal organization, or individual and collective choice has generated a sea of contradictory arguments in normative and positive social and political theory.[1] Overall, these debates suggest that, up to a certain threshold, equality and liberty mutually presuppose each other; but beyond that threshold, the two principles are associated with rival forms of organization. For our purposes, it suffices to say that those who rank liberty higher than equality tend to favor market institutions that allocate scarce resources among groups and individuals spontaneously. In contrast, proponents of equality over liberty prefer central political mechanisms for allocating (redistributing) scarce resources. In the political struggle, therefore, the pursuit of the spontaneous allocation of wealth through markets and the planned redistribution of resources through political decisions have constituted polar opposites on a continuous dimension of programmatic alternatives. I will refer to these two programmatic alternatives as liberal capitalism and socialism.

The third ultimate value, fraternity, and the axiological principle that drives its institutionalization, community, cannot be accommodated within the same ideological continuum as equality and liberty, but constitutes an independent dimension that cross-cuts alternatives on the "distributive" axis of political conflict. Fraternity is realized in a communitarian social order that relies on face-to-face contact within small decentralized units governed by shared norms.[2] Communitarians reject the dominance both of markets and of central organization

---

1 Among the more recent influential normative and positive contributions, see Hirschman (1970), Lindblom (1977), Miller (1990), and Williamson (1985).
2 For an exploration of the concept of community, see Taylor (1982: 25–33).

because the latter undercut the normative integration of collectivities. Markets and formal organizations are said to generate instrumental relations among citizens, they treat individuals' goals as given and examine how each actor maximizes payoffs under the constraint of formal rules (exchange, command and compliance, voting). Instead, communitarians call for a communicative process of interaction in which participants come together to identify common goals and institutional rules. Liberals and socialists are primarily concerned with the *nature of outcomes* of the social process (allocation of resources), whereas communitarians focus on the *quality of the process* in which collective outcomes are brought about.

Advocates of a communitarian social order, however, have envisioned both the internal structure as well as the relationship among the small units that are expected to deliver fraternity in starkly contrasting ways. At one extreme, the libertarian pole, the idea of community is associated with the voluntary and equal participation of all citizens in the community and the loose association of communitarian units in a federation. Libertarian advocates of community presuppose the full realization of equality and liberty in the construction of a communal order. At the opposite extreme, the authoritarian pole, the idea of community is associated with a rejection of equality and liberty. Community involves compulsory membership in internally hierarchical units and a stratified ordering among communitarian units. Whereas European anarchism most clearly embodies the libertarian vision of fraternity, paternalist and corporatist ideologies express the authoritarian extreme.

Communitarians thus are sharply divided over the significance of liberty and equality for the realization of fraternity. Are socialists and capitalist liberals also divided over the cross-cutting dimension of community in its two polar authoritarian and libertarian modes? It appears that socialists and liberals have an ambivalent and noncommittal relationship to the idea of community and fraternity. Market liberals, for example, often are vague about whether individuals or families (communities) are the basic units of market society. They tend to ignore that citizens' conception of individual rights, liberties, and principles of justice is rooted in community experience (Sandel 1982). Similar ambiguities characterize socialist visions. Marx's idea of socialism calls for a social organization based on a "definitive plan," but also a "free association of men," pointing toward a libertarian social organization (Marx 1867/1967: 78–9). In the same vein, Marx's concern with alienation and the commodification of social relations in capitalism suggests that he attributed considerable importance to community, yet he did not develop a theory of communitarian social relations. Twentieth-century socialists have by and large divided into a "cultural" wing most concerned with a libertarian-communitarian critique of alienation under capitalism and a "political economy" wing confined to questions of property rights and income distribution while ignoring the problem of community.[3]

---

3 The first wing is represented by the Lukacs and the Frankfurt schools of (post-)Marxist thinking. The second by Anglo-Saxon political economy from Sweezy (1942) to Przeworski and Wallerstein (1982) and Roemer (1985).

Figure 1.1 summarizes the relationship among ultimate values and institutional forms of social organization I have outlined. Moreover, it suggests that different options on the distributive and the communitarian dimension of political alternatives may give rise to hybrid views of ultimate goals. Anarcho-syndicalism, in the upper left corner, blends fraternal and socialist demands into a vision of order that calls for workers' self-management in firms and communities. Libertarian market anarchism, in the upper right corner, hopes to realize a free association of individuals primarily via an unconstrained reign of market exchange.[4] Authoritarian capitalism, in the lower right corner, stipulates that traditional hierarchical practices of communitarian integration, such as patriarchalism, church authority, and patriotism/militarism, are critical cornerstones for free market capitalism. In the lower left corner, finally, Stalinism would be a prime example of efforts to blend the redistributive allocation of resources with hierarchical principles of social order.

It would require an entire book on political ideology to elaborate and defend the internal logical consistency, exhaustiveness, plausibility, and theoretical fruitfulness of the typology of ultimate values and related institutional forms I offer.[5] Since my primary task is to reconstruct political preference formation in advanced capitalism in order to understand the strategic options and dilemmas of contemporary social democracy, I will propose a more modest test of the pragmatic fruitfulness of my typology in subsequent sections of this chapter. The typology is valuable if it allows us to develop theoretically interesting and empirically testable propositions about the formation of individual and collective political ideas and the relation of competition among rival political programs. Citizens' experiences in their work and social life generate political predispositions that can be mapped onto the two-dimensional space created by the socialist–capitalist and the libertarian–authoritarian dimensions, and party strategies situate themselves in this field of competing programs.

In the following two sections, I develop a theory of citizens' preference forma-

---

4 This uniquely American blend of libertarianism is represented by Rothbard (1973) and is clearly set apart from European libertarianism in the anarchist and syndicalist tradition.

5 The closest competitor for my typology derives from the research program pursued by Mary Douglas and Aaron Wildavsky (see Douglas and Wildavsky 1982; Wildavsky 1987; Thompson, Ellis, and Wildavsky 1990). Basically, this research program distinguishes forms of social organization based on the permeability of the boundaries of institutions within which individuals are placed ("group") and the extent to which such institutions prescribe the individual's internal life within institutions ("grid"). Where boundaries are permeable and normative descriptions weak, for example, market-based individualism prevails. The schema, however, cannot clearly place socialism in its bounds. Because Marxist socialism is concerned with equality and human empowerment, overcoming external constraints, yet also instituting community, it is said to be a manifestation of egalitarianism (strong group, weak grid) (Thompson et al. 1990: 157). Yet Marxist theory never emphasized strong group boundaries and always insisted on the need for internal structure (gridness) to bring about equality. Equally awkward is Wildavsky's identification of communitarianism in the grid–group framework. Douglas and Wildavsky emphasize equality as the discriminating property of "sects" and communities, but the theory and practice of communitarianism shows that stable sects may be hierarchical, a point emphasized by Kanter (1972).

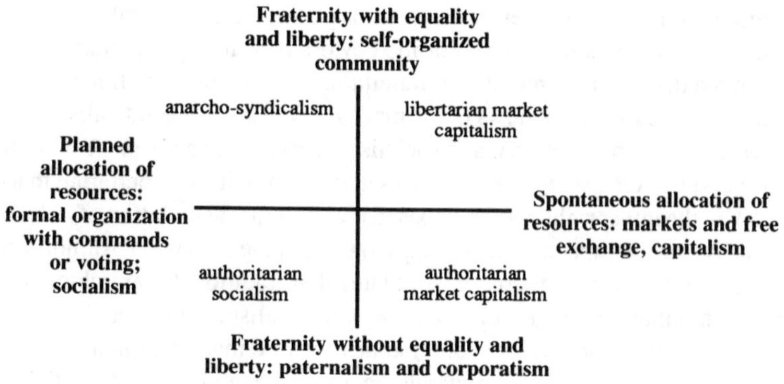

**Fraternity with equality
and liberty: self-organized
community**

anarcho-syndicalism | libertarian market
capitalism

**Planned
allocation of
resources:
formal organization
with commands
or voting;
socialism**

**Spontaneous allocation of
resources: markets and free
exchange, capitalism**

authoritarian
socialism | authoritarian
market capitalism

**Fraternity without equality and
liberty: paternalism and corporatism**

Figure 1.1 Ultimate values, ideologies, and forms of social order

tion that relies on two master hypotheses. First, people's experiences in their everyday lives shape their rank ordering of political preferences concerning liberty, equality, and community (this is the micro-logic of preference formation). Second, the preferences that will be politicized most intensely are those that are individually salient *and* appear to be least realized in the existing order (this is the macro-logic of preference mobilization). Given the limited complementarity and the trade-offs among the ultimate values of liberty, equality, and fraternity that drive modern visions of the good society, *political challenges of the status quo tend to call for institutions that realize those values which are least satisfied within the existing social order.* Primarily communitarian orders are subject to market-liberal or socialist attacks; market-liberal orders, in turn, are challenged by communitarian and socialist contention; and socialist orders have to defend themselves against liberal and communitarian critics.

## 1.2  SOCIAL EXPERIENCES AND POLITICAL PREFERENCE FORMATION: THE MICRO-LOGIC

Political preference and group formation is a multilayered process in which a variety of experiences shape individuals' orientations and beliefs. Katznelson (1986: 14–21) provides a sophisticated frame of reference for the formation of social classes as political actors that specifies four different levels and types of experiences: (1) economic class positions, as defined by fundamental property relations; (2) concrete social transactions in capitalist work settings, characterized by authority relations and labor markets, but also "away from work" experiences in the sphere of consumption; (3) interactive processes among people in everyday life that generate the "cultural configurations" or beliefs and dispositions on which people act; and (4) collective action and politics itself. Class formation, then, is the "conditional (but not random) process of connection between the four levels of class" (p. 21). Class formation involves a process of "structuration" unfolding in the interplay between objective conditions and intentional choice (Giddens 1973: 105). In this process, the collective actor develops a sense of common identity (Who are we and what are we striving for?), an awareness of opponents (Who works to prevent us from realizing our identity and objectives?), and beliefs about the nature of the social order in which the political struggle takes place.[6]

While class formation is a special case, Katznelson's four "layers" of collective mobilization may be applicable to other instances in which political groups emerge as well.[7] I will argue below that political class formation, in the Marxian sense, is extremely unlikely in advanced capitalism. Nevertheless, Katznelson's framework of collective political mobilization remains useful for reconstructing the emergence of political preferences over the socialist/capitalist and libertarian/authoritarian alternatives. First, I examine property relations. Then I turn to people's market and occupational experiences in their concrete work environment. Finally, I discuss the sphere of social consumption.

### *Class and exploitation: Weak bases for collective mobilization*

Conventional Marxist views of class formation short-circuit the complex multi-layered process of collective mobilization by focusing only on the first and the last of the four levels distinguished by Katznelson: economic property relations and collective political action. As a consequence, Marxist debates have often engaged in a sterile confrontation between objectivist and voluntarist class conceptions. Objectivists claim that the property relations of social categories ("class in itself") eventually give rise to conscious class mobilization under the impact of increasingly bitter distributive struggles with capital and a general decline of the economy.[8] Voluntarists, in turn, claim that classes are constituted by political struggles alone, with the class party providing the leading role.[9] But such economic determinism has failed to predict empirical class action adequately. Conversely, political voluntarism renders class theory tautological; whenever political actors define themselves as classes, social classes exist and make a difference.

Class analysis based on property relations is implicitly or explicitly grounded in three basic propositions. First, human beings primarily wish to maximize their control over property and income. Class theory here relies on an anthropology of human labor and a utilitarian theory of economic self-interest (cf. Lockwood

6 Here I am following Touraine (1977, 1981), who defines "class actors" not by reference to particular economic groups, but as groups with a sense of identity, opposition, and totality of the social order in which they are immersed. For a similar view, see Giddens (1973: 112–13).

7 Contemporary research on social movements, for example, realizes that a satisfactory account of social mobilization presupposes the analysis of (1) social structure, (2) recruitment networks, (3) formation of shared beliefs, and (4) group organization within a political opportunity structure. Cf. Klandermans, Kriesi and Tarrow (1988) and Morris and Mueller (1992).

8 This was the dominant Marxist view in the Second Socialist International. Cf. Giddens (1973: ch. 1) and Przeworski (1985: 48–9).

9 One early supporter of the voluntarist position is E. P. Thompson (1963), although he also relies on the actors' experiences in their everyday lives. More radical voluntarist positions have been adopted by Touraine (1971: 33) and in a quasi-Leninist mode by Przeworski (1985: 67).

1985). Second, rational individuals will eventually organize their cognitive map of the social world around the division between owners and nonowners of means of production. And third, members of a class will develop basic normative and cognitive capabilities to overcome *free-rider problems* by developing a sense of solidarity and institutions that enforce collective action. The Marxist tradition justifies none of these propositions adequately.

One avenue for reconstructing collective action within the Marxist framework is through the concept of *exploitation*. In Marx's labor theory of value, workers are exploited because they produce a surplus which is appropriated by the capitalist. Although the labor theory of value has been discredited (cf. Elster 1985: 127–41), neo-Marxists have insisted on the strategic role of exploitation for political class action. Roemer (1982), for example, redefines exploitation as a group's ability to receive greater benefits from its endowments by withdrawal from rather than compliance with existing contractual arrangements. This conception of exploitation not only draws on untestable counterfactual assumptions (Elster 1985: 203), but also yields a multiplicity of asset holders who exploit or are being exploited in the marketplace, not a division of society into two major classes. Exploitation thus cannot serve to explain class formation. Roemer already takes a step in the direction of a Weberian reconstruction of concrete market positions in order to explain the empirical political consciousness of individual actors.

A different (neo-)Marxist approach links class action to productive labor. Only productive, surplus-producing, laborers are exploited. Such individuals are involved in the creation of material products (Poulantzas 1978: 216–21), and are technically indispensable for the production process, whereas unproductive workers only police property rights and assist in the circulation of commodities (Przeworski 1985: 84–5). Unproductive workers are less able to develop socialist consciousness, because they will disappear with the demise of capitalism. Unfortunately, it is all but impossible to draw a line between the creation and the policing of property[10] so that the theory gives us no means to account for class formation.[11] Moreover, the shrinking proportion of "productive" workers in advanced capitalism bodes ill for the process of class formation.

Theories of exploitation or productive labor thus do not show how and why workers can define their collective identities based on property relations while overcoming all other differences among them that might undercut the process of class formation.[12] Moreover, Marxist theory focuses exclusively on the capitalism–socialism axis of preference formation and says nothing about workers' class views on the communitarian dimension. Elster (1985: 354–7) has shown

---

10 The distinction between manual and nonmanual labor provides no basis for identifying productive workers. If, following Williamson (1985), production concerns only technically inseparable processes and everything else is transaction, most manual workers would be nonproductive.

11 For a critique of Marx's conception of productive and unproductive labor, see Giddens (1973: 95–98).

12 T. H. Marshall (1977: 180) defined class formation as a mechanism for producing a collective consciousness that *overrides* all differences among people.

that Marx provides more phenomenological ad hoc observations about workers' mobilization in his historical writings that address what Katznelson has termed the intermediate levels of class formation. For example, Marx suggests that physical proximity, social homogeneity, and temporal continuity of employment facilitate a sense of collective identity among workers and the discovery of a (class) adversary. Which of these or any other industrial conditions affected workers' collective mobilization has never been settled.[13] The critical point, however, is that a phenomenology of work conditions leads away from class formation based on property relations to a greater appreciation of the concrete market and occupational experiences of wage earners. Ownership or nonownership of the means of production may orient individuals in a vague way toward more pro-capitalist or anti-capitalist positions. But a full account of individual preference formation and readiness for collective action must take other conditions into account.

### *Markets and work organizations: A phenomenology of preference formation*

Because markets stimulate the self-attribution of success and failure, market experiences increase people's cognitive sophistication and rationality and enable them to act on self-regarding preferences (cf. Lane 1991). The medium of market transactions is money, which is the measure and store of value. In this sense, market experiences are likely to shape the orientation of rational, self-regarding individuals to the pursuit of money income as the overriding instrumental preference. Whether this general preference translates into support for institutions of spontaneous capitalist market allocation or of centralized socialist redistribution, however, depends on market participants' expectations of which institutions are likely to maximize their discounted stream of future income, given their prevalent market position and experience.

This conception of social stratification originates in Weber's work on market locations rather than in Marx's class theory. Marxists propose that people who derive their income from profit and interests will be more inclined to support capitalist markets than those who earn wages. But this is only one of three aspects of citizens' market situation that shapes their interests over alternative distributive institutions. The second aspect is the location of an individual's source of income in the private or in the public sector. Public employment in a competitive democracy is much less exposed to the vagaries of the marketplace and to the pressures of competition and productivity than private employment. Private sector employers and wage earners, therefore, may welcome subsidies for their particular industry, but they will be more opposed to general redistributive policies (subsidies, public services) that lower their own industry's profitability and capacity to invest through higher taxes. Public sector employees, in contrast, will be less

---

13 For a list of variables, see Giddens (1973: 107–10) and for a more sophisticated view based on recent historical empirical studies, Marks (1989).

troubled by general concerns of productivity and investment in the private market sector and tend to benefit from a growing size of the public sector.

A third aspect of individuals' market experience concerns the extent to which their jobs and assets are exposed to competitive pressures. With some simplification, one may distinguish sectors exposed to international competition (most manufacturing and an increasing share of financial services) and sectors oriented toward domestic or local markets (retail, construction, personal services). Employers and wage earners whose well-being depends on the global marketplace are especially likely to prefer smaller bundles of public goods, such as public social services, and to oppose domestic redistributive measures (e.g., taxes) that may hobble a company's international competitiveness. In contrast, domestic sector companies may offset new tax burdens by price increases and thus protect their owners and workers.

Market experiences are thus characterized not just by property relations, but also by employment and location in production sectors. Jointly these market structures shape people's self-interested choices over policy alternatives ranging from spontaneous market allocation to redistributive, socialist policies.[14] Historically, the dividing line between public and private, domestic and international sectors has been fluid. But with decreasing transaction costs, precipitated by improved information technology and other breakthroughs, there has been a distinctive shift toward the private sector and international competition in all advanced capitalist countries. This is likely to promote capitalist market policies over socialist redistributive programs.

Political preference formation, however, is not confined to market experiences. Marxist and neoclassical economists presume that people worry about their market situation all the time, but other experiences in the daily environment of work organizations and the sphere of social consumption may be more important (Lane 1991: 25). Psychological research suggests that personal satisfaction with one's life derives less from market success than from these other spheres of social experience (Lane 1991: part VII). While markets affect people's affluence, organizational experiences contribute to their personal satisfaction and happiness. My contention is that experiences in the occupational world primarily influence people's communitarian political preferences.

People's control over their work environment and opportunities to participate in a communicative social process are critical factors shaping occupational experiences. Work environments that offer job autonomy and involve communicative skills reinforce preferences for social reciprocity and individual creativeness over monetary earnings. Moreover, such work profiles instill a sense of competence in citizens that encourages them to demand more participation in collective affairs,

---

14 A market-based notion of class formation that is not confined to property relations was first proposed by Weber (1920/1968: 177–9) and has even influenced Marxian theories of class formation (cf. Edwards 1979; Wright 1985). The not so hidden Weberianism in Erik Olin Wright's (1985) reframing of Roemer's theory of exploitation has drawn reproaches from more orthodox Marxists. See the debate in Wright (1989).

including politics. Organizational experiences, then, are not primarily related to people's political dispositions on the distributive, socialist versus capitalist dimension, but to a libertarian versus authoritarian dimension that relates to cultural conceptions of identity and appropriate political collective decision-making structures.

Libertarians value creative self-fulfillment, self-determination, and participatory decision making or social processes that are intrinsically rewarding. They view social interaction as a communicative process in which preferences, identities, and actions are developed in an open dialogue. In contrast, authoritarians attribute little significance to such objectives, favor social compliance, unambiguous standards of behavior, and rewards external to the social process. Social action is conceived as a monologue in which standards of social rectitude are adopted upon the command of a higher authority. Work experience, then, is a critical force shaping citzens' relative awareness of and preference for libertarian or authoritarian objectives within the political process.[15] The intellectual origin of this hypothesis can be traced to Habermas's (1985) distinction between strategic and communicative action. In contrast to Habermas, however, I do not attribute strategic action to the sphere of work and administration and communicative action primarily to the sphere of sociocultural reproduction. Both styles can be found in all arenas of social action.

One indicator of organizational experiences is education, because job autonomy and education are highly interrelated. Highly educated individuals typically have greater control over their job environments and therefore are inclined to develop participatory demands. Higher education predisposes individuals toward a more libertarian view of community than the view held by less educated individuals.

An indicator of communicative involvement is the kind of *work situation* individuals encounter in their daily occupational tasks. Where employees face other human beings and their emotional dispositions as the primary "task structure" and deal with clients' individuality or with cultural symbols that invoke the development of human individuality (in education, art, communication, health care, counseling, social work), communicative experiences are most intense. The greater the clients' "communicative claims" to individuality in the work setting, the more uncertain and nonroutine is the work process. Nonroutine client-interactive labor individualizes workers' occupational experience and dilutes authority relations.[16] It is likely to instill an antiauthoritarian vision of work autonomy and a greater sense of other-regardingness and reciprocity with interaction partners than does work on objects and documents.[17] Communicative experi-

---

15 Of course, socialization research could trace individuals' choice of occupation back to family settings in which particular predispositions are nurtured or discouraged.

16 Such hypotheses can be derived from contingency theories of organizational structure, such as those of Thompson (1967) and Perrow (1986).

17 This orientation yields well-researched conflicts between formalized bureaucratic oversight and professional claims to autonomy, for example in social service administrations where employees wish to treat clients as individuals, but bureaucratic imperatives of cost and expediency force them to treat clients as cases. See Hummel (1982).

ences are less pronounced where clients are treated as standardized cases (retail, finance, insurance, general public administration, police, and many legal services), or where material commodities and documents are the objects processed through the work organization (manufacturing, communications/transportation, engineering design, research).

A third indirect indicator of organizational experience is *gender.* Women tend to be overwhelmingly employed in people-processing organizations and, if they have higher education, primarily in symbol-producing and client-interactive jobs. Women are thus more likely to support libertarian orientations. Moreover, women's socialization experiences and involvement in reproductive activities may predispose them to giving greater priority to communicative reciprocity.

There is yet another prominent division among members of work organizations noted by non-Marxist sociologists, that of *authority relations,* and also traceable to Weber's sociology (cf. Dahrendorf 1959; Goldthorpe 1987). Authority structures, however, are a derivative of two market and organizational experiences I have already introduced, asset control over capital or knowledge. Thus, a recent Swedish study of social stratification found fairly high correlations between authority and capital ownership ($r = .58$), authority and knowledge ($r = .68$), yet not capital ownership and knowledge (Petersson, Westholm, and Blomberg 1989: 183–6). Authority was also unrelated to various measures of employment sector. Authority relations, therefore, are no substitute for measuring most of the divisions I have introduced.

### Styles of consumption and personal habitus

Marxist and Weberian theories of stratification and political consciousness generally share the premise that individuals' work experiences are the primary forces shaping their political outlook. As a consequence of increased disposable free time and technologies that have improved physical and intellectual mobility (automobile, mass media), the close linkage between job, residence, family structure, and subcultural activities that was so common for working-class constituencies in the first half of the twentieth century has been attenuated. Instead, personalized "consumption styles" have developed that yield an individualized "habitus" not easily captured by structural class or occupational categories.[18] Sociocultural experiences, crystallized around styles of conduct and consumption, become independent forces impinging on people's political orientations. While economic inequality persists, the individualization of life-styles has proliferated (Beck 1983, 1986).

Life-styles and styles of consumption are particularly likely to affect individuals' positions on the libertarian–authoritarian dimension, whereas market experiences and calculations tend to prevail on the distributive socialist–capitalist

18 Bourdieu (1977) introduced the concept of habitus to distinguish the analysis of social conduct from reductionist economic and structural sociology.

dimension.[19] *Age* and *life cycle,* in interaction with *gender,* affect predispositions toward libertarianism. Young people who lack family commitments and women who are only now claiming some of the personal autonomy enjoyed by men are particularly likely to support libertarian, participatory political ideals.[20] More generally, individuals who have not lived in the standard family consisting of parents and children for most of their lives tend to emphasize libertarian values often at odds with the discipline imposed on emotions in the conventional family.

The experience of one's physical environment also affects orientations toward libertarian as well as distributive values. Citizens who have disposable time and money to take advantage of the aesthetics of nature by moving into suburbs or countryside or by travel and outdoors activities, as well as those who are directly physically threatened by environmental aggravations are likely to call for more participatory, libertarian politics and may even demand the limitation of private investment rights exercised in competitive markets in order to protect the environment. Thus, people's involvement in work life and the consumption sphere may yield contradictory orientations and "role conflicts." Even those whose work experiences predispose them to more capitalist or authoritarian politics may waver when they try to preserve their consumptive experiences and find that the politics for doing so leads them to libertarian and redistributive market-constraining alternatives.

The experiential correlates of consumption styles that promote authoritarian and pro-capitalist views are the mirror image of libertarian dispositions. Individuals who have lived most of their lives in standard households, particularly homemakers and pensioners, are least likely to support libertarian values. Among younger individuals, men may be expected to express a more pronounced authoritarian orientation than women. Furthermore, those who do not perceive physical threats to the environment because they live in a comparatively undisturbed area or cannot afford to seek out enjoyment of nature will give least priority to libertarian demands.

The critical point of my discussion is that consumptive styles are irreducible to market and occupational experiences. Consumption experiences are organized through a system of social stratification involving physical space, subjective time (life cycle), and gender, all categories that have found no place in conventional Marxist and bourgeois analyses of social stratification. In order to keep the complexity of the argument to a minimum, however, I will advance my theoretical argument about political preference formation in advanced capitalist democracies

19 Dunleavy and Husbands's (1985: esp. 19–25) approach to employ citizens' reliance on public or private consumption of education, health care, housing, transportation, and general income as predictors of political preference goes beyond conventional class measures of voter behavior, but does not entail a consumption-based theory of preference formation in the same way I propose here. Dunleavy and Husbands's indicators measure the direct or indirect market experiences of individuals and therefore relate to the distributive dimension of preferences. As Scarbrough (1987: 229–30) has argued, Dunleavy and Husbands's theory therefore has difficulties to test the impact of public consumption on voting independent of more conventional class measures.

20 In part, this hypothesis is overdetermined by the distribution of education across age cohorts.

exclusively with respect to citizens' market and occupational experiences. It should be kept in mind, however, that the predictive power of that theory is limited by the fact that politically relevant experiences in the consumptive sphere may cut across the lines of division that are rooted in market and occupational roles.

### 1.3 POLITICAL PREFERENCES AND GROUP MOBILIZATION: THE MACRO-LOGIC

The micro-logic of experiences that shape dispositions toward ultimate values and political belief systems leaves us with a rather disjointed view of political preference formation. Ideally, the hypotheses introduced above help us to reconstruct the political orientations of particular individuals in light of their market, occupational, and consumptive experiences. I now turn to aggregate level macro-processes and examine how socioeconomic change and political institutions impinge upon the overall salience of politically relevant experiences for the occupationally stratified population of advanced capitalist democracies. Next, I will explore how different market and organizational experiences cluster around prevalent types in everyday life. Change in social stratification and institutions makes some clusters of market and organizational experiences more prominent. This process permits us to develop hypotheses about the changing distribution of political preferences and the potential for political group formation.

### Economic change, institutions, and collective preference formation

Socialist and capitalist, libertarian and authoritarian orientations are not unique to advanced capitalism. Yet the relative salience of such views for citizens' political self-definition and the quantitative distribution of such preferences is correlated with economic and institutional changes that affect the balance of citizens' everyday experiences. Changing market and organizational experiences, in turn, affect the aggregate distribution of political preferences. In advanced capitalist democracies, change brings about a marginal net shift of preferences from socialist to capitalist views, but also a greater salience of citizens' preferences on the "communitarian" dimension. Libertarian views of community become most pronounced, but are mirrored by an authoritarian backlash.

The economic change that most strongly promotes a surge of capitalist political commitment is the breakdown of national market barriers and the acceleration of global competition to which a lengthening list of industrial and service sectors is exposed. With capital becoming internationally more mobile and trade expanding, the autonomy of national governments to choose domestic economic policy, even in the larger capitalist countries, has dwindled. Economic policy is required to enable domestic corporations to earn internationally competitive profit rates in order to prevent them from relocating to foreign countries (Scharpf 1987a).

At the sectoral level, workers and employers in industries that thrive only by remaining internationally competitive have become increasingly averse to government regulations and taxes that impose global market disadvantages. At the occupational level, the introduction of sophisticated electronic production systems has put a premium on high skills and has made conventional unskilled and semiskilled workers more and more obsolete.[21] The "winners" of the industrial modernization process are particularly likely to support international market competition, while the "losers" call for protection and subsidies. New sectoral and occupational divisions contribute to a growing lack of solidarity among wage earners and a breakdown of centralized industrial relations regimes. They undermine the process of comprehensive class formation and stimulate pro-market sentiments within considerable segments of the labor force.

Probably the most important institutional change in advanced capitalism is the rise of social policy and the welfare state. Although its qualitative and quantitative development varies across countries (cf. Esping-Andersen 1990), it has affected capital accumulation and industrial relations in the entire Western Hemisphere. But large welfare states have contributed only marginally to the shift of political preferences toward capitalism. The primary bone of contention is the size and salary level of the public sector, whereas most wage earners fully support the universalist social insurance systems that protect them from the vagaries of the labor market. On the one hand, skilled blue-collar and white-collar workers in internationally competitive sectors call for containing public sector employment and wages to preserve their own market position. Moreover, such groups support efforts to expose public sector employees to more market competition or to privatize public sector corporations. On the other hand, a growing proportion of wage earners are employed in the public sector and constitutes a significant lobby for public sector preservation.

Overall, then, advanced capitalist welfare states experience a *renewed challenge of market efficiency and productivity.* Radical socialist appeals for nationalization, economic planning, and income leveling began to fade in the 1970s, and have been all but abandoned after the collapse of the communist bloc. Politically serious positions range from a new economic liberalism demanding more market competition, lower taxation, and reduced public spending to a moderate defense of the accomplishments of the welfare state.

Citizens' orientations over libertarian and authoritarian alternatives have been affected by four macro-developments: increasing affluence, greater educational accomplishments, changes in the sectoral composition of labor markets, and again the welfare state. The relationship between affluence and libertarian–authoritarian orientations is probably most tenuous. A great deal has been made of the association between affluence and "post-materialist" orientations that measure primarily libertarian predilections for self-realization and political participation (Inglehart 1990). People who are affluent or were brought up in affluent homes are expected to gain marginally declining satisfaction from further income increases and there-

---

21 This process was first described in detail by Kern and Schumann (1984).

fore become more interested in libertarian values. But for two reasons, affluence, taken by itself, is likely to be a relatively weak predictor of libertarian preferences. First, not the absolute level, but differentials of income relative to other groups affect personal satisfaction most (Lane 1991).[22] If income thus is a "positional good" (Hirsch 1976), competition for more income is unlikely to wane with rising average earnings and access to consumer goods. Second, material affluence is at best an indicator of consumption styles, but does not sufficiently characterize individuals' everyday experience in market and occupational environments that shape political consciousness. Much of the relationship between affluence and libertarian values may be due to intervening variables, particularly education and work situation.

The increasing demand for sophisticated education in advanced industrial economies, together with the shift from manufacturing to financial and personal services, has probably given the most powerful boost to libertarian political preferences. "Post-Fordist" economies rely less on the provision of standardized mass consumer goods and services than flexible, computer-aided production runs and variable services matched to highly versatile and sophisticated consumer demands.[23] Capitalist markets thrive increasingly on the cultural manipulation of symbols and client relations (Baudrillard 1975; Bell 1976). This development reinforces the salience of libertarian orientations.

The growth of the welfare state is caught up not only in the preference formation over the "distributive" capitalist–socialist alternatives, but also the "communitarian" libertarian or authoritarian orientations. Most welfare state employees regularly encounter work situations with nonroutine communicative interactions with clients and colleagues. Even where bureaucratic rules force employees to process clients as standardized "cases," the incommensurability of human experience with bureaucratic rules leaves their mark on the employees' political consciousness (Hummel 1982). Finally, an overproportional share of public sector employees in human services are women. For this reason, many public sector employees, primarily in social services, but not in general administration, police, or the justice system, are likely to express libertarian preferences. The growth of public social services thus contributes to the salience of libertarian orientations in contemporary politics.

In addition to the challenge of market efficiency, modern capitalism is also characterized by a challenge of libertarian politics. Libertarian politics envisions autonomous institutions *beyond* state and market (negative freedoms) that endow individuals with citizens' rights to participate in the governance of collective affairs (positive freedoms). Libertarians demand greater individual autonomy in

---

22  In the same vein, Inglehart (1990: 241–2) shows that overall life satisfaction and happiness are influenced more by recent *changes* in one's financial situation rather than by levels of family income.

23  This view of advanced industrial economies borrows from the French "regulation" school that developed since the mid-1970s (for an overview, see Boyer 1988 and Noël 1987), and its American counterpart, Piore and Sabel (1984).

shaping personal and collective identities, the transformation of gender roles, and an ethic of enjoyment rather than of accumulation and order.

Although structural and institutional forces strengthen both capitalist and libertarian orientations in advanced industrial democracies, they also create a backlash potential from individuals whose experiences have left them out of the mainstream. The "losers" of economic modernization and workers in domestically protected sectors are least likely to endorse capitalism. The growing salience of libertarian orientations among professionals, personal service employees, and women also is likely to prompt authoritarian responses from less educated, typically male workers in manufacturing sectors, clerks or small business owners. The new authoritarianism values a "natural" hierarchical community, deference to political authority, the return to a stable patriarchal division of labor between the sexes, and an ethic of personal discipline.

At the institutional level, free marketeers, libertarians, and authoritarians target the existing Keynesian welfare state (KWS) as the source of their dissatisfactions. After World War II, the KWS represented a compromise between the principles of market efficiency and liberty, on the one hand, and that of citizens' equality and security, on the other. Macro-economic state intervention through fiscal and monetary policies to promote growth, low unemployment, and low inflation, and comprehensive social policies extended bureaucratic governance in mass parties, centralized interest groups, and state agencies at the expense of the free reign of markets and communitarian forms of social association.[24] The "class compromise" of the KWS contributed to a reduction in overtly disruptive conflict about property rights and converted conflicts over economic distribution from a zero-sum, single-shot confrontation between capital and labor into an iterative, incremental positive-sum game. But it also produced the bureaucratic centralization that is now targeted by market-capitalist and communitarian challengers.

### *The interdependence of market and organizational experiences in political group formation*

If structural changes in advanced capitalism reinforce capitalist and libertarian preferences among citizens, will the strongest political groups combine both orientations? More generally, what are the typical "clusters" of preference-forming experiences that create opportunities for political group formation in this new historical situation? Identifying such clusters permits us to map the range of strategic avenues from which politicians may choose to build electoral coalitions.

One path for exploring the clustering of preferences is to examine the normative and logical compatibility between positions on the libertarian–authoritarian and the capitalist–socialist axis. Is the division between socialist libertarians and capitalist authoritarians more *intellectually coherent* or less than the division between socialist authoritarians and capitalist libertarians? Although capitalism is

---

24 This story has been told from Marshall's "Citizenship and Social Class" (reprinted in Marshall 1977) to Offe's (1984) analysis of the Keynesian welfare state.

a necessary historical correlate of political democracy (Dahl 1971), the logic of democracy tends to interfere with dispassionate processes of market allocation (Weber 1920/1978: 94). For this reason, some liberal capitalist theorists advocate authoritarian restraints on democratic choice (Hayek 1977). Moreover, numerous theorists from Schumpeter (1975: 127, 157) to Bell (1976) have held libertarian, cultural, and political orientations, such as hedonistic individualism and women's emancipation, to be responsible for the decline of the capitalist ethic of accumulation that has the multigenerational family as its ultimate beneficiary.[25] This complementarity between authoritarian institutions and capitalist markets applies only up to the threshold at which authoritarian command would infringe on the formal freedom of commodity owners in the marketplace. Similarly, leftist socialist and libertarian institutional preferences appear compatible only up to the point at which equality undermines the individuals' capacity for free association. Overall, an argument based on the *coherence of ideas* suggests some affinity between libertarian and socialist views, on the one hand, and authoritarian and capitalist views, on the other, but ultimately remains inconclusive.

The second avenue for investigating the clustering of preferences is empirical and examines the actual combination of everyday life experiences shared by large groups in advanced capitalism. The task then is to determine which of the six market and organizational experiences I have employed to characterize distributive and communitarian orientations typically go together and provide the foundations of group formation. We thus move from a logic of ideas to a logic of material or nonmaterial preferences and interests. In modifying Weber's (1915/1958a: 280) famous dictum, ideas about ultimate values (liberty, equality, fraternity) and corresponding institutions (markets, organization, community) may, like switchmen, still determine the tracks along which actors proceed, yet concrete human experiences and interests always directly govern political conduct. To explore the clustering of political dispositions, I will now present several hypotheses about the dominant configurations of experiences that shape the distribution of political preferences in advanced capitalism.

Public sector employees and workers in domestic industries are segments of the labor force that are likely to be unenthusiastic about market capitalism because their jobs are protected from the risks of the marketplace and the global pressure of competition and investment. In addition to more anti-capitalist inclinations, public sector personnel also tend to be libertarian because many jobs involve communicative client-interactive experiences, require advanced education, and attract women. Public sector employees in general administration and law enforcement are a different story. These groups are on average less educated, more involved in processing material objects, and more predominantly men. For this reason, employees in this sector would be expected to have a significant authoritarian potential.

---

25 A leftist argument about the erosion of the (authoritarian) moral foundations of capitalism can be found in Habermas (1975).

Private sector employees, regardless of whether they are white or blue collar, can also be divided according to the work situation they encounter. Individuals in people-processing occupations with higher education tend to be more libertarian, but their orientation on the capitalist–socialist dimension depends very much on their employment sector (domestic versus competitive). Overall, the number of employees situated in occupations involving the manipulation of symbols or client-interactive communications while also located in the international competitive sector is relatively small (consultants, advertising agencies, mass media, etc.). Even if we throw in a significant share of the liberal professions and managers, the size of the occupational groups combining capitalist and libertarian predispositions is likely to be much smaller than that of the group with more socialist and libertarian orientations.

Employees in object-processing organizations are differentiated by skill level and sector and therefore may express rather different orientations. Highly skilled industrial workers, for example, may assume an intermediate position on the libertarian–authoritarian dimension, yet are pulled toward the center-right of the capitalist–socialist dimension. They know that world markets are vital for the survival of their companies and that the growth of public expenditure may hurt them. Less skilled white and blue collar workers in object-processing job situations tend to be more authoritarian and, depending on the international competitive exposure of their firm, more or less pro-capitalist. It is uncontroversial, however, that the number of labor-market participants who have low skills, work on objects, and are situated in the domestic sector is shrinking. The combination of authoritarian and socialist politics thus should become comparatively less common and remain typical only among older workers, low-skilled clerical employees, and retirees rather than in the younger labor force.

Corporate organization people – managers and owners of larger businesses – are clearly most committed to capitalist preferences, yet their orientation on the libertarian–authoritarian axis may vary. Since they tend to work on documents and objects or treat people like cases who must contribute to the external objectives of an organization, they may have a penchant for authoritarian views of social order. At the same time, however, such individuals usually have received a sophisticated education making them sensitive to libertarian claims. Moreover, their experiences in the sphere of social consumption may temper their demand for more authoritarian politics.

The clusters of occupations that share a dominant political outlook cut across familiar sectoral divisions, such as that between "manufacturing" and "services." There is no unity to the vast residual category of the "service sector" and different job profiles within that sector promote rather divergent political orientations.[26] A theory of group formation based on market and occupational experiences also

26 An interesting differentiation of jobs in the service sector was attempted by Esping-Andersen (1990: ch. 8). While his categories are useful to predict different national occupational profiles based on the type of welfare state in a country, I doubt, however, that they are also useful to characterize patterns of political consciousness.

suggests that the popular concept of the "new middle class" or the "service class," as defined by high education but no capital ownership, is deeply flawed, because it subsumes heterogeneous experiences and life-styles under a single category.[27] The range of new middle-class positions encompasses a continuum that is bounded by the polar opposites of cultural symbol producers (Kirkpatrick 1976) and strategic organization persons, with each occupational group distinguished by task structure, gender composition, property regimes, and market sector. [28] Members of the new middle class thus vary in their politics over the entire space of distributive and communitarian politics and are unlikely to coalesce around a joint political perspective (Berger 1986: 125–7).

Overall, the greatest capitalist-authoritarian potential is shared by a now small social group that traditional Marxists refer to as the petty bourgeoisie of shopkeepers, craftsmen, independent salespersons, and farmers. These individuals strongly defend private property, and their orientation to the marketplace has become more favorable with rising tax burdens, although they often call for the protection of their own businesses from market pressures. At the same time, the petty bourgeoisie combines comparatively low education with object-processing task structures and is thus quite strongly predisposed to authoritarian views.

If all six attributes that characterize the experience of individuals in the social structure – ownership, public or private sector, international or domestic sector, task structure, education, gender – were independent of one another and individuals could assume one of two values on each dimension, the population of advanced capitalist societies would be divided into no fewer than sixty-four groups. Fortunately, a number of combinations are empty or occupied by very small groups.[29] Conversely, there are clusters of attributes that yield rather large numbers of citizens. In Figure 1.2, I have mapped the seven groups that appear to be quantitatively and qualitatively the most important categories.

Figure 1.2 simplifies reality by depicting the main areas of ideological space in which sizable occupational groups are expected to cluster. Note that the extreme socialist–authoritarian and capitalist–libertarian regions of the space are empty, reflecting my argument that the choice of political alternatives is constrained by considerations of intellectual coherence and material self-interest.

Figure 1.2 ignores a number of forces outside market and organizational experiences that may affect the location of groups and individuals in the political

---

27  Giddens (1973: 187) aptly criticized the concept of the service class because "it does not distinguish adequately between class and the division of labor." For empirical distinctions in the service class, see Brint (1984).

28  Moreover, the whole class metaphor is inadequate. Classes are characterized by collective continuity and intergenerational "entrapment" that foster mobilization. Recruitment into the ranks of symbol producers rather than that of strategic organization persons is by and large a voluntary decision. This point has been emphasized by Parkin (1972: 185) and Kriesi (1987; 1989).

29  For example, public sector employees in internationally competitive industries (combined with the other criteria, sixteen cells) or women capital owners (combined with other criteria, sixteen cells) do not exist or represent extremely rare cases.

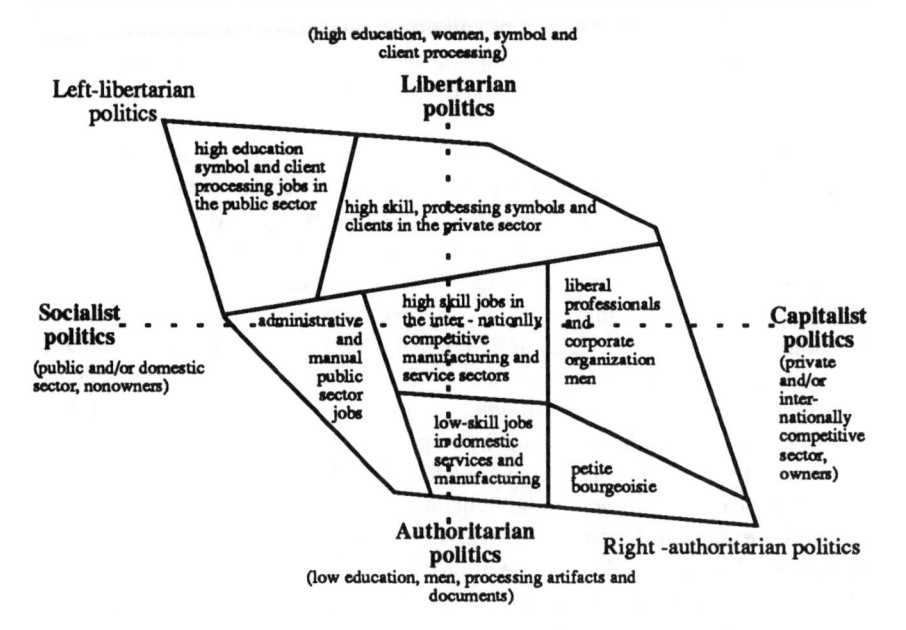

Figure 1.2. Ideology and occupational groups in advanced capitalist democracies

space. First, as I have emphasized, experiences in the sphere of social consumption have an independent impact on preferences. Second, my occupational model is static and does not take into account *occupational mobility* of individuals across different clusters of occupational experiences. As long as it is empirically plausible to assume that people spend most of their occupational life in one general occupational location, however, the model still may have predictive power for political consciousness formation. Third, *conjunctural effects,* such as a sharp economic crisis that reduces the salience of the libertarian–authoritarian dimension, or conversely a highly charged environmental, gender, or cultural conflict that temporarily eclipses issues of distributive politics, are likely to alter the position of individuals and groups in the space. Fourth, the exact slope of the left-libertarian versus right-authoritarian main distribution varies with a country's economic structure, political institutions (welfare state), and the politicians' appeal in the arena of party competition. Nevertheless, the model reflects a general distribution of preferences that are found to a greater or lesser extent in most advanced capitalist countries.

### Theoretical model and empirical referents

A drawback of the theoretical model I have proposed is that not all of its components are easily measurable. The choice of indicators is particularly constrained by a lack of data sets that permit direct comparisons of citizens' political preferences for most of the European countries examined in subsequent chapters.[30] I will assess these problems and some recent empirical findings before continuing my theoretical outline.

Efforts to measure libertarian or authoritarian orientations in political psychology go as far back as Adorno et al.'s (1950) study of the authoritarian character. In existing cross-national data sets that include most European countries, however, the only option to identify such orientations is the "materialism–post-materialism" index (MPM). It asks respondents to rank order the importance of four government tasks: (i) providing for more citizens' participation in government, (ii) protecting freedom of speech, (iii) fighting inflation, and (iv) maintaining law and order. A respondent giving priority to participation and free speech is scored high on post-materialism, one giving priority to stable prices and law and order is scored high on materialism. Actually, only one of the four items directly measures materialism (fighting inflation), and even here, it is conceivable that the item taps a *distributive* issue that divides economic left and right rather than (post-)materialism.[31] Capitalists prefer to fight inflation (at the expense of jobs), whereas socialists prefer to fight unemployment (at the expense of profits). The other three items of the index also do not relate to the extent of materialism, but to *citizens' views of political authority* either positively (law and order) or negatively (participation, free speech).[32] A broader, twelve-item post-materialism index also shows that support for participatory and antiauthoritarian policies define the post-materialist extreme (with additional items being "more say on the job," "ideas count"). In addition, a directly communitarian objective loads highly on post-materialism ("less impersonal society").[33] The materialist end of this index now includes endorsement of two additional authoritarian issues (fighting crime, strong defense) together with the only two clearly materialist issues (economic growth, stable economy).

In conclusion, the MPM index primarily measures libertarian versus authoritarian views. Only three of twelve items of the scale concern economic materialism or distributive views, although libertarian positions are associated with more leftist economic views and also rather weakly with a preference for a more nonmaterialist, simple life-style, post-materialism is not the central concept measured by the scale.[34] The empirical use and the theoretical interpretation of the MPM index

---

30 A richer data file that will overcome some of the problems I mention in this section will become available with the publication of the 1990 World Values Survey in 1994.

31 A test of this proposition is that post-materialists may not value fighting inflation, but fighting unemployment.

32 My interpretation of the post-materialism index has some similarity to Flanagan's (1987) argument that the link between post-materialism and libertarianism is artificial. This enables us to say that there is a nonmaterialist or now better: authoritarian New Right. See also Savage (1985) and, for a further disaggregation of issue dimensions, Knutsen (1990a).

33 For these findings see Inglehart (1990: 136–41). Inglehart gives a different and in my view less adequate interpretative spin on these indicators on p. 134.

34 The only item directly related to post-materialist, aesthetic life-styles, "making our cities more beautiful," loads only weakly on the post-materialism factor that Inglehart has identified.

have been subjected to a deluge of other criticisms, but it strikes me as valid for the purposes of measuring libertarian versus authoritarian orientations.[35]

Other cross-nationally comparable measures of the libertarian–authoritarian dimension are harder to come by, but they include the willingness to join libertarian social movements (ecology, antinuclear, peace, feminist movements), attitudes about racism and cultural pluralism, and views of women's social freedoms (abortion, political involvement, role in labor markets).[36] A further widely available indicator of political orientations – religiosity, as measured by the frequency of attending religious services – is also likely to tap communitarian divisions as well as distributive preferences. Strong Christian religious affiliation typically teaches compliance with established social norms and practices and subordination of individual aspirations to those of the religious community. At the same time, a status quo orientation also promotes a defensive attitude about the existing distribution of property rights and thus a pro-capitalist disposition.

Unfortunately, the most critical socioeconomic predictor of communitarian orientations – client-interactive occupations versus occupations that process clients as standardized cases or manipulate objects and documents – cannot be measured directly with available survey evidence because the disaggregation of occupations is not sufficiently fine-grained to track this theoretical distinction.[37] Nevertheless, education and white collar or professional occupation can serve as indirect indicators of occupational experience. Educated white collar professionals are most likely to engage in client-interactive tasks and, therefore, also to support libertarian orientations. Furthermore, age may offer an even more indirect tracer of libertarian attitudes. Younger age cohorts, particularly women, are more likely to be involved in communicative-interactive jobs because of the structural and generational change of the labor force. Gender, by itself, is not a viable measure of libertarian or authoritarian values, unless the interaction with age is taken into account.[38]

35 A good summary of the critical issues is presented by Clarke and Dutt (1991), who argue that individuals' MPM values are volatile and that there is no clear cross-sectional or intertemporal evidence for PM to covary with affluence and economic growth. The individual-level volatility of opinion survey instruments, however, is endemic to survey research in general. As far as cross-sectional and intertemporal comparisons go, my analysis does not assume that Western publics should become progressively more "post-materialist," a hypothesis Clarke and Dutt reject, but only that libertarianism versus authoritarianism is a strong and salient structuring feature of political divisions in advanced capitalism, but varies in significance from country to country.

36 In this study, I will confine my empirical analysis to the indicator "readiness to join social movements." In another research project on the New Right in Western Europe, indicators on racism, family norms, and the evaluation of sexual conduct yields closely consistent results (Kitschelt forthcoming).

37 Inglehart's (1990: 324) analysis of the balance between materialism and post-materialism among German social elites, however, is quite instructive as indirect evidence for my contention. At the post-materialist end of the scale, there are presidents of universities and research institutions, journalists, and intellectuals; at the materialist end, we encounter officers of business and farm associations, directors of major industrial concerns, and military generals.

38 An empirical corroboration of these linkages for Scandinavia can be found in Knutsen (1990b).

Cross-nationally comparable indicators of the capitalism–socialism division and its expected experiential correlates in markets and occupations also are difficult to find. Specific issue items such as support for the nationalization of industry or the welfare state rarely appear in surveys that also include measures of communitarian political preferences, and therefore the linkage between the dimensions cannot be studied satisfactorily.[39] A general and widely available indicator, individuals' self-placement on the left–right scale has been found to relate to *both* distributive and communitarian issues (Inglehart 1990: 274, 297; Kitschelt and Hellemans 1990a,b). In such studies, leftist self-placements appear to remain strongly associated with defense of the welfare state, whereas support for nationalization has generally declined.

Among the everyday life experiences likely to generate stances on distributive politics, neither property ownership nor work in the internationally competitive or the domestic market sector are directly measurable without confounding influences. Data on property ownership and sectoral employment can be only indirectly inferred from very crude occupational categories. Blue collar workers are somewhat more likely to work in the internationally competitive sector than white collar employees, who constitute much of the public sector. Managers of firms probably have more property rights in the means of production than other individuals. Also, data about private or public sector employment as predictors of political dispositions on distributive issues are rarely available in systematic cross-nationally comparable data sets. Existing evidence, however, indicates that public sector employees have moved toward leftist positions on the distributive dimension and toward libertarian positions on the communitarian division.[40]

Overall, a full empirical exploration of the linkages between citizens' market and organizational experiences, on the one hand, and political preference formation, on the other, awaits surveys guided by the theoretical propositions I have advanced above. My own empirical investigation in Chapter 4, therefore, has a necessarily explorative and illustrative character.

## 1.4 DILEMMAS OF SOCIAL DEMOCRACY IN ADVANCED CAPITALISM

In the transformation of capitalism since World War II, the rise of the Keynesian welfare state, together with the transformation of the economic structure that expanded the proportion of labor market participants who are highly educated, work with clients, and are female, has shifted the main axis of voter distribution from a simple alternative between socialist (left) and capitalist (right) politics to a

39 Among European biannual Eurobarometers, only the 1979 Eurobarometer 11 includes both distributive and communitarian issue items. But this survey is too old to represent issue preferences and mean positions of parties' supporters in the 1980s. This weakness will be remedied when the 1990 World Values Study that includes most European countries is published and freely available for analysis.

40 See the instructive study by Goul-Andersen (1984) on Danish voting behavior and social structural correlates.

more complex configuration opposing left-libertarian and right-authoritarian alternatives. Figure 1.3 reflects this shift by rotating the voter distribution from an area that envelops the socialist–capitalist axis of ideological division to an orthogonal axis that is limited by the new left-libertarian and right-authoritarian extremes. The new axis of voter distribution does not intersect the socialist–capitalist axis at its midpoint, but to its (capitalist) right and does not extend all the way to the socialist extreme. Since the 1970s, pure socialist alternatives have lost their political attractiveness, a process that has been accelerated by the collapse of East European socialism. This has shortened the axis of competition over alternative economic modes for allocating scarce resources. Further, Figure 1.3 reflects the argument that political agendas inspired by libertarianism and socialism at the left extreme and those inspired by authoritarianism and capitalism at the right extreme are compatible only up to a point beyond which libertarianism works against socialism and authoritarianism against capitalism.

I want to emphasize that the extent to which the main axis of voter distribution and party competition has shifted from the horizontal to the diagonal or the vertical axis in Figure 1.3 varies across countries and depends on a number of factors, among which social structure and basic institutions are only the most important. Others include the mobilization of libertarian or authoritarian social movements and the issue leadership of political parties. In this sense, Figure 1.3 represents an idealization that does not reflect the conditions existing in any individual country.

The stage on which politicians try to win over an electoral following is now set. Politicians' strategies depend on the behavior of voters within the two-dimensional policy space and on their own objectives. To begin with a first rough theoretical approximation, if voters act rationally in a Euclidean space and only support parties close to their own ideal position, and politicians primarily strive to maximize their electoral support, most but not all parties would locate their strategic appeals within the ideological range covered by each time period's main area of voter distribution.[41] Only parties representing small pressure groups on specific secondary issues would be able to garner limited electoral support with positions outside these basic regions of the space in Figure 1.3.[42] This hypothesis ignores the fact that a large share of the electorate votes on party identification rather than issue positions. Such voters are impervious to party strategy, but their proportion in the overall electorate appears to be falling.[43]

Consider now the strategic choices social democrats face relative to the chang-

---

41 If voters behave strategically, i.e., they do not vote for parties, but for governing coalitions closest to their ideal point, the rationale of party politics would be more complicated. Particularly in multiparty systems, however, strategic voting involves such complex calculations about the reasoning of voters and parties that it probably has only marginal influence. Strategic voting is most important in party systems clearly dominated by two parties, a limiting condition that applies only in a few empirical instances.

42 One may think of farmers or other rent-seeking economic status groups.

43 The increasing role of issues in voter choices has been demonstrated by Franklin et al. (1992) for a comprehensive set of advanced democracies.

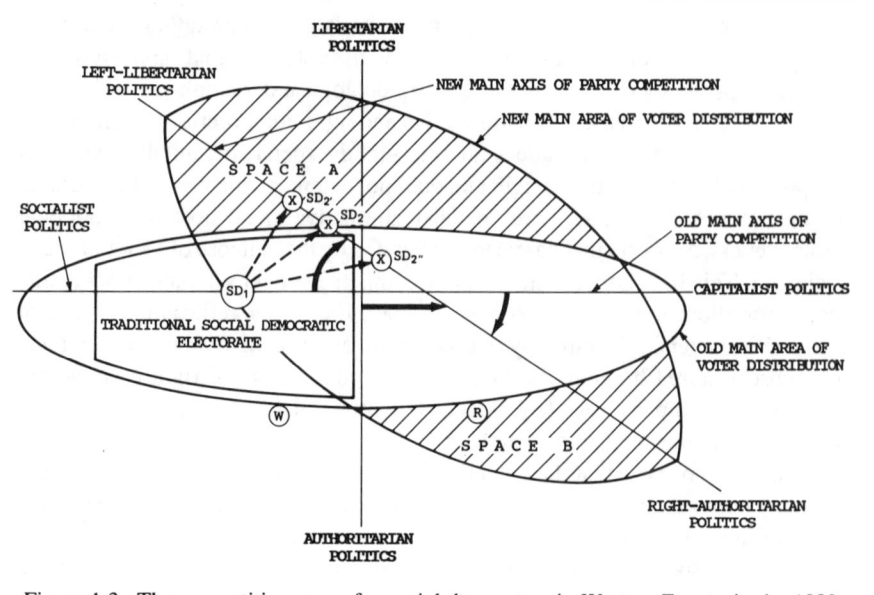

Figure 1.3. The competitive space for social democracy in Western Europe in the 1980s

ing main space of voter distribution in an advanced capitalist democracy.[44] In the first decades after World War II, a position close to $SD_1$ in Figure 1–3, on the moderate left of the socialist–capitalist axis, but neutral on the libertarian–authoritarian axis, tended to be electorally advantageous. With the rotation and rightward shift of the main area of voter distribution since the 1960s and, consequently, also the shift of the main axis of party competition, social democratic parties are well advised to move toward (i) more libertarian and (ii) more capitalist positions, for example near locations $SD_2$, $SD_{2'}$, or $SD_{2''}$.

Superimposing Figures 1.2 and 1.3 reveals that the range of new social democratic strategies involves a substantial transformation of the electoral coalitions on which social democrats have relied. Given the declining number of blue collar workers in manufacturing, electorally rational social democratic parties will increasingly rely on white collar constituencies, with some emphasis on the public sector and generally individuals in symbol-producing and client-interactive professions.

Social democratic strategies affect the political behavior of traditional working-class clienteles. Social democrats here face a double trade-off. First, by moving along the vertical libertarian–authoritarian dimension, social democrats must decide whether they will rely more on traditional less educated blue collar, working-class voters or more on highly educated white collar employees. Consider, for example, worker W in Figure 1.3 who might be a semiskilled male

44 A refinement of this simple model with hypotheses predicting variance across countries will be presented in Chapter 4.

automobile worker with a high school diploma. Because of the changing occupational stratification and experiences, he is located at the periphery of the main area of voter distribution in "post-Fordist" capitalism. The more the social democratic party he supported in the past moves from $SD_1$ to $SD_2$, the more alienated this worker is likely to feel from his party and the more he may be tempted to vote for, say, racist and xenophobic party R, which appeals to his unhappiness with libertarian policies, although party R is unsympathetic to his commitment to the welfare state and redistributive economic policy.

Social democrats also face a second trade-off within the working class itself, contingent upon their distributive economic stance. If they move to the socialist left, they will lose the growing pool of highly educated, predominantly male workers in internationally competitive manufacturing and service industries who no longer support further growth of the public sector and may even advocate marginal reductions of public employment and expenditure. Leftist policies are likely to preserve support among less educated workers in industries that are protected from international competition. Socialist appeals to class politics thus do not unite the working class, but divide it in different ways than a more moderate pro-capitalist program. On the socialist–capitalist axis, then, social democrats choose not between a pure class and a cross-class strategy, but between mobilizing different segments of the working class. As a consequence, class politics is no longer the foundation of a broadly successful social democratic electoral coalition.

Because of changes in citizens' market and occupational experiences, social democratic strategic choices have thus become considerably more complex than in previous decades. The complexity of building a social democratic political coalition is even greater when one also factors in the heterogeneity of consumptive lifestyles. The transformation of social democracy is thus a process of strategic adjustment to an electoral marketplace characterized by changing socioeconomic settings, citizens' political preferences, and patterns of party competition. Because the working class, conceived in Marxist terms of exploitation and nonownership, has become an empty category to which no collectively shared daily experiences correspond, social democrats are confronted with the difficult task of combining coalitions among bits and pieces of the working class with various occupational segments of the white collar constituencies. Politics can no longer act on preexisting collective identities, but parties are compelled to manufacture political coalitions in an economically, socially, and culturally more heterogeneous environment (cf. Beck 1983: 58; Hellemans 1990: 233–36). Since parties can count less and less on the loyalty of solid blocs of "core clienteles," electoral competition becomes a matter of *managing the variety* rather than contriving the homogeneity of electoral constituencies (Streeck 1987).

Let us now examine the individual strategic options social democrats face since the late 1970s. In the transition from $SD_1$ to $SD_2$, social democrats can become both more pro-capitalist *and* more libertarian. Once they are close to the new main axis of party competition, however, further strategic moves are likely to be *either* toward a more left-libertarian ($SD_{2'}$) *or* centrist appeal ($SD_{2'''}$). Where social democrats will strategically locate depends on their electoral objectives and their competitors' positions.

In a simple spatial model of multiparty competition among short-term vote maximizers, parties have an incentive to spread out across the ideological space rather than to gravitate toward the median voter (Cox 1990a; Shepsle and Cohen 1990). The more a market segment is crowded with serious competitors who can cope with the costs of entering the game, the less attractive it is for parties to approach that segment. Rational parties locate themselves in the middle of their market, as far away from competitors as possible.[45] For social democrats, the most profitable electoral stance depends on the "crowdedness" of the competitive space to the party's libertarian Left and its authoritarian Right.

Rather than short-term vote maximizing, social democrats may wish to maximize their chance of holding executive office. If the party manages to capture the pivotal voter in the main dimension of party competition, no government coalition can be formed against it. Social democrats would pursue such a "pivoting" strategy by moving to position $SD_{2''}$. While increasing the social democrats' bargaining power over policy and government formation, on balance, this strategy may cost the party votes, because left-libertarian voters will be tempted to support more radical parties.[46] Another possible objective of social democratic strategy is to preempt or destroy a new left-libertarian competitor first and then resume a strategy of maximizing votes or office holding. In this case, the party would lose votes by moving toward a more extreme left-libertarian position at $SD_{2'}$, but would hope to regain market shares by renewed moderation once the new competitor has been eliminated ("oligopolistic competition"). Office-maximizing strategies or oligopolistic competition are not rational strategies per se, but depend on circumstances that make pursuing such objectives feasible.

The theory of social democratic choice in the arena of party competition I have sketched in anticipation of a fuller discussion of the model in Chapter 4 explains the electoral consequences of parties' strategic choices, but can it explain the choices themselves? How, for example, do social democrats choose among objectives of party competition when there are several plausible avenues of action? And why do they sometimes opt for unworkable objectives and strategies that cost votes but do not deliver the gains expected from oligopolistic competition and office-seeking appeals?

Sometimes, strategic failure may result from a "tragic" competitive situation, in which changes in the lineup of competing parties, voter distribution, or rules of the game would have thwarted *any* systemic strategy, be it short-term vote maximization, office seeking, or oligopolistic competition. In many instances, however, the choice of strategies translating into electoral decline can be explained only in terms

---

45 All these conjectures depend on certain further assumptions I discuss in Chapter 4.
46 For an analysis of the interaction between electoral competition and government formation, see Laver (1989).

of the internal dynamic of political coalition building inside social democratic parties, a task I address in Chapter 5.

Simple models of party organization construct an antagonism between radical, ideological rank-and-file activists, and moderate, electorally minded party leaders who intend to abide by systemic objectives of party competition. Such models predict that parties with strong autonomous leaders who decide strategy and subordinate rank-and-file activists to their views tend to be strategically most flexible and successful. This argument, however, does not explain why autonomous leaders sometimes become formidable obstacles to a party's advantageous strategic adjustment, why parties that make the leadership accountable to the rank and file to a large degree have often been electorally successful, and why rank-and-file militants sometimes engineer breakthroughs to new and electorally successful strategies by installing new leadership groups.

A contingency theory of party organization I develop in Chapter 5 can relate the relative autonomy of leaders vis-à-vis activists and the patterns of membership recruitment and internal participation to changing conditions of party competition. For example, the greater the heterogeneity of a party's electoral constituency, the less viable are mass party organizations that emphasize solidarity, identity, and discipline at the expense of more participatory, purposive modes of incorporating political activists, because the former fail to register the highly differentiated demands of the electoral target audiences. Flexible framework parties that give voice to small groups of activists who can effectively reach out to the party leadership are better adapted to coping with diversified electoral demands. Also, the more a party's electoral and office payoffs are sensitive to strategic appeals of competitors because citizens vote more on issues than party identification, the more important is the ability of party leaders to set and revise party objectives during campaigns and in legislative politics. Strategic mobility becomes an essential ingredient of political success.

In the past when challenges to the Keynesian welfare state revolved around *transform* distributive conflicts, social democratic parties usually performed quite well with encompassing mass parties and accountable leaders enjoying limited strategic capacity. With the transformation of social structure and the rotation of the main axis of party competition toward the polarity between left-libertarians and right-authoritarians, however, both of these organizational features are impediments to strategic capacity. Successful party organizations, therefore, must change from internally consensual and solidary mass organizations to stratified internal conflict systems whose activists articulate the heterogeneity of a party's constituencies, but whose leaders have the capacity to manage internal political variety.

In this process, the working-class rank and file is displaced by new activists from white collar professionals, particularly those who work in client-interactive occupations. At the same time as bureaucratic rules of accountability erode, party leaders gain greater autonomy for staking out strategies, but also develop new channels of communication with the rank and file and engage in more intraparty

Social dem: gradually luring blue collar in favor of white collar

debates. In the new strategic environment, social democratic parties thrive on internal conflict, not consensus, as long as they are able to find collectively binding solutions to the ongoing discord about strategy. Parties must manage heterogeneity and strategic capacity simultaneously. They can bind electorates only by mapping societal conflicts and resolving them case by case. Whereas social democratic parties of the past often treated political currents and tendencies as reprehensible signs of political decay, in the new environment they may actually be indicators of the parties' vitality and capacity to build more encompassing political coalitions. The pressures toward adopting the stratified cadre party as a model increases with the realignment of party competition away from purely distributive conflict toward conflict along the left-libertarian versus right-authoritarian axis and with the strategic feasibility of pivoting (executive office seeking) as an alternative to vote-maximizing party objectives. These conditions put a premium on new inputs from below and on strategic autonomy from above.

Conventional models view leader–activist relations as a zero-sum game: If the rank and file are empowered, party leaders are weakened and vice versa. In contrast, I see other possible combinations and outcomes. Both rank-and-file dominance over a weak leadership and leaders' autonomy over a docile mass membership promote strategic inertia, which keeps a social democratic party from adapting to the new challenges of the electoral marketplace in postindustrial capitalism. Where the recentering of political competition around left-libertarian and right-authoritarian challenges is strong, only those social democratic parties which find a more productive linkage between innovative political inputs from the membership and strategic capacities of the leadership are likely to succeed. A party faces greater adjustment problems of its organizational structure to new competitive conditions the more entrenched the historically grown structures of mass party organization are that resist debureaucratization (path dependent learning). Often only momentous electoral crises enable party activists to mobilize around new political visions and leaders, who then refashion a party's formal statutes and actual power distribution.

The process of organizational and strategic choice, however, is not just constrained by systemic competitive conditions and internal rules of party politics, but also by the less tangible influence of the political language and ideas that have informed social democratic politics in preceding decades. Established modes of political discourse affect the range of arguments that can count on acceptance from party activists and prestructure avenues of ideological innovation that result from the creative recombination of often time-honored ideas in light of new political experiences.

Social democratic party fortunes are particularly affected by the availability of alternatives to the discourse about distributive politics that has been defined by Marxian socialism, at one end of the political spectrum, and market liberalism, at the other. In countries where communitarian ideologies on the Left and the Right, such as anarchism and Catholic corporatism, have been of marginal importance in the twentieth century and where the primary political debates have always revolved around the polarity between rival distributive programs, social democratic parties find it particularly difficult to meet the new challenges of left-libertarian and right-authoritarian politics, because their vocabulary has no terms for capturing the new communitarian demands and aspirations. Decisive evidence of the role of ideas in shaping social democratic party fortunes is furnished by cases in which parties have failed to realize their strategic objectives in the 1980s. The direction of their deviation from more promising paths typically betrays the impact of ideology and organizational form on strategic choice.

## 1.5 THEORY AND PRACTICE OF EUROPEAN SOCIAL DEMOCRACY

Because a party's competitive situation, objectives, organization, and discursive universe affect its electoral performance, no simple formula does justice to the fortunes of any social democratic or socialist party in the 1970s and 1980s. What is required is a careful reconstruction of the dynamics in each party in light of these theoretical considerations. I conclude this chapter with a schematic overview of the main forces and choices that have influenced social democratic party fortunes in the nine countries I examine in detail in later chapters. I emphasize cross-sectional contrasts rather than each party's dynamic over time, the topic of detailed case studies in later chapters.[47]

Socialist parties who won votes in the 1980s faced highly varied competitive environments. In France, the left-libertarian political challenge remained modest after a brief surge in the mid-1970s, whereas the challenge of market liberalization and later of authoritarian and racist politics was far more important. Since the French socialists faced strong incentives for pivoting, there was a strong pull to win elections and assume executive power with a "centrist" strategy, which was foreshadowed by the 1981 presidential campaign but fully implemented only after 1983. This competitive situation placed a premium on the strategic autonomy of party leaders and a fairly fluid party organization. The combined effect of autonomous leaders and of cadre-like party structures held entrenched working-class organizations at arm's length from the party and kept it sensitive to periodically resurgent left-libertarian stirrings, although it failed to prevent the eventual rise of a new Green challenge.

In the 1980s, the Spanish socialists also faced a strategic situation making centripetal competition attractive. The Spanish socialists switched to a moderate strategy when technocratic constituencies entered its small cadre organization and displaced leftist currents, thus allowing the party leadership to refashion the party's governance structure in 1979. Yet the realignment of left-libertarian political forces around a new leftist electoral alternative made the socialists' centripetal office-seeking strategy costly in the 1986 and 1989 parliamentary elections, although the socialists continued to control the pivot of the system.

47 As the case studies will show, both strategic choices and competitive settings varied in each country from election to election.

Finally, in Italy, socialists faced a crowded field of leftist and libertarian competitors that ruled out a shift in that direction. The party's switch to a new centripetal strategy was preceded by organizational reform in the late 1970s. Yet the Italian socialists' success remained limited by its still large patronage-oriented mass party organization that slowed the party's strategic flexibility, eventually involving it in political scandals, and limited by the difficulties of winning a pivotal position in the highly fragmented competitive space of the Italian party system.

Nevertheless, all socialist "winners" in the 1980s diluted their organizational and electoral linkages to working-class constituencies, failed to develop or weakened the existing mass party organization, and moved away from leftist distributive appeals.

Socialist "stabilizers" in the 1980s pursued contrasting strategies in response to different competitive settings. At one extreme is the Dutch Labor Party. It abandoned mass party organization in the early 1970s and moved to a fluid cadre organization with little leadership autonomy. In an electoral environment with a highly mobilized left-libertarian cleavage and relatively few electoral incentives for centripetal competition, intraparty politics led to the adoption of an "oligopolistic" strategy directed against leftist competitors. At the other extreme, the Swedish social democrats faced both strong left-libertarian challenges and incentives for pivoting (executive office seeking) in the 1980s. Their entrenched mass party organization, which limited leadership autonomy, and a political discourse that contrasted state and market to the exclusion of communitarian concerns, made it difficult to abandon the party's distributive agenda in favor of either or both libertarian and market-capitalist challenges. Eventually, these difficulties led to the electoral defeats of 1988 and 1991.

The Belgian socialist parties also tended to stave off electoral instability in the 1980s by resisting strategic innovation in a competitive environment characterized by weak left-libertarian and right-authoritarian challenges. The parties' bureaucratic mass organization cemented this strategic commitment. The competitive situation changed only at the end of the decade as ecologists and parties of the New Right strengthened and created serious electoral difficulties for the Belgian socialists.

The three socialist "losers" in the 1980s all failed to gear their strategies to new conditions in the electoral marketplace, yet in each country different organizational and competitive conditions prevailed and were associated with unique ways of refashioning socialist strategies. The Austrian socialists adhered to an outmoded strategy for too long, the German social democrats wildly varied their strategies within too short a period of time, and the British Labour Party committed itself to a dramatic strategic reversal in the late 1970s.

In Austria, an entrenched mass party organization with limited leadership autonomy made it difficult for the socialists to respond to the emerging challenges of left-libertarian and right-authoritarian politics in the 1980s. Only once the party was caught up in a full-fledged electoral crisis, could a new leadership set the party on a course of organizational reform and strategic change.

In Germany, social democrats were torn between intense left-libertarian and right-authoritarian challenges that provided incentives for very different strategies of pivoting, vote maximization, and oligopolistic competition. At the same time, the moderately entrenched mass party organization, headed by a leadership constrained in its strategic autonomy, made it difficult to find a new strategic equilibrium with a consistent approach. As a consequence, party strategies oscillated over the entire range of alternatives without persevering with any particular course of action.

In Britain, finally, the Labour Party combined a fluid cadre organization with an accountable, constrained leadership. Because political alternatives in the competitive arena have remained centered around distributive conflicts more than in any other country with the possible exception of Belgium, a rather different organization with mass membership would have been more beneficial for the choice of electorally successful strategies. As things evolved in the 1970s, the party was captured by radical socialist minorities whose ideology was focused on the polarity between state and market to the exclusion of new communitarian issues. The radical strategy led the party into the electoral wilderness, because the competitive situation offered strong incentives for centripetal competition around vote- and office-seeking objectives. Efforts to reverse party strategy in the second half of the 1980s met limited success in part because the party's internal structure and methods of political coalition building were not radically changed.

## CONCLUSION

In this opening chapter, I have developed a theory of political preference formation in advanced capitalist democracies that sets the stage for parties to compete. I have also analyzed the general structure of competition in which socialist parties are immersed, the internal process of political coalition building within party organizations, and the ideological legacies that influence party strategies and ultimately affect their electoral payoffs. The applicability of my argument is not confined to social democratic parties, but can be extended as well to the strategic problems faced by moderate conservative parties competing against the new extreme Right in many European countries (see Kitschelt 1991d; forthcoming).

The theoretical model I employ to account for socialist party fortunes privileges forces and determinants internal to the arenas of party competition. To buttress the plausibility of this approach, it is instructive to review existing explanations of socialist politics that are more parsimonious and rely on variables external to the competitive electoral arena. The critique of external theories should demonstrate not only that such explanations are empirically inadequate, but also that their shortcomings can be traced to the omission of precisely those variables that are most prominently featured in my own analysis of social democratic party fortunes.

# 2

# Class structure and left party performance

In the previous chapter I proposed a new account of voter preference formation based on citizens' market and organizational experiences in the production sector and age or life cycle, gender, and experiences in the reproduction sector rather than on economic class. Moreover, parties' fortunes are not bound to particular socio-economic groups, but depend on parties' strategic choices in the arenas of interparty competition and intraparty decision making. Because this complex, non–class-based argument about voter alignments and party competition goes against the grain of much work in this area, in this chapter I examine the limitations that traditional class structural approaches building on stratification research and Marxist class theory encounter when they attempt to explain social democratic party fortunes in the 1970s and 1980s. Class approaches are more parsimonious than my own theoretical account. Yet my analysis in this chapter shows that any effort to remedy the theoretical and empirical flaws of class-based accounts of party fortunes calls for consideration of those popular political demands and those attributes and forces internal to the field of political competition I have proposed. The constructive purpose of this chapter on class theory is to illustrate the transformation of social structure in contemporary democracies and the ability of many social democratic parties to transcend a narrow working-class base. Social democrats do not face a simple "trade-off" between working-class and non–working-class support, but a considerable range of choices to assemble electoral coalitions.

I first examine a naive theory of class politics that contends socialist parties weaken in direct correspondence to the contraction of the blue collar industrial working class in advanced capitalism. In the main body of this chapter, however, I focus on the sophisticated class analysis of left party performance as it has been presented in *Paper Stones* (1986), a brilliant book by Adam Przeworski and John Sprague. That study provides the best conceivable case for a Marxist class analysis of political alignments. Przeworski and Sprague amend naive class theory by including some of the forces impinging on social democracy I feature in my own explanatory framework, most notably the formation of political preferences, party competition, and political organization. In the end, however, *Paper Stones* still remains much too wedded to conventional class analysis to make full use of party competition and party organization as determinants of left party fortunes.

## 2.1 CLASS AND PARTY PERFORMANCE: THE NAIVE THEORY

A naive theory of left party politics treats socialist electoral support as directly corresponding to the proportion of blue-collar workers in the labor force. Most electoral studies define the working class as manual occupations. If the main breadwinner in the household is or was a worker, all nonemployed household members are also counted as workers (homemakers, retirees, the unemployed). As this "core" constituency of social democratic politics becomes smaller, socialist parties inevitably lose electoral support.

Cross-national data of employment structure are usually not fully comparable, as even authors of published data sets emphasize (Flora, Kraus, and Pfennig 1987).[1] In order to increase the robustness of my inferences, Table 2.1 presents several data sets measuring the relative size of the working class. Furthermore, the decline of manufacturing in the sectoral composition of the labor force in Table 2.2 provides an indirect measure of working-class contraction. Sectoral change, however, may understate the decline of manual labor, as white collar employees replace workers within manufacturing at a higher rate than workers are added to growing service industries.

Even a cursory inspection of the tables shows that the varying electoral fortunes of socialist parties are all but unrelated to cross-national differences in the size of the working class or working-class decline over time. In Germany, the Sozialdemokratische Partei Deutschlands (SPD), for example, should have been electorally strong when its working class peaked in the 1950s and 1960s. Yet the SPD was at that time much weaker than social democratic parties in Austria, Denmark, Norway, and Britain and strengthened only at a time when the size of the German working class began to contract. Further, the SPD's decline in the 1980s cannot be attributed to change in social structure, because the French, Spanish, and Italian socialists won votes in that decade, although their working classes were shrinking as well. Similarly, the Swedish working class has contracted considerably since the early 1970s, yet change in the occupational structure left few traces in the party system until the late 1980s. Overall, deindustrialization from the early 1970s to the late 1980s is most pronounced in Belgium, Denmark, Norway, Sweden, and the United Kingdom, but each country's left parties had rather different careers.

To generalize the argument, we can explore for all cases how frequently changes in the strength of manufacturing industry and of blue collar occupations coincided with changes of left party strength in the periods from the early 1950s to the early 1980s and from the early 1970s to the most recent available data. After eliminating Spain, where left parties began to compete in free elections only in 1977, Tables 2.1

---

1 Przeworski and Sprague (1986: 194–200) describe the difficulties of constructing cross-nationally and intertemporally comparable measures of class structure.

Table 2.1. *Workers in the occupational structure, 1950s–1980s (percentage of the active work force)*

| | | Early 1950s | Early 1960s | Early 1970s | Early 1980s | Latest |
|---|---|---|---|---|---|---|
| Austria | A | 44.4 | 45.0 | 43.3 | — | — |
| | B | 37.4 | 39.6 | 39.6 | 37.0 | 35.0 (1988) |
| Belgium | A | 52.3 | 46.6 | 44.2 | — | — |
| | B | — | 47.1 | 45.2 | 32.1 (U: 10%)[a] | 30.2 (1988) |
| Denmark | A | 50.6 | 49.7 | 44.9 | — | — |
| | B | — | 38.7 | 38.6 | 27.2 (U: 9.3)[a] | 31.5 (1986) |
| France | A | 43.5 | 41.8 | — | — | — |
| | B | — | 38.5 | 34.6 (1968) | 30.9 (1982) | — |
| Germany | A | 50.9 | 50.9 | 45.6 | 40.0 | — |
| | B | — | 44.7 | 35.8 | 36.7 | 33.3 (1986) |
| Italy | A | 47.0 | 54.1 | 50.5 | (39.9) | |
| | B | — | 39.7 | 42.0 (U: 4.9)[a] | 36.0 (U: 10.6)[b] | — |
| Netherlands | A | 48.3 | 49.6 | 44.9 | — | — |
| | B | — | 42.8 | 35.4 | 27.0 (U: 7.4)[a] | 26.3 (1985) |
| Norway | A | 46.0 | n.d. | 48.0 | 45.0 | — |
| | B | — | 44.9 | 42.8 | 31.9 | 27.7 (1989) |
| Spain | A | — | — | 40.3 | — | — |
| | B | — | — | 39.7 | 38.0 | 37.1 (1988) |
| Sweden | A | 54.0 | n.d. | 52.0 | 43.0 | — |
| | B | — | 43.2 | 39.2 | 29.5 | 29.4 (1988) |
| United | A | 41.7 | 42.7 | 36.2 | 29.5 | — |
| Kingdom | B | — | 48.8 | 40.0 | 30.8 (U:10.8)[a] | — |

[a] A considerable portion of the unemployed (U) are (potentially) workers.
*Source:* Series A. Flora, Kraus and Pfennig (1987) for Austria, Belgium, Denmark, Germany, Italy, Netherlands, Norway, 1950s–1970s; Germany 1980: Cerny (1990: 274); Italy 1980: calculated from Biorcio and Natale (1989: 407–8); France: Jaffe (1980: 39); Norway: Esping-Andersen (1985: 52, 56); Spain 1970: Gunther, Sani, and Shabad (1986: 191); Sweden: Holmberg and Gilljam (1987: 185); United Kingdom: Crewe (1990: table 5). Series B. International Labour Office 1990a,b.

and ⧉    yield a total of twenty comparisons each. Parallel movements of class and party occur in exactly half of these comparisons, while the other half disconfirms the naive theory of class politics.

One can derive more precise estimates of the influence of class structure on left party strength from Eurobarometer surveys available for six of the countries in Tables 2.1 and 2.2 since 1976. These surveys employ identical definitions of occupational categories.[2] For each occupational group, the disposition to vote for a left party in a given survey can be employed to forecast a party's support at a later time assuming that the political dispositions of occupational groups remain the same as in the prior time period but the relative size of the groups changes. Thus, if

2 Definitions were changed in 1988. My comparison, therefore, includes only surveys taken between 1976 and 1987.

Table 2.2. *Percentage of the work force employed in industry*

|                | Early 1950s | Early 1970s | Latest 1985–87 |
|----------------|-------------|-------------|----------------|
| Austria        | 37.1        | 41.6        | 37.7           |
| Belgium        | 48.3        | 43.7        | 28.7           |
| Denmark        | 34.1        | 37.7        | 26.5           |
| France         | 35.7        | 34.7        | 30.9           |
| Germany        | 42.3        | 48.9        | 40.5           |
| Italy          | 30.4        | 42.2        | 32.6           |
| Netherlands    | 35.0        | 36.2        | 27.1           |
| Norway         | 36.5        | 37.3        | 26.5           |
| Spain          | 25.1        | 38.1        | 32.5           |
| Sweden         | 40.6        | 40.3        | 29.8           |
| United Kingdom | 49.2        | 42.2        | 30.2           |

*Source:* 1950 and 1970 data, except Spain: Flora, Kraus, and Pfennig (1987); Spain: Lieberman (1982: 88). 1985–87 data: Statistical Office of the European Community (1989: 117).

workers are most predisposed to support left parties but their electoral proportion declines, left parties should suffer electorally.

To eliminate fluctuations in party support over the course of electoral cycles, I compare average values of multiple surveys taken in the four-year periods of 1976–79 and 1984–87. Table 2.3 provides the average percentage of workers in each set of surveys [column (1)],[3] the percentage of workers voting for left parties [column (2)], and the actual support of these parties in both periods [column (3)]. Column 4 represents the expected left party support in 1984–87, had workers and nonworkers maintained the same disposition to support the Left as in 1976–79. Changes in the expected left electoral support from 1976–79 to 1984–87, then, are entirely based on changes in the class structure. Finally, I calculate the percentage of the actual changes in left electoral support between the two time periods that is actually accounted for in terms of class structure [column (5)].

Except for the case of the Italian Communist Party (PCI), changes in class structure account for only a minute share of left party electoral fortunes. In Britain, the decline of the working class accounts for 24% of the observed decline in Labour Party support. Socialist party performance in Belgium, France, Germany, Italy, and the Netherlands is unrelated to change in class structure. Given that survey results in all but two instances closely reflect the socialists' actual election results, these findings are plausible. As the first exception, survey support for the German social democrats rose from 43.1% (1976–79) to 47.1% (1984–87), while the party declined in the elections from about 43% (1976) to 37 percent (1987). The party was indeed more popular than its opponents during much of the 1984–87

3 The working class includes only respondents actually employed in blue collar jobs, not individuals inactive in labor markets, even though they may be dependent on working-class breadwinners.

Table 2.3. Changes in class structure as predictor of left party performance

| | (1) Percentage of workers in samples | | | (2) Percentage of workers voting for left parties | | (3) Total support for left parties (% of all respondents) | | (4) Expected support for the left in 1984–87 based on 1976–79 dispositions | (5) Percentage of difference between actual and expected left vote, 1984–87, explained by change in the class structure since 1976–79 |
|---|---|---|---|---|---|---|---|---|---|
| | 1976–79 | 1984–87 | | 1976–79 | 1984–87 | 1976–79 | 1984–87 | | |
| Belgium (PSB/BSP) | 29.1 | 29.9 | | 38.1 | 41.8 | 26.9 | 30.8 | 26.9 | 0 |
| France (PS/PCF) | 26.2 | 24.8 | PS: | 44.1 | 38.8 | 39.0 | 34.9 | 38.9 | 2 |
| | | | PCF: | 23.1 | 12.6 | 13.0 | 7.0 | 12.8 | 3.3 |
| Germany (SPD) | 31.3 | 24.1 | | 53.4 | 54.8 | 43.1 | 47.0 | 42.0 | 0 |
| | | | | | | | (37.0) | | (18) |
| Italy (PSI/PCI) | 23.9 | 20.9 | PSI: | 21.3 | 17.3 | 19.1 | 18.0 | 19.1 | 0 |
| | | | PCI: | 45.3 | 46.9 | 28.1 | 27.6 | 27.4 | 71 |
| | | | combined: | 66.6 | 64.2 | 47.2 | 45.6 | 46.5 | 0 |
| Netherlands (PvdA) | 31.6 | 21.5 | | 53.3 | 49.8 | 34.3 | 36.1 | 31.5 | 44 |
| United Kingdom | 47.8 | 39.7 | | 54.4 | 41.5 | 42.3 | 33.9 | 40.3 | 24 |

*Source:* All calculations are based on the average percentage of voters expressing a party preference in the Eurobarometers 5–12 (1976–79) and 21–28 (1984–87). Workers are a percentage of the active population, excluding homemakers and retirees.

term, yet it was defeated in the election. Class dispositions to vote social democratic in 1976, however, predict only 18% of the party's correct result in 1987. The first exception is the Italian Socialist Party (PSI), whose electoral support is vastly overstated in the 1976–79 surveys. Given that Communist Party support is understated, but joint support about accurately represented, one could employ the political dispositions of occupational groups in 1976–79 to vote for PSI or PCI in order to predict the support of both parties in 1984–87. Even then, however, class structure explains only a fraction of the Left's electoral change.

Other electoral studies confirm the validity of the findings in Table 2.3. Even though support for the British Labour Party fell when the working class contracted, studies by Rose and MacAllister (1986) and Crewe (1990) found that only about half of Labour's long-term decline can be accounted for by changes in the social structure. Changes in Swedish class structure since 1956 would have led to a decline of the Swedish Social Democrats (SAP), had not both workers and nonworkers become more disposed to vote for the Left (Holmberg and Gilljam 1987: 186).

If working-class size does not explain trends in left party voting, changes in working class and non–working-class *dispositions* provide the key for understanding electoral outcomes. Studies of voter behavior in fact show not only that class *varies* as a determinant of voting behavior across countries, but also that in most countries the class structuring of the vote has progressively declined over time, though with a different pace and rhythm.[4]

In Sweden especially, but also in Britain and Austria, class was traditionally the strongest predictor of voting behavior. Yet in Sweden the predictive value of class fell from 53% of the variance in 1956 to 34% by 1985 (Holmberg and Gilljam 1987: 223), with young and female voters being least influenced by class position. At the same time, the predictive power of opinions on issues has risen from 23% to 57% of the variance (p. 292).[5] Similarly, in Britain, manual workers are increasingly less inclined to support Labour. Secondary class attributes, such as union membership or residence in public housing, have a more resilient, but still declining influence on voting decisions.[6] In the 1983 election, the Labour Party suffered a much worse drop in electoral support among labor union members and manual workers than among the professional and managerial occupations. Also, by the early and mid-1980s, issues and ideologies influenced voting much more than did

4 The most comprehensive evidence for such trends has recently been presented by Franklin et al. (1992).
5 This trend was continued in the 1988 election. Cf. Gilljam and Holmberg (1990: 269–75).
6 Important studies are Särlvik and Crewe (1983: 103), Crewe (1985a: 134), Franklin (1985: 110), and Crewe (1990). The only dissenters from this line of reasoning are Heath, Jowell, and Curtice (1985), who in turn were criticized by Crewe (1986) and Scarbrough (1987). Claims advanced by Dunleavy and Husbands (1985: 142) that differences in public or private consumption (housing, health care, transportation, etc.), have so far been insufficiently substantiated because the explanatory power of class and consumption theories has not been directly compared (cf. Scarbrough 1987: 229–30).

occupation, income, union membership, or housing.[7] Austrian investigations, too, conclude that issue orientations and party identification explain considerably more variance in voting behavior than the socioeconomic or religious attributes of voters (cf. Haerpfner 1985; Plasser, Ulram, and Grausgruber 1987: 249). By the mid-1980s, workers' households accounted for only 53% of the socialists' electorate (Plasser 1989: 47).

In a second group of countries, which includes France, Germany, and Italy, class has been a moderately powerful socioeconomic determinant of voting behavior. Yet, here too, class lost ground in the 1970s and 1980s. In all three countries, religion tends to be the strongest predictor of voting behavior. In France, occupation is a close second (Mayer 1986: 162) or even slightly ahead of religion (Lewis-Beck 1984), yet both pale in importance compared to left–right self-placement (Lewis-Beck 1988: 82). Furthermore, in the 1986 and 1988 elections the class distinctiveness of French party electorates continued to decline, while the division between private and public sector employees became more pronounced.[8] In Germany as well, class has declined as a voting determinant, especially among younger citizens (Dalton 1984: 129), whereas religion has continued to hold its own.[9] Union membership is a class residual that is a better predictor of voting behavior than occupation (cf. Berger et al. 1987: 267). Similar observations apply to Italy, where religion and class or union membership have been displaced by left–right self-placement (Allum and Mannheimer 1985; Lewis-Beck 1988: 82).

In a third group of countries, which includes Belgium and the Netherlands, class has always been a weak structuring element of the vote, and ideological voting tends to supplant whatever is left of socioeconomic determinants. In the Netherlands, common socioeconomic and cultural voter attributes, such as income, occupation, education, religion, or age, play at best an indirect role when compared to strong voting predictors, such as left–right self-placement, post-materialism, or attitudes toward the legalization of abortion.[10] In Belgium, class has often been overwhelmed by religious and ethnolinguistic divisions (Hill 1974; Frognier 1975) and has remained a weak structuring element of the vote (Knutsen 1988). Finally, in Spain, which has experienced competitive democracy only recently, class, religion, and labor union membership appear to play some role, but are dwarfed by the impact of citizens' positions on the left–right scale on voting behavior.[11]

7 Relevant findings are reported in Robertson (1984: 203, 219), Franklin (1985: ch. 6), Rose and McAllister (1986: 115–37), and McAllister and Mughan (1987, 57). Lewis-Beck (1988: 82) finds that class is a weaker predictor of voting than ideology or economic voting.

8 For opinion polls of recent French elections backing these arguments see Bell and Criddle (1987; 1988), Guyomarch and Machin (1989: 199), Levy and Machin (1986: 277) and Le Gall (1986: 14).

9 The decline of class relative to religion is documented by Baker, Dalton, and Hildebrandt (1981: 170, 190, 285), Pappi (1984), and Schmitt (1989).

10 This result can be gleaned from studies that vary in their research strategy and specific conclusions: Van der Eijk and Niemöller (1987), Irwin et al. (1987), Irwin and Holsteyn (1989), and Van Deth and Geurts (1989).

11 See Barnes, McDonough, and Pina (1985), Lancaster and Lewis-Beck (1986), and Gunther, Sani, and Shabad (1988).

In the six countries where the class structuring of the vote has declined from high or intermediate levels of determination, left party performance has varied considerably in the past two decades. In France and Italy, socialists have benefited from class destructuration. In Austria, Britain, and Germany, they have lost, and in Sweden, the result was mixed until the end of the 1980s. Analyses of the class structure and past class voting, taken by themselves, offer no clue as to why parties have had particular electoral fortunes in an environment of class decomposition.

## 2.2 CLASS AND PARTY STRATEGY: THE SOPHISTICATED THEORY

In *Paper Stones,* their analytically incisive and methodologically elegant study of electoral socialism, Przeworski and Sprague, in the future abbreviated as P/S (1986), forcefully argue that class position is not a brute determinant of left political fortunes. Instead, class is politically constructed in a complex process in which political actors create class identities and orientations that override other identities based on religion, ethnicity, or race (P/S 1986: 7–8). Przeworski and Sprague thus squarely call for a *theory of political preference formation* that does not confine itself to property relations. In contrast to sociological reconstructions of political preference formation, including my own account in the first half of the preceding chapter, the authors emphasize the role of *parties* in political class formation. Yet while parties shape classes, they do not do so under freely chosen conditions. Institutional arenas, occupational structure, and the history of past class formation constrain the strategic alternatives of politicians.

According to Przeworski and Sprague, the act of voting isolates individuals and thus has a profoundly disorganizing effect on the working class (P/S 1986: 54). For socialist politicians, the decision to participate in the electoral institutions removes the option of revolutionary struggle and makes it harder to build class unity. It opens the door for cross-class strategies based on appeals to "the people," "the masses," or "the poor." Electoral cross-class strategies are tempting for socialist politicians because the working class is usually in the minority. Hence, electoral majority support hinges upon cross-class appeals that necessarily dilute the ideological salience of class (P/S 1986: 45). Electoral socialism thus faces an unavoidable trade-off between the goal of workers' socialism and the democratic takeover of executive power. If socialists appeal to non–working-class "allies," they trade off the support of workers who become less motivated to vote on class identity and now are more likely to abstain or vote for parties with nonclass appeals.

Thus, in the initial process of class formation, electoral institutions and occupational class structures, mediated by politicians' preferences over electoral outcomes, shape voters' class orientations. Once preferences have been shaped, institutions and political power relations also determine the severity of electoral trade-offs between class and cross-class strategies. Trade-offs between workers and allies in the social democratic electorate are exacerbated if workers perceive an effective "exit option" to support other political forces when social democrats engage in cross-class appeals. Workers have more opportunities to exit from the social democratic fold when (1) strong communist parties are present, (2) ethnic and religious parties offer collective identifications other than class, and (3) labor unions lack encompassing organization and tight linkages to social democratic parties that would make it costly for workers to abandon their class ties.

Based on econometric models estimating the class composition of left party electorates over several decades, Przeworski and Sprague identify two corporatist countries with weak communist parties and hence minimal electoral trade-offs, Denmark and Norway. The two other Scandinavian countries, Sweden and Finland, have intermediate trade-offs. Three additional European countries – Belgium, France, and pre-1933 Germany – have the most severe trade-offs because corporatism is absent, communists are serious electoral contenders, and nonsocialist competitors campaign on religious or ethnic cross-class appeals.

After the conclusion of initial class formation, Przeworski and Sprague see workers' preferences and electoral trade-offs as constants. Socialist politicians then can decide only whether and how to choose a strategy that reaches the party's maximum electoral "carrying capacity" with the existing trade-off parameter at the point where the marginal gain of allies is exactly offset by the loss of workers. Parties actually pursue sub-optimal strategies because internal constituencies, such as party activists and labor unions, may prevent party leaders from choosing the optimal strategy or because leaders have a short tenure and focus on short-term electoral gains that undermine long-term success (P/S 1986: 119–25).

Because trade-off parameters remain constant, however, party leaders' deliberate choices and mistakes have only a modest influence on the parties' electoral fate over the long run (P/S 1986: 126). With fixed trade-offs, a party's carrying capacity and constraint on electoral success depends on the proportion of workers in the population alone. A voluntarist view of class formation thus leads Przeworski and Sprague to a pessimistic and determinist view of the future of socialist parties as captives of socioeconomic change:

And they do not have much of a choice: their organizational links, their ideological commitments, their daily habits, and their political projects tie them to their working-class roots. They are thus more likely to turn inward, to their working-class base, and suffer the electoral consequences. . . . Ashamed of looking too far forward, mortally afraid of appearing irresponsible, left-wing political parties view socialism with embarrassment. Thus the era of electoral socialism may be over. (P/S 1986: 185)

While *Paper Stones'* melancholy conclusion has contributed much to its provocative appeal, the book's analytical model deserves serious attention. Przeworski and Sprague emphasize the significance of a Marxist conception of class, while at the same time introducing constitutive elements of the theoretical account of social democratic party fortunes I have proposed in Chapter 1: political preference formation, interparty competition, and intraparty political conflict and coalition building. But Przeworski and Sprague cannot take advantage of the full potential of this richer theoretical framework because class enjoys explanatory priority. This results in two major weaknesses in their work. First, which political appeals shape class formation and electoral trade-offs remains unclear. Second, the nature and the effects of party competition and working-class organization for social democratic electoral payoffs in varying societal settings is not sufficiently explored. If these criticisms are correct, class trade-offs in socialist parties' electorates, in the way conceptualized by Przeworski and Sprague, are empirically improbable. The ultimate objective of my critique, then, is to show the absence of class trade-offs and to interpret the socioeconomic class composition of social democratic electorates within a non-Marxist and explicitly political theoretical framework.

## Class appeal and preference formation

Although Przeworski and Sprague place great emphasis on a voluntarist political theory of class formation, they do not specify (1) what programmatic appeals promote a sense of class identity among workers and (2) why a class appeal simultaneously repels potential allies and results in a trade-off. As a consequence, the theory of party strategy lacks micro-foundations (Panitch 1987: 491; Burowoy 1989: 64).

Leftist parties must teach workers to *see* society in terms of class relations (P/S 1986: 48) and to "struggle for those interests that are attached to workers as a collectivity – those that constitute public goods to workers as a class" (p. 54). Revolutionary socialism evidently does not meet these criteria because it appeals to the good of humanity, a benefit to virtually everyone rather than to a particular class. As Przeworski elaborates elsewhere, workers themselves may be opposed to socialism because (1) its benefits are distant and uncertain and (2) it would impose the task of promoting the good of *society at large* on the working class (Przeworski 1985: ch. 5, 6).[12]

Przeworski and Sprague evidently search for appeals that offer particular "club goods" that accrue *only* to workers and thus create a working-class consciousness. Yet even parties with strong working-class support, such as the Swedish SAP, in fact have appealed to the electorate on the basis of universalistic claims to promote economic security and minimum standards of living for all, not special benefits to the working class (cf. Tingsten 1941/1973; Sainsbury 1980; Tilton 1990). Welfare state programs *either* help constituencies much broader than the working class (family benefits, health insurance, social security), *or* they benefit particular sectors and occupations that cross cut class divisions (e.g., unemployment insurance schemes, public housing).

12 King and Wickham-Jones (1990: 394) have argued that Przeworski and Sprague's reconstruction of the socialist parties' strategic dilemma is inconsistent with Przeworski and Wallerstein's theory that the working class refrains from pursuing socialism. Whereas the former presupposes that workers want socialism, the latter shows that they do not. But Przeworski and Sprague never argue that workers want socialism. They claim only that workers are attracted to socialist parties by the prospect of particular "appeals" and "visions" that are never identified with socialism or anything else. Socialism presupposes a revolutionary party, abandoning the democratic majority principle, *outside* the electoral arena. For this reason, it is not an argument against P/S to point out that workers abandon left parties when their socialist appeals radicalize. What saves P/S from King and Wickham-Jones' critique is their vagueness about working-class "appeals" by left parties.

Przeworski and Sprague's archetype of the workerist party appeal appears to be the SPD in Weimar Germany, which even after 1927 "continued to behave as an electoral pressure group of unionized workers" (P/S 1986: 72). The authors do not identify the particular appeals that were designed to target only workers, nor do they consider whether it was the historical conjuncture that made unionized workers especially amenable to the party's otherwise universalist demands for state-regulated wage settlements, unemployment insurance, and public housing.

The identification of class strategy with pressure group politics in pursuit of particular club goods reveals a contradiction in Przeworski and Sprague's account of class. If class formation results from political appeals, as a voluntarist account would hold, it is not obvious why ambitious socialist politicians would want to forge "classness" around club goods delivered to a narrow occupational category of blue collar workers. Yet at the same time, Przeworski and Sprague advance a highly restrictive and objectivist definition of the working class as "manual wage earners in mining, manufacturing, construction, transport and agriculture and their inactive household members" (P/S 1986: 35), excluding even manual workers in "unproductive" sectors and white collar employees. Przeworski and Sprague thus postulate a *social* formation of the working class that precedes politics, but they never explain which social experiences and dispositions constrain politicians' voluntarist efforts to shape *political* class formation.

The emergence of "trade-offs" between workers and allies in socialist electoral strategy remains in doubt as long as it is unclear which club good appeals and party self-interests promote narrow political class formation confined to productive blue collar workers. Moreover, the existence of electoral trade-offs may be contingent upon the specific nature of socialist party appeals and the time and places when they were issued and cannot be generalized over long periods of time and wide variations of party strategies.

To illustrate this argument, consider Figure 2.1 where a hypothetical socialist party's electoral payoffs among workers and allies are contingent upon its strategic stance. Should the party adopt a radical revolutionary strategy, it is likely to draft more intellectuals than workers into its ranks.[13] If the party were to abandon sectarian politics, its support among both workers and allies might gradually pick up (Bandwagon I). Beyond a certain point, however, the party's workerist appeal may demobilize intellectuals without attracting other allies, thereby generating an electoral trade-off. If the party were to move beyond narrow laborist concerns to the bread-and-butter issues of social reform politics, it might gradually attract greater numbers of workers, but also less educated allies among lower salaried employees, artisans, or farmers (Bandwagon II). Such a supraclass strategy, however, may cross into a region where further gains of allies come only at the expense of workers' support levels, generating another trade-off zone. Finally, party strategy may become so indistinguishable from bourgeois competitors that workers and allies alike abandon the party ("negative" Bandwagon III).

---

13 This hypothesis is consistent with the electoral composition of many radical revolutionary parties, e.g., in Italy and France during the 1970s.

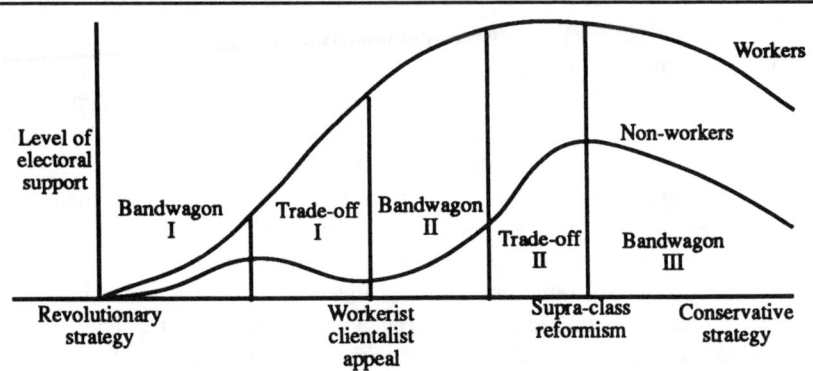

Figure 2.1. The relationship between workers' and allies' support for left parties

Over time and across countries the same socialist strategy may be perceived by workers and allies in different ways and thus yield different bandwagons and trade-offs. For example, the transformation of occupational experiences, standards of living, and social security in advanced capitalism make it implausible that workers and nonworkers are politically mobilized by the same issues as fifty years earlier and that the *relationships* among the political interests of various occupational groups have remained the same. Policies concerning the scope and structure of the welfare state, industrial development, foreign trade, the environment, or the family are more likely to divide broad class categories into fragments than to pit workers against allies. Hence, socialist party fortunes cannot be accounted for by the mechanics of class trade-offs.[14]

### Class organization and party strategy

Once parties have gone through a particular trajectory of political class formation over a number of years, Przeworski and Sprague see them as captives of their

14 Because Przeworski and Sprague insist on reading class trade-offs into socialist party strategies in the 1970s and 1980s, they arrive at entirely misleading interpretations, such as the claim that the German SPD lost the 1983 election because of its cross-class strategy (P/S 1986: 64). In fact, the SPD lost an equal share of workers (from 62% to 55% of this group) as of white collar employees (from 50% to 43%), indicating a negative bandwagon rather than a trade-off. In a similar vein, Przeworski and Sprague's (1986: 72) claim that in France "the Socialist Party continues to be pinched between the need for middle-class support and the threat that workers might defect to the Communists" is misleading. In fact, the workerist rhetoric of the French Communist Party (PCF) did most to antagonize its own working-class clientele, which fell in absolute and relative terms in the Communist electorate; conversely, the PS increased its share of workers in the 1981 elections despite its moderate supraclass appeal in the campaign year, as documented in the party's election manifesto, the *110 Propositions* that superseded the brief interlude of radical rhetoric, the *Projet Socialiste* of 1979. Moreover, contrary to Przeworski and Sprague's claim of a strong trade-off between workers and allies, workers did not return to the PCF once the PS government began to pursue a supraclass policy.

historical strategies, prisoners of the "cumulative consequences of the strategies pursued by political parties of the Left" (P/S 1986: 9) that cement the trade-offs between workers and allies in socialist party electorates. These authors ignore the fact that for trade-off parameters to persist over long periods of time, conditions that shape the severity of trade-offs must remain stable, such as the existence of strong communist parties, ethnic or religious parties, and labor corporatism. Not only changes in the socioeconomic organization of society, however, but also changes in the field of party competition and the organization of parties themselves may undercut the inexorable and constant electoral trade-offs that are said to preside over left party fortunes. Although such institutions as well as the strategies of socialist competitors are subject to flux, Przeworski and Sprague never model the variable ways socialist parties may respond to changing opportunity structures to prevent workers from exiting from their political camp.

Furthermore, as a consequence of the socioeconomic transformation of advanced capitalism the causal impact of the institutions and constraints that determine trade-offs on the electoral consequences of social democratic party strategies itself has changed. Przeworski and Sprague postulate that socialist parties that enjoy close ties to encompassing and centralized labor unions and face no communist or culturally based party competitors have the greatest capacity to fight electoral decline and have the mildest trade-offs in the class composition of their electorate. I argue the contrary. It is the organizational encapsulation of shrinking traditional low-skill manufacturing constituencies and the absence of competitors with cross-class appeal that reduce the strategic flexibility of contemporary socialist parties and prevent them from producing electoral bandwagons among critical segments of the high-skill blue collar and white collar work force. This constraint operates *regardless* of the severity of electoral trade-offs predicted by Przeworski and Sprague's model.[15] Contrary to their predictions, socialist parties have been more successful where they have been able to exploit a declining communist party, weak labor unions, and a new electoral configuration in which it pays for both socialist and bourgeois parties to package their appeals into programs that are more complex than those based primarily on class and economic redistribution.

Hence, socialists tend to perform better in those competitive systems where Przeworski and Sprague would predict the most severe constraints on their electoral maneuverability. Among the cases Przeworski and Sprague discuss in their book, the alternative hypothesis is borne out by the spectacular rise of the French socialists in the 1970s and 1980s, a party expected to face severe trade-offs, as well as the extraordinary performance of the German SPD in the 1960s and 1970s. Conversely, in countries with mild to moderate trade-offs located in Scandinavia, social democrats have barely held on to their electorates in the 1970s and 1980s

---

15 Przeworski and Sprague (1986: 115–19) argue that the encapsulation of the working class prevented Scandinavian social democracy from pursuing an electorally optimal cross-class strategy mandated by a small trade-off between workers and allies. But if institutional constraints override opportunities and limits set on socialist party strategy, why then construct the conditions of socialist party success around trade-off parameters at all?

(Sweden until 1985) or suffered serious losses (Denmark, Finland, Norway, and lately also Sweden). These electoral trajectories cannot be accommodated in Przeworski and Sprague's model and call for an alternative explanation.

## Trade-offs: Conceptualization and evidence

In spite of the theoretical problems of *Paper Stones,* Przeworski and Sprague generate some empirical evidence that at least partially appears to corroborate the trade-off argument. I show now, however, that these empirical plausibility probes employ inadequate mathematical models. Moreover, they cannot explore whether trade-off parameters change over time. In order to estimate trade-off parameters among classes and thus party strategies with econometric techniques, the time series of left party electoral support must be sufficiently long. A purely methodological constraint compels Przeworski and Sprague to assume, without further empirical and theoretical justification, that workers' and allies' preferences remain fixed over many decades. Furthermore, the authors calculate each country's trade-off parameters from a limited range of observations about left party support and class composition up to about 1970. Yet they extrapolate about ideal points outside that range ("carrying capacities"). Counterfactual propositions about party strategy and performance, however, become less reliable as they move further away from the actual range of observations employed to estimate a theoretical model (Lichbach 1984: 447).[16] The occupational structure of advanced capitalist countries has undergone considerable change since the last time points Przeworski and Sprague include. For this reason, estimates based on elections between the 1920s and 1960s are not a good predictor of developments in the 1970s and 1980s.

The most serious empirical problem, however, is the mathematical modeling of the constraint hypothesis. The change in the proportion of workers supporting left parties ($W$) between election $t$ and $t + 1$ [$W(t + 1) - W(t)$] is a function of the proportion of all workers ($X$) at $t + 1$ that had not yet been recruited to vote for the Left at $t$ (i.e., [$X(t + 1) - W(t)$] and the *level* of allies' left party support in election $t$ [$N(t)$]. A trade-off exists if the parameter $d$ estimating the influence of allied support at $t$ on the ability of left parties to recruit new workers at $t + 1$ is negative:

$$W(t + 1) - W(t) = p \ [X(t + 1) - W(t)] - dN(t)$$

Przeworski and Sprague do not explain why the *change rate* of worker support for the Left between two elections should be modeled as a function of the *level* of allied support in the earlier election. Closer examination reveals that their choice biases the model in favor of finding a trade-off, as the example depicted in Table 2.4 shows. From election to election, the proportion of the working class and of allies moves closely in tandem, revealing no trade-off, *provided* we measure trade-off as the change rate of the proportion of voters in each group that supports the Left in one election as compared to the preceding one. In contrast, with Przeworski

16 This is not to deny that counterfactual arguments are often critical for comparative political analysis, as Fearon (1991) has recently argued.

and Sprague's equation using levels of allied support in the preceding election as a predictor of change rates of working-class support to the next election, the very same figures lead us to conclude that there is a fairly strong trade-off; the higher allied support is in the preceding election, the more workers' left party support declines in the subsequent election. And since good elections are often followed by bad elections and vice versa, it is likely that Przeworski and Sprague's model yields a negative trade-off.[17] Yet given that *change rates* of both workers' and allies' support move in parallel, there is no reason to call the observed pattern a trade-off between different class constituencies.[18]

Even though Przeworski and Sprague employ statistical models that bias results in favor of their conclusion, their own empirical evidence supports the hypothesized trade-offs only weakly. Primarily, *Paper Stones* provides no independent empirical data on the parties' class composition. Parameters for the parties' ability to gain voters among workers and allies are those "which best reconstruct the historical record of votes obtained by particular parties or the Left as a whole in each country" (P/S 1986: 66). Estimating the parties' class composition is thus an exercise in curve fitting to a biased model. This explains why the claimed results do not hold up well when confronted with the evidence generated by voter surveys.

For example, survey evidence shows that the Swedish and Norwegian social democrats have a similar electoral class composition, yet according to Przeworski and Sprague, they have profoundly different carrying capacities, strategic payoffs, and class compositions of their electorate (cf. Sainsbury 1990). Moreover, in France, Germany, and Belgium, Przeworski and Sprague estimate socialist carrying capacities that are far lower than actual electoral results in the 1970s or 1980s. Also the survey data Przeworski and Sprague (1986: 149–58) employ in a later chapter provides little support for their theory. For example, their model predicts that the French, German and Swedish parties in the post–World War II period rely on increasingly workerist strategies, signaled by a rising Alford index of class voting measured by the difference between the percentage of workers and non-workers supporting socialist parties (P/S 1986: 165). Instead, surveys show a continuous decline of Alford indices in these countries (cf. Franklin et al. 1992).

17  Michael Wallerstein has pointed out to me that Przeworski and Sprague's "trade-offs" then follow as a consequence of a simple "regression toward the mean." "If social democratic election results are a stochastic process with $v(t) = F(x(t)) + u(t)$, where $F(x(t))$ represents the predictable aspects of the vote (based on the class structure and past party strategies or whatever you like) and $u(t)$ is a random variable with a mean of zero, then an unusually good election is likely to indicate a high value of $u(t)$. The probability that $u(t + 1) < u(t)$, and therefore that $v(t + 1) < v(t)$ if $x$ doesn't change very much, will be high. When $u(t)$ is unusually low, then it is likely that $u(t + 1) > u(t)$ and the social democrats will do better in the subsequent election" (personal communication).

18  Other ways to measure class trade-offs yield results no more promising for Przeworski and Sprague's thesis than my own. Thus, Lichbach (1984) models trade-offs as the impact of left party class composition $[q \{W(t) - N(t)\}]$ on both workers' and allies' left party support at election $t + 1$. In contrast to Przeworski and Sprague, he discovered that working-class strategies are best for the Swedish, Danish, and British Left and worst for their German comrades. None of these strategies involved trade-offs between workers' and allies' support, a configuration he found only in Australia.

Table 2.4. *Trade-off or not? Hypothetical example of left party class composition in seven elections*

| Election | Proportion of a class supporting the Left | | Change in the proportion of a class supporting the Left | |
|---|---|---|---|---|
| | Workers | Allies | Workers | Allies |
| 1 | 55 | 22 | — | — |
| 2 | 58 | 23 | +3 | +1 |
| 3 | 62 | 28 | +4 | +5 |
| 4 | 57 | 23 | −5 | −5 |
| 5 | 59 | 25 | +2 | +2 |
| 6 | 52 | 19 | −7 | −6 |
| 7 | 56 | 23 | +4 | +4 |

## 2.3 ELECTORAL TRADE-OFFS AND BANDWAGONS

Przeworski and Sprague's *Paper Stones* is an impressive achievement because it provides the most rigorous comparative framework for analyzing left party fortunes to date. My critique has shown, however, that there are empirical and theoretical reasons for questioning its validity. In particular, the trade-off hypothesis is theoretically unfounded and empirically unproven, provided we employ unbiased estimation models. I now explain why, according to the theoretical framework I outlined in the first chapter, one would not necessarily expect class trade-offs. I then test the rival accounts of left party class composition with aggregate survey data.

The critical reason why there is no simple trade-off between workers and white collar allies in social democratic electorates in the post–World War II period is that social democratic parties cannot appeal to "club goods" exclusively benefiting blue collar workers in "productive" industries because such club goods simply do not exist. The main party planks of moderate social democratic parties – particularly full employment policies and comprehensive welfare states – attract a much broader audience. Conversely, revolutionary rhetoric or radical programs calling for the expropriation of capitalists antagonize large segments of blue collar workers and are more appealing to certain fringe constituencies (intellectuals, small peasants). As social democratic parties move along the economic policy dimensions between extreme left expropriatory and moderate left redistributive policies, their support among blue collar workers and white collar employees thus tends to change *in tandem*.

The same dynamic applies in the 1970s and 1980s as well, but it is further complicated by the increasing salience of communitarian issues on the libertarian-versus-authoritarian policy dimension. Figure 2.2 simplifies the analytical schemes presented in the first chapter by distributing high-skill client-interactive non–working-class jobs and low-skill object-processing mostly working-class jobs, but also white collar jobs, over the two-dimensional ideological space.

Assuming the absence of other competitors in the lower left sector of the electorate, a social democratic party that attempts to maximize workerist support would probably locate in a moderate redistributive, but slightly authoritarian position at $W^*$.[19] Workers' constituencies are effectively lost by moving away from authoritarian positions toward more libertarian stances at $SD_{2''}$. In contrast, by moving only along the economic policy dimension from $W^*$ to $W^{**}$, the party would first appeal to different groups of workers (intraclass trade-offs), but then more extreme redistributive positions would lead to a net loss of workers. Social democratic parties would incur the greatest losses among workers if they moved to socialist *and* libertarian positions at $SD_{2'}$. At the same time, social democrats would probably maximize their overall electoral support by taking positions somewhere between $SD_{2'}$ and $SD_{2''}$.[20]

At least in the 1970s and 1980s, social democratic parties thus are likely to perform best if they are least captured by blue collar working-class constituencies. The lower the Alford index of working-class support, the more social democratic parties enjoy strategic flexibility. This is typically the case in party systems with cross-class cleavages that highlight the communitarian political dimension. Moreover, an ailing communist rival and weak organizational linkages to labor unions promote the socialists' strategic capacity. Hence, socialist parties are bound to thrive just under those conditions where Przeworski and Sprague are led to expect the most severe trade-offs, the most constrained "carrying capacity" and the greatest potential for the demise of socialist parties. Whether or not socialist parties take *advantage* of such strategic opportunities, however, is yet another matter and requires close analysis of the structure of party competition and the internal organization of the parties. For this reason, I do not expect a direct positive linkage between lack of external constraints and electoral bandwagons.

In order to test Przeworski and Sprague's hypotheses and my alternative, I have selected two types of data sets. One is composed of national election studies which provide information on the patterns of class voting. Data of this type are available for at least nine elections covering the period of the 1950s to the mid-1980s for Britain, Denmark, France, Germany, and Sweden. I have added data on seven Norwegian elections. For Italy, three time points are available, a number too small for statistical analysis.[21] The working class is generally defined as manual work-

---

19 It is well possible that parties of the authoritarian New Right force themselves into a space where they become attractive to authoritarian workers. This, of course, would change the strategic consequences of social democratic appeals.

20 Again, this conjecture is contingent upon the location of the party's competitors, a topic discussed in detail in Chapter 4.

21 Data sources are as follows:
Britain (1951–87): Särlvik and Crewe (1983: 87) and Crewe (1990: 7)
Denmark (1964–84), Norway (1957–85), and Sweden (1956–85): Sainsbury (1990)
France: entire Left, legislative elections 1956–88 in Dalton (1988: 156); and Le Gall (1988: 21); socialists: (1956–68) in P/S (1986: 154) and Le Gall (1988: 19), 1988 with presidential election

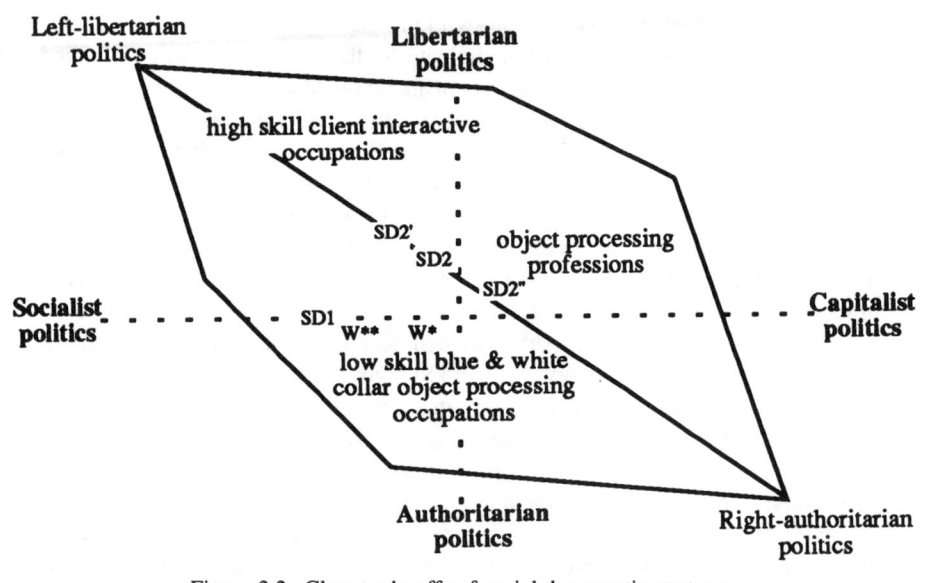

Figure 2.2.  Class trade-offs of social democratic strategy

ers, but also includes workers in the "unproductive" service sector. The definition of "allies" includes white collar employees and civil servants and, in some instances, all other non–working-class occupations. Individuals without occupation are classified by their former occupation or that of the household breadwinner. I could obtain no comparable data sets for Austria, Belgium, and the Netherlands. In Spain, too few elections have taken place to warrant analysis.

The second data set I have selected is composed of Eurobarometer surveys taken every six months from 1976 to the second half of 1987 or a total of twenty-four surveys each covering six of the nine countries that are at the center of my attention: Belgium, France, Germany, Italy, the Netherlands, and the United Kingdom. I have calculated the averages of manual working-class and white collar voting patterns for groups of four consecutive Eurobarometers each in order to overcome problems of small sample size and short-term volatility of parties' electoral support. With twenty-four Eurobarometers, this procedure yields six time points per country. In contrast to the elections data set, the working class and the salariat (allies) are defined here only as those who actually exercise an occupation. Homemakers, retirees, the unemployed, and students cannot be distributed onto the two main classes.

We can first test Przeworski and Sprague's biased mathematical model of trade-offs expressing left parties' ability to mobilize *more* workers at election $t + 1$ as a

only; communists (1981–88) in Le Gall (1988)
Germany (1957–87): Pappi (1973:191) and Berger et al. (1987: 267)
Italy (1963, 1968, 1976): calculated from Farneti (1985: 98)

negative function of the *level* of non–working-class allies' support at election *t* (Table 2.5). With the exception of the Italian PSI, the parameter estimate of allied support has the correct negative sign, yet in all but two instances, the correlation is weak and insignificant. The exceptions are the French Communist Party (data set I) and the Italian Communist Party (data set II).[22] Moreover, the data suggest that trade-offs are more severe in countries where Przeworski and Sprague would expect mild trade-offs, such as in Norway and Sweden, which have high socialist entrenchment in the working class. Conversely, the trade-offs appear to be mild for the German Left and the French Socialist Party (PS), where they hypothesize sharp trade-offs because the working-class is only weakly tied to socialist parties. Even the biased model indicates that party entrenchment in working class constituencies is a liability, not the asset Przeworski and Sprague claim.

The bias in Przeworski and Sprague's mathematical model of trade-offs yields theoretically strange results. This can be shown by regressing *levels* of working class support at election *t* on *change rates* of working class support from *t* to *t* + 1. Even this regression yields consistently negative and often significant coefficients.[23] Adopting Przeworski and Sprague's reasoning leads to the conclusion that the more workerist a party was at the previous election, the more workers it will lose at the next election. In reality, regressing levels of group support for socialist parties on change rates of group support only shows that good electoral times (high working-class *and* allied support for the Left) are inevitably followed by bad times (declines of support in both groups).

A more appropriate specification of class trade-offs relates change rates of workers' support for the Left to change rates of allies' support from one election to the next. A strategic trade-off requires significantly negative relations between the two change rates. A glance at Table 2.6 confirms the absence of trade-offs and instead the existence of positive bandwagons. Depending on the data set, the unstandardized regression coefficients reveal that such bandwagons are particularly strong among socialists in Norway, Britain, Denmark, Germany, and France. Only the Italian socialists experience a mild trade-off. The greatest (negative) bandwagon is experienced by the French Communist Party. It has suffered dramatic declines in voter support among *both* workers and allies in the last several decades. The relative strength of the bandwagons experienced by parties of the Left, however, can be explained only in light of a detailed analysis of their strategic appeals to distributive and communitarian issues and their politics of internal coalition building.

Przeworski and Sprague's theory of class trade-offs yields several further

22  Przeworski and Sprague (1986: 175) report much stronger correlations. In Norway the correlation is −.65 and in France −.88 for the entire Left and in the same range for the socialists. The authors, however, include only four to seven time points, compared to the seven to thirteen time points in my own data set.

23  Data can be obtained from the author. The negative relationship is significant for Denmark, France (PCF), and Germany in data set I, and for Belgium, France (PS and PCF), Germany, and the Netherlands in data set II.

Table 2.5. *The trade-off between workers and allies: changes in workers' support for the Left as a function of levels of allies' support for the Left in the previous election*

| | Data set I: 1950s–1980s | | | Data set II: 1976–1987 | | |
|---|---|---|---|---|---|---|
| | Intercept (t-value) | b (t-value) | Adjusted $R^2$ | Intercept (t-value) | b (t-value) | Adjusted $R^2$ |
| Belgium (PSB/BSP) | | | | 20.4 (1.31) | −.81 (−1.36) | .18 (N = 5) |
| Denmark (Left) | 10.1 (.65) | −.38 (.49) | .07  2255](N = 9) | | | |
| France (PS) | 7.0 (.60) | −.24 (−.60) | .05 (N = 8) | 41.2 (1.69) | −1.06 (−1.72) | .33 (p < .19) (N = 5) |
| (PCF) | 36.0 (39.9) | −3.18 (−51.3) | .99** (p < .01) (N = 3) | −.37 (−.09) | −.22 (−.44) | .06 (N = 5) |
| Germany (SPD) | 14.1 (1.47) | −.32 (−1.35) | .11 (N = 8) | 12.7 (.22) | −.28 (−.21) | .01 (N = 5) |
| Italy (PSI) | | | | −37.3 (−.94) | +1.87 (+.92) | .22 (N = 5) |
| (PCI) | | | | 20.3 (2.06) | −1.00 (−1.99) | .42 (p < .14) (N = 5) |
| Netherlands (PvdA) | | | | 2.6 (.69) | −.85 (−.73) | .15 (N = 5) |
| Norway (Left) | 67.9 (1.68) | −2.14 (−1.74) | .29 (p < .16) (N = 6) | | | |
| Sweden (Left) | 21.7 (1.64) | −.60 (−1.69) | .19 (p < .14) (N = 8) | | | |
| United Kingdom (Labour) | 22.2 (1.71) | −1.03 (−1.85) | .18 (p < .18) (N = 12) | 6.84 (.29) | −.35 (−.42) | .05 (N = 5) |

*Source:* Data set I: National Election Studies data (see fn. 21). Data set II: Eurobarometers 5–28.

Table 2.6. Change rates of allies' support for the left parties as predictor of change rates of workers' support

| | Data set I: 1950s–1980s | | | Data set II: 1976–1987 | | |
|---|---|---|---|---|---|---|
| | Intercept (t-value) | b (t-value) | Adjusted $R^2$ | Intercept (t-value) | b (t-value) | Adjusted $R^2$ |
| Belgium (PSB/BSP) | | | | -.33 (-1.03) | .34 (.77) | .17 (N = 5) |
| Denmark (Left) | -1.24 (-.75) | 1.23 (3.96) | .65 (p < .01) (N = 9) | | | |
| France (PS) | -1.23 (-.74) | 1.16 (5.84) | .83 (p < .001) (N = 8) | -.54 (-.34) | .76 (3.69) | .76 (p < .04) (N = 5) |
| (PCF) | -4.84 (-.72) | 2.84 (1.13) | .13 (N = 3) | -1.93 (-2.14) | .44 (1.38) | .19 (N = 5) |
| Germany (SPD) | .80 (.43) | .46 (1.66) | .20 (p < .15) (N = 8) | -2.05 (-1.56) | 1.62 (3.60) | .75 (p < .04) (N = 5) |
| Italy (PSI) | | | | 11.9 (.98) | -.63 (-1.07) | .03 (N = 5) |
| (PCI) | | | | 1.34 (.69) | .70 (1.44) | .21 (N = 5) |
| Netherlands (PvdA) | | | | -2.04 (-1.05) | +1.47 (4.41) | .82 (p < .02) (N = 5) |
| Norway (Left) | -.23 (-2.12) | 1.11 (1.75) | .29 (p < .16) (N = 6) | | | |
| Sweden (Left) | -.70 (-.70) | .27 (.64) | .06 (N = 8) | | | |
| United Kingdom (Labour) | -.74 (-.60) | 1.21 (2.62) | .35 (p < .03) (N = 12) | -.97 (-.32) | 1.29 (2.20) | .49 (p < .12) (N = 5) |

Source: Data set I: National Election Studies data (see fn. 21). Data set II: Eurobarometers 5–28.

testable propositions that can be confronted with rival predictions consistent with my alternative framework. According to *Paper Stones,* where trade-offs are mild and workers tend to have few exit options from the socialist camp because unions are tightly linked to left parties and serious communist or religious, ethnic, and communitarian parties do not compete for the workers' allegiance, socialists have the ability to pursue cross-class strategies with little loss of workers' support. Hence, a decline in the Alford index measuring the difference between the proportion of workers and allies supporting socialist parties should be accompanied by overall electoral success. Yet at the same time, because mild trade-offs presuppose strong union linkages and because unions insist on workerist party strategies, socialist parties should never stray far from workerist strategies. Over time, the proportion of workers in the socialist electorate will, therefore, remain high. Countries with few exit options for workers from the socialist camp are Denmark, Norway, Sweden, and Britain.[24] Indeed, in these countries the Alford index of socialist electoral support has been high.[25]

Przeworski and Sprague predict a different configuration for socialist parties in countries with strong incentives for workers to exit from the socialist camp and therefore severe class trade-offs in socialist electorates. Here weak linkages to labor unions enable socialists to pursue cross-class strategies yielding low Alford indices of the electorate's class composition. But strategic moves to cross-class strategies produce stiff electoral penalties when trade-offs are severe, because the gain of new allies is offset by the exit of a large number of workers. A decline of the Alford index should therefore be associated with electoral decline of socialist parties. In addition to the cases of Belgium, France, and Germany that Przeworski and Sprague discuss, electoral trade-offs would tend to be severe also in Italy and the Netherlands because workers can exit from the socialist coalition given the presence of cross-class appeals, strong communist parties, and weak union linkages. In all these instances, Alford index values tend to be low.[26]

In both groups of countries, for one reason or another Przeworski and Sprague believe parties cannot change their strategies dramatically and should be prepared to appeal to a fairly constant share of workers. Yet, contrary to their predictions, Table 2.7 demonstrates the existence of trends rather than equilibria in the percentage of workers supporting socialist and communist parties. Oddly, countries and parties where mild trade-offs indicate strong working-class loyalty to socialist parties, such as Denmark, Norway, Sweden, and Britain, working-class left sup-

24 Przeworski and Sprague do not include Britain, but the British Labour Party does not face a communist competitor or a party with strong cross-class appeals and has close ties to the labor unions.

25 Based on the national election studies from the 1950s to the 1980s, the average Alford index for the Swedish Left has been 28.2, for Britain 37.5, for Norway 37.6, and for Denmark 39.7.

26 National election studies show an average Alford index of 1.8 for the French socialists, 6.0 for the Italian socialists, 12.0 for the French communists, 17.0 for the Italian communists, and 17.8 for the German SPD. Eurobarometer Alford indices for the 1976–88 period are 12.8 for the Belgian socialists, 17.3 for the Dutch Labor Party, 1.1 for the French socialists, 0.5 for the Italian socialists, 10.4 for the French communists, and 21.7 for the Italian communists.

Table 2.7. *Deterioration of workers' support for the Left, 1950s–1980s*
*(percentage of workers supporting the Left as a function of the time period)*

| | Data Set I: 1950s–1980s | | | |
| | Intercept (*t*-value) | *b* (*t*-value) | Adjusted $R^2$ | |
| --- | --- | --- | --- | --- |
| Denmark (Left) | 87.3 | −3.37 | .20 | (*N* = 10) |
| | (8.60) | (−1.81) | (*p* < .11) | |
| France (PS) | 20.6 | +1.92 | .05 | (*N* = 8) |
| | (2.28) | (1.19) | (*p* < .28) | |
| (PCF) | 130.5 | −14.5 | .98 | (*N* = 4) |
| | (14.7) | (−11.9) | (*p* < .01) | |
| Germany (SPD) | 50.7 | +1.38 | .26 | (*N* = 9) |
| | (13.4) | (1.97) | (*p* < .09) | |
| Norway (Left) | 83.9 | −2.60 | .86 | (*N* = 7) |
| | (36.4) | (−6.18) | (*p* < .002) | |
| Sweden (Left) | 83.5 | −1.55 | .59 | (*N* = 9) |
| | (38.4) | (−3.73) | (*p* < .006) | |
| United Kingdom | 67.5 | −2.76 | .54 | (*N* = 13) |
| (Labour) | (21.3) | (−3.89) | (*p* < .003) | |

*Source:* National Election Studies data (see fn. 21).

port deteriorated from the 1950s to the 1980s. Such parties have either declined electorally (negative bandwagons) or have been able to replace workers by other social groups, primarily through libertarian political appeals. These findings show the malleability of electoral coalitions and an interaction among voter groups faced with socialist party strategies that is not sufficiently captured by Przeworski and Sprague's theoretical framework.

Przeworski and Sprague's prediction that parties with severe trade-offs and low Alford index values of electoral support can improve their electoral position only by "workerist" strategies, whereas parties with mild trade-offs can engage in cross-class strategies that increase their proportion of allies and thus lower the Alford index also is not borne out. To test this proposition, one may predict a party's overall electoral return based on its Alford index in the same election. A more demanding test regresses the Alford index in election *t* on a party's overall support at *t* + 1, assuming a lag between the party's strategic posturing, revealed by its class composition, and its electoral results.

Application of both models to national election data yields the same results and the left part of Table 2.8 shows estimates only for the more demanding test. Contrary to Przeworski and Sprague's implicit hypothesis, it demonstrates that among parties with high Alford index values and mild trade-offs, overall electoral support is positively related to high workers' support.[27] The same applies to the two communist parties with intermediate Alford index values. Such socialist and

27 Denmark is the only outlier.

Table 2.8. Afford index of left party support at election t as a predictor of the Left's electoral performance at election t + 1 (data set I) or at election t (data set II)

| | Data set I: 1950s–1980s | | | Data set II: 1976–1987 | | |
|---|---|---|---|---|---|---|
| | Intercept (t-value) | b (t-value) | Adjusted R² | Intercept (t-value) | b (t-value) | Adjusted R² |
| **Group I: High Alford index values** | | | | | | |
| 1. Norway (Left) | 30.6 (3.09) | .42 (1.60) (p < .18) | .21 (N = 6) | | | |
| 2. Sweden (Left) | 39.8 (11.0) | .27 (2.91) (p < .02) | .45 (N = 8) | | | |
| 3. United Kingdom (Labour) | 10.1 (1.74) | .86 (5.44) (p < .001) | .72 (N = 12) | 18.3 (7.78) | .99 (2.48) (p < .07) | .51 (N = 6) |
| **Group II: Intermediate Alford index values** | | | | | | |
| 4. Denmark (Left) | 47.9 (7.85) | -.06 (-.40) | .02 (N = 9) | | | |
| 5. France (PCF) | 9.1 (3.55) | .23 (1.58) | 43 (N = 3) | 2.77 (.85) | .72 (2.33) (p < .08) | .47 (N = 6) |
| 6. Italy (PCI) | | | | 23.2 (2.19) | .10 (.22) | .01 (N = 6) |
| 7. Netherlands (PvdA) | | | | 24.4 (3.66) | .47 (1.25) | .10 (N = 6) |
| **Group III: Low Alford index values** | | | | | | |
| 8. Belgium (BSP) | | | | 28.1 (5.90) | -.06 (-.16) | .01 (N = 6) |
| 9. France (PS) | 29.3 (10.8) | -1.46 (-2.48) (p < .05) | .42 (N = 8) | 36.9 (2.19) | -.60 (-.61) | .08 (N = 6) |
| 10. Germany (SPD) | 43.8 (9.37) | -.21 (-.83) | .09 (N = 8) | 49.9 (8.24) | -.26 (-.46) | .05 (N = 6) |
| 11. Italy (PSI) | | | | 18.3 (27.6) | -.12 (-.50) | .06 (N = 6) |
| **All countries, separate time periods** | | | | | | |
| 12. 1950–69 | 35.8 (15.6) | .27 (4.24) (p < .001) | .39 (N = 28) | | | |
| 13. 1970–latest | 41.4 (11.26) | .07 (.56) | .01 (N = 32) | | | |

Source: Data set I: National Election Studies data (see fn. 21). Data set II: Eurobarometers 5–28.

communist parties do not substitute workers by allies in their electorates, but face bandwagons in which workers' support climbs or descends faster than allied support. In those cases, however, where Przeworski and Sprague identify severe trade-offs and low Alford index values and hence expect electoral decline through cross-class strategies, electoral support improves, as parties abandon a class-pure strategy and Alford index values fall (French and German socialists). Since these socialist parties also experience electoral bandwagons (see Table 2–6), the result indicates that nonworkers' support increases and decreases faster than workers' support in the electorates of socialist parties with generally low Alford index values.[28]

The short-term Eurobarometer data set in Table 2.8 suggests similar patterns of class support and electoral success. Because the number of time points is small, however, only the weak formulation of the hypothesis, employing Alford index values at time *t* to predict electoral performance at time *t*, could be tested and most results remained insignificant, although coefficients have the correct sign.

Findings in Table 2.8 lend support to the hypothesis that those socialist parties which have never been wedded to dominant working-class support, in principle, can best take advantage of new electoral coalitions that emphasize non–working-class constituencies. Actually such strategies often boost workers' support, although at a lower rate than that of nonworkers. The strong entrenchment of socialist parties in the working class is no longer an automatic electoral asset. This message is also confirmed by lines 12 and 13 in Table 2.8, where Alford index values for all left parties combined are regressed on left party electoral success in two time periods. The relation between class purity of socialist strategies and electoral support is clearly subject to *period effects*. Thus, high Alford index values were positively associated with electoral success in the 1950s and 1960s, but the relationship essentially vanished in the 1970s and 1980s. The working class has become less crucial for the electoral success of leftist parties. More complex calculations enter the choices of socialist strategists. Whether and how parties were able to take advantage of such opportunities can be explained only in terms of a closer analysis of party competition and party organization, an investigation not undertaken by Przeworski and Sprague.

The difference in regression coefficients for different time periods suggests that Przeworski and Sprague's conceptualization of class and party relations *may have been correct* for certain periods in the past, although even there the evidence is weak, but is definitely inadequate for the past twenty years. This interpretation would be consistent with the theory of changing market and organizational relations in advanced capitalism I have presented in Chapter 1. Left parties now appear to possess considerable and growing freedom in choosing their strategies and electoral coalitions. If there is any relation between patterns of class trade-offs, based on a party's union linkage, the existence of cross-cutting cleavages, and the

28 Alford index values (percentage of workers minus percentage of nonworkers supporting a left party) decline, while workers' support increases, because the support of allies rises even more rapidly.

Table 2.9. *"Class trade-offs" in socialist strategy and the Left's electoral success from the 1970s to 1980s*

| Change in the electoral performance from 1970s to 1980s | Average level of support 1981–90 | | |
|---|---|---|---|
| | Less than 30% | Less than 40% | More than 40% |
| **Loss of more than 3%** | British Labour: −8.6% | West German SPD: −6.6% | Austrian SPÖ: −5.7% |
| Trade-off: | Mild | Mild | Mild |
| Party–union linkage: | Strong | Strong | Strong |
| Cross-cutting cleavages: | No | No | No |
| Communist competitor: | No | No | No |
| **Gain/loss less than 3%** | Belgian BSP/PSB: +1.6% | Dutch PvdA: +2.4% | Swedish SAP: +1.3% |
| Trade-off: | Intermediate | Intermediate | Mild |
| Party–union linkage: | Medium | Medium | Strong |
| Cross-cutting cleavages: | Yes | Yes | No |
| Communist competitor: | No | No | No |
| **Gain of more than 3%** | Italian PSI: +3.2% | French PS: +9.5% | Spanish PSOe: +14.3% |
| Trade-off: | Strong | Strong | Strong |
| Party–union linkage: | Weak | Weak | Medium |
| Cross-cutting cleavages: | Yes | Yes | Yes |
| Communist competitor: | Yes | Yes | Yes |

*Source:* Predictions are based on what can be inferred from Przeworski and Sprague's analysis.

presence of strong communist competitors, and parties' electoral success in the 1980s, it is the opposite to that predicted by Przeworski and Sprague. Parties that operate in an environment prone to yield severe trade-offs have improved their electoral performance most. Conversely, parties facing intermediate or mild electoral trade-offs performed worst (Table 2.9).

## CONCLUSION

In the preceding section I offered a preliminary test of Przeworski and Sprague's model and sketched the outlines of an alternative explanation. Table 2.9 suggests there is a correlation between party union linkages, cross-cutting cleavages, communist competition, and electoral success that is different from what Przeworski and Sprague would expect. To illuminate the micro-mechanisms that allow leftist parties with weak union linkages in environments with historically strong cross-cutting cleavages to thrive electorally, subsequent chapters will further flesh out the theoretical model of party competition that situates socialist parties in a space characterized by distributive and communitarian political alternatives.

What should be clear from this chapter's discussion is that conventional class categories no longer enable us to reconstruct accurately how parties build and change electoral coalitions. The whole enterprise of tieing left parties' electoral fortunes to their voters' class position, defined in terms of property, exploitation, and "productive" labor becomes questionable. Occupational structures and life chances in modern capitalist societies yield patterns of political preference formation that can be traced only in very fragmentary ways through class categories. This weakness of class analysis is not substantially remedied by adding parties and politicians as agents of class formation, as Przeworski and Sprague suggest. Neither a determinist nor a voluntarist class conception is able to shed much light on the trajectory of the Left in advanced capitalist democracies. Nevertheless, the admirable analytical clarity and rigorous comparative design of Przeworski and Sprague's *Paper Stones* has enabled us to see this weakness better than ever before.

# 3

# Political economy and left party fortunes

Even though the change of class structure, conceived in conventional terms of economic property rights, does not, by itself, account for the electoral fortunes of socialist parties, left parties are exposed to elementary social and economic forces by running for and holding office. These forces may shape their political fortunes. First, the mere fact that a party heads the government, regardless of specific government policies and policy outcomes, may subject it to a particular responsibility for a variety of social developments in the eyes of the voters. Government incumbency endows a party with vulnerabilities vis-à-vis competitors that may affect its subsequent electoral performance. Second, a governing party's achievements in economic and social policy-making may shape the electorate's voting intentions. Institutional features of government formation and authority may intensify or reduce the electorate's awareness of government policy and willingness to attribute policy outcomes to party actions. Third, the electoral fortunes of governing parties may also depend on political-economic institutions, such as the organization of interest intermediation in economic policy-making between business, labor, and the government and the scope and design of welfare states. Such institutions affect citizens' trust in the long-term feasibility of a party's general economic policy approach and citizens' economic self-interests.

In a brief formula, three social and institutional conditions may be hypothesized to help social democratic parties in the electoral competition. They are likely to thrive electorally if they are in the opposition and do not have to justify a government track record, if they face incumbents who have governed during bad economic times, and if they operate in the institutional environment of centralized industrial relations with strong labor unions, a comprehensive welfare state, and a large public sector. Conversely, socialist parties face the most serious uphill struggle where they are in government, have presided over a weakening economy, and find themselves in a decentralist system of industrial relations with a weak welfare state and a small public sector.

Of course, whether socialists are in the most or the least fortunate position is not simply a matter of political fate, but also a consequence of politicians' choices. A party's government status, economic performance, and political-economic institutions are all not only potential *causal* determinants of its electoral performance. As strategic actor, a party *intentionally* attempts to adapt to and to manipulate the impact of incumbency, economy, and institutions in order to optimize future electoral performance or policy influence. For instance, if government office is a liability, a party may opt for the opposition benches, particularly if policy influence in government is also limited. If high unemployment depresses support before an election, a left government may attempt to boost employment. If centralized industrial relations and comprehensive welfare states promote trust in social democracy, socialist governments may act to strengthen and deepen such arrangements. I therefore explore the extent to which parties anticipate the electoral consequences of economic and institutional forces and adjust their strategies accordingly.

The varying electoral experience of socialist parties in the nine countries suggests that not all parties have strategically reckoned with the consequences of economic conditions. Either the political-economic theories I have just sketched are incorrect, although party strategists act upon them in their own calculations, or parties are unable to respond strategically to the political-economic environment confronting them. In either event, the failure of parties to optimize performance requires a causal rather than a strategic explanation of why party decision makers held false beliefs or failed to act on correct beliefs.

In this chapter, I argue that political-economic factors are more useful in exploring socialist electoral fortunes than class theories but nevertheless fall far short of a satisfactory account of the political mechanisms that bring about the highly divergent careers of the nine socialist parties I examine. Government incumbency pure and simple has the least significant causal association with social democratic party trajectories. Socialist politicians also appear not to act intentionally on government status. Economic developments under socialist parties in government or opposition have *some* influence on party performance, but there are many exceptions. Economics cannot explain dramatic socialist electoral losses or gains and it is often tied to socialist party careers in ways that appear counterintuitive from the perspective of run-of-the-mill political-economic theories.

Most important, where socialist or bourgeois governments lost when presiding over a weak economy in the 1980s, the main winners were not in the opposite political camp, but parties running primarily on noneconomic platforms. One may claim that disgust with the major economic policy alternatives advanced by conventional parties in the political arena and hence support of newcomers as protest voting is one way the electorate votes on economics. This still leaves the difficulty of explaining why particular noneconomic party appeals become attractive for electoral constituencies. A more straightforward interpretation of such electoral realignments follows from the theoretical framework I sketched in Chapter 1. Social change is one critical force that explains why economics is no longer the only critical question salient in party competition. The configuration of party systems and the internal organization of socialist parties explains why socialist parties often cannot take advantage of the new configuration of political demand and supply.

Like economic performance, political-economic institutions, particularly the scope and organization of the welfare state, appear to be associated with social democratic electoral fortunes to a limited extent, yet not in ways predicted by conventional theories. A comprehensive welfare state no longer benefits socialist parties. Conversely, socialist governments have little incentive to shore up weak welfare states to boost their long-term electoral constituency. Again, such findings make theoretical sense only within the framework of the theory of political preference formation and strategic choice outlined in Chapter 1 and closely examined in Chapters 4 through 6.

### 3.1 LIABILITIES OF GOVERNMENT PARTICIPATION

Government incumbency may either help or hurt a party. A party in office may gain electorally because it has more media exposure and is in a position to promote policies popular with its voters. Or a party in office may suffer because it is exposed to the pendulum effect of voters supporting the underdog opposition party. Most important, a government party will be held responsible for policy outcomes, whereas an opposition party may be free to attract voter support with alternative programs that gloss over hard choices. Rose and Mackie (1983: 125) showed that between 1948 and 1979 governing parties lost votes in about two thirds of all elections. This propensity was particularly high in the 1968–79 period in Scandinavia and the Anglo-Saxon countries but much less so on the European continent.

Table 3.1 reports electoral consequences of left party government status for the left parties themselves in the 1970s and 1980s [columns (1)–(4)] and for the major bourgeois competitors in the 1980s columns (5) and (6)]. Consistent with Rose and Mackie's conclusions, government status on average depressed subsequent electoral support, while opposition status boosted it. The liabilities of incumbency and the benefits of opposition markedly increased in the 1980s. Yet a close look at individual countries for the two decades reveals that there are numerous exceptions to this general pattern (italicized in Table 3.1). Moreover, the major bourgeois parties often lost votes in the 1980s *even if* left parties were in government.[1]

What is most puzzling, however, is the remarkable deterioration of some left opposition parties, such as in Britain (1974/I, 1983), the Netherlands (1981, 1989), and Germany (1987; 1990). Overall, the substantial variance in electoral performance among parties with the same government status and the large number of inconsistent election outcomes exhibited in Table 3.1 does little to shore up confidence in the government liability thesis. A simple regression of left party electoral change on government status in the nine countries for the period from 1970 to 1990 (N = 54) explains very little variance, even though the sign of the

---

1 Of course, this finding is particularly striking for elections in Austria (1983, 1986), Sweden (1985, 1988), and France (1986), because bourgeois parties were in the opposition at that time. In the other cases, major bourgeois parties participated in the government together with social democrats.

Table 3.1. *Electoral fortunes and parties' government status in the 1970s and 1980s (average change in percent electoral support over subsequent elections)*

| Change of electoral performance from 1970s to 1980s | Left party electoral performance | | | | Electoral performance of the major bourgeois parties in the 1980s | |
|---|---|---|---|---|---|---|
| | 1970s | | 1980s | | Left government participation | Left parties in opposition |
| | Government | Opposition | Government | Opposition | | |
| *Losers* | | | | | | |
| Britain | -1.7 (70, 74/II, 79) | -5.9 (74/I) | — | -3.1 (83, 87) | — | -0.8 (83, 87) |
| Germany | -0.1 (72, 76) | — | -2.2 (80, 83) | -1.3 (82) | +0.1 (80, 83) | -2.5 (87, 90) |
| Austria | +1.0 (71, 75, 79) | +4.8 (70) | -2.4 (83, 86, 90) | — | -3.2 (83, 86, 90) | — |
| *Preservers* | | | | | | |
| Sweden | -2.5 (70, 73, 76) | +0.5 (79) | -1.2 (85, 88) | +2.4 (82) | -1.6 (85, 88) | -4.0 (82) |
| Belgium | -0.9 (78) | -1.0 (78) | -0.3 (81) | +2.8 (85, 87) | -3.9 (82) | +0.2 (85, 87) |
| Netherlands | +6.5 (71, 74, 77) | +1.3 (71, 72) | +2.1 (82) | -1.3 (85, 87) | +4.4 (82) | -1.8 (85, 87) |
| *Winners* | | | | | | |
| Italy | -0.4 (72) | +0.1 (76, 79) | +2.3 (83, 87) | — | -2.0 (83, 87) | — |
| France | — | +6.2 (73, 78) | -8.3 (86) | +8.5 (81, 88) | -0.1 (86) | -3.4 (81, 88) |
| Spain | — | +1.2 (77, 79) | -4.4 (86, 89) | +17.3 (82) | +0.6 (86, 89) | -8.6 (82) |
| Average change/Elections | -.40/16 | +1.34/11 | -1.78/14 | +2.27/13 | -1.15/14 | -2.38/13 |
| Communist Party performance | | | | | | |
| France | | +0.3/2 | | -3.1/3 | | |
| Italy | | +1.2/3 | | -1.9/2 | | |
| Spain | | +1.6/1 | | -0.6/3 | | |

association is correct (adjusted $R^2 = .094$).[2] Furthermore, the incumbency effect appears to be a function of the duration of a party's status as government or opposition. (See Figure 3.1.) For all elections between 1948 and 1989, left parties benefit from opposition status typically after five to six years, yet even parties locked into the opposition for seven to ten years have lost votes more often than not. The same erratic distribution of expected payoffs applies to governing left parties. The downside is greatest after four to six years, but parties with longer government incumbency often do well, indicating a hegemonic government position.[3]

While government status is generally a weak electoral liability, its electoral risk may be greatest if the incumbent is a highly visible player in policy formation. Where socialists govern as majority party or lead a majority coalition, their electoral risk may therefore be greater than where they participate in minority governments or oversized coalitions. Voters can attribute responsibility for policy outcomes more easily to incumbents in the first two cases. The data for the nine countries, however, provide little support for this hypothesis. The probability that socialist parties in majority governments lose votes or socialist opposition parties faced with a bourgeois majority government win votes is barely better than chance between 1980 and 1990 (57.6% of 33 cases). In oversized governments, social democratic electoral change is correctly predicted by government status 44.4% of the time (4 of 9 cases). Strangely, socialists most frequently benefit from opposing minority governments and lose from minority government incumbency (10 of 12 cases).[4]

Democratic institutions may affect the risk socialists take on by opting for government status. If political authority is centralized in the national government and the opposition has little parliamentary influence over public policy, voters tend to attribute policy responsibility to government parties more than in federal states and parliamentary systems with strong opposition power over the legislative process, for example where opposition parties are represented on and may even chair specialized parliamentary committees that match the jurisdiction of ministries. Government status may also influence voter decisions more profoundly where elections are decisive in the sense that voters are able to identify the shape of the future government alternatives before elections from the announcements of politician and where the losers of elections are generally relegated to the opposi-

---

2  Interestingly, a similar regression of changes in the electoral support of major bourgeois parties on government status generates a somewhat stronger linkage (adjusted $R^2 = .13$).

3  Most of the cases in this category are from Austria, West Germany, and Sweden.

4  This finding appears to be inconsistent with Strom's (1990a: 124) more general result for fourteen countries and more than three decades that minimum winning majority coalitions incur the greatest losses (−4.26 % per election), followed by majority governments (−2.23 %) and then formal and substantive minority governments (−2.10% and −1.24%). Not only the time period covered and the parties studied but also the countries included or excluded may account for this difference. For reasons not entirely clear to me, Strom's study of government formation does not include Austria and West Germany, two countries in which government formation appears to disconfirm a number of his hypotheses.

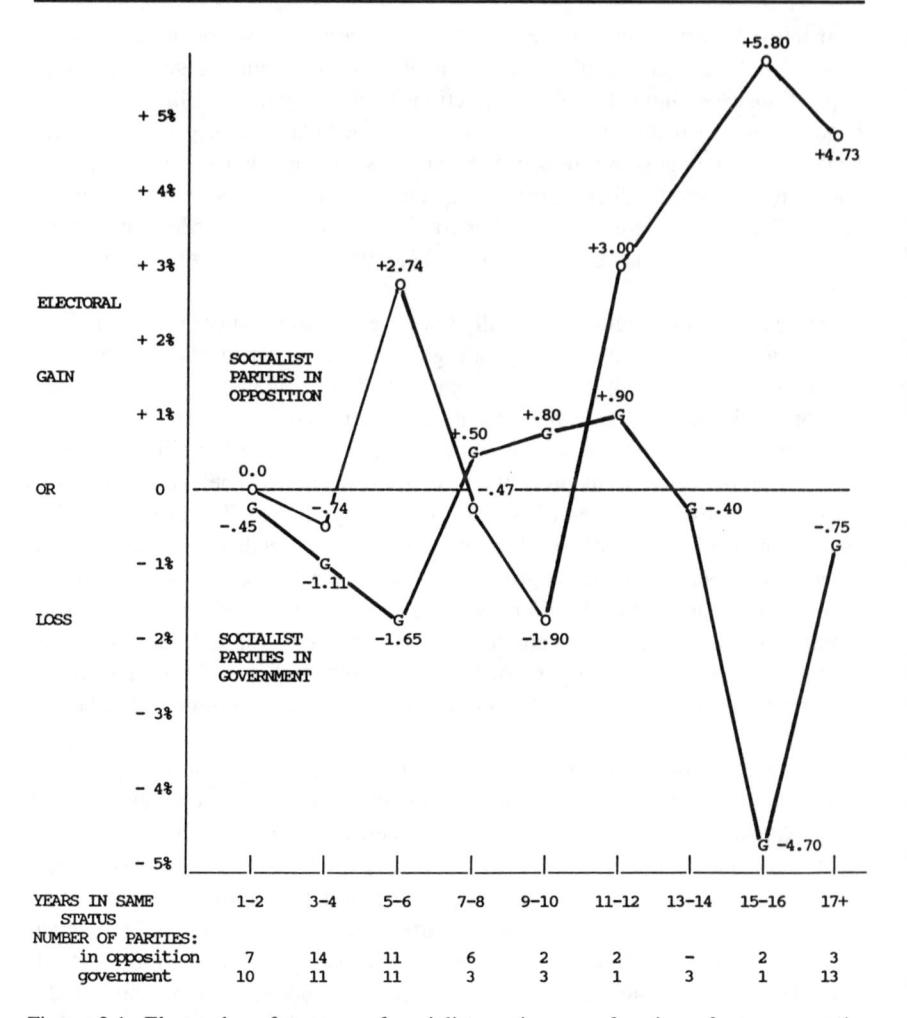

Figure 3.1. Electoral performance of socialist parties as a function of years spent in government or opposition

tion benches (Strom 1990a). Parties face lesser risks of executive office holding if alternative future government coalitions are not identifiable before elections and losers of elections may stay in office.

Strom's (1990a) ingenious study provides measures for three of the four variables affecting the political risks of government status (opposition influence over public policy; identifiability of future governments; electoral gains or losses determining government status). Lijphart (1984) offers a measure for a fourth variable, centralization of government. Table 3.2 combines these four variables in an additive index of overall electoral risk of government status and correlates this with the electoral consequences associated with socialist parties' government or opposition status.

Table 3.2 demonstrates that, on average, socialist parties' electoral swing contingent upon their government status is greatest in the two countries with high risks of office holding, France and Britain. French and British socialist government incumbents are punished by an average loss of 3.35% voter support per election, whereas the equivalent loss for social democrats in five countries with intermediate risks of office holding is 1.0%. In low-risk countries, socialist government participants can even expect a slight gain of 0.13%. Conversely, the average electoral gains of opposition status increase from 0.94% (low-risk cases) to 2.49% (high-risk cases).

Unfortunately, the general risks of office holding do not explain why socialist parties belong to the group of losers, preservers, or gainers in the 1980s. The big electoral losers, Britain, Austria, and Germany, face rather different institutional risks from government participation. They are long-term electoral losers because they defy the logic of office payoffs. British and German social democrats lost votes regardless of whether they were in or out of office. Austrian socialists sustained slight average losses in office, but had no periods in opposition to offset this erosion of voter support. Similarly, the socialist winners of the 1980s are distributed across the spectrum of institutional risks from government office (France, Spain, and Italy). The Italian case is clearly inconsistent with the logic of the incumbency argument. While institutional conditions of executive–legislative relations and government (coalition) formation *in general* are important to explain average electoral gains or losses sustained by political parties, this theoretical proposition does not shed much light on the secular trends of socialist party support in the nine countries.

Up to this point, I have considered a party's incumbency as a causal determinant of its electoral performance. Following Strom (1984, 1990a), however, government status may be interpreted from a choice-theoretic perspective. Since party leaders understand the consequences of office holding in different institutional settings, they may avoid government status where costs appear to be high, but seek it where costs are likely to remain low. If Strom's theory of the rational choice of government participation is correct, no systematic link between government status and left party performance should occur because rational parties would join only when incumbency poses few risks for the party's political future.

In order to test this argument, two further distinctions are relevant. First, parties may primarily seek electoral or policy success. Vote-seeking parties view entry into a government with great capacity for centralized policy formation as an electoral liability. In contrast, policy-seeking parties see such government participation as an opportunity, regardless of electoral cost. Second, one must distinguish situations where left parties were presented with a real choice for joining government from situations where they became "natural" parties of government or "natural" opposition parties. In a rough approximation, socialist parties are natural government parties, if they, together with parties *further* to their left,

Table 3.2. *The risks of executive office and electoral payoffs of government and opposition status: Socialist parties 1970–90*

| | Capacity of policy formation | | High decisiveness of elections | | | Electoral payoffs 1970–90, contingent upon status (average percentage change and number of elections) | |
| --- | --- | --- | --- | --- | --- | --- | --- |
| | (1) Executive hegemony over legislature | (2) Centralization of government | (3) Future government alternatives identifiable before election | (4) Losers of elections go into opposition | (5) Electoral risk index of government participation | Government | Opposition |
| *High risk* | | | | | | | |
| Britain | 1.0 | 1.0 | 1.0 | 1.0 | 4.0 | −1.7/3 | −4.0/3 |
| France | 1.0 | 1.0 | 1.0 | 1.0 | 4.0 | −8.3/1 | +6.4/4 |
| Average change | | | | | | −3.4/4 | +2.5/7 |
| *Medium risk* | | | | | | | |
| Spain | 0.5 | 0.0 | 1.0 | 1.0 | 2.5 | −4.4/2 | +9.3/2 |
| Austria | 1.0 | 0.0 | 1.0 | 0.0 | 2.0 | −0.7/6 | – |
| Sweden | 0.0 | 0.5 | 1.0 | 0.5 | 2.0 | −2.0/5 | +1.5/2 |
| Germany | 0.0 | 0.0 | 1.0 | 0.5 | 1.5 | −1.2/4 | −1.3/3 |
| Netherlands | 0.5 | 1.0 | 0.0 | 0.0 | 1.5 | +4.3/2 | −0.2/5 |
| Average change | | | | | | −1.0/19 | +1.3/12 |
| *Low risk* | | | | | | | |
| Belgium | 0.0 | 0.5 | 0.0 | 0.0 | 0.5 | −0.8/4 | +1.5/3 |
| Italy | 0.0 | 0.5 | 0.0 | 0.0 | 0.5 | +1.4/3 | +0.1/2 |
| Average change | | | | | | +0.1/7 | +0.9/5 |

*Source:* Party scores in columns (1), (3), and (4) are based on a division of Strom's (1990a: 73, 75) scores into low (0.0), medium (0.5) and high (1.0) values. Column 2 is based on an equivalent division of Lijphart's (1984: 216) scores for government centralization based on a factor analysis.

control more than 50% of the seats in a legislature.[5] Conversely, they are natural parties of opposition if the strongest bourgeois competitor, together with parties *further* to its right, controls more than 50% of the seats. Socialist politicians choose government status only if there are parties between them and their major bourgeois competitors that are available for coalition with either side (such as in West Germany or in Austria after 1983) or the largest bourgeois competitor is small enough to require broad-based coalitions to obtain a government majority (such as in Belgium, Italy, and the Netherlands). In the other countries, the socialist or the nonsocialist camps usually have held clear-cut majorities so that opportunities for choice did not arise (Britain, France, Spain, and Sweden before 1976 and after 1982).

If socialist parties are vote seeking and are able to choose government entry, they appear not to avoid government participation *even if* the liabilities of executive office, as measured by the four indicators in Table 3.2, are moderately high.[6] In Austria since 1983 socialists have stayed in office although they face intermediate incumbency risks of electoral losses. The German and Dutch left parties face similar incumbency risks, yet the German social democrats stayed in office for 65% of the 1970s and 1980s, whereas the Dutch Labor Party participated in governments for only 35% of the time. Similar variance can be found among socialist parties facing low electoral incumbency risk: Belgium (45% socialist government participation) and Italy (65% government participation).

If socialist parties are policy seeking and able to choose government entry, again Strom's logic of strategic party action is not confirmed. In this instance, the attractiveness of office is the difference between the benefits of government control over policy formation (as indicated by little opposition power in parliament and centralized government) and the electoral costs of decisive elections (identifiability of government coalitions before elections and the probability that electoral defeat results in loss of incumbency status). In three countries, the attractiveness of incumbency for policy-seeking parties is moderate, either because both benefits and costs of executive office are high (Austria) or both are low (Belgium, Italy). Yet the frequency and duration of socialist government participa-

---

5 The logic behind this proposition is that the bargaining power of any nonsocialist party taking the lead role in a government would be extremely constrained if the Left occupied a near hegemonic position. The same logic applies to the opposite configuration. Any centrist or moderate social democratic party, when faced with right-wing parties that control a majority of the seats in the legislature, would abstain from government for want of bargaining power.

6 A critic of this analysis may argue that it is tautological to employ the risks of executive office holding in the 1970s and 1980s as a predictor of the parties' actual participation in governments, since the independent variable derives from the dependent variable. First of all, only one component of the index of incumbency risk in Table 3.2, losers of elections go into opposition, taps party decisions to change government status based on electoral performance. The results of my analysis would not be substantively different if that component were dropped. Second, the controversial component of the independent variable measures the behavior of all parties, not just that of socialists. Third, the values of that variable would not be significantly different, if party behavior in the 1950–70 time period had been used to predict 1970–90 choices.

tion varies between 100% of the time (Austria 1983 and after) and 45% (Belgium 1970–90).

Even more instructive are two extreme cases where the liabilities of office for policy-seeking parties are either very high (Germany) or very low (Netherlands). In Germany, a weak federal government and decisive elections should discourage the government participation of policy-seeking parties. Nevertheless, the German SPD chose to remain in office after the onset of the 1974 oil crisis in the face of overwhelming obstacles that hobbled its policy program and future reforms.[7] In the Netherlands, stronger government capacity and less electoral decisiveness should have made government office attractive for a policy-seeking Labor Party, yet in 1977 and 1982, the PvDA retreated into the opposition after lengthy negotiations with the Christian Democrats.

By opting out of government, the Dutch Labor Party acted irrationally in light of *both* vote- and policy-seeking objectives. Conversely, the German social democrats tended to be irrational from both perspectives by staying in government. In Austria and Italy, one or the other objective suggests government participation and in the Belgian case both predict preference for opposition status. Overall, parties do not appear to choose government participation based on anticipated electoral losses or policy influence. Government participation may depend more on the competitive strategy socialists choose in the electoral arena (Chapter 4) and on the outcomes of internal decision-making processes that determine parties' overall strategic preferences (Chapter 5).

## 3.2 ECONOMIC PERFORMANCE AND PARTY SUCCESS

Causal-determinist and intentional strategic hypotheses of government participation and electoral payoffs lack not only explanatory power but also a clear micrologic that explains when and why voters punish government parties for their office performance and when and why party leaders seek votes, policy, or neither of these objectives. The theory of retrospective economic voting provides a micro-logic that links the liabilities of government status to individual voter choices. According to the theory formulated by Anthony Downs (1957), rational voters assess the relative utility of voting for a party largely based on that party's past track record, because uncertainty about the future and about the sincerity of candidates makes past action the best guide to assessing a party's future utility. A decisive, though probably not exclusive, component of retrospective voting is the voters' perception of economic performance during a party's term in government office.

If the Downsian theory is correct, the electoral success of a socialist party should be sensitive to office holding and economic performance. Socialist incumbents during a period of economic weakness will lose votes to the main bourgeois

7 Following Strom's logic, the party's left wing was correct in calling for a withdrawal into the opposition with the onset of the world economic crisis in 1974 and the fall of Chancellor Brandt. Over the ensuing eight years, the SPD under Schmidt could do little to implement its program and has slid into a severe electoral crisis since then.

opposition parties. Conversely, if socialists are in opposition and bourgeois governments experience economic decline, socialists should benefit. If there is *no symmetry* between the gains and losses of socialist and bourgeois parties contingent upon government status and economic performance, one of two phenomena may occur. First, voters may attribute blame and praise to parties of different ideological stripes asymmetrically. For example, one might derive from Budge and Farlie's (1983a) salience theory of voting that socialist governments suffer *more* from a worsening economy than bourgeois governments, because voters attribute more economic competence to bourgeois parties. Second, asymmetries or a lack of systematic relationship between government status and party performance may be an indirect indicator that voters emphasize *other issues than the economy.* Surveys and expert judgments help us to assess the relative salience of policy issues in electoral campaigns.

Institutional conditions, such as a government's capacity to control policy-making, may determine the extent to which the electoral performance of government and opposition parties is sensitive to economic performance. I will first examine evidence for social democratic party performance bearing on the non-institutional theory of economic voting. Then I will draw on institutional arguments to account for cross-national variations in parties' sensitivity to economic voting. Overall, my conclusion is that economic performance and economic voting explain the trajectory of socialist parties in the 1970s and 1980s only to a limited extent. On the one hand, such theories provide scant insight into how voters form expectations about parties' government performance and how they determine the relative salience of issues (Kiewiet and Rivers 1985: 219; Simon 1985; Visser and Wijnhoven 1990).[8] On the other, the economic effects that can be identified tend to be inconsistent with run-of-the-mill political economic theories.

### Economic voting in the nine countries

Economists and political scientists usually seek to establish the linkage between economic indicators (inflation, unemployment, growth, and so on) and party fortunes through time-series regressions of "party popularity functions" for individual countries. These functions employ economic variables to predict voter sympathy with government or opposition parties. The number of such studies skyrocketed in the late 1970s and early 1980s, but since then it has declined due to their methodological and conceptual problems.[9] While most analyses find some kind of effect of economic variables on party support, estimates are highly sensitive to the specification of time periods for which coefficients are calculated,

8 Studies emphasizing voter expectations include Whiteley (1985, 1986a), Clarke, Stewart, and Zuk (1986a,b), Sanders, Ward, and March (1987), and Clarke and Whiteley (1990).

9 For an instructive survey of economic voting studies in five of the nine countries included in my study, Britain, France, Germany, Italy and Spain, see Lewis-Beck (1988: 13–31). A fair number of studies is also available for Sweden. An overview of the entire field through the mid-1980s can be found in Schneider and Frey (1988). There are no comparable studies for Austria, the Netherlands, or Belgium.

the intervals at which variables are measured (months, quarters, years), the choice of independent and dependent economic and noneconomic variables, and the time lags that are presumed to exist between economic developments and voter reactions.[10] Furthermore, predictors of party support are unstable over time and across countries, and models do not explain how governments' instrumental variables, such as fiscal and monetary policy, relate to economic outcomes (cf. Alt 1985: 56–7). The models also assume that voters have a realistic view of economic affairs. They rarely adopt the less demanding assumption that voters are "cognitive misers," who update preconceptions only when new experience is highly inconsistent with them.[11] With the exception of Kiewiet's (1983) and Lewis-Beck's (1988) studies, there are few individual-level analyses of economic voting. These investigations often find that voters' choices are influenced by ideological preconceptions to a much greater extent than by voters' perception of the economy.[12]

Given these technical, conceptual, and theoretical problems in time-series popularity functions, I have chosen a simpler tool to explore the dependence of social democratic electoral support on the economy. I will first visually inspect the time series of an economic misery index, measuring an annual inflation plus unemployment minus real growth in gross domestic product (GDP), and its association with socialist parties' performance while paying special attention to the critical elections in each country during the 1970s and 1980s. To test the robustness of my general findings, I will then examine change rates of social democratic voter support in all nine countries, regressing them on change rates of overall economic misery, inflation, or unemployment. If economic voting theory is correct, increasing economic misery should drive down left electoral support, where socialists are in office, while boosting it where socialists are in opposition.

*Electoral losers.*    Figure 3.2 depicts the evolution of economic misery in the three countries where moderate left parties lost a significant share of their voters from the 1970s to the 1980s. For each country, I will ask three questions. First, did changes in the year preceding each election affect electoral behavior? Second, did change in economic misery from the previous election to the next election affect the fortunes of socialists as incumbents and as opposition parties? Third, were changes of socialist and main bourgeois parties *symmetrically interrelated* in the instances where socialists suffered or benefited from economic voting?

West Germany is the case where the data presented in Figure 3.2 most consistently support the theory of retrospective economic voting. Here, social democratic

10  For a critical review of the literature on economic popularity functions see Paldam (1981), Whiteley (1984), Kiewiet and Rivers (1985), Lewis-Beck and Eulau (1985), Toinet (1985), and Lewis-Beck (1988: 16–18). The only study explicitly modelling voters' "memory" and the time lag of economic data is Hibbs (1982).

11  For an empirical critique of this assumption, see Peffley (1985) and Peffley, Feldman, and Sigelman (1987).

12  It is well known that sympathizers of governing parties often use their responses to opinion polls to register their protest against particular government policies, but then in the final analysis cast their votes in favor of the incumbent.

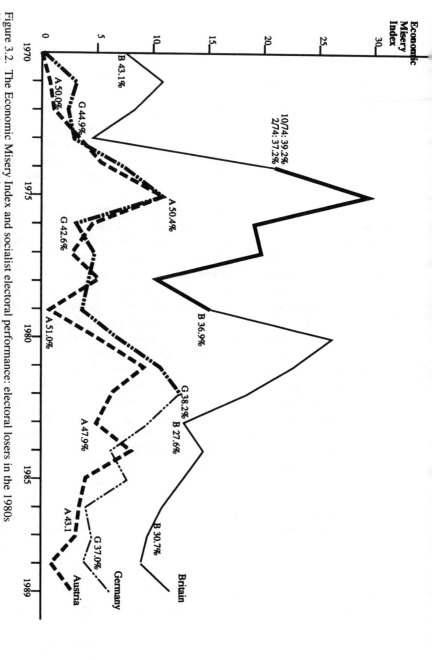

Figure 3.2. The Economic Misery Index and socialist electoral performance: electoral losers in the 1980s
*Notes and sources:* bold lines signify party in office. Economic Misery Index = % Consumer Price Index + % unemployment – % real GDP growth. Calculated from OECD Historical Statistics, 1989

gains or losses were in accordance with economic growth or decline and government status in four of six elections, regardless of whether we examine economic change over entire election periods or in the preelection year. Yet in only two instances (1976 and 1983) did economic voting also coincide with a symmetrical change of voter support between SPD and Christian Democratic Union (CDU). In the 1987 and 1990 elections, the incumbent Christian Democrats lost votes in spite of a relatively good economic climate, but the social democratic opposition did not benefit from this development. Estimates of government popularity functions find generally weak, though consistent effects of economic performance on voter support in the 1970s, though *not* in the 1980s.[13] The asymmetry of parties' electoral payoffs and the insignificance of economic predictors of government popularity in the 1980s suggest that economic concerns were not voters' primary motivation in these elections.[14]

The British results are even less consistent with economic voting. Only three of six elections show a change of Labour Party support consistent with retrospective economic voting based on the party's government status and economic performance since the preceding election or the preelection year. And in only two instances, the October 1974 and the 1979 elections, were Labour's and the Conservatives' changes in electoral support both symmetrical and consistent with economic voting. Furthermore, Labour's dramatic drop in 1983 appears unwarranted in light of the weak overall economic improvement and much higher unemployment compared to the 1979 election. Given that the working class is particularly sensitive to unemployment,[15] it is unintelligible why it abandoned the party in greater numbers than the middle class in 1983.[16] Individual-level voter studies show that both Labour and Conservatives would have received about 35% in 1983, had voters cast their ballot based on six economic issues (Heath et al. 1985: 96–8). In a 1984 survey, Lewis-Beck (1988: 82) found that expectations about future economic performance and anger about the government are more important than retrospective economic evaluations. Other studies emphasize the benefits the conservative government drew from the Falklands War (Clarke, Stewart, and Zuk 1986a; Norpoth 1987), although the magnitude of that effect is disputed (Sanders, Ward, and Marsh 1987).

Socialist party performance in Austria appears almost entirely at odds with economic voting theory. Six of seven election outcomes are inconsistent with economic performance in the preelection year. The same applies to five of seven elections when economic performance over the entire electoral term is considered.

13  For analyses covering the 1970s see Peretz (1981), Hibbs (1982), and Whiteley (1984). Economic voting is insignificant in the 1960s (Baker et al. 1981: 102, 280) and the 1980s (Kirchgässner 1989).

14  Budge and Farlie's (1983a) salience theory is not very convincing since the conservatives who are said to "own" economic issues (inflation, growth, fiscal stability) also lost votes in spite of good economic news.

15  On the class relatedness of economic voting, compare Hibbs (1987) and Scarbrough (1987: 234).

16  Crewe (1985a,b) critiques the validity of economic voting theory to account for the 1983 British election results.

Whereas the Austrian Socialist Party (SPÖ) government strengthened its electoral support in a climate of economic deterioration, especially in 1975, it did not benefit from good economic news throughout the 1980s. Moreover, in the 1980s, its main bourgeois competitor also suffered electoral losses, yielding an asymmetry that suggests the importance of other than economic issues on the voters' agenda.[17]

Comparing the three countries, economic voting theory sheds little light on the *critical elections* in which social democratic support declined dramatically, most notably the Austrian elections of 1983 and 1986 and the British election of 1974/I. Even in instances where social democratic decline is consistent with retrospective voting theory, established bourgeois competitors were not the primary beneficiaries, as is shown by the 1983 British election as well as the 1983 German election when the SPD lost votes primarily to the Greens.

*Electoral stabilizers.* Sweden, Belgium, and the Netherlands, where socialist parties generally held on to their 1970s vote share in the 1980s, economy voting theory reveals little about electoral outcomes. Both in the twelve-month run-up to elections as well as over the entire electoral term retrospective economic voting is the exception. Moreover, socialist and bourgeois party gains or losses are distributed asymmetrically. The annual economic performance of the three countries, as measured by the composite misery index (inflation + unemployment − GDP growth), is presented in Figure 3.3.

In Sweden, short-term retrospective economic voting is borne out only by the socialists' losses in 1976 and 1985.[18] Economic performance over entire electoral terms appears to affect the party in three of seven elections. The accelerating erosion of social democratic support in the 1980s is unexpected, because unemployment fell throughout this period in an overall solid economic environment.[19] In 1988, social democratic losses did not symmetrically benefit bourgeois parties, one of several indicators that social democrats lost the election on noneconomic issues.[20] Even in 1991 in a deteriorating economic climate heavy social democratic losses (− 5.5%) did not yield corresponding gains for the traditional bourgeois parties (− 2.2%), which promised voters a new economic strategy. The main beneficiaries were new entrants into the Swedish parliament that ran their campaigns focusing on noneconomic appeals. The Christian Democrats gained 4.2%

---

17 In fact, surveys show that environmental problems, clean government, and microeconomic questions concerning the rationalization of state-owned companies were much more important than economic questions in 1983 and in 1986. Cf. Traar and Birk (1989: 130) and Ulram (1989: 206).

18 Even for 1976, however, Korpi (1983: 142–3) argued that the Swedish Social Democratic Party (SAP) lost on the noneconomic issue of nuclear power rather than its economic record.

19 This is particularly noteworthy, given that econometric popularity functions for the 1970s have singled out unemployment as the key economic determinant of elections. See Frey (1979), Jonung and Wadensjö (1979), Hibbs and Madsen (1981), and Sigelman (1983).

20 The campaign issues are described in Micheletti (1989), Sainsbury (1989), and Wörlund (1989). For a survey of issue salience in 1988, see Gilljam and Holmberg (1990: ch. 2).

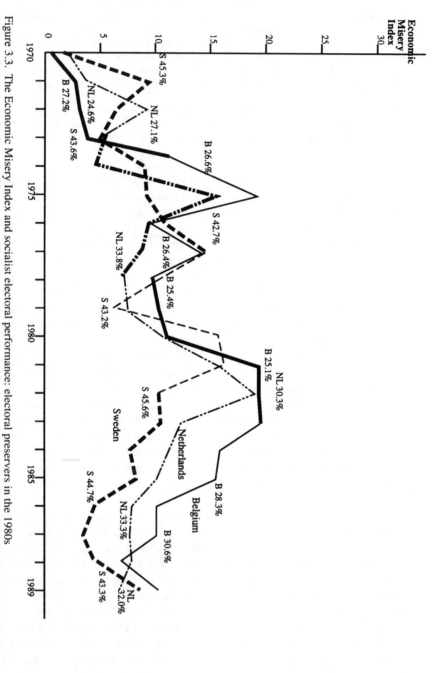

Figure 3.3. The Economic Misery Index and socialist electoral performance: electoral preservers in the 1980s
*Notes and sources:* bold lines signify party in office. Economic Misery Index = % Consumer Price Index + % unemployment – % real GDP growth. Calculated from OECD *Historical Statistics,* 1989

of the vote, while the anti-immigrant and anti-establishment New Democracy attracted 6.7%.

In the Netherlands, four of seven elections are consistent with short-term economic voting for or against the Dutch Labor Party, but only three elections are consistent with voters' long-term economic assessments over entire electoral terms. Yet most political analysts agree that the elections of the 1970s and of the second half of the 1980s were rarely fought over economic issues.[21] The PvdA's greatest successes came after years of lackluster economic performance, with unemployment going from 2.2% to 5.3% under a socialist prime minister (1977: +6.7%) and after a prolonged economic stabilization led by a bourgeois government with Labor in the opposition (1986: + 5.0%). Not surprisingly, socialist gains and losses rarely corresponded symmetrically to electoral changes of the two leading bourgeois parties, the Christian Democratic Appeal and the Liberals.

The same is true of Belgium. The socialists' electoral performance has rarely been consistent with short-term retrospective voting over the twelve-month period preceding the election (two of seven elections) or long-term economic voting over the election term (three of seven elections). In the 1970s, Belgian voters were preoccupied with the regional and linguistic question. In the 1980s, when linguistic issues subsided, the socialist opposition gained votes, although the Christian-Liberal government engineered economic stabilization. The logic of retrospective economic voting cannot explain why the incumbent bourgeois government failed to benefit from an improving economic environment.

In the three countries where socialists held on to their electoral support throughout the 1980s, then, most key elections in which socialists lost or gained votes significantly are not explained by economic voting theory. This applies to all relevant elections in Belgium (1985, 1987), the Netherlands (1977, 1981, 1986), and in Sweden at least to the 1988 election. The consistency of the Swedish election of 1976 with economic voting theory is disputed. Only the 1991 Swedish election appears to confirm economic voting, but even here the lack of symmetric losses and gains raises doubts.

*Electoral winners.* The careers of winning French, Italian, and Spanish socialist parties in the 1980s are also insufficiently explained by retrospective voting based on economic misery (Figure 3.4). This general conclusion stands even if the electoral performance of each country's *entire* left block is calculated, although communists and socialists were usually at odds over policy and coalition strategy.

In France, election results in 1973, 1978, and 1981 are consistent with the predictions of short-term and long-term retrospective economic voting. The socialist opposition gained at the expense of the bourgeois government in an era of weak economic performance. The 1986 and 1988 election results, however, are

---

21 Individual-level analysis suggests that in the late 1980s, no more than 10% to 15% of the electorate was influenced by economic perceptions. See Middentorp and Kolkuis Tanke (1990).

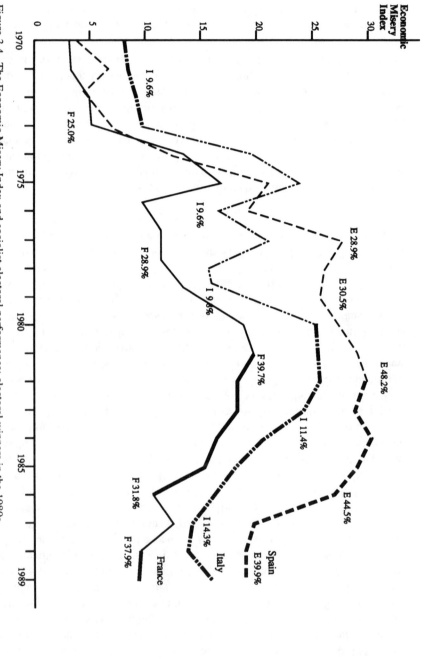

Figure 3.4. The Economic Misery Index and socialist electoral performance: electoral winners in the 1980s
*Notes and sources:* bold lines signify party in office. Economic Misery Index = % Consumer Price Index + % unemployment – % real GDP growth. Calculated from OECD Historical Statistics, 1989

inconsistent with economic voting. In 1986, a relatively successful socialist government lost the election. The same fate befell the bourgeois government two years later. Voter research shows that ideology, followed by class, anger at the government, and future expectations far outweighed the influence of retrospective economic voting in France (Lewis-Beck 1988: 82–4).

Some estimates of popularity functions have found that it is the unemployment rate that drives French party performance[22] and Lewis-Beck (1988: 10–11) reports a correlation of +.93 between unemployment and the vote for the main opposition party in legislative elections from 1958 to 1981. Based on this reasoning, the bourgeois Right should have received upward of 60% in the 1986 election, yet actually received just above 40%. Conversely, in 1988, the Left's opposition vote at 49% falls more than 10 points short of what the 1958–81 correlation would lead one to expect.

In Spain, two elections are consistent with short-term and long-term economic voting, while two are not. In 1979, the Spanish Socialist Party (PSOE) actually lost votes in a slightly improving economic environment. Its electoral support looks better because it absorbed a previously independent small socialist party. The PSOE's gain in 1982 is consistent with retrospective voting, although its magnitude (+ 17.7%) is hardly warranted by the modest intensification of economic misery after 1979. The PSOE's persistent electoral decline in 1986 and 1989 also is difficult to reconcile with the improving economic environment. Still, the PSOE ended the 1980s far better off than it had begun the decade and the main bourgeois parties did not benefit from its losses. Spanish popularity functions for the 1970s found personal income growth to be the sole economic predictor of the prime minister's popularity (Lewis-Beck 1988: 26).[23] Yet on that base, one would have expected a consistent improvement for the socialists throughout the 1980s.

In Italy, efforts to find traces of economic voting are complicated by the small size of the Italian socialist party. Surprisingly, the party's changes in electoral support are always consistent with short-term economic voting, yet only in two of three instances with long-term economic voting (1972 and 1987). In 1983, the party made electoral headway after supporting a government that presided over Italy's worst recession since World War II. Given the party's small size, its electoral changes are rarely reflected in symmetrical movements of the main bourgeois party.

The overall performance of retrospective voting theory applied to socialist winners in the 1980s is mixed at best. Many elections cannot be explained by the argument, such as the 1986 and 1988 French elections and the 1986 and 1989 Spanish elections. Nevertheless, the socialists' breakthrough in France (1981) and Spain (1982) is consistent with retrospective voting.

---

22 This is suggested by Lafay (1985), while others see unemployment as one of several significant economic variables (cf. Lewis-Beck 1980, Hibbs 1981).

23 Surveys show some economic voting, yet little party identification, class or ideological voting in the early 1980s. See Lancaster and Lewis-Beck (1986) and McDonough, Barnes, and Pina (1986).

*Retrospective voting and political business cycles*

The limits of retrospective economic voting theory can also be explored by a summary test that classifies socialist electoral change contingent upon short-term and long-term economic misery changes from the pre-election year and the year of the previous election (Table 3.3). Consistent with the theory are outcomes where left parties in government win votes in a stable or improving economy (A1 cells) or lose in a declining economy (C2 cells). Also consistent are cases where left opposition parties lose in a stable or improving economy (B1 cells) or gain in a declining economy (D2 cells). Yet short- or long-term economic performance predicts socialist party fortunes in only 25 of 54 elections. Results are no better if one makes similar calculations for individual components of the misery index, such as inflation or unemployment as predictors of party performance.

Table 3.3 permits a crude test of political business cycle theories, the intentional-strategic transformation of the causal-determinist retrospective economic voting argument. If parties know how economic performance will affect their electoral payoffs, they will attempt to schedule elections in periods of good economic performance or make sure that economic performance is improving in the election campaign. Of course, this presupposes that voters are myopic and do not discount government economic strategies shortly before an election.[24] If the economic business cycle argument is correct, elections should cluster in years when economic performance improved in the twelve months preceding the election (cells A1, A2, B1, and B2 of part I, Table 3.3). Yet only 32 of 54 elections fall into those cells, a ratio only slightly better than chance given the distribution of years with improving or deteriorating economic performance in the nine countries. If similar calculations are performed for inflation or unemployment – the strategic variables that politicians wish to influence – the results are no better.[25]

Damaging for political business cycle theory is also the observation that even after pre-election years with an improving economy, socialist incumbents are less likely to gain than to lose votes (5 gains versus 11 losses). In the same economic situation, socialist opposition parties more often improve than give up electoral support (10 gains versus 6 losses). The business cycle theory's argument that improving economies help incumbents is not borne out.

Overall, the evidence of nine European countries from 1970 to 1990 does not

---

24 I am relying here on the basic elements of business cycle theory reported by Alt and Chrystal (1983: 105–12), who primarily draw on Nordhaus (1975). The business cycle literature must be clearly separated from the "partisan politics" argument according to which left governments attend to their core constituencies *after* winning elections (cf. Alt 1985; Alesina 1989; Alvarez et al. 1991).

25 Findings are even less supportive of political business cycle theory if politicians are expected to time elections in years that show an improvement over the year of the previous election. Only 26 of 54 elections took place under such circumstances. In 17 of these 26 cases socialist incumbents lost or socialist opposition parties gained votes.

Table 3.3. *Economic performance and socialist party electoral fortunes*

| | I. Change of economic misery from the pre-election year | | II. Change of economic misery from the previous election | |
|---|---|---|---|---|
| | Left in government | Left in opposition | Left in government | Left in opposition |
| **Stable or improving economy** | | | | |
| Left gains votes | *A1:* 5 Elections (A79, G72, G80, I87, NL 77) | *B1:* 10 Elections (A70, B85, B87, F73, F78, F88, NL86, S79, S82, UK87) | *A1:* 2 Elections (A79, I87) | *B1:* 8 Elections (A70, B85, B87, F88, I79, NL86, S79, UK87) |
| Left loses votes | *A2:* 11 Elections (A83, A86, A90, B78, F86, G70, S70, S73, S88, SP86, SP89) | *B2:* 6 Elections (G87, G90, I76, NL89, SP79, UK83) | *A2:* 9 Elections (A86, B78, F86, S70, S85, S88, SP86, SP89, UK79) | *B2:* 7 Elections (G87, G90, NL71, NL72, NL89, SP79, UK83) |
| **Declining economy** | | | | |
| Left gains votes | *C1:* 5 Elections (A71, A74, G80, NL82, UK74/II) | *D1:* 5 Elections (F81, I79, NL71, NL72, SP82) | *C1:* 7 Elections (A71, A75, G72, G80, NL77, NL82, I83) | *D1:* 6 Elections (F73, F78, F81, S82, SP82, UK74/II) |
| Left loses votes | *C2:* 9 Elections (B71, B74, B81, G83, I72, S76, S85, UK70, UK79) | *D2:* 3 Elections (B77, UK74/I, NL81) | *C2:* 11 Elections (A83, A90, B71, B74, B81, G76, G83, I72, S73, S76, UK70) | *D2:* 4 Elections (B77, I76, NL81, UK74/I) |

*Note:* A stable or improving economy is defined as a misery index declining from the pre-election year to the election year (columns I) or from the previous election (columns II) to the election year. A = Austria; B = Belgium; F = France; G = Germany; I = Italy; NL = Netherlands; S = Sweden; SP = Spain; UK = United Kingdom.

support the claims of political business cycle theory.[26] Elections often take place in a declining economy and even if the economy improves, incumbents frequently lose votes. More attention must be paid to the institutional conditions that help voters to frame the attribution of political responsibility for the economy.

26 See the findings surveyed by Schneider and Frey (1988: 239–40) and the recent tests of the argument in comparative studies by Schmidt (1983), Lewis-Beck (1988: 142–46), and Alesina (1989: 75). For Britain, however, a study by Clarke and Whiteley (1990) has found supporting evidence.

### The structural vulnerability of governments to economic voting

Based on a sample of five countries, Lewis-Beck (1988: 105) infers that the extent of economic voting in a country depends on its coalition complexity and rate of growth. While the substantive interpretation of his analysis is debatable,[27] I endorse the thrust of Lewis-Beck's argument to search for institutional and structural circumstances that influence the salience of economic performance for voters' choices. But governments' vulnerability to economic voting can be explored with more refined instruments than the one constructed by Lewis-Beck. The more central governments control public policy and the simpler the party composition of the cabinet, the easier it is for voters to attribute economic performance to political parties. Table 3.4, column (1), employs a measure of government control over policy previously introduced in Table 3.2, and a measure of government simplicity [column (2)]. Beyond such institutional factors, high levels of economic misery and great magnitudes of economic fluctuation may influence voters' attribution of salience to economic issues. Columns (3) and (4) in Table 3.4 thus add the average of economic misery and its standard deviation to the aggregate index of a government's structural vulnerability to economic voting reported in column (5).

Figure 3.5 shows the association between the structural vulnerability of governments to economic voting and the actual incidence of economic voting in each country, as measured by the difference between the number of elections consistent and inconsistent with retrospective economic voting theory, when voting is predicted by economic changes from the time of the previous election. The figure reveals a weak association between structural vulnerability and economic voting. Outliers are Austria, which has too little economic voting in light of its structural conditions, and Germany, which has too much.

### Retrospective economic voting and "pure" socialist governments: A regression analysis

In order to explore the role of retrospective economic voting further, I have regressed the change of electoral support for socialist and bourgeois government or opposition parties on economic misery, unemployment, and inflation. For each of these economic indicators, I have created three independent variables as predictors of electoral fortunes: first, the level of economic performance in the pre-election year; second, short-term changes from the pre-election to the election year; third,

---

27 Lewis-Beck claims that in 1984 France had a government coalition more complex than that of Germany and therefore provided little evidence of economic voting. Given that the socialist party alone held an absolute majority of seats in the National Assembly, I do not see how economic voting was measurably more complex than in Britain or Germany, countries in which Lewis-Beck detected a somewhat greater voter propensity to support parties based on retrospective economic assessments.

## Table 3.4. Structural vulnerability of governments to economic voting

| | (1) | (2) | (3) | | (4) | | | (5) |
|---|---|---|---|---|---|---|---|---|
| | Government influence on policy | Simplicity of government coalition | Average economic misery 1969–88 | | Standard deviation of economic misery | | | Structural conduciveness to economic voting index of (1) + (2) + (3b) + (4c) |
| | | | (a) | (b) | (a) | (b) | (c) | |
| United Kingdom | 2.0 | 2.0 | 14.6 | 2.0 | 6.69 | .49 | 0.0 | 6.0 |
| France | 2.0 | 2.0 | 11.4 | 1.5 | 5.37 | .47 | 0.0 | 5.5 |
| Spain | 0.5 | 2.0 | 18.8 | 2.0 | 10.2 | .54 | 0.5 | 5.0 |
| Austria | 1.0 | 1.5 | 4.1 | 0.0 | 3.22 | .79 | 2.0 | 4.5 |
| Netherlands | 1.5 | 1.5 | 8.4 | 1.0 | 4.65 | .55 | 0.5 | 4.5 |
| Germany | 0.0 | 2.0 | 5.1 | 0.0 | 4.02 | .74 | 2.0 | 4.0 |
| Belgium | 0.5 | 1.0 | 10.7 | 1.5 | 6.25 | .59 | 1.0 | 4.0 |
| Sweden | 0.5 | 2.0 | 8.0 | 0.5 | 4.10 | .55 | 0.5 | 3.5 |
| Italy | 0.5 | 0.0 | 15.9 | 2.0 | 6.23 | .39 | 0.0 | 2.5 |

*Sources and coding:*

Column (1): Addition of values in Table 3.2, columns (1) and (2).

Column (2): Dominant type of (coalition) government in country
- 0.0: Complex oversized or undersized governments.
- 1.0: 2 major parties in majoritarian coalition.
- 1.5: Coalitions of type 1.0 and 2.0 occur frequently.
- 2.0: Single-party government or one major party.

Column (3): a: Averages of data employed in Figures 3.2–3.4.
b: Transformation of intervals in column (3a) into values in (3b).

| (3a) | <6.0 | <8.0 | <10.0 | <12.0 | >12.0 |
|---|---|---|---|---|---|
| (3b) | 0.0 | 0.5 | 1.0 | 1.5 | 2.0 |

Column (4): a: Standard deviations of values employed in Figures 3.2–3.4.
b: Ratio of standard deviation (4a) to mean value of economic misery (3a).
c: Transformation of (4b) into intervals ranging from 0.0 to 2.0.

| (4b) | <.50 | <.55 | <.60 | <.65 | >.65 |
|---|---|---|---|---|---|
| (4c) | 0.0 | 0.5 | 1.0 | 1.5 | 2.0 |

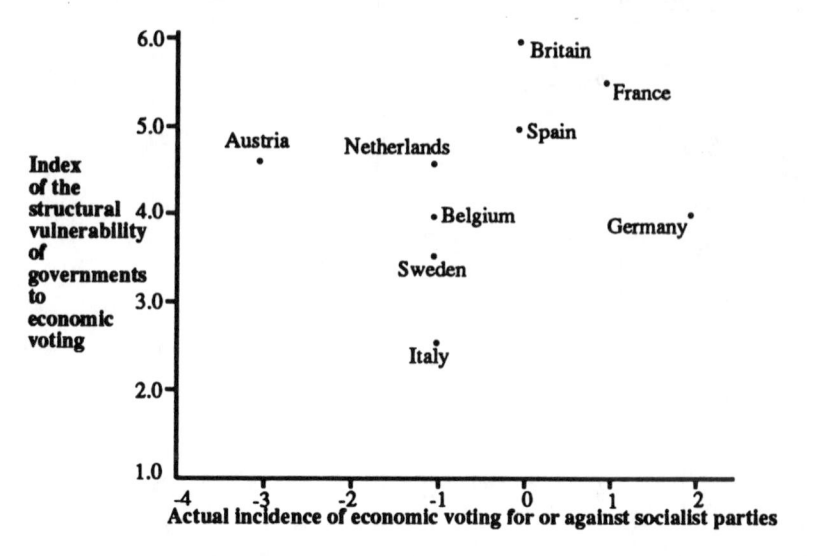

Figure 3.5. The structural vulnerability of governments to economic voting and socialist party exposure to economic voting
*Notes and sources:* Index of Structural Vulnerability: see Table 3.5. Incidence of Economic Voting: number of elections between 1970 and 1990 in which gross change of socialist electoral support in accordance with economic voting minus number of elections in which this was not the case (derived from Table 3.3, columns B).

long-term change from the previous election to the present election.[28]

Regression of these economic variables does not explain socialist electoral performance when bourgeois parties are in office. Also bourgeois party performance in government proves to be by and large immune to changing economic fortunes. Whenever socialists are in government, however, and particularly when they govern as "pure" socialist cabinets without the support of major bourgeois parties, economic performance has a statistically significant impact on the parties' subsequent electoral performance, as regression equations in Table 3.5 demonstrate. The signs of the coefficients in these equations, however, often reveal a rather different relationship between economic performance and electoral fortunes of the Left than one might expect from retrospective economic voting theory.

In the period from 1970 to 1990, socialist governments generally *benefited* at the polls when economic misery worsened over the preceding electoral term (equation 1). This holds true even once levels of economic misery in the pre-election year have been controlled.[29] Socialist governments suffered, however, when levels of

28 By differencing most independent variables and the dependent variable, problems of autocorrelation can be minimized. Moreover, change rates have a clear substantive meaning for the theory I am testing.
29 Change rates of economic misery from the preelection year to the election year have insignificant effects no matter what the specification of the statistical model is. The relationship between economic changes over the entire electoral term and socialist party performance remains when the level of economic misery is deleted as an independent variable.

Table 3.5. *The effects of economic performance on socialist electoral fortunes*

|  | Parameter estimate | *t*-value |
|---|---|---|
| 1. Economic misery: Socialist electoral payoff in "pure" socialist governments ($N = 19$) | | |
| Intercept | −.93 | −1.020 |
| Misery level in the pre-election year | −.09 | −1.079 |
| Change of misery level from past election year | +.22 | +2.768 |
| Adjusted $R^2$: | .27 | ($p < .03$) |
| Durbin-Watson: | 2.40 | |
| 2. Unemployment: Socialist electoral payoff in "pure" socialist governments ($N = 19$) | | |
| Intercept | −.32 | −.410 |
| Unemployment level in the pre-election year | −.27 | −2.705 |
| Change of unemployment from the past election | +.12 | .419 |
| Adjusted $R^2$: | .23 | ($p < .05$) |
| Durbin-Watson: | 2.02 | |
| 3. Inflation: Socialist electoral payoff in "pure" socialist governments ($N = 19$) | | |
| Intercept | −1.27 | −2.65 |
| Change of inflation from the past election year | +.47 | +3.888 |
| Adjusted $R^2$: | .44 | ($p < .001$) |
| Durbin-Watson: | 2.32 | |
| 4. Joint impact of inflation and unemployment: "Pure" socialist governments ($N = 19$) | | |
| Intercept | −1.410 | −2.950 |
| Level of unemployment in pre-election year | −.143 | −1.517 |
| Change of unemployment from the past election | +.33 | +1.230 |
| Level of inflation in pre-election year | +.02 | +.090 |
| Change of inflation from the past election | +.42 | 2.454 |
| Adjusted $R^2$: | .48 | ($p < .01$) |
| Durbin-Watson: | 2.33 | |

unemployment were high, even though they may not have risen under socialist governments in the short or long term (equation 2). Inflation, finally, exercised a much stronger effect on socialist party performance than did unemployment, yet it is contrary to the predictions of retrospective economic voting theory. Pure socialist governments benefited from rising inflation and suffered when inflation fell (equation 3). Equation 4 provides a more complete picture pitting unemployment and inflation against each other. The significant and negative intercept indicates that socialist government parties slightly lost votes, no matter what their economic performance. If the general liability of incumbency is not the major cause of this result, noneconomic issues are likely to contribute to such losses.[30] Further, equation 4 shows that socialist governments' efforts to lower inflation hurt them most. A second (and not quite significant) negative factor is a constant high unemployment rate, but it is offset by a statistically insignificant tendency that rising unemployment boosts socialist government fortunes. Changes in inflation

30 In the theoretical model sketched in Chapter 1 and elaborated in Chapter 4, such issues are likely to relate to the libertarian–authoritarian components of the parties' competitive dimension.

remain the strongest predictor of left party electoral performance. Regression diagnostics show that this finding is not driven by any single case.[31]

Employing the structural vulnerability of governments to economic voting (Table 3.4) as an interactive term does not substantially increase the variance of socialist government performance explained by economic variables. Dividing the sample into socialist governments in the 1970s and governments in the 1980s, however, reveals that all significant correlations between economic performance and socialist governments' electoral fortunes occur only in the 1980s, whereas such relations are statistically insignificant for the 1970s.[32]

It is not difficult to make sense of these findings. Lowering inflation and increasing unemployment involve a monetarist philosophy of economic belt tightening and austerity that hurts groups in vulnerable labor market positions. This is exactly what left governments delivered in the early 1980s in Germany, throughout the 1980s in Austria, France, or Spain, and, to a lesser extent, in the late 1980s in Sweden. Where socialist governments implemented this strategy over a longer period of time, they were electorally *punished* by voters disappointed by an insufficient reduction of unemployment. At the same time, this strategy enabled socialist parties to *prevent* a lasting electoral resurgence of bourgeois competitors who were unable to offer a substantively different economic strategy. The major bourgeois opposition parties thus did not substantively gain when the Austrian, French, or Spanish socialists lost votes in elections during the 1980s. In an environment where the main competing parties could not offer economic policy alternatives, it became easier for disappointed voters to justify their choice *by noneconomic issues.* The socialists' policy may thus have indirectly and unintentionally contributed to the increasing salience of the communitarian dimension of party competition. Thus political strategies, not just socioeconomic change, affect the nature of the issues politicized in the electoral arena.

Why are socialist governments punished for the pursuit of economic austerity policies, while bourgeois governments can count on neutral voter reactions to the same bitter medicine? As Scharpf (1987b: 245–6) has argued, bourgeois governments are in a secure position as long as inflation is low even if unemployment is high. This combination satisfies business and the middle salariat, whose members, at least until recently, have occupied recession-proof jobs. Conversely, a socialist government pursuing the same policy may maintain its electoral support in the middle salariat yet endanger the loyalty of its blue collar core constituency. Scharpf here restates Przeworski and Sprague's theory of strategic trade-offs between the working class and allied support for the Left, but overlooks the fact that the division between winners and losers of monetarist austerity policies may

31 All the countries where socialists remained in office in the 1980s – France, Italy, Spain, and Sweden – show the same link between declining inflation and declining social democratic electoral fortunes.

32 For the 1980s decade taken by itself, the change rate of inflation over the entire electoral term predicts as much as 62% of the variance in socialist electoral change. Adding the unemployment level in the preelection year increases the explained variance to 70%.

cut across class lines and affect sectors, occupational groups, and regions within each economic class in different ways. Even if we drop the class trade-off hypothesis,[33] however, it is clear that socialist governments are hurting some of their vital constituencies by economic austerity policies. Nevertheless, they may hope to hold on to enough economic winners of austerity policies to prevent the resurgence of a bourgeois party majority.

In the new environment of liberalized capital markets and intensifying international competition in the 1980s, socialists apparently faced a Catch-22 situation between outright electoral decline and ephemeral, transitory electoral success. Either they promised economic austerity policies that initially boosted their support but contributed to their later gradual electoral decline when enacted; or they remained true to their run-of-the-mill Keynesian economic prescriptions and were kept on the opposition benches.[34] Socialist opposition parties that promised reflation never got a chance to govern, as the cases of Belgium, Britain, Germany, and the Netherlands in the 1980s demonstrate.

An economic analysis of the electoral performance of pure socialist governments in the 1980s reveals the fleeting nature of left electoral success in France, Italy, and Spain, but sheds little light on what causes parties to pursue such strategies. One key question is why some socialist parties, but not others, were willing to subscribe to austerity policies and, in some instances, even to announce them before elections to take advantage of the electoral marketplace. The other key question is why socialist parties were unable to seize on the new communitarian issues that inspired voters who were disaffected by the socialists' conventional Keynesian or new monetarist economic policies to support new parties. As I will show later, social democratic strategies and outcomes are accounted for by the structure of party competition (Chapter 4), social democrats' intraorganizational decision making (Chapter 5), and each party's ideological traditions and innovations (Chapter 6).

My discussion of the electoral consequences of economic policy strategies for socialist government incumbents has revealed weaknesses of retrospective economic voting theory, but also an interesting result which is at first sight counterintuitive given the basic assumptions of economic voting. The theory can show why socialist governments that pursued austerity policies in the 1980s faced an uphill electoral battle. It cannot explain, however, why these parties attract voters in the first place and where voters went once they withdrew from the socialist camp. The theory has nothing meaningful to say about the performance of nonsocialist parties. Overall, it lacks an argument accounting for the preferences and economic interpretations of voter groups characterized by different market and occupational

33  As I have shown in Chapter 2, there is no empirical or theoretical reason to believe that socialists suffered from a class trade-off in the 1970s and 1980s.

34  As Luebbert (1991: 227–32) has shown, a similar problem beset socialist governments in liberal democracies in the late 1920s. They obtained government office only where they abandoned their more ambitious programs, but precisely the compliance with the liberal economic order also precipitated their political decline.

positions. Finally, the theory does not explain why socialist parties choose different electoral appeals and policy options in West European countries and often cannot seize upon the noneconomic political issues that have gained salience in the electoral arena. Taken by themselves, economic parameters account for the trajectory of socialist parties in the 1970s and 1980s only to a very limited extent.

### 3.3 POLITICAL-ECONOMIC INSTITUTIONS AND LEFT PARTY PERFORMANCE

Two sets of economic institutions are said to have boosted socialist electoral strength in Western Europe over the past decades. Centralized labor unions with close ties to the Left ("labor corporatism") permit socialist governments to pursue expansionary fiscal policies in order to promote growth and employment while simultaneously restraining the demands of labor representatives in collective bargaining and thus dampening inflationary pressures. Moreover, the organizational centralization of unions allied to left parties binds voters to the socialist block and thus stabilizes its electoral performance. Social democrats should also derive electoral benefits from a comprehensive, egalitarian welfare state with a wide array of public services that creates a vast constituency beholden to social democratic parties because they have been instrumental in building and guaranteeing such institutions.[35]

Labor corporatism and the welfare state play a dual role in shaping the electoral fortunes of socialist parties. On the one hand, they extend or constrain socialist government capabilities in economic policy-making and thus affect the parties' vulnerability to *retrospective* economic voting. On the other, a long-term proven track record of socialist government capacity may generate *prospective* voter expectations that are independent of recent socialist government performance and in fact *protect* socialist governments from the potentially negative effects of retrospective economic voting. In other words, corporatist and welfare state institutions may affect not only the odds that economic decline hurts socialist parties, but also the salience of macro-economic performance for socialist electorates.

I will argue in this section, however, that this conventional theory is not borne out by the facts. In the 1980s, socialist parties appear to be more likely to suffer electorally precisely where the institutional configuration looks favorable to them. While welfare states and labor corporatism may have been designed to serve social democratic interests in the past, they now bring about unintended consequences that render the relationship between political-economic institutions and socialist party performance indeterminate, if not negative. Because the welfare state and

35 The influence of social democracy on creating the welfare state has often been indirect. For example, nonsocialist parties often promoted the welfare state to preempt more extreme economic and political demands advanced by the Left (cf. Flora and Alber 1981). And it is more the power configuration between the Left and its bourgeois competitors than absolute electoral strength that accounts for the shape of the modern welfare state (cf. Castles 1978; Schmidt 1982; Esping-Andersen 1990).

labor corporatism are no longer decisive for socialist success, left parties situated in similar institutional environments have experienced rather different electoral careers in the 1970s and 1980s.

### *Labor corporatism, economic success, and left party fortunes*

Contrary to the institution-free world of economic theories of party competition (Downs 1957) and to rational partisan governance theories that attribute policy outcomes to the ideological convictions of governing parties (Hibbs 1977; Castles 1982; Roubini and Sachs 1989), research in the 1980s has linked the economic performance of leftist governments to the existence of labor corporatism with centralized unions that restrain the wage demands of their rank and file (Schmitter 1981; Cameron 1984; Lange 1984). Lange and Garrett (1985) argue in their general model that, on average, economies perform well only if there is a close match between the political composition of a country's government and the institutions of economic interest intermediation.[36] According to this congruency theory, left governments in polities with labor corporatism may stimulate economic growth through expansive fiscal policies that promote full employment without fueling inflation because such governments can secure union support for modest nominal wage increases. Centralized unions agree to such strategies because they can discipline radical rank-and-file opposition whose members cannot defect to more radical unions. Conversely, where labor unions are decentralized and organize only a small share of all employees, expansionary policies are inflationary. Under these circumstances, only the opposite congruous arrangement – bourgeois governments choosing fiscal austerity policies and avoiding cooperation with the fragmented sector of labor representatives – can achieve good economic results. The worst of all possible worlds is realized in regimes where the partisan color of government is incongruous with the structure of interest intermediation or where interest intermediation and government coalitions have a mixed complexion.

Scharpf (1987a: 26–8) has objected to this congruency model that the nature and effects of actual government policies cannot be gleaned from the correlation of regime configurations and economic results. According to Scharpf, the simple congruency model presupposes that (1) left governments indeed resort to expansionist fiscal policies together with restrictive incomes policies with corporatist management and (2) the character of economic growth problems is Keynesian. Only in a Keynesian world is the mixture of government expansion and income restriction viable, because economic crises are due to a shortfall of demand, and inflation is driven by a wage–price spiral under conditions of full employment. What, however, if the underlying economic problem is not Keynesian, but classical, as Scharpf maintains for the period of the 1980s? In a classical crisis, depressed profit levels and high wages, not demand shortfall, cause economic stagnation and

---

36 For elaborations of this argument see Garrett and Lange (1986, 1989), Hicks (1988), Alvarez, Garrett, and Lange (1991), and the debate between Jackman (1987, 1989), a critic of the argument, and Lange and Garrett (1987) as well as Hicks (1988) and Hicks and Patterson (1989).

cannot be remedied by the array of policy instruments associated with social democratic corporatism.

In the 1980s, the reemergence of a classical economic crisis was caused by the increasing mobility of capital, flowing to countries and investment opportunities offering the highest return, and the technology-induced restructuring of companies that puts pressure on an increasing differentiation of wage scales to attract scarce highly skilled specialists. These changes, in turn, generated a growing pool of unskilled excess labor. In this situation, national economic policymakers lost their fiscal and monetary policy autonomy and were compelled to engage in supply-side policies that lower taxes on profits and cut back on subsidies, deregulate the economy, and abstain from industrial policy in order to promote efficient market allocation and to redistribute resources from consumption to investment and from individuals holding abundant skills to those having scarce skills. Scharpf argues in favor of a "complex" congruency theory, according to which governments reap economic benefits only if they seize (1) on the correct economic theory that (2) matches the economic situation to (3) the institutional restrictions. Hence, in the 1980s social democratic governments were forced to pursue austerity policies to tackle a classical economic crisis. Corporatism plus demand-side Keynesianism was a successful recipe only for the 1970s.

My goal is not to decide whether Lange and Garrett or Scharpf provide the better political explanation of economic outcomes in the 1980s.[37] Instead I wish to expand the two theories beyond the range of application intended by their authors in order to explore whether labor corporatism can account for the electoral fortunes of social democracy in the 1980s. If voters act on rational expectations that are driven by a model of partisan government and political-economic institutions, they would commit themselves to different electoral strategies, depending on whether they subscribe to Lange and Garrett's simple congruency theory or to Scharpf's complex alternative.

If Lange and Garrett are correct and congruous political regimes outperform incongruous or mixed regimes, socialist governments in corporatist countries should, on average, remain electorally strong, at least as long as they remain faithful to Keynesian fiscal policies and to wage moderation because voters have incorporated expectations about the institutional efficacy of such policies into their voting calculus (hypothesis 1.1). Moreover, if a socialist government's recent economic record has been weak, voters should be less willing to abandon it in a

---

37 As Garrett and Lange (1991) show themselves, *change rates* in the employment of economic policy instruments by governments of different partisan complexion in the 1980s can hardly be explained in terms of the simple congruency theory. What can still be explained in such terms, of course, are *levels* of economic instrument variables, such as budget balance and government expenditure, social wage and public employment, tax revenue and income tax, that have their origins in economic periods preceding the 1980s. Crepaz (1992) has shown that corporatist configurations still depress inflation, unemployment, and strikes in the 1980s, but do not boost GDP growth. Given the low levels of unemployment and strike activity in corporatist countries in the 1970s, a better test for the continuing effect of corporatism may be to account for the change rate of economic performance indicators from the 1970s to the 1980s.

corporatist regime than in mixed or in fragmented, pluralist systems of interest intermediation that undercut the effectiveness of Keynesian policy. In general, congruous regimes should experience *less* retrospective economic voting as punishment of government incumbents than mixed or incongruous regimes (hypothesis 1.2). Moreover, whether retrospective economic voting takes place or not, voters should favor parties that reestablish regime congruency (hypothesis 1.3).

If Scharpf's complex congruency theory is correct, in the 1980s social democratic governments should have electorally performed badly even in corporatist regimes with Keynesian strategies because the latter have been rendered ineffective (hypothesis 2.1). In the 1980s, only voters in pluralist-bourgeois regimes had an incentive to ignore short-term economic performance and to confirm bourgeois parties in office regardless of short-term economic results because socialists could not offer an alternative to austerity policy in a classical economic crisis (hypothesis 2.2). In labor corporatist regimes with socialist governments, bourgeois parties should have benefited from retrospective economic voting and done well even if the governing labor parties enjoyed some economic successes, because confidence in corporatist strategies was shaken (hypothesis 2.3).

Cross tables of labor regimes and social democratic electoral success (Table 3.6A) and of retrospective economic voting for left parties in the 1980s contingent upon regime congruency (party complexion of government consistent with labor regime) provide a first test of these hypotheses. In Table 3.6A, two different indicators of corporatism were employed to assess the character of labor regimes, one developed by Lijphart and Crepaz (1991), based on twelve previous studies, and one by Alvarez, Garrett, and Lange (1991), based on union density and centralization. No data are available on Spain and in two instances, Germany and the Netherlands, the latter index would indicate a pluralist labor regime while the former identifies a mixed regime, a difference that does not significantly alter the interpretation of the table for my purposes.

Contrary to the first hypothesis, derived from the extension of Lange and Garrett's theory, socialists in corporatist countries suffered electoral losses in the 1980s or remained level.[38] The only socialist winners are located in pluralist labor regimes. The second hypothesis, that congruous labor and government regimes experience less economic voting than mixed and incongruous regimes, also receives little support from the evidence presented in Table 3.6B. In congruous regimes, 4 of 10 elections evidence economic voting, in all other regimes, 8 of 16 elections (hypothesis 1.2). Even less supportive of the simple congruency theory is the fact that, contrary to hypothesis 1.3 and regardless of whether economic voting took place, in most elections where voters had a choice between congruous and incongruous regimes [columns (1) and (3)], socialist gains or losses overwhelmingly tended to support incongruous governments (7 of 10 elections without economic voting; 3 of 6 elections with economic voting). Most disturbing, in Austria (1986, 1990) and in Sweden (1985, 1988) congruous social democratic

---

38 This tendency would be more articulated had other medium to high corporatist cases, particularly Norway and Denmark, been included in this study.

Table 3.6. *Labor corporatism, regime congruency, and socialist economic voting*

A. Labor regime and socialist performance in the 1980s

| | Labor corporatism | Mixed labor regime | Pluralist labor regime |
|---|---|---|---|
| Socialist winners | | | Italy (LC: −.851; AGL: 1.58) France (LC: −.725; AGL: .81) Spain: no data |
| Socialist stabilizers | Sweden (LC: 1.40; AGL: 3.62) | Netherlands (LC: 1.00; AGL: 1.89) Belgium (LC: .258; AGL: 2.77) | |
| Socialist losers | Austria (LC: 1.60; AGL: 3.19) | Germany (LC: .48; AGL: 1.73) | Britain (LC: −.862; AGL: 1.93) |

*Source:* Rankings of labor regimes are from Lijphart and Crepaz (1991), abbreviated LC, and from Alvarez, Garrett, and Lange (1991), abbreviated AGL. Note that the metric for each of the sources is different and that the labor regimes can be compared only within the same metric.

B. Retrospective economic voting for socialist parties in the 1980s and congruency between Labor regime and government party[a]

| | Congruous regime | Mixed regime | Incongruous regime |
|---|---|---|---|
| Consistency of socialist electoral performance with retrospective economic voting[b] | | | |
| Consistent | *Austria 1983* Britain 1983 *France 1981* *Spain 1982* | Belgium 1981 Germany 1983, 1987, 1990 Netherlands 1981, 1989 | *Italy 1987* Sweden 1982 |
| Inconsistent | *Austria 1986, 1990* *Britain 1987* *France 1988* *Sweden 1985, 1988* | Belgium 1985, 1987 Netherlands 1982, 1986 | France 1986 *Italy 1983* Spain 1986, 1989 |

[a]Italicized entries are elections where the vote went against congruency between labor regime and government party.
[b]Consistency with retrospective economic voting is based on Table 3.4, columns (b).

governments were weakened *although* they had improved the economy. Conversely, socialists in the pluralist countries of France and Italy gained votes *although* incumbent congruous bourgeois governments had improved the economy or socialist incumbents had contributed to worsening it (France 1988; Italy 1983).

Overall, these findings do not substantiate the simple congruency theory. The extension of Scharpf's complex congruency theory, however, fares only marginally better. The failure of Keynesian policies in congruent labor corporatist regimes in the 1980s is evidenced by the decline of Austrian and Swedish left governments and the stagnation or decline of left governments in mixed regimes (hypothesis 2.1). It is puzzling, however, that socialists performed so well in pluralist labor regimes. Moreover, the cases of France (1981) and Spain (1982) show that bourgeois governments pursuing austerity policies in pluralist regimes in the face of a classical economic crisis could not maintain electoral strength, even though rational voters should have expected no improvement from a socialist government. Most surprising is that in an environment of favorable economic performance bourgeois incumbents in pluralist regimes lost votes and office to socialists (France 1988) (hypothesis 2.2). Finally, in congruous labor corporatist regimes, the main bourgeois parties advocating economic austerity policy rarely benefited to any appreciable extent from socialist losses, thus indicating that voters did not abandon socialist parties because of their economic policies (hypothesis 2.3). This is illustrated by elections in Austria (1983, 1986, 1990) and Sweden (1988).[39] It is also true that in mixed and incongruous regimes, bourgeois parties advocating a rational strategy of economic austerity often do not benefit from socialist losses, as is shown by elections in France (1986), Germany (1987, 1990), and Spain (1986, 1989).

If Scharpf's theory is correct, socialist governments should experience the greatest electoral decline in the 1980s in pluralist regimes, when accelerating economic misery, and inflation in particular, call for economic austerity programs. Bourgeois parties typically have the reputation for enacting such programs. My discussion of retrospective economic voting, however, showed that the electoral fortunes of socialist government parties actually declined the more successful they were in implementing austerity programs and the more they reduced economic misery and inflation. Socialist government support declined with decelerating inflation in Austria (1986, 1990), France (1986), Spain (1986, 1989), and Sweden (1985, 1988), with only Italy (1983, 1987) representing an outlier.

If we include the institutions of the labor regime as an interactive term impinging on change rates of economic misery or inflation, does this complex relationship at least *depress* the perverse negative relation between economic improvement and socialist electoral decline in office detected in Table 3.5? Following the extension of Lange and Garrett's argument, *only* in labor corporatist regimes, where voters have little trust in bourgeois parties, might socialist governments be expected to benefit from higher economic misery and inflation, whereas in pluralist regimes bourgeois parties offer a better alternative to fight economic ills. As equations in Table 3.7 demonstrate, however, the reverse is true. The interaction between economic misery (inflation) and pluralist labor regimes actually strengthens the explanatory power of the linkage between economic improvement and the elec-

---

39 The same rationale applies to Sweden in 1991 where the three established bourgeois parties lost 2.2% compared to 1988, while the social democrats lost over 5%.

toral decline of socialist incumbents. In the 1980s, socialist governments in the pluralist French and Spanish regimes lost most when they accomplished the greatest reduction in inflation. This observation is inconsistent with the extension of Scharpf's complex congruency theory as well which would predict governments that succeeded with anti-inflationary austerity policies in the 1980s to win.[40]

To conclude this discussion, a brief glance at the actual policies pursued by socialist governments in the 1980s may lend some descriptive plausibility to the cross tables and statistics I have presented so far. Consistent with Scharpf's analysis, the main message is that socialists could assert their electorally dominant position in the 1980s only where they abandoned Keynesian demand side policies. Yet contrary to Scharpf's expectation, even in these circumstances and in the face of considerable success with fighting inflation and budget deficits, socialist governments with austerity policies tended to lose voters, although their electoral decline often left them above their 1970s support levels.

The Austrian and Swedish social democratic governments, situated in congruent regimes with labor corporatism, were slow to abandon Keynesian demand-side strategies in the early 1980s. In Austria, a deep crisis of the technically and managerially outmoded public industrial sector eventually brought about a change of heart (cf. Müller 1988), but only after the SPÖ had gone through two consecutive elections in which it sustained severe losses. By the late 1980s, the government focused on supply-side measures to improve the competitiveness of Austrian industries, a policy that bore electoral fruit only in the party's relative stabilization in the 1990 election.

Also in Sweden, the incoming socialist government relied on tried quasi-Keynesian instruments when it came back to office in 1982. Its drastic devaluation of the Swedish Krona amounted to a Keynesian export demand boost with inflationary domestic consequences that were to be fought by wage restraint, but precisely this part of the policy package ran into mounting difficulties. The centralized Swedish labor unions and employers' organizations began to show signs of internal division, with significant suborganizations willing to defect from peak bargaining to seek wage settlements for particular sectors or occupational groups. The government's traditional policy of refraining from direct incomes policy was gradually eroded by indirect exchanges in which governments promised tax reductions in exchange for wage concessions and by the government's confrontational bargaining strategy in public sector wage negotiations.[41]

---

40 At the same time, it would be wrong to conclude that rising unemployment rates really explain the decline of social democratic governments in an environment of decelerating inflation. There is a comparatively weak and often insignificant negative association between *levels* of unemployment in the preelection year and the electoral performance of socialist government incumbents (cf. Table 3.5), but that linkage is not improved by a labor regime interaction term.

41 The difficulties of Swedish labor relations in the 1980s and the decline of corporatist interest intermediation have been analyzed in a literature too broad to review here. Instructive recent contributions are Ahlen (1989), Elvander (1990), Micheletti (1990; 1991), Michels and Slomp (1990), Pontusson (1990), and Swenson (1990).

Table 3.7. *The performance of socialist government incumbents in incongruous pluralist labor regimes: Interaction of economic predictors with regime status*

Change of economic misery over socialist term in office, "pure" socialist governments (N = 19)

| | Without regime interaction term | | With regime interaction term | |
|---|---|---|---|---|
| | Parameter estimate | t-value | | Parameter estimate | t-value |
| Intercept | -.93 | -1.020 | Intercept | -.88 | -1.054 |
| Misery in pre-election year | -.085 | -1.079 | Misery in pre-election year × pluralist labor regime | -.084 | -1.173 |
| Change of economic misery over electoral term | .217 | 2.768 | Change of economic misery over electoral term × pluralist labor regime | +.149 | 3.545 |
| Adjusted R²: .27 | (p < .03) | | Adjusted R²: .40 | (p < .01) | |
| Durbin-Watson: 2.41 | | | Durbin-Watson: 2.28 | | |

Change of inflation over socialist term in office, "pure" socialist governments (N = 19)

| | Without regime interaction term | | With regime interaction term | |
|---|---|---|---|---|
| | Parameter estimate | t-term | | Parameter estimate | t-value |
| Intercept | -1.55 | 1.260 | Intercept | -1.667 | -1.497 |
| Misery in pre-election year | .041 | 0.243 | Misery in pre-election year × pluralist labor regime | .065 | 0.424 |
| Change of economic misery over electoral term | .456 | 3.240 | Change of economic misery over electoral term × pluralist labor regime | .258 | 3.740 |
| Adjusted R²: .41 | (p < .007) | | Adjusted R²: .48 | (p < .004) | |
| Durbin-Watson: 2.32 | | | Durbin-Watson: 2.13 | | |

In the second half of the 1980s, the SAP government began to make belated efforts to search for innovative answers to the new challenge of international market competition and capital mobility. The government decided to give the economy no further demand-side boosts from Krona devaluations, to facilitate international capital flows, and to expose public sector companies to more competition (Andersson 1987; Mjøset 1987; Pontusson 1988b). The social democrats, however, embarked on a decisive policy break only in 1990 when Sweden was embroiled in a deep economic crisis with increasing unemployment. In this environment, the SAP government declared that fighting inflation would henceforth have priority over maintaining employment, enacted cuts in social expenditure and health care, revised its energy policy to keep nuclear power plants operating, and eventually applied for membership in the European Community in a dramatic reversal of traditional interpretations of Swedish neutrality. All these measures, however, came too late to reestablish confidence in the social democratic government in the 1991 general election.

The French, Spanish, and Italian socialist parties, situated in pluralist systems of interest intermediation, learned to appreciate the liabilities of demand-side Keynesian policies in the 1980s much faster than their colleagues in Austria and Sweden. In France, the socialist government engaged in two years of Left–Keynesian fireworks with fiscal expansion, industrial planning, and social policy reform before changing its interpretation of the economic situation and embarking on a course of fiscal austerity (Bell and Criddle 1988: ch. 8; Hall 1987). In Spain, the socialists participated in economic austerity policies even before assuming office in 1982 and intensified their commitment after taking power (cf. Share 1989: ch. 4). They immediately set out on a policy of rationalizing the large Franquist state-owned industrial sector and spinning off components into an open market environment (Williams 1989). In the area of social policy, reforms fell short of voters' expectations, such as in the health care sector (Gillespie 1989: 423) or in the pension system, where the party withdrew from promises made to the labor unions (Radice and Radice 1986: 133; Gillespie 1989: 429–30). Even in Italy, where the PSI always remained a junior partner of a broad bourgeois dominated coalition government, the PSI championed economic austerity policies in a profound reversal of policies the party had advocated in the 1970s (cf. DiScala 1988: ch. 11–14).

In all three countries, the rapid move toward supply-side economics paid off in the electoral arena, although economic stabilization without a significant reduction in unemployment resulted in some electoral erosion for the French and Spanish socialists. By 1987 the Italian party reached its highest level of voter support in more than two decades. The Spanish socialists preserved their hegemony throughout the 1980s, although some electoral losses from the dizzying heights of the 1982 election (+17.7% compared to 1979) were inevitable. In France, the socialists suffered electoral defeat in 1986 but still maintained a higher support level than in the 1970s, and came back to win the 1988 election, although the economy had improved under the bourgeois government incumbents from 1986 to 1988. As indicated before, what is particularly interesting is that the main French and Spanish bourgeois parties did not gain votes, even in elections that generated considerable socialist losses.

The opposite situation prevailed in the four countries where socialist parties spent much of the 1980s in the opposition. Here socialists often could not significantly improve their electoral support base even when bourgeois government parties lost voters. This occurred in Germany in 1987 and 1990, in the Netherlands in 1989, and in Britain in 1983. What made socialist parties so unattractive and motivated former bourgeois voters to support third parties rather than the left opposition? While neither simple nor complex congruency theory can explain this movement to third parties, one fact consistent with Scharpf's approach is that socialist parties in all four countries remained faithful to a rather conventional Keynesian demand-side economic policy in their appeals as opposition parties until near the end of the decade.

During a short period in government at the beginning of the 1980s, the Belgian socialists participated in quasi-corporatist policies of income restraint that remained by and large fruitless (cf. Deweerdt and Smits 1982: 265–6). While in opposition, the parties' main economic plank was to attack the Christian-Liberal government's austerity policy (Fitzmaurice and Van den Berghe 1986). Modest steps toward "updating" the parties' socioeconomic alternative met with stiff intraparty resistance, particularly in Wallonia (Deweerdt 1987). In the Netherlands, the Labor Party fought the electoral campaigns of the 1980s primarily on noneconomic issues. In 1986, the party decried the redistributive consequences of the Christian-Liberal coalition policy, but made no promise to reflate the economy (Van der Eijk, Irwin, and Niemöller 1986: 294; Gladdish 1987: 117). By 1989, the party accepted the need to improve market capitalism and to keep the public sector within bounds (Wolinetz 1990: 282). In neither country did the left parties' economic stance attract many voters.

The German social democrats had moved toward accepting the new realities of international competition and vulnerability already in the last years of the Schmidt government by adopting elements of fiscal austerity policy (cf. Scharpf 1987a: ch. 10). But it relapsed into traditional demand-side formula during the party's first years in opposition. The party lost the 1983 and 1987 elections to the conservatives both on economic issues, floating the loose concept of an "ecological market economy," and on noneconomic issues on which it could not stake out convincing and distinctive new positions (cf. Padgett 1987; Müller-Rommel 1990: 99). In the late 1980s, the party did not suffer from a shortage of new ideas but from an internal disarray that prevented it from focusing these ideas into a clear program and electoral message.[42] The party's vague economic policy profile, among other and probably more important reasons I will discuss in the next chapters, contributed to the string of electoral defeats from 1983 to 1990.

42 Indicative of this situation are the debates during the preparation of the new Basic Program of December 1989 and the difficulties of leading personalities to agree on an operational government program. Cf. *Die Zeit,* May 12, 1989: 29.

The party that undoubtedly experienced the greatest difficulties in coping with the new economic realities of the 1980s was the British Labour Party. Rather than responding vigorously to the challenge of supply-side market efficiency, the Labour Party withdrew into the intellectual ghetto of traditional socialist visions of nationalizing industry, economic planning, expansionary fiscal policy, and incomes policy. Labour's radical stance could be put to practice only at the local level in efforts to counteract the austerity policy of the Thatcher government (cf. Gyford 1985). The oft told story of how Labour's strategy contributed to its devastating electoral performance in 1983 does not bear repeating here.[43] By the end of the decade, the Labour Party was still suffering from the reputation it acquired during long years of leftist official party stances, although it began to move away from conventional socialist ideas.

I prefaced my discussion of left party strategy and political-economic institutions with the remark that I would not seek to decide whether Lange and Garrett's simple congruency theory or Scharpf's complex alternative is correct. What I hope to have shown, however, is that, when extended to explain left parties' electoral performance, Scharpf's theory provides a marginally superior analytical framework. Yet Scharpf's complex congruency theory is also faced with a number of empirical anomalies, such as bourgeois parties not gaining from the losses of socialist incumbents (Austria, Sweden) or socialists defeating economically successful bourgeois incumbent governments (France). Moreover, Scharpf's theory does not provide a micro-logic of why left parties learn about changing economic environments at different speeds. But the causality could also be the other way round. Parties that internally learn to cope with a new economic situation in creative ways are more likely to get to and to survive at the helm of government. Political economic institutions and government incumbency, taken in isolation, do not help us to understand the dynamic that encourages or stifles political learning in parties. In order to make further headway on these fronts, one must analyze the competitive situation in which parties are placed and their internal processes of strategic choice.

*The welfare state: Asset or liability for socialist party fortunes in the 1980s?*

Aside from corporatist labor regimes, the scope and structure of the welfare state may shape voters' expectations vis-à-vis left parties and governments. The modern welfare state protects citizens against the vagaries of capitalist market economics by expanding public employment opportunities and providing for private consumption irrespective of earned income. Most public employment is in the area of social services; high social benefit levels protect citizens' living standards and security even if they lose their jobs in the private sector. Social democratic parties have always been the main proponents of an encompassing and egalitarian welfare state. Where such institutions exist, they should also generate a loyal electoral

43 See Butler and Kavanagh (1984: ch. 4), and Seyd (1987), and Hamilton (1989: 128–50).

constituency for socialist parties in hard economic times, regardless of left government parties' short-term economic performance (cf. Esping-Andersen 1985: 241). Thus, a comprehensive, redistributive welfare state desensitizes electorates to short-term retrospective voting and boosts socialist electoral support. At a time when bourgeois parties call for retrenchment, socialist parties will have a greater capacity for fighting the erosion of their voter base in countries where the public sector serves a large and growing constituency (Alber 1988: 463). At the operational level, social democratic success in the 1980s should covary with (1) the size of public sector budgets and particularly their social policy components, (2) the egalitarian structure of social programs, and (3) the extent of public employment. Table 3.8 presents some basic information pertaining to these three dimensions as well as standardized ratings for each of them that are summarized in a combined index of social policy protection (column 4).

In the mid-1980s, Sweden and the Netherlands had by far the largest budget outlays for social security programs (including medical care). They were followed by Belgium and France, which had considerably less generous programs. Further behind were Austria, Germany, and Italy. The entire field is trailed by Britain and Spain, the latter of which only began to build a comprehensive social security policy in the late 1970s and 1980s. A similar distribution applies to Esping-Andersen's index of social policy "decommodification" [column (2)]. Higher values indicate that key social policy insurances (pension, sickness compensation, unemployment), weighted by the share of the population covered, are less income dependent and disbursed more in terms of services than cash benefits. Both techniques increase the redistributive impact and thus the generosity of social programs.

Esping-Andersen (1990: 69–77) also discovered that the countries with very high levels of generosity tend to have universalist and egalitarian programs. Countries at the intermediate level tend to be "conservative" welfare states that are encompassing, but based on particularistic social policy programs creating status hierarchies among occupational groups. Finally, "liberal" welfare states are located at the low end of the index of generosity and primarily provide need-based flat benefits whose recipients often must pass means tests.[44]

One might expect expensive, encompassing, and redistributive social policies to promote the fortunes of left parties, particularly in an environment where bourgeois parties call for retrenchment, but in the 1980s this is clearly not the case. In countries with the most elaborate welfare states, social democrats could only preserve their electorates in the 1980s, regardless of whether they were in government or in opposition. Behind these lead countries, we find a random patchwork of

---

44 As World Bank figures show, the articulation of the welfare state is closely tied to patterns of income inequality in advanced capitalist democracies. Belgium, the Netherlands, and Sweden are the most egalitarian, with the top quintile of household incomes having on average 4.9 times the income of the bottom quintile, whereas the ratio between highest and lowest quintile is 5.8 in Spain, 6.0 in Italy, and 6.8 in Britain, if we examine countries ranked near the bottom of the scale with index values of welfare state generosity (World Bank 1990: 237).

Table 3.8. *Structure and scope of the welfare state and socialist electoral performance*

| | Budget outlays for social security (percentage of GDP 1983) | | Decommodification and generosity of social policy | | Public sector employment (percentage of population age 15–64 in 1984) | | Combined index of social protection | Socialist electoral fortunes in the 1980s |
|---|---|---|---|---|---|---|---|---|
| Sweden | 33.3 | (2.0) | 39.1 | (2.0) | 25.7 | (2.0) | 6.0 | Preserver |
| Belgium | 28.0 | (1.5) | 32.4 | (1.5) | 11.0 | (2.0) | 3.5 | Preserver |
| Netherlands | 31.9 | (2.0) | 32.4 | (1.5) | 8.3 | (0.0) | 3.5 | Preserver |
| Austria | 24.2 | (1.0) | 31.1 | (1.5) | 12.8 | (0.5) | 3.0 | Loser |
| France | 29.4 | (1.5) | 27.5 | (1.0) | 13.2 | (0.5) | 3.0 | Winner |
| Germany | 24.3 | (1.0) | 27.7 | (1.0) | 9.5 | (0.0) | 3.0 | Winner |
| Italy | 25.7 | (1.0) | 24.1 | (0.5) | 9.1 | (0.0) | 2.0 | Loser |
| Britain | 20.5 | (0.5) | 23.4 | (0.5) | 14.4 | (0.5) | 1.5 | Loser |
| Spain | 17.7 | (0.0) | [Low] | (0.0) | 6.1 | (0.0) | 0.0 | Winner |

*Source:*

Budget outlays: International Labor Office (1988: 673–74), includes medical care, benefits in kind other than medical care, all other cash benefits, administrative expenses, transfers to other schemes. Index values: <18% of GDP = 0.0; 18–22% = 0.5; 22–26% = 1.0; 26–30% = 1.5; 30% = 2.0.

Social policy generosity: Esping-Andersen (1990: 50, 52, 74); no data for Spain. Index values: <20% = 0.0; 20–25% = 0.5; 25–30% = 1.0; 30–35% = 1.5; >35% = 2.0.

Public sector employment: calculated from OECD, *Historical Statistics* (1987: 30, 38). Index values: <10% of working age population = 0; 10–15% = 0.5; 15–20% = 1.0; 20–25% = 1.5; >25% = 2.0.

socialist winners and losers with different patterns of welfare state generosity. It is safe to conclude that there is no clear-cut relationship between comprehensiveness of the welfare state and socialist party fortunes in the 1980s, other than that a large welfare state may have been conducive to a certain "inertia" of socialist voter movements.

Similarly, socialist governments appear not to benefit from a large public sector, although comparative studies have gathered evidence that such governments promoted public sector growth in the 1970s and 1980s (cf. Masters and Robertson 1988a,b; Schmidt 1988; Cusak, Notermans, and Rein 1989). With the exception of Sweden, public employment is too limited to influence the electoral fortunes of the Left decisively. Moreover, educated public sector employees are likely to abandon socialist parties in favor of left-libertarian competitors and thus depress the electoral payoff socialists derive from expanding the public sector.

Hence, in light of the three indicators of welfare state development – public budgets, structure of benefits, public employment – a summary index of social policy protection that weighs each of these three dimensions equally [Table 3.8, column (4)] displays only a weak pattern relating the elaboration of the welfare state and left party performance in the 1980s. Countries with the most comprehensive welfare states tend to have socialist parties that maintained their electoral support in the 1980s. Behind this lead group, however, there is no consistent pattern linking welfare state development to socialist success.

In countries where citizens depend to a considerable extent on a comprehensive welfare state, security concerns may uphold socialist support. Yet this "security hypothesis" does not explain the diverse fortunes of left parties in other countries, where the expansion or preservation of more modest welfare states are subject to dispute among contending political parties. In particular, it is implausible that a "need hypothesis" may explain the rising fortunes of social democracy in Spain, Italy, or France. While at least Spain and perhaps Italy have less comprehensive welfare states than most other European countries, socialist governments in the 1980s undertook little effort to catch up with northern European levels. Upon coming to office in 1982, the Spanish socialist government took some timid steps toward social reform of the pension system and of health care, but these measures fell far short of the expectations the party had created beforehand (cf. Share 1988a: 51; 1988b: 417). The Italian socialists abandoned an expansive welfare state program in the early 1980s (cf. Merkel 1985: 366–73). The rise in social expenditures in Italy and Spain during the 1980s was due less to social policy initiatives than to the extraordinary depth of their economic crises, which generated levels of unemployment approaching or exceeding the 20 percent mark by the mid-1980s and required a very large budget allocation to unemployment compensation schemes, even at reduced benefits levels. For France, the need hypothesis is less plausible than for Spain or Italy. The French socialist government as well abandoned social policy reform and redistribution toward the less well-off two years into its electoral term (Hall 1987: 66–8).

One might argue that in Britain, Germany, and Austria left parties could have supported welfare state cutbacks because of the structure of social policy programs. In Britain, which has a liberal need-based and egalitarian welfare state, the middle class receives relatively little except health care from social policy. This enabled the conservative government after 1979 to cut back on means-tested benefits and public housing expenditures. These measures, however, reinvigorated the Labour Party's welfare state rhetoric. The view from the opposition benches kept Labour from appreciating economic and political realities that had undermined the electoral appeal of the welfare state in the eyes of all but a limited and decidedly lower income constituency.

The conservative Austrian and German welfare states also have a vertical stratification of benefits across status groups which reduces the loyalty of the broad middle strata to only those programs that benefit this vocal constituency. While still in office, the German SPD came close to a rigorous policy to contain social expenditures by cutting back on benefits accruing to the weakest constituencies of the welfare state, particularly the unemployed and the recipients of means-tested welfare (Alber 1988). Yet its policy was too indecisive to build a new electoral coalition once social policy cuts had antagonized some of its traditional electoral constituencies. And after being forced out of office, the party returned to a rhetoric of social protection and welfare state growth that made it difficult to reach out to new voter groups. In Austria, the socialist government maintained social policy expenditures with minor cutbacks of benefits levels throughout the economic crisis and continued to increase expenditures moderately after a brief interruption in 1979–80 (Alber 1988; Talos 1988: 261–3).[45]

The operational social policies intentionally called for or enacted by socialist parties in the 1980s are not generally consistent with need- or security-driven social policy demands. Socialist governments did not appreciably expand the welfare state, where the narrow scope or the inequality of existing benefits helped them to mobilize voters against bourgeois governments (France, Italy, Spain). Conversely, left parties have not withdrawn from a rhetoric of comprehensive, universalist welfare, where elements of this program became manifestly unpopular in the 1980s (Britain, and to a lesser extent Austria and Germany). Only in Sweden, Belgium, and the Netherlands did the long-term development of comprehensive welfare states generate expectations that maintained socialist voter support and that forced bourgeois parties to keep social programs in place.

The lack of a clear-cut relationship between welfare state size and socialist electoral fortunes has to do with the endogenous change of preferences and interests that is generated by large welfare states (cf. Chapter 1). The resource requirements of a large public sector divide the traditional blue collar electorate of socialist parties into social policy opponents and advocates. The former work for internationally competitive private sector industries and worry about social overhead costs. The latter have jobs in the public sector or in domestic private

---

45 Public housing, for example, increased from 31.7% (1980) to 35.9% (1988) of all residential construction. See United Nations (1990).

industries that are not exposed to tough foreign competition.[46] Yet even public sector employees are not a natural clientele for socialist parties. Especially for highly educated and female public employees, characteristics of the work environment, such as client-interactive task structures, generate libertarian and non-economic preferences for personal autonomy and democratic self-control that are usually at odds with the bureaucratic conception of social democratic welfare states. As a consequence, these voters are often inclined to support new left-libertarian parties.[47]

For these reasons, a comprehensive welfare state is a mixed blessing for social democracy. It may reduce the persuasiveness of bourgeois arguments to gear public policies to the challenges of international market efficiency. Yet at the same time it amplifies the left-libertarian political challenge to social democracy. This micro-logic explains why the size and shape of the welfare state alone reveal little about the electoral paths followed by socialist parties in the 1980s.

### 3.4 IMPACT OF INSTITUTIONS ON ECONOMIC VOTING

The relationship between voter expectations vis-à-vis social democratic parties, institutional setting and the incidence of retrospective economic voting can now be pushed one step further than in previous discussions. We have already seen that pluralist relations of interest group intermediation increase the vulnerability of socialist incumbents to retrospective economic voting, but in highly counterintuitive ways. We would expect that in less extensive welfare states, voters should evaluate socialist government incumbents more critically on the basis of retrospective economic voting. A weak welfare state exposes citizens to the risks of the labor market, makes them less confident in the capacity of social democratic policy making, and sensitizes them to the Left's economic performance.

Governments' structural vulnerability to economic voting, noncorporatist labor regimes, and weak welfare states can be compounded in an overall additive index high values of which indicate that the institutional environment promotes citizens' propensity to act in terms of retrospective economic voting.[48] This index may serve as a variable interacting with changes in economic misery and inflation

46 Thus, public sector employees have represented an increasing share of socialist voters. See Plasser and Ulram (1989: 74) for Austria; Le Gall (1986: 14) and Guyomarch and Machin (1989: 199) for France; Dunleavy and Husbands (1985: 132–3) for Britain; and Goul-Anderson (1984) and Thomas (1986: 192–3) for Scandinavia. Particularly in Scandinavia, left parties' electoral gains among public sector employees have for this reason been outweighed by losses in the private sector (cf. Marklund 1988: 479).

47 On the public sector support of left-libertarian parties see Holmberg and Gilljam (1987: 195) for Sweden; Brinkmann (1988) for Germany; and Guyomarch and Machin (1989: 199) for France.

48 Operationally, the index combines each government's structural vulnerability to economic voting [Table 3.5, column (5)], a dummy variable for the congruency or incongruency of economic-political regimes when socialists are in office, and the comprehensiveness of welfare states [Table 3.8, column (4)]. Each of the three additive index components is weighted equally, with higher values always indicating increased institutional exposure of socialist governments to economic voting.

Table 3.9. *The performance of socialist government incumbents: Economic predictors interacting with overall institutional conduciveness to retrospective economic voting*

|  | Parameter estimate | *t*-value |
|---|---|---|
| Change of economic misery over socialist term in office, "pure" socialist governments ($N = 19$) | | |
| Intercept | −.88 | −1.072 |
| Misery in pre-election year | −.075 | −1.064 |
| Change of economic misery over electoral term × overall institutional conduciveness to retrospective economic voting | .0056 | 3.66 |
| Durbin-Watson: 2.18 | Adjusted $R^2$: .42 | ($p < .006$) |
| Change of inflation over socialist term in office, "pure" socialist governments ($N = 19$) | | |
| Intercept | −1.836 | −1.722 |
| Inflation in pre-election year | .095 | 0.646 |
| Change of inflation over electoral term × overall institutional conduciveness to retrospective economic voting | .009 | 3.917 |
| Durbin-Watson: 2.09 | Adjusted $R^2$: .50 | ($p < .002$) |
| Joint impact of unemployment and inflation over socialist term in office, "pure" socialist governments ($N = 19$) | | |
| Intercept | −1.336 | −3.17 |
| Change of inflation over electoral term × overall institutional conduciveness to retrospective economic voting | .012 | 5.205 |
| Change of unemployment over electoral term × overall institutional conduciveness to retrospective economic voting | .007 | 1.931 |
| Durbin-Watson: 1.80 | Adjusted $R^2$: .58 | ($p < .001$) |

identified earlier as determinants of pure socialist governments' electoral performance (Table 3.5, equations 1, 3, and 4). In Table 3.9, this interactive term increases the variance of left party fortunes explained by changes of economic misery over the period of an electoral term from 27% (without interactive term) to 42% and that of inflation over the same period from 44% to 50%. The joint impact of changes of inflation and unemployment, finally, improves from 47% to 58%.

The findings of this analysis still remain counterintuitive from the point of view of the retrospective economic voting literature. Socialist parties in the 1980s suffered when they pursued austerity policies that drove down inflation and improved economic growth. At the same time, it is *only* in countries where socialists have chosen such strategies that they have remained above their 1970s support levels. The success of the Left in the 1980s thus appears to be self-destructive. In order to increase their electorate, socialist parties had to engage in policies that subsequently eroded their voter support base gradually, as they implemented their policy program. Neither the theory of retrospective economic voting nor the institutional arguments I have explored explain why socialist parties were able to choose such strategies and actually preferred them to alternative courses of action.

## CONCLUSION

The key puzzle emerging from my review of political-economy arguments that can be brought to bear on socialist electoral performance is why socialist parties in environments that appear to be most adverse to socialist "class politics," traditionally conceived, appear to have reaped substantial, though possibly fleeting, electoral benefits in the 1980s. Conversely, the theories I have employed cannot explain why left government parties presiding over relatively good economic performance and located in corporatist labor regimes with strong welfare states failed to benefit electorally from conditions that have been generally considered to favor left parties.

Conventional political economy provides no micro-logic that could reconstruct such findings. Moreover, it furnishes no arguments that would explain the socialists' choice of strategy in the electoral competition and in public policy making. A first step toward a new account that renders electoral outcomes and their linkage to political-economic conditions more intelligible has been made in Chapter 1. We must abandon a class-based reconstruction of voters' demands and replace it by a subtler reconstruction of citizens' political preferences and interests in the light of market, occupational, and consumption experiences. Starting from this premise, I will next present a model of electoral party competition and intraparty decision making that explains why some socialist parties have been able to free themselves more quickly and completely from traditional socialist programmatic appeals than others. Initially, this model treats parties as unitary actors faced with varying electoral constraints (Chapter 4). In a second step, I open the black box of party organization to examine how different forces interact within parties to shape strategies and the potential for policy innovation (Chapter 5). Finally, I examine semantic constraints and opportunities that have influenced socialists' strategic flexibility and electoral appeal (Chapter 6).

# 4

# Social democratic strategy and electoral competition

In the preceding chapters, I primarily explored the extent to which class structure, economic performance, and political-economic institutions affect the electoral support of socialist parties. I considered the role of social democratic party strategy in the mobilization of electoral constituencies only indirectly when I examined whether left parties strategically act on a class trade-off (Chapter 2), choose to join or abstain from governments, manufacture political business cycles, or manipulate institutions of interest intermediation or of the welfare state to their electoral advantage (Chapter 3). In all these instances, there is little evidence that parties were able to act strategically or, if they did, their actions often did not yield the desired results. For example, most socialist governments failed to bring about political business cycles and even where they were successful, they were likely to lose elections. Similarly, corporatist intermediation and comprehensive welfare states in the 1980s had ambiguous or clearly negative consequences for social democratic electoral support. In the 1980s, several socialist governments engaged in successful economic austerity policies that eventually cost them votes but kept their main bourgeois competitors weak. Without examining the strategic context of party competition, however, one cannot explain why some socialist parties were able to choose this strategy and win executive office.

In this chapter, therefore, I will examine the direct impact of left parties' strategic appeals on voters' electoral choices. With the decline of party identification and class voting (Franklin et al. 1992), an increasing share of the electorate becomes sensitive to the explicit political messages and appeals issued by parties in the competitive game. Rather than the historical weight of political-economic institutions, parties' immediate electoral and legislative activities and future commitments affect their electoral performance (prospective voting). My first objective is to explain parties' strategic appeals in terms of the competitive configuration within European party systems. I assume the existing distribution of popular political preferences as a given although, in the long run, it is shaped not only by societal change but also the trajectory of party competition and social movements. My second objective is to account for electoral outcomes in terms of the rationality or irrationality of the strategies socialist parties chose to compete with their rivals. In this analysis, I treat parties as unitary actors. In the next chapter, I explore whether variations in the parties' electoral rationality are due to differences in their internal decision-making structures and modes of coalition-building. In Chapter 6, I examine the semantic codes and ideologies on which parties draw in their efforts to build intraparty and electoral coalitions.

Party systems, party organization, and semantic codes constitute the immediate contexts of politicians' strategic choices. Such features relate social democratic electoral success to proximate causes under the direct purview of political action rather than to distant structural conditions in a country's political economy and social stratification. If proximate causes permit us to develop a convincing account of socialist party strategies and electoral outcomes, the view that socialist party decline is inevitable becomes implausible.

Given that parties select strategies in an *interactive* environment where they are confronted with rationally calculating competitors with often explicit, consistent, and relatively stable preference schedules, the purpose of my discussion is *not* simply to show that all socialist parties which barely preserved their electorates or lost market shares in the 1980s were "irrational." Any conclusion about the efficacy of party choices can be made only after determining whether short-term electoral vote maximization is in fact a party's overriding goal or whether alternative goals may be just as plausible. Moreover, since electoral outcomes derive from the interaction of numerous parties, the relationship between a party's rational choice of strategic stances and electoral success is mediated by its competitors' moves. A party may be successful because it is lucky that competitors have made strategic mistakes. Conversely, a party may be in a tragic situation because its competitors' strategies make it virtually impossible to preserve its electoral market share with any conceivable strategy. From the perspective of parties as unitary actors, electorally unsuccessful strategies may be attributed to strategic irra-tionality only once alternative rational explanations have been exhausted.

In this chapter, I first flesh out a theory of multiparty competition that prescribes different rational strategic positions contingent upon a party's preferences. I then operationalize the strategic environment and incentives socialist parties are facing in the countries included in my comparison. The main empirical burden of proof for this model rests on a set of comparative case studies that explains socialist parties' strategic choices and electoral performance in light of systemic incentives. I have added Denmark as a tenth case to the list of social democratic parties considered in preceding chapters because its social democratic party strategy offers interesting contrasts to several of the corresponding parties in other coun-tries. In addition to the case studies, I discuss a limited amount of survey evidence and expert judgments of parties' strategic appeal to back my argument. This analysis is more exploratory than conclusive, particularly the factor analyses that show the mean positions of each party's voters in the competitive space. In an addendum to this chapter, I briefly consider how my results are likely to stand up in light of alternative theoretical assumptions about party competition.

### 4.1 SPATIAL THEORY OF PARTY COMPETITION AND THE EUROPEAN LEFT

A party system is "in equilibrium" if neither parties and candidates nor voters have incentives to change their behavior. No one can unilaterally choose a strategy that makes himself better off. Given the complexity of political situations, however, an equilibrium may not exist, it may be unattainable, or there may be multiple equilibria. In each of these cases it is difficult, if not impossible, to sort out rational from irrational strategies. To do so, theoretical models must simplify reality and introduce behavioral and institutional constraints on competition that are still sufficiently plausible to preserve the model's empirical relevance for actual party strategy and electoral payoffs. This section is meant to detail such idealizations that drive my analysis of rational party strategies in alternative competitive environments.

### *Voter choices*

While spatial models of voter orientation have recently been challenged by salience and directional theories,[1] the spatial imagery may still serve as a rough approximation of the realities of party competition and as guide for the positioning of parties.[2] Four assumptions underlie spatial theory of party competition that were elaborated by Downs (1957). First, voters have little information about political alternatives and primarily vote on simplified ideological cues offered by parties and candidates, cues that evoke recollection of past political experiences among voters. Second, in light of such information constraints, party competition has a very low dimensionality. In most instances, a single dimension of alternatives (left versus right, liberal versus conservative, or left-libertarian versus right-authoritarian) suffices to map the voters' conceptualization of party choices. Third, voters are situated along the relevant dimension(s) in a uniform or a single-peaked distribution, with most voters amassed somewhere in the center of the political space. Fourth, rational voters support the party or candidate that is perceived to be *closest* to their own positions. Voting is therefore a sincere and deterministic act of rationally pursuing one's preferences.

The reason why the dimensionality of the electoral space relevant for parties' strategic appeals is so limited has to do with the distinction between domains of voter identification and domains of party competition (Sani and Sartori 1983: 330). Voters' party preferences may be guided by a particular issue dimension such as religion, but if voters identify with parties on that dimension and are not available for competitive appeals, other parties will see few opportunities to compete on that issue. Instead, they will stress the salience of issues that offer a reasonably open

---

1 See especially Budge and Farlie (1983a,b) and Rabinowitz and MacDonald (1989), Listhaug, MacDonald, and Rabinowitz (1990), and Rabinowitz, MacDonald, and Listhaug (1991).
2 I discuss in an addendum to this chapter whether and to what extent my findings could be challenged from the vantage point of an alternative model of voter behavior.

electoral market of uncommitted voters. Rational parties will orient their appeals to the distribution of voters and that of competing parties on such dimensions. Larger parties definitely have to compete on the most salient dimension. Small parties may find market niches outside the main dimension of competition.

The rational position of parties is affected by the location of the median voter on the relevant dimension(s) and by the dispersion of voters, provided that party systems offer incentives for the ideological dispersion of parties. If there are such incentives, a wider distribution of voters around the median will also lead to greater distances among the parties and between parties and median voter thus generating more extremism in the party system. In other words, a higher level of cleavage mobilization (Kitschelt 1989a: ch. 2) or ideological polarization may affect the positioning of parties (cf. Sartori 1976: ch. 6, 10).

A cross-sectional analysis of party strategies simply takes voter distribution as given and examines whether parties respond to it with an intelligible rationale. It is irrelevant whether that distribution was brought about by social mobilization and institutional change outside the electoral arena or endogenously through past competitive appeals of the parties. As soon as the longtudinal dynamic of parties and party systems comes into view, however, alternative mechanisms for influencing the voter distribution become relevant for party strategy. Parties may exercise "issue leadership" in promoting a new dimension of competition or at least in changing voters' distribution over an existing dimension. In general, parties should anticipate that changes in the dimensionality and distribution of voter positions, whether exogenously induced or endogenously triggered, involve glacial movements that promise no quick electoral payoff.[3] Hence, parties' efforts to change voter distributions may only become attractive if particular competitive conditions prevail.[4]

### *Party preferences*

The Downsian model of party competition assumes that electoral candidates maximize short-term office winning. Parties are coalitions of candidates who seek political office. Following Strom (1990b), one should distinguish, however, among at least three different preferences that may motivate politicians and then consider circumstances under which these preferences are likely to come to the fore. First, a party may desire to maximize its legislative representation. Although electoral systems affect the conversion of votes into seats, by and large the desire to increase a party's legislative representation involves a "vote-seeking" strategy to maximize that party's share of the vote. Second, a party may desire to maximize its chance of holding executive office. "Office-seeking" motivation is a narrower motivation than the general pursuit of legislative representation. Depending on the

3 Of course, sudden dramatic changes of world historic proportions, such as the collapse of communism and German unification, have an immediate and unanticipated impact on voter distributions and the dimensionality of party competition.
4 I will elaborate on these conditions in my analysis of "oligopolistic" competitive strategies.

ideological position of parties and the distribution of voters, seeking government office and seeking to maximize the number of legislators in parliament may require quite different party strategies (cf. Laver 1989). A party may be compelled to take a political stance that reduces its voter appeal in order to increase its chances to participate in the formation of a coalition government. Third, a party may desire to subordinate its vote or office seeking to the higher goal of policy. A party may be sufficiently policy seeking to reject concessions required to gain votes or government office.

Theories of party competition must be careful to specify the preference schedule for which an electoral strategy is rational under given circumstances. Further, such theories may generate propositions about the formation of parties' preference schedules and assess *how "rational" in a broad sense* it is for parties to pursue a certain objective. Thin conceptions of rationality usually assume that rational calculation concern only the optimal choice of means for given ends, whatever they may be. But in a broader sense, theories of rationality also presuppose that actors collect information about alternative ends and then choose among them in light of what is feasible with given means and constraints (Elster 1986). For party competition, institutional constraints and opportunities may affect the probabilities that a certain objective can be met and thus render its pursuit more or less attractive.

I will next flesh out a theory of multiparty competition around progressively more complex electoral objectives. The simple model assumes short-term vote and legislative seat maximization only. I will then introduce trade-offs between vote- and office-seeking strategies and specify conditions under which a party may be willing to sacrifice legislative seats in order to win office. Finally, I will examine oligopolistic strategies of competition that *look* like pure policy seeking without electoral or executive ambitions, but are intended to have vote- or office-seeking consequences in the long run.

Pure policy-seeking behavior without electoral or executive objectives, however, cannot be explained in terms of a theory of party competition. Theories of party competition examine a party's rational strategy in light of the strategies of all other parties in pursuit of common scarce resources up for grabs in the competitive game (legislative seats, executive office). If a party is purely policy seeking, it declares that it is not intrinsically interested in the stakes of the electoral game. Hence, its behavior cannot be explained in terms of aspirations to win such stakes. While its behavior is irrational in light of what it means to play the electoral game, it may nevertheless be rendered intelligible in terms of other preferences, conditions, and arenas of political action. For example, the intraparty struggle for power may yield an uncompetitive electoral strategy (Chapter 5).

Rationalist theories of party competition may identify the conditions under which the choice of a seemingly irrational policy-seeking strategy that does not maximize the tangible rewards of the electoral game may nevertheless be a reasonable one. Parties may pursue policy maximization at the expense of other objectives if their supply of voters or their chance of winning government office is *inelastic* to incremental changes in the party's policy positions.[5] This is typically the case with parties catering to specialized economic pressure groups or cultural pressure minorities and with antisystem parties whose missionary zeal may boost their efforts to change voters' preference distribution.[6]

### Party strategy in simple spatial competition

According to Downs's (1957) median voter theorem, two parties competing in a unidimensional competitive space will converge to the position of the median voter. This theorem holds only if numerous behavioral and institutional restrictions are imposed. Voters cannot abstain because they are alienated or indifferent toward converging parties. The entry of new parties is prohibited, particularly that of radical parties which may not win political office, but are able to blackmail the dominant parties into taking more radical stances than they otherwise would in order to prevent new entrants from attracting radical, alienated voter groups. Moreover, the median voter theorem assumes that parties do not have a reputation to defend and can freely move in the electoral space. These are some of the more important conditions limiting the median voter theorem.[7]

While much of the rational choice literature on spatial competition in the last several decades has relaxed the assumption that party competition is unidimensional, it has maintained the scenario of two parties vying for votes (cf. Enelow and Hinich 1984). Beyond informal accounts in Downs (1957: ch. 8, 9) and Sartori (1976: ch. 10), multiparty competition has been rigorously treated only in recent analyses that usually presuppose unidimensional competition and a uniform or a single-peaked voter distribution. If these assumptions are dropped, there may be little hope for general results from formal analysis (Shepsle and Cohen 1990: 37). Even in such constrained settings, however, equilibria may be rare (Cox 1990a: 183). Nevertheless, the formal literature comes to the conclusion that under conditions of multiparty competition, whether in systems with proportional representation or with plurality voting, rational vote maximizers have incentives to spread out over the competitive space, provided voters act sincerely.[8]

5 Other contingencies promoting more policy- than office-seeking behavior of parties may include opposition influence over government policy (Strom 1990b), party size, and party ideology (cf. Laver and Hunt 1992: ch. 4).
6 Voluntaristic theories of preference formation liken voters' preferences and interpretative frames to clay ready to be shaped by the hands of a potter (Riker 1986; Przeworski and Sprague 1986). This completely ignores the societal bases of preference formation. In the end, also Przeworski and Sprague (1986: 73–8), however, are compelled to admit that the potential for class formation is limited by pre-existing religious and ethnic cleavages. A more plausible model of issue evolution for party competition has been presented by Carmines and Stimson (1989).
7 Furthermore, absence of knowledge about the voters' true position may drive parties away from the median voter (Chappell and Keech 1986). For a summary of arguments undermining the general applicability of the median voter theorem in two-party competition, see Garrett and Lange 1989: 678–9.
8 I am relying here on Greenberg and Weber (1985), Greenberg and Shepsle (1987), Shepsle and Cohen (1990), Cox (1990a,b), and Shepsle (1991).

The extent to which parties spread out depends on the *effective number of parties* competing in a system. This number includes not only formally declared parties that are competing, but also *potential* entrants that may be attracted depending upon the positions the actual competitors assume. The cost of entry thus affects the actual competitors' incentives to disperse over the electoral space. At a minimum, such costs are determined by the quota of votes a party must get in order to receive legislative representation. Beyond that, the difficulty of entry is also affected by the start-up cost of advertising a new party's position and gaining a reputation for the truthful representation of voters. Moreover, the new party must be able to maintain a minimum ideological distance from established parties to convince voters it is sufficiently different from existing ones. In fact, equilibria in party systems with entry may presuppose entry thresholds and reputational effects (cf. Shepsle 1991: 56–9).

In equilibrium, parties spread out so much that no new entrant, whether considering entry at the extremes or in the middle of the competitive space, could expect to gain the quota of votes needed to obtain legislative seats. A large number of parties is an indication of low entry cost. With an identical distribution of voters, a more fragmented system will support relatively more extreme electorally significant parties than a less fragmented one.[9]

Entry is one of several conditions affecting the dispersion of parties in an ideological space. If the distribution of voters is uniform across a unidimensional space, even with a fixed number of parties, Cox (1990b) has shown that "product differentiation" is a superior strategy both under conditions of proportional representation and plurality voting if the number of candidates or parties in each district ($m$) exceeds more than twice the number of votes ($v$) cast by each voter ($m > 2v$).[10] Under such circumstances, candidates or parties can meet the quota and win representation even if they do not win a majority of votes and capture the median voter.

Based on formal theories of spatial competition in economic markets, Shepsle and Cohen (1990) have argued that three-party systems (with a single vote cast by voters) are generally unstable. In four-party systems, however, vote-seeking parties bunch around positions at 0.25 and 0.75 of a competitive space defined by the endpoints [0,1] and uniform voter distribution. Under these conditions, each party can expect one fourth of the entire market. This result, however, prevails only when there is "agency conjecture." In this context each competitor individually assumes that the adversaries will stay put and not retaliate by modifying its

9  The correlation between the distribution of parties in the electoral space and the number of parties thus does not imply Sartori's (1976: 43) hypothesis of "space stretching," according to which a large number of parties is causally responsible for a wider distribution of voters in the competitive space. Empirical analyses that relate the number of parties in a system of voters' left–right positions to the parties' election manifestos have found only a very weak association between party system format and extent of polarization. See Bartolini and Mair (1990: 199). A similar point about the independence of fragmentation and polarization has been made by Sani and Sartori (1983).

10  Votes are assumed to be equally weighted.

strategic stances once it has chosen its own position. If vote-seeking parties mutually respond to each others' moves and try to inflict maximum electoral damage on each other, competitors will be evenly spread out over the entire electoral market and be located in the middle of their market segment. A similar logic of dispersion applies to systems with more than four vote-seeking parties as well. The general hypothesis is that parties engage in product differentiation under conditions of multiparty competition with $m > 2v$.

The entry cost for potential competitors and the number of actual competitors are the key variables that determine party positions when voters are uniformly distributed. To illustrate this argument, consider party systems with a uniform distribution of voters on one dimension ranging between the endpoints [0,1], with a possibility of new parties entering, costless movement of all competitors across the electoral space, and no agency conjecture. Moreover, parties are able to leapfrog other parties' positions within certain limits.[11] Under these circumstances, each party will locate in the middle of its own market, provided the number of parties is sufficiently large ($m \geq 4$).[12] In Figure 4.1, the first diagram, which has only two parties, represents Downs's median voter theorem with both competitors, social democracy (SD) and conservative party (C) bunching around the median voter. In the next diagram, two more parties have entered the competitive field, the radicals (R) to the left of SD and the liberals (L) to the left of the conservatives. Being faced with two parties to the right and one party to the left and each party seeking to attract maximum electoral support, the rational strategic stance of SD shifts to the left into the center of a substantially smaller market. At the same time, C has been displaced to the right. The third diagram has six parties, and each controls one sixth of the market. Now the liberals have split and spawned another party, the radical liberals (RL); at the same time, a national front (NF) has gained electoral support on the far right. This further crowding on the right drives a vote-seeking SD to the left in order to protect its market share. In the final diagram, a further division of the radical Left now has pushed SD toward the center.

Several circumstances, however, counteract strategic dispersion in multiparty systems. For example, if voters have several votes that can be cumulated on one candidate or they are entitled to partial abstention, parties have incentives for moving toward the median. Further, if voters are strategic rather than sincere, they may choose a second-best party or candidate if that choice promises to yield final results in a legislative assembly and government coalition that are closer to their ideal points than if they voted sincerely. Since government coalitions usually include the median voter, strategic voting may create a tendency toward concentration in the party system, because voters will refrain from supporting radical parties that have no chance to enter a government coalition. Even in one-dimensional competition, however, it may require too much knowledge about the strategic

---

11 For example, a socialist party being squeezed by a radical party moving toward the center can shift its position marginally and emerge on the left of its previously more radical competitor.
12 Specifications of this model are again taken from Shepsle and Cohen's (1990) rendering of recent contributions to the economics of spatial competition.

a. two-party competition: minimal differentiation

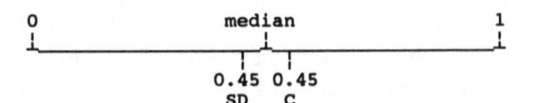

b. four-party competition (without agency conjecture)

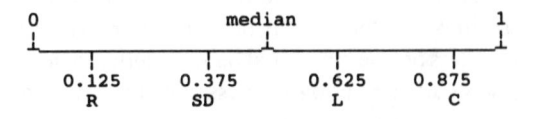

c. six-party competition (without agency conjecture)

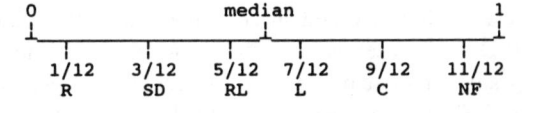

d. seven-party competition (without agency conjecture)

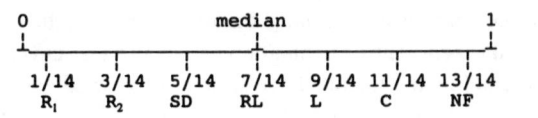

Figure 4.1. Rational party strategies and the number of competitors (uniform distribution of voters)

calculations of everyone else to identify an optimal course of strategic voting if four or more parties and their potential electorates interact in a competitive system.

All the models discussed so far assume not only unidimensional competition, but also uniform voter distributions. But what if the voter distribution is bell shaped with most voters bunching around the median? Would not then parties have an incentive to move toward the median voter regardless of the number of competitors, because they will always offset losses of extreme supporters by greater gains of moderate voters? Under such circumstances, no equilibrium would ever occur (cf. Shepsle 1991: 18). Successive generations of parties would appear at the radical fringes of the electoral space, but gradually moderate their positions in search of electoral success and eventually disappear in the "black hole" of the median voter into which they are pushed by more radical, but also gradually moderating competitors (Rabinowitz, MacDonald, and Listhaug 1991: 155).

In reality, however, we do observe stability in multiparty systems for at least two reasons. A *psychological* argument is that voters' choice is not based on ideological proximity to a party, but the salience and direction of issues featured by parties (MacDonald et al. 1991; Rabinowitz et al. 1991). Hence, parties never have an incentive to be right in the center on every dimension and will attempt to multiply the competitive dimensions when favorable positions on existing dimensions are occupied by competitors.[13] There is, however, also an *institutional* argument based on entry costs that preserves the spatial imagery, but yields equilibrium solutions, provided one adds some further relatively weak and plausible specifications concerning the distribution and behavior of voters. This argument is fleshed out in Figure 4.2 and the associated table.

Figure 4.2 shows the left half of a unimodal, symmetrical, and unidimensional voter distribution ranging from an extreme position 1, supported by two voters, to the median position 19 supported by 28 voters. There is a total electorate of 564 voters distributed over the entire space of 37 ideological positions. In order to make the black hole of competition disappear, while preserving most of the usual premises of spatial models, I make three additional assumptions. First, for a new party to win seats in the legislature, it must receive 5% of the overall electorate (29 voters). Second, parties are required to maintain a minimum distance of four units in the ideological space bounded by positions [1, 37]. If they move closer together, their voters will become indifferent and abstain in increasing proportions. Parties separated by only three units lose 25% of the voters whose ideal point is closest to the parties' announced position, parties with two units of distance lose 33% and those separated by only one unit 50%. Finally, *new* entrants must control at least *some* electoral terrain that is at least four units removed from an existing competitor or they will never be attractive for defectors from established parties.

If one imagines the competitive situation in scenario I with the parties of the Left and the Center-Left evenly distributed across the left half of the competitive space (B: 5; C: 10; D: 15; on the Center-Right E: 23), the strategic distribution is obviously not in equilibrium. B and C can make gains at the expense of their most centrist competitor D, who can be pushed further to the center to reach a position of "minimum distance" from its Center-Right competitor E (scenario II). At this distribution, a potential entrant A at the extreme would never marshal enough support to meet the quota of representation.[14] Furthermore, no new entrant between B and C or between D and E could appeal to a core electorate at least four units removed from the next competitor's position. Beyond the new location of the parties in scenario II, however, no competitor can expect to make further gains by altering its ideological position. Consider D. Its position is constrained by E's location at a minimum distance on the Center-Right. In a similar vein, if C moved in on D, C would violate the minimum distance rule and therefore lose votes, while

---

13 Directional theory of party competition is innovative but faces a number of objections I will sketch in the addendum to this chapter.
14 At the most profitable positions 4 and 5, that entrant would suffer penalties due to violations of the minimum distance rule and never collect more than twenty-three or twenty-four votes.

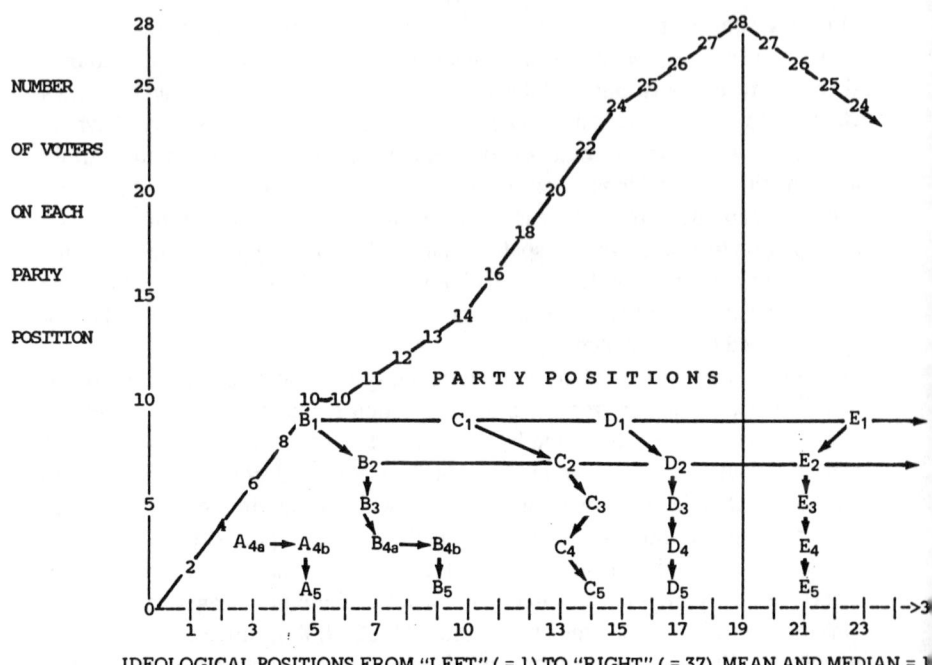

Figure 4.2. Rational multiparty competition in a symmetrical unimodal and unidimensional voter distribution
*Notes:* Rules for the payoffs of parties: 1. Minimum entry of parties: 5% of 564 votes = 29. 2. Market between two parties is split evenly. 3. If parties are closer to each other than four units distance on the ideological scale: At distance 3, 25% of each party's voters abstain at distance 2, 33%; at distance 1, 50%; 4. No new party can enter without controlling a space at least four space units removed from the next party.

only B would reap benefits (scenario III). But returning to scenario II, does not B have an incentive to move from position 7 to 8 or 9, because it would still stay outside the necessary minimum distance range of party C? Yet as soon as B moves to position 8, let alone position 9, the number of voters at the left extreme of the competitive space becomes sufficiently large to attract a more radical entrant A who can now capture anywhere from 35 to 45 voters contingent upon B's position (scenario IVa and b). Even if simultaneously C had been foolish enough to move in on D, a more moderate position would still not pay for party B (scenario V).

Plausible and simple model constraints thus show that multiparty competition in a spatial world with a single-peaked distribution of voters is unlikely to lead to a situation in which competitors are sucked into a black hole near the median voter in a centripetal competition without equilibrium.[15] Behavioral assumptions about the capacity of voters to discriminate party positions and institutional assumptions about cost of entry prevent this.[16] With reasonable assumptions about voter distribution and orientation to parties, the *balance of fractionalization* to a party's left and right determines its electorally rational appeal on the main dimension of competition. The greater the number of significant competitors to a party's right relative to the number of its competitors on the left, the further that party will be driven toward a left strategy abandoning the median voter.[17] Most favorable for a centrist strategy is an even balance between competitors on left and right. What drives this model is a logic of product differentiation in which parties can count on voters' support only as long as they supply a distinctive message on the main dimension of competition and exploit areas of the electoral market difficult to cover by their competitors.

In equilibrium, then, the position of parties as rational short-term vote maximizers reflects the distribution of voters across the main ideological spectrum (hypothesis 1) and the balance of party fractionalization on a party's left and right competitive frontiers (hypothesis 2). This is the core of a simple theory of spatial competition that can be employed to compare party strategies and electoral payoffs. Before moving on to a more complex model of spatial competition, two difficulties must be addressed. First, if parties choose strategic positions that are vote maximizing and the electoral distribution remains fixed, new parties would never appear because established rational parties would have removed any opportunity for entry of a new competitor. Second, how far does the model carry us if we permit more than one competitive dimension?

In order to explain change in the competitive system, either parties are not rational short-term vote maximizers or the distribution of voters changes such that *at least for a transition period* each party's existing position is in disequilibrium.

---

15 The black hole theory also does not hold if we permit parties to leap beyond each other's position. Centrist parties that are threatened by formerly radical, but increasingly moderate competitors, may then simply leap over their challengers to a more radical position.

16 As Tovey (1991) has shown, also in two-dimensional competition chaos is likely to be averted if institutional and behavioral constraints are fleshed out. For Tovey, a reasonable minimum distance between parties to permit voter discrimination and incumbency advantages/entry costs are only two of six possibilities to bring about stability. Others concern the cost of changing one's party identification, bounded rationality, and the uncertainty of the payoffs derived supporting a new party.

17 Of course, a party D pays most attention to its neighbors C and E on the competitive space. If C and E act rationally, however, their position is influenced by the strategies of their neighbors B, D, and F, whose position will be affected by their neighbors A, B, C, E, F, and G. Hence, the overall distribution of parties affects each party's position.

This is so because either voters have moved along the existing dominant competitive dimension *or* that dimension itself has changed.[18] In this instance, entry takes place under one of three conditions. Either existing parties may fail to register the electorate's shift quickly enough to adjust their position, or each party's reputation is so entrenched in voters' minds that new strategic stances are given little credence, or the new distribution of voters would require existing parties to spread out over an ideological space so large that few voters would find it attractive. Given the distribution of voters and the competitive rules assumed in Figure 4.2, for example, it is impossible for just two parties C and D to capture all voters on the left side of the competitive space. They could never prevent a third party B from entering and acquiring more than the required quota of votes to be represented in the legislature.[19] In this instance, parties are faced with tragic choices. Although they are electorally rational, they are destined to lose votes, because under existing rules of competition they cannot possibly hold on to their previous market share.

New parties may also enter the electoral arena if a new dimension of competition emerges which the established parties will not or cannot take into account. Major parties calculate how many voters they might lose on the existing major competitive dimension by taking a stance on a new minor dimension. For the big vote-getting parties, diverting their energies from the main dimension does not pay because it risks disorganizing their core constituencies. As a new dimension grows in importance, major parties *will attempt to assimilate the new dimension into the major dimension of competition.* In this sense, multidimensionality tends to be unstable in party systems when rational major parties aspire to incorporate new themes. In contrast to larger parties, smaller parties may develop special voter appeals that create minor second or third competitive dimensions catering to well-defined and limited electoral constituencies such as farmers, professionals, or sociocultural minorities. Such parties are often crowded at the center of the main competitive dimension. Multidimensionality can be sustained if only minor parties compete on subordinate dimensions.

We may now apply the model of simple spatial competition to the problems faced by European social democracy in the 1980s and 1990s. In advanced industrial democracies, as I have argued, the main dimension of competition stretches from left-libertarian to right-authoritarian voter positions, although the extent of the incorporation of communitarian alternatives into the distributive political division varies from country to country. The fusion of distributive and libertarian issues has taken place due to social change, the mobilization of social movements, and the response of the established major parties to the new challenge (cf. Kitschelt 1988). By the mid-1980s, socialist parties in all countries in my comparison except Britain faced serious left-libertarian competitors able to mount national electoral campaigns. The socialists' electoral fortunes were contingent upon the interdepen-

---

18 At this time, I am not concerned about the sources of changing voter positions.
19 Depending on where C and D are located, that entry might occur on the extreme left, between C and D, or in the center region.

dent strategic choices they and their established and new competitors made in light of the given voter distribution.

To analyze socialist party electoral payoffs and rational strategic choice under these circumstances one must address three questions. First, what is the overall mobilization of left-libertarian sentiments in a country? If the competitive configuration of a multiparty system stays the same, the more voters favor left-libertarian policies, the greater is the incentive for socialist vote maximizers to cater to such preferences (hypothesis 1). Second, what is the balance of party system fractionalization? Assuming identical voter dispersion across the main dimension of party competition, socialist parties should be more inclined to support left-libertarian positions rather than stances close to the median voter, the more crowded the party spectrum is in the center-right of the competitive space and the less crowded the system is on the party's libertarian left (hypothesis 2). Third, given the constraints elaborated in hypotheses 1 and 2, do the socialists' main competitors assume electorally rational positions? Were this not the case, socialists might gain votes, *even though* they pursue suboptimal strategies, were all other parties to choose optimizing strategies. If socialist party positions and payoffs are not rationally explicable when voter distributions, balance of fractionalization, and the stances of their competitors are taken into account, then more complex strategic rationality may decide the parties' political stances.

## *Complex spatial competition I: Office seeking*

If parties seek government office as their most important priority, they will sacrifice votes and legislative seats to improve their chances to obtain a pivotal position in the process of government coalition formation. A party is pivotal if no majority coalition can be formed against it. In a unidimensional competitive space with coalition formation according to the principle of "connected" coalitions that minimize the ideological distance among coalition partners (cf. Dodd 1976), a party controls the pivotal position if it captures the median voter, regardless of the proportion of votes won by more radical parties on either side of the competitive space.[20]

To illustrate how a party's vote and office maximizing strategies may diverge, consider the two possible payoff matrices in Table 4.1. A left-libertarian party (LL) is located at the extreme left of the competitive space and the conventional socialist or social democratic party (SD) is situated directly to its right. There are other competitors further to the right of the two parties, but for the sake of this scenario I assume their distribution remains the same in all alternatives. Let I, II, III, and IV represent increasingly extreme left-libertarian strategic stances in the competitive space. Social democrats choose between centrist and moderately leftist positions (I and II), left-libertarians choose between intermediately and extremely leftist stances (III and IV). For each pair of strategic choices, Tables 4.1A and 4.1B

20 In multidimensional competitive spaces, in contrast, most of the time there is no pivotal position in the party system.

present the percentage of votes that social democrats or left-libertarians can expect. I assume that the parties' vote shares directly translate into seats.

If the conventional Left maximizes votes, it simply strives for the largest share of the electorate it can attract on its own. If it maximizes office, then it will seek out that stance which allows left-libertarians and social democrats together to exceed 50% of all voters. Under the assumption that coalition governments can be formed only among ideologically neighboring "connected" parties and LL and SD together control over 50% of the votes and seats, no government can be formed against SD. This makes SD the "pivotal" party and endows it with the greatest bargaining power in the party system.[21] In contrast, LL has little bargaining power because it can coalesce only with SD.

In Table 4.1A, a vote- *or* an office-maximizing-SD would always choose strategy I and LL would always endorse strategy III. By selecting these strategies, both parties maximize their worst payoffs. They also have no incentive to defect from this strategy. The situation is markedly different in configuration 4.1B. Here, SD is compelled to choose between vote and office maximization. Vote maximizing strategy II will keep LL and SD in the minority so that SD is unlikely to emerge as the pivotal party.[22] Conversely, the office-maximizing strategy I will weaken SD electorally but enable it to become the pivot of the party system.

Individualist rational choice theories based on "thin" rationality assume preferences to be exogenous. A mixture of "structuralist," behavioral, and rational choice considerations, however, opens the way for endogenizing the choice of party preferences and understanding the circumstances that persuade a party to move from a vote-maximizing to an office-maximizing strategy. The greater the *operational feasibility and the payoffs* and the more limited the *electoral cost* of an office-maximizing strategy are, the more palatable party strategists might find an office-maximizing approach. Opportunities thus affect not only strategies, but also preferences office or vote-seeking preferences.

The feasibility and benefits of office seeking depend on four conditions. Most important, a party's closeness to the pivotal position in the preceding election affects its intention to compete for office rather than votes in the subsequent election. If the combined payoff of LL and SD parties is 45%, SD is more likely to be office seeking at the next election than if the combined payoff is less than 40%. Second, the more parties are crowded in the center of the competitive space, the harder it may be for SD to gain the additional support required to capture the pivot, regardless of how many votes SD is willing to sacrifice to LL. Crowded centers discourage office-seeking ambitions and multiply the options for coalition formation. Third, a large number of centrist parties frequently indicates the presence of secondary dimensions of competition. Multidimensional competition, in turn, discourages centrist office-seeking strategies, because there may be no pivot under

21 For efforts to conceptualize the power of the pivotal party, see Daalder (1984), Remy (1985), and Roosendahl (1990).

22 Unless at the extreme rightist end of the political spectrum there is a party that is unacceptable as a coalition partner to all moderate rightist and centrist parties.

Table 4.1. *The strategic game between left-libertarian and conventional left parties*

A. No trade-off between office- and vote-seeking party strategies from the perspective of the conventional Left

| | | Strategic stance of left-libertarians | | Combined electoral payoffs contingent upon conventional left strategies only |
|---|---|---|---|---|
| | | III | IV | |
| Strategic stance of conventional left parties | II | 39, 4 | 41, 2 | 43/43 |
| | I | 42, 9 | 45, 6 | 51/51 |
| Combined electoral payoffs contingent upon left-libertarian struggles only | | 43/51 | 43/51 | |

B. Trade-off between office and vote seeking from the perspective of the conventional Left

| | | Strategic stance of left-libertarians | | Combined electoral payoffs contingent upon conventional left strategies only |
|---|---|---|---|---|
| | | III | IV | |
| Strategic stance of conventional left parties | II | 40, 6 | 42, 4 | 46/46 |
| | I | 35, 16 | 38, 13 | 51/51 |
| Combined electoral payoffs contingent upon left-libertarian strategies only | | 46/51 | 46/51 | |

these circumstances.[23] Finally, while party strategists may value office for its own sake, they will be more attracted to an office-seeking strategy if their influence over public policy is significantly increased in comparison to going into the opposition (Strom 1984).

The cost of office-seeking strategies is a function of the expected loss of votes incurred in comparison to a vote-seeking strategy. In the first place, these costs depend on the distribution of voters. The greater the proportion of radical voters, the greater the likely electoral losses from office-seeking strategies. Second, easy entry of new competitors into the electoral arena discourages seeking office,

23 On the role of multidimensional competition and party strategy see also Strom (1990b: 586).

because it raises the probability that new parties will harness an office-seeking party's alienated constituencies. Serious obstacles to the entry of new competitors due to electoral thresholds or plurality-majority formula, in contrast, will make office-seeking more attractive when compared to vote seeking (Greenberg and Shepsle 1987; Strom 1990b). This does not apply, however, when the electoral losses incurred by office-seeking strategies are a step function: Up to a certain point, moderation will translate into only minor losses; beyond that point, however, a new entrant will be successful and reduce an office-seeking party's electorate by a huge margin.

Finally, the probability that parties seek office rather than electoral gains may be a consequence of the iterative nature of the electoral game and the *fatigue* created by long-term opposition status. If social democratic parties are repeatedly locked into the opposition while pursuing vote-maximizing strategies that keep them out of office, over time they may begin to discount the value of votes relative to that of office. Simultaneously, they may become more charitable to their radical left-libertarian competitors who stand to benefit from an office-seeking stance of their social democratic neighbor.

Office-seeking strategies may not be simply a matter of rational choice by party leaders, but they may also be furthered by strategically motivated voters. If parties in multiparty systems give signals on potential coalitions, voters may vote on entire coalitions rather than sincerely support the individual party with which they sympathize (Austen-Smith and Banks 1988; Kitschelt 1989a: ch. 9; Laver 1989: 309–10). In other words, office-seeking parties may generate strategic voters and strategic voters may induce parties to seek office.

Office-seeking strategies are "rational" in a broader sense than permitted by thin theories of rationality, *provided* most structural conditions indicate that the electoral costs of seeking office are limited, while the probabilities of success are high. In addition, fatigue with the opposition role adds a purely behavioral element to the analysis of complex spatial competition.

### *Complex spatial competition II: Oligopolistic competition*

While a party's office-seeking strategy implies a position closer to the median voter than required by a vote-seeking strategy, a strategy of oligopolistic competition moves a party's stance further from the pivot. Oligopolistic competition presupposes a long-term view of the electoral game and is akin to a dumping strategy in oligopolistic markets.[24] It sacrifices votes at the next election for the sake of long-term office or vote maximization. If a firm or party has reasonable confidence that it might be able to eliminate a close competitor by forgoing short-term profit or vote maximization, it may opt for a strategy of lowering prices now and recouping lost profits later on when the challenger has vanished.

24 As Budge and Keman (1990: 28) remind us, Downsian political entrepreneurs in simple party competition do not care about their long-term electoral chances or reputation.

Again using Table 4.1A, assume that a country's electoral system bars parties with less than 5% of the popular vote from legislative representation. Decision makers in SD might reason that if the party succeeded in pushing LL out of parliament by assuming the suboptimal strategy II, LL's resources and media exposure would sufficiently deteriorate to prevent it from being a serious future competitor. Meanwhile SD could safely return to vote-maximizing strategy I, while effectively attracting most of those voters who supported LL as long as it was a viable alternative.

As in the case of office-seeking strategy, a rational choice analysis cannot explain why parties may prefer a longer time horizon that sacrifices votes in the short run. Yet again, a number of structural and behavioral circumstances affect a party's rational considerations about embarking on the path of oligopolistic competition. First, since oligopolistic competition makes entry into government coalitions less likely than vote- or office-seeking strategies, it is attractive to parties if (1) chances for government participation are small regardless of strategic choice or (2) if government status promises little additional influence over policy, either because of the institutional weakness of government or because of the policy compromises that would be extracted by coalition partners. Second, fatigue with opposition status, as a residual factor, again plays its role. Parties locked into opposition may become restless and prey on more radical competitors to change their lot.

Party strategists must also carefully consider the institutional susceptibility of the target party to oligopolistic competition. If the start-up costs of new parties are high, electoral dumping strategies by a would-be oligopolist may be attractive. High electoral thresholds, the established parties' control over mass media (radio, TV), and restrictive conditions of public party finance create obstacles to new parties. Moreover, a centralist state structure with infrequent elections at the national level makes it more difficult for a challenging party to stage a comeback and defeat oligopolistic competition than a federal system where threatened parties can play in numerous regional secondary elections. Further, if a party targeted for oligopolistic competition is older and has an entrenched protective belt of loyalists and party identifiers who will stand by their party, even as an opposing party adjusts its appeal to draw their support, oligopolistic strategies are unlikely to succeed.

Finally, the greater the proportion of voters concentrated in the center of the electoral space, the more voters will be lost by the party that embarks on an oligopolistic strategy with a more extreme voter appeal. Conversely, conditions are also unfavorable when there is a sizable constituency of highly mobilized, radical voters. Attracting these voters may require a drastic shift of oligopolistic appeals and heavy losses among moderate voters. More important, oligopolistic strategies involve *consequences for voters' preference formation* that may impede future plans for returning to a moderate competitive strategy. In order to wipe out a more radical competitor, an oligopolist will intensify the salience of radical issues and risk increasing the dispersion and polarization of voters across the competitive space. Radicalized voters may abandon the oligopolist party as soon as it returns to a more moderate vote- or office-maximizing strategy. The net voter gain of oligopolistic strategies may be zero or negative.

To sum up, parties are more inclined to pursue oligopolistic strategies where there are high start-up costs for new parties, a strong central government, low entrenchment of target parties, a small core of radical voters, but also no dense concentration of voters around the median, and little gain of control over policy through government status (hypothesis 4). Nevertheless, given that oligopolistic competition endogenizes the voter distribution and may actually polarize the electorate, payoffs of such strategies are highly uncertain. Oligopolistic strategies have less chance of success and involve greater uncertainties than short-term vote- and office-seeking strategies. Given the damage oligopolistic strategies can inflict on a party, party decision makers are likely to choose them only if intraparty coalitions favor such a stance, regardless of systemic opportunities.[25]

## 4.2 SOCIAL DEMOCRATIC STRATEGIC RATIONALITY AND ELECTORAL PAYOFFS: THE CONSTRAINTS ON STRATEGIC CHOICE

In the previous section I argued that socialists pursuing a short-term vote-maximizing strategy assume comparatively more radical left-libertarian stances when the distribution of voter sentiment is favorable to left-libertarian appeals (hypothesis 1) and when the balance of party system fractionalization places a relatively larger crowd of competitors for social democrats in the center of the party system than at the left-libertarian periphery (hypothesis 2). Further, there is a range of conditions that may persuade social democratic party strategists to prefer either an office-seeking and pivoting strategy of competition (hypothesis 3) or a long-term vote-seeking strategy of oligopolistic competition (hypothesis 4).

These four hypotheses explain strategic stances and only indirectly predict electoral payoffs. My ultimate goal, however, is to account for socialist electoral fortunes. The first two hypotheses imply that parties failing to choose appropriate responses to the voter distribution and to the balance of party fractionalization will suffer electoral losses. Parties, however, may be *willing* to suffer such losses if they are seeking office or competing oligopolistically (hypotheses 3 and 4). Even parties subscribing to short-term vote-maximizing rationality may suffer electorally if they are faced with tragic choices due to changing conditions of competition that permit the entry of another party, as is the case with B in the scenario outlined in Figure 4.2. Conversely, parties pursuing nonequilibrium strategies may be lucky and gain votes if their competitors also diverge from the prescriptions of the simple spatial theory of multiparty competition. In other words, a test of the theory requires a rather detailed and sophisticated case-by-case analysis of competitive configurations.

The spatial theory I have outlined would be *partially* refuted if it failed to account for a party's position *either* in terms of short-term vote seeking (taking

25 This intraparty dynamic will be considered in Chapter 5.

"tragedy" and "luck" into account) *or* in terms of office-seeking or oligopolistic competition. The theory would be *fully* refuted if electoral payoffs are *also* inconsistent with its predictions about the effects of the parties' competitive configuration.

Even the complex model and any empirical exploration of its usefulness as an interpretative scheme for mapping social democratic strategic positions and electoral payoffs, however, make a number of idealizing heroic assumptions that limit its empirical punch. Most important, it expects voters' choices to be motivated by party appeals and to support the party that is closest to their own stance on the dominant competitive dimension while in fact many voters choose according to party identification. Moreover, the theoretical model allows for little history and dead weight in party positions and ignores that a party's reputation may limit its strategic flexibility. Further, the model presupposes that parties know voters' ideal positions, an assumption that is hazardous even if voter movements are slow and monitored by frequent polling. Nevertheless, rather than throwing our hands up in despair, it is worthwhile to explore whatever explanatory mileage the theory helps us to extract, while keeping in mind that many voters commit themselves based on party identification, a party's past reputation, or complex strategic calculations not reflected in spatial models of multiparty competition.

It is now time to operationalize the theory's key independent variables with (quasi-)quantitative measures. In doing so, several issues must be explored: (1) the construction of the main competitive dimension in each country and its relationship to the theoretically postulated left-libertarian versus right-authoritarian dimension introduced in Chapter 1, (2) the parties' strategic stances on that dimension, (3) the balance of party system fractionalization with which socialists are faced, (4) the composite incentives for pivoting and office-seeking strategies; and (5) the overall incentives for oligopolistic competition. Since most of the quasi-quantitative indicators measure the theoretical concepts only indirectly, I will "test" the theory primarily through comparative case studies in which I analyze the trajectory of each European socialist party with a blend of narrative accounts of party strategy and electoral payoffs. Quantitative indicators of party stances have a merely illustrative purpose.

### *Left-libertarian versus right-authoritarian cleavage mobilization*

Political cleavages in a population combine (1) group divisions in the social structure with (2) general ideological divisions and (3) participatory dispositions toward political action.[26] In order to explore the existence of a dominant political division and, more specifically, the relevance of a left-libertarian versus right-authoritarian cleavage dimension, I have chosen voters' attributes from these three aspects of cleavage formation.

26 In contrast to older approaches that distinguish ascriptive trait, opinion, and act cleavages (Rae and Taylor 1970), this approach examines cleavages as a *combination* of these attributes. See Kitschelt (1989a: ch. 2) and especially Bartolini and Mair (1990: 213–20).

As socioeconomic traits, I include citizens' age, occupational status (dummy variable for white collar or student) and education. Such attributes are likely to register ideological predispositions and political expectations. To single out left-libertarians, one would preferably identify occupations in the public client-interactive service sector, but data limitations permit only blunt measures such as white collar employment and student status.

For general ideological divisions, I will employ the popular ten-point scale of left-right self-placement, a ten-point scale of religiosity, and the familiar, though controversial measure of materialist versus post-materialist orientation. As I discussed in Chapter 1, this last scale would better be characterized as a libertarian versus authoritarian scale because it primarily taps respondents' attitudes toward state authority.

To identify participatory dispositions, existing cross-nationally comparative surveys include questions on the readiness of respondents to join peace, ecology, or antinuclear movements. Though each of these movements attracts a somewhat different clientele, all three are associated with left-libertarian concerns.[27] At least involvement in peace initiatives, however, may also relate to a traditional economic left–right dimension, given the almost century-old pacifism of working-class organizations.

The nine indicators measuring the dimensionality of citizens' cleavages are constrained by the availability of comparative data in the Eurobarometer surveys in the 1980s that cover eight of the ten countries I examine. It should be emphasized that the indicators do not prejudice the analysis toward a dominant left-libertarian versus right-authoritarian dimension. It is also conceivable that class politics emerges as the dominant dimension that would combine people who place themselves on the left, are less religious, support the peace movement, have less education, and are less likely to be white collar employees against a polar opposite with more rightist white collar employees who are more religious and oppose the peace movement. Furthermore, the data could yield a religious cleavage that combines more religious practice with less education and more rightist self-placement. On the face of it, only *three* of the nine indicators appear to be directly related to recent changes in political mobilization that involve the libertarian versus authoritarian dimension (post-materialism, readiness to participate in ecology, and antinuclear movements).

If a factor analysis of the nine measures shows that the empirical correlates of established cleavages do *not* relate to the three core measures unique to the libertarian versus authoritarian dimension, then it is likely that party competition is multidimensional. If, however, *all nine variables load in the appropriate way on the same factor,* we have fairly strong evidence for the overriding importance of the postulated dominant cleavage. I should add that factor analyses of the dimensionality of party systems are obviously sensitive to the number and nature of variables employed. Yet the results I present are robust to variations of the

27 Similarities and differences in social movement constituencies have been analyzed by Rohrschneider (1990b).

variables. Equivalent factor analyses with rather different measures I have employed elsewhere yield almost identical results.[28]

Table 4.2A and 4.2B presents findings from a principal components analysis of respondents' values on all nine variables in each of eight countries for which comparable survey data are available. The data are from 1986 (Eurobarometer 25) and thus represent the predominant voter outlook in the middle of the critical decade for which I intend to trace socialist party strategy. The analysis generates two interpretable factors. In all countries, the first factor is clearly identifiable as the left-libertarian versus right-authoritarian dimension. All variables, with one partial exception, load strongly on this factor in every case. Individuals who tend to support one of the three social movements *also* tend to support the others (behavioral dispositions). Moreover, they tend to be more post-materialist, secular, and to the left (ideological dispositions) as well as to be young, highly educated white collar employees or students (social structure).[29] The spread of the factor loadings on each variable across the eight countries is small. It ranges from a mere 0.14 (peace movements) to 0.41 (left–right self-placements), the one partial exception to the commonality of patterns. While in six of the eight countries, the general left-libertarian syndrome is rather strongly related to leftist self-placements (−.33 to −.55), this is much less the case in Italy (−.17) and Belgium (−.14). In these two countries, the left–right cleavage appears to be primarily based on traits, opinions, and readiness to mobilize that are distinct from the left-libertarian dimension.

This is confirmed by a glance at the factor loadings on the second component in Table 4.2B. The six countries that had close to identical patterns of factor loadings on each variable for the first factor component also reveal a similar convergence on the second factor component, which loads strongly on behavioral dispositions and moderately on social position. It pits an older, less educated working class moderately predisposed to supporting social movements against a cluster of young, educated white collar individuals who oppose the movements. We may call this the "yuppie" syndrome. Upwardly mobile young urban professionals care little about broader political movements and prefer centrist technocratic politics. The division between yuppies and an older working class is only weakly associated

---

28 See Kitschelt (1991d) and (forthcoming) on the rise of the New Radical Right in Western Europe. In this study, I employed several different variables for occupation (blue collar worker, business), gender, income, and cognitive mobilization, while all three behavioral dispositions toward left-libertarian politics (willingness to join social movements) were not included. Also Knutsen's (1989) analysis based on an older Eurobarometer survey from 1981 shows the overriding importance of what he terms the materialist–post-materialist cleavage in at least Denmark, Italy, Germany, and the Netherlands. In France it is the second strongest cleavage dimension and in Britain it is fused with a conventional left–right division. Only in Belgium, Knutsen finds a comparatively low importance of the left-libertarian versus right-authoritarian cleavage, although it exists even here.

29 This configuration also tends to confirm that left–right self-placements are not simply a matter of party identification, but in fact relate to issues and ideological predispositions that include nonmaterialist items. See Huber (1989). Further studies on the linkage of left–right self-placements to left-libertarian politics include Inglehart (1984, 1990), Savage (1985), Schmitt (1987), Van Deth and Geurts (1989), and Kitschelt and Hellemans (1990b).

Table 4.2. Political divisions in eight democracies (principal component analysis, just two components)

Component I: Left-libertarian politics vs. right-authoritarian politics

| | Belgium | Denmark | France | Germany | Italy | Netherlands | Spain | United Kingdom |
|---|---|---|---|---|---|---|---|---|
| *Socio-demographics* | | | | | | | | |
| Age | -.48 | -.70 | -.64 | -.60 | -.65 | -.50 | -.64 | -.56 |
| Education | +.65 | +.68 | +.60 | +.57 | +.68 | +.53 | +.56 | +.58 |
| White collar/student | +.52 | +.61 | +.49 | +.45 | +.58 | +.39 | +.50 | +.44 |
| *Dispositions* | | | | | | | | |
| Being on the right | -.14 | -.42 | -.39 | -.49 | -.17 | -.55 | -.38 | -.33 |
| Religiosity | -.29 | -.40 | -.45 | -.48 | -.38 | -.50 | -.54 | -.22 |
| Post-materialism | +.37 | +.49 | +.50 | +.55 | +.45 | +.54 | +.58 | +.49 |
| *Readiness to join social movement* | | | | | | | | |
| Ecology movement | +.61 | +.47 | +.51 | +.69 | +.63 | +.54 | +.71 | +.59 |
| Antinuclear movement | +.74 | +.62 | +.54 | +.70 | +.59 | +.64 | +.74 | +.70 |
| Peace movement | +.62 | +.62 | +.64 | +.68 | +.69 | +.70 | +.76 | +.73 |
| Explained variance | 27.3% | 31.3% | 28.6% | 34.4% | 31.5% | 30.1% | 37.3% | 28.3% |
| Eigenvalue | 2.46 | 2.82 | 2.57 | 3.09 | 2.84 | 2.71 | 3.36 | 2.54 |

Component II: Yuppies versus working-class sympathizers of social movements

| | Belgium | Denmark | France | Germany | Italy | Netherlands | Spain | United Kingdom |
|---|---|---|---|---|---|---|---|---|
| *Sociodemographics* | | | | | | | | |
| Age | +.14 | +.42 | +.43 | +.54 | +.41 | +.58 | +.43 | +.56 |
| Education | -.14 | -.39 | -.48 | -.56 | -.54 | -.56 | -.59 | -.58 |
| White collar/student | +.02 | -.39 | -.46 | -.58 | -.56 | -.66 | -.58 | -.60 |
| *Dispositions* | | | | | | | | |
| Being on the right | +.64 | +.01 | -.02 | -.29 | -.33 | -.28 | +.05 | -.24 |
| Religiosity | +.69 | +.21 | +.19 | -.04 | -.01 | +.11 | +.12 | +.04 |
| Post-materialism | -.47 | -.18 | -.15 | -.10 | -.07 | -.10 | -.26 | +.08 |
| *Readiness to join social movement* | | | | | | | | |
| Ecology movement | +.28 | +.49 | +.50 | +.40 | +.45 | +.35 | +.40 | +.23 |
| Antinuclear movement | +.37 | +.58 | +.60 | +.43 | +.55 | +.47 | +.54 | +.46 |
| Peace movement | +.36 | +.60 | +.57 | +.33 | +.46 | +.43 | +.50 | +.45 |
| Explained variance | 17.0% | 16.7% | 18.1% | 16.7% | 17.4% | 19.2% | 19.3% | 16.6% |
| Eigenvalue | 1.53 | 1.50 | 1.63 | 1.50 | 1.61 | 1.73 | 1.74 | 1.50 |
| Number of respondents | 771 | 888 | 850 | 891 | 887 | 924 | 627 | 1162 |
| Missing cases | 236 | 155 | 153 | 96 | 215 | 95 | 381 | 217 |

*Source:* Eurobarometer 25.

with ideological dispositions. Almost everywhere, yuppies tend to be slightly more post-materialist and secular, whereas working-class supporters of social movements are more religious and materialist. On the left–right scale, factor loadings are extremely weak and exhibit no uniform tendency.

The two outliers are again Belgium and Italy. In Belgium, something approximating an "old" left–right dimension emerges on component II that links leftism, secularism, and post-materialism but is not particularly associated with social background (older, less educated working class) or sympathy to social movements. In Italy, a similar phenomenon emerges as the second component, yet it is more closely linked to the pattern common to the six other countries. Here predisposition toward social movements and social background are related to ideological self-placement. Yuppies are more to the right, while the older working class sympathetic to contemporary movements is more to the left. This pattern exhibits consequences of the particular issue leadership of the Italian Communist Party I will discuss in the case study.

Although my analysis confirms the importance of the left-libertarian dimension, the relative strength of a second unrelated and clearly interpretable dimension arguably undermines the assumption that voter preferences can be mapped in terms of a unidimensional distribution. Even where factor analytic techniques reveal numerous dimensions of voter preference, one must keep in mind, however, that (1) voters do not take all of these dimensions into account when voting and (2) parties may not compete on all dimensions but systematically highlight particular cleavages. The cleavage space ("domain of identification") and the competitive space of political parties may be different (cf. Sani and Sartori 1983: 330).

A final problem revealed in Table 4.2 concerns missing values. In most countries, between 10 and 15 percent of the observations are missing, yet there are two outliers, Belgium and Spain with 23.6% and 38.1% of all respondents missing. Cross-checking of missing data on individual variables reveals that nonresponses are not randomly distributed. In particular, individuals are *more* likely not to reveal their willingness to affiliate with social movements, if their responses on other variables exhibit a more right-authoritarian tendency. Thus, it is safe to conclude that in Spain and to a lesser extent in Belgium left-libertarians are overrepresented in the factor analysis and all other calculations based on this data set, a problem I will take into account in testing my theory.[30]

With the partial exception of Belgium, the factor analysis overall reveals that (1) the factors are by and large the same in all countries and (2) the left-libertarian versus right-authoritarian dimension emerges as the strongest division, with a second dimension dividing an older working class mildly sympathetic to contemporary movements from technocratic yuppies. In addition to the "new" left-libertarian dimension traces of the old distributive left–right division are still present. When mapping party positions, it will be vital to check whether alternatives vary more on the first or the second dimension and how parties' positions on

---

30 In Spain, this self-selection of respondents may also explain the extraordinarily high variance explained by the first factor.

both dimensions relate to each other. When running a second factor analysis excluding left–right self-placements, as the one variable where the Belgian and Italian first factor scores diverged from the common pattern, the Belgian and Italian "exceptionalisms" disappear and in all countries the two factors are unambiguously defined in the terms just described.

The extent of left-libertarian cleavage mobilization determines the incentive socialist parties face in moving their strategies toward left-libertarian appeals. I have pooled all eight countries in a factor analysis of the eight variables that produced similar results when run in individual countries (Table 4.3). Each country's average factor score on the first left-libertarian versus right-authoritarian factor provides a crude measure of cleavage mobilization.[31] If we partition the space between the country with the lowest left-libertarian propensity (Belgium, −.35) and the country with the highest propensity (Germany, +.39) into four equal sections, German and Dutch voters are clearly in the highest group of left-libertarian mobilization. They are followed by Spain, but it must be recalled that Spanish cleavage mobilization is probably overstated due to the nonresponses of interviewees unwilling to participate in social movements. In the third group are Britain and Denmark. Italy is situated on the margin to the lowest quartile with France and Belgium trailing everyone else in left-libertarian mobilization.

Other techniques for measuring the average position of a national electorate and its distribution on the left-libertarian versus right-authoritarian dimension yield similar results. For example, one could sum up the percentage of voters on each of the nine key variables who have favorable predispositions to left-libertarian politics (cf. Kitschelt 1993: table 2). Again, Germany and the Netherlands show the highest average cleavage mobilization, followed by Spain and Denmark. Britain, France, and Italy are behind at some distance, trailed by Belgium with even lower left-libertarian mobilization.[32]

For the two nonmembers of the European Community (EC), Austria and Sweden, data comparable to the Eurobarometer survey are not available. Other fragmentary survey evidence, however, permits us to gauge their left-libertarian cleavage mobilization in a rough way. In Sweden, structural conditions for left-libertarian politics are generally favorable because a comparatively high share of the population has advanced education and white collar occupations (cf. Holmberg and Gilljam 1987: 179–81, 213–18). At the same time, secularism, post-materialism, and leftist self-placements appear to be somewhat more widespread than in Denmark (cf. Bennulf and Holmberg 1990; Knutsen 1990a,b). There are no surveys on the willingness of Swedes to associate with social movements corre-

31 Of course, also the distribution of values over the cleavage dimension is important. The distribution, however, is single-peaked and similarly shaped in all countries.
32 The high level of left-libertarian mobilization in Germany and the Netherlands as compared to Britain, Austria, and the United States can also be gleaned from an analysis of unconventional political activism by Kaase and Marsh (1979: 154–5). Also studies of environmental consciousness in Europe found Germany, the Netherlands, and Denmark in the lead, Italy in an intermediate position, and Belgium, Britain, France, and Spain far behind (Hofrichter and Reif 1990).

Table 4.3. *Principal component analysis of political cleavages: Pooled analysis of eight variables in eight countries*

| | Factor I<br>Left-libertarians vs. right<br>authoritarians | Factor II<br>Yuppies vs. working class<br>sympathizers of social<br>movements |
|---|---|---|
| *Sociodemographics* | | |
| Age | −.50 | −.48 |
| Education | +.49 | +.52 |
| White collar/student | +.44 | +.57 |
| *Dispositions* | | |
| Religiosity | −.36 | −.26 |
| Post-materialism | +.49 | +.22 |
| *Readiness to join social movement* | | |
| Ecology movement | +.67 | −.41 |
| Antinuclear movement | +.72 | −.48 |
| Peace movement | +.75 | −.44 |
| Explained variance | 32.2% | 19.0% |
| Eigenvalue | 2.57 | 1.57 |
| *Average factor scores* | | |
| Belgium | −.35 | +.18 |
| Denmark | −.04 | +.36 |
| France | −.19 | +.18 |
| Germany | +.39 | −.25 |
| Italy | −.15 | −.14 |
| Netherlands | +.27 | +.11 |
| Spain | +.12 | −.33 |
| United Kingdom | −.02 | −.10 |

*Source:* Eurobarometer 25.

sponding to the questions asked in Eurobarometer studies. Yet Knutsen's studies of post-materialism in Scandinavia (1990a: 267; 1990b: 88), on balance, suggest that Swedish and Danish public opinion and associational dispositions are not all that different. The level of left-libertarian cleavage mobilization in Sweden is, therefore, similar to that of Denmark.

In terms of social structure, Austria in the mid-1980s had unfavorable conditions for left-libertarianism because of its voters' demographic, educational, and occupational profile (cf. Plasser 1985). Similarly, its level of post-materialism fell short of the mean value of the other European countries covered in this study (Plasser 1985) and leftism and secularism are less pronounced than elsewhere as well. Nevertheless, environmental questions made it to the top of the list of salient issues in the second half of the 1980s (Ulram 1989: 200) and the controversy about nuclear and hydroelectric power plants was among the most polarizing conflict in Austrian politics in the 1980s. Still, the proportion of individuals willing to participate in unconventional action may lag compared to many other countries. Overall, given positional, ideological, and associational elements, Austria probably ranks somewhere between Belgium, at the low end of left-libertarian mobilization, and the lower middle group of countries that includes France and Italy.

If hypothesis 1 is correct, socialist parties should be most inclined to pursue left-libertarian strategies in Germany and the Netherlands and least inclined to follow that strategy in Austria and Belgium. Left parties in Spain and Sweden should be closer to the first pole and parties in France and Italy closer to the second pole. The Danish and British parties should be in an intermediate range.

I account for party strategy by employing the distribution of voters on the left-libertarian versus right-authoritarian axis as an independent ("exogenous") variable. While this is unproblematic in a purely cross-sectional analysis of party strategies at one time point, a longitudinal analysis must entertain the possibility that voter distribution across the main competitive dimension may be in part endogenous to party competition. Even though there is evidence of a secular shift from a purely economic-distributive left-right competitive dimension to the left–libertarian versus right-authoritarian dimension in response to rising affluence and a changing socialization of young age cohorts,[33] the wide dispersion of the average positions of national electorates on the cleavage dimension, however, appears to remain insensitive to converging economic conditions.[34]

Such cross-national differences in left-libertarian politics may be indeed related to political rather than to economic factors alone. For example, the centrality of highly organized political camps in Austria and Belgium around religious and class politics may impede the recentering of the political space. More broadly, the strategy and impact of social movements around left-libertarian or right-authoritarian issues is mediated through existing political institutions and configurations of the party system (cf. Kitschelt 1986; Tarrow 1990a; Kriesi et al. 1992). Such conditions shape the extent to which new conflicts are politicized and affect a general restructuring of the perceived political alternatives. For example, where political elites and interest groups were able to crush antinuclear power protests or to coopt the opposition by policy compromise, this particular left-libertarian issue lost salience whereas it stayed alive in countries where the (party) elites countered the mobilization of antinuclear forces with inconclusive policies (Jasper 1988). Aside from political opportunity structures, sudden shocks, such as the collapse of communism, after a period of long-run intellectual decline of Marxist thinking in Western Europe, also may influence voters' political orienta-

---

33 This, at least, is the argument that has been substantiated by Inglehart (1977, 1990) for one important element of the left-libertarian versus right-authoritarian dimension, propensity toward post-materialism. See also Inglehart and Abramson (1992a,b).

34 For a longitudinal and cross-sectional analysis criticizing Inglehart's hypothesis of growing post-materialism, see Clarke and Dutt (1991). I have also run factor analyses of the items represented in Tables 4.2 and 4.3 for the Eurobarometer Surveys 17 (1982) and 21 (1984) in addition to the main survey 25 (1986) employed in my analysis. At least over this four-year time span, competitive spaces and party positions have remained by and large stable in the various countries. For a critique of Clarke and Dutt, see Inglehart and Abramson (1992a).

tions. The longitudinal case studies of socialist electoral fortunes presented below consider the interaction between citizens' issue mobilization, political opportunities, and party strategies.

## *Party strategy*

In the eyes of the voters, party strategy is expressed in the public pronouncements of party leaders and their actions in the legislative and government arena. Because such actions and statements are difficult to compare, studies have relied on content analyses of parties' electoral platforms (cf. Robertson 1976; Thomas 1982; Budge, Robertson, and Hearl 1987). Unfortunately, the reliability and validity of the only comparative data set on election manifestos is so questionable that this data source is not useful for my purposes.[35] Furthermore, content analyses do not measure the leaders' positions in terms of the same indicators employed above to measure the voters' positions (e.g., left–right self-placement, stance on religion, post-materialism, etc.).[36]

As a consequence, I construct two alternative, indirect measures of parties' strategic stances. First, I rely on a country-expert survey of party positions conducted by Laver and Hunt (1992) in the late 1980s. Experts assessed parties' issue positions such that they can be combined in scales. In my individual country analyses, I examine each party's position on a "conventional" economic left-right dimension, tapping parties' positions on the nationalization of enterprise and on support for a comprehensive welfare state, and a "libertarian" dimension, measured by parties' moral "permissiveness" and the rank order given to environmental protection and economic growth. If party competition is unidimensional, parties' stances on each of these dimensions should covary or one of the dimensions alone should systematically differentiate party positions.[37]

35 Budge, Robertson, and Hearl (1987) intend to operationalize not the position of parties on issues, but only the relative salience of issues as measured by the proportion of a manifesto devoted to a particular topic. In practice, however, some items are coded in a positional mode, while others are coded in a salience mode (See coding categories in Budge et al., pp. 459–64). Furthermore, the factor analyses of national party positions are not comparable cross-nationally because the content of factors varies widely. Finally, the characterization of parties' ideological appeals is often highly implausible. For example, the Belgian Christian Democrats at times appear to be more anti-clerical than the socialists (Hearl 1987: 247). In several elections, the Danish social democrats are depicted as more "New Left" than the Socialist People's Party (Holmstedt and Schou 1987: 200) and both in Sweden and Denmark party positions are highly volatile (pp. 202–5). The Dutch data do not reveal the Labour Party's move to radical libertarian positions in the 1970s (Dittrich 1987: 221). In the 1970s, the French socialists come out further on the left than the communists (Petry 1987: 342), and the German Christian Democrats appear to favor international solidarity and domestic quality of life more than the social democrats (Klingemann 1987: 319).

36 Data where identical issue cues were given to political leaders and the general electorate are available only for a very restricted set of questions included in a 1979 Eurobarometer survey and the European Political Parties Middle Level Elites survey of the same year (cf. Dalton 1984; Iversen 1991). Unfortunately, such data are unavailable for any time point in the 1980s.

37 Other measures in Laver and Hunt's (1992: ch. 3) study include religion, government decentralization, view of the Soviet Union, and urban–rural interests. As Laver and Hunt's factor analyses of

Second, I employ voters' positions in the 1986 Eurobarometer surveys to assess party strategies. If a voter's position in the electoral space is related, though not necessarily identical with her preferred party's ideological appeal, the average scores of a party's supporters on the two strongest issue dimensions yielded by the factor analyses reported in Table 4.2 constitute a tracer of that party's strategy.[38] In line with "directional" theories of voting, we may even concede that parties' strategic positions are not identical with their voters' mean positions. But as long as there is a systematic relationship between voters' positions and party appeals rather than a random variation in the distance between the two, voter preferences still serve as tracers of party strategy. Laver and Hunt's (1992) data set with expert judgments on the position of party leaders and party electorates provide at least some hints that this presumption is warranted. Moreover, Iversen's (1991, 1992) studies of party and voter positions in the late 1970s also serve as checks for assessing the validity of my claims.

Policy-defined competitive spaces in which voters are placed in relation to parties may provide a misleading image of the political process because voters' perceptions of policy issues are already contaminated by party strategies. For my purposes, the existence of such contamination is not a flaw, but a welcome effect, because it will bring voters' and parties' positions closer together.[39]

Although the factor analytic representation of voter positions in Table 4.2 requires at least a two-dimensional space, parties may not compete in two separate dimensions. In fact, "multi-dimensional issue-preference space becomes irrelevant, if the parties' ordering on each of these dimensions is approximately similar, which is frequently the case" (Van der Eijk and Niemöller 1983: 208). Below I explore the extent to which unidimensionality of competition applies once parties' positions are inscribed in the policy-defined electoral space.

### The balance of party system fractionalization

Hypothesis 2 in the simple theory of spatial competition states that the optimal location of parties depends on the balance of fractionalization in the system of

party positions show, introducing these issues does not significantly affect the dimensionality of the issue space. In most countries, the space is by and large unidimensional, although the Benelux countries and Germany require a second dimension to place liberal parties, a finding confirmed also by other investigations.

38 Of course, alternative techniques such as likelihood ratio space analysis (Budge and Farlie 1977: ch. 2 and 9) or discriminant analysis (Knutsen 1988; 1989) perform the same job of locating groups of individuals in a multidimensional space. Explorations with discriminant analysis yielded similar results as those I will report from a simple principal components factor analysis and are therefore not presented here.

39 The alternatives to policy-defined spaces are party sympathy ratings to generate party-defined spaces, e.g. in the interesting study by Listhaug et al. (1990a). Such spaces, however, are difficult to interpret and to compare cross-nationally.

party competition encountered by socialist parties. If the difference between the number of competitors to a party's right and left is about the same, the party should be in a centrist position. The greater the difference between the two values, the more a party should be located to the left or right periphery of the political spectrum. Operationalizations of this hypothesis depend on how we "count" relevant parties and no unambiguous, generalizable rule is available to yield such a calculus (cf. Sartori 1976: 121–4). In general, all those parties count that are sufficiently important to be potential coalition partners, as do parties with a potential to blackmail parties considering government participation. Particular institutional rules (e.g. electoral thresholds and other barriers to entry) and the party system format determine which parties should be included or excluded.

Table 4.4 reflects the balance of fragmentation in the ten party systems in the mid-1980s. It also provides abbreviations of all parties that will be referred to in this study. In general, relevant parties managed to gain at least an average of 2% of the vote in national parliamentary and presidential elections or in European elections in the 1980s. Whether parties are truly located to the left or the right of socialists along the main dimension of party competition, of course, is an empirical matter that will be explored in detail below.

In Belgium, the communists are excluded from consideration because they played an insignificant role, although they had been represented in Parliament until 1987. The Flemish Block (VB), a racist and nationalist party had yet to make electoral inroads sufficient to qualify it as an influential party in the 1980s. In Denmark, the political spectrum to both the right and the left of the social democrats is extremely crowded. While the Socialist People's Party averaged 12.6% in the 1980s, Left Socialists began the 1980s as a marginal blackmail party at 2.7% and then dwindled to insignificance, while the Greens rose to 1.4% by 1988 and replaced the former as a libertarian blackmail party.

In France, in the 1980s ecologists never managed to gain more than 1% of the vote in parliamentary elections. They received about 4%, however, in the 1981 and 1988 presidential elections, and became a significant factor in the run-offs among the lead candidates. In the Italian party system, counting rules are complicated because the Center and the far Left are so fragmented. I have decided to count the small secular centrist parties, Social Democrats and Republicans and omit the Liberals, a party that has hovered around barely 2%. On the Left, I count Radicals, Greens, and Demoproletarians, all of whom increased their electoral support between 1983 and 1987 to at least 2% of the vote. In the Netherlands, I have counted the "Green Progressive Accord," composed of Communists (CPN), Pacifist Socialists (PSP), and Radicals (PPR) as a single party, although they officially merged into the Green Left only in 1990. For similar reasons, I have also counted the three formally independent Protestant fundamentalist parties, the Evangelical People's Party (EVP), the Reformed Political Union (GVP), and the Reformed Political Federation (RPF), as a single entity. In Spain, the socialists faced competition on the left primarily from an electoral alliance between a major faction of

Table 4.4. *Party system fractionalism in ten European democracies:*
*unidimensional representation*

| | Competitors to the (libertarian) "left" of social democrats | Competitors to the (authoritarian) "right" of socialist parties | Balance of party system fractionalization |
|---|---|---|---|
| Austria | United Greens (VGÖ) | People's Party (ÖVP), Free Party (FPÖ) | +1 |
| Belgium | Agalev,[a] Ecolo[a] | Christian Democrats (CVP, PSC), Flemish People's Union (VU) Liberals (PRL, PVV) | +2 |
| Britain | – | Conservatives, Liberal Democrats (consisting of Liberals, Social Democrats in the Alliance) | +2/0 |
| Denmark | Socialist People's Party (SPP), Left Socialists (VS), or Greens (G) | Radicals (RV), Liberals (V), Conservatives (KF), Progress Party (FP), Center Democrats (CD), Christian Democrats (KRF) | +4 |
| France | Ecolo, Communist Party (PCF) | Gaullists (RPR), Liberals (UDF/Dem. Center/Indep. Republicans), National Front (NF) | +1 |
| Germany | Greens (G) | Christian Democrats (CDU/CSU), Free Democrats (FPD) | +1 |
| Italy | Ecologists (V), Radicals (PR), DemoProletarians (DP), Communist Party (PCI) | Social Democrats (PSDI), Republicans (PRI), Christian Democrats (DC), Italian Social Movement (MSI) | 0 |
| Netherlands | Green Progressive Accord (GPA), since 1990 Green Left, consisting of Communists (CPN), Pacifist-Socialists (PSP), Radicals (PPR) | Democrats '66 (D '66), Liberals (PVV), Christian Democrats (CDA), Protestant Fundamentalists (GPN+RPF+SGP) | +3 |

Table 4.4. *(cont.)*

|  | Competitors to the (libertarian) "left" of social democrats | Competitors to the (authoritarian) "right" of socialist parties | Balance of party system fractionalization |
|---|---|---|---|
| Spain | United Left (IU), consisting of Communists (PCE), ecologists, and independent Left; small regional Left: Herri Batasuna (HB) | Regionalist Center (Convergence and Unity, CIU), Democratic and Social Center (CDS), Popular Party (PP) | +2 |
| Sweden | Left Party (Communists) (VPK) Greens (MP) | Center Party (CP), Christians (KDS), People's Party (PP), Moderates (M) | +2 |

*<sup>a</sup>An ecology party.

the former Spanish Communist Party (PCE), the ecologists, and other left-libertarians. The regionalist Left, particularly the Basque Herri Batasuna, is too small to count in national party strategy. On the right of the PSOE, however, Catalan regionalists receive a significant proportion of the centrist vote and must be counted in addition to the two national parties, the Democratic and Social Center and the Popular Party. In Sweden, social democrats faced not only the four established competitors in the 1980s, but also the Greens and the Christian Democrats as new entrants with at least blackmail potential. An additional party, New Democracy, appeared on the scene in 1991 and does not figure into this analysis.

In the British case, finally, I have omitted regionalist parties and the Ecologists because they have been too insignificant or regionally confined to affect Labour Party strategy. This leaves only three significant British parties. Since the entire argument about strategic dispersion applies only to multiparty systems with at least four parties, the balance of party fractionalization is meaningless as a predictor of Labour's vote-maximizing strategy. Given that Liberals and Social Democrats cannot leapfrog Labour's stance on the left, Labour's dominant strategy is always moderation, equivalent to a reading of 0 on balance of party system fragmentation, unless we presume that Labour responds to as yet nonexisting radical blackmail parties.

In light of hypothesis 2, the overall balance of party system fragmentation leads to the prediction that vote-maximizing socialists will pursue fairly extreme left-libertarian strategies in Denmark and the Netherlands, moderately left-libertarian strategies in Belgium, Spain, and Sweden, more moderate strategies in Austria, France, and Germany, and clear-cut centrist positions in Italy and Great Britain.

*Incentives for pivoting (office seeking)*

Pivoting or office-seeking strategies are affected by a number of contingencies that can be specified in a straightforward manner, but that are difficult to *weigh* in a combined index of the overall incentive for pivoting. I have chosen to count each of five indicators equally with values on each ranging from 0 to 2. The index for the attractiveness of pivoting thus varies between a minimum of 0 and a maximum of 10 (see Table 4.5). High electoral thresholds [column (1)], the close proximity of socialist parties to the median voter in the main competitive space [column (2)], an uncrowded center of the political space [column (3)], actual unidimensionality of party competition [column (4)], and a significant increase in a party's influence over policy-making through government status [column (5)] render pivoting attractive. In addition, of course, fatigue (long duration of opposition status) may contribute to the lure of office seeking, a factor I have discounted for the purposes of this discussion.

Austria, Britain, France, and Spain offer socialists great incentives for pivoting. This strategy is mildly attractive for German, Swedish, and Danish social democrats. In Italy, Belgium, and the Netherlands, conditions for pivoting are unpromising.

*Incentives for oligopolistic competition*

Table 4.6 shows the incentives for oligopolistic competition – that is, long-term vote seeking at the expense of short-term vote or office seeking – as a function of five variables. Oligopolistic competition is made more attractive by high electoral thresholds [column (1)] and the absence of federalism [column (2)], a weak entrenchment of left-libertarian alternatives to social democracy [column (3)] and small stakes of government status [column (4)]. The fifth variable, cleavage mobilization, is related in a curvilinear way to oligopolistic competition. Where radical left-libertarians are numerous, oligopolistic competition is just as costly as in a system where only few of them exist. If the pooled factor analysis reported in Table 4.3 measures the incidence of left-libertarian radicalism,[40] oligopolistic competition is least promising in countries that have the lowest mobilization (Belgium, France, Italy, and without comparable data support, Austria) or the highest mobilization (Germany, Netherlands). Spain is a difficult borderline case. Oligopolistic competition should be more attractive in countries with intermediate mobilization, such as Denmark, Britain, and Sweden. Of course, the absence of a left-libertarian competitor in the British case makes oligopolistic competition a viable strategy only if the counterfactual argument is valid that a new left-

40 Mean scores for each country do not reflect the dispersion of ideological positions that should be measured, but standard deviations for each country and the analysis of the actual national distribution of sentiments in section 3 justify the conclusion that higher left-libertarian mean values indicate a larger number of radical left-libertarians.

Table 4.5. Incentives for office seeking and pivoting rather than short-term vote-seeking strategies

| | (1) Electoral thresholds | (2) Distance of social democracy from the center | (3) Crowdedness of the center | (4) Dimensionality of competition | (5) Stakes of government status | Aggregate circumstances favorable to pivoting |
|---|---|---|---|---|---|---|
| *Highly favorable* | | | | | | |
| France | 1.5 | 2 | 1 | 2 | 2 | 8.5 |
| Austria | 1 | 2 | 2 | 2 | 1 | 8.0 |
| Britain | 2 | 0 | 2 | 2 | 2 | 8.0 |
| Spain | 1.5 | 2 | 1 | 2 | 0.5 | 7.0 |
| *Medium favorable* | | | | | | |
| Germany | 1.5 | 1 | 2 | 1 | 0 | 5.5 |
| Sweden | 1 | 2 | 0 | 2 | 0.5 | 5.5 |
| Denmark | 0 | 2 | 0 | 2 | 1 | 5.0 |
| *Unfavorable* | | | | | | |
| Italy | 0 | 2 | 0 | 2 | 0.5 | 4.5 |
| Netherlands | 0 | 1 | 0 | 1 | 1 | 3.5 |
| Belgium | 1 | 0 | 1 | 0 | 0.5 | 2.5 |

*Scoring:*

Column (1): PR with thresholds ≤2% = 0; thresholds ≤4% = 1; PR thresholds >4% or majoritarian run-off = 1.5; plurality voting = 2.

Column (2): Distance of social democrats from the 50th percentile >10% = 0; 5–10% = 1; <5% = 2; (1980s averages)

Column (3): Crowdedness of the Center-Right (excluding extreme Right): 1–2 parties = 2; 3 parties = 1; 4 or more: = 0. (For party system format, see Table 4.4.)

Column (4): Judgmental scoring of dimensionality, see Figures 4.3–4.13. Two full dimensions = 0; multidimensionality on one side of the political spectrum = 1; unidimensionality = 2.

Column (5): Summed values of government's capacity of policy formation, from Table 3.2, columns (1) and (2), data for Denmark added.

libertarian party *would* surge were the Labour Party to adopt a short-term vote- or office-maximizing strategy.

The overall opportunities for successful oligopolistic competition are greatest for the Spanish, Swedish, and British socialists. They are moderate in Denmark, France, and Germany. Conditions in Austria, Belgium, Italy, and the Netherlands hold out the least promise for this strategy. Note that the conditions for oligopolistic competition are *not* a mirror image of conditions for pivoting. In fact, there are several countries where neither pivoting nor oligopolistic competition are promising for socialist parties (Belgium, Italy, Netherlands) and others where *both* strategies have comparatively strong (Britain, Spain, France, Sweden) or moderate (Germany) advantages. In Austria, only pivoting makes sense and in Denmark there are marginal incentives for engaging in oligopolistic competition.

### The strategic situation of West European socialist parties in the 1980s

Table 4.7 depicts the entire strategic situation of socialist parties. The margins are defined by each country's scores on the key variables that determine their strategic position were they to follow a short-term vote-maximizing strategy. The more even the balance of party system fractionalization (columns) and the more subdued left-libertarian cleavage mobilization (rows) is, the more socialist parties should be inclined to a moderate strategy (upper-left corner of the table). Countries' positions in the cells of Table 4.7 depend on their summed scores on each of these two dimensions (values are given in brackets) and are based on Tables 4.3 and 4.4. Austria, France, Britain, Italy, and Belgium have very low summed scores (1 or 2) and socialists here are expected to pursue moderate strategies. Socialist parties in a second group of countries – Sweden, Spain, and Germany – face incentives for maximizing votes by pursuing a mixed left-libertarian strategy. Finally, in Denmark and even more so in the Netherlands, vote-maximizing social democrats should opt for a radical left-libertarian strategy.

Preferences may rationally diverge from the vote-maximizing strategy toward moderation if incentives for pivoting are strong. Conversely, they may veer off toward radical strategies if incentives for oligopolistic competition look attractive. In Table 4.7, pivoting incentives are represented by arrows running toward the upper left corner of the table (moderate strategies). These arrows have negative values that correspond to a socialist party's scores for pivoting in Table 4.5 and are depicted only if they reach at least intermediate scores for the attractiveness of that option, i.e., a value of 5. Arrows running toward the lower right corner of Table 4.7 (radical strategies) indicate incentives for oligopolistic competition.

The table illustrates that socialist parties are distinguished not only by their short-run vote-maximizing stances, but also by their opportunities for choosing "complex" strategies of multiparty competition. Particularly the British, French, Swedish, and Spanish parties face a wide range of choices and may therefore engage in *volatile strategies*. The theory of party competition I propose can predict only the electoral consequences of such choices, yet not the particular option that is

Table 4.6. Incentives for oligopolistic competition (long-term vote seeking) rather than short-term vote-seeking strategies

| | (1) Electoral thresholds | (2) No federalism | (3) Weakness of left-libertarian party entrenchment | (4) Stakes of government status | (5) Left-libertarian cleavage mobilization | Aggregate circumstances favorable to oligopolistic competition |
|---|---|---|---|---|---|---|
| *Highly favorable* | | | | | | |
| Sweden | 1 | 2 | 0 | 1.5 | 2 | 6.5 |
| Britain | 2 | 2 | 2/0 | 0 | 2 | 6.0 |
| Spain | 1.5 | 1 | 1 | 1.5 | 1 | 6.0 |
| *Medium favorable* | | | | | | |
| Denmark | 0 | 2 | 0 | 1 | 2 | 5.0 |
| France | 1.5 | 1 | 2 | 0 | 0 | 4.5 |
| Germany | 1.5 | 0 | 1 | 2 | 0 | 4.5 |
| *Unfavorable* | | | | | | |
| Belgium | 1 | 0 | 1 | 1.5 | 0 | 3.5 |
| Italy | 0 | 2 | 0 | 1.5 | 0 | 3.5 |
| Austria | 1 | 0 | 1 | 1 | 0 | 3.0 |
| Netherlands | 0 | 2 | 0 | 1 | 0 | 3.0 |

*Scoring:*

Column (1): PR with thresholds ≤2% = 0; thresholds ≤4% = 1; PR thresholds >4% *or* majoritarian run-off = 1.5; plurality voting = 2.

Column (2): No regional parliaments = 2, weak regional parliaments = 1; strong regional parliaments = 0.

Column (3): Relevant left-libertarian parties founded before 1975 = 0; parties founded before 1980 =1; parties founded after 1980 = 2.

Column (4): Inverse value (2 − x) of Table 4.5, column 5 (government stakes).

Column (5): Scores of left-libertarian cleavage mobilization from Table 4.3. Mean country values on the left-libertarian/right-authoritarian factor for scoring, see text; countries with low and high mobilization = 0; intermediate mobilization = 1 or 2.

## Table 4.7. Incentives affecting socialist parties' strategic choices

| | Left-libertarian cleavage mobilization | | | |
| --- | --- | --- | --- | --- |
| **Balance of party system fractionalization** | Low (0) | Moderately low (1) | Moderately high (2) | High (3) |
| Even (0) | | −8 / Italy (1)    Britain (1) / +6 | | |
| Close to even (1) | −8 / Austria (1) / −8.5    France (1) / +4.5 | | | −5.5 / Germany (4) / +4.5 |
| Moderately uneven (2) | Belgium (2) | | −5.5 / Sweden (4) / +6.5    −6.5 / Spain (4) / +6.0 | |
| Uneven (3) | | | −5 / Denmark (5) / +5 | Netherlands (6) |

Incentive for the most moderate strategy and pivoting

Incentive for radical left-libertarian strategy and oligopolistic competition

chosen. Since any of the strategies, especially pivoting and oligopolistic competition, requires a certain stability over time to yield desired results, a rapid succession of contradictory stances indicates "irrational" party behavior that can be explained only in terms of intraparty coalition building.

## 4.3 HOW RATIONAL IS SOCIALIST PARTY STRATEGY?

I now turn to the ten cases of European socialist party strategy in the order they are shown in Table 4.7, beginning with parties where the simple theory of spatial competition predicts radical strategies and then moving to parties where conditions suggest moderate ones. If a party fails to adopt the electorally efficient short-term strategy or its electoral returns diverge from the theoretically expected payoffs, I address three additional questions. Did the party choose strategies of pivoting or oligopolistic competition and were such strategies warranted in light of the conditions present in that country? Did competitors fail to abide by a logic of short-term electoral maximization and enable socialists to pursue a favorable disequilibrium strategy ("luck")? (3) Or, did changes in the competitive environment cause socialists to lose votes *regardless* of the strategy they might have chosen ("tragedy")? Only when all three questions have been answered negatively system-level rationality does not explain the performance of socialist parties.

I wish to emphasize that the reconstruction of party strategies and electoral payoffs in these case studies is critical for the assessment of the theoretical argument. The accompanying quasi-quantitative evidence from Laver and Hunt's expert surveys and the Eurobarometer factor analyses I have already introduced above have only illustrative value because they rest on strong methodological assumptions that make them too weak to carry the weight of testing the theory I have proposed.

*Incentives for radical left-libertarian strategies of short-term vote maximization: Dutch and Danish socialists*

Although circumstances made fairly radical left-libertarian strategies of short-term vote maximization attractive for both Danish and Dutch social democrats, the parties actually pursued very different strategies in the 1970s and 1980s. The Dutch party more or less consistently followed a left-libertarian course and had its best decade since World War II in the 1980s, while the Danish social democrats chose a more centrist strategy and lost ground until 1990.

*Netherlands.* Starting in the mid-1960s, New Left and radical-libertarian parties emerged as serious challengers of the PvdA. First, the Pacifist Socialist Party (PSP) split off from the radical fringes of the PvdA in the late 1950s. Next, the Democrats '66 combined a centrist program for constitutional reform and strengthening of the executive with libertarian policy demands. Further, left dissenters of the Catholic People's Party (KVP) founded the Party of Political Radicals (PPR) in

1968. On top of these developments, the Dutch communists gradually evolved into a New Left party. By the early 1980s, the left-libertarian "Small Left" including PSP, PPR and Dutch Communist Party (CPN) had converted greatly. This process climaxed in the Green Progressive Accord (GPA), an electoral alliance of the three parties in the 1984 European election. Since then, this alliance also competed in national elections and finally formed a single party in 1990 (Rüdig 1985: 13–26; Lucardie, Vanderknoop, van Schuur, Voermann 1991).

Beginning in the late 1960s, the PvdA responded to this challenge with a new strategy of polarization aimed at the established religious and liberal parties. Rather than building centrist government alliances with them, the PvdA sought electoral strength with a leftist program of state economic intervention and a libertarian social and cultural agenda that would resonate with the growing left-libertarian voter sector in the Netherlands. They also undertook efforts to build a coalition with the other libertarian parties, primarily the Democrats '66 (D '66) and the PPR.[41] The new strategy of the PvdA was reflected in the progressively more leftist self-placement of its supporters (cf. Irwin and Dittrich 1984: 273). In the 1971 and 1972 elections, this strategy increased the PvdA's and its New Left alliance partners' popular support, eventually enabling them to form a coalition government. The new PvdA prime minister, however, needed support from the Catholic party. PPR and Democrats '66 became increasingly disaffected with the coalition in which they felt the PvdA monopolized the political stage. At the same time, Christian and liberal competitors tried to counter the PvdA bloc by their own bloc strategy.

With its new left-libertarian stance, the PvdA surged from 23.6% in 1967 to a high of 33.8% in 1977, when its reputation as a left-libertarian party crested. After four years of lackluster performance as an opposition party, it ceded half of these gains in 1981 (28.3%). In 1986, its support bounced back to 33.3%, largely because of the party's role as a spokesperson for the highly mobilized Dutch peace movement. The successes of 1977 and 1986, however, were limited in that almost all of the PvdA's gains came at the expense of the other libertarian and left-libertarian parties. Taking the parties of the Small Left, the Democrats '66, and the PvdA together, their combined voter share hardly changed from 1972 (42.3%) to 1986 (42.5%) and reached a high in 1981 when the PvdA lost to the benefit of D '66 and the Small Left (45.6%).

In other words, the game the PvdA played with its close left-libertarian competitors was zero-sum or even negative-sum. All shared the same pool of voters, but were unable to tap into the crowded center of the political space. In the eyes of spokespeople of Dutch environmental organizations, for example, the PPR was perceived as only slightly more pro-environmentalist than the Democrats '66 or PvdA, and all of these parties ranked far ahead of Christian Democrats and Liberals (Dalton 1990). Since the PvdA actively participated in these movements (cf. Rochon 1989: ch. 7), most left-libertarian sympathizers saw no reason to

41 On changing strategies of coalition building in the Netherlands, see De Swaan (1982), Vis (1983), Daalder (1986), Jong and Pijnenburg (1986), and Wolinetz (1988).

support the small parties of the Green Progressive Accord (GPA). Most electoral gains of the Dutch Labor Party in 1986 therefore came at the expense of their potential coalition partners.[42]

The PvdA's position was rational from the perspective of short-term vote maximization. At the same time, the party's structural position provided it with little incentive to adopt a centrist strategy of pivoting. This is so because the party was located too far from the median voter and faced too many obstacles en route to conquering the crowded political center. As a further consequence of the party's short-term strategy of vote maximization in a time of increased left-libertarian mobilization, the PvdA's programmatic radicalism was reinforced. This confined the party to the opposition, separated by a wide gulf from the Christian-Liberal coalition governing from 1977 to 1981 and from 1982 to 1989. The long-term opposition role, however, began to generate *fatigue* with the party's strategy and started party members on the road to revaluate the polarization strategy in the mid-1980s. After 1986 the party attempted to reclaim the political center by shedding many of its radical positions (see Kalma 1988; Partij van de Arbeid 1988a,b; Tromp 1989). As a result of this move from vote maximizing to a new office-seeking strategy, the left-libertarian GPA and the Democrats '66 saw their combined share of votes rise from 9.2% in 1986 to 12.0% in 1989, while the PvdA fell back slightly to 31.9%. The small growth of the left-libertarian bloc deprived the Christian-Liberal government of its parliamentary majority and enabled the PvdA to join a lasting coalition government with the Christian Democrats for the first time in more than two decades.[43]

This analysis is borne out by the configuration of each party's mean voter positions derived from the factor analysis reported in Table 4.2 (Figure 4.3A). This figure and similar figures for other countries discussed below report each party's mean voter position (factor scores) on the first and the second factor in the two-dimensional space. For example, the voters of the Socialist Pacifists have a value of +1.54 on the vertical axis, the factor that divides left-libertarian voter opinions at the positive upper end of the dimension from right-authoritarian positions at the negative lower end of the dimension. Thus, together with the PPR, the party is at the extreme left-libertarian end of the scale, whereas the fundamentalist Protestant parties RPF, GPV, and SGP are at the right-authoritarian opposite pole. The second coordinate for the PSP, +.29, reports this party's mean voter position on the horizontal second dimension, dividing workers with pro-movement sentiments from yuppies. Here, the PSP is no further to the left than the PvdA, whereas the liberal PVV is closest to the yuppie extreme of the scale.

Figure 4.3A also shows that there is an association between the parties' mean positions on the left-libertarian versus right-authoritarian dimension (factor 1) and the working-class sympathizers of social movements versus yuppies dimension

---

42 Voter flows from 1982 to 1986 are analyzed by Van der Eijk, Irwin, and Niemöller (1986: 297). The strong ideological overlap between PvdA and GPA voters has been demonstrated by Irwin and van Holsteyn (1989: 116).

43 The 1973–77 PvdA government had Catholic support, but no Catholic cabinet participation.

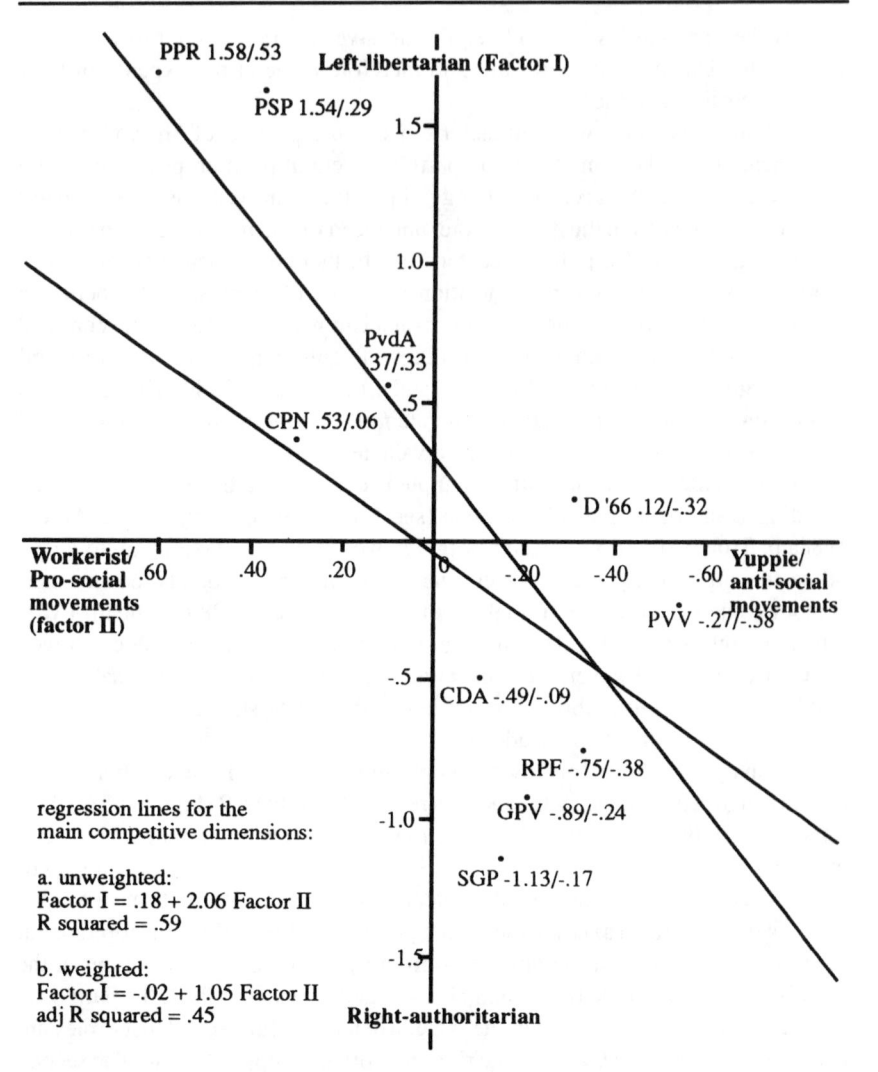

Figure 4.3A. The political space of Dutch party competition:
Parties' mean position on two factors in the Netherlands (1986 Eurobarometer data)
*Source:* Party supporters' mean factor scores calculated from principal component analyses
reported in Table 4.3. Eurobarometer 25 data set.

(factor 2). This association is depicted by regression lines in two different ways.
$E_{uw}$ measures the association between party positions on both dimensions if one
assigns no weights reflecting the size of a party's support base to each party's
position. $E_w$ indicates the regression line, if weights for the size of each party are
taken into account. With weights the regression line is generally closer to the
positions of the largest parties, but does not change its location in the space

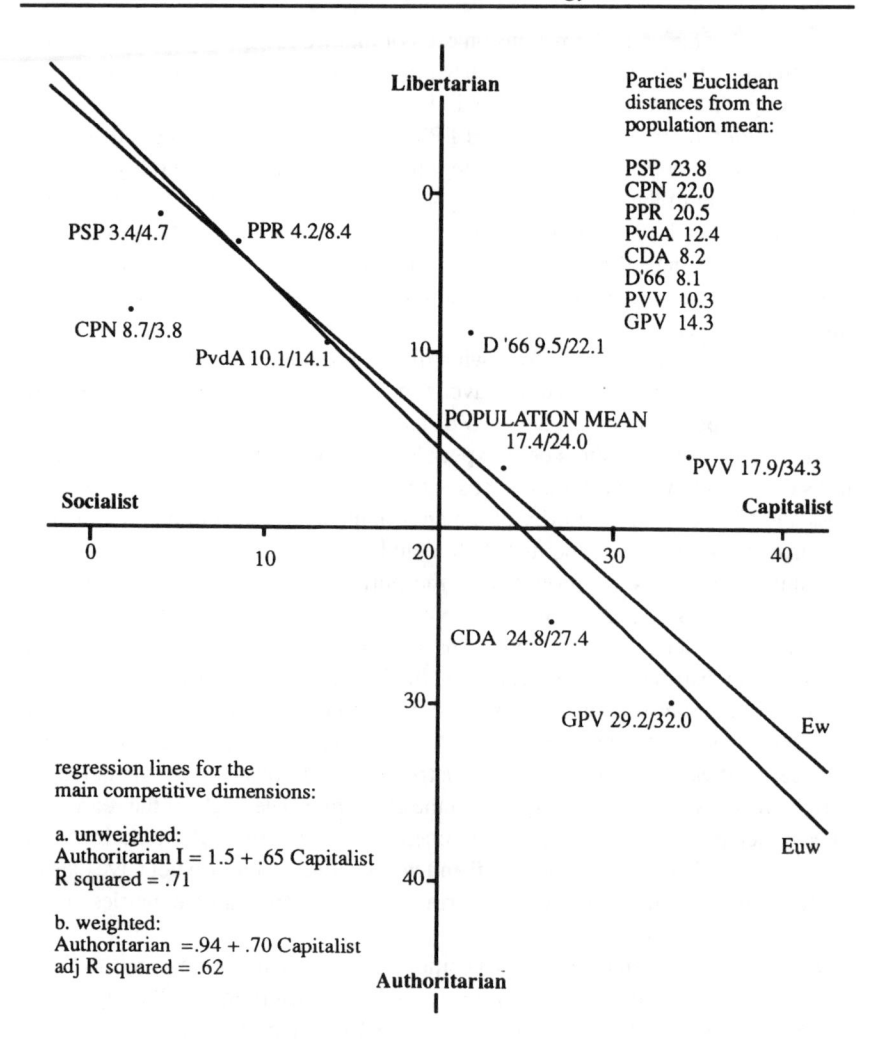

Figure 4.3B. The political space of Dutch party competition:
Parties' mean positions according to expert judgments on two dimensions in the Netherlands
*Source:* Expert judgments on parties' positions on libertarian-authoritarian issues (2 items: abortion, environment) and socialistic-capitalist issues (2 items: nationalization and welfare state), collected by Laver and Hunt (1992).

dramatically. $E_{uw}$ and $E_w$ are approximate measures of the main competitive dimension in the Dutch party system.

In the Netherlands, both regressions exhibit a strong association of party positions on the two dimensions, thus supporting the interpretation that there is one dominant dimension of party competition. This should not conceal, however, that the Democrats '66 and the liberal PVV are more clearly distinguished from the other major parties on the second factor than the first. Individual level regressions also show that the voters' positions on each of the two factors explains a considerable amount of variance in voters' party preferences, with the first factor exercising stronger influence than the second.[44]

Although the Small Left (PSP and PPR) is at the extreme of the left-libertarian versus right-authoritarian dimension, the PvdA is also considerably removed from the center of the space and its major competitors. In 1986, Christian Democrats and Liberals were close to each other and constituted the government coalition. In the late 1980s, a mutual rapproachment of CDA and PvdA made it possible to displace the CDA–VVD alliance that governed the Netherlands for much of the decade.

A similar story is told by a somewhat different rendering of the spatial dimensions in the Netherlands based on Laver and Hunt's (1992) expert assessments of Dutch party positions in the late 1980s. Note that here, unlike Figure 4.3A, the vertical dimension measures only experts' judgments on the Dutch parties' positions defined by two libertarian versus authoritarian issues, (1) social permissiveness and (2) the relative priority of the environment over economic growth. This dimension does not combine distributive and communitarian questions. Parties' distributive positions are provided on the horizontal dimension, measuring experts' judgments of parties' positions vis-à-vis (1) social policy and (2) public property. In practice, parties' positions on communitarian issues predict their positions on distributive issues rather well. The three small left parties are at the extreme libertarian-socialist pole of the competitive space, whereas fundamentalist Protestants are at the opposite pole. Again, regression lines for the association between parties' communitarian and distributive positions can be calculated unweighted and weighted for party size in the electorate. The angle of the regression lines indicating the main competitive dimensions in Figure 4.3B differs from that in Figure 4.3A because the horizontal and vertical dimensions do not have exactly the same meaning in both figures. Nevertheless, the configuration of parties in both figures is very similar.

The expert assessments of party positions also allow us to measure the Euclidean distance between the mean voter (population mean) and each party's position.[45] It shows that in the second half of the 1980s the PvdA was significantly further removed from the population mean (Euclidean distance: 12.37) than were either the much smaller Liberals (10.21) or the Christian Democrats (8.19). These figures again underscore the left-libertarian radicalism of the PvdA.

*Denmark.*   Beginning in the late 1960s, the Danish social democrats faced the dilemma of being squeezed between the challenges of left-libertarian politics

44 For the sake of brevity, I am not reporting various linear and log-linear ways to calculate the explained variance of voting behavior, if voting for socialists, bourgeois parties, or left-libertarian parties are treated as dummy dependent variables and individuals' factor scores on the two factors are employed as independent variables. Detailed results can be obtained from the author or can easily be run on the original Eurobarometer data sets.

45 The population mean is calculated based on the summary of all parties' positions, weighted by the percentage of votes each party received in the last election before Laver and Hunt's survey was performed.

represented by new and rapidly growing left parties and a reinvigorated market-oriented Right. On the left, the originally blue collar oriented Socialist People's Party (SPP) rapidly transformed itself into an advocate of left-libertarian politics and attracted educated white collar personal service sector voters and activists (cf. Logue 1982; Togeby 1990).[46] Since 1966 when the SPP had its first substantial electoral breakthrough, the Danish social democrats have had a choice between two strategies of competition (cf. Bille 1989). On the one hand, they may directly compete with the SPP by adopting a left-libertarian appeal. Though the strategy risks alienating moderate voters and driving both left parties into the opposition, it may maximize the vote, giving the large size of the left-libertarian political sector. Moreover, since government status provides only marginal gains in policy control, social democrats may choose left-libertarian appeals as an oligopolistic strategy of competition.

Alternatively, social democrats may compete for moderate voters and tolerate expansion of the left-libertarian party sector in order to win the pivotal position in the party system. In the 1960s, the attractiveness of pivoting was initially great because all parties of the Left, taken together, usually received close to 50% of the votes and the political space to the right of social democrats was not yet as crowded as it would become in the 1970s and 1980s. Social democrats, therefore, at first chose pivoting strategies that allowed the New Left to grow. Once the social democrats became the pivot in 1966 and 1971, however, their strategic dilemma reappeared on a different scale in the legislative arena. Either they chose a leftist alliance with the Socialist People's Party, a strategy that alienated centrist voters and thus undermined the party's pivotal position or they joined or tolerated centrist (minority) governments and alienated more radical voters who proceeded to defect to the SPP.

Social democrats have pursued both principal strategies of competition with varying success. In 1966 and 1971, a left bloc of social democrats and SPP survived only for short periods of time until leftists in the SPP and moderates in the Social Democratic Party broke loose and formed their own parties, the Left Socialists (VS) in 1968 and the Center Democrats (CD) in 1973, precipitating major electoral losses for both coalition partners in the subsequent elections.[47] Thus both alliance partners faced a negative-sum game over the two election rounds that marked the beginning and the end of their cooperation (cf. Thomas 1977: 251).

Later in the 1970s and 1980s, social democrats therefore opted for the alternative strategy of centripetal competition in order to (re)gain the pivot of the party system. In 1979, Danish social democratic functionaries were less willing to endorse left-libertarian post-materialism than most other socialist parties except those of Belgium and Italy (Iversen 1991). In environmental politics, the party provided little leadership and postponed a clear negative decision on nuclear

---

46  As a consequence, there has been little room in Danish politics for an additional Green party. The support of the Greens remained below the 2% electoral threshold. See Schüttemeyer (1989).

47  Voter flows between 1966 and 1968 and between 1971 and 1973 are reported in Berglund and Lindström (1978: 94, 97).

power until the mid-1980s (Goul-Andersen 1990b: 187).[48] Moreover, the Danish social democrats endorsed a more liberal market orientation in their social and economic policies than any of their Scandinavian sister parties (Esping-Andersen 1985: ch. 7). This strategy, however, resulted in escalating electoral losses benefiting the libertarian Left.[49]

In the 1980s, the SPP moderated its stance, as the social democrats moved to the center, and proceeded to whittle away at its competitor's electorate. The SPP's moderation was facilitated by the disintegration of its own radical competitor, the Left Socialists, amid acrimonious internal disputes (Lund 1982). By the late 1980s, however, the party had difficulty in sufficiently distinguishing itself from the social democrats. In the 1988 campaign, the SPP for the first time accepted Danish NATO and EC membership, and promptly lost votes both to the social democrats and to more radical left-libertarian splinter parties (Smith-Jespersen 1989: 191–2). The SPP's difficulties increased because the social democrats, under the leadership of a young intellectual, Sven Auken, recharted their strategy of competition from a centripetal to a centrifugal direction and targeted the SPP as the main competitor.

By the 1990 election, the SPP experienced its most serious defeat in decades, losing 4.7% of the vote because of its strategic rapprochement to the social democrats, the latters' new appeal, and the negative fallout from the collapse of East European socialism for formerly Marxist parties (Borre 1991: 134). At the same time, the social democrats benefited not only from the SPP's weakness, but also from combining Auken's left-libertarian aura with a last minute skillful strategic withdrawal from radical positions in its new 1989 program (Maor 1991: 210). This experience shows that *socialist parties can maximize voter support at a "crossover" point when they switch from oligopolistic competition to a strategy of pivoting while confined to the opposition benches.* At that juncture, socialist parties still command the loyalty of their more radical supporters, but begin to woo moderate voters as well. Given the nature of Danish party competition, however, the electoral leap from 29.8% to 37.4% in 1990 did not move social democrats much closer to the pivotal position in the Danish coalition game than they had been in 1988. In Denmark, the crowdedness of the center makes it difficult for social democrats to succeed with a strategy of office seeking. The party remained confined to the opposition benches despite its electoral improvement at the expense of the SPP.

While a mixture of luck (the SPP's strategic mistakes, external "shocks" influencing the voter distribution) and strategic maneuvering helped the Danish

---

48  This analysis is at variance with findings of the party manifestos project according to which the Danish social democrats, not the SPP or other left-libertarian parties, had the most pronounced New Left position (cf. Holmstedt and Schou 1987: 200, 203).

49  During social democratic governments from 1975 to 1981, the combined electoral share of SPP and VS grew from 7.1% (1975) to 14.0 (1981), while the social democrats' share initially increased from 29.9% (1975) to 38.3% (1979), but then slumped to 32.9%.

social democrats in 1990, the main question is why they pursued an electorally inefficient strategy of centripetal competition and allowed the SPP to grow unchecked throughout the 1970s and 1980s. Only an analysis of intraparty politics, not of systemic constraints, can shed light on the party's choice of strategy.

My reconstruction of Danish social democratic party strategy is borne out by data on the electoral and competitive spaces in which the party is immersed. The factor analysis of social democratic voters' mean positions (Eurobarometer data) shows them close to the center of the political space, yet on the side opposite to the SPP, Greens, and VS, to whom the party has conceded much left-libertarian electoral territory by moving rather close to its bourgeois competitors (Figure 4.4A). Moreover, one of the "bourgeois" parties, the radical liberals (RV), is clearly located on the left-libertarian side of politics and thus has leapfrogged over the social democrats.

The Danish competitive space approximates unidimensionality, dominated by the left-libertarian versus right-authoritarian polarity identified by factor I. Factor II does not very clearly discriminate among party positions, which are located along a narrow band. Traditional working-class voters are slightly closer to right-authoritarian political conceptions than are yuppies. Danish politics thus probably reveals less of conventional class politics than any other country compared here. The left-libertarian pole is dominated by young educated voters in tertiary employment. Whereas an individual's score on the two factors explains a considerable share of the variance of bourgeois and left-libertarian voting, it does not predict social democratic voting very efficiently because social democrats now take an undistinguished middle-of-the-road position on both dimensions. Throughout much of the 1980s, the Danish social democrats were a centrist party without clear ideological profile.

The one-dimensional nature of Danish party competition is also reflected in Laver and Hunt's expert assessments of party positions in the 1980s. Given the substantive meaning of the axes in Figures 4.4A and 4.4B, the location of the competitive dimension differs as well. Compared to the Netherlands, where the Euclidean distance between the PvdA's position on socialist-libertarian issue positions and the population mean was 12.4, the Danish social democrats are only 7.6 units from the Danish population mean. Pivoting strategies are likely to be unsuccessful, however, because several other parties are almost as close or even closer to the mean voter (CD: 3.1; KRF: 8.1; RV: 8.6). All the evidence suggests that office-seeking centripetal strategies are not only electorally costly for Danish social democrats, but unlikely to come to fruition.

The Danish and Dutch social democrats, who are located in an environment favoring more radical left-libertarian vote-maximizing strategies, signal an interesting contrast in strategic choices that cannot be explained in terms of the simple or the complex theories of spatial competition. What the theory does explain very well, however, are the electoral payoffs that each party has reaped from its strategic stances.

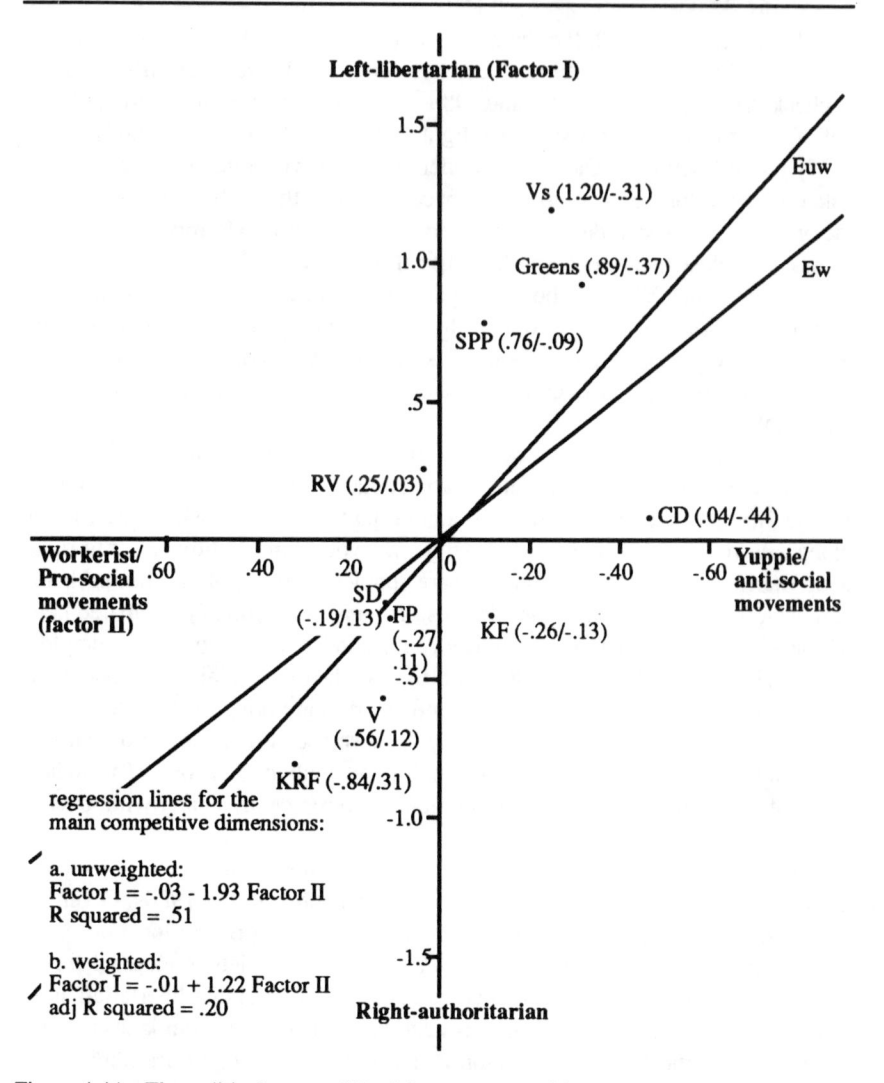

Figure 4.4A. The political space of Danish party competition:
Parties' mean position on two factors in Denmark (1986 Eurobarometer data)
*Source:* Same as Figure 4.3A

*Incentives for intermediate left-libertarian strategies of short-term vote maximization, yet strong opportunities for pivoting or oligopolistic competition: Spain, Germany, Sweden*

The Dutch and Danish electoral environment is relatively simple because it favors a single radical social democratic strategy of instant vote maximization and offers the parties not much leeway for more sophisticated strategies of pivoting or oligopolistic competition, although the parties opted for such avenues on some

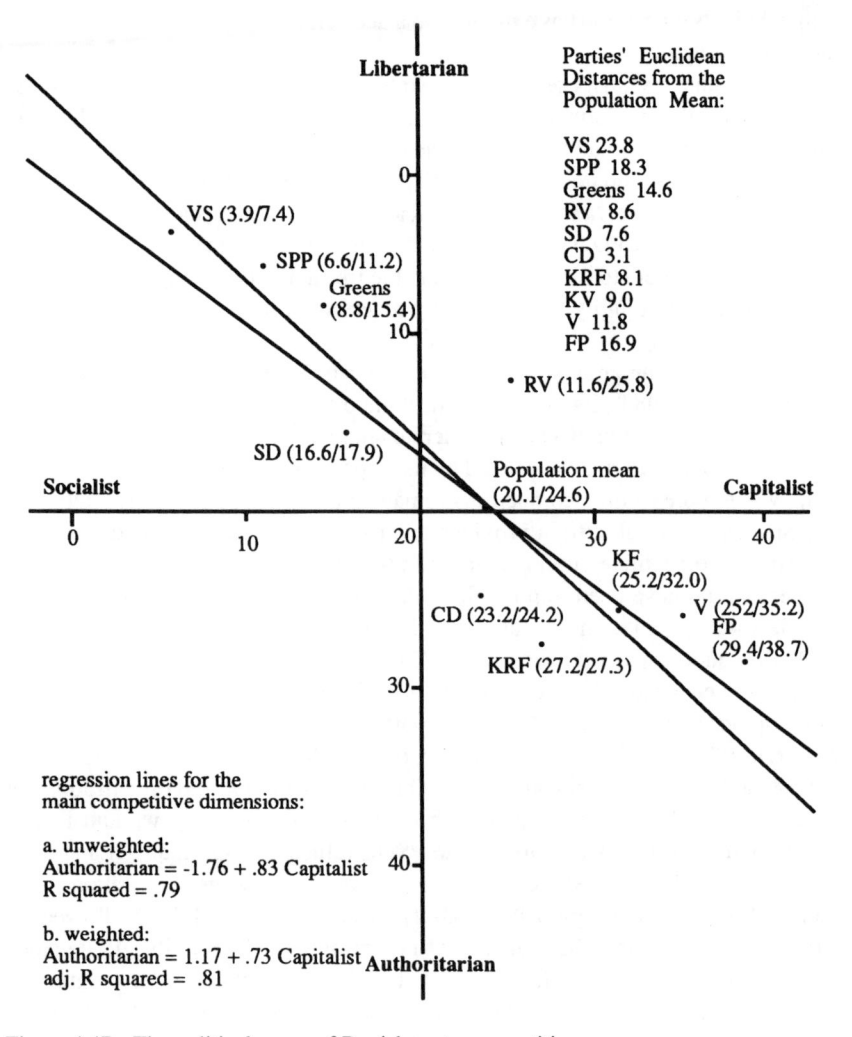

Figure 4.4B. The political space of Danish party competition:
Parties' mean positions according to expert judgments on two dimensions in Denmark
*Source:* Same as Figure 4.3B

occasions. The opposite is true for the next three cases. All share in common a mixed structure of incentives encouraging medium radical left-libertarian strategies of short-term vote maximization and moderate to strong opportunities for office seeking or oligopolistic competition. Yet each party has achieved different electoral results because it has actually chosen fundamentally different strategies. The Spanish socialists were, on the whole, extremely successful at the polls in the 1980s. In contrast, the German social democrats declined to their lowest support level in decades. While it seemed in the mid-1980s that Swedish social democracy might hold its own, it too has experienced a deep electoral crisis beginning in 1988 and worsening in 1991.

The Spanish socialists sequentially exploited every strategic opportunity that presented itself. The German social democrats, in contrast, failed to take advantage of the competitive situation and vacillated between incompatible strategies. The Swedish party also did not seize upon electoral opportunities in the second half of the 1980s and suffered a momentous defeat in 1991 after a decade of immobility. While the German SPD became hyperactive in opposition, the Swedish SAP was slow to respond both to the libertarian and the free market challenge and could not regain popular credibility when it finally reversed its strategy in 1990.

*Spain.*    In part, the great success of the Spanish PSOE is due to *strategic luck.* Throughout the 1980s, its potentially most important contenders on the right were unable to coalesce around a clear moderate alternative. The strongest party of the Right, the Popular Party, was tainted by its association with the Franquist dictatorship, while more centrist competitors remained divided and ineffective, although the Spanish electoral system provides great rewards for consolidated blocs and centripetal competitive strategies (cf. Gunther 1989). Nevertheless, the PSOE's success would have been impossible without the party's skilled manipulation of the electoral space that marginalized both left and right competitors.

As the country democratized from 1975 to 1977, the Spanish communists (PCE) at first seemed to have the edge against the PSOE because of their entrenchment in labor unions and their large clandestine party organization. To gain acceptability, the CE in 1977 participated in the quasi-corporatist Moncloa economic pact, which was signed by the provisional center-right government and the organizations of business and labor to ensure a smooth transition to democracy without further strikes and inordinate wage hikes. The PSOE refused to sign the pact and leap-frogged the PCE with a strategy of leftist opposition to wage moderation (Middlemas 1980: 232; Gillespie 1989: 303–4). In some ways, the PSOE followed the strategy of a farsighted oligopolist. By first crushing the PCE to its left, it gained electoral maneuverability after the PCE had lost its viability as a progressive alternative. High electoral thresholds, the absence of strong regional parliaments and the weakness of voters' party identification made it plausible that the PCE, once sufficiently undermined, would be permanently impaired, regardless of subsequent socialist party strategies.

In the first free election of 1977, the PSOE became the largest party of the Left with about three times the vote of the PCE (28.3% compared to 9.2%). The communists were hurt by deeply rooted popular distrust, particularly in light of efforts by the Portuguese communists to thwart liberal democracy in their own country in 1974–75, but also by the PSOE's militant leftist rhetoric. After the 1979 election, in which neither PSOE nor PCE made any electoral headway, several developments occurred which allowed the PSOE to alter its electoral appeal drastically and to adopt a strategy of moderate reform in the 1982 electoral campaign.

First, the governing Democratic Center Union (UCD) disintegrated, giving way to a transitional executive of politically unknown technocrats. Second, the conservative Popular Alliance could not fill this void on the Right because of its Franquist connections. Third, the PCE's electoral stagnation in 1979 precipitated intense intraparty conflicts between advocates of a workerist-Stalinist orthodoxy, an Eurocommunist center, and reformist intellectuals (cf. Middlemas 1980: 234; Timmermann 1987: 174–6). As a consequence, the PSOE could invade the PCE's electoral space and attract more than half of the PCE's former voters in the 1982 election (Mujal-Leon 1983: ch. 7; Maraval 1985: 151–3). Much of the PSOE's success in 1982, however, was due to its *strategic moderation,* which allowed it to exploit the cross-over point from an oligopolistic to a vote-maximizing strategy. While still relying on the loyalty of a radical following that had supported the PSOE or the PCE in the late 1970s, it also reached out to voters in the center of the competitive space who were up for grabs because of disarray to the Right.[50]

The new PSOE government pursued social and economic austerity policies gradually alienating the socialist labor union, the General Workers' Union (UGT). At the same time, it paid relatively little attention to the typical concerns of the libertarian Left. The party liberalized abortion laws and legalized contraceptives, yet did relatively little to improve women's opportunities in the labor market (Kedros 1986: 218; Threfall 1989: 235). After initially opposing Spain's membership in NATO, the PSOE government reversed itself and engineered Spain's full membership in both NATO and EC. The socialist government also gave short shrift to environmentalist concerns, judged by expenditures on environmental research and emission control standards (cf. Organization of Economic Cooperation and Development 1987: esp. pp. 57, 103, 157, 301).

In the second half of the 1980s, the PSOE faced stiffer electoral competition as the far Left reconstituted itself. Two major factions of the PCE entered a "United Left" (IU) alliance that also included dissatisfied socialists, supporters of contemporary peace and ecology movements, and Green lists (Timmermann 1987: 180). This new formation strengthened its ties to social movements, particularly the Spanish women's movement. Moreover communist unions joined hands with the formerly socialist UGT that had been alienated by the PSOE government (Gillespie 1988: 338–9). Thus, the PCE's crisis brought about a left-libertarian realignment of the radical Left unequaled by that of the PCE's French or Italian Communist sister parties. Eventually, the PSOE's failure to satisfy its socialist and left-libertarian constituencies benefited the new United Left in the 1989 election, when the latter doubled its voter share from 4.6% in 1986 to 9.1% (Amodia 1990).

Why did the PSOE prefer to adhere to a centrist stance that made little concessions to workerist or libertarian demands instead of meeting the growing chaⁱenge of the libertarian Left? Is the socialists' centrism an *irrational* posture needlessly sacrificing leftist voters, given that most centrist voters are likely to remain loyal to the socialists as long as the disarray of the Right continues? The PSOE's strategy

50 Voter flow studies show that in 1982, the PSOE gained 58% of the PCE's 1979 voters, 60% of all new voters, and 40% of the center-right vote (Lopez-Pintor 1985: 298).

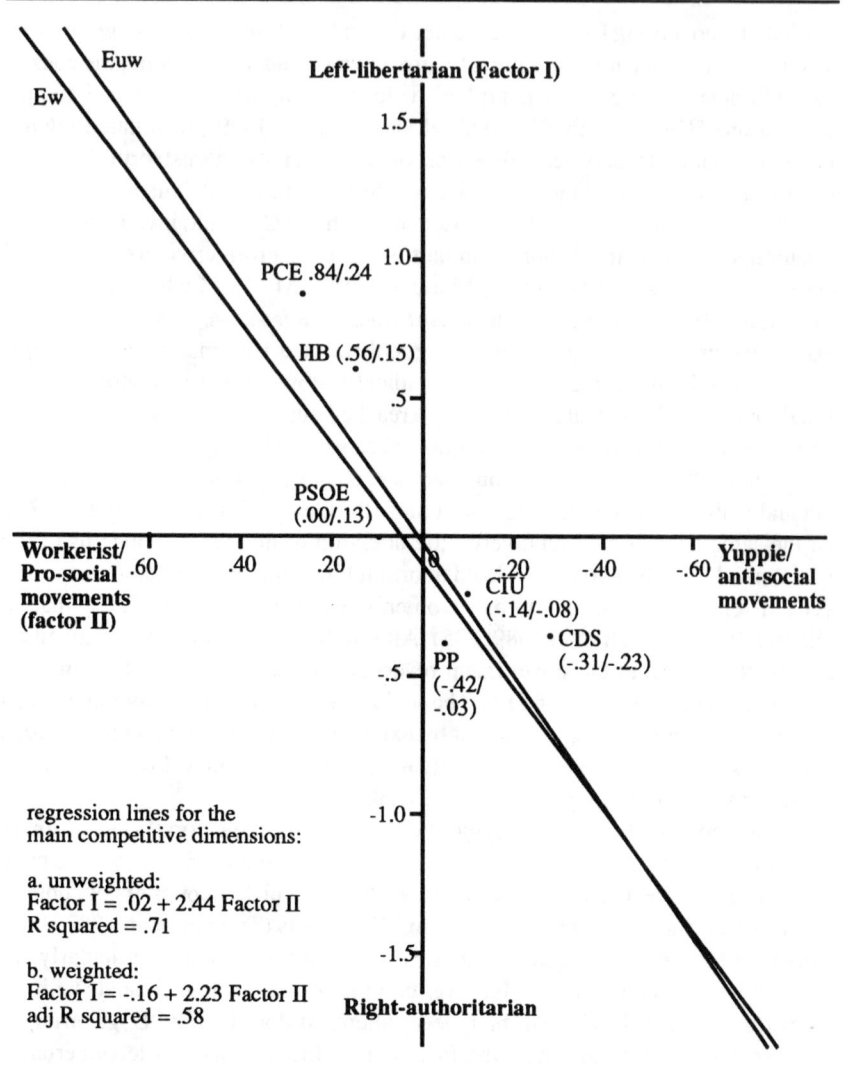

Figure 4.5A. The political space of Spanish party competition:
Parties' mean position on two factors in Spain (1986 Eurobarometer data)
*Source:* Same as Figure 4.3A

represents a switch from the objective of maximizing votes to controlling the pivot
in the party system. Pivoting is attractive because the electoral system discrimi-
nates against smaller parties, the existence of essentially only one cleavage
dimension highlights the importance of a pivot, and the combined left parties are
close to the 50% mark (1989: 39.9% for the PSOE plus 9.1% for the UI). Moreover,
given the relative weakness of the Spanish parliament in the policy-making
process (cf. Strom 1990a: 73) and Spain's incomplete federalism, the influence
differential between government and opposition is fairly large, making pivoting

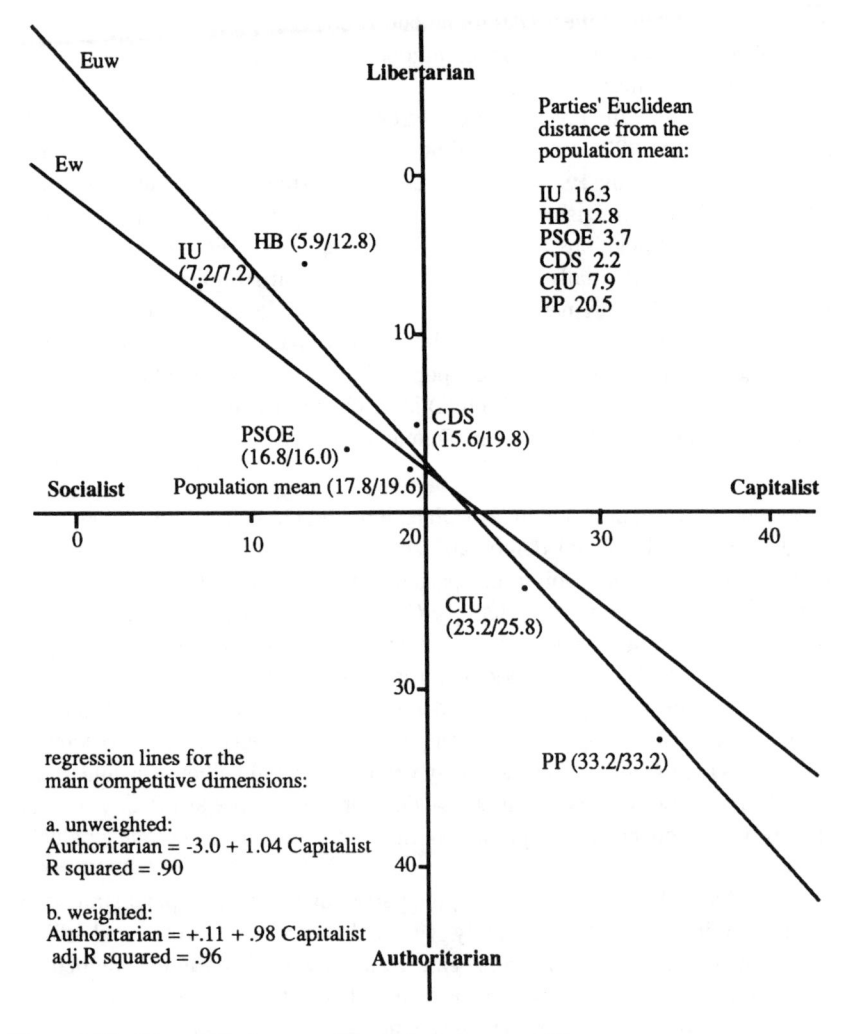

Figure 4.5B. The political space of Spanish party competition:
Parties' mean positions according to expert judgments on two dimensions in Spain
*Source:* Same as for Figure 4.3B

even more attractive. Thus, while the PSOE pursued a classic strategy of vote maximization in the first half of the 1980s, by the late 1980s it was well on its way to a pure strategy of office seeking and pivoting that conceded more electoral territory to the reconstituted libertarian Left.[51] The sequence of PSOE strategies

51 The PSOE's strategy is also revealed by the cabinet reshuffle in early 1991. Many portfolios were redistributed to technocrats who often were not even members of the PSOE. This has given rise to speculations that the PSOE will seek out the centrist regional Catalan party as a coalition partner, should the PSOE's dominant electoral position weaken in future elections. Cf. *The Economist*, March 16, 1991: 46.

from the second half of the 1970s to the late 1980s thus pursued all objectives of electoral competition outlined above: oligopolistic competition, followed by vote maximization, and then pivoting.

Survey data show the position of the PSOE in the Spanish party system in the second half of the 1980s well. According to the factor analysis of Eurobarometer 1986 voter positions, the PSOE's supporters are on average just about in the center of an essentially unidimensional competitive space (Figure 4.5A). Parties have not taken pronounced positions on the familiar workerist–yuppie second dimension making the latter essentially irrelevant in the electoral struggle. The Laver and Hunt (1992) expert judgments of party positions yield similar results (Figure 4.5B). The parties compete in a unidimensional space in which the PSOE is situated near the mean position of the population. The party's Euclidean distance from the mean Spanish voter (3.7 units) is much smaller than that of the Danish social democrats, let alone that of its Dutch sister party.

*Germany.*   In Germany, an intermediate left-libertarian strategy theoretically would maximize the social democrats' short-term electoral yield because left-libertarian mobilization is high, but partially offset by a fairly even balance of fractionalization in the party system. In Germany, structural conditions are also conducive to pivoting and, to a lesser extent, to long-term oligopolistic competition. Moreover, the SPD's strategic opportunities were enhanced by the failure of the Greens to choose comparatively moderate strategies of short-term vote maximization. At least in federal electoral competition, the Greens always projected an image that was too radical to attract many voters who would otherwise vote for the party.[52] All this should have led the social democrats to choose an effective course, yet they vacillated between options, as their share of the electorate gradually shrank.

Under Chancellor Helmut Schmidt, the party pursued a centripetal strategy of competition in the 1970s and early 1980s that was both vote- and office-maximizing *as long as no competitor entered to the party's left* in the competitive space. But the emergence of the Greens in 1978 began to change the game. Figure 4.6 traces the strategic interaction between the two parties by showing the share of SPD and Green supporters who locate themselves on the left of a ten-point self-placement scale from 1976 to 1988. The Greens entered the scene after a prolonged period in which the social democrats had moved to the right, engaged in economic austerity policy, and disregarded genuinely left-libertarian feminist and ecologist demands (cf. Braunthal 1983).[53] The Greens initially entered politics with a moderate program, but soon radicalized, as they strengthened their voter appeal. When the Schmidt government fell in 1982, the social democrats began to move back to the left to retrieve some of the lost electoral terrain. At this

52  For an analysis of Green party strategy at the federal and the state level, see Kitschelt (1989: ch. 9).

53  The nuclear power conflict (Kitschelt 1980: ch. 5) and the SPD's hesitation in the legalization of abortion (Ferree 1987) as well as its opposition to the peace movement express this strategic thrust (cf. Brand, Büsser, and Rucht 1983).

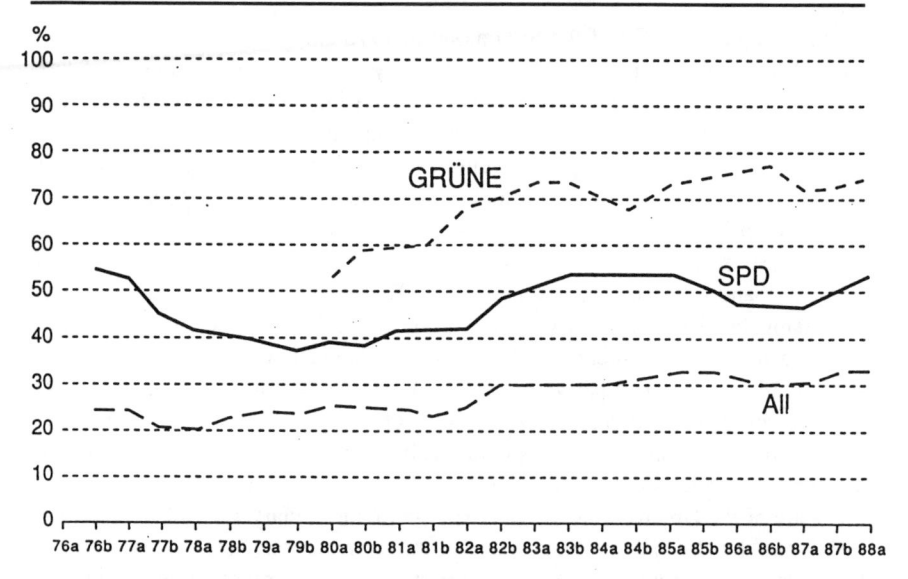

Figure 4.6. Self-placement of West German Green and Social Democratic voters on the Left (moving averages 1976–88)
*Notes:* Lines show the moving averages of the percentage of each party's voters who locate themselves on the political left. As 'left' self-placements are considered scores from 1 (extreme left) to 4 (moderate left) on a ten-point scale ranging from 1 (extreme left) to 10 (extreme right).
*Source:* Schmitt (1990: 136), moving averages of the Eurobarometer data include two data points each.

point, the party began grappling with the choice between strategies of pivoting, vote maximization, and oligopolistic competition.

Advocates of oligopolistic competition proposed eliminating the Green threat by suddenly turning the SPD toward the left-libertarian agenda. This would be followed by a gradual return to a vote-maximizing strategy, once the Greens had vanished from the party system. At the opposite end of the spectrum, proponents of a pivoting strategy pushed the party to write off left-libertarian voters and to concentrate on the business of regaining government office with centrist voters.[54] In the 1983 campaign, the oligopolistic strategy prevailed, and the party ran on peace and ecology issues rather than on issues of economic renewal and growth. In Figure 4.6, this tendency is expressed in the pronounced leftward shift of SPD voters from 1982 to about 1984. Most likely, this strategy limited the share of the social democratic electorate that fell to the Greens, but could not ultimately stop the entry of the Greens into the German *Bundestag*.[55] In spite of the SPD's losses in 1983, the Green and social democratic share of the vote, taken together, was

54 This option was outlined in an important strategy paper authored by Richard Löwenthal and widely discussed in the early 1980s.
55 In polls throughout 1982 the Green party ran closer to 10%, but actually managed to win only slightly more than the required quota of 5% for parliamentary representation in the March 1983 election.

actually larger than that of the SPD alone in 1976 and 1980, suggesting that the overall left sector had not shrunk significantly.[56] Because the intensity of left-libertarian social mobilization, which was in part triggered by the intransigence of the Schmidt government to social movement demands, had opened up a political space that permitted a new party to enter, the SPD was in a "tragic" situation in which a new competitor was destined to decrease its electoral support *no matter how rationally it chose its voter appeal.*

The party's losses in 1983 and its failure to regain government office led the SPD to abandon the oligopolistic strategy. Before the 1987 election, the party leadership, headed by a new candidate for the chancellor's office, moved toward a pivoting strategy, documented in Figure 4.6 by the decline of leftist SPD support from 1984 to 1986. The party's halfhearted commitment to centripetal competition, however, was too ambiguous to win back many voters who had previously supported the Christian Democratic and Liberal government coalition. Yet SPD supporters with left-libertarian leanings now abandoned the party and increased the share of the Greens at the SPD's expense in the January 1987 election.[57] The SPD's and the Greens' combined share of the German vote, however, was greater than that of any previous group of left parties. An SPD pivoting strategy was a positive sum game for the Left as a whole, but damaged the SPD's share of the electoral market.

In the aftermath of the 1987 defeat, the SPD switched back from a centripetal pivoting strategy to a more libertarian appeal to compete with the Greens. At the same time, however, the party under the leadership of Oskar Lafontaine advocated more free-market economic policies to compete with the government parties. Party leaders expected a strategy combining sharp libertarian and moderate redistributive appeals to make inroads into the Green electorate *as well as* white collar support of the bourgeois coalition, but to risk the continued loyalty of some traditional blue collar and labor union clienteles.[58] The electoral efficiency of this potentially vote-maximizing strategy could not be put to a full test because German unification overwhelmed all other issues in the final run-up to the December 1990 election. The SPD in fact gained voters at the expense of the Greens, but due to its lack of enthusiasm for rapid unification, it not only performed disastrously in the new German states, but also alienated many traditional SPD voters and centrist voters who otherwise might have abandoned the Christian Democratic–Liberal coalition parties.[59] In order to become the pivot of the

56 Some of the social democratic votes, of course, were defectors from the social-liberal wing of the FDP. At the same time, the SPD lost a significant number of both blue collar and white collar workers to the CDU/CSU. Cf. Berger, Gibowski, Roth, and Schulte (1983) and Schmitt (1990: 146). The SPD essentially lost voters to the government camp who were concerned about economic issues. See Irwing and Paterson (1983: 481), Müller-Rommel (1990: 97–9) and Schultze (1987: 7).

57 On the 1987 election, see Berger et al. (1987) and Padgett (1987).

58 For example, Lafontaine offended powerful labor unions by suggesting the introduction of flexible work time and shorter work hours without full pay compensation.

59 For a detailed analysis of the 1990 election in the context of German electoral history, see

the party system or even to maintain its vote share compared to 1987, the party would have had to endorse national unification wholeheartedly and leave the antinational libertarian campaign to the Greens.

The volatility of SPD strategy appears even greater when one examines the party's appeals in German state elections. Between 1987 and 1990, the party ran on a strong left-libertarian agenda in some states where the weakness of Christian Democrats and Liberals was pronounced enough so that even an oligopolistic strategy with left-libertarian appeals directed against the Greens would still ensure a pivotal position for the SPD (Saar, Lower Saxony, Schleswig-Holstein). In other states where the Greens were too caught up in internal disarray to become a serious electoral threat, the SPD ran a campaign based on pivoting strategy (Hamburg, Bremen, Rhineland Palatinate, North Rhine Westphalia). Finally, in the German Southwest, where the Greens were well entrenched, the SPD opted for a strategy of pivoting and "division of labor" with the Greens (above all in Hesse and Baden-Württemberg).

My description of SPD strategy and its electoral payoffs is borne out by voter flow analyses. In 1983, the party was abandoned not only by young educated voters who went to the Greens,[60] but also by white collar voters, the technical intelligentsia and blue collar workers, who switched sides and supported the liberal-conservative government which emphasized economic recovery and growth. In 1987, when the SPD backed away from left-libertarian themes, it lost an additional 600,000 votes to the Greens (Schultze 1987: 12), but it was unable to win back all the workers and white collar voters it had ceded to the government parties four years earlier. In 1990, with its most pronounced libertarian strategy to date, the SPD regained 600,000 votes from the Greens, but heavily lost voters to the CDU, the FDP, and to abstention.[61]

The puzzle, then, is why the SPD did not become more willing to commit itself to a centripetal strategy of pivoting. Electoral losses from consistent pivoting hardly could have been worse than the results of oscillation between contradictory strategic stances. Before the 1990 election, the electoral and parliamentary support of the leftist bloc was also sufficiently close in size to that of the Christian Democratic–Liberal alliance to make an SPD strategy of pivoting attractive. The oligopolistic strategy of the early and mid-1980s did not succeed in preventing the entrenchment of the Greens in state parliaments and at the federal level.[62] More-

---

Kitschelt (1991c). SPD losses were particularly great among West German blue collar workers and members of the labor unions (cf. Gibowski and Kaase 1991).

60 Ninety-two percent of the Green voters who were predominantly young and well educated indicated that their second party preference was the SPD (cf. Pappi 1984: 24).

61 These data are based on an Infratest voter flow analysis reported two days after the election. See *Frankfurter Allgemeine Zeitung*, December 5, 1990: p. 5. For a more detailed statistical analysis of the 1990 election see especially Gibowski and Kaase (1991) and Pappi (1991).

62 Also the failure of the Greens to surmount the 5% hurdle of federal parliamentary representation in 1990 does not change this fact, given the Greens' impressive electoral performance in all state elections in the subsequent electoral term.

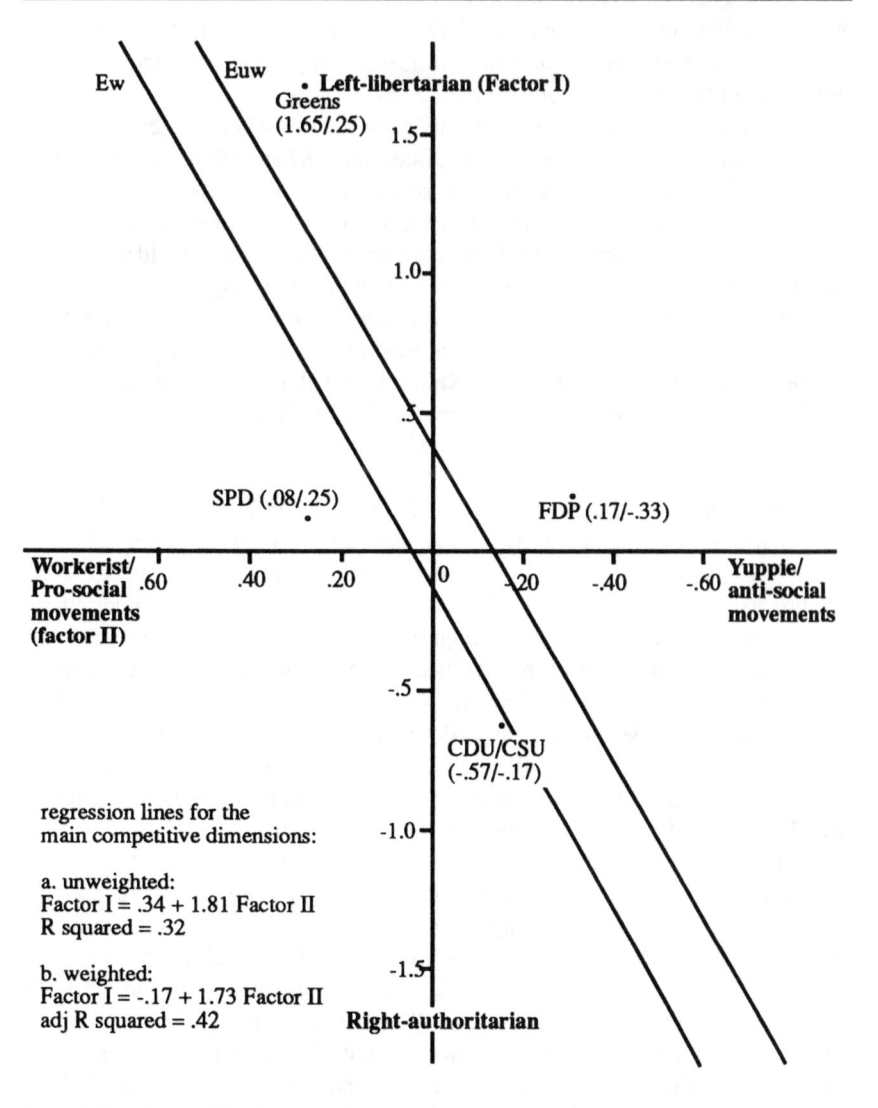

Figure 4.7A. The political space of German party competition:
Parties' mean position on two factors in Germany (1986 Eurobarometer data)
*Source:* Same as Figure 4.3A

over, the electoral threshold makes the entry of further competitors on the libertarian left unlikely, thus giving Greens an incentive to compete centripetally.[63]

Survey data may summarize my analysis of SPD strategy. Figure 4.7A reflects
the SPD's strategic position in 1986 Eurobarometer data on party supporters at a

63 When faced with the opportunity of a Green–social democratic coalition, most Greens are
   sufficiently tempted to give up fundamentalist strategic concerns. Cf. Kitschelt (1989a: ch. 9).

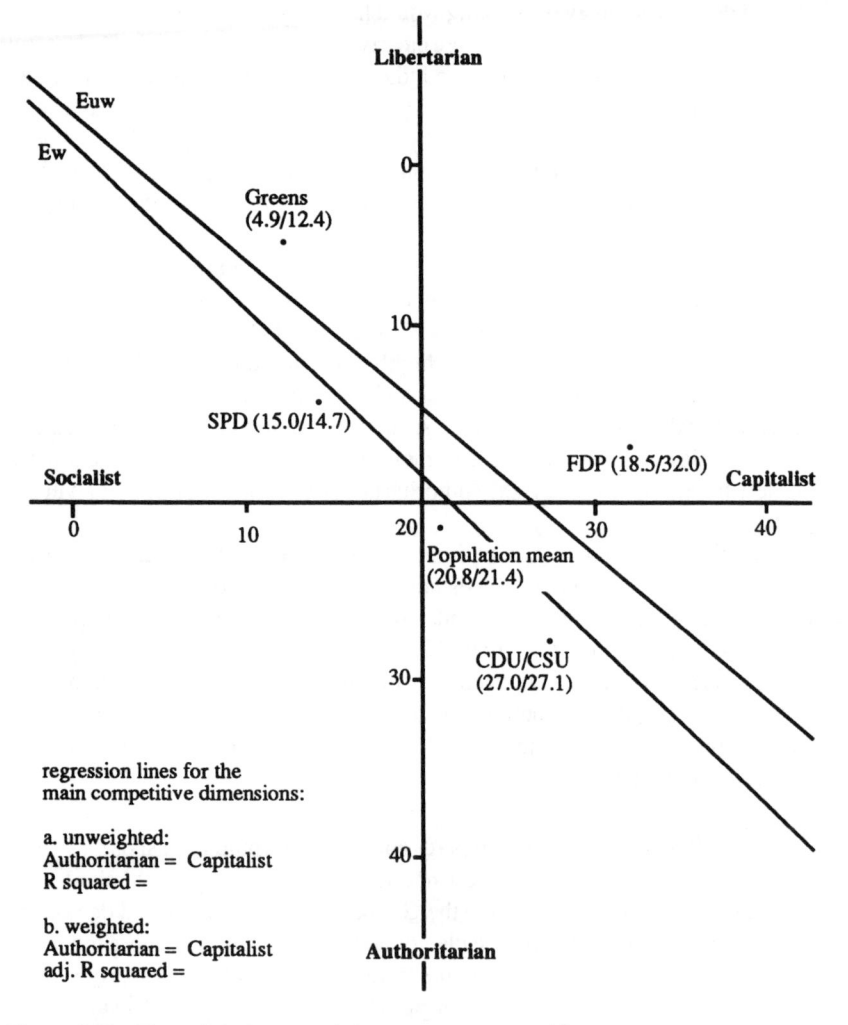

Figure 4.7B. The political space of German party competition:
Parties' positions according to expert judgments on two dimensions in Germany
*Source:* Same as Figure 4.3B

time when the party pursued a centripetal strategy. On the left-libertarian versus right-authoritarian axis, the party was relatively close to the CDU and less libertarian than the Free Democratic Party (FDP).[64] A strategy of voter maximization, let alone oligopolistic competition, might have required a more left-libertarian, but also less conventionally leftist, blue collar oriented stance. Con-

64 When the individual respondents' factor scores are regressed on party preference, they yield a rather considerable explained variance for bourgeois voters and Green voters, yet not for SPD supporters. Moreover, whereas bourgeois and Green support is predicted primarily by the voters' positions on Factor I, social democratic support is predicted slightly better by voters' positions on Factor II.

versely, a decisive strategy of pivoting would have suggested a further rapprochement to CDU and FDP. The Greens were clearly too extreme for their own electoral good. The Laver and Hunt (1992) expert judgments of party elite appeals in the late 1980s show that the SPD had backed away somewhat from the center of the party space toward the strategy advocated by Lafontaine.[65] The party's Euclidean distance from the population mean (8.9 units) is greater than that of the Danish or Spanish socialists, indicating that the party had little chance to win the pivot of the system.

Both Figures 4.7A and 4.7B also show that the German competitive space is not fully one-dimensional. At least on the right side of the space, there is two-dimensional product differentiation between CDU and FDP. For a relatively small, but sharply distinguished electorate of highly educated professionals, the FDP's package of moderately libertarian policies combined with a capitalist economic program is highly attractive. Given the specialized nature of the FDP's clientele, the other parties compete along a common dimension that divides voters more along left-libertarian versus right-authoritarian issues than workerist or yuppie appeals.

A systemic theory of party competition fails to explain why neither the SPD nor the Greens were able to choose consistent, rational courses of vote maximization or office seeking that would have mandated the pursuit of centripetal competition with the government camp. It is implausible to assume that SPD leaders simply did not understand the trade-offs between pivoting, short-term vote maximization, and long-term oligopolistic competition in the German party system. Strategic instability is more likely attributable to shifting intraparty coalitions, a dynamic I will discuss in the next chapter.

*Sweden.*    The structure of Swedish party competition would predispose a socialist party to adopt an intermediate left-libertarian stance if it pursued short-term vote maximization. In comparison to the German SPD, Swedish social democrats face a less mobilized left-libertarian electorate and thus should be more moderate on that critical dimension of party competition. Yet the balance of party system fractionalization with a crowded center pushes a vote-seeking SAP away from a centrist position toward a more left-libertarian stance. As in Germany, oligopolistic competition and pivoting are strategically attractive, because the electoral threshold is relatively high, new parties cannot entrench themselves easily at the sub-national level, and the stakes of government status are limited. Unlike the German SPD, however, the Swedish SAP actually occupied the pivotal position in the party system throughout the 1980s. Whereas the German SPD in opposition vacillated among strategies, the SAP remained ultrastable and shifted direction only almost imperceptibly before it lost its dominant position before the 1991 election. The SAP responded late to left-libertarian and free-market challenges and

65 It goes without saying that the numerical values in Figures 4.7A and 4.7B are based on different metrics and therefore cannot be compared. All that counts is the relative distance of the mean party position from the mean or the median voter.

therefore could not curb growing competition from both sides on the main competitive dimension.

In the early 1970s, with the rise of the left-libertarian challenge, the SAP's electoral position began to erode as the communist Left Party (VPK) took up a left-libertarian appeal to social decentralization, participation, and environmental protection, issues raised first by the former agrarian Center Party (C) and clearly popular with the protest generation of 1968.[66] Although the SAP had moderated its economic stance in order to preserve its pivotal position (Krauss and Pierre 1990: 240–1), its failure to embrace an antinuclear power stance enabled the VPK and the Center Party to capitalize on this issue in 1976.[67] The SAP's position was further complicated by the labor unions' call for the introduction of wage earners' funds that would redistribute wealth and gradually socialize Swedish industry (cf. Lewin 1988: 274–304; Pontusson 1988a: ch. 3; Steinmo 1988). The party's tacit and later explicit endorsement of this neosocialist demand was certain to maneuver the SAP into strategic difficulties because wage earners' funds ran counter not only to bourgeois visions of market efficiency, but also to libertarian calls for citizens' participation and political decentralization. The SAP promptly lost the 1979 election when it gave in to wage earners' funds. Even when the party was voted back into office in 1982 after several years of bourgeois government instability and economic decline, its own voters perceived an increasing gap between its leftist economic program and their own preferences.[68] After regaining office, the party was sensible enough to pass legislation on a scaled-back version of wage earners' funds and to remove the issue from the agenda.

In the 1982 election, the SAP benefited from an electoral campaign waged primarily on economic issues. Prior to the election, the nuclear conflict had cooled off because a national referendum had placed a moratorium on the construction of new nuclear power plants and committed the government to dismantling all existing plants by 2010 (cf. Lewin 1988: ch. 8). In time, however, left-libertarian themes resurged to threaten the SAP's competitive position. While the party still fought the 1985 campaign on the issue of economic recovery (Sainsbury 1986), it lost votes in major urban areas where voters perceived the SAP as not sufficiently antinuclear. This should have served as an early warning to SAP politicians.[69] After six years of social democratic government incumbency and economic

66 On the gradual transformation of the VPK toward ecologism and feminism see Hermansson (1988).

67 Nevertheless, the SAP engaged in an environmental policy that reduced pollution per capita to levels significantly lower than those in most other more densely populated countries (cf. OECD 1987).

68 Holmberg and Gilljam (1987: 303) show that the gap between socialist voters' left–right self-placements and their perception of the party's stance grew between 1979 and 1985. At the same time, the average left–right self-placements of VPK and SAP voters drifted significantly to the right from 1979 to 1985 (ibid., p. 258). For a different and misleading representation of the SAP's position, see results of the party manifesto project in Holmstedt and Schou (1987: 205).

69 Holmberg and Gilljam (1987: 25, 34) document changing voter concerns. In 1985, the typical SAP voter was as pro-nuclear as the conservative party voter (ibid., 269).

stability, the 1988 election campaign focused on noneconomic themes, most importantly environmental protection, nuclear power in the post-Chernobyl era, and public dissatisfaction with elite-dominated democracy (cf. Micheletti 1989; Sainsbury 1989; Bennulf and Holmberg 1990: 165). In this climate, the SAP lost left-libertarian voters to the VPK and a hitherto unsuccessful Green party.[70] What permitted the party to retain its pivotal position and government status were heavy electoral losses of an internally divided bourgeois camp. The Greens certainly benefited from the Center Party's inability to maintain its reputation as an environmentalist party. Moreover, liberals and conservatives were unable to seize on the new concerns as well because such issues were at odds with their pro-business stance.[71]

The SAP's support among voters in the postindustrial metropolitan areas declined further as the party began to grapple with problems of economic governance and market efficiency when the Swedish economy quickly deteriorated in 1989 and 1990. The bourgeois opposition seized upon the economic crisis to persuade voters of the declining capacity of the domestic economic policy institutions built by SAP governments. The SAP government's modest measures to adapt the Swedish economy to international competition in the 1980s failed to stem the bourgeois parties' challenge to its economic policies and a shift of voters toward their position.[72] In 1990–91, the SAP responded to the economic and electoral realities by reversing its economic and social policy in favor of fiscal austerity and opening the Swedish economy to more international competition.[73] Though this course was sure to alienate leftist party loyalists, it was meant to preserve the party's pivotal position in the electoral space against a bourgeois camp increasingly unified on basic demands for economic reforms. With the intensifying economic policy debates, the party also abruptly reversed itself on membership in the European Community and adopted a pro-EC position when the bourgeois parties threatened to make the EC a campaign issue in 1991.[74]

70 Gilljam and Holmberg (1990: ch. 4) demonstrate the failure of the social democrats to appeal to left-libertarian themes in an empirical analysis of voters' perception of parties' issue positions.

71 The Swedish Greens made their biggest gains in 1988 from the Social Democrats (21% of the Greens' 1988 voters), the Center Party (13%), nonvoters and first-time voters (10%), and the Left Party (9%), 26% of its supporters had already voted for the party in 1985 and the remaining 19% were accounted for by voters coming from Moderates, Liberals, and Christians. See Gilljam and Holmberg (1990: 108).

72 Thus, not only increasing unity of the bourgeois camp, but also a net shift of voters from left-libertarian to more free-market positions affected the SAP's strategic position. As argued above, voters do not stay fixed over time, but respond to party strategies and external shocks, such as an economic crisis and the collapse of communism.

73 A survey of the initial austerity measures passed in the spring of 1990 can be found in Pontusson 1990: 23–33. A number of further measures followed in Fall 1990. See Sainsbury 1991: 36–9.

74 In 1988–89, opinion surveys showed that more than two thirds of the respondents who had an opinion on EC membership (60% of the survey) were in favor of joining. The pro-membership sentiment ran especially high in the bourgeois parties, but also social democratic voters supported EC membership by a majority. Opposed were only the left-libertarian VPK and the Greens (see Lindström and Svasand 1990: 10–11).

By the early 1990s the SAP faced the strategic dilemma of an intensifying two-way battle for votes experienced by so many other socialist and communist parties in Europe. Even though the VPK and the Greens lost voters in 1991, the libertarian Left still represents 8% of the Swedish electorate, compared to 4%–5% in the 1970s.[75] On the right, the SAP was squeezed by the surging populist New Democrats, who attracted many new voters and a considerable share of the SAP's former blue collar supporters. Throughout the 1980s and early 1990s, the SAP consistently opted for a *rational pursuit of pivoting*, but the party's appeals to voters lacked enough strategic mobility to maintain its dominant position despite the changing electoral agenda of the late 1980s and early 1990s.

Swedish social democratic party strategy can be illustrated with data on the Swedish parties' strategic appeals. Lacking Eurobarometer surveys from Sweden, I have supplemented Laver and Hunt's expert judgments of Swedish party positions in the late 1980s (Figure 4.8B) by a survey among Swedish members of parliament exploring their parties' programmatic stance around the 1985 election (Figure 4.8A). Both figures show that Swedish party competition proceeds in a basically unidimensional space.[76] Yet, in contrast to the previously discussed countries, that space accommodates little variance on the authoritarian–libertarian dimension and instead still runs predominantly from the economic left to the economic right.[77] In both representations of the Swedish party system, the SAP is situated on the economic left, signaling little inclination to embrace libertarian themes. Moreover, the party is located further from the population mean in Figure 4.8B than is the Spanish PSOE in Figure 4.6B, the only socialist party that successfully defended its pivotal position.

In both 1988 and 1991, the SAP could probably have strengthened its electoral support base *and* its hold on the pivot by a more libertarian position. At least in 1991, an economically more pro-market position would also have benefited its performance. The SAP's abrupt adoption of a new economic policy in 1990 came too late to be understood by party loyalists or to win the confidence of voters who mistrusted the party's previous economic strategy. Party loyalists stayed home or voted for the populist New Democracy.[78] The inability of the four established bourgeois parties to attract the bulk of SAP defectors and to reach a majority of the

75 Whereas in 1988 many former voters of the bourgeois parties supported the Greens, the party became increasingly identified with the Left through its parliamentary record (Sainsbury 1992: 162).

76 The exception is the Greens in 1985 (Figure 4.8A). By the early 1990s, the Greens had moved closer to the VPK.

77 Compare the angles especially of the regression lines based on the parties' *weighted* mean positions in Figure 4.8A and 4.8B with that of the preceding Figures 4.4 through 4.7.

78 Social democrats sustained their greatest net losses to abstention (– 68,000 votes) and to New Democracy (– 55,000 votes). Most of these losses may be due to disgruntled blue collar party loyalists. They outweigh the parties' combined losses to all four bourgeois parties (– 113,000). The inability of the SAP to stake out innovative positions is also reflected in the fact that the party attracted less than 25% of the first time voters in 1991. For a voter flow analysis of the 1991 election, see *Från Riksdag & Departement* 16, no. 31 (1991): 17–21.

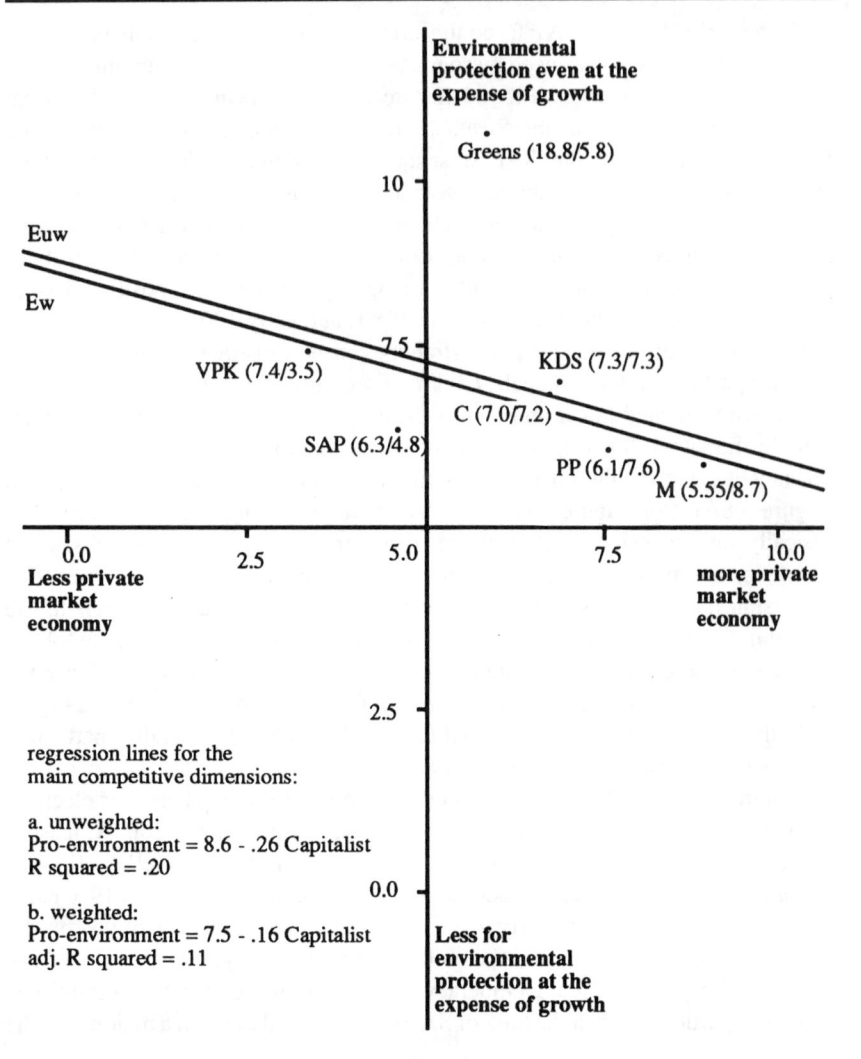

Figure 4.8A. The political space of Swedish party competition:
Parties' mean position on two factors in Sweden: elite assessments of Swedish political party locations in 1985
*Source:* Gilljam and Holmberg 1990: 277)

electorate on their own suggests that a more vigorous and carefully crafted innovative strategy might have preserved the party's pivotal position. It remains puzzling why the Swedish social democrats were unable to opt for a consistent pivoting strategy that combined a libertarian with a more moderate economic appeal. The SAP's strategic immobility may have internal causes that can be identified only by an analysis of the party's internal coalition politics and decision rules.

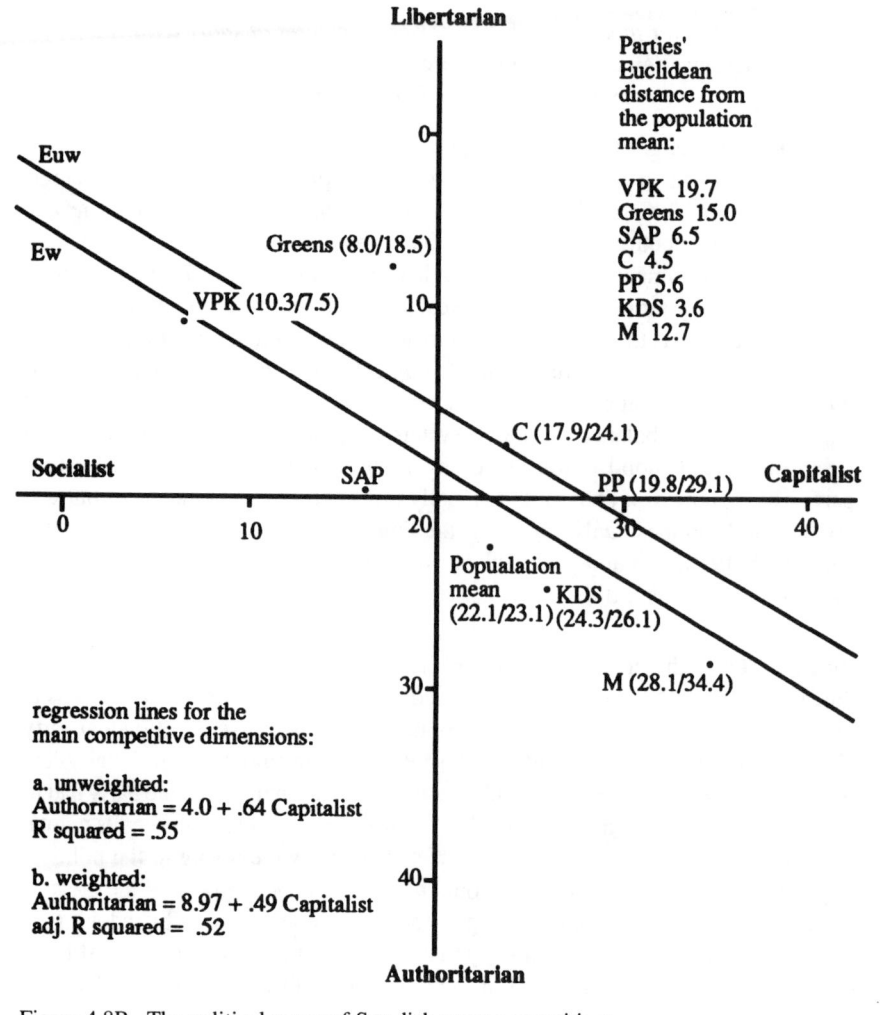

Figure 4.8B. The political space of Swedish party competition:
Parties' mean positions according to expert judgments on two dimensions in Sweden
*Source:* Same as Figure 4.3B

Among the three social democratic parties facing medium incentives for left-libertarian strategies of short-term vote maximization and strong incentives for either pivoting or oligopolistic competition, only the Spanish PSOE chose a rational course that maximized one of these three possible ends. Nevertheless, the complex theory of party competition is only partially refuted by evidence in the other two countries. While the theory fails to predict strategic choice in these instances, it accurately accounts for the gains or losses accruing to parties as a result of their choices.

*Incentives for moderate left-libertarian strategies of short-term vote
maximization and strong incentives for pivoting or oligopolistic
competition: Austria, Britain, and France*

Like the previous group of socialist parties, Britain, France, and Austria face a
strategic situation in which there is a wealth of plausible alternative strategic
objectives (see Tables 4.5 through 4.7). In Britain and France, pivoting *and*
oligopolistic competition are strategic objectives that may be attractive alternatives to vote maximization. In Austria, at least pivoting may displace a short-term
vote-maximizing rationale. What makes these parties different from the ones
already discussed is that the baseline short-term vote-maximizing strategy clearly
calls for an unambiguously moderate ideological stance, one that avoids vigorous
leftist-redistributive appeals as well as libertarian positions. This is the case
because an even balance of party system fragmentation and subdued left-
libertarian social mobilization are unfavorable to radical strategies. The three
parties have, however, chosen dramatically different strategies yielding contrasting electoral fortunes. Only one party, the French socialists, thrived in the 1980s,
while both the British and Austrian socialists committed themselves to strategies
that resulted in electoral decline.

*Austria.*   Once the environmental conflict had gained momentum in Austria in
the late 1970s, the SPÖ could have avoided losses to the left-libertarian Greens in
1983 by consciously abandoning its pivoting strategy, a course of action that party
clearly was not prepared to follow. The SPÖ's failure to hold on to its absolute
majority in 1983, therefore, is a result of a tragic situation in which the party had to
choose between losses to a new left-libertarian entrant, while preserving its pivotal
position, and efforts to preempt the new challenger, while losing to the political
Right. It is unclear which position would have, on balance, produced the greatest
losses. The party's hesitation to fight for its pivotal position by adopting a
determined centrist economic strategy to counter the challenge of market efficiency that ÖVP and FPÖ articulated in 1986 is quite a different story and does not
involve a strategic dilemma.[79]

The SPÖ coming to office in 1970 embarked on a reform policy to modernize
the Austrian welfare state, the legal system, the penal code, as well as family
legislation. An equalization of women's wages, the legalization of abortion in the
first trimester, and other measures designed to improve the status of Austrian
women catered to the emerging feminist movement (cf. Köpl 1984; Pircher 1984).
These changes brought Austria into the mainstream of modern West European
countries (cf. Hartl 1986: 71–82). By the late 1970s, however, the SPÖ's reformist
energies dissipated, as new left-libertarian challengers battled with traditional

79  The SPÖ was less affected by an increasingly xenophobic and populist FPÖ in the late 1980s. The
    FPÖ did benefit from the SPÖ's gradual change toward more libertarian and free-market appeals,
    especially among workers, but the bulk of its growth comes from the ailing Austrian People's
    Party.

representatives of the party's labor clientele (Mayr and Seitlinger 1989). In the 1970s, environmental legislation and its implementation had a slow start (cf. Christian and Welan 1985; Glatz 1988). The SPÖ also endorsed construction of a nuclear power plant that triggered intense protest and precipitated the government's defeat in a close national referendum in 1978 (Kok and Schaller 1986). Nevertheless, by confining the nuclear issue to a referendum, the SPÖ chancellor Kreisky managed to isolate it from the arena of party competition and won the 1979 election. The environmental conflict, however, did not subside with nuclear power, but reached another climax in the conflict over a new hydroelectric plant on the Danube supported by SPÖ and labor unions. After vigorous public protests, the government eventually abandoned the plant (cf. Gusenbauer 1988; Pelinka 1987, 1989).

The salience of left-libertarian issues, such as environmental protection and government accountability in an elite-controlled polity, helped new Green parties to gain support in the late 1970s first at the local level (cf. Merli 1984; Nick 1986) and later in state and national elections, when the two ideologically diverging Green parties finally united. Much of the SPÖ's losses in 1983 was due to voters switching over to the ecologists (Neuwirth 1983: 268). In 1986, at least 1% of the SPÖ's total loss of 4.8% is accounted for by former SPÖ voters moving to the ecologists (Plasser and Ulram 1987: 66). Since the ecologists also gained a substantial share of first time voters and previous nonvoters, the SPÖ's true loss was probably significantly greater.[80] Comparing electoral districts in 1971 and 1986, the Greens' gains almost directly mirrored the SPÖ's losses over this period (Plasser 1989: 58).

The SPÖ's 1986 losses, however, also show that many former SPÖ voters now opted for the bourgeois parties. Not ecology, but the impending crisis of national enterprises had intensified calls for a decentralization and privatization of the public sector the SPÖ failed to address in time. Only after the 1986 defeat, in a new coalition government with the ÖVP, did the socialists change course (cf. Müller 1988). The SPÖ opened to the center under the new leadership of Franz Vranitzky, a technocrat from Austria's central bank who entered politics as the replacement for a socialist finance minister who resigned under a cloud of scandal (Mayr and Seitlinger 1989: 25). In 1989, the party installed a new program entitled *Social Democracy 2000*, which called for an "ecological market society" with more individual choice (Ernst 1988; Sozialistische Partei Österreichs 1989). This change, the personal charisma of the party leader and chancellor Franz Vranitzky, the internal divisions of the Greens (Haerpfner 1989) and the conflict between the Austrian People's Party and the revitalized xenophobic Freedom Party helped the party to avert further losses in the 1990 national election.

---

80 To be sure, at least in 1986, the Greens also won significant support from former ÖVP voters (−0.8%) and the Free Party (−0.3%), demonstrating that the Greens appealed to a wide range of predominantly young voters. Nevertheless, the SPÖ sustained the largest actual losses and opportunity cost among new voters.

To a considerable extent, the SPÖ's electoral decline in the 1980s was due to the party's delayed strategic response to the challenge of market efficiency. By the end of the decade, however, the party appeared to have committed itself to a strategy of pivoting in a competitive environment, a strategy made easier by a fragmented right and a left-libertarian challenger that competes for a rather limited electorate.

Laver and Hunt's expert survey (Figure 4.9) demonstrates the SPÖ's recent accomplishment, particularly if one compares the party's position with that of its sister parties in other countries. The SPÖ's small Euclidean distance from the estimated population average in a by and large unidimensional space highlights its ability to remain pivotal.[81] Only the Spanish PSOE achieved a similar position (distance: 3.7, Figure 4.5B), whereas social democrats in Sweden (distance: 6.5, Figure 4.8B) and Germany (distance: 8.9, Figure 4.7B) were less successful in controlling the pivot. In the later 1980s, the SPÖ moved more rapidly to international market liberalization and EC membership than the Swedish SAP, although public opinion polls showed less support for European integration in Austria than in Sweden (cf. Lindström and Svasand 1990: 10). After an unavoidable loss of votes to the libertarian Left, the SPÖ appears to have stabilized its new position close to the pivot of the Austrian party system, although at a level of electoral support lower than it enjoyed in the 1970s.

*Britain.*    In Britain, the Labour Party's competitive situation suggests a strategy similar to that of the Austrian socialists in the 1970s and 1980s. The absence of a credible left-libertarian competitor made an oligopolistic strategy unnecessary.[82] At the same time, the structural incentives for pivoting strategies were extremely strong in a two-party system with plurality electoral laws. Instead of pursuing Austrian-style centripetalist strategies, however, Labour fell back on an old workerist left appeal, bypassing options for centripetal competition.

After the loss of government office in the 1970 election, the Labour Party moved closer to socialist economic positions, a move documented in *Labour's Program for Britain* (1973). It called for unilateral demilitarization, more nationalizations, and Britain's exit from the European Community. This stance contributed to another drop at the polls in February 1974. Labour regained government office only because voters were even more disaffected with the Conservatives. Labour's spell in office was not a total economic failure, though the strike wave in the winter of discontent preceding the 1979 election turned Labour's lead in the opinion polls into a hefty deficit at the ballot box.

After this defeat, the party never looked back as it accelerated its move to old-style socialist appeals enshrined in Labour's 1983 election program, *The New Hope for Britain*. This document set the party on a course opposite of that chosen

81 Compared to the Netherlands and Germany, where the liberal parties required a "half" second dimension, in Austria the Freedom Party is much closer to the dominant political dimension.
82 As Rüdig and Lowe (1986) and Rootes (1992) have argued, the British Greens never attracted significant support in the 1970s and 1980s because they failed to reach out to the new social movements or were preempted by Labour, particularly in the case of the peace movement.

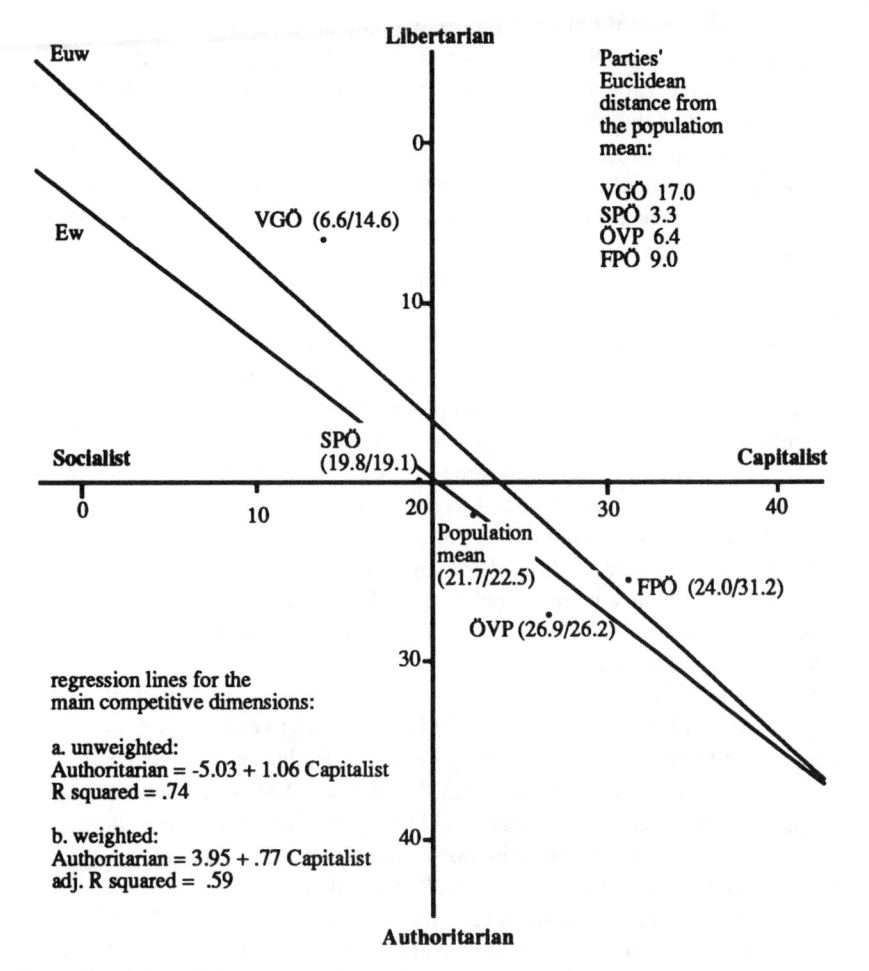

Figure 4.9. The political space of Austrian party competition: parties' mean positions according to expert judgments on two dimensions in Austria
*Source:* Same as Figure 4.3B

by Labour's voters, who progressively drifted to the right in the 1970s (cf. Kavanagh 1987: 169). At the same time, the party's purist socialist program made few efforts to cater to libertarian concerns. Labour embraced the British disarmament movement (Rochon 1989: ch. 7) but failed to address feminism (Ruggie 1987) or the ecology movement in any serious fashion. Above all, the party opposed shutting down the nuclear industry to placate Labour's powerful union allies. According to a 1985 survey, leaders of British environmental organizations judged the Labour Party to be only slightly less unfavorable to ecological concerns than the Conservatives. Only the Liberals obtained a moderately positive rating (Dalton 1990).

As a consequence of Labour's increasing radicalism, in 1981 moderates broke away and founded the Social Democrats. The new party eventually pooled resources with the Liberals in an electoral alliance. In all these conflicts, the distributive left–right dimension played the critical role, whereas the adversaries addressed libertarian issues only in a subdued way.[83] Labour's strategic shift to radicalism is reflected in the tendency of its dramatically reduced electorate to place itself further on the left of an ideological self-placement scale in the 1982–87 period than in 1976–81.[84] At the same time, radicalism among its party activists accelerated at a greater pace than among voters, increasing the gap between activists and voters (Crewe 1985a: 140).

In 1983, Labour suffered its greatest electoral defeat since the 1920s. Even though issues whose salience normally would have been favorable to Labour dominated the campaign, such as unemployment, social security, and housing, the incumbent Conservative government had little to fear, because Labour's old-style leftist appeal lacked credibility and antagonized its former working-class constituency even more than its middle-class supporters.[85] By 1979, many unionized workers had already abandoned the party because of its leftist leanings (Särlvik and Crewe 1983: 85, 98, 137). Its 1983 losses were again greatest among workers (−11%) and especially labor unionists (−16%) (cf. Crewe 1985b: 166, 170–1). Most of the defectors (22% of Labour's 1979 electorate) proceeded to support the Liberal–Social Democratic Alliance.

Before the 1987 election, Labour, under a new leadership presented a mixed program that still included enough "Old Left" themes to enable the Conservative government to attack Labour's "loony Left" (cf. Butler and Kavanagh 1988). It was only after another electoral defeat that the new Labour leadership began a decisive return to a centripetal strategy. This triggered an almost immediate rise of Labour's fortunes in the opinion polls and precipitated Margaret Thatcher's eventual fall in 1990. The rise of the SDP–Liberal alliance served as a catalyst to force Labour to adopt a new moderate strategy that contributed to the subsequent relative decline of the Alliance (Crewe and King 1992). Yet even after years of trying, the Labour Party of 1992 had not changed its political image with voters sufficiently to defeat a Conservative government at the depth of a long and painful economic recession period.

The situation of the British Labour Party is illustrated by the competitive spaces generated from Eurobarometer data and Laver and Hunt's expert survey (Figures 4.10A and 4.10B). Both data sets show that in Britain, like Sweden, the main axis of party competition is primarily configured around the economic capitalism-

---

83  For the 1979 election, Särlvik and Crewe (1983: 170) found almost no linkage between left-libertarian issues and voting behavior. Later, some left-libertarian demands were assimilated into the classical economic left–right division (Heath, Jowell, Curtice, and Evans 1990).

84  The average Eurobarometer value of Labour sympathizers' self-placement on a ten-point left–right scale was 4.63 in the first six-year period and 4.38 during the second period.

85  Thus, Robertson (1984: 132) found that middle-class Labour supporters were still most likely to support a comprehensive leftist program that included both economic and cultural radicalism.

socialism alternative rather than the libertarian-authoritarian axis.[86] The competition between the three major parties demonstrates how party leaders can defy salient voter divisions, although the Alliance and the successor Liberal Democrats slightly accentuate libertarian positions. Conventional distributive politics has remained critical for the British parties and libertarian-authoritarian alternatives have remained relatively subdued *although* they structure the electorate to a significant extent. The Laver and Hunt expert survey demonstrates that even in the late 1980s the Labour Party was situated further from the British population mean in the two-dimensional issue space than socialist parties in every other country, including the Netherlands (Euclidean distance for Labour: 12.9; and for the Dutch PvdA: 12.4).

The Labour Party adopted a stance so radical and out of mainstream on the economic dimension that it was virtually doomed to electoral failure. Moreover it failed to seize on communitarian appeals. Theories of simple or complex spatial competition can account for the results of Labour's strategy, but not for the process that led the party to adopt a manifestly irrational stance from either a short-term vote maximizing or pivoting perspective. It was also gratuitous from the perspective of oligopolistic competition, because there was no radical competitor in sight that was worth destroying.

*France.* The competitive environment of the French Socialist Party (PS) in the 1980s shares some remarkable similarities with that of the Labour Party. In both countries, left-libertarian mobilization was relatively subdued and parties faced a strong centripetal pull toward the pivot of the party system. In both, ecologists failed to build a "second Left" revolving around left-libertarian themes rather than single-issue appeals to environmental protection. Yet in France, the socialists won votes, while in Britain they lost.

Throughout the 1970s, several circumstances allowed the French socialists to perform well even with a fairly radical socialist and at times libertarian appeal. To the right, they faced an increasingly divided bourgeois government coalition, which failed to adopt a clear pro-market position. France, therefore, lacked an advocate of market efficiency that would have posed as serious a challenge as the British Labour Party faced from the Conservatives. On the left, the French socialists were protected from the demise of the old workerist Left because its devolution took place in a separate Communist Party (PCF). Overall, the PS benefited not only from a more benign competitive configuration (divided Right), but also the good luck of dealing with leftist competitors unable to act rationally on their opportunity structure (Communists, extreme Left, ecologists). French socialists succeeded because they demonstrated flexibility at critical turning points in 1971–72, 1978–80, 1983–84, and 1988. The party's sequence of strategic shifts is similar to that followed by the Spanish socialists some years later.

The French socialist party began the 1970s in disarray facing an overwhelming communist competitor on the left. In order to carve out its own electoral space in

86 A similar competitive dimension emerges also in Belgium (see below).

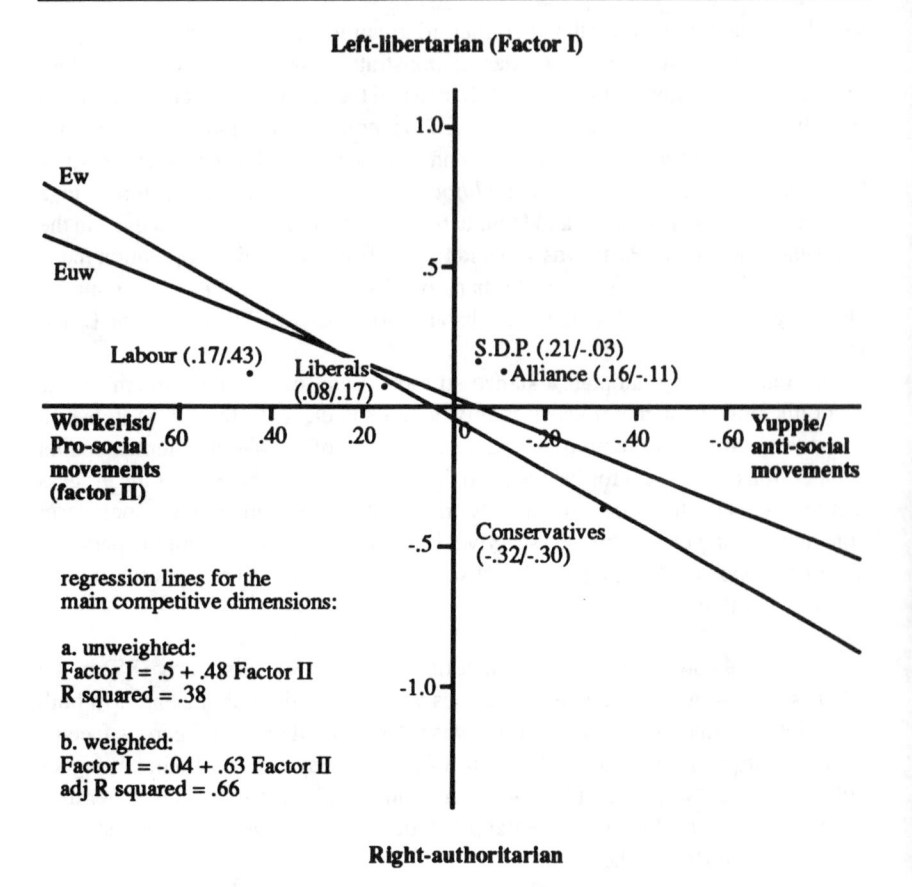

**Left-libertarian (Factor I)**

Figure 4.10A. The political space of British party competition:
Parties' mean position on two factors in Britain
*Source:* Same as Figure 4.3A

the initial phase of its reconstitution from about 1971 (Epinay Congress) to the signing of the Common Program with the PCF in 1973, it pursued a strategy of oligopolistic competition with a radical socialist rhetoric.[87] The sheer size of the prospective bounty of communist voters who might switch over to the socialist party made it likely that the oligopolistic strategy, at least initially, satisfied the criteria of both short-term and long-term electoral gain. The socialists engaged in product differentiation from the authoritarian antifeminist and antiecological PCF by blending libertarian themes into the socialist-redistributive message. The PS announced workers' self-governance ("autogestion") as a socialist goal and also made advances to embrace left-libertarian social movements, such as feminists

---

[87] The best general overview of the Parti Socialiste is Bell and Criddle (1988).

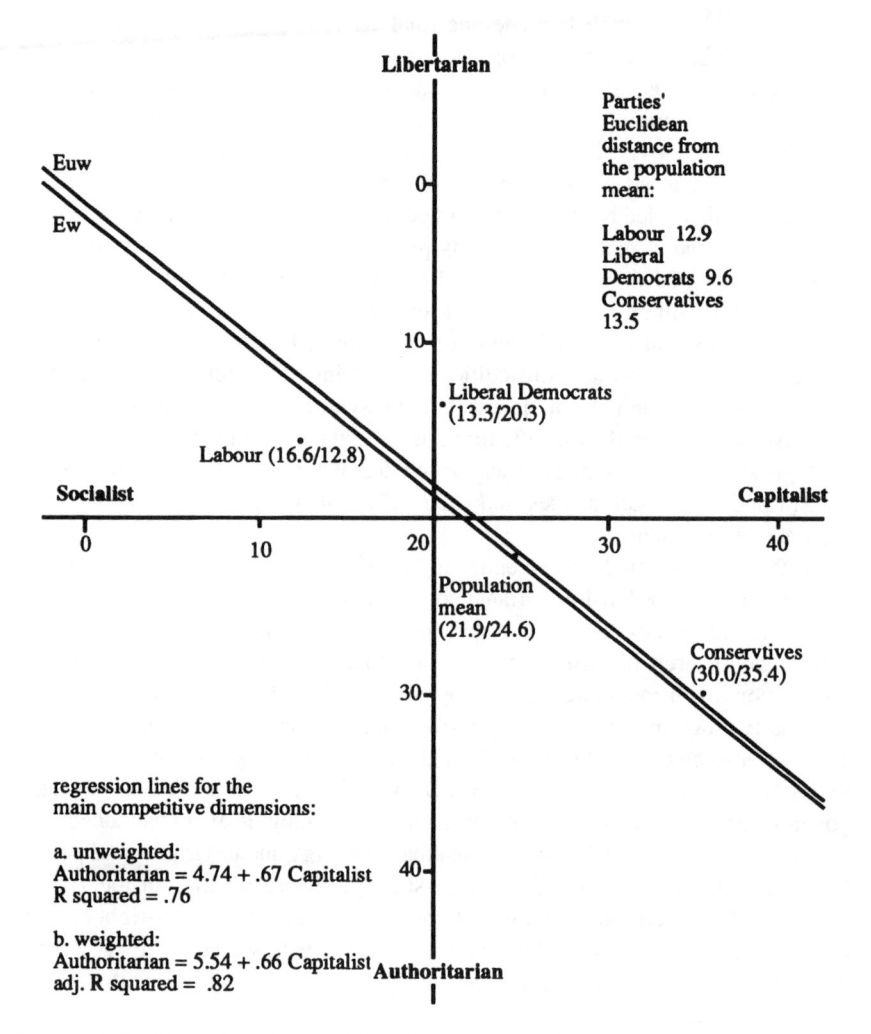

Figure 4.10B. The political space of British party competition:
Parties' mean positions according to expert judgments on two dimensions in Britain.
*Source:* Same as Figure 4.3B

and, to a lesser extent, adversaries of nuclear power.[88] As the PS gained electoral weight relative to that of the PCF in the 1973 parliamentary and in subsequent local and national elections, it moved to dilute its programmatic posture. In 1977, the PCF, stung by the socialists' relative success, took the PS's moderating strategic adjustments as a pretense to opt out of the Common Program and step up its rhetoric against PS "social democratism." After narrowly losing the 1978 parliamentary elections, but nevertheless establishing their electoral superiority vis-

88 See Nicolon and Carrieu (1979) and Ladrech (1989: 269–75). The absorption of a major part of the PSU was instrumental for this opening. For a somewhat more guarded assessment compare Lewis and Sferza (1987: 100).

à-vis the PCF, the socialists made one final effort to preempt charges of social democratism in the new 1979 program, *Projet Socialist*.

In the early 1980s, favorable circumstances weakened the PCF's ability to force the socialists toward more radical stances. The PC's orthodox rhetoric and strategic dilemma vis-à-vis the PS led the party into a programmatic and strategic paralysis that reduced its voter appeal (cf. Penniman 1988: 96–7; Ross 1992).[89] The PS was also aided by the inability of ecology lists to go beyond vague center-left positions and to make a convincing pitch for the libertarian Left, and by the ecologists' internal divisions (Prendiville 1989: 97–8). Under these conditions, voters with left-libertarian preferences expected the socialists to be the more effective representative of their views (cf. Kitschelt 1988). As a consequence, the French ecologists had many difficulties in salvaging a distinctive electoral space for its candidates and the majority of their sympathizers regularly supported socialist candidates in the run-offs for seats in parliament or the presidency.[90] The ecologists' failure can be traced back to their denial of a linkage between economic leftism and libertarian stances and their efforts to treat the environment as a separate issue dimension.

In 1981, the PS won the presidential and legislative elections by default. Neither the communists, the left-libertarians, nor the divided and demoralized conservative governing parties were able to stake out viable alternative political appeals.[91] Mitterrand secured his party's victory by running on a set of 110 campaign propositions with moderate reform appeal instead of the comparatively radical 1979 party program. The sharp policy reversal two years into his electoral term in 1983–84 also highlights Mitterrand's willingness to trade programmatic commitments for votes. After a brief experiment with left Keynesianism, his socialist government then adopted an economic austerity policy. It also abandoned left-libertarian promises, particularly in the areas of energy and environmental policy. Given the weakness of the PCF and the strategic disorganization of the various Green lists,[92] Mitterrand's hand was strengthened against the center-right opposition. The PS survived the 1986 election relatively unscathed with a centrist political appeal, although the parliamentary majority narrowly reverted to the bourgeois parties.[93]

---

89 The literature on the electoral "suicide" of the PCF is too large to incorporate in this book. By 1989 Bell and Criddle (1989) found no less than 120 papers that address this question. As a general overview, see Courtois and Peschanski (1988).

90 On the French ecologists in the 1970s see Parodi (1978), Boy (1981: esp. 396), and Capdeville et al. (1988: 254, 256–7).

91 As Pierce and Rochon (1988) show, Mitterrand did not really attract new voters, but benefited from a low turnout resulting from more than proportional abstention among former conservative voters.

92 The inability of the ecologists to develop a strategy of the "second left" is discussed in Jenson (1990: 18–19) and Machin (1989: 72–3).

93 To a considerable extent, the themes the PS and the liberal–conservative opposition parties highlighted during the campaign overlapped. In all parties the economic crisis, unemployment,

Mitterrand pursued the same centrist strategy in the 1988 parliamentary and presidential election. Lacking a viable left-libertarian policy mix, communist and ecologist competitors again posed no serious threat to the socialists. The PCF's strategic paralysis was sufficiently strong to create a breakaway faction headed by Pierre Juquin, who ran for president on an ad hoc left-libertarian platform (Raymond 1988: 177–9).[94] At the same time, Mitterrand's party was aided by the reappearance of a deep political and personal split inside the bourgeois party camp, in part precipitated by the growing competitiveness of the National Front on the radical right. In this situation, Mitterrand could play on popular disaffection with the left–right polarization, project an image of the presidency as being situated above the parties and present the PS as the lesser political evil.[95]

Overall, voter movements between 1978 and 1988 show that those who selectively supported ecological lists or the PCF in critical elections returned to the socialist party, because the PCF and ecologists could not build an electoral reputation around left-libertarian positions. This pattern began to change for the first time in the 1989 local and European elections.[96] After almost a decade of socialist rule, the still divided ecologists made a breakthrough and benefited from the left-libertarian voters' disaffection with the government. This new dynamic of voter movements was confirmed in the 1992 regional elections in which the socialists lost almost half of their voters primarily to two competing ecology lists.[97]

and the situation of young labor market entrants were at the top of the list (Levy and Machin 1986). Only behind these main points issues are diversified by party (cf. Missika and Bregman 1988: 104).

94  The data presented below in Figure 4.11A based on a Eurobarometer 1986 voter survey still claim a moderate PCF commitment to left-libertarian causes. In part, this is due to the PCF's support for the French peace movement, which, because of the PCF's leading role, never gained the stature of equivalent mobilizations in other European countries. In part, it reflects overreporting of left-libertarian inclinations by Communist voters, whereas party elites remained staunchly opposed to the left-libertarian agenda.

95  For an analysis of Mitterrand's campaign strategy, see Cole (1988: 85–8). In Daniel Singer's words: "To say that the French Socialists mellowed is an understatement. The concept of class and capitalism, even the very word *socialism,* had disappeared from their vocabulary. The epitome of radicalism is a Socialist meeting, and the party's one remaining link with the Left was the assertion that social justice and solidarity are necessary in order to carry out the indispensable economic reforms" (Singer 1988: 267).

96  The movement of ecologists and PCF to socialists is visible in the 1981 elections (cf. Boy 1981: 397; Cayrol 1988: 148), in the 1986 parliamentary election and the 1988 presidential and parliamentary elections (cf. Dupoirier 1986; Frears 1988: 245; Guyomarch and Machin 1989: 299. In contrast, in the 1989 European elections, the breakthrough of the ecologists goes mostly at the expense of the conventional Left (PCF and PS) which lost about 8% of all voters (or one sixth of all left voters) to the ecologists, and less at the expense of the UDR/RPR (– 4%) and the National Front (– 0.4%). See Le Gall (1989: 19). I have discussed changing opportunities for the French ecologists in Kitschelt (1990a).

97  This result is particularly remarkable because the voter turnout was very high for French standards (77%). The regional elections should thus not be discounted as a "secondary" election with little predictive power for national elections.

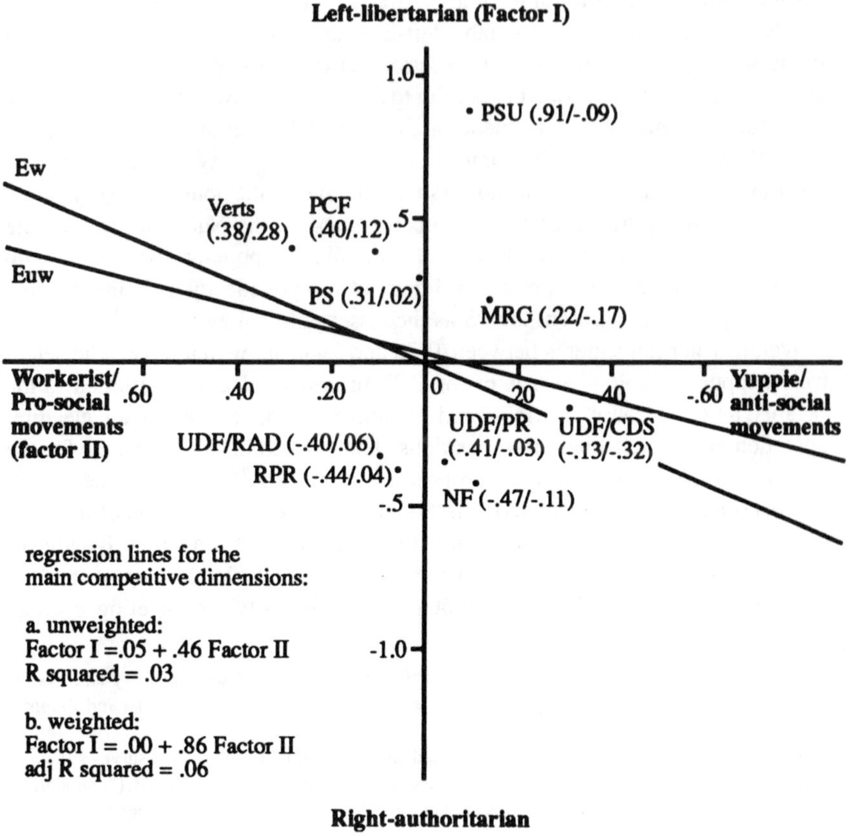

**Left-libertarian (Factor I)**

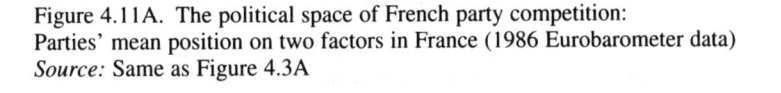

1.0—

• PSU (.91/-.09)

Ew

Verts   PCF
(.38/.28)  (.40/.12) .5—

Euw

PS (.31/.02)

MRG (.22/-.17)

**Workerist/**                  0                     **Yupple/**
**Pro-social** .60    .40    .20          .20    .40    -.60 **anti-social**
**movements**                         UDF/PR  UDF/CDS **movements**
**(factor II)**    UDF/RAD (-.40/.06)  (-.41/-.03) (-.13/-.32)
               RPR (-.44/.04)•
                     -.5— NF (-.47/-.11)

regression lines for the
main competitive dimensions:

a. unweighted:
Factor I =.05 + .46 Factor II    -1.0—
R squared = .03

b. weighted:
Factor I = .00 + .86 Factor II
adj R squared = .06

**Right-authoritarian**

Figure 4.11A. The political space of French party competition:
Parties' mean position on two factors in France (1986 Eurobarometer data)
*Source:* Same as Figure 4.3A

Ironically, the French socialists helped to build up one strand of the French
Greens, *Génération Ecologie,* by coopting its leader, Brice Lalond, into the 1988
socialist cabinet, not anticipating that the Greens would become the socialists'
fiercest competitor for votes by the 1993 parliamentary election. The bland
technocratic concern with industrial modernization that helped the socialists in
elections during the 1980s by limiting the electoral attractiveness of the liberal-
conservative opposition was ineffective in preventing the rise of a strong Green
party, once Green activists could overcome their internal divisions. By the early
1990s, the socialists could no longer thrive on the mistakes of their competitors.

In the French case, party positions derived from their voters' dispositions
expressed in the 1986 Eurobarometer survey (Figure 4.11A) require special
interpretation. Two party blocs emerge that are clearly set apart on the left-
libertarian versus right-authoritarian dimension. Yet because each party's position

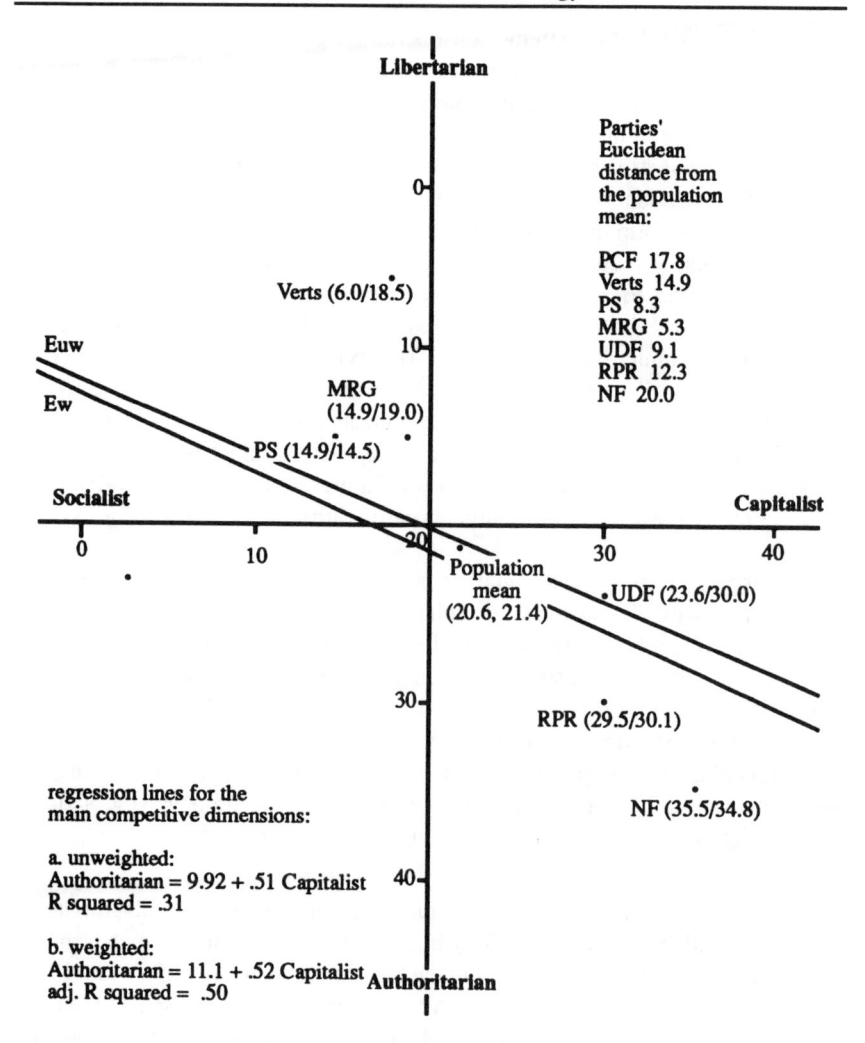

Figure 4.11B. The political space of French party competition:
Parties' mean positions according to expert judgments on two dimensions in France
*Source:* Same as Figure 4.3B

on the workerist–yuppie dimension almost randomly varies within each camp, the regression line linking the parties' mean positions on the two factors has no explanatory power. The left-*libertarianism* of the PCF is probably overstated, because the party's voter positions reflect the elite's strategic appeal less than in almost any other party.[98] The failure of the ecologists within the left camp to differentiate themselves from the other parties suggests why they remained elec-

98 I draw this conclusion from Laver and Hunt's expert judgments on party elite and voter positions that demonstrate a sharp divergence between the two in the French PCF. In fact, hardly any party in Laver and Hunt's European survey shows a sharper divergence between elite and mass on economic and libertarian issues than the PCF.

torally unsuccessful. An extreme left-libertarian position is only taken by the Unified Socialist Party (PSU), a survivor of 1968 with little credibility, promise, or support in the eyes of most French voters.[99]

The spatial representation of party elite positions based on Laver and Hunt's expert survey shows the relative location of ecologists, communists, and socialists on the left-libertarian versus right-authoritarian dimension more clearly. If the winning electoral formula of the Left in the 1980s was a *combination* of moderate calls for economic redistribution (socialism) with libertarian politics, then the communists failed to address libertarian issues and insisted on too radical a Marxist position, while the Greens focused on libertarian questions without considering economic-distributive issues. The PS ended up in a position of relative strength and pivotal importance for coalition making, although it is fairly far removed from the mean national voter (Euclidean distace: 8.3), compared to the Spanish, Austrian, or even Swedish social democrats, all of whom occupied a pivotal position at the time of the survey (cf. Figures 4.5B, 4.8B, and 4.9B). In all those countries, however, some bourgeois parties are situated closer to the average voter than in France.[100]

The success of the French socialists is largely predicated on its competitors' strategic mistakes. These mistakes enhanced the party's early success with a strategy of oligopolistic competition. Later, in the early 1980s, the socialists pursued a vote-maximizing strategy that might have generated electoral losses had other parties taken advantage of their opportunities. And in the late 1980s and early 1990s, the socialists tried to pursue a new strategy of pivoting that tolerates losses to strong ecology lists attracting left and libertarian voters, as long as the bourgeois party camp was divided and engaged in a centrifugal competition with the National Front, which impeded its ability to recapture the median voter.

In spite of the similarity of party system fractionalization and muted left-libertarian cleavage mobilization, Austrian, British, and French socialists have chosen distinctly different strategic courses. Only the Labour Party strategy of the late 1970s and the first half of the 1980s and the Austrian strategy of the mid-1980s can be qualified as outrightly irrational in light of all the theoretical expectations based on simple and complex models of party competition. The Austrian SPÖ, however, soon moved to a new strategy of pivoting and even the British Labour Party made energetic efforts to return to an electorally more rational strategy in the late 1980s.

99  Note that within the bourgeois camp, the position of the National Front is not clearly differenti-
     ated from that of the other parties, yet, in contrast to the ecologists in the left camp, the NF was
     electorally successful. The factor analysis picks up the relative position of bourgeois, conven-
     tional left, and left-libertarian parties fairly well, but not that of the New Right because it does
     not include statements about racism (see Kitschelt 1991d).

100  The German socialists are only slightly further from the mean voter than their French colleagues
     (cf. Figure 4.11A), yet German bourgeois parties are closer to the mean voter than the SPD
     or their French counterparts. Hence, the SPD is considerably further removed from the mean
     voter *relative* to the position of its competitors in the German party system than is the PS in
     France.

The French socialists, finally, benefited from a great deal of luck that enabled them to succeed with a nonequilibrium strategy because of strategic errors committed first by the communists and ecologists, and later also their bourgeois competitors. By the late 1980s, however, the socialists' streak of luck was running out.

*Incentives for moderate left-libertarian strategies of short-term vote maximization, and no incentives for pivoting or oligopolistic competition: Belgium and Italy*

The Belgian and Italian socialists share with the previous group of socialists the same incentives for centrist vote maximization. Left-libertarian mobilization is relatively subdued and the parties are located on the center-left of their balance of political fractionalization. In contrast to the situation in Austria, Britain, or France, the Belgian and Italian party systems are unfavorable to socialist strategies of pivoting and oligopolistic competition. Finally, the factor analysis of voter traits and attitudes presented earlier in this chapter (Table 4.2) shows that Belgium and Italy are the only countries in which the left-libertarian dimension is weakly associated with left–right self-placements and religion. This suggests that old cleavages are still salient and pattern party competition and the left-libertarian versus right-authoritarian axis is of limited relevance for the electoral success of socialist or communist parties. In this systemic configuration, left parties are more likely to succeed at the polls if they take a noncommittal, moderate position on the new cleavage dimension.

*Belgium.* In the 1970s, the Belgian socialists appealed to traditional economic and social positions, but their main task was to adapt to the highly salient ethnolinguistic cleavage dividing the country's two language communities, a problem that was solved by the eventual separation into two socialist parties, one Flemish and one Walloon. The different weight of each socialist party in its regional party system generated some strategic differences among them, although without altering their principal commitment to conventional social democratic economic and social policies.[101]

In the old industrial regions of Wallonia, the socialists were the dominant party. By the early 1980s they had managed to absorb ethnolinguistic parties by calling for interregional redistribution. In an environment of comparatively high labor unionism, the Walloon socialists continued to insist on a conventional leftist program with few concessions to left-libertarian concerns (cf. Fitzmaurice and Van den Berghe 1986: 75).[102] Not surprisingly, the Walloon party lent only lukewarm

101 In the late 1970s, Belgian socialist party activists took more moderate economic and left-libertarian positions than those of socialist parties in other countries. Moreover, judged by the small distance between socialist activists' and voters' preferred policies, activists in the Flemish and Walloon socialist parties engaged in very little issue leadership vis-à-vis their own electorates (cf. Iversen 1991).

102 A change was initiated only with the speech of the party leader, Guy Spitaels, at the 1990 party conference in which in he emphasized gender relations, new social movements, and ecology.

support to the peace movement against stationing new medium-range nuclear missiles on Belgian soil in the early 1980s, a demand firmly endorsed by its Flemish sister party (Dewachter 1987: 185). Mirroring the Walloon socialists' position, the left-libertarian competitor, Ecolo, assumed a moderate position out of rational electoral considerations because limited popular left-libertarian orientation could not support a more radical stance. Ecolo is attracted to a moderate position because the ecologists have the potential for playing the role of pivot in the Walloon parliament between the socialists on the left and the liberal and Christian Democrats on the right (cf. Deschouwer 1989; Kitschelt 1989a: ch. 9).

The Flemish socialists are a minority party facing a hegemonic Christian democracy and a firmly entrenched ethnoregional party, the Volksunie. To escape from its permanent minority position, the party attempted to open to the Catholic working class by toning down its secular and socialist ideology in the 1970s. Modest socialist efforts to embrace the left-libertarian issues of citizens' participation, ecology, and peace did not prevent the formation of a successful new ecology party, Agalev, that became highly efficient in attracting, particularly, young white collar voters whose family background was in the established Catholic pillar. With its strategic maneuverability restricted, the leadership of the Flemish socialists began to withdraw from the party's cautious left-libertarian overtures in the early 1980s and to insist on a moderate economic and social policy that enabled it and its Walloon sister party in 1987 to enter a government coalition with the Christian Democrats after six years in opposition (cf. Dewachter 1987; Leonard 1989).

As in Sweden and Britain, Belgium's large political parties are still primarily configured along an economic left–right dimension that also has a religious aspect. The ecologists are the only party that has taken a pronounced stance on a cross-cutting communitarian dimension that divides libertarian versus authoritarian issues. This is shown quite clearly by the mean location of each Belgian party's voters in the two-dimensional space based on the factor analysis of Eurobarometer data (Figure 4.12A). Laver and Hunt's expert survey suggests a somewhat greater alignment of parties along a left-libertarian versus right-authoritarian dimension (Figure 4.12B). In part, this is due to the increasing salience of left-libertarian issues and the strengthening of a new authoritarian Right in the late 1980s at the time of Laver and Hunt's survey. The socialists' relative neglect of left-libertarian issues may explain why the Belgian socialist parties lost heavily to the libertarian Left when such issues gained salience before the 1991 election.[103] In previous elections, studies of voter flows discovered considerable gross turnover of voters between ecologists and socialists, but traced back most of the ecologists' net gains

---

103 Especially in Wallonia, where Ecolo surged from 6.5% (1987) to 13.5% (1991), the socialists lost almost 70,000 votes or more than 3% of their 1987 voters to Ecolo, whereas the main bourgeois parties lost only 1.9% to Ecolo (cf. Rihoux 1991). The socialists' losses are probably greater given that an overproportionate share of new young voters supported Ecolo rather than the socialists. In Flanders as well, 1991 surveys indicate that Agalev and the socialists had become zero-sum competitors for the same pool of voters. See "De Campagne: Wie zoekt war kiezers?" *De Morgen* (June 20, 1991).

to new voters, former voters of the extreme Left, and surprisingly also to former supporters of the Christian Democrats and the Volksunie.[104]

The application of spatial competition theory to the Belgian case suggests that the Walloon and Flemish socialists were right to pursue a rather noncommittal course on libertarian issues in the 1980s. At the same time, Figures 4.12A and 4.12B indicate that the socialists could have watered down their socioeconomic position in order to gain more votes from their bourgeois competitors. The parties' Euclidean distance from the hypothetical mean voter is rather large in cross-national comparison (11.9 compared to 3.8 in Italy, 6.5 in Sweden and 7.6 in Denmark). Nevertheless, the Belgian socialists proved that parties could be moderately successful in the 1980s *without* showing extraordinary strategic flexibility, provided that the constraints of party competition did not require policy innovation. The 1991 results demonstrate that this important condition no longer holds. In the 1990s, strategic immobility has begun to haunt socialists in Belgium as it does socialists in other countries, and has benefited the new left-libertarian parties.

*Italy.*    Compared to Belgium, the situation of the Left in the Italian party system was complicated by the rivalry between socialists and communists and numerous left-libertarian splinter parties. The socialists chose a strategy of centripetal competition and pivoting that largely ignored the left-libertarian challenge. The communists, however, reacted with much greater sensitivity to the emerging new challenge. Given the easy entry of new parties all around them, however, they found themselves in the tragic situation that no conceivable strategy would preserve their electoral market share. This may have contributed to the PCI's extraordinary volatility and indecision throughout the 1980s.

In contrast to the French or Spanish socialists, the PSI fought most elections in the post–World War II era as the minority party of the Left.[105] When participation in the center-left coalitions of the 1960s failed to halt the party's electoral decline, it swung to the left and into the opposition under DeMartino in the 1970s. Like Spanish and French socialists, the PSI adopted a rhetoric of autogestion and feminist politics that was designed to appeal to the small noncommunist parties of the Left and an emerging left-libertarian constituency around the Radical Party (cf. Merkel 1985: 339–55; Nielsson 1987: 79; DiScala 1988: 171). This strategy of leapfrogging beyond the Italian communists on left-libertarian issues failed, however, to improve the party's electoral standing because the PCI also seized on these issues at the same time it moderated its economic stance. The new strategic configuration on the Left precipitated a flow of voters from PSI to PCI, losses the PSI could barely offset by gains from the radical-liberal political spectrum (cf. Corbetta, Paris, and Schadee 1988: 423). Unlike its larger French and Spanish sister parties, the PSI lacked the electoral weight to engage in a successful strategy

104 For Flanders, see Swyngedouw's (1986) voter flow analysis of the 1985 election and an equivalent analysis for the 1987 election by Swyngedouw and Billiet (1988).
105 On the history of the PSI's strategy stances, see Farneti (1985), Merkel (1985), DiScala (1988), and Hine (1989).

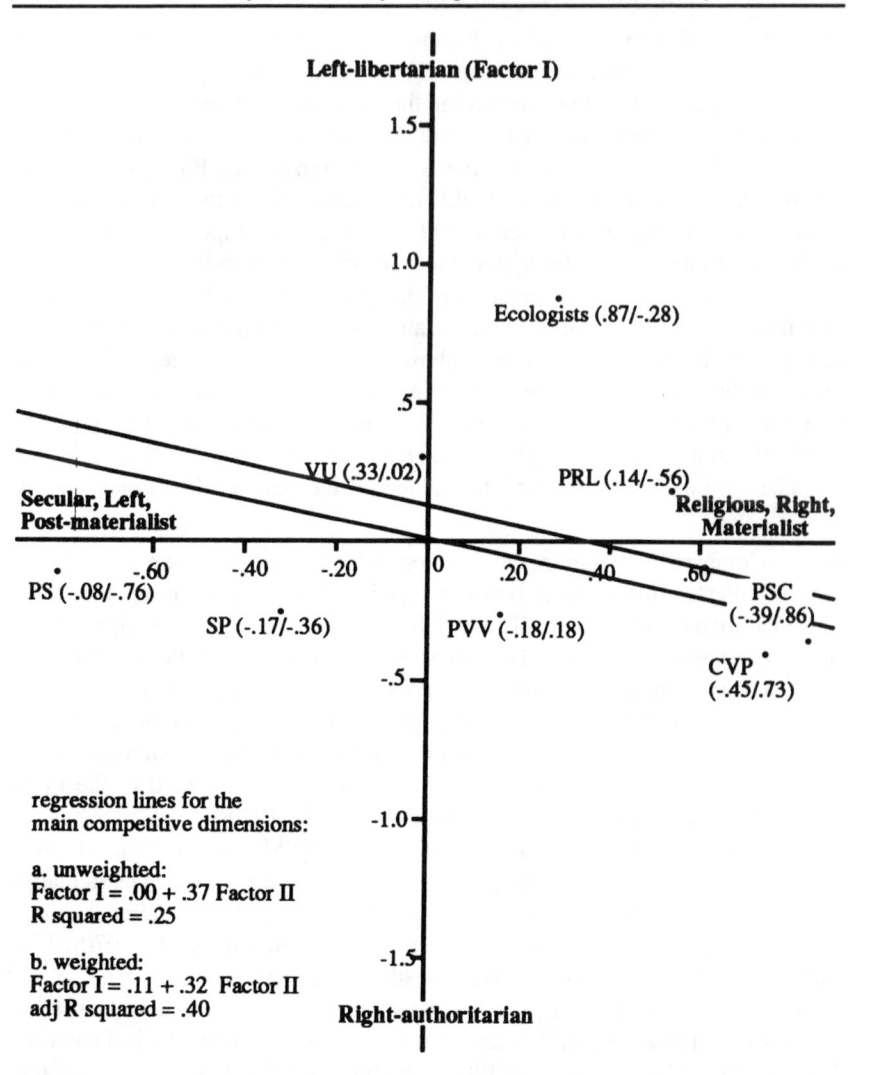

Figure 4.12A. The political space of Belgian party competition:
Parties' mean position on two factors in Belgium (1986 Eurobarometer data)
*Source:* Same as Figure 4.3A

of oligopolistic competition of first destroying the communist competitor by adopting a radical rhetoric and then moving back to a more centrist stance after the communists' defeat.[106] Moreover, the Italian communists proved to be strategically more versatile than their French or Spanish comrades.

After 1976, with the DeMartino strategy defeated and the PSI in opposition to a

106 Structural conditions, such as low electoral thresholds and the PCI's regional entrenchment also made an oligopolistic strategy not promising.

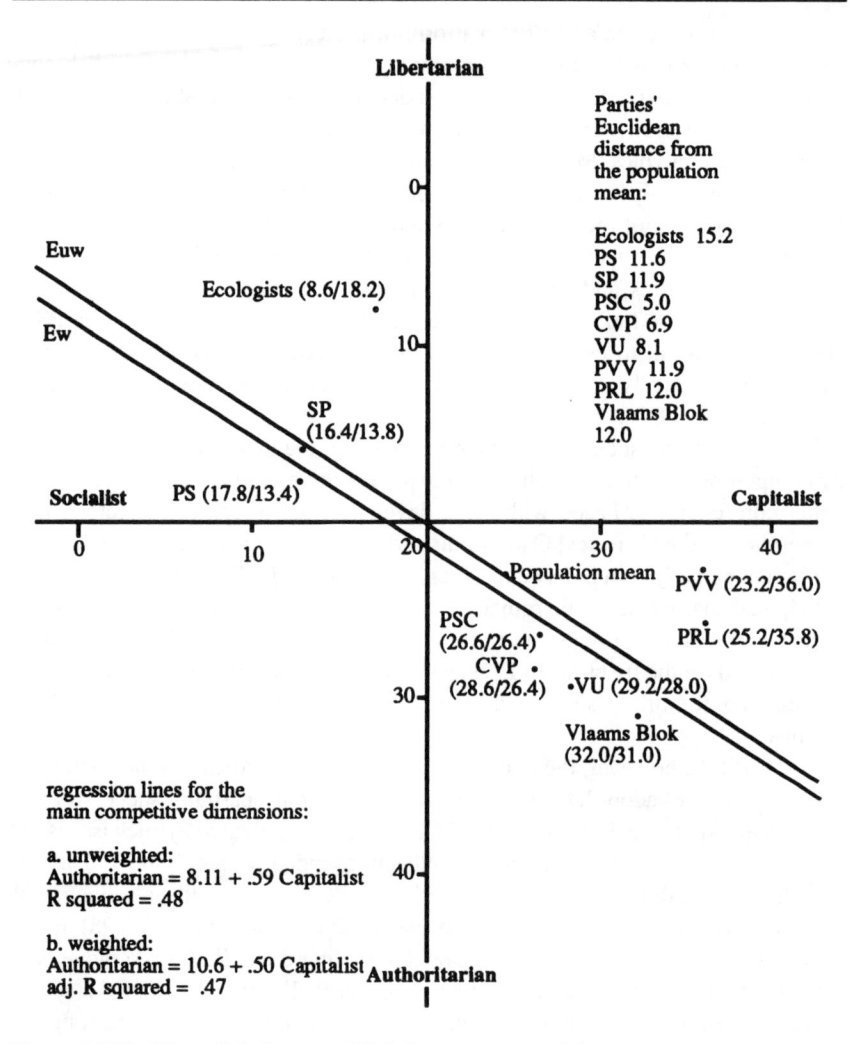

Figure 4.12B. The political space of Belgian party competition:
Parties' mean positions according to expert judgments on two dimensions in Belgium
*Source:* Same as Figure 4.3B

quasi-coalition of the Christian Democrats (DC) and the PCI, a fundamental strategic reversal took place. The PSI largely abandoned most conventional leftist and left-libertarian appeals and endorsed basic capitalist institutions and economic austerity policies. It also lent little support to ecological, antinuclear, and disarmament movements, with the exception of a late and purely tactical environmentalist turn in 1987 (cf. Hine 1987: 268; Nielsson 1987; DiScala 1988: 207. 242).[107]

107 The Radical's efforts to blackmail the PSI to adopt a left-libertarian stance failed in 1982 when the PR split and some of its parliamentarians were absorbed by the PSI (Panebianco 1988b: 133).

Instead, the PSI ran on a centrist platform of protecting liberal rights (due legal process, gender equalization) and improving Italy's governability through constitutional change creating a stronger presidency, higher electoral thresholds as an antidote to party system fragmentation, and more parliamentary party discipline by abolishing secret votes. Moreover, the party attacked the fusion of party and state apparatus commonly referred to as partitocrazia and reinforced by the DC and the PCI during the era of the Historical Compromise (cf. DiScala 1988: ch. 14, 15).

The new strategy electorally benefited the PSI by gaining votes from the small laicist center parties and from the communists who were caught between the libertarian extreme Left and the new centrist PSI strategy.[108] Overall, the PSI's strategy turned out to be both vote and office maximizing. Although the party stayed comparatively small, it occupied the pivot in the Italian party system throughout the 1980s.

In the 1970s, the socialists' main left contender, the PCI, found itself engulfed by competitors on all sides, while also experiencing a gradual erosion of its blue collar core clientele. Faced with these developments, the party correctly chose moderation in the Historical Compromise with the DC. Given the crowdedness of the Italian party system in its centrist region, however, PCI strategists could have anticipated that whatever marginal gains the party would make by its moderate stance would be offset by losses to new extreme competitors. When these losses materialized for the first time in 1979, party leaders were unwilling to give up vote maximizing for office seeking and therefore abandoned the Historical Compromise.

In the 1980s, however, the party was unable to find a consistent new strategic appeal. Efforts to adopt left-libertarian issues were only partially successful and never firmly tied constituencies to the PCI, who were motivated by such issues.[109] In the 1970s the party was ill at ease with the independent women's movement and only the surge of the Radical Party compelled the PCI to support the introduction of divorce and abortion rights (Panebianco 1988b: 124–5; Pasquino 1988: 28). In the 1980s, the PCI's tactic of embracing and dominating the Italian peace movement actually stifled the movement's growth. And the PCI's late adoption of a stance against nuclear power in a close vote at the 1987 party congress was not enough to restore the party's credibility with the libertarian Left (cf. Hine 1987: 268; Sani 1987: 22; Ceri 1988; Pasquino 1988: 28–9; Maguire 1990: 11). In 1985–86, environmentalists rated the PCI's ecological credentials considerably lower than

---

108  This argument is borne out by individual and constituency level voter flow analyses of the 1979, 1983, and 1987 elections. See Merkel (1985: 286), Corbetta et al. (1988: 423), and Biorcio and Natale (1989: 133).

109  See Della Porta and Rucht (1991). In contrast, Tarrow (1989: 268–9) claims that the PCI successfully associated itself with new left-libertarian currents. Also claims that the PCI had essentially assimilated left-libertarian demands because many of its activists came from the 1960s movements (Lange et al. 1990) may be misleading. Many left-libertarian voters, but particularly the leaders of the social movements, associated themselves with the left-libertarian Proletarian Democracy, Radical Party, and eventually the Greens. See Pasquino (1988: 26, 29).

those of the Radical Party and not much higher than those of the Republicans or the PSI (Dalton 1990).

At the same time, Italian voters had moved away from radical socialist stances, a process that surfaced in opinion surveys showing that PCI voters progressively placed themselves further to the right on a ten-point self-placement scale from 1976–77 to 1985–86.[110] This tendency further restricted the PCI's strategic range of maneuverability.

By the early 1980s, the PCI was squeezed both by small parties of the extreme Left as well as by centrist parties, including the PSI (Donovan 1989), leaving it unable to formulate a winning strategy for replacing the Historical Compromise (Hellman 1990). The 1986 PCI congress at Florence self-critically recognized the party's problems. By then it was clear to members that the party lacked any specific alternative to the left-libertarian parties, on the one side, and the PSI, on the other. It had ignored changes in the working class, done little to reach out to technical cadres and the rising education and service sector, and developed weak linkages to social movements (Timmermann 1987: 133).

Predictably, in the 1987 election, the PCI lost votes to all of its competitors on the libertarian left and in the center. The party had been locked into a tragic position, besieged by old and new competitors. Yet given the PSI's centripetal strategy in the 1980s, the PCI might have fared better by earlier and more vigorous efforts to shed its communist legacy in favor of social democratic stances that began to take shape only after the party split and turned away from Marxian socialism at the beginning of the 1990s.[111]

The strategic configuration of Italian party politics in the second half of the 1980s is illustrated by the factor analysis of party supporters' mean positions in the 1986 Eurobarometer surveys and Laver and Hunt's expert judgments of party positions in the late 1980s (Figures 4.13A and 4.13B). Figure 4.13A shows that the main axis of party competition, weighted by the relative voter support for each party, was still situated closer to a socioeconomic left–right dimension than a left-libertarian versus right-authoritarian axis.[112] The configuration also highlights that the PSI and PCI had made little effort in the mid-1980s to reach out to libertarian voters. While the PSI was close to the center region of the competitive space, the PCI remained wedded to the workerist pole. Moreover, the figure suggests that communist losses might have been even greater had the new left-

---

110 The following figures are based on the average self-placements for each party's supporters on four Eurobarometer surveys in each of the two time periods:

|  | 1976–77 | 1985–86 |
| --- | --- | --- |
| Extreme Left | 1.46 | 2.10 |
| PCI | 2.02 | 2.53 |
| Radical Party | 2.53 | 3.60 |
| PSI | 3.35 | 3.91 |

111 The PSI's identification with the partitocrazia establishment and the postcommunists' new stance may have contributed to the PSI's electoral decline from 14.3% (1987) to 13.6% (1992).

112 As shown in Table 4.3, voters' left–right self-placements are wedded more to the socioeconomic than the libertarian–authoritarian dimension.

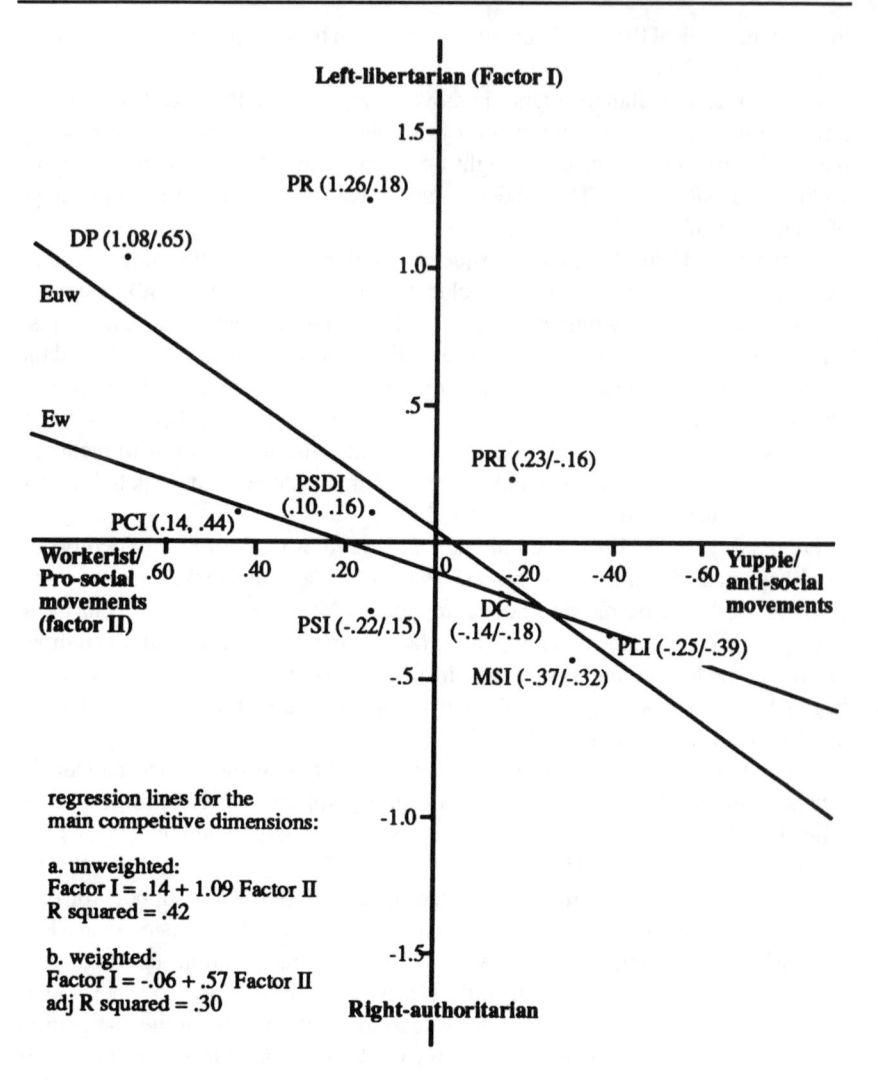

Figure 4.13A. The political space of Italian party competition:
Parties' mean position on two factors in Italy (1986 Eurobarometer data)
*Source:* Same as Figure 4.3A

libertarian parties not taken such an extreme stance. Since 1986, the rise of the Italian Greens in fact has increased the menu of left-libertarian options and has provided yet another and somewhat less radical alternative (Diani 1989).

Laver and Hunt's expert survey quite closely matches the configuration revealed by the factor analysis. In the late 1980s, the PSI was in the center of the political space, while the PCI continued to emphasize anti-capitalist themes, though with more concessions to libertarian issues. Demo-Proletarians, Greens, and Radicals

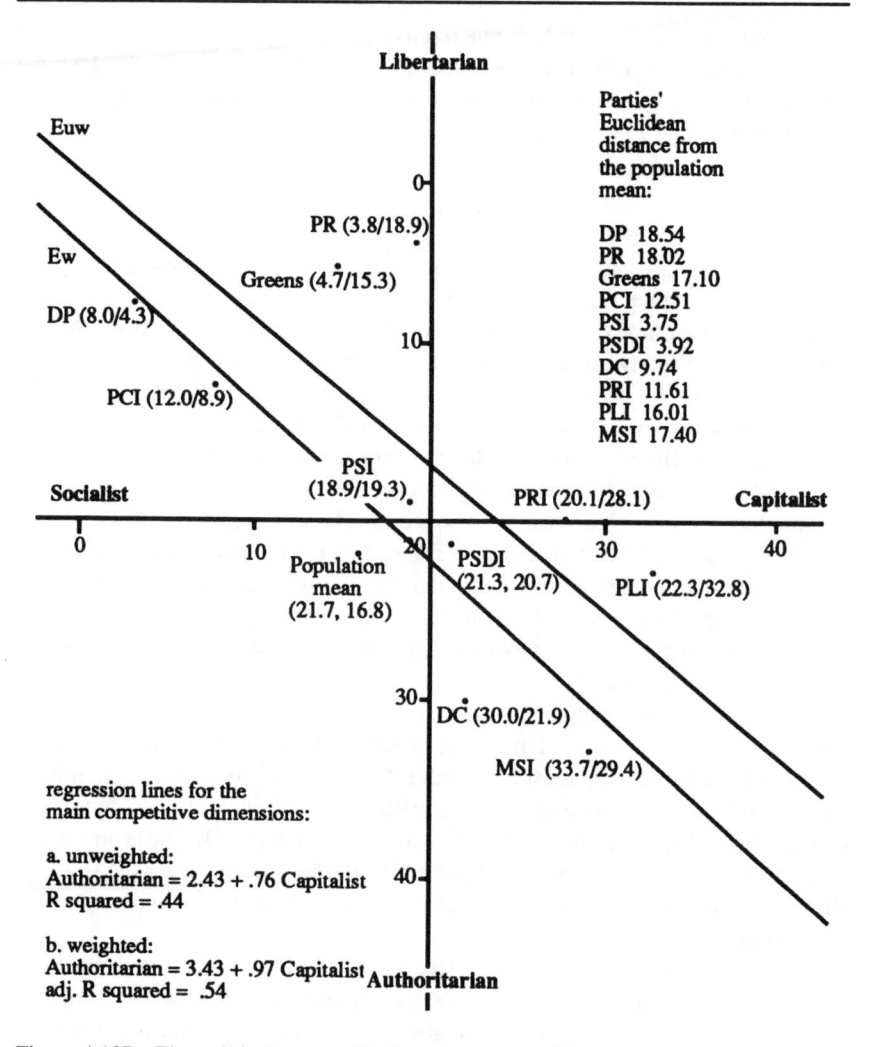

Figure 4.13B. The political space of Italian party competition:
Parties' mean positions according to expert judgments on two dimensions in Italy
*Source:* Same as Figure 4.3B

adopted libertarian positions, mixed with varying doses of economic leftism. The Italian socialists rationally abandoned most remnants of economic leftism, but also had few incentives for embracing left-libertarian politics, given the crowdedness of the competitive arena. The communists, in turn were engulfed by old and new competitors who whittled away at their share of the electoral market.

Both the Belgian and the Italian socialists had every incentive to assume moderate positions on the left-libertarian versus right-authoritarian dimension. Not only the balance of party system fractionalization, but also the relatively low left-libertarian ideological mobilization made it unattractive for these parties to choose a more radical strategy. The lack of intense cleavage mobilization, in turn, also kept the salience of conventional socioeconomic left–right competition at a higher level than in many other European countries.

## CONCLUSION

The analytical case studies of socialist party strategies in competitive party systems demonstrate that simple spatial theories have considerable power in accounting for parties' actual electoral payoffs, once strategies have been chosen. The selection of party strategies themselves, however, often follows a different logic. Very roughly, socialists or communist parties fought at most half of the elections held during the 1970s and 1980s in the ten countries with strategic stances predicted by a logic of short-term vote maximization (cf. Figure 4.14). This includes cases where socialist parties benefited from the strategic "mistakes" of competitors and were able to exploit a nonequilibrium strategy (e.g., the French PS in 1981 and probably also in 1988). Further, this list includes cases where vote maximizing stances also had office maximizing or oligopolistic consequences. For example, in the Dutch PvdA, the vote-maximizing strategy in an environment of high left-libertarian cleavage mobilization also happened to meet the criteria of oligopolistic competition.[113]

Where vote- and office-maximizing goals require different strategies, the rationale of choosing a strategy of pivoting depends on structural conditions. Such conditions were unambiguously favorable for socialists in only two countries, Austria and Spain. But pivoting has also influenced the choices of the Danish and Dutch social democrats and even the Italian communists. In these instances, fatigue with long-term opposition status may have been decisive for the strategic choice. Further, intraorganizational factors of coalition building I will explore in the next chapter were critical.

Parties may also resort to oligopolistic competition as an alternative to short-term vote or office maximizing. This strategy is rational only if structural opportunities are favorable, such as when socialist parties could exploit the existence of a large and strategically immobile or internally divided communist party (France and Spain in the 1970s). Efforts to pursue oligopolistic competition by the British Labour Party, the Italian socialists in the 1970s, or the Danish and German social democrats in brief episodes in the 1980s, however, were nonrational because structural conditions offered little hope that such strategies would succeed in the long run.

In a residual group of cases, party strategy has remained too volatile to qualify either as a serious attempt at sophisticated competition through pivoting or oligopolistic competition, or as consistent effort to pursue short-term vote maxim-

---

113 Of course, my generalization for the 1972–86 period ignores the 1981 election in which the PvdA lost considerably to the libertarian Left and the Democrats '66 after a bland performance in opposition that undermined the party's issue leadership.

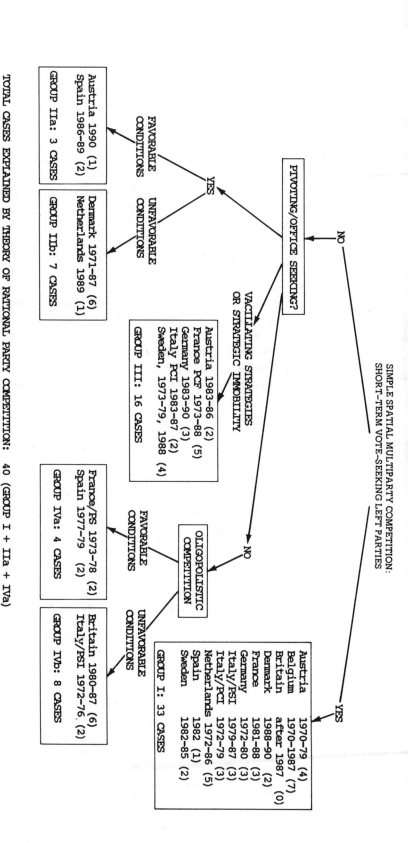

SIMPLE SPATIAL MULTIPARTY COMPETITION:
SHORT-TERM VOTE-SEEKING LEFT PARTIES

PIVOTING/OFFICE SEEKING?

NO

YES

FAVORABLE CONDITIONS

Austria 1990 (1)
Spain 1986-89 (2)

GROUP IIa: 3 CASES

UNFAVORABLE CONDITIONS

Denmark 1971-87 (6)
Netherlands 1989 (1)

GROUP IIb: 7 CASES

VACILLATING STRATEGIES
OR STRATEGIC IMMOBILITY

Austria 1983-86 (2)
France PCF 1973-88 (5)
Germany 1983-90 (3)
Italy PCI 1983-87 (2)
Sweden, 1973-79, 1988 (4)

GROUP III: 16 CASES

NO

OLIGOPOLISTIC COMPETITION

FAVORABLE CONDITIONS

France/PS 1973-78 (2)
Spain 1977-79 (2)

GROUP IVa: 4 CASES

UNFAVORABLE CONDITIONS

Britain 1980-87 (6)
Italy/PSI 1972-76, (2)

GROUP IVb: 8 CASES

YES

Austria         1970-79 (4)
Belgium         1970-1987 (7)
Britain         after 1987 (0)
Denmark         1988-90 (2)
France          1981-88 (3)
Germany         1972-80 (3)
Italy/PSI       1979-87 (3)
Italy/PCI       1972-79 (3)
Netherlands     1972-86 (5)
Spain           1982 (1)
Sweden          1982-85 (2)

GROUP I: 33 CASES

TOTAL CASES EXPLAINED BY THEORY OF RATIONAL PARTY COMPETITION: 40 (GROUP I + IIa + IVa)

TOTAL CASES NOT EXPLAINED BY THE THEORY OF RATIONAL PARTY COMPETITION: 31 (GROUP IIb + III + IVb)

Figure 4.14. Explanatory power of systemic theories of party competition for socialist party strategy

ization. The volatility of strategic appeals most clearly beset the German SPD in the 1980s. Strategic immobility is a more common problem in the West European Left. It characterized the predicament of the Austrian socialists and the Italian communists for much of the 1980s and of the French PCF and the Swedish SAP, in different ways, throughout the 1970s and 1980s. The ultrastability of the Swedish SAP translated into rather serious electoral losses in the 1970s from levels reached in the 1960s. The SAP's brief electoral recovery in the early 1980s occurred only by default due to the strategic disorganization of the competing bourgeois camp.

Following the theoretical argument of this chapter, these immobile left parties would have had to adopt less socialist-redistributive stances, while simultaneously catering to more libertarian electoral sensitivities, in order to remain short-term vote maximizers or successful office seekers or both. Systemic theory of party competition, by itself, does not explain, however, why the parties failed to choose such trajectories.

Based on Laver and Hunt's (1992) expert judgments of party positions, the rationality of the socialist parties' strategies can be also compared in light of each party's Euclidean distance from its country's mean voter, as calculated in Figures 4.3B through 4.13B. A strategy of pivoting would require a party stance close to a country's mean voter.[114] Figure 4.15 shows that the logic of pivoting is most clearly expressed by the Austrian, Italian, and Spanish socialists in the late 1980s.

The most efficient position of short-term vote-maximizing parties is not determined by the position of the median voter, but the balance of party system fractionalization and the intensity of left-libertarian cleavage mobilization, as measured by the index provided in Table 4.7. As index values rise, vote-maximizing socialists should distance themselves from the median voter somewhere within the corridor bounded by the lines b and c in Table 4.15. On that account, the Dutch Labor Party pursued a policy of vote maximization in spite of its decided radicalism throughout much of the 1970s and 1980s. Similarly, the German social democrats began to settle on a new strategy of vote maximization with intermediate libertarian and only moderately economic left positions at the end of the 1980s that was upset by the external shock of national unification in 1990. The French socialists also may have been within the corridor of vote maximization, although they benefited a great deal from the irrational positions and the strategic predicaments of just about all of their competitors. Finally, the Danish socialists at the end of the decade had temporarily abandoned efforts to win the pivot of the party system and moved toward a vote-maximizing strategy under Sven Auken. The Swedish SAP may have been stuck in an intermediate field between vote maximization and pivoting in the late 1980s and early 1990s and achieved neither.

Beyond the upper bound of vote-maximization strategies (line c), one would

114 Strictly speaking, pivoting parties would want to capture the *median* voter. Eurobarometer data show, however, a fairly symmetric bell-shaped distribution of respondents on the left-libertarian versus right-authoritarian dimension so that it may be reasonable to treat median and mean voter as identical.

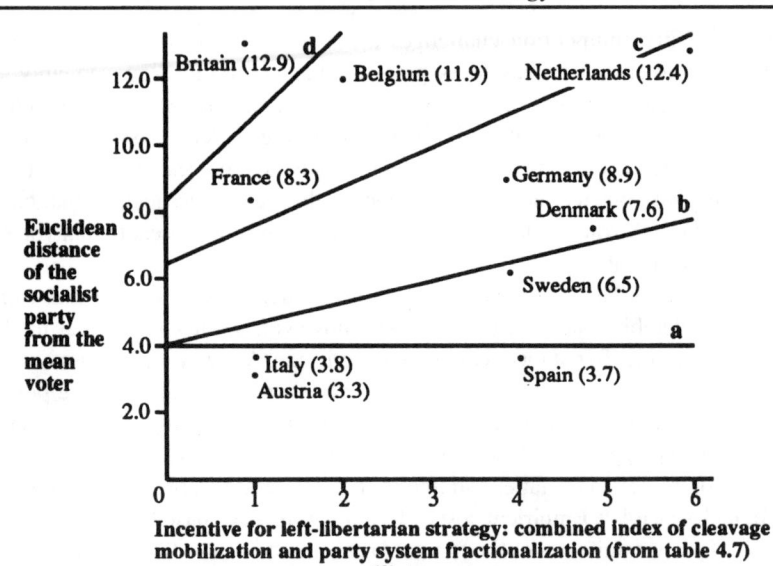

Incentive for left-libertarian strategy: combined index of cleavage
mobilization and party system fractionalization (from table 4.7)

Figure 4.15. Socialist party strategy in the 1980s: Euclidean distance from the mean voter
*Source:* For measures of socialist party distance from mean voter, see Figures 4.3B through
4.13B; for measure of index of incentives for left-libertarian strategy, see Table 4.7.

find strategies of oligopolistic competition that go at the expense of vote maximization. The German social democrats halfheartedly and briefly attempted to venture
into that region after losing power in the early 1980s. The single clear-cut case of a
party that pursued a quasi-oligopolistic strategy is the British Labour Party, which
operated in a system that otherwise favored pivoting. This strategy was manifestly
nonrational, given that the party had no need to displace a more radical challenger.
The strategically immobile Belgian socialists are stuck somewhere between vote
maximizing and oligopolistic competition in a party system that did not impose
high demands on strategic mobility.

Figure 4.15 again shows that a systemic theory of party competition cannot fully
account for the socialists' strategic choices. The explanatory gaps left by systemic
theories set the theoretical agenda for the final two chapters of this study. Why are
some strategies not accounted for in terms of systemic constraints? Further, why do
parties choose differently between short-term vote maximization, office seeking,
or oligopolistic competition when each of these objectives has some rational
plausibility? To explore such choices, I will abandon the systemic and structural
level of analysis and examine the internal process of party politics in both
organizational and ideological terms.

## ADDENDUM: ALTERNATIVES TO SPATIAL MODELING IN
### THE ANALYSIS OF PARTY COMPETITION

Since the 1970s, spatial models of party competition have come under fire because
they are said to provide an inadequate reconstruction of rational voter choices and,
hence, also of parties' best strategies to attract electoral support. A "salience

theory" of party competition challenges the assumption made by most spatial analysts that voter preferences are of great simplicity and low dimensionality.[115] Whereas the spatial model sees all issues as "positional" in the sense that voters take pro or contra positions, in reality many issues are "valence" issues on which most voters are in agreement. What decides voters' choices, then, is not the position they take on an issue, but the salience of that valence issue in a situation of political choice. A voter endorses the party whose appeal is closest to that voter's rank order of salient issues.

Salience theory has presented an ingenious model of voter choice that commands considerable plausibility. It is likely, however, to alter the spatial model only at the margins. To put the theory to work, one must know what a separate issue is for voters and how issues are related to each other. Are issues discrete policy questions or are they linked through some kind of overarching cognitive map? Salience theory appears to lean toward the former alternative, whereas spatial theory is committed to the latter and implies that issues are mapped onto a broader ideological space.[116] Empirical tests of salience theory, based on the content analysis of party manifestos or the campaign pronouncements of politicians, do not inspire confidence in the actual discreteness of policy issues. Not only are many issues coded in positive and negative terms and thus reintroduce the spatial-positional analogy directly,[117] but critical issues that may be coded as salience questions are substantive alternatives on a single ideological dimension.[118] The salience of issues is subordinated to the positionality of the ideological dimensions on which issues are mapped. It is no wonder, then, that empirical studies informed by salience theory tend to find a single overarching left–right dimension that appears to structure party manifestos, with a "new politics" dimension coming in second in a substantial number of countries (Budge and Robertson 1987). Because issues are not discrete appeals, but come in structured clusters and polarities, one ends up where one began at a spatial model. Party positions can be mapped according to the spatial imagery on one or two dominant competitive dimensions.[119]

115 Salience theory was developed by Robertson (1976) and Budge and Farlie (1983a: ch. 2).
116 For a formalization of this argument, see Enelow and Hinich (1990) and Hinich and Munger (1990).
117 I am referring here to the roster for the content analysis of party manifestos employed in Budge et al. (1987: 459–64) where a large number of items is coded in positive and negative terms, e.g.:

| 107. internationalism: positive | 109. internationalism: negative |
| 406. protectionism: negative | 407. protectionism: positive |
| 506. education: anti-expansion | 507. education: pro-expansion |
| etc. | |

118 Examples from the same content analysis (fn. 5) are enterprise (401), regulation of capitalism (403), incentives (402), economic planning (404), and controlled economy (412), economic orthodoxy and efficiency (414), and nationalization (413), etc.
119 The credibility of a party in the voters' eyes is based on issue linkage. Only if parties command a web of popular positions are they able to attract voters. In the 1983 British election, Labour was clearly identified with fighting unemployment, the most important issue on the voters' agenda. But the party did not benefit from this issue conjuncture because it lacked credible policy

According to salience theory, a party must seize on valence issues, promote the salience of such issues, and induce voters to identify the party with them. Parties are expected to make investments in new issues after losing elections focused on other issue dimensions.[120] In the 1980s, left parties that have experienced a losing streak should be particularly eager to identify new issues. But most issues are linked to ideological dimensions and are not discrete items. Hence, new competitive dimensions cannot be created simply because of the whims of vote-seeking rational politicians. Moreover, if there are discrete valence issues, this is a transitional stage of competition until rational politicians have linked them to broader positional ideological alternatives.[121] Rational incumbents will do everything to assimilate valence issues to the existing patterns of directional competition either by adopting them or by linking them to adverse positions on the already existing ideological dimension(s) of competition. This process is illustrated by feminism and ecology, topics that began their career as valence issues but have become enmeshed in overarching left-libertarian and right-authoritarian ideological positions over the past two decades.

My case studies have demonstrated that socialist parties on a losing trajectory are typically unable to reposition themselves on an entirely new dimension of competition. They recover votes only if they discover a more profitable position on the left-libertarian versus right-authoritarian competitive dimension. In this sense, socialist parties are compelled to face up to ecology or feminism and cannot simply choose to ignore them in order to compete on a more convenient issue agenda. As Laver and Hunt's (1992) expert judgments show, in almost all countries ecology and sociocultural issues have gained high salience for socialists' electoral appeal in Western Europe. Socialists have to fight over "occupying" these themes and absorbing them into a more encompassing structured set of appeals.

Party competition is thus much less disjointed than salience theory suggests. Of course, it must be granted that there are phenomena spatial theory clearly misses in its reconstruction of party strategies and that have an impact on electoral success at the margin. I am thinking here of the electoral impact of leadership personality or the management of crises by a government party, such as political scandals, wars, or natural catastrophes. Such issues inevitably influence voters, even though they cannot be brought into a spatial representation of party competition.

A recent proposal to model voter choice and party competition combines elements of spatial and salience approaches in a "directional" theory of party

solutions (Crewe 1985b: 179). Labour's problem was that it linked its popular stance on unemployment to an array of unpopular leftist economic policy proposals.

120 In Riker's (1986) language, losing parties engage in a "heresthetic" of reshaping the electoral competition, "structuring the world so that you can win."

121 Moreover, as Laver (1989: 321) has pointed out, parties that emphasize their uniqueness in the electoral arena face a dilemma in the legislative arena: "[O]ther things being equal, a party will want to manipulate salience in order to develop dimensions that isolate itself from others in the electoral party system, but [that] quite the reverse applies in the legislative party system since ideological isolation reduces bargaining power."

competition.[122] Voters not only choose the issue dimensions they find salient but respond to the spatial location of parties within each dimension as well. In line with salience theory, directional theory holds that (1) there may be a multitude of dimensions that inform voters' choices and (2) voting is not a matter of choosing the party that is closest to one's own position on a continuum of alternatives, but the party that articulates a salient position in the same *direction* of one's own policy inclinations. Nevertheless, directional theory accepts spatial imagery in at least two critical respects. First, voting is positional rather than purely salience-based, although not governed by the minimum-space theorem. The intensity of the party's positions motivates participation in elections. Hence, the attractiveness of a choice is the scalar product of the voter's and the candidate's position, as measured by the distance of each position (in the same direction) from a neutral mean. Second, however, voters do not reward the intensity of a party's position beyond a certain threshold of acceptability and responsibility. On each relevant issue dimension, there are optimal positions sufficiently intense to motivate voter choice, yet not so radical as to deter voters who lean only mildly toward a party's position. If directional theory is correct, there will be two parties on each competitive dimension that occupy optimal positions on each side of an issue. Further, there may be room for two other small radical parties that attract voters with less sensitivity to the optimal position on the dimension. If the system has more than four parties, however, they will compete on different dimensions.

The problem with the directional model is that the optimal intensity of a party's position may vary depending on the individual voter's preferences. Hence, while salience theory may predict that parties cannot take bland centrist positions on all issues, there is no single pair of optimal positions in each direction on any dimension of party competition, but a wide range of positions that attract different groups of voters depending upon how much intensity of political appeals they find acceptable. Rabinowitz and MacDonald (1989) are probably correct in claiming that a purely centrist position will not attract voters and that parties will have to display some issue leadership. But even if the very center of a competitive space is empty, the spatial imagery may still apply to all other positions, as long as we assume with directional theory that voters' and parties' positions are systematically linked.[123]

As a further difficulty, directional theory, like salience theory, has to come to grips with the problem that parties' strategic interaction in a dynamic setting may undermine multidimensional competition.[124] Vote-seeking parties will compete

122 The theory was developed by Rabinowitz and MacDonald (1989) and has been further fleshed out in Listhaug, MacDonald, and Rabinowitz (1990a,b) and Rabinowitz et al. (1991).

123 Iversen (1992) has shown that in fact both directional and spatial elements explain voting behavior. In a similar vein, Shaffer (1992) develops a "congruence" model that postulates spatial proximity as the rationale of voters' decisions, *as long as* parties and voters are on the same side of an issue.

124 Maybe for this reason, in an empirical analysis of six European party systems, Listhaug et al. (1990a) were unable to identify a second dimension that yields sufficient variance of party position in at least three countries (Denmark, France, and the Netherlands). To be fair, the article

not only by defending dimensions on which they hold optimal positions, but they will also compete over the *relationship among salient dimensions.* If parties compete across dimensions and even try to merge and appropriate dimensions, their positions may be mapped on a single superdimension, with weights given to their positions on each of its subcomponents.[125] In this superdimension, which actually reflects their overall competitive position and interests, parties will, of course, be lined up from extreme to centrist positions in both directions. The spatial analogy again would approximate a correct interpretation of party competition.

If we remain true to the pure formulation of directional theory, rational parties would maintain the optimal position on at least that dimension which is most salient to their cause. In other words, parties will not move contingent upon other parties' strategic stances on that dimension, but only respond to changing voter demands and perceptions of optimality. Thus, in contrast to spatial interpretations, we do not expect a linkage between costs of entry or the crowdedness of the competitive space and party positions. Moreover, crowded party systems should be more complex in the dimensionality of competition that characterizes them.

Calculations of the correlation between parties' positions on the two dimensions of voter identification that emerged from the factor analyses of Eurobarometer data, the left-libertarian versus right-authoritarian and the yuppie versus working class movement sympathizers dimensions, showed, however, that the linkage between parties' mean positions on the two dimensions is insensitive to the number of parties in a system. Thus, an extremely crowded system, such as Denmark's, comes very close to a purely uni-dimensional configuration of party competition, whereas a less crowded system, such as Germany's, does so only to a more limited extent. Further, in some countries parties are indeed located close to the center, such as the Italian and Spanish socialists, and it is unlikely that they compete on other dimensions not included in the analysis.[126] Moreover, it would be difficult to state that parties are located at an optimal distance from the center on their competitive dimension. Even in countries where the center area of the competitive space is empty, parties are located at widely varying distances from the neutral position. Even if issue leadership matters, it matters in different ways that can be represented spatially.

Listhaug et al. (1990a) map the competitive spaces of European democracies based on party sympathy ratings of survey respondents, without relying on particular issues or voter attributes. Although their data analysis shows that the center is usually empty,[127] in a number of instances the party systems are all but unidimen-

does convincingly underpin their main point that parties take more extreme positions than their voters supporting the basic proposition of directional theory.

125 This is essentially the strategy of "space squeezing" that Sartori (1976: 338) recommended.

126 A potential counterargument that "centrism" or "governability" itself becomes an issue dimension on which these parties take a radical position begs the question.

127 Without denying the drawbacks of constructing spaces from sympathy ratings that are difficult to interpret in substantive terms, they defend the superiority of this procedure compared to policy-based party spaces because the latter are based on the arbitrary choice of stimuli (Listhaug et al. 1990a: 230). Nevertheless, it is likely that sympathy ratings pick up emotional antagonisms that

sional with a large number of parties close to a single dimension (Denmark 1979, Netherlands 1971, France 1967). Moreover, parties' relative distance from the center varies from country to country and from party to party. Whereas salience theories claim that only *one* party can be accommodated on each (valence) dimension and directional theory posits that only *two* parties fit on a dimension (one in each direction), it is actually often the case that *many* parties compete close to a dominant competitive dimension.

All this is not meant to deny that directional theories of competition deliver insightful and important arguments to *modify* spatial analysis of party strategies. At the same time, they do not warrant to discard the latter. The validity of directional theory is ultimately an empirical question and in the few cases where adequate data are available to compare spatial and directional theories rigorously, the latter appears to have only a slight edge over the former in accounting for voters' choices (cf. Rabinowitz and MacDonald 1989; Listhaug et al. 1990b).[128] In many instances, spatial theories will deliver explanations that are difficult to improve by directional reconstructions. For practical purposes of cross-national comparison and the explanation of parties' strategic positions and electoral payoffs, it may be premature to give up the spatial imagery.

are irrelevant for the competitive positioning of parties yet overstate the actual distance from centrist positions.

128 Shaffer's (1992) test of spatial, directional, and congruence models of voting does not show any superiority of the directional approach.

# 5

## Internal politics in socialist parties: Preference formation, aggregation, and strategic choice

The theory of party competition explored in the previous chapter can explain how party strategies translate into electoral payoffs within a competitive situation. But the theory only insufficiently illuminates the parties' choice of strategy itself. How do social democratic parties choose among the potential goals of oligopolistic competition, short-term vote seeking, and office seeking? And why are their strategies sometimes irrational in light of the feasible courses of action?

In this chapter, I argue that intraparty decision-making processes and coalitions explain the parties' strategic appeal. Because systemic considerations account for the electoral consequences of parties' stances, my dependent variable here is the party strategy itself, not electoral performance. Once parties are viewed as miniature political systems with contending actors, electoral strategies may make sense when they would not if parties were unitary actors. Party organization and internal politics affect a party's effort to seek votes as well as its strategic view of office seeking and coalition building with other parties.[1]

Party organization affects two different attributes of party strategy that are often distinguished insufficiently, the *substantive direction* and the *temporal stability, flexibility,* or even *volatility* of party appeals. Organizational rules directly affect a party's temporal strategic flexibility vis-à-vis new competitive challenges. They determine how quickly "dominant coalitions" inside parties can be displaced by new contenders. The substantive direction of a party's strategic appeal, however, depends more on the distribution of political sentiments among party activists that are by and large shaped by the political setting in which a party operates. Because party activists change organizational rules and because organizational rules bias the effectiveness of intraorganizational group mobilization and coalition building, there is, of course, an indirect interaction effect between the substance and stability of a party's strategic appeal.

The theoretical thrust of my argument is to show that many contemporary social democratic parties inherited organizational structures that reinforce stability, but undercut strategic flexibility. On the one hand, such organizations cut down on

---

1 On vote-seeking, see Aldrich (1983), Aldrich and McGinnis (1989), and Robertson (1976); on coalition theory and party organization, see Laver and Shepsle (1990a,b), Panebianco (1988a: 215), and Pijnenburg (1987).

flexibility by building encompassing, entrenched bureaucratic mass organizations that give little weight to innovative new participants. On the other, they restrict the autonomy of the party leadership by formalizing rules of leadership recruitment, accountability, and strategic choice and thus setting up highly cumbersome patterns of decision making. Particularly in situations where social democratic parties are faced with new competitive challenges, both bureaucratic mass party organization and formal patterns of leadership accountability and decision making impede the choice of new and electorally beneficial strategic stances.

A more flexible organizational form enhances the chance that a party seizes on new strategic opportunities, but it also increases the risk that it is captured by unrepresentative groups choosing strategic appeals that undermine a party's attractiveness to substantial segments of its previous electoral market. Flexibility implies risk. Whether or not a party's organizational form leads to its capture by special interests, however, depends less on the organizational form itself than the political climate and social divisions into which it is immersed.

## 5.1 PLAYERS, RULES, AND DECISIONS: RECONSTRUCTING THE DYNAMICS OF INTRAPARTY POLITICS

The one parsimonious analytical reconstruction of intraparty politics first proposed by Michels and Weber and then elaborated from Duverger to contemporary rational choice theory rests on two basic propositions.[2] First, party leaders are motivated primarily by elected office, whereas rank-and-file activists are driven by ideology or group solidarity. In a unidimensional competitive space with a bell-shaped distribution of the electorate around moderate positions, party activists are therefore "preference outliers" when compared to a party's leaders and voters. Second, organizational form determines the substance of party strategy. The more leaders are in control of their party, the more vote seeking or office seeking will be its strategy.

The two propositions tie a party's organizational form closely to the substantive direction of its strategy. Organizational roles ("leaders" and "followers") determine actors' preferences. Hence, the more power is exercised by the followers, the more radical and ideological will be the party's strategy. In practice, the propositions of this model are rarely supported by data on party strategy. In most instances, either party activists are not preference outliers at all, or both activists and party elites are issue leaders who differ from the voters' more moderate position.[3] It is also incorrect that authoritarian, elite-centered party structures translate into more moderate vote-seeking strategies, as is demonstrated by the demise of European communist parties. Conversely, parties with highly fluid and decentralized structures often are electorally opportunistic.

2 In recent years, the most important original contributions include Gaxie (1977), Robertson (1976), Schlesinger (1984), and Wellhofer and Hennessey (1974). For an older literature on amateurs and professionals in political parties, see Wilson (1962) and Hofstetter (1971). For a more extensive critical discussion of these works, see Kitschelt (1989a,b).

3 For evidence in European parties, see Dalton (1984), Holmberg (1989), and Iversen (1991).

The absence of a clear rift between party activists and leaders is not surprising. Since leaders must want to remain party leaders, no matter what other objectives they have in mind, they will strive to minimize party disunity (Luebbert 1986: 46). Hence, they will express the policies and strategies of the *dominant coalition* of activists inside a party, because even if the organizational division of power gives them autonomy from internal dissenters ("voice"), their party's strength will always be threatened by the exit of activists willing to support other parties if their preferences are ignored. The ideological composition of a party's rank and file cannot be deduced from a party's organizational form, but must be treated as a largely independent determinant of party strategy.[4]

The dominant theory about party activists and leaders also yields an inadequate reconstruction of organizational and strategic change in parties. The theory proposes that parties learn from mistakes and reestablish their competitiveness after electoral defeats by designing "electorally efficient" organizations or they will be eliminated over time. This functional and evolutionary view does not account for the varying *pace* nor the *substantive direction* of "learning" in parties that often leads them to adopt a different trajectory than predicted by a logic of vote seeking or office seeking.[5]

The problem of rationalist theories of party organization, then, is twofold. Such theories do not conceptualize players and rules of intraparty decision making as separate determinants of strategy. Furthermore, they do not distinguish between the *substantive direction* of political competition that emerges from intraparty selection of external competitive strategies and the party's *procedural flexibility* in choosing strategies. These distinctions are the starting point for my own alternative.

### Intraparty players and the substantive direction of competitive strategy

The party activists' preferences are shaped by external political conditions that affect the *recruitment* of new activists and by internal debate. The overall party strategy depends on the relative composition of activists with different preferences. This distribution, together with the rules of decision making, delimits the range of feasible intraparty strategic coalitions.[6]

Party activists subscribe to one of three ideal-typical preference schedules.[7] First, "ideologues" value the pure blueprint of a future society and the internal solidarity benefits of party organization because its arrangements anticipate institutional aspects of the promised "good society." In strategic terms, ideologues tend to be issue leaders and advocate oligopolistic competition. Second, "pragmatists" endorse marginal social reforms providing collective goods that will attract

4 I will qualify this statement below in my discussion of *selective recruitment* into parties.
5 The functionalist view of party organization is represented by Kirchheimer (1966), Epstein (1967) and Wright (1971). For a critique, compare Schonfield (1983).
6 A more detailed analysis of my theoretical model can be found in Kitschelt (1989a: ch. 2).
7 In contrast to simple rational choice accounts, I allow for a heterogeneity and contingency of the rank and file's interests. A similar assumption is made by DeNardo (1985).

new voters to the party, but do not find party organization itself a source of satisfaction. They tend to be vote seeking or office seeking. Finally, whereas ideologues and pragmatists are both primarily concerned with private benefits (organizational satisfaction or office holding) and general collective benefits (moderate or radical social reform), "lobbyists" are preoccupied with selective benefits or "club goods" that accrue to specific external party constituencies. Lobbyists will ally with ideologues or pragmatists depending on the likelihood of either group delivering or defending club goods. If the value of government office is high and the party is in a competitive position, lobbyists are likely to throw in their lot with pragmatists, otherwise they may prefer ideologues.

Even if activists were not ideologically and strategically divided and valued electoral success or office holding across the board, this, by itself, would not produce unity within parties, because in addition to the "hot" *motivational* differences of actors' orientations there are also "cold" *cognitive* predispositions that reinforce the divide between ideologues, lobbyists, and pragmatists.[8] Each group provides a different strategic "road map" of the routes likely to maximize votes or office. For ideologues, a purist appeal to party objectives will eventually convince voters of the party's correctness. Ideologues, therefore, tend to subscribe to a pure directional theory of party competition in which voters' preferences are changed by the activists' appeals. Pragmatists, in contrast, prefer a moderate stance lest the party isolates itself from the values and beliefs of its potential electorate. Pragmatists, then, endorse a spatial theory of competition and assume that voters' positions are fixed, that voters support parties close to their own positions, and that parties, therefore, must adapt their strategies to these circumstances. Lobbyists, finally, claim that catering to the needs of a firm, clearly delineated loyal core electorate is the keystone for success with marginal floating voters. This view is close to the idea of salience theories of competition that parties defend valence issues they "own" in the mind of most voters.[9]

The relative strength of each group and their capacity for coalition building depends on at least three types of external conditions familiar from the preceding chapter: (1) the societal mobilization of the cleavage represented by a party[10]; (2) institutional features of party competition (electoral laws and entry costs, value of government office, etc.); and (3) a party's competitive position (party system format, number of feasible government coalitions, etc.). Conditions (2) and (3) affect the incentives for pivoting and oligopolistic competition directly, condition

---

8  On the distinction between "hot" motivational and "cold" cognitive mechanisms that shape actors' orientations, see Elster (1985: 465–68).

9  The linkage between ideological preferences and a cognitive map of political competition offers only one of many examples showing that social theories are Janus-faced: They are scholarly interpretations of social reality, but also represent secondary codings of social processes that first have been interpreted by the actors themselves.

10  This does not preclude that popular mobilization at time $t_n$ has been prepared by a party's issue leadership at time $t_{n-1}$. No pure sociologism is thus implied by viewing cleavage mobilization as a determinant of party activism.

(1) affects them indirectly. The micro-level mechanisms that translate external conditions into internal party alignments are the *recruitment* of new activists and the *internal socialization and debate* among activists. In this sense, intraparty politics is more "dialogical" than "monological" (cf. Offe and Wiesenthal 1980).

In an environment of high cleavage mobilization, favorable conditions for oligopolistic competition and disincentives for pivoting, the ranks of ideologues are likely to grow disproportionately inside the party. Under inverse conditions, pragmatists will grow in number. The quantity of lobbyists is likely to be a function of past organization-building efforts among core electoral target groups more so than current environmental conditions. Since organization building is most on the minds of ideologues, past political conditions favoring radicalism stimulate political organization building and increase the proportion of lobbyists at a later stage.[11] If at that later stage, however, strategies of office seeking and pivoting are attractive, it is likely lobbyists will throw their lot in with pragmatists, who are then expected to deliver club goods for organized constituencies. Only when parties are politically isolated and ineffective in public policy-making, is it likely that lobbyists will team up with ideologues.

My argument is not simply that party activists adjust their positions to external constraints in a rational fashion, but that *the extent to which certain preferences (oligopolism, vote seeking or office seeking) count in parties' strategic choices is influenced by such constraints.* In other words, external constraints are here treated not as separate from actors' preferences,[12] but as stimuli shaping such orientations.[13] Hence, some systemic configurations will lead to intraparty coalitions that undermine what is usually regarded as the archetype of rational politics, the prevalence of vote or office seeking.

Party activists, of course, choose not only preferences and strategies, but also organizational vehicles for coordinating their political struggle. Because social cleavage mobilization influences the outlook of individual activists and the proportion of different intraparty groupings, at least at a party's inception, ideology has an important impact on the party's basic organizational shape, although political institutions and a party's competitive position may already loom large.[14]

11 In the labor movements, for example, large cohesive union organizations emerged in an environment where labor parties were excluded from political participation or power sharing, such as Austria, Germany, and the Scandinavian countries before World War I.

12 The separation of preferences and constraints is one basic assumption of the rational choice approach. From its perspective, interaction of preferences and constraints, as illustrated by the phenomena of wishful thinking, sour grapes adjustment of aspirations, or cognitive dissonance reduction, indicates a failure of rationality (cf. Elster 1983: ch. 3, 4).

13 This perspective is also taken in Strom's (1990b) analysis of party strategies. It is quite misleading, therefore, to call his approach a "rational choice" theory of party strategy, because preferences are not separated from constraints.

14 Following Panebianco (1988a), neither a purely sociological account of party organization as an expression of values and ideologies nor a purely functionalist approach viewing party organization as a rational response to a party's institutional opportunities and competitive position is sufficient to explain party organization.

Once the party's initial organizational format has been chosen, however, *party organization also becomes an independent variable.* Selective recruitment and socialization of activists under the auspices of existing organizational rules limit the search for and implementation of organizational alternatives. Moreover, the persistence of institutional rules permits only "path-dependent" learning of new political preferences and strategies (March 1978). Party organization thus has a profound influence not only on a party's choice of substantive preferences, but also on the form of strategic innovation (pace, volatility) that parties may undertake when the conditions of political competition change.

### Party organization and the procedural capacity for strategic innovation

I have argued that the substantive distribution of opinions inside a party is primarily influenced by the external political setting and a party's competitive situation. The pace and the fashion of a party's strategic responses to such conditions, however, also depend on its organizational structure, which influences how effectively different groups of activitists can push for their own vision of party strategy and convince other activists to join an emerging intraparty coalition. Strategic choice is thus also a matter of internal structure and political debate. A party's strategic flexibility or inertia is shaped by at least two organizational features, membership entrenchment and leadership autonomy.

Organizationally "entrenched" parties exhibit a cluster of structural properties that includes mass membership, the formalization of internal interactions among members, the functional specialization of roles, and the emergence of a specialized bureaucratic staff. Bureaucratization encourages a standardization of members' involvement and discourages ideological factionalism and intensive debates about a party's policy objectives. For this reason, entrenched mass organizations tend to rely on selective material incentives (patronage) rather than purposive ideological appeals to attract members and activists.

Organizational entrenchment limits the influx of new demands into the party "from below" through recruitment and restricts the party's sensitivity to new inputs from civil society and public opinion in its internal debates. Individuals who seek an outlet for political activism but do not conform to a party's dominant strategy will be discouraged from joining or will leave a party if that party is a bureaucratic mass organization. Bureaucratic mass parties thus experience little "innovation from below."

Innovation from below is likely to be critical for a party's performance in a rapidly changing electoral market place characterized by new political cleavages and dealigned voters. Under these circumstances, a vote- or office-seeking party is well advised to diversify its appeal and represent popular debates and ideological variety within the microcosm of the party. An interesting corollary follows from this argument. Ideological factionalism in political parties is not always a bad thing for the pursuit of electoral objectives, particularly when it is treated as a legitimate and even formally sanctioned mode of intraparty debate that is supplemented by clear-cut internal mechanisms of interest aggregation.[15] Under these circumstances, rational voters can take factionalism into account because it is transparent. In contrast, where ideological factionalism is partially submerged in the organization, confined to informal divisions among "currents," and repressed by the party's organizational rules and external self-representation, rational voters have little information on which to base their support of a party and thus face uncertainty over a party's true strategic orientation that discourages electoral support.

Aside from innovation through popular mobilization from below, parties may also institute "innovation from above," whereby party leaders act autonomously from a party's internal process of interest aggregation. The bureaucratic entrenchment of party organization, taken by itself, neither promotes nor undercuts the autonomy of leadership. Only where leaders themselves are subjected to a plethora of rules of decision making ("accountability") does their strategic flexibility tend to be inhibited.[16] Accountability is enhanced by division of leadership positions into competing offices, internal recruitment filters of party career patterns that instill conformism in aspiring future leaders, and rules requiring leaders to submit their political pronouncements to internal scrutiny and formal votes by representatives of the rank and file. Moreover, leaders may be accountable not only to intraparty constituencies, but also to external, organized clienteles that have power over the appointment or activities of party elites.

Leaders' strategic autonomy becomes particularly important in situations where the transaction cost of internal strategic discussions is exceedingly high because parties have to make stragetic choices quickly. This is typically the case when a party is in a strong competitive position and small changes in its strategic appeal may result in great differences in its success in vote seeking or office seeking.

Cross-tabulating parties' openness to new demands from below (absence of bureaucratic mass party entrenchment) and to new ideas from above (elite autonomy and lack of accountability to internal and external party constituencies) yields four ideal-typical organizational alternatives depicted in Figure 5.1. The theory underlying the four models has the form of an organizational contingency theory. *If* a party's environment has certain properties, *then* particular structural arrangements are appropriate for coping with and controlling sources of environmental uncertainty.[17] Changing voter cleavages call for the displacement of an inert

15 This has also been recently argued by McAllister (1991) in a study of the Australian Labor Party and Maor (1992) in an analysis of coalition bargaining. More generally, Lipset, Trow, and Coleman (1956) showed political associations divided by internal competition can achieve effectiveness.

16 Many contingency theories of formal organization therefore have found an inverse relationship between bureaucracy and leadership centralization.

17 In principle, this model could be fleshed out in terms of an application of transaction cost institutional economics (Williamson 1985) to political organization. The basic idea is that efficient organizations develop the "requisite variety" to respond to sources of uncertainty in their environment. This argument was anticipated by contributions to organization theory such as those of Thompson (1967) and Perrow (1986).

bureaucratic mass organization and channels for new citizens' interests to express themselves inside parties from the bottom up. High party competitiveness in the electoral arena, indicated by strong incentives for pivoting strategies, gives an advantage to parties where the elites are autonomous and can rapidly adjust their appeal to the strategic moves of their competitors.

Loosely coupled networks of grassroots organizations operating under an autonomous central leadership (cell 1), a system of semiautonomous "clubs" under a centralized leadership, maximize a party's responsiveness to changing environmental conditions. Flexibility is not impaired by a paralyzing stand-off between leaders and followers, because each organizational level is able to operate in its own way. Rank-and-file mobilization can set new issues on the agenda. Party leaders are confronted with new demands, but are not forced to match them one by one in their own strategic appeals. This organizational configuration is likely to be most appropriate for social democratic parties that face a high mobilization of left-libertarian and liberal market challenges and also have the opportunity to capture the pivot in the space of party competition. Such parties must free themselves from the constraints of the old social democratic "culture" of mass party organization and responsible leadership. To remain politically successful, such parties must cope with the task of converting solidary mass organizations into stratified internal conflict systems incorporating heterogeneous constituencies, but permitting party leaders to manage the internal plurality of political voices.[18]

In contrast to clubs under centralized leadership, "decentralized clubs" (cell 3) confer innovative capabilities only on the rank and file, while the leadership is constrained by rules of accountability to the basic units. Under these circumstances, the party generates strategic volatility through new inputs "from below," that may internally pluralize its political process, but gives leaders little opportunity to express a unified stance in interparty competition. For social democratic parties, this model may work best, where new citizens' preferences challenge conventional ideas, but where parties are in a weak competitive position and therefore can afford ambiguity about their stances at the leadership level without losing critical resources in the struggle for executive power.

Where only leaders to the exclusion of the rank and file have strategic capabilities, the organizational configuration resembles a Leninist cadre party. It has a small, tightly knit network of political leaders at the helm and, beneath them, a vast transmission belt of party-subordinated and incorporated mass organizations (cell 2). Innovative capacity is limited to the top and guarantees that parties operate as corporate actors. This model may be efficient as long as a socialist party can rely on a homogeneous and stable electoral following that does not generate new demands. Autonomous leaders can then devote their full attention to the struggle for executive power either by trying to capture the pivot of the party system in

---

18 This model is reminiscent of Eldersveld's (1964) view of American party organization as "stratarchal," comprised of relatively autonomous clubs and elites at different hierarchical levels.

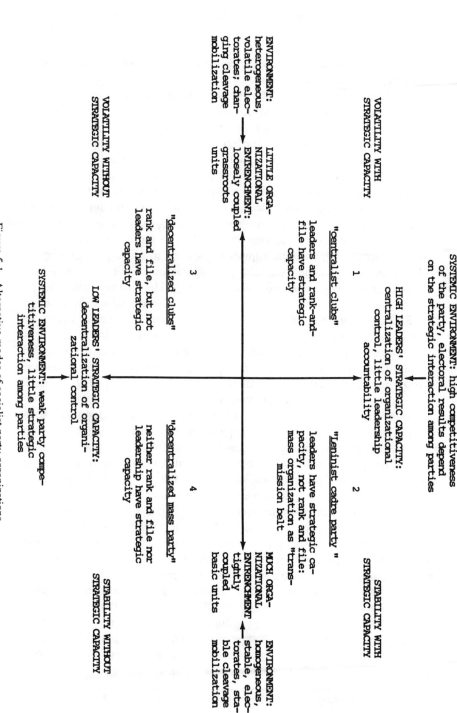

Figure 5.1. Alternative modes of socialist party organizations

electoral competition or – in the Leninist version – by trying to bring about and act upon a revolutionary situation.[19]

In the final configuration, the rank-and-file party organization has no strategic capacity, but neither has the leadership (cell 4). This situation prevails in decentralized mass parties with a large bureaucratic apparatus and strict rules of leadership accountability. The strategic inertia of such parties is not necessarily counterproductive in electoral terms, as long as electoral demands remain stable and a party is insufficiently competitive to capture the pivot of the electoral system. Under such circumstances, parties perform well if they encapsulate their constituencies with bureaucratic mass organizations (cf. Duverger 1954; Wellhofer 1979). Historically, many communist, social democratic, and Christian Democratic parties thrived on such organizational models until the 1970s.

Organizational contingency theory does not necessarily assume that parties must adjust to their environment. As strategies of encapsulation show, parties sometimes actively shape their environment to fit their internal structure. The theory, therefore, is about the correspondence between systemic environment and party organization, *not* about the origins and the direction of the adjustment process. An organizational contingency theory of strategic choice in parties yields a concise hypothesis about the circumstances under which parties are likely to behave in nonrational ways, although it cannot determine in which direction parties will diverge from the appropriate strategies. If there is a mismatch between systemic contingencies and organizational arrangements, parties tend to adopt electorally nonrational stances in terms of vote seeking, office seeking, and oligopolistic competition.

This correspondence hypothesis is relevant not only for cross-sectional comparison, but also for understanding the longitudinal process of strategic change inside parties. Theories of bounded rationality stipulate that organizations will follow routine operations as long as their performance is not deeply disturbed (March and Simon 1958). Moreover, organizational routines will prevent strategic adjustments the greater the sunk costs of past investments into organizational structure. In political parties, the existence of bureaucratic mass organizations and the application of elaborate rules of leadership accountability are typical sunk costs. Thus, a party may not instantly modify its strategy in light of changing cleavage mobilization or the party's competitive position. Even if the party suffers electoral defeat or loses executive office, the key intervening variable is a party's organizational structure that facilitates or impedes strategic flexibility. Decentralized mass parties may be slow in responding even to severe defeats. Conversely, centralized clubs potentially overreact even to mild defeats and engage in wild swings of strategy because their sunk costs in party organization are modest.

The recruitment of new members and electoral defeat are the mechanisms that may lead to change in a party's organization and strategic flexibility. But both

19 For an analysis of Leninist party doctrine from a contingency theory perspective, see Kitschelt and Wiesenthal (1979).

mechanisms work best in parties with a relatively small membership and un-bureaucratic structures. In contrast, bureaucratic mass parties may not attract innovators, but lower class militants who seek small status gains that reinforce more authoritarian and rigidly institutionalized organization (Panebianco 1988a: 32, 277). Also the impact of electoral defeat that often triggers a decline in party membership (Bartolini 1983a: 194) is mediated by party organization. At one extreme, defeat and exodus of activists may lower a mass party's strategic mobility to the vanishing point. At the other extreme, if membership is small and competition between intraparty groups is close, a party may become ripe for takeover by new entrants and a new challenging coalition, as the ranks of a party's core coalition thin out.

Where recruitment or electoral defeat triggers a profound change of a party's dominant coalition, its first target is usually the existing institutional structure that supported the dislodged leadership. In a process of "organizational learning," the new coalition will modify a party's internal decision rules to consolidate its own power and enable the party to pursue new strategies. Most likely, these changes do not amount to a wholesale replacement of existing arrangements, but an incremental adjustment that blends existing routines with new operating procedures.[20] In this sense, organizational structures in parties are both independent variables shaping a party's internal politics, as well as dependent variables affecting entry and exit of activists, electoral defeat, and changing intraparty coalitions.

To sum up, by spelling out the complex interaction between systemic contingencies, organizational structures, and properties of party strategy (flexibility, direction of competition), my approach moves away from misleading models that stipulate an immutable contrast between the preferences of party leaders and followers and try to identify a single "electorally efficient" form of party organization (e.g., Kirchheimer 1966; Wright 1971). Instead, organizational structures and strategic choices must be placed within a framework of variable systemic conditions that include cleavage mobilization and the competitive position of individual parties. These systemic conditions affect the actors' rational choice of strategies in light of preconceived preferences, but also the nature of the preferences themselves. Party organization is a critical intervening variable that is shaped by intraparty coalitions of ideologues, lobbyists, and pragmatists. Conversely, existing party organization affects the mechanisms of recruitment and internal socialization.

The overall theoretical argument is condensed in Figure 5.2. As with all visual representation, the figure does not fully capture the dynamic interaction among components of the model over time. I will now apply the most critical part of the model to the choice of strategic positions in European left parties: Can organizational features explain the socialists' pathways of strategic choice? More specifically, can discrepancies between the systemic environment of party action, as detailed in Figure 5.1, and the mode of socialist party organization (entrenchment,

---

20 On the logic of organizational change, compare Panebianco (1988a: 243–4).

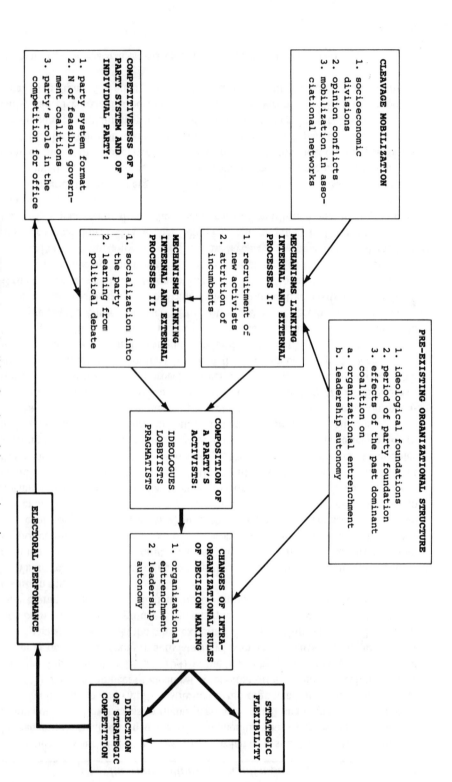

Figure 5.2. The internal politics of parties and the systemic environment

leadership autonomy) account for socialist strategic stances in the 1980s that are nonrational when viewed from the systemic perspective of party competition?

## 5.2 SOCIAL DEMOCRATIC PARTY ORGANIZATION AND STRATEGIC CHOICE

If the general argument I have just outlined is correct, social democratic parties which have chosen electorally rational strategies in the 1980s – especially the parties in Belgium, France, Italy, the Netherlands, and Spain – should evidence a better match between organizational features and systemic contingencies than do socialist parties whose strategic stance in at least certain periods of the 1980s is difficult to account for by the rational choice of short-term vote-seeking, office-seeking, or oligopolistic strategies. This is the case primarily for the Austrian, British, German, and Swedish social democrats.

The critical task, then, is to construct measures of organizational entrenchment and leadership autonomy in left parties that can be related to the political environment characterized by political cleavage mobilization and a party's competitiveness in the fashion proposed in Figure 5.1. My initial analysis adopts a comparative-static design that disregards dynamic organizational change in each party over time. Because measures of party organization tend to be rather crude, they may also overstate contrasts among left party organization. I have nevertheless chosen this technique of comparison to further the clarity of my explanation. The case studies presented later in this chapter add qualifications and consider dynamic processes in socialist party organization that affect their strategic capacity over the course of the past two decades.

I will not discuss the internal groups and currents within socialist parties in detail. There is little doubt that internal conflicts and factionalism in left parties intensified when the left-libertarian cleavage became increasingly relevant in party systems and affected the internal organization of socialist parties starting in the late 1960s (cf. Hine 1986: 263). My theory does not try to reconstruct the development of intraparty politics in terms of concrete factions and currents in socialist parties, but employs abstract clusters of cognitive and motivational orientations – ideologues, lobbyists, pragmatists – to characterize a party's internal balance of power. Yet in the case of socialist parties, it is not difficult to relate these analytical concepts to actual political groups. Ideologues in most contemporary socialist parties are no longer orthodox Marxist intellectuals and workers, but left-libertarians who support ecology, peace, or feminist movements, place themselves on the left, hold secular and antiauthoritarian views, and work in client-interactive or symbol-producing occupations.[21] These ideologues are pitted against a group of pragmatists that consists of market-liberal technocrats. Sometimes technocrats emerge from the same stratum as left-libertarians, but more often they are rooted in

---

21 For evidence that traditional Leftists have increasingly given way to a new left-libertarianism in socialist parties, see Schmitt (1987: esp. ch. 3) on political opinions within the German social democracy and Whiteley (1983: 42, and ch. 3) on the British Labour Party.

the technical-administrative professions (law, business). Whereas radicals vigorously respond to the left-libertarian challenge, technocrats are more eager to address the challenge of market efficiency and productivity and wish the party to compete for the voters of the nonsocialist parties.

The generic group I have called lobbyists can most readily be identified with the socialist parties' unionized blue collar clientele and its intraparty spokespersons, who are usually functionaries and leaders of labor unions. These "traditionalists" defend the welfare state and its core institutions that protect workers from the uncertainties of the marketplace. Traditionalists are not responsive either to left-libertarian or to market-liberal challenges. As a consequence, they ally themselves with one or the other group case by case, depending on the payoffs of coalitions and strategies for their core clientele. In the final section of this chapter, I will demonstrate how the flow of individuals belonging to different categories of activists in and out of socialist parties has influenced their organization and strategic stances.

The three groups of activists advocate structures of party organization that cohere with their political preferences and convictions. The traditionalists seek to preserve bureaucratized mass parties with considerable leadership accountability to the rank and file. This model has sometimes been called "social democratic centralism" as opposed to the Leninist "democratic centralism" with greater leadership autonomy. Left-libertarians, in contrast, often wish to abandon the inflexible mass party with local branch organizations in favor of a more fluid structure of "clubs" organized around political issues and the concerns of specific target groups within the party membership. These mobilized groups, in turn, should control party leadership and legislative groups by a variety of means, including intraparty primaries and referenda. Pragmatists with a technocratic outlook, finally, wish to increase the autonomy of the party's legislative representatives from party executive and other intraorganizational bodies of oversight and to devolve more authority over the party's policy program and public self-presentation to staffs of hired policy experts who are often unaffiliated with the party. They also see traditional mass organization as a political obstacle to their strategy.

The organizational vision advocated by different intraparty groups does not necessarily benefit that group if implemented. Left-libertarians in the Dutch PvdA, for example, ran into the dilemma that they had installed a decentralized, activist-controlled framework party organization making internal interest aggregation so volatile that it undermined the left-libertarians' own efforts to stabilize their hegemony and build an alternative ruling coalition (cf. Boivin, Hazelhoff, Middel, and Molenaar 1978: 53).[22] Conversely, the example of Southern European communist parties in the 1980s shows that a firmly centralized party with considerable

---

22 Similarly, the very informal decision-making structures that were advocated by "fundamentalists" in the German Greens prevented them from gaining a firm grip on the party organization. Thus they were easily swept from power when the party's improving competitive situation led to an influx of pragmatic activists. Cf. Kitschelt (1989a: ch. 7–9).

leadership autonomy does not necessarily favor pragmatic electoralist stances.[23] Because party organization is hard to change and generates unintended consequences, it is not simply the product of internal group interests. Instead, it has its own dynamic and consequences for the emergence of party coalitions and strategies. I will therefore now specify aspects of socialist party structure that affect their ability to cope with changing electoral demands and patterns of party competition.

### Organizational entrenchment in socialist parties

"Entrenched" parties make it difficult for small groups of new entrants and small shifts in the convictions of existing participants to bring about significant changes in the party's strategic orientation. As a rule, the sheer size of a party's organization, the complexity of its routines and its division of labor, the availability of patronage incentives, and the relationship among political currents affects its strategic volatility or stability. Small parties with little formal bureaucratic apparatus, internal ideological pluralization, and little control of patronage in civil service or the quasi-public sector are strategically most flexible and permit small groups of rank-and-file activists to exercise considerable influence over strategic questions. In contrast, large party organizations with a sizable staff of middle-level functionaries, little factional division and extensive control over patronage are most difficult to affect by the turnover of activists or internal debates. Overall, tightly coupled organizational structures confer little power on individual members or small groups to alter a party's strategic course. I will represent the dimension of *organizational entrenchment* by four indicators each of which may assume a low (0.0), a medium (0.5), or a high (1.0) value. The values for each party will be justified in the case studies presented in section 5.3.

*A party's member/voter ratio.* The member/voter ratio measures the "encapsulation" of a party's electorate and thus the relative size of a party vis-à-vis its electoral constituency. I have given high values to parties where the member/voter ratio exceeds 20% (Austria, Sweden) and intermediate values where it is at least 5% (Belgium, Italy, West Germany). Parties with less enrollment approximate the type of "framework party" with a modest membership (Britain, France, Netherlands, Spain). Member/voter ratios, of course, are not a direct measure of the number of internal party activists or of turnover rates, the really crucial actors who determine the strategic influence of new groups joining and old ones leaving a party. Comparable figures on membership turnover are all but impossible to obtain and estimates of levels of intraparty activism are sufficiently similar to justify using member/voter ratios as a reasonable approximation of the actual size of a

---

23 Thus Fedele (1987: 62–5) argues that the functionaries and the leadership of the PCI were a greater stumbling bloc to a rapid strategic adjustment of the Italian communists in the 1980s than the rank and file, particularly in the big cities.

party's activist core. As a rule, no more than 10–20% of a socialist party's members regularly participate in its meetings and debates.

*The availability of patronage.*   Patronage, primarily in the form of party-dependent civil service or nationalized industry appointments and promotions, is a key material incentive for party entry and is widely available in Austria, Belgium, and Italy. Patronage not only inflates the membership of a party, but also makes the members impervious to citizens' challenges of patronage systems, whether they are pushed by left-libertarians or populist free marketeers. Patronage has an inherently conservative character that favors a depoliticized, reactive mode of strategic choice in which beneficiaries of the system oppose any move to rock the boat (Müller 1989: 346). While patronage has the greatest impact in the Austrian, Belgian, and Italian parties, it is also an incentive of intermediate importance for socialist parties in France, the Netherlands, Spain, and West Germany, particularly with respect to the appointment of state officials. Only in Britain and Sweden does patronage appear to play a marginal role for the ability of political parties to attract members.

*The size of the party's middle-level apparatus.*   The larger the number of part-time or full-time functionaries in a party, situated in district, regional, or national party offices, the more decisions will be prepared and influenced by employees who establish routines and standard operating procedures. Even though function-aries are not the dominant group in any socialist party, the relative size of the administrative apparatus is a factor stabilizing strategic choice. Reliable data on the effective number of party functionaries, including civil servants who may carry out party work in practice, and reliable data on party finance, including public subsidies, are difficult to obtain and to compare across countries. Nevertheless, available data suggests that Austria, Belgium, Italy, Sweden, and West Germany have relatively strong party apparatuses or public funding or both (Nassmacher 1987, 1989). The Spanish party holds an intermediate position on this continuum, while the British, French, and Dutch socialists have very small administrative staffs and limited funds.

*Ideological integration or pluralization.*   Turnover of party activists and electoral defeats have a greater impact on changes of party strategy, if the party has been open to ideological pluralism already at an earlier point of time. Parties without pronounced wings, but with broad intellectual uniformity, are least likely to succumb to new challenges, one reason why strategic inertia is likely to be high in Austria, Belgium, and Sweden. Strategic continuity or fluidity within a narrow band is also moderately high in pluralist parties with numerous countervailing factions, because each group has only limited bargaining clout in altering a party's overall appeal, a situation that characterizes the German SPD throughout much of the 1980s. The French, Italian, and Spanish parties moved from a situation of open pluralist competition in the 1970s to that of an imbalance between a hegemonic faction and a scattering of minority groups in the 1980s. Also here, it is difficult to displace an existing strategy. Strategic flexibility tends to be greatest in sharply polarized parties in which two or three groups are pitted against each other in a zero-sum game for strategic control. In the 1970s and 1980s this situation prevailed in the British and, to a lesser extent, the Dutch left parties.

Overall, entrenched socialist mass party organizations existed during the 1980s in Austria, Belgium, Italy, and Sweden (Table 5.1). Also the French and Italian communist parties approximated the model of mass organizations. West Germany and Spain had moderately entrenched socialist party organizations, whereas the British, French, and Dutch socialists had the least entrenched small framework parties.

### Leadership accountability or autonomy in socialist parties

The second dimension of party organization that affects strategic volatility, the autonomy or accountability of the top leadership, can also be disaggregated into four indicators of party structure, each of which receives a low, medium, or high value for each party. Recruitment of candidates for electoral office, control of conference schedules, domination of the legislative leadership over the party executive and the party's distance to labor unions provide the critical variables to gauge leadership autonomy.

*Central control of recruitment for national electoral office.*     Based on comparative studies of political recruitment (e.g., Gallagher and Marsh 1988), I infer a curvilinear relationship between local control of nominations and strategic flexibility. Central control of recruitment permits leaders to exercise some strategic autonomy, for example, by nominating party "outsiders" to important offices who would otherwise not survive a selection process controlled by the rank and file. With the possible exception of Spain, elite control over the recruitment of socialist parliamentarians is nowhere very pronounced, yet central party boards clearly have some influence over the process in Belgium, France, Italy, and Germany. Local control of nominations for electoral office can imply *either* great strategic stability *or* high flexibility, depending upon the nature of grassroots organization. In mass parties, grassroots control of nominations usually reinforces structural inertia and the dominance of traditionalists, a situation prevalent in Austria and Sweden. In framework parties, such as the British and Dutch labor parties, local control can produce innovative impulses as a consequence of changing rank-and-file coalitions that put either radicals or technocrats in charge. In these instances, leadership autonomy is obviously low.

*Control of party conferences.*     Conferences can be one important arena in which to constrain the strategic choices open to party elites. For this reason, autonomous elites will want (1) to schedule conferences infrequently, (2) to time them, if unavoidable, close to elections because this may cut down on the delegat s'

Table 5.1. *Organizational entrenchment in socialist parties*

| | (1) Member/ voter ratios | (2) Importance of patronage in government | (3) Size of the party apparatus | (4) Ideological intergration or diversity | (1)–(4) Summary index |
|---|---|---|---|---|---|
| Austria | 1.0 | 1.0 | 1.0 | 1.0 | 4.0 |
| Belgium | 0.5 | 1.0 | 1.0 | 1.0 | 3.5 |
| Britain | 0.0 | 0.0 | 0.0 | 0.0 | 0.0 |
| France | 0.0 | 0.5 | 0.0 | 0.5 | 1.0 |
| Germany | 0.5 | 0.5 | 1.0 | 0.5 | 2.5 |
| Italy | 0.5 | 1.0 | 1.0 | 0.5 | 3.0 |
| Netherlands | 0.0 | 0.5 | 0.0 | 0.0 | 0.5 |
| Spain | 0.0 | 0.5 | 0.5 | 0.5 | 1.5 |
| Sweden | 1.0 | 0.0 | 1.0 | 1.0 | 3.0 |

*Scoring:*
Column (1): Member/voter ratio >20% = 1.0; m/v >5% = 0.5; m/v <5% = 0.0.
Column (2): Judgmental assessment, see discussion and references in section 5.3 of this chapter.
Column (3): Judgmental assessment, based on extent of public financing (cf. Nassmacher 1989), size of professional party staffs, probability of civil servants working on party business; large apparatus = 1.0.
Column (4): Judgmental assessment – absence of factional conflicts = 1.0; pluralist factionalism or one dominant group = 0.5; polarization between alternative factions = 0.0.

willingness to criticize the leadership, and (3) to control the agenda and the motions by a powerful conference committee framing the delegates' choices in detail. Although in-depth comparative studies are lacking, the centralized management of national party conferences appears to have been perfected in Austria, Italy, Spain, and Sweden. Less centralized control is exercised in Belgium, France, and West Germany. In the 1980s, the greatest grassroots leverage over conference proceedings prevailed in Britain and the Netherlands.

*The domination of the parliamentary leadership over the party executive.* A party's legislative leadership is usually in an advantageous position to develop an integrated strategy that exploits a party's bargaining position in the legislature and its competitiveness in the electoral arena. In contrast, party executives tend to be more accountable to intraparty currents. A party's legislative leadership is most powerful when it is identical with the executive leadership. A factor contributing to the further centralization of leadership is the absence of strong regional party federations equipped with independently elected elites who can challenge the national leadership. A centralist fusion of intraparty leadership, under the dominance of the party in legislature and government, prevails in France, Italy, Spain, and Sweden. Austria, Belgium, and Germany have essential elements of this pattern as well, but in each case there are critical countervailing forces (strong federations, some separation of party executive and leadership in electoral or government office). The separation of party executive and legislative leadership is most pronounced in Britain and the Netherlands.

*Party autonomy from the labor unions.*  Strong linkages to labor unions privilege traditionalists in the party leadership who are unwilling to take on *either* the challenge of market efficiency *or* the challenge of left-libertarian politics. There are at least three structural configurations in union–socialist party linkages. At one extreme, labor unions dominate the party elite by controlling key appointments and placing their own leadership in important executive and legislative party offices. This situation was most closely approximated by the Austrian and British Left in the 1970s and well into the 1980s. In a second type, there is close communication between the major union federation and the socialist party, yet both are intent on some distance both in terms of overlapping leaderships as well as strategic maneuverability. This configuration can be encountered in Belgium, Sweden, and West Germany, although in each case the union–party linkages exhibit unique features. Finally, there are socialist parties which have all but cut their formal organizational linkages to the labor movement and permit comparatively little personnel overlap at the level of the party elite. This arrangement prevails in France, Italy, and Spain, with the Netherlands constituting a case located between this and the intermediate pattern of party-union linkage.

In the 1980s, socialist parties with a strong autonomous leadership existed in France, Italy, and Spain, as the summary index of leadership autonomy in Table 5.2 shows. Socialist party elites reached intermediate levels of autonomy in Belgium, Sweden, West Germany, and, at the lower bound of this middle group, in Austria. Leadership autonomy was highly constrained in Britain and the Netherlands during that period. Turning to communist parties that follow the Leninist model of democratic centralism, they have obviously preserved strong leadership control of the rank and file, though challenges from below and internal divisions at the top have increased in the 1980s.

### The "match" between organizational forms and leadership autonomy

If each socialist party's values on the composite indices of organizational entrenchment and leadership autonomy are represented in a two-dimensional space, three clusters emerge (Figure 5.3). The first cluster encompasses conventional social democratic mass party organizations with comparatively high entrenchment, but only intermediate leadership autonomy. A second cluster involves Mediterranean socialist cadre parties with high leadership autonomy ("centralized clubs"). Finally, the British and Dutch labor parties constitute a residual category of "decentralized clubs" that have low leadership autonomy and organizational entrenchment. Outside these three clusters I provide a generic location for commu-

Table 5.2. *Leadership autonomy in socialist parties*

|  | (1)<br>Central<br>control of<br>leadership<br>recruitment | (2)<br>Leadership<br>control of<br>party<br>conferences | (3)<br>Integration<br>of party<br>executives<br>and<br>legislatures | (4)<br>Looseness<br>of the<br>linkage<br>between<br>party union<br>leadership | (1)–(4)<br>Summary<br>index |
|---|---|---|---|---|---|
| Austria | 0.0 | 1.0 | 0.5 | 0.0 | 1.5 |
| Belgium | 0.5 | 0.5 | 0.5 | 0.5 | 2.0 |
| Britain | 0.0 | 0.0 | 0.0 | 0.0 | 0.0 |
| France | 0.5 | 0.5 | 1.0 | 1.0 | 3.0 |
| Germany | 0.5 | 0.5 | 0.5 | 0.5 | 2.0 |
| Italy | 0.5 | 1.0 | 1.0 | 1.0 | 3.5 |
| Netherlands | 0.0 | 0.0 | 0.0 | 0.5 | 0.5 |
| Spain | 0.5 | 1.0 | 1.0 | 1.0 | 3.5 |
| Sweden | 0.0 | 1.0 | 1.0 | 0.5 | 2.5 |

*Scoring:*Column (1): Judgmental data (cf. Gallagher and March 1988): local control in an otherwise highly entrenched party = 1.0; mix of local and central control = 0.5; local control in another, nonentrenched party = 0.0.
Column (2)–(4): Judgmental data, see description in sections 5.2 and 5.3 of this chapter.

nist mass parties in Western Europe. They are about equidistant from the midpoints of the clusters around conventional socialist party organization and the Mediterranean centralized organizations.

The robustness of this assessment can be tested by a second analysis of party organization that is derived from Laver and Hunt's (1992) expert survey of socialist party structure. Country specialists were asked to assess the power of the leadership and of the rank and file over party's policy choices on a scale ranging from 0 to 20.[24] To compare relative power relations across countries, I have calculated a mean "power value" for party leaders (15.80) and activists (9.33) in all countries. The organizational structure of each socialist party can then be represented as the divergence of leaders' and followers' power from the overall mean, with positive values indicating greater than average power for a group and negative values lesser power (Figure 5.4).

The vertical axis in Figure 5.4, power of the party leadership, is directly comparable to Figure 5.3, and the vertical rank ordering of the parties is similar, with the exceptions of the French and the German social democrats. Italian and Spanish socialists concentrate the most power in the leadership, whereas there is little leadership autonomy in Britain and the Netherlands. The remaining countries are in the intermediate range. Also in Figure 5.3, France registers lowest on

24 Experts also assessed the relative power of party leaders and followers over the choice of government coalition. The results reveal a similar cross-national pattern as the assessments of power over policy choices.

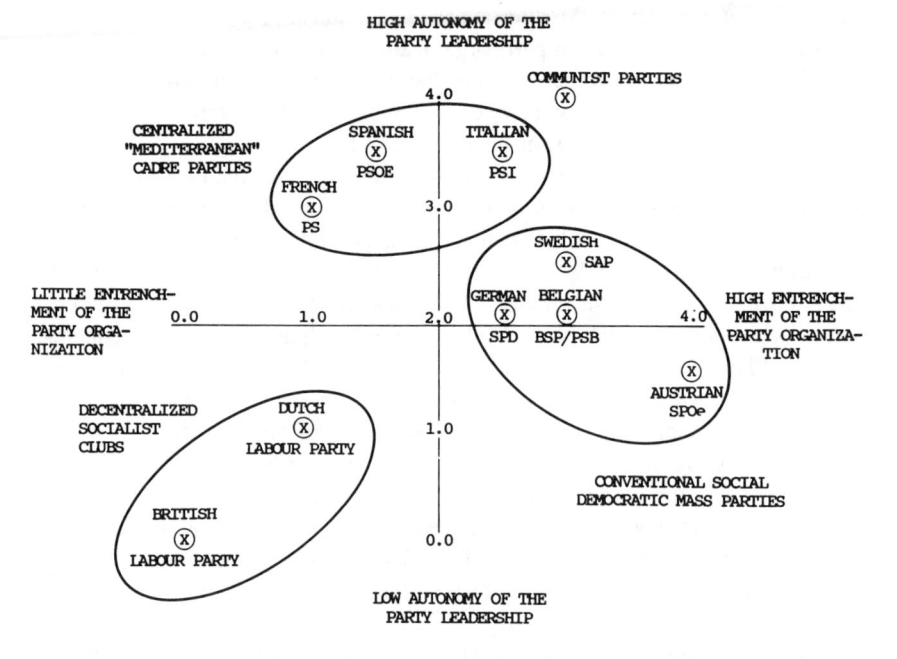

Figure 5.3. The organizational structure of left parties in comparative perspective

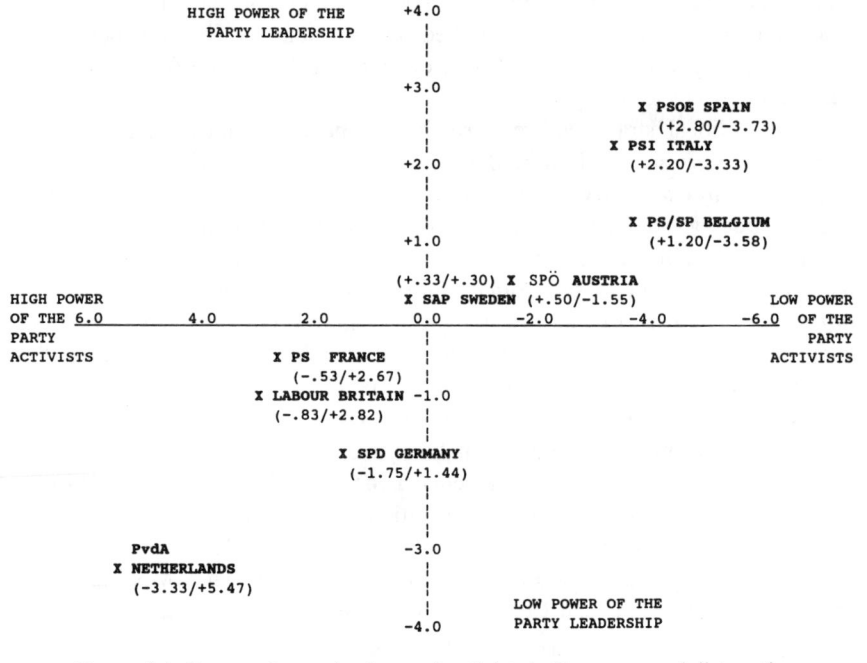

Figure 5.4. Power of party leaders and activists in European socialist parties

leadership autonomy in the Mediterranean cluster and slips even further in Figure 5.4. Among conventional mass party organizations, rank orders differ slightly with Austria much closer to Sweden's levels than in Figure 5.3, a judgment that may result from changes in Austrian party organization in the late 1980s. German party elite autonomy is distinctly lower than in Figure 5.3.

The horizontal axis in Figure 5.4 measures the power of the rank and file, not organizational entrenchment as in Figure 5.3. Nevertheless, there is some resemblance of rank orderings between power and entrenchment measures as well. Generally, in parties with less entrenchment, rank-and-file activists have more power (Britain, Netherlands, France, Germany), whereas they have less power in parties with more entrenchment (Austria, Belgium, Italy).[25] As a consequence, Laver and Hunt's expert judgments reproduce two of the three clusters in Figure 5.3 quite well (decentralized socialist clubs, conventional social democratic mass organization), yet bisect the centralized Mediterranean cadre parties.

Returning to Figure 5.3, within each cluster, in the 1980s there was a fairly tight linkage between the parties' organizational structure and strategic choice. The Dutch and British labor parties with decentralized club organization were most willing to engage in radical policies of a left-libertarian or a traditional socialist kind. Social democratic parties with conventional mass organization proved to be least able to adopt strategies going beyond left social and economic policies defending the status quo of the Keynesian welfare state. The Mediterranean centralized club parties, finally, dropped much of the conventional socialist agenda and were most willing to tackle the challenge of market efficiency. The Mediterranean communist parties with entrenched organizations, but autonomous elites, declined as important segments of their elites resisted rank-and-file pressures to stake out new electoral appeals.

While political strategies are fairly homogeneous within each cluster, the *electoral payoffs* are much more diverse. *This is so because the systemic challenges faced by each party within each cluster vary.* Because the electoral success of party strategy and organizational form depends on systemic contingencies, such as cleavage mobilization and the socialists' capacity to capture the pivot of the party system, one and the same organizational form may be associated with very different electoral consequences. Table 5.3 therefore compares environmental challenges to the organizational structures of socialist parties and assesses the "match" between environment and intraparty politics.

Environmental challenges for social democratic parties are left-libertarian cleavage mobilization, electoral competitiveness, and, associated with the latter, the intensity of the liberal market challenge in the political arena. The measure of a country's left-libertarian cleavage mobilization is derived from the pooled factor analysis of voter positions reported in Chapter 4 (Table 4.3). Values for Austria and Sweden are approximated, based on more limited survey evidence. Mobilization is high in the Netherlands and Germany, intermediate in Spain and Sweden, and

---

25 Discrepancies between the two measures surface especially in the case of Spain and – to a lesser extent – Sweden.

Table 5.3. *The match between systemic challenges and organizational structure*

| | Environmental challenges | | Organizational form | | |
| --- | --- | --- | --- | --- | --- |
| | Left-libertarian cleavage mobilization | Opportunities for conquering the pivot of the party system | Mass level entrenchment | Leadership autonomy | Strategic match between organization and systemic context |
| **Close match between environment and organization** | | | | | |
| Belgium (BSP/PSB) | Weak | Weak | High | Medium | Adequate |
| France (PS) | Weak | Strong | Low | High | Adequate |
| Italy (PSI) | Weak | Weak | Medium | High | Adequate |
| Netherlands (PvdA) | Strong | Weak | Low | Low | Adequate |
| Spain (PSOE) | Medium | Strong | Low | High | Adequate |
| **Mismatch between environment and organization** | | | | | |
| Austria (SPÖe) | Weak | Strong | High | Medium | Deficient in leadership autonomy |
| Britain (Labour) | Weak | Strong | Low | Low | Deficient in leadership autonomy |
| Germany (SPD) | Strong | Strong | High | Medium | Too much entrenchment, too little leadership autonomy |
| Sweden (SAP) | Medium | Strong | High | Medium | Too much entrenchment, too little leadership autonomy |

*Scoring:* For the environmental challenges, see Tables 4.4 to 4.6. For the organizational properties of socialist parties, compare Tables 5.1 and 5.2.

more muted in the remaining countries. If party organizations match their environment, parties placed in an environment with high left-libertarian mobilization should display fewer mass bureaucratic structures.

The second environmental condition, the socialists' competitiveness in the party system, that is, their opportunities for pivoting and office seeking – has also been operationally defined in Chapter 4. It is strong where a socialist party in a multiparty system, together with all other parties to its libertarian left, comes close to 50% of the total vote or where social democrats compete in a two- or three-party system for the median voter. According to this rationale, socialists in Belgium, Italy, and the Netherlands were in a weak competitive position in the 1980s, but in a strong competitive position everywhere else.

Where socialists were in a strong competitive position in the 1980s, they also tended to confront an intense challenge of market efficiency articulated by a consolidated bourgeois party (bloc) that was not internally divided by religious, urban versus rural, or ethnic divisions.[26] A unified bourgeois bloc can devote more attention to economic issues and will try to capture the pivot of the party system in the competition with social democrats based on economic policy appeals. If party organizations match their competitive environment, one would expect more autonomous party elites where the social democrats' competitiveness is high and liberal challenges of market efficiency are intense.

Inspecting Table 5.3 reveals that Belgium, France, the Netherlands, and Spain display a close match between organizational forms and environmental challenges. These are also the countries in which socialist parties performed well or at least held on to their share of the electoral market in the 1980s. The successful organizational forms and strategies, however, differ from party to party. In Belgium, even an entrenched, decentralized bureaucratic mass party could perform well electorally, because it was placed in an environment with little left-libertarian mobilization and socialist competitiveness. Conversely, in Spain, intermediate left-libertarian mobilization and intense competition mandated a centralized club organization. The configuration is similar in the case of the French socialists. In the Netherlands, the Labor Party did not operate in a highly competitive environment and therefore could perform relatively well with little leadership autonomy, but its electoral success was based on its fluid organizational form that allowed the party to incorporate left-libertarian movement supporters in a highly mobilized political climate. A fairly good match between organizational form and political environment is also evidenced by Italy, where weak left-libertarian mobilization did not compel the party to abandon organizational entrenchment, but where leadership capabilities were well developed to cope with a situation in which the party enjoyed little competitiveness.[27]

---

26 The only exception is Sweden, where the SAP successfully competed for the pivot of the party system but faced a divided bourgeois opposition unable to mount a strong free market challenge at least until 1988.

27 Nevertheless, Craxi's PSI has of course taken advantage of electoral changes and movements of its competitors. At the same time, its electoral gain is much less pronounced than that of parties

For the remaining four parties, there is a serious mismatch between environmental challenges and organizational form. These parties saw their market share erode in the 1980s. In Austria, muted left-libertarian mobilization limited the stress to which the party's mass organization was exposed, but leadership autonomy clearly fell short of what would have been desirable for the party to engage fully in short-term vote maximization and pivoting. The same configuration of challenges with the opposite organizational structure generated mismatches for the British Labour party. Here organizational entrenchment was much weaker than called for and leadership autonomy was too constrained to take advantage of strategic opportunities. This predisposed the party to highly volatile strategy in response to pressure from the rank and file. This is illustrated by the party's radical shift to the left in the 1970s and early 1980s, as well as its rather dramatic strategic reversal in the late 1980s, when leftist grassroots activism subsided in the face of a string of electoral defeats.

In Germany, the SPD's entrenched party organization has remained at odds with strong left-libertarian mobilization. Considerable leadership accountability also has undercut the party's strategic maneuverability in a competitive system with favorable opportunities for pivoting. With somewhat different weights, a similar mismatch holds true for Sweden. Here, the entrenched party organization was exposed to the strains of left-libertarian mobilization and the limits of leadership autonomy have delayed strategic adjustments to pivoting opportunities.

The predicaments encountered by the German and Swedish social democrats are evident in even starker terms in the French and Italian communist mass parties in the 1980s. Their impressive organizational entrenchment, maintained by a vast middle tier of full-time party functionaries, combined with a bureaucratic centralization of authority, undercut the parties' adaptability to new challenges (cf. Jenson and Ross 1984; Pridham 1988: 280–96; Waller 1988).

When the mismatch between environmental challenges and party organization gives rise to strategies that cause the party to suffer dramatic electoral losses, activists and leaders try to respond. In this sense, party organization is not simply an exogenous parameter that mediates between systemic contingencies and strategic choice, but also an endogenous variable that is transformed *over time* by (1) the experience of electoral crisis and (2) the related ebb and flow of entry and exit of activists. It is these forces that allow us to move from a comparative-static analysis of internal party politics to a dynamic analysis of change over time.

When a party has lost votes over a considerable period of time, eventually resulting in the loss of government office and long-term exclusion from government participation, dominant coalitions within socialist parties are likely to erode and give way to new coalitions that eventually establish a new internal organizational regime associated with a new strategy of party competition. This happened in France and in the Netherlands in the late 1960s and in Italy, Spain, and the

operating in a strategically more complex environment of party competition, such as the French or Spanish socialists.

United Kingdom in the late 1970s.[28] To a lesser extent, upheavals have also taken place in Sweden (after 1976) and in Germany (after 1983). Left parties turned out of office are usually marred by intensified internal conflict (Hine 1986: 276). As we shall see, an organizational reversal, by itself, does not necessarily enhance a party's competitiveness and rationality in choosing vote- or office-seeking strategies and will not always produce changes that moderate a party's appeal. In most instances, electoral losses have led to an initial radicalization of socialist parties with varying electoral results. This is true for the Netherlands, France, and Italy in the early 1970s, for Britain and Sweden in the 1970s, and for West Germany in the early 1980s.

### 5.3 PARTY ORGANIZATION AS CAUSE AND CONSEQUENCE OF PARTY STRATEGY: NINE CASE STUDIES

The comparative-static analysis of the linkage between environmental contingencies and a socialist party's organizational form has proved useful in explaining strategic choices. It still leaves us, however, with several tasks I will address in the case studies below. Empirical assessments of party structures proposed in Tables 5.1 and 5.2 must be justified. Moreover, I wish to qualify some of my categorical assertions about party structure and to place party organization within a dynamic framework of change through electoral crisis and turnover of activists. This analysis will remove the impression created by the simple cross-sectional comparison that party organizations are immutable exogenous constraints on political action.

#### *Electoral victors*

The three socialist winners of the 1980s – the French, Italian, and Spanish socialists – were much more exposed to the political challenge of market efficiency that was expressed by fairly consolidated, but temporarily weakened bourgeois parties than to left-libertarian mobilization. In this environment, all three parties eventually moved to a centripetal strategy of competition with clear vote- or office-seeking objectives. The adoption of such strategies was facilitated by a high degree of leadership autonomy and comparatively low levels of party entrenchment. The most successful party, the Spanish PSOE, engaged in a dramatic strategic reversal in the late 1970s that led the party toward moderation and an organizational structure dominated by a technocratic leadership. In France, low levels of organizational entrenchment initially favored a radical strategy, but it was eventually counteracted by a leadership steering the party toward support of a socialist government that had abandoned many of its initial radical promises. Once in government office, however, the leaders of both socialist parties began to promote party entrenchment in order to foreclose a future radical strategic reversal that may

28 In a sense, the Italian socialists had two strategic turns, one in the early 1970s when they withdrew from the center-left and the second when they realized the failure of their new radical strategy in the late 1970s.

be initiated by a defection of moderate rank-and-file supporters or the influx of a new wave of radical activists. Organizational change in the Italian socialists also focused on increasing the level of leadership autonomy, while organizational entrenchment always remained much higher than in France or Spain. In all three socialist parties, efforts of the new technocratic leadership to maintain or to increase organizational entrenchment have recently turned into an electoral liability rather than an asset.

*Spain.*   When Franco's regime came to an end, the Spanish PSOE emerged as a small party of radical Eurosocialists who had freed themselves from the old emigrant PSOE leadership residing in France and embraced a participatory socialist restructuring of the political economy.[29] The party's strategic reversal to a moderate approach became possible because it lacked organizational entrenchment but was swamped with new pragmatic activists, primarily employees in the civil service, who began to enter the party once democracy was established and began to displace the radical core membership from the resistance era. With the aid of these new members, the leadership engineered a basic change in intraorganizational relations in 1979. After the 1979 election, which was widely perceived as a defeat, the party's secretary, Gonzales, established the undisputed hegemony of the moderate pragmatists cemented by rule changes that reduced the representation of minority currents at the national party conference. Henceforth, delegates were chosen in regional party conferences based on a winner-take-all scheme rather than in district elections with proportional representation of different currents.

After the party's victory in 1982, the leadership attempted to increase its entrenchment with mixed results. Although in 1983 the PSOE set a goal for the party of raising its membership to 500,000, by the late 1980s the party still had only about 215,000 members or a member/voter ratio of about 2%. Entrenchment, however, increased in less desirable ways because the governing PSOE attracted growing numbers of patronage seekers. By the late 1980s, close to half of all members were civil servants (Pridham 1989: 149) and 70% of the delegates to the 1988 party conference either held electoral office or were civil servants (Gillespie and Gallagher 1989: 173).[30] Simultaneously the party's central and regional apparatus of functionaries was strengthened. The influx of new pragmatic civil servants weakened the initial radical party core and eventually pushed factional divisions to the margins. The increasing uniformity of the party rank and file has reinforced the party's ability to hold on to power and maintain its moderate strategic appeal, but also cuts down on its strategic flexibility and makes it vulnerable to patronage scandals.

The PSOE's strategic capacity derives primarily from the centralization of authority around the party's former general secretary and then long-time prime

---

29  The best sources on the history and the organization of the Spanish PSOE are Gillespie (1989) and Share (1989). For a comparative assessment of the PSOE, see Gillespie and Gallagher (1989).

30  The PSOE activists, in general, are older, better educated, have a higher income, and are more often male than the party's voters (Maraval 1985: 152–3).

minister Felipe Gonzalez, who built the party's new managerial structure together with his closest allies. The PSOE government firmly controls both the party's executive and its legislators. The preferences of the leadership considerably influence the recruitment of candidates for national legislative office (cf. De Esteban and Lopez Guerra 1985: 70–2). The leadership now orchestrates conference proceedings to an extent that even the prime minister has advocated some minimum representation for his opponents to save the party's democratic reputation and ideological inclusiveness.

At the same time, the socialist labor union UGT has become increasingly estranged from the party, so much so that the union's leadership organized a general strike against the PSOE government in 1988 and endorsed support of the United Left in the 1989 election (Gillespie 1990). Union traditionalists inside the party had first teamed up with the dominant technocratic coalition, but defected when the party failed to meet their demands. Weak labor unions and the dominance of civil servants within the PSOE have made the party's alienation from the union movement less a threat to its electoral viability than an opportunity for moving the party's strategy further toward a moderate position, forestalling efforts by right-wing parties to win over pivotal voters and build an alternative majority. Consistent with this logic, Gonzalez revamped his cabinet and the party leadership by appointing technocrats who were not even party members to key economic ministries and by removing his ally Alfonzo Guerra, a left-wing populist, from the office of party secretary. This change of personnel was widely interpreted as preparing the PSOE for a centrist alliance with the Catalan regionalists in case of a further loss of PSOE voters on its left fringe in the 1993 national election.[31]

In spite of the PSOE's success in the 1980s, the increasing entrenchment of its middle-level party apparatus based on government control and patronage may undermine the strategic flexibility of the party to respond to new signals and demands from civil society in the long run. Patronage scandals have begun to taint the party's popular reputation seriously in the early 1990s. This could precipitate the party's electoral defeat, if not only leftists, but also moderate voters begin to abandon the party.

*France.*     After a series of disastrous electoral defeats in the late 1960s, Mitterrand engineered the French socialists' rejuvenation based on a new set of rules to select the party directorate. This change was supported by varied intraparty tendencies that rallied around the shared desire to replace the strategic immobilism of the incumbent leadership around Guy Mollet (Bell and Criddle 1988: 65). This coalition for renewal abandoned the majoritarian system in which the strongest faction, then headed by foes of a popular alliance strategy, occupied most positions in the party's steering body in favor of the proportional representation of all currents with at least 5% of the conference delegates. Like its predecessor, however, the new PS under Mitterrand remained a loose-knit cadre organization with local notables and political clubs that fed into a variety of political currents

31 Cf. *The Economist,* March 16, 1991: 46.

represented at the level of the party directorate.[32] The assumption of government power in 1981 precipitated some changes in the relationship between national leadership and political currents.[33]

Similar to the Spanish PSOE, the French PS organizes few voters. At its high point in 1983 the party barely exceeded 210,000 members, less than 2% of its voters.[34] Moreover, the party has continued to rely on fluid political clubs and tendencies rallied around charismatic leaders as well as on networks of local clientelism tied into the party's national legislative group. Most socialist members of the National Assembly are also mayors or municipal councilors of their hometowns, who plead for their local constituencies in Paris, thus opening avenues for patronage and material advantages to local party followers. Despite certain opportunities for patronage, the party has overall developed little organizational entrenchment and remains halfway between a mass and a cadre party (Panebianco 1988a: 96). With a small membership and limited public party finance, the PS developed a weak apparatus of functionaries.

Since its rebirth in 1971, the socialists' system of currents and tendencies, encompassing an old workerist Left, a New Left, southern socialist notables, and northern social democrats, has kept the party sensitive to changing political demands in society. On the one hand, factionalism has been the core of the PS's internal democracy (Roucaute 1983: 82–3). On the other, it has enhanced Mitterrand's ability to bolster his own position as party leader by coalescing various currents (Cole 1989). Throughout the 1970s, Mitterrand governed his party with a center-left coalition against the party's right wing headed by Michel Rocard, who challenged Mitterrand in 1979.

Since the beginning of the 1980s, with Mitterrand in the presidency and socialist majorities governing in the National Assembly for all but two years, the nature of the factions has changed. The Left organized by the Centre d'Études, de Recherches et d'Education Socialistes (CERES) has been weakened as ideologues have withdrawn from party activism and all currents have undergone a transformation from ideological groupings to political machines that serve their leaders' presidential ambitions and claims to cabinet positions (cf. Roucaute 1983; Lagroye 1989; Ladrech 1990). By the late 1980s, finally the PS had exhausted the innovative momentum of a self-limiting intraparty pluralism and lost touch with important new political currents (Sferza 1991).[35]

While preserving factional pluralism, the PS, however, has experienced an increasing centralization of political power around an autonomous leadership since Mitterrand's takeover in 1971. It may be too sweeping, however, to characterize the party as a monocracy, as Schonfield (1980, 1985) has suggested. Local

---

32 The structural diversity of the party has been analyzed by Sferza (1991).
33 Useful overviews of the French socialists' organization can be found in Kergoat (1983), Roucaute (1983), Hanley (1986), Bell and Criddle (1988), and Thiebault (1988).
34 By 1985, the party membership was down again to the 190,000 (Bell and Criddle 1988: 261).
35 Indicative is the strong performance of the ecologists in the local and the European elections of 1989.

party sections still dominate the recruitment of legislative candidates, even though the leadership intervenes in case of conflicts (Thiebault 1988). Party conferences require a process of compromise formation. In the 1970s, when Schonfield originally formulated the monocracy hypothesis, survey evidence showed that socialist militants attribute more influence to the rank and file than those of the other major French parties (cf. Lagroye, Lord, Mounier-Chazel, and Palard 1976: 114, 121). And with the end of the Mitterrand era in sight, the 1990 party conference at Rennes was characterized by sharp internal disagreements and competition among leaders positioning themselves for the next presidential race. Nevertheless, it is obvious that the Mitterrand government "decapitated" (Roucaute 1983: 139) the party by appointing its leadership to government offices. Moreover, Mitterrand has since 1974 consistently distanced himself from the party manifestos in his presidential campaigns (cf. Roucaute 1983: 93; Cole 1988: 70).

The tenuous relationship between PS and the French labor movement has further enhanced the party leader's autonomy. In 1981, less than one sixth of the socialist parliamentarians had made their career through labor unions (Collovald 1985: 28). Even the labor union most sympathetic to the socialists, the Confédération Française Démocratique du Travail (CFDT), maintained only loose links to the most workerist party current, CERES (Hanley 1986: 164–6). Thus, labor traditionalists and radicals in the PS had little power to constrain the party's move toward market-liberal policy. The socialists in government did little to redeem their promise to strengthen workers' self-management and the role of unions in the collective bargaining system (Lewis and Sferza 1987: 107–10).

Overall, the French socialists' flexibility for engaging in strategic change was buttressed by a malleable, decentralized, and loosely coupled grassroots structure and a highly autonomous, mobile party leadership, which was constrained only by pluralist factionalism and the need to hammer out compromises among the various intraparty forces. The competition among factions made leaders who can overcome divisions indispensable (Bell and Criddle 1988: 237). Given the complexity of power relations within the PS, it is not surprising that scholars have called the party a monocracy (Schonfield 1980), an oligarchy of faction leaders who consult their followers (Bell and Criddle 1988: 210, 236) or a decentralized democratic party with internal political debate (Thiebault 1988: 87). At least in the 1970s, the party's secret was its *ability to combine all these elements simultaneously,* thus enhancing its capacity for strategy at both the rank-and-file level and the elite level. In this sense, the PS resembled a "stratarchal" organization with multiple leaderships at different organizational and electoral levels (Eldersveld 1964) more so than conventional European social democratic mass bureaucratic parties.

*Italy.*    The Italian PSI enacted organizational reforms in the late 1970s that moved it closer to the French model. Nevertheless, the Italian socialists were building on a legacy of mass party organization and local entrenchment, particularly in the Italian South, that has been difficult to undermine. Whatever organizational and strategic changes were brought about in the transition from the 1970s to the 1980s presupposed a serious electoral crisis of the party and the ascent of a dynamic leader, Bettino Craxi, who undercut some of the pillars of organizational entrenchment and increased the autonomy of the national party leadership.[36]

The PSI's local entrenchment has remained a problem for the party leadership. Because party membership and electorate declined in tandem, the member/voter ratio remained at about 1 to 7 from the 1960s to the early 1980s (Hine 1989). Yet the structure of the membership changed significantly. Working-class membership fell to only about 20% of the total by the early 1980s (Merkel 1985: 318). Instead, Craxi's centripetal government strategy attracted patronage hunters with middle-class background, professional credentials, and appointments in the municipal government (DiScala 1988: 241). Under Craxi the PSI in fact engaged in an aggressive penetration of the state apparatus and enhanced opportunities for its followers to obtain patronage (Donovan 1989: 124). Patronage initially reinforced internal support for a moderate strategy, but then hampered the leadership through scandals, particularly since the party ran on a clean government platform (cf. DiScala 1988: 212). Mass organization, public party finance, and patronage have also preserved an entrenched middle-level party bureaucracy in the party's county and regional federations.

In the past, factionalism fed on local entrenchment and patronage appointments, yet its ideological tenor also tended to boost the party's strategic flexibility. By the 1970s, however, pluralist factionalism led the party into a strategic stalemate (cf. Pasquino 1977: 190; DiScala 1988: ch. 11). While undermining the power of factions, Craxi did not create a new mechanism to generate political input from the party's rank and file and to revive intraparty debates.[37]

In 1976 a motley coalition of the right wing and left wing chose Craxi as party secretary because they reckoned he, as the leader of the smallest faction, would be too weak to upset the balance of power inside the party. Yet the party's strategic paralysis and electoral crisis enabled him to consolidate his power within five years and to increase the party's strategic flexibility at the top, though not at the bottom (Hine 1989: 122). The national leadership increased its influence over the choice of the party's candidates in national elections, although the provincial party organization remains important (Wertman 1988). In the 1980s, rule changes enhanced Craxi's autonomy vis-à-vis party conferences and executive. Congresses met only once every three years and were increasingly choreographed by the national leaders (Merkel 1985: 106–10). In 1984, Craxi was successful in abolishing the party's central committee and in limiting the power of the conference to electing a very large and therefore ineffective national assembly with several hundred members. At the same time, Craxi enhanced his personal power by asking the conference to elect him as general secretary. This separated his office and

---

36 The most informative studies on the new PSI organization and strategy are Merkel (1985), DiScala (1988), and Hine (1989).
37 Craxi considered a network of "clubs" based on the model of the French socialists or primaries in the nomination of parliamentarians (cf. DiScala 1988: 243), but these initiatives appear to have stalled.

power base from the party executive that in the past had the power to appoint the secretary. Moreover, Craxi engineered a large-scale turnover on the party executive and packed it with his supporters. Since Craxi began to take an interest in the regional nomination of electoral candidates, membership in the party executive has become a career steppingstone toward parliamentary office (Massari 1989).

As in the French and Spanish parties, the decline of the labor unions and their increasingly tenuous linkage to the party enhanced the strategic autonomy of the Italian socialist leader. Before Craxi's ascent, the party's dominant coalition consisting of radicals and left traditionalists maintained close links to the socialist minority in the communist dominated Italian General Confederation of Labor (CGIL) (cf. Merkel 1985: 250–6; Kreile 1988). Not surprisingly, Craxi's new moderate coalition cut the influence of labor unions on the party's strategy and attenuated party-union linkages.

The partial modernization of the PSI at the top, but not at the bottom, left the party with two organizational problems. Internally, the autonomy of party leaders did not mesh entirely with the realities of a strongly entrenched patronage party, particularly in southern Italy. Externally, the extension of socialist patronage control was one motivation for the PSI's alliance with the Christian Democrats, but it counteracted the PSI's efforts to dissociate itself from the "old" politicians and build a credible centrist alternative (cf. Hine 1989). The party's ties to the old patronage politics, together with the extreme crowding of the centrist political space in Italian politics, explain why the Italian socialists experienced more limited electoral success in the 1980s than their counterparts in France or Spain.

In summary, all socialist winners of the 1980s shared some common organizational traits. They either lacked mass party entrenchment or made efforts to abandon the mass party trappings typical of most other continental socialist parties. Yet at the same time, all three parties resorted more or less to patronage networks and subnational party notables to stabilize a moderate strategy. At the elite level, the three parties were characterized by tenuous linkages to generally weak and divided labor unions and power highly centralized around leaders who subdued the party executive, the legislative party, and the party conferences. Overall, this pattern is most pronounced in Spain, while the French PS leans more in the direction of a fluid decentralized cadre party, and the Italian PSI has preserved elements of mass organization.

### Electoral stabilizers

Socialist parties that went through the 1970s and 1980s without definite voting trends do not share a common organizational form because they have coped with very different strategic environments. The Belgian and the Dutch socialists accomplished a reasonable, though not perfect fit between external challenges and internal organization. Yet in maintaining this match, the Belgian socialists have remained a semicentralized social democratic mass party, whereas their Dutch colleagues have moved toward a decentralized framework party. In the second half of the 1980s, the Swedish social democrats experienced the comparatively greatest stress on their organization in an environment that called for both less organizational entrenchment and more leadership autonomy.

*Belgium.* The Belgian socialists faced a weak mobilization of the libertarian Left, particularly in Wallonia, and found few opportunities for increasing their electoral support in a crowded party system or for office-seeking strategies because they were in a weak competitive position. Within this placid environment, they experienced little pressure to innovate in organizational and strategic respects.

The Belgian socialist parties are typical mass organizations.[38] They enroll about one in every six socialist voters, have extensive bureaucratic machines that are partially submerged in the public administration. The Belgian socialists are one of the few European left parties with increasing membership since 1970 (cf. Bartolini 1983b). Since party-affiliated organizations administer public services (health care, public sector jobs, unemployment benefits), this trend may be due to material incentives.[39] "Particracy," the centrality of political patronage in all walks of life, has sustained the dominance of the established parties, especially after the temporary ethnoregionalist challenge of the 1960s and 1970s subsided.

Given the importance of parastate organizations run by party-affiliated bodies, it is difficult to determine the size of the socialist party apparatus. Moreover, Belgium has no public party finance and parties are not financially accountable in any meaningful way (Van Haegendorn 1981: 42–3). Nevertheless, it is safe to presume that the Belgian parties belong to the most entrenched mass organizations in West European politics.

Patronage and close ties between party and state apparatus have prevented ideological factionalism and the influx of the New Left into the Belgian parties (see Mabille and Lorwin 1977: 402). In the 1970s, the socialist party was split into a Walloon and a Flemish wing to resolve the main internal conflict about language. Differences between the two halves illustrate the linkage between party organization and strategy. The Walloon party has been more closely linked to the labor movement and maintains a more entrenched organization. Its strategy has been more workerist in comparison to the Flemish social democrats, who are less entrenched and have reached out to white collar employees, Catholic voters, and even some elements of the New Left.[40] At the elite level, party–union linkages have therefore constrained the leadership autonomy of the Walloon socialists more than that of their Flemish counterparts (Rudd 1986: 131–2).

---

38 The literature on Belgian party organization is exceptionally limited. See Obler (1974), Ceulers (1977, 1981), Dewachter (1987); and De Winter (1981, 1988).

39 Studies of the Belgian welfare state argue that the ideological bases of traditional political "pillarization" have been replaced by material organizational incentives and maintain the coherence of the institutional fabric surrounding the major parties (cf. Billiet and Huyse 1984; Huyse 1984).

40 In 1982, the member/voter ratio was 22.9% in Wallonia and 16.1% in Flanders (cf. Dewachter 1987: 314–15).

Within the bureaucratized party organizations, socialist party leaders enjoy only a moderate degree of autonomy. Candidates for national parliament are selected in an interactive process involving county party organizations and national headquarters. As one might expect, the Walloon socialists, with their greater organizational entrenchment, the selection powers of the party leadership are more constrained by requiring many candidates to be approved in local membership polls. In both parties, delegate conferences are not the true center of power (Dewachter 1987: 319). The timing of key conferences, for instance, before elections or after the completion of negotiations over government coalitions strengthens the hand of the leadership. Party leaders also firmly dominate the socialist legislative group (Witte 1980; Van Haegendorn 1981: 38), although there is usually a formal division between party executive and party leaders with cabinet posts that poses a potential for internal friction.[41]

Differences in the organizational structures of the two Belgian socialist parties reflect the Flemish social democrats' greater willingness to embrace left-libertarian themes, although their innovative efforts are more limited than those of socialists in other countries, for example the Netherlands. The Walloon party, in contrast, has remained wedded to a workerist organization and strategy until the end of the 1980s.[42]

*Netherlands.* In contrast to Belgium, the Dutch PvdA has undergone a process close to an organizational revolution since libertarian New Left adherents entered the party in the late 1960s.[43] In the preceding decade the party's membership had fallen precipitously from 143,000 (1959) to 98,700 (1971). The decline made the party receptive to the new ideas and demands of small yet critical new groups of activists. These forces were able to reshape the party organization by expanding the power of the rank and file at the expense of the leadership. The changed balance of power enabled a new coalition of hard-line socialists and left-libertarians to push the party toward a course of polarization against its main political contenders, the Christian Democrats and the Liberals.

After 1971, stagnating membership enrollments, but rising electoral support led to a fall of the party's member/voter ratio from 6.3% in 1971 to only 3.3% in 1986 (PvdA 1988a: 54). Unlike Belgium, party membership in the Netherlands became less attractive, because social depillarization coincided with a depillarization of the state that limited parties' access to state patronage.[44] At the same time, Dutch parties receive only modest state funding (Koole 1990) and make do with small

---

41 Conversely, this division may strengthen the hand of a party's government representatives in coalitional bargaining because they can always claim their hands are tied by their party.
42 As discussed in Chapter 4, this may have contributed to its particularly severe losses in the 1991 general election.
43 On the Dutch socialists see Wolinetz (1977, 1988), Boivin et al. (1978), Daalder (1987), and Koole and Leijenaar (1988).
44 On these limits, see Daalder (1987: 246) and Koole and Liejenaar (1988: 199).

staffs of party functionaries.[45] Against this background, it took only a small critical group of innovators amounting to only 1% to 2% of the membership in the late 1960s and early 1970s to initiate strategic change (Boivin et al. 1978: 43–9). At that time, technocrats and traditionalists were weakened in number and dispirited by past strategic failures. They could not effectively counter the sudden assault of highly motivated New Left radicals who eventually entered a new dominant coalition together with Fabian guild socialists and left-libertarians.

The new intraparty coalition increased the power of local activists by giving them the decisive say in the nomination of legislative candidates (Boivin et al. 1978: 51). Even in 1986–87, when the New Left agenda appeared to have been exhausted and almost a decade in the opposition had converted many former leftists into supporters of a new moderate course, the party executive failed to reinforce its grip over the selection process (Koole and Leijenaar 1989: 199). In the 1970s, party activists were also strengthened at the expense of party leaders by scheduling national conferences as often as once a year, a frequency matched only by the British Labour Party among European socialists. Moreover, responsibility for conference preparation and management was taken away from the party executive and given to ad hoc appointees (Daalder 1987: 252). A firm separation of party executive from legislative group and party leaders in government further cut down on the strategic autonomy of the party leaders.

The three rule changes, taken together, had profound strategic consequences for the PvDA. In 1977, after its electoral victory, the sitting PvdA prime minister, den Uyl, engaged in lengthy coalition bargaining with the Christian Democrats that ultimately failed because of the inflexible position of the PvdA's left-leaning party executive (Daalder 1986: 519). Similar problems contributed to the quick demise of the coalition between PvdA, CDA, and Democrats '66 in 1981.

The rapid strategic change of the Dutch socialists was further facilitated by the weakening bonds between party and labor unions (PvdA 1988a: 40). In the process of depillarization, Dutch socialist and Christian unions increasingly cooperated with each other and eventually formed a single bargaining unit. This required the unions to loosen their respective party affiliations. On the socialist side, the decreasing linkage to labor unions made the party more vulnerable to a left-libertarian takeover.

Left-libertarian party structures, however, are inherently unstable because they make choices contingent upon the mobilization of small critical groups of activists. By the late 1980s, the left-libertarian strategy had reached a dead end because it had kept the party out of power for over ten years, although it yielded a historically high level of socialist voter support. Many former left-libertarians who had obtained legislative office retreated into regional and municipal executive appointments to overcome the frustrations of opposition life.[46] As the political pendulum began to swing back toward advocates of a centripetal strategy of competition,

---

45 This arrangement is also reflected in the relative inexpensiveness of Dutch electoral campaigns (cf. Daalder 1987: 239).

46 Cf. *Vrij Nederland*, July 2, 1988: 3–4.

Wim Kok, a former chair of the Dutch labor unions, was brought to the helm of the party. Kok wasted no time reversing the left-libertarian strategy and began steering the party toward a renewed coalition with the Christian Democrats. Given the close interaction between party strategy and organizational structure in the PvDA, a strengthening of the party leadership is the likely consequence of the change in the party's dominant coalition.

*Sweden.* The Swedish social democrats have been situated in a fragmented party system with considerable left-libertarian mobilization like their Dutch counterpart, but they have faced different strategic incentives because they can effectively compete over control of the pivot in the party system. In contrast to the Dutch party, the Swedish SAP has been characterized by an extraordinary organizational entrenchment and by greater autonomy of its leadership. This organization has facilitated a very different strategic approach than that of the PvdA.[47]

Next to the Austrian socialists, the Swedish SAP is the European party with the highest member/voter ratio. In 1985, more than one third of all SAP voters were directly or indirectly (through unions) affiliated with the party. Even excluding all indirect collective associates, the member/voter ratio was still about one sixth of the voters. Membership, however, leveled off and began to decline in the second half of the 1980s, primarily because of a shortfall of young and female entrants (Socialdemokraterna 1989a: 14). The traditional mass organizations surrounding the party – labor unions, the cooperative movement, youth and women's organizations – are no longer able to instill the sense of solidary and purposive commitments that used to promote party affiliation.[48] In Sweden, membership also cannot be maintained by patronage incentives to attract materially motivated members. Organizational entrenchment, however, is furthered by a relatively large apparatus of party functionaries that is financed by an efficient system of dues collection, considerable public subsidies (Nassmacher 1987), and unpaid party officials doubling as full-time salaried union functionaries. These functionaries tend to subscribe to a social democratic traditionalism that has been insensitive to new issues.[49]

Conventional views of the Swedish SAP stress the absence of factionalism as a cause of the party's stability.[50] Nevertheless, in recent years, internal differentiation of opinions can be clearly discerned. On the one side, there are intraparty groups with left-libertarian inclinations, such as the youth, women's, and Christian

---

47  Few studies deal with Swedish social democratic organization. See especially Elvander (1980: ch. 6), Esping-Andersen (1985: 118–20), Pierre (1986), and Thomas (1986) and my own investigation based on elite interviews with Swedish party officials (Kitschelt 1994).

48  This problem was exacerbated by the abolition of collective membership affiliation in January 1991. I do not have data on the percentage of former collective members who have become individual members.

49  This judgment relies on interviews with Swedish party functionaries. See Kitschelt (1993).

50  Pierre (1986) found no sustained organization of leftist currents at SAP party conferences. Hine (1986: 281–2) argues that the party's internal cohesion enabled it to avoid the bruising struggles within other European social democratic parties in the 1980s.

temperance organizations. These groups are pitted against the traditional party core around labor union functionaries, who are themselves divided along industrial sectors and public or private employment. Unions in the private and internationally competitive economic sector, such as the metal workers, are most opposed to the left-libertarian agenda (Kitschelt 1994). Overall, then, Swedish social democracy is still marked by an extraordinary level of organizational entrenchment, but the organization shows distinct signs of decay and internal dissolution.

At the same time, the autonomy of the party leadership appears to have increased over time, although it is still more constrained than that of Southern European socialist parties. The parliamentary and government leadership has always exercised central strategic control and also has managed the party conferences. Final political authority rests with the governing committee of the national party executive, the *verkställende utskott* (VU), a small inner circle of the government and parliamentary leadership, supplemented by a few regional party leaders and the chairman of the main union federation. The parliamentary group almost always complies with the wishes of the party leadership, as do party conferences. The timing of conferences, once every three years about twelve months before the next parliamentary election, certainly helps to establish delegate compliance. Party conferences vote on a slate of propositions that have been submitted by the party executive. Other motions generally have little prospect of success (Pierre 1986: ch. VI).

The SAP leadership is more constrained in matters pertaining to the party's union linkage and its recruitment of parliamentary personnel. But both restrictions have gradually been relaxed in recent years. Important policy initiatives, such as the party's opening toward more sectoral economic planning, industrial democracy, and collective ownership funds were prepared in response to union demands. More recently, however, the internal divisions among unions and their intensifying concerns with narrow sectoral advantages have driven a wedge between the party and a number of sectoral unions.[51] Given the diversification of union demands, it has become more difficult for the party to represent a generalized working-class interest. Moreover, the unions have blocked the party from taking a lead on the new "libertarian" issues of the 1970s and 1980s, such as nuclear power, citizens' participation, citizens' choice over public services, and feminism. The weakening party–union linkage was highlighted by the decision of the labor union federation in the mid-1980s to phase out the collective affiliation of its constituent members with the SAP by the end of 1990 and to recommend its members to join the SAP as a matter of individual affiliation.

The predicament of the unions has also influenced recruitment to high electoral, party, and government office. The party's county organizations still control the nomination of parliamentary candidates and the SAP caucus in the Swedish legislature has a larger proportion of parliamentarians with a working-class occupational background than any other European socialist party but the British Labour

51 The politics of sectoral coalition building within Swedish unions has been exhaustively analyzed by Swenson (1990, 1991a,b).

Party. Union–party conflicts have recently diminished the unions' ability to impose their functionaries on the party. This has permitted SAP government leaders to tap more technocrats who are unaffiliated with the conventional mass organizations to fill key political appointments. Nevertheless, both SAP parliamentarians and senior party leadership are still recruited through conventional socialist career tracks, making it difficult for outsiders to rise to positions of prominence.

As the 1980s progressed, the Swedish social democrats found it increasingly difficult to respond to a strategic environment in which organizational flexibility both at the grassroots as well as at the leadership level was becoming critical for the party's performance. Because of its organizational inertia, the party was unable to cope with the left-libertarian challenge in the 1980s or to confront the challenge of market efficiency and international competitiveness early enough to prevent a consolidation of the bourgeois bloc around such issues. Hence, the crisis of Swedish social democracy in the 1990s not only affects its policy stance, but is also likely to precipitate a sharp reversal of its organizational format to enable the party to make a serious bid to regain its power with a new strategy.

In socialist parties that exhibited no dramatic changes in electoral support from the 1970s to the 1980s, different patterns of environmental challenges, organizational structure, and strategic choice prevail. In Belgium, entrenched and decentralized mass organization with little leadership autonomy worked quite well in an environment that required few strategic initiatives. In Sweden, a similar organizational form increasingly became a burden on the social democrats' strategic flexibility in the 1980s. In the Netherlands, finally, entrenched mass party organization was unable to cope with changes in Dutch politics in the early 1970s and was rapidly dismantled in the course of the PvDA's electoral crisis. With a delay of about two decades, the Belgian and Swedish socialists may also be forced now to cut back on entrenched mass party organization to forge a new intraparty coalition that can cope with new political challenges.

### Electoral losers

Left parties in Austria, Germany, and the United Kingdom all failed to adopt structures and strategies that would have preserved their electoral market in the 1980s. Again, however, systemic contingencies were so different that any one organizational formula would have produced different results in each country. In Austria, the party leadership lacked sufficient autonomy to respond to the challenge of market efficiency with a strategy aimed at preserving its pivotal competitive position. In Germany, the SPD's moderately entrenched mass party organization could not cope with an intense left-libertarian challenge and also lacked enough leadership autonomy to reconquer the pivot of the party system by addressing the challenge of market efficiency. In Britain, finally, the Labour Party's loose cadre organization made it overly responsive to radical leftist stirrings promoted by activists who proceeded to dismantle leadership autonomy and prevent the party from choosing a vote- or office-seeking strategy against its major conservative antagonist, which emphasized the agenda of market efficiency.

*Austria.* The Austrian SPÖ probably has Europe's most entrenched party organization, surpassing even that of the Swedish SAP. Together with restrictions on the operational flexibility of its leadership, this format has amplified the party's inertia vis-à-vis new political demands.

Even in the early 1980s, the SPÖ still counted one third of its voters as party members. From 1980 to 1988, however, the party's membership declined by more than 10% primarily due to its inability to attract young, educated, and female members. These constituencies typically supporting left-libertarian causes did not join the SPÖ because they saw no possibility of reversing the party's organizational routines and political appeal.[52] The party's entrenchment is reinforced by a patronage system that includes the civil service, the large sector of nationalized industries, public housing, and many other opportunities for disbursing material privileges to party loyalists.[53] The patronage system depoliticizes the party's internal debates because it is based on an elaborate system of benefit sharing with the SPÖ's main conservative competitor, the Austrian People's Party. Throughout the late 1970s and all of the 1980s, patronage scandals tainted the SPÖ's image and it took the party more than a decade to confront this problem by instituting a new organizational discipline.[54]

The patronage system has been tied into an extensive local and regional party bureaucracy with legions of minor functionaries who often hold additional appointments in public administration or labor unions. The dues of more than 600,000 members and the generous flow of public party subsidies have promoted the proliferation of salaried party officials. Critics within the ranks of the party see party functionaries as a major obstacle to change in party organization and strategy. Moreover, the political functionary, oriented toward personal gain, symbolically highlights the party's increasing distance from the average citizen. The party's size, structure, and material incentives dampen the influx of individuals motivated by a desire for change. The small leftist intraparty opposition was eliminated in the 1950s (Shell 1962) and the party apparatus has continued to keep a close eye on the socialist youth organization, which at times has displayed radical leanings (cf. Keller 1988). Even in the 1980s, left-libertarian internal opposition never seriously

---

52 In an interview, one Austrian party functionary remarked that the same number of young left-libertarians could cause havoc in the German SPD's less entrenched local organizations, say in Frankfurt or Munich, but would be marginalized in a party the size of Vienna's SPÖ (cf. Kitschelt 1994).

53 Surveys among SPÖ members show that at least one third joined the party because of career concerns and one quarter because of the prospect of public housing (cf. Luther 1987: 380; Müller 1989: 342).

54 These difficulties are discussed in Hartl (1986) and Leser (1988). Leser reports an exchange of letters with Chancellor Bruno Kreisky in which the latter admitted to Leser that he could do little to attack the intraparty forces that maintained the patronage system.

threatened the party's incumbent elites. This is a consequence of the party's organizational entrenchment as much as of the relatively limited left-libertarian cleavage mobilization in Austrian society.

At the top of the party, while the SPÖ leadership has maintained an extraordinarily strict regime at party conferences, its autonomy in almost every other respect was limited in the 1980s. Party conferences always included motions, votes, and speeches evidencing some internal dissent, but these voices never came close to winning majorities in a party where the leadership has always closely watched the selection of delegates and in which a commission appointed by the party executive prepares a tight conference agenda.

Obstacles to leadership autonomy and strategic innovation stem primarily from the federal organization of the party, which creates influential regional leaders who dispense patronage benefits and control much of the flow of public party finance. Party organizations in the individual states thus impede a sweeping organizational change in the party. The SPÖ parliamentary caucus, in contrast, represents no challenge to the party's leadership, because parliamentarians have little independent access to information and usually hold appointments in the regional and national party executive.

The national party executive also has little control over the nomination of parliamentary candidates or regional party executives. It is entitled to appoint up to 20% of the parties' candidates in national elections and place them on regional lists. But this prerogative enables only a few policy experts, who lack political backing by powerful local and regional clienteles to gain parliamentary seats.[55]

The most important constraint on leadership autonomy in the SPÖ has been the Austrian Federation of Labor Unions (ÖGB). Although the union is nominally nonpartisan, historically a tight linkage to the SPÖ has bordered on an organizational symbiosis, evidenced by the overlap between the leaders and functionaries of both entities. The ÖGB chairman was traditionally elected by the SPÖ as the speaker of the Austrian parliament and many union leaders have held cabinet office in national and regional SPÖ administrations, a practice unknown even in Swedish, British, or Belgian socialist parties. Moreover, the "etatization" of the Austrian labor unions has been furthered by their crucial role in the management and the patronage system of the state industries. Close union linkages have delayed the SPÖ's efforts to rationalize state industries in the 1980s, thus contributing to the party's electoral decline. Unionists also forced an antiecological policy onto the party that helped the Austrian Greens. Finally, union scandals have also tainted the party's image, because the exposed individuals usually combined union and party offices.

In view of the unions' strong influence, the capacity for strategy at the helm of the SPÖ was quite limited, although some have attributed a "quasi-bonapartist" style to the SPÖ's chancellor from 1970 to 1983, Bruno Kreisky (Löw 1988: 66). Only with the weakening of the labor movement by deepening divisions between

55  On Austrian candidate selection procedures, see Shell (1962: 115–18), Konecny (1980: 382), and Stirnemann (1989).

public and private sectors in the 1980s, after more than a decade of organizational drift, a new party leadership under chancellor Franz Vranitzky staked out a more independent strategic profile that ventured to overcome the party's dependency on the unions.

The appointment of Vranitzky, who had devoted little attention to party activities during his time as a technocrat at the Austrian central bank, as finance minister, then as chancellor, and finally as party leader, represented a clear break with the past practice of recruiting leaders from the party apparatus, a process in which regional party organizations played a major role (Müller and Meth-Cohn 1991). With this break, more voices within the party have called for such reforms as abandoning the traditional entrenched mass party organization, moving to a system of internal primaries to nominate candidates for electoral office, and increasing the distance between party and labor unions. The SPÖ's electoral crisis in the mid-1980s thus triggered efforts to bring about organizational change.

*Germany.* The German SPD combines some of the limitations on leadership autonomy faced by SPÖ and SAP with the vulnerability of a less entrenched party apparatus. Weaker entrenchment invited left-libertarians to enter the party in order to change its strategy, but unlike the Dutch PvdA, the organization proved resilient to a leftist takeover attempt. At the same time, the leadership could not free itself from the powerful countervailing forces struggling inside the party and stake out a consistent strategy. As a consequence, the SPD experienced organizational and strategic paralysis and indecisiveness throughout the 1980s.

The SPD's member/voter ratio of 10% is less than that of the most entrenched European socialist parties. The SPD electorate's lower degree of organizational encapsulation has to do with the less ample opportunities for patronage in German local politics and civil service appointments than, for example, in Austria or Belgium.[56] Membership is further limited by weaker local linkages between party and union sections and the lack of collective union affiliation with the party. Compared to Austria or Sweden, the stratum of full-time SPD functionaries also is thin (cf. Aleman 1990) and does not carry much political weight.

Because of limited organizational entrenchment, the SPD was a more attractive target for the precursors of the left-libertarian challenge, the New Left, in the aftermath of the 1968 movements. The SPD membership increased in the early 1970s, particularly among young educated individuals whose New Left inclinations drew them closer to the party (Kolinsky 1984: 88). As a consequence, many big city party sections went back and forth between leftist and moderate control, a process that was accompanied by fierce intraparty polarization that led to heavy electoral losses.[57] In every instance, however, the Left was too weak to overcome

56 Nevertheless, there is considerable patronage also in Germany (cf. Dyson 1977) and patronage scandals damaged the SPD's image in a number of cities, such as Berlin (Hess 1984: 242–62). Local politics was often identical with personnel appointments (Raschke 1974: 95).
57 Studies of local politics in the SPD include Raschke (1974) and Hess (1984) on Berlin; Pumm (1977) on Hamburg, Meng (1985) on Hesse, and Kronawitter (1979) and Koelble (1991) on Munich.

the resistance of the dominant moderate forces at the regional *Land* or district level and it never came close to a majority at national party conferences. In the late 1970s, the Left moved from a more conventional Marxist appeal to a left-libertarian one (cf. Schmitt 1987) and the absolute number of members with "Green" leanings in the mid-1980s may well have been greater than Green party membership itself (Greven 1987: 192). But these forces failed to bring about a decisive breakthrough. Hence, by the 1980s, local party life was in decay (Becker and Hombach 1983) and younger people were disproportionately drawn to the Greens (Michal 1988; Schmitt 1990; Wiesendahl 1990: 9). The exodus of many left-libertarians led to the virtual collapse of the party's youth organization, the Jungsozialisten, which had been a stronghold of the SPD Left.

In the 1980s, the SPD reached an equilibrium of political currents which made it imperative to find a compromise formula that undercut efforts to select and carry out a firm, consistent strategy. The need for compromise in the party was further enhanced by the constraints on leadership autonomy which placed the SPD somewhere between such extremes as the Dutch PvDA, on the one hand, and the Spanish PSOE, on the other. Based on Germany's mixed electoral system with individual member constituencies and regional party lists, power over the nomination of candidates for national parliament is widely distributed (cf. Roberts 1988). The constituency organizations jealously guard their local decision-making autonomy, and it is here where most leftist members of parliament have been nominated. In contrast, the regional party lists emerge from elaborate negotiations between party subdistricts and regional and national party executives, giving the party establishment the edge.

The management of conferences has also yielded mixed results. National conferences are usually scheduled biannually and, in spite of complex procedures of agenda setting and efforts at hammering out disagreements in advance, different currents time and again have been able to make their voices publicly heard. Compromise among different currents therefore characterizes major strategic or programmatic resolutions and the election of the party executive. Clear leadership autonomy exists only in the day-to-day governance of the party by the Parteipräsidium, a select committee of the party executives which has been the dominant institution since the early 1960s (cf. Klotzbach 1982: 571–2). It works out relations between parliamentary party, party executive, and party in government and prestructures major decisions, such as choosing the nominee for the chancellor's office, before an electoral campaign.

A major constraint on the party has been the German Federation of Labor Unions (DGB). Although formally nonpartisan and less closely linked to the social democrats than its Swedish or Austrian counterpart, the DGB has influenced the SPD's strategy, a process highlighted by the presence of DGB officials in the party leadership and in SPD cabinets when the party was in government under Chancellor Schmidt until 1982. In the last several years of his reign, union pressure kept Schmidt from catering to such left-libertarian demands as imposing a moratorium on nuclear power plants, but also from more decisive austerity measures to combat the second oil crisis (cf. Padgett 1987: 336). The relationship between SPD and DGB cooled when the party ran on a mildly left-libertarian agenda in the 1983 electoral campaign and improved only when the candidate for the chancellor's office in 1987, Johannes Rau, catered to the party's core blue collar constituency. Party–union relations reached their nadir in 1990 with the party's most left-libertarian lead candidate ever, Oskar Lafontaine.[58]

In conclusion, ties to the DGB curtailed the party leadership's freedom to respond to left-libertarian or market-efficiency challenges. Together with the party's other structural handicaps, these constraints made it all but impossible to stake out a clear, consistent course throughout the 1980s that would have followed an electoralist logic of vote maximization and/or pivoting in order to regain government office.[59] Only in 1991, after the party's third electoral defeat, did internal forces appear to shift toward a centripetal strategy targeting moderate white collar voters and the technical intelligentsia, groups that are likely to endorse a new center-left coalition between social democrats and liberals[60] or even a grand coalition with the Christian Democrats to address the economic and political crisis of German unification.

*Britain.* In the late 1970s, the British Labour Party succumbed to pressures from below to increase rank-and-file influence over strategy and actually empowered a coalition of radical and semiradical socialists who temporarily emasculated the party's leadership in the legislature. After the disastrous electoral consequences of this experiment, the leftist assault quickly receded, but the structural conditions that made the party strategically volatile remained. This episode in Labour's history was made possible because the party is only "incompletely institutionalized" (Panebianco 1988a: 166–7), with a small direct membership and a weak party apparatus, and is financially and in its internal decision-making process dependent on its external sponsor, the British labor unions organized in the Trades

---

58  Also in local politics, the DGB has often energetically influenced party strategy. For example, in the Munich municipal council, it blocked a coalition between SPD and Greens (cf. Michal 1988: 80).

59  The party's collective strategic indecisiveness is reflected well in the statement of a regional party manager reported by Meng (1985: 347–8): "I have the impression that with almost sympathetic sincerity our party has no relationship to power. That is, the question concerning the extent to which I have to accept certain necessities because of power considerations involves an assessment of trade-offs I can never determine in abstract terms. Our party often sees the necessities of power politics much too late. . . . In its whole structure, our party has no rational strategically justified relationship to power. It has a relationship to the exercise of power in many individual respects, but a grand rational-strategic consideration of trade-offs, deciding when policies and objectives should be deferred in order to remain in power or when power should be released or risked intentionally, because one does not want to sacrifice political objectives, this is something I do not see in most instances."

60  The party's coalitions with the liberals at the *Land* level in Rhineland Palatinate and Hamburg are a good indicator of the new strategy. All major coalitional realignments in German politics have been preceded by changes in coalition politics at the regional level.

Union Congress (TUC). Both attributes are unique among West European socialist parties and are due to the founding of the party by the British labor unions.

External union sponsorship explains the modest number of individual party members, though it does not account for the decline of individual members. Similarly, the absence of patronage opportunities and the lack of public financing cannot explain the precipitous fall in membership enrollment. The party reached its nadir in 1982 with about 274,000 direct members, reflecting a member/voter ratio of 2% to 3%, as low or lower than that of the French and Spanish socialists. There are, of course, millions of members collectively affiliated through the labor unions, but they play no role in party life. The party's incomplete institutionalization, by itself, also does not account for the decline in the number of Labour's staff of paid functionaries. In the 1950s, between 200 and 300 agents worked for the party full time, but this number declined to about 50 in the 1980s (Byrd 1987: 222).

The key reason for the decline of party membership and staff has to be sought in the changing ideological complexion of the constituency of the Labour Party. Moderate and instrumental blue collar activists gradually dropped out of the party when they became disappointed with Harold Wilson's Labour government in the late 1960s. They were partially displaced by an influx of young middle-class radicals, particularly those holding public sector appointments (Whiteley 1983: 61–5; Seyd 1987: 45–50; Hamilton 1989: 127). A comparison of Labour constituency organizations shows that working-class constituencies remained more moderate, whereas organizations dominated by white collar workers were taken over by radicals (Seyd 1987: 63–71). Such radicals could win because they had to overcome only small numbers of committed activists and functionaries to alter local intraparty power balances in a decisive way.[61]

Labour was not always characterized by a deep rift between moderate party leaders and radical constituency activists.[62] Quite to the contrary, the left currents grew from the 1960s onwards, when the "soft" Left Tribune group was complemented by a "hard" Trotskyist faction called "Militant," the Campaign for Labour Party Democracy (CLPD) and a small socialist-feminist current, to name only the most important groupings. These activists made their first inroads after Labour had lost office in 1970 and then strengthened their presence during the Callaghan premiership (cf. Kogan and Kogan 1983). By the late 1970s, hard and soft Left had taken over key local party organizations, particularly in the large cities (cf. Gyford 1985; Kogan and Kogan 1983: ch. 10, 11; Seyd 1987: 37–58; Shaw 1988: 218–53). In Liverpool, the Militant leadership even surrounded itself with a paramilitary guard that bullied recalcitrant party members and city councilors into compliance with the group's wishes (cf. Shaw 1988: 277–90).

---

61 Comparing French communists and the British Labour Party, Newman (1987) argues that the structural vulnerability to the New Left made Labour fare especially badly.

62 Proponents of the leader–follower division are McKenzie (1955) and Robertson (1976). Opponents, able to master a considerably more solid array of empirical data, include Rose (1974), Minkin (1978), Seyd (1987: 37–8), Shaw (1988: 51–114), and Hamilton (1989: 102).

The high water mark of radicalism was the election of Michael Foot, a soft leftist, as party leader in 1981. At the same time, Tony Benn, the head of the hard left, martialed almost enough votes to become deputy leader. After the 1983 electoral defeat, first the hard and then the soft Left receded (Seyd 1987: 159–71) and the party leadership finally began to move against Militant's quasi-Leninist constituency organizations. The temporary victory of Labour's hard Left was possible only because of the structural weaknesses of Labour's decision-making process and the unions' influence over strategic choices. The labor unions are not only the major party financiers, but also control the Conference Arrangement Committee, which sets the agenda at national party conferences, and the bulk of the conference votes, which are cast in blocs by the leaders of individual unions. Moreover, the unions elect a majority of the party's national executive council (NEC). The separation of NEC and the parliamentary party constitutes an element of divided leadership that has restricted the autonomy of Labour's parliamentary leader. Finally, unions have considerable influence over the party's process of nominating candidates for the House of Commons. They submit their own candidate slates to the constituency labor parties. In contrast to the practice of most other socialist parties, the role of labor unions in the recruitment of legislators has kept the proportion of workers in the parliamentary Labour Party fairly high.[63]

In the late 1970s, a coalition consisting of New Left constituency activists and unions dissatisfied with Labour's economic austerity policy emerged to replace the incumbent leadership. After the moderate leadership's electoral defeat in 1979, a critical mass of labor unions had defected from the dominant intraparty coalition and the New Left was sufficiently established in the constituencies to create an alternative winning power bloc. This new bloc succeeded in pushing through structural changes designed to displace the existing leadership. The first and perhaps most significant change removed the selection of the party leadership as a prerogative of the parliamentary party and gave it to a tripartite assembly composed of the party constituency organizations, the unions, and the parliamentary party. Second, sitting members of parliament had to submit to mandatory reselection procedures in each electoral term. This made installing replacements more congenial to radical local party elites a great deal easier.[64] Third, the NEC gained final say over the party's election manifesto, previously a prerogative of the party leader in the House of Commons (Seyd 1987: 120–4).

While these rule changes cemented the new dominant leftist coalition, after its defeat in the 1983 election the pendulum began to swing back toward a more moderate coalition reestablishing the supremacy of the parliamentary leadership in the House of Commons over the party executive, constituency organizations, and

63 In contrast to the French PS, where only 2% of all socialist legislators were workers in 1981, 35% of all Labour members of parliament in 1979 and 45% of all candidates were workers in Britain (cf. Bell and Criddle 1988: 201–3; Denver 1988: 52–4).

64 Only eight sitting members of parliament were deselected before the 1983 election (Seyd 1987: 129–33), but a number of more conservative MPs had switched over to the Social Democrats or resigned from their seat in anticipation of not being reselected.

labor unions (cf. Brand 1989). The party's lingering problem, however, is that the structural bases that permitted strategic volatility remain largely untouched. Foot's successor Kinnock, sensing this problem, encouraged a membership drive to rebuild the party organization. Yet structural change has encountered obstacles. After initial resistance,[65] local constituency party electoral colleges and primaries were introduced to determine the (re)selection of parliamentary candidates, thus cutting back on the power of left-dominated local party executives and labor union affiliates (Seyd and Whiteley: 1991: 8). Similarly, the labor unions have taken a lower profile in party strategy and electoral campaigns since 1983 (cf. Taylor 1987: 199–241; Minkin 1989), and the 1990 party conference decided that after the next election new rules of conference decision making should go into effect that reduce the power of activists and labor unions to the benefit of rank-and-file members. At the same time, the leadership proposed standing policy committees that make recommendations to conferences and thus defuse controversies in conference debates (Seyd and Whiteley 1991).

As long as these and other organizational changes are not firmly instituted, the Labour Party, in principle, remains vulnerable to strategic swings, provided a political conjuncture of grassroots radicalism yields the right circumstances. Survey evidence among party activists suggests that the radicalized groups are demobilized for the moment, but that they have not abandoned their traditional socialist inclinations (Seyd and Whiteley 1992: ch. 6).

A problem common to all socialist electoral losers in the 1980s was an overly strong dependence on labor union lobbies in the intraparty decision-making process (cf. also Koelble 1987, 1991). But this is only part of the story. The development of the Austrian, British, and German Left shows that strategic choices can be accounted for only by examining the complex configuration of organizational mechanisms that permit new inputs from below and elite effectiveness from above. While leadership autonomy was a problem in all three parties, the Austrian socialists permitted too little input from activist citizens and the British Labour Party too much. The SPD, finally, lacked a mechanism to forge lasting coalitions out of the variety of inputs it received.

## CONCLUSION

In Chapter 4, not all strategies of socialist parties could be accounted for solely in terms of systemic contingencies (left-libertarian mobilization, patterns of party competition) and one of three systemically rational strategic objectives, vote seeking, office seeking, or oligopolistic competition. Moreover, systemic contingencies could not explain why some parties followed one strategic objective, while others chose another. In this chapter, I have shown how internal party organization and intraparty coalition building intervene between systemic con-

---

65 At the 1984 Labour conference, a proposal to take away authority over local candidate selection from the left-dominated GMCs and rely on a poll of all party members was rejected by a majority of labor union and Left constituency votes (cf. Butler and Kavanagh 1988: 192).

tingencies and parties' strategic appeals. My central argument is that parties identify systemically advantageous strategies only if there is a match between environmental conditions and party organization. Left-libertarian demands are articulated inside socialist parties most effectively if the parties lack an entrenched organization and mass membership. Social democrats are most able to respond to a highly competitive situation and a strong challenge of market liberalism if they have an autonomous leadership. Where parties provide the appropriate match of organizational forms and systemic conditions, they have chosen successful strategies. Among the parties compared here, this applies primarily to the Belgian, French, Italian, Dutch, and Spanish socialists.

Party organization theory has its strongest analytical bite where socialist parties have not chosen the rational strategies mandated by systemic competition theory, but where the internal process of coalition politics can explain the actual choice of a systemically nonrational strategy. This applies primarily to the Austrian, British, German, and, more recently, the Swedish social democrats. In all four cases, the autonomy of the party leadership was too constrained to permit it to address the challenge of market efficiency in a highly competitive situation. At the same time, however, the nature of membership recruitment and the level of organizational entrenchment affected the parties' capacity for strategic innovation and consistency. Austrian and Swedish social democrats were almost impervious to new left-libertarian inputs, the German social democrats were unable to organize them into a new dominant coalition, and the British Labour Party with small constituency organizations proved vulnerable to the takeover by small radical groups who teamed up with disgruntled labor unions.

Given the complex interaction between the contingencies and the mechanisms that link party organization to strategy and electoral success, simplistic generalizations – such as universal formulas about the appropriate relationship between leaders and party activists – do not tell us enough about what helps socialist parties to thrive in different competitive settings. In this sense, one should also caution against idealizing the model of "Mediterranean" French, Spanish, or Italian party organizations as a general recipe for success (cf. Hine 1986: 287). The plebiscitarian democracy inspired by men like Gonzalez, Craxi, and, to a lesser extent, Mitterrand has a tendency to resort to patronage strategies to increase their parties' entrenchment. That such efforts may come to haunt their creators has been recently highlighted by Papandreou's experience in Greece. Moreover, a patronage-oriented organization is ill equipped to meet the left-libertarian challenge that has affected social democratic and socialist parties in the most advanced northern European democracies, as the example of Austria may teach. Meanwhile, the latter are still searching for a promising way out of the dilemma posed by the simultaneous challenge of left-libertarian politics and market efficiency.

# 6

# The socialist discourse: Political semantics and party strategy

In the preceding chapters I have shown that socialist parties' competitive strategies and their electoral payoffs can be explained primarily in terms of a *logic of interests* where actors strive to obtain given objectives (votes, office) in light of realistic beliefs about the constraints set by electoral institutions, the strategic moves of other parties and the voter distribution.[1] Where parties do not follow this logic, organizational constraints on the competition among intraparty groups typically explain departures from vote- or office-seeking strategies. Nevertheless, organizational processes in socialist parties also involve a *logic of ideas* in which the recruitment or exit of party members and internal debates in light of a party's experience of crises in the electoral and the legislative arena bring about changes in the objectives and beliefs that guide a party's strategy.

In Chapter 5, I characterized the formal mechanisms of membership turnover and crisis debates according to which a logic of ideas influences party strategy, but I did not account for the substantive beliefs of activists who join and leave socialist parties and who engage in debates about responses to electoral decline. Why, for example, were "leftist" challengers of the dominant intraparty coalition in the Swedish social democrats or the British Labour Party inspired by a fairly orthodox economic Marxist socialism in the 1970s and the 1980s, whereas their counterparts in the Dutch Labor Party and the German Social Democrats increasingly subscribed to a strong cultural, ecological, communitarian, and libertarian discourse during the same time? The extent of each country's left-libertarian cleavage mobilization, by itself, explains these differences insufficiently. Both in Sweden and in the Netherlands, communitarian issues gained salience in public opinion in the early 1970s, yet social democratic intraparty debates and strategic appeals reflected these changes in different ways in the ensuing decades. In this chapter, I will propose that political traditions identifying acceptable arguments and ideas shape the internal discourse in political parties and limit the range of strategic choices when parties are faced with new challenges.

---

1 I omit rational strategies of long-term oligopolistic competition, the third option explored in Chapter 4, because where parties pursued such strategies they were rarely rational given the circumstances of competition in which they were chosen.

Where politicians engage in strategies consistent with a logic of interests, it is impossible to separate out independent ideas as an identifiable force shaping political action. The task of this chapter, then, is to show the independent contribution of substantive political ideas to the choice of party strategies in those instances where parties abandoned a vote- or office-maximizing logic of interests. Ideas are critical for explaining the *direction in which parties diverge from rational strategies*. Rational action provides the baseline against which to measure the efficacy of ideas.[2]

Ideas have cognitive and normative components that are closely intertwined. Ideas result from diagnostic debates among party activists about the nature of society and its political divisions and from therapeutic discussions about desirable objectives of social change. Material and nonmaterial interests directly govern human conduct, but ideas constitute cognitive and normative frames for interpreting the content of interests and for determining effective ways to pursue them.[3] Ideas are created by individuals, but against the background of an existing fund of linguistic concepts and stock of arguments that are held to be acceptable within a given community and that are updated in light of a continuous flow of new experiences. Ideas thus impose "semantic constraints" on what actors may think and do and on how they interpret their experiences. Ideas are social constructs that guide action, they are not part of a "natural" ordering of political interests or of an "objective" political road map that exists in a prelinguistic world.

Epistemologically, semantic constraints on actors' strategic capabilities may have no other explanatory status than previously discussed external constraints on political action, such as the rules of inter- and intraparty competition. All constraints are constructed through "talk" and social scientists can usually identify them only by careful analysis of linguistic practices.[4] Nevertheless, there are three reasons why it is difficult to employ ideas in explanations of political processes.

First, debates about the nature of "political culture" show that talk about citizens' beliefs and aspirations is less accessible to empirical analysis than talk about following behavioral rules in institutions. Cultural analyses of beliefs and aspirations tend to be few and far between, impressionistic, speculative, or arbitrary. They often rely on educated guesswork based on reading secondary accounts of people's orientations.[5] Other studies engage in a more or less rigorous content

---

2 For a similar methodology in demonstrating the role of ideas in political life, see Lewin (1991).

3 I am obviously influenced here by Weber's analysis of "world images" and ideas that I have already invoked in the first chapter (Weber 1915/1958a,b).

4 Above all, this applies to the exploration of a country's political space of competition through surveys or content analyses. In a subtler way, an organization's rules, "institutions," and power relations are also constituted through linguistic practices analysts cannot divorce from concept formation in the social sciences. Even the political-economic realities discussed in Chapter 3 have a linguistic base. Problems of measuring unemployment, inflation, or growth, let alone structures of the welfare state, show how closely any representation of social reality is tied to linguistic practices.

5 An example is Wildavsky's (1987) effort to link political cultures to alternative strategies of

analysis of texts that are said to reveal actors' interpretations of political reality, but they use questionable coding categories.[6] The most detailed analyses draw on in-depth semistructured interviews or videotapes of group discussions and also suffer from problems of analytical conceptualization and intercultural comparability.[7]

The second problem with semantic analysis is the absence of conceptual schemes that would allow one to compare the content of citizens' orientations. Probably the greatest weakness of the political culture literature is that it has identified alternative practices primarily in terms of proper names ("French" or "German" political culture) or ad hoc concepts ("culture of deference," "amoral familism," etc.) which are difficult to apply and to compare across settings.

The third problem is the difficulty in assessing the *causal efficacy of ideas* in comparison to the external constraints of a situation. For this reason, Elkins and Simeon (1979) recommend employing political culture explanations only as a matter of last resort.[8] In principle, comparison should enable us to distinguish situations where our reading of actors' ideas and of the external constraints with which they are faced produces *convergent* predictions about actors' strategies from situations where ideas and external constraints produce *divergent* predictions about actors' behavior. While it is logically impossible to determine the causal efficacy of ideas in the first instance, the second opens the door for causal analysis.

My analysis of the influence of ideas on social democrats' strategic choices offers no solution to the problem of rigorous data collection on political orienta-tions. By relying on secondary accounts of parties' ideas and justifications for alternative strategies, I do not improve on the weak empirical grounding in the comparative studies of political ideas. But I do address the second problem of cultural analysis by outlining general conceptual tools for distinguishing types of arguments and beliefs in the political discourse in the first section of this chapter. I then explore semantic constraints that account for the ideological direction in which socialist parties' strategies diverged from "rational" office- or vote-maximizing objectives in the 1970s and 1980s. I argue that the possibilities for divergence were limited by the ideological alternatives that had become part of each party's political history of internal and external debate *long before* the strategic challenges of the 1970s and 1980s emerged. These older debates and alternatives played a role in determining whether a social democratic party in the 1970s and 1980s veered from vote- or office-maximizing strategies toward an Old

environmental movements and public policy. The same applies to Thompson et al.'s (1990: 223–60) critical reinterpretation of classics in the study of political culture.

6 Examples are Budge, Robertson, and Hearl's (1987) content analysis of party programs the empirical problems of which I have discussed in Chapter 3. A less rigorous cross-national comparison and explanation of the semantic content of debates on energy policy can be found in Kitschelt (1984). Impressionistic content analysis also drives most cognitive studies of foreign policy-making and strategic thinking.

7 Such explorations in the semantic analysis of citizens' and politicians' interpretations of political life and decision problems include Putnam (1973), Hochschild (1981), Touraine, Dubet, Hegedus, and Wieviorka (1980), and Luker (1984).

8 On the difficulties of employing political culture as a causal variable, see Barry (1980: ch. 3).

Left fundamentalism primarily concerned with property rights and income distribution, or toward the libertarian objectives of the New Left.

## 6.1 STRUCTURING THE SEMANTIC UNIVERSE OF SOCIALIST AND SOCIAL DEMOCRATIC DEBATES

In order to compare ideas in the political discourse with some measure of clarity, I make the controversial assumption that somehow cognitive propositions and normative justifications come in recognizable "packages" and "patterns" of beliefs and orientations that involve coherent sets of postulates and impinge upon social practices.[9] Such packages are often referred to as "ideologies." They explain the actors' situation, define goals, demands and aspirations, and provide arguments and standards of justification for values and beliefs.[10]

At the beginning of Chapter 1, I suggested a typology of alternative political beliefs as the basis for constructing a two-dimensional space of political alternatives to which parties can appeal. On the first dimension, ideologies differ over the relative emphasis placed on institutions of individual or collective choice, markets or formal organization. These alternatives are associated with differences in the emphasis on liberty or equality as ultimate values. On the second dimension, ideologies differ over the nature of and emphasis placed on social reciprocity in face-to-face human interaction and in broader participatory collective institutions governed by shared norms that maximize social "fraternity." Committed communitarians reject both markets and formal organizations as central modes of institutionalization, but express rather different views on the underlying values of liberty and equality. At one extreme, libertarian (anarchist) communitarians wish to establish a spontaneous fraternal order that accommodates both liberty and equality. Within this group, we can distinguish more socialist equality-seeking from more free-market liberty-seeking anarchists. At the other extreme, authoritarian communitarians reject individual freedom and equality in favor of a hierarchical vision of fraternal normative integration.[11] Liberals and socialists generally take a neutral stance on the fraternal foundations of society because their analytical reference point is *not* a distinctly bounded group of human beings tied together by bonds of face-to-face interaction and participatory decision making, but either the

---

9 Thompson et al. (1990: 1) refer to the ensemble of beliefs, values ("cultural bias"), and social relations as "ways of life."

10 In the context of party politics, see Sainsbury (1980: 15–17) for a definition of ideology. I have no intention of pursuing the key questions of ideology theory here, namely whether ideology is false belief and whether ideology has rational or nonrational origins. Among the recent literature on this subject, see especially Boudon (1989: ch. 2–4) and Thompson (1990: 52–67).

11 This option is represented by varieties of Catholic, statist, or fascist corporatisms that call for pyramidally organized, internally solidary, and egalitarian collectives. See Williamson (1986: 19–80). Unlike Streeck and Schmitter (1985), I see no need to introduce corporatism and "private interest government" as a principle of organization independent of markets, formal organization, and community.

abstract individual, stripped of her ties to her associates, or the universe of all citizens and mankind.[12]

Historically, social democracy is situated closer to the pole of formal organization and material equality than the pole of markets and individual liberty on the first "distributive" dimension of this two-dimensional division of modern ideologies. It combines the demand for an egalitarian material baseline for all citizens with the respect of personal freedom in a liberal-democratic order instituting both collective decision making and individual contracting (Padgett and Paterson 1991: 1). Social democracy thus constitutes a synthesis between liberalism and socialism, and, like its intellectual ingredients, it takes no strong position on the second "communitarian" dimension at all.[13]

In contrast to earlier chapters, where I used the concepts of socialism and social democracy *without* drawing a semantic distinction between them, in this chapter I formally separate them. Socialism is more uncompromising than social democracy in its call for the priority of collective decision making and formal organization over markets and individual liberty. Let me emphasize, however, that this ideological difference often is *not* reflected by programmatic differences between parties that carry the notions of socialism or social democracy in their labels. Parties calling themselves socialist are often no less social democratic in their programmatic appeal than parties carrying the social democratic label.

Situating socialism and social democracy within the two-dimensional space of ideological alternatives also sheds light on the various historical traditions of thought in which modern socialist thinking is placed (cf. Eley 1991: 35–45). In the late eighteenth-century and first half of the nineteenth century, early utopian socialism was primarily driven by a communitarian vision of a decentralized social order that implicitly idealized the image of the more or less self-sufficient village economy and called for the preservation of the special life-style and privileged status of crafts occupations. Beginning in the 1860s, political socialism sharply differentiated itself from the older communitarian utopian traditions. Its new doctrines and party organizations firmly linked the objective of material equality for all members of society to institutions of central planning. In the emerging new

---

12 In modern positive theories of institutions inspired by liberal and mildly socialist thought, community therefore appears as a residual category under the ill-explored cover of "loyalty" and "atmosphere." See, e.g., Hirschman (1970) and Williamson (1975).

13 The two-dimensional typology of social institutions and ultimate values I have suggested allows us to locate European social democracy in a more clear-cut way as the grid–group scheme in cultural theory that has been suggested by Aaron Wildavsky and his associates based on the work of the anthropologist Mary Douglas. See esp. Thompson et al. (1990: 157), who try to force socialism into the category of a strongly communitarian egalitarianism. Wildavsky (1987: 82) sees social democracy as a hybrid between a hierarchical collectivism and a sectarian (communitarian) striving for equality. This interpretation does not do justice to social democracy's concern with individual choice and antisectarian universalism. Wildavsky and his associates overrate social democracy's emphasis on fraternity and community, a judgment derived from the close linkage they see between community and equality. I find this association tenuous and analytically misleading.

Marxist socialist discourse, direct democracy and community had little importance and were replaced by a discourse emphasizing the centrality of party and state organization as the guarantors of material equality and citizenship rights: "In other words, there was little interest in the official counsels of the pre-1914 socialist parties in decentralized forms, whether in the shape of cooperative and communitarian self-management schemes pioneered by their early socialist predecessors, or in that of the soviets and workers' councils that emerged from 1917 to 1921" (Eley 1991: 38).

In much of the twentieth century, we encounter three rather sharply distinguished strands of reasoning within labor movements and leftist parties broadly defined. First, a minority communitarian strand was transformed into an anarcho-syndicalist ideology that stressed direct industrial action and workers' self-organization without the intermediating role of parties and state bureaucracies. Second, a dominant Marxist socialist strand emphasized the centralization of property rights and collective redistribution of scarce goods by hierarchically organized agents (state and party). Later on, with the stabilization of liberal-democratic regimes, a third social democratic variant of the labor movement diluted socialist thinking by accepting elements of political and economic liberalism and calls for a combination of centralized coordination and markets.

The key principles of what became the dominant socialist discourse in Western democracies are the priority of collective choice over individual choice or fraternal group consensus, an egalitarian provision of life chances within the framework of centralized societal concertation, and the priority of collective production and distribution over private and personal concerns with consumption and social reproduction. Even in its attenuated, more flexible social democratic version, this discourse has promoted social equality over individual liberty or communal fraternity.

Social democracy is distinct from socialism not only by its concessions to the principles of individual liberty and freedom of contract, but also in a number of other respects. Whereas socialists endorsed a realist and technocratic epistemology according to which the correct Marxist social theory enables them to engage in a large-scale reorganization of society without having to fear unwanted and unintended outcomes, social democrats subscribe to a fallibilist epistemology teaching mistrust of grand theories and advocating incremental trial-and-error techniques of social change. Further, whereas socialism is concerned with the redistribution of property rights as the key problem of justice, social democrats place greater emphasis on the rules for distributing scarce resources. While socialists endorse full economic equality, social democrats support a version of Rawls's second principle of justice, according to which equality should be pursued within the limits of efficiency; inequality is acceptable to social democrats as long as it helps the worst-off in society to improve their lot, provided a minimum standard of living guarantees the primary goods underlying human dignity and self-respect to all citizens. Finally, whereas socialists have expressed an anthropology of work as self-realization, social democrats are more inclined to hope for a reduction of the chores of work life through more leisure activities.[14]

The New Left that developed first in the 1960s and then fed into the "libertarian Left" of the 1970s and 1980s can be understood as a response to the success of the social democratic vision of society. Three ideas drive the left-libertarian challenge, all of which are directed against the absence of communitarian elements in conventional socialist and social democratic theory. First, the socialist discourse has neglected what precedes and what follows the process of material appropriation and distribution – that is, the relationship of human beings to nature and to the sociotechnical organization of production, on the one hand, and the process of social consumption and enjoyment, on the other. For socialists, nature is primarily a raw material, a "human laboratory"; sociotechnical organization is a question of efficiency; and styles of social consumption and aesthetic enjoyment, as well as human reproduction through gender relations, have played only a subterranean, rarely emphasized role in socialist discourses (Baudrillard 1975: 22–47). Second, socialists have privileged relations of production over "relations of social recognition" among human beings. As a consequence, socialists have not developed an adequate grasp of social community and of the construction of individual and collective identity.[15] Third, lacking a full appreciation of the bases of human autonomy and collective identity, socialists have also been unable to develop a satisfactory theory of political democracy that would recognize the importance of citizens' participatory involvement.

Within this framework of ideological coordinates, contemporary socialist and social democratic parties may remain committed to the compromise between liberalism and socialism embodied in the Keynesian welfare state. Alternatively, they may adopt a traditional socialist discourse that emphasizes equality, restrictions on private property, and the priority of collective decision making over individual choice and communal reciprocity. Further, social democratic parties may opt for a mixed strategy of incorporating libertarian and communitarian elements into their programmatic appeals and tone down central collective decision making. Finally, they may take a more explicitly communitarian stance, one directed at incorporating anarcho-syndicalist principles of reciprocal social organization at the expense of a social order based on markets and central collective choice.

I have argued in previous chapters that the extent of popular left-libertarian cleavage mobilization, the balance of fractionalization in the party system, and intraparty organization affect the rational choice of social democratic parties' ideological appeals. What I have not explained, however, is the *ideological direction* in which parties' appeals may diverge from rational competitive strategies. I now argue that this direction is influenced by the historical trajectory of socialist thinking *and* of adversarial ideologies in a country.

---

14 For a further elaboration of these points, see Kitschelt (1991a: 199–202).
15 This is Jürgen Habermas's (1985) key complaint about the Marxist legacy.

## 6.2 THE CAUSAL EFFICACY OF IDEAS: EXPLAINING THE ELECTORALLY NONRATIONAL SOCIAL DEMOCRATIC PARTY APPEALS

The causal efficacy of ideas can be demonstrated only where party strategies diverge from a logic of interests, based on self-regarding vote- and office-maximizing objectives, toward a logic of ideas that inspires party stances that undercut vote- or office-seeking ambitions. Table 6.1 identifies the ideological content of party strategies in all those instances where parties pursued the type of suboptimal electoral strategies identified in Chapter 4. The table includes all those instances in which (1) socialist and social democratic parties were vacillating or strategically immobile in the face of left-libertarian and free-market challenges, (2) engaged in office-seeking strategies of pivoting under unfavorable conditions, or (3) ventured into oligopolistic competition under unfavorable conditions.[16] Although conditions for oligopolistic competition were favorable for the French and the Spanish socialists in the 1970s, I have also included these cases because the substantive ideological direction of oligopolistic competition – conventional socialist or libertarian leftism – requires explanation. Here, as well as in all other cases listed in Table 6.1, the critical question is: Why did whole parties or influential internal minority currents appeal to a traditional socialist discourse on property rights and income distribution in some instances, to a conventional social democratic Keynesian welfare state program in others, and to a libertarian leftism in yet others?

The party strategies listed in Table 6.1 can be divided into three groups. First, some parties did not respond to changing voter demands for more libertarian politics or market efficiency. Instead, they adhered to suboptimal positions ranging from a defense of the Keynesian welfare state to traditional socialist ideas about workers' empowerment and income redistribution. The Swedish social democrats and the British Labour Party fit this pattern. In both instances, no left-libertarian opening occurred and influential party currents engaged in a socialist discourse about property rights and economic redistribution. A second group of parties tried to hold on to social democratic positions, but was more tempted by left-libertarian alternatives than a recourse to traditional socialism in the 1980s. This trajectory characterizes the German SPD and, to a lesser extent, the Austrian SPÖ of the 1980s. The Danish social democrats are somewhere between the two groups, generally displaying a great deal of ideological immobility around traditional social democratic doctrines with intermittent gestures toward socialist ideas (Esping-Andersen 1985: 213). In a final group of parties, the political discourse ranges from traditional socialist to left-libertarian positions. This configuration characterized Southern European parties in the 1970s and the Italian PCI in the first half of the 1980s. In general terms, Group I deviated from vote- or office-maximizing strategies in favor of a traditional socialist stance in the 1970s and 1980s. Group II only debated the extent to which left-libertarian deviations might

16 I omit here the cases of the French and Italian communists that are included in Chapter 4.

Table 6.1. *Logic of ideas over logic of interests in socialist parties 1970–90*

Group I: Socialist vs. social democratic discourse

Britain

| | | |
|---|---|---|
| (Labour Party) | 1970–87 | Party position is considerably too socialist to be vote- or office-seeking. |
| Sweden (Social democrats) | 1970s–1980s | Party position insists too much on socialist issues of property rights and too little on libertarian positions to be vote- or office-maximizing. |

Group II: Social democratic vs. left-libertarian discourse

| | | |
|---|---|---|
| Germany (Social democrats) | 1983–90 | Party position vacillates between left-libertarian oligopolistic position (1983) and a conventional social democratic program (1987). |
| Austria (Social democrats) | 1983–86 | Party position incorporates too little market efficiency and shows little flexibility to libertarian minorities to be vote- or office-maximizing. |
| Denmark (Social democrats) | 1970–87 | Mixed case: Party strategy stays with dominant social democratic strategy and resists left-libertarian politics until the late 1980s; brief excursion into socialist appeals in the 1970s. |

Group III: Socialist vs. left-libertarian discourse

| | | |
|---|---|---|
| France (Socialists) | 1973–78 | |
| Spain (Socialists) | 1976–79 | Left-libertarian appeals in a strategy of oligopolistic competition with the communists. |
| Italy (Socialists) | 1972–76 | |

be embraced in the 1980s. Group III deviated from maximizing strategies in favor of socialist and left-libertarian stances in the 1970s but turned to rational strategic stances in the 1980s.

The difference between countries with socialist deviations and all others surfaces in the expert judgments gathered by Laver and Hunt (1992) on socialist parties' positions on economic issues (nationalization of industry, welfare state) and libertarian issues (ecology over economic growth, moral permissiveness). Based on calculations presented in Chapter 4, we can measure each social democratic party's distance on each dimension from a country's imputed mean voter position (Figure 6.1).[17] Starting at the lower left, party positions along the diagonal line become progressively more socialist and libertarian. Parties' positions on both dimensions are highly correlated and most parties are situated within a narrow interval around that diagonal line, an interval that becomes wider as one moves to more extreme positions.[18]

The first group of countries listed in Table 6.1 with socialist "deviations" from

17 The data on which Figure 6.1 is based are drawn from Figures 4.3B through 4.13B.
18 Without knowing the balance of fractionalization in the party system, the competitors' strategic stances, and the level of left-libertarian cleavage mobilization, of course, we cannot say whether a position is electorally rational or not.

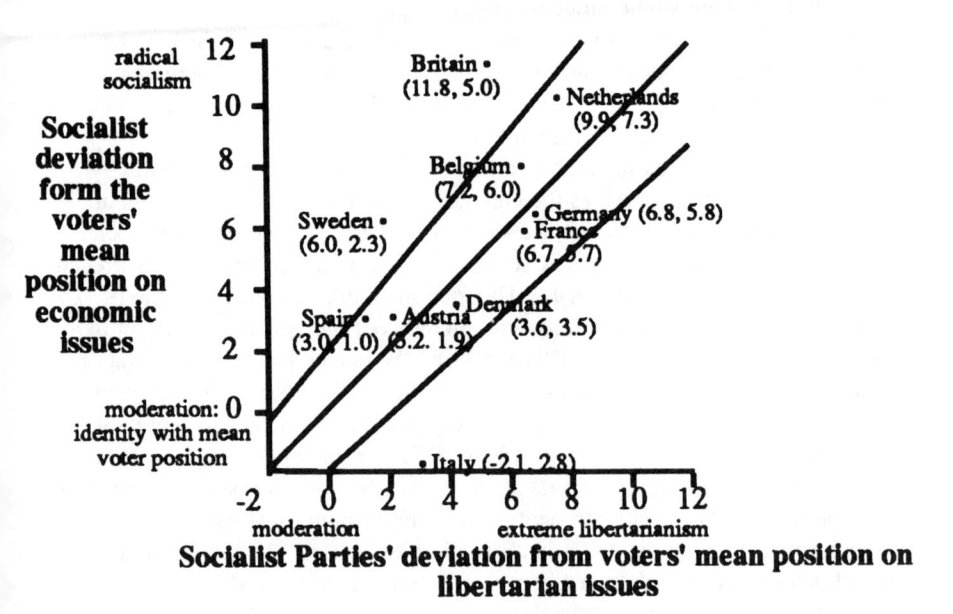

**Socialist Parties' deviation from voters' mean position on libertarian issues**

Figure 6.1. Socialist parties' position on libertarian and economic issues: deviation from a country's mean voter position
*Source:* Based on Laver and Hunt's (1992) expert judgments of socialist party positions on economic and libertarian issues reported in Figures 4.3B through 4.13B (Chapter 4). Scores in Figure 6.1 represent the difference between a party's position on economic or libertarian issues and the hypothetical mean voter position in a country; e.g., in Figure 4.3B, the PvdA's score on socialist economics is 14.1, the mean voter score is 24.0, and the difference score reported in Figure 6.1 is 9.9.

vote- or office-maximizing strategies – Britain and Sweden – are clearly set apart by being located *outside* the region proximate to the diagonal. The British Labour Party is moderately libertarian, but extremely socialist; the Swedish social democrats are moderately socialist but lack any libertarian issue leadership. Both parties have relatively more pronounced socialist economic positions than libertarian appeals. The second group of countries in Table 6.1, including Germany, Austria, and, with greater qualifications Denmark, is characterized by traditional moderate social democratic positions (Austria, Denmark) or by slightly more intense socialist and libertarian positions (Germany). Note that Laver and Hunt collected their assessments at a time when the SPD was moving from a decisively moderate libertarian and social democratic appeal in the January 1987 electoral campaign to a more libertarian position under the leadership of Oskar Lafontaine in 1990.

The final group of parties including the "Mediterranean" deviations toward socialism and libertarianism in the 1970s no longer comprises a coherent group in the late 1980s, when all the relevant parties had adjusted to rational party positions within the peculiar systemic opportunity structures of their countries. In this vein, the Italian socialists now have abandoned just about every remnant of socialism and engaged in a mildly libertarian appeal, the Spanish socialists have embraced a centrist social democratic strategy of pivoting, and the French socialists have pursued an intermediate socialist-libertarian appeal that has held the communists at bay and promised success as long as the party's bourgeois competitors proved unable to reclaim the political center and the ecologists were unable to establish themselves as a "second" libertarian Left.

What accounts for the singularity of British and Swedish socialist debates? Why did continental parties, such as the German or Austrian socialists, struggle more with libertarian issues from the second half of the 1970s on than with socialist policy debates? And why was it so easy for the Italian, Spanish, and French socialist parties to put aside leftist and libertarian programs at the end of the 1970s? Only the final question can be answered in terms of the systemic theory of party competition I have detailed in Chapter 4 and the account of intraorganizational dynamics in Chapter 5. In Southern Europe, the left-libertarian strategy paid off only as long as it weakened communist support, and party leaders were able to abandon it when this objective was achieved (France and Spain) or clearly missed (Italy). But even this argument does not reveal why genuinely libertarian concerns became so important in the competition with the communist parties in the 1970s.

One simple hypothesis that might explain the different ideological content of social democratic, socialist, or libertarian visions in the parties' deviations from vote- or office-maximizing strategies is based on cleavage mobilization. In countries with intense left-libertarian cleavage mobilization, the main axis of party competition is centered *more* on the left-libertarian versus right-authoritarian alternatives than in other countries, where the socialist versus capitalist alternative remains prominent. Only where left-libertarianism is strong and defines the main axis of party competition may socialist parties be inclined to deviate from vote- or office-maximizing policies toward left-libertarian alternatives. Translating this hypothesis into the actions of individual party members, in countries with a broad left-libertarian infrastructure it is more likely that left-libertarians will be recruited into socialist parties and work to recast the party discourse than in countries with thriving working-class labor organizations and subcultures that supply activists favoring socialist rather than moderate social democratic positions. Where working-class socialism has remained entrenched and parties have appealed to such sentiments, it is also likely that the main axis of party competition is still closer to the dimension of distributive conflicts between market and state than the communitarian dimension between libertarian and authoritarian positions.

The discussion in Chapter 4 showed that countries with high left-libertarian mobilization, such as the Netherlands, Denmark, or Germany, also exhibit a distinctive recentering of party competition from pure issues of economic distribution to the continuum ranging from left-libertarian to right-authoritarian positions. This general rule, however, does not apply in all cases. In Britain, for example, left-libertarian cleavage mobilization is intermediate, yet the major parties have by and large refused to compete on "communitarian" issues on the libertarian–authoritarian dimension. A similar process took place in Sweden, where left-libertarian mobilization in the 1980s was fairly strong, yet the major bourgeois and social democratic parties still almost exclusively emphasized and competed on distributive issues.

If a sociological argument that traces the ideological (re)configuration of party competition back to left-libertarian popular mobilization and to the underlying postindustrialization of contemporary Western societies fails to account for the content of socialist parties' ideological deviance from vote- or office-maximizing strategies, an explicitly political account of party strategy that focuses on the nature of political alternatives debated in each country may do better. The *continuity of ideas* over time is a critical factor influencing the ways parties stake out electoral appeals and hammer out intraparty consensus. Past ideological debates within and among competing parties pattern the range of appeals parties may issue with some promise of political acceptance at a later point in time. A logic of ideas thus identifies a historical stock of political arguments available to parties in the competitive struggle if they wish to remain credible. Innovative strategies are framed within the available stock of ideas, although they may incrementally recast such ideas. The credibility of ideas is analogous to the notion of "reputation" in iterated games. Actors are able to make certain strategic moves with some prospect of success only because they have accumulated a reputation among other players through the behavior (and talk) they have exhibited in the past. Political parties maintain a continuity of ideas and credible positions, even across generations, through institutions such as journals, newspapers, party training centers, programmatic documents, and rules of intraparty promotion. The logic of ideas thus materializes in lived political practices, institutions and corresponding intellectual artifacts that can be examined by conducting content analyses.

A comparison of socialist parties in Scandinavia and Britain to those in continental Europe highlights one overriding difference in each region's available stock of political arguments. In Scandinavia and Britain, liberalism and social democracy have been hegemonic ideological forces in the arena of political reasoning for close to a century. They have structured the political dialogue around questions of liberty and equality, individual property rights and the central government's power to intervene in the marketplace, social class and citizenship. This hegemonic discourse has by and large marginalized concerns with the preservation of individual and collective identities or the conditions for community and fraternity in modern society. In contrast, in most continental European polities, the importance of the communitarian discourse has historically surfaced in at least two influential political currents. On the political right, various statist and Catholic-corporatist political visions have always posed a strong challenge to political-economic liberalism. On the political left, undercurrents of anarchist and anarcho-syndicalist thinking and political practices have accompanied working-class movements from their inception to the interwar period and have left their imprints on divisions within and between working-class parties and labor unions. In some countries, such as France, the Netherlands, and Italy, Catholic social thinking and communitarian-anarchist currents came together in New Left organizations in the 1960s.[19]

The existence of ideological traditions and arguments beyond liberalism and socialism have made continental European socialists more susceptible to the distinctive communitarian impetus of left-libertarian politics. The absence of socialist-liberal hegemony has contributed to the breakdown of class-based politics in European social democracy, even in those instances where political activists manifestly opposed vote- and office-maximizing strategies. The class background of the new radicals in the 1960s and 1970s does not explain their ideological outlook. In all countries, the vanguard advocating social democratic strategies deviating from vote- or office-maximizing objectives typically were not working-class stalwarts or labor unionists, but individuals with an occupational background in the new personal service sector salariat. In Britain these individuals veered to the socialist Left (cf. Whiteley 1983; Seyd and Whiteley 1991, 1992), elsewhere they subscribed to left-libertarian ideas. In continental social democratic parties, whose intellectuals have always been intimately familiar with the heterodoxies of paternalist and anarchist communitarian discourses, the new libertarian demands struck a more responsive chord than in the Anglo-Saxon and Scandinavian region where liberalism and socialism have reigned supreme. In all countries, however, working-class stalwarts and labor unionists inside socialist parties remained wedded to the conventional Keynesian welfare state agenda and rarely supported the libertarian Left or neosocialist appeals.

Differences in the range of arguments acceptable within socialist parties in the 1980s thus can be accounted for in terms of the salience of paternalist and anarchist communitarian discourses cutting across the liberalism–socialism polarity and its compromise formula, conventional social democracy, in previous decades. This hypothesis is consonant with the conclusions of many observers about the career of working-class politics. Przeworski and Sprague (1986), for instance, emphasize that cross-class political appeals, particularly those of religion or ethnicity, undermine class unity and offer alternative principles of collective self-identification. Both of these cross-cutting principles are clearly related to communitarian conceptions of particularist, bounded collectivities. The rivalry between class and other nonliberal principles of political mobilization has also been relevant for the construction of the welfare state. Both Wilensky (1981) and Esping-Andersen (1990) highlight the Catholic contribution to social policy but point out that Catholic welfare states on the European continent are based on status-related and hierarchically stratified benefits systems accruing to occupational groups as opposed to the more egalitarian social democratic welfare states in Scandinavia and Britain.

The heterogeneity of discursive traditions within the working class movements of different countries has long been recognized (cf. Katznelson and Zolberg 1986; Eley 1991). It is therefore not surprising that past debates within working-class

---

19  This applies, for example, to the French PSU (Hauss 1978) and the Dutch Radical Political Party (PPR).

movements, particularly between socialists, anarchists, and Catholics, still leave their imprint on the strategic choices and practices of contemporary socialist parties when vote- and office-seeking are not the overriding political rationales. In the next section, I document the cross-national differences in the strategic debates of those socialist parties that have failed to pursue vote- or office-maximizing courses of action in the 1970s and 1980s. I place special emphasis on the British and Swedish parties, both of which operate in an ideological environment characterized by a liberal–socialist hegemony.

## 6.3 SOCIALIST DISCOURSES AND THEIR IDEOLOGICAL COMPETITION

In Britain and Sweden, where socialist parties have been immersed in a discourse dividing liberalism from socialism, they have encountered particular difficulties in incorporating libertarian themes into their strategic appeals (group I). In other countries, the experience of Catholic and anarchist political counterparts generally facilitated socialist parties' acceptance of the libertarian discourse. Even here, however, the extent and the role of libertarian politics varies between a Northern European pattern, including Austria, Germany, and the Netherlands,[20] and a Southern European alternative with France and Italy. It is important to emphasize that the ideological appeals parties have endorsed in their pursuit of strategies diverging from vote or office seeking show no correlation with party organization. Decentralized framework parties that have empowered their rank and file and that have weak leaders have shifted toward a left-libertarian stance (Netherlands) or a socialist stance (Britain). Conversely, among the Northern European mass parties, only the Swedish social democrats incorporated a neosocialist thrust into their electoral appeal in the late 1970s and early 1980s, whereas their continental competitors vacillated between conventional social democratic and libertarian programs.

*Group I: Social democratic versus socialist discourse*

Although the Swedish and British labor parties encountered different left-libertarian and market-efficiency challenges, both parties revived the socialist distributive discourse. Both parties faced incentives to engage in pivoting strategies, but in the Swedish case, the realization of that goal required a stronger commitment to libertarian politics (e.g., ecology, feminism, decentralized administration, and citizens' participation) than in Britain. In both instances, however, the parties failed to move to a strategically rational position. The British Labour Party experienced an intense socialist revival, whereas the Swedish social democrats succumbed to a relatively mild resurgence of the redistributive agenda around the Meidner plan's profit sharing and "cold socialization" schemes to shift ownership in productive assets to the working class (cf. Chapter 3). In both

20 The Danish social democrats are a borderline case between the first and the second group of parties.

countries the peace and student movements of 1968, which presaged libertarian political initiatives elsewhere, were unable to mobilize a large segment of the generation born after World War II.

A brief review of the two parties' ideological development shows the historical absence of libertarian themes. Although the British Labour Party and the Swedish social democrats emerged from different origins and have always faced constitutional arrangements and labor relations that have promoted different party organizations, both parties rejected orthodox Marxist socialism and arrived at essentially pragmatic, doctrineless, and populist redistributive programs by the 1920s. This was possible in large part because they never had to confront any significant communitarian challenges.

In Britain, Marxism was limited to one strand of debate within the Independent Labour Party (ILP), a precursor organization to the Labour Party whose activists never gained much influence. More important than Marxism were purely ethical socialism and Fabian reformist socialism (Foote 1986: 19–36), a "gospel of discipline, efficiency and order" with "stifling, joyless austerity" espoused especially by Sidney and Beatrice Webb (Morgan 1987: 54). Labour did face a syndicalist challenge in the first decades of the century, primarily in the guise of "guild socialism," which sought not so much to overcome existing property relations as to abolish the existing industrial autocracy in favor of a libertarian system of occupational and industrial self-organization (cf. Foote 1986: 85–125; Pierson 1979: 202–26). The emotive, fraternal quality of the guilds was particularly important for this strand of reasoning. Overall, however, the challenge of guild socialism remained confined to a few intellectuals.

In Sweden, social democracy had firmer roots in Marxism, although the party's early doctrinal orthodoxy before World War I is easily overstated.[21] Like its British counterpart, the Swedish SAP was exposed to communitarian ideas, particularly through the programmatic thinking of Ernst Wigforss, one of the party's important politicians, who also was impressed by guild socialism. Nevertheless, this impulse left no enduring legacy in the party.[22] While it had initially taken a negative position on consumer cooperatives, it moved to a stance of benevolent neutrality later on (Tingsten 1973: 686–92). By the early 1940s, the "ideological heritage of Swedish social democracy was a mixture of Marxist thought, reformism, strands of guild socialism, and a self-devised variant of Keynesian economic theory infusing the party's notion of economic planning" (Sainsbury 1980: 21). It practiced a nonclass appeal to equalization and to a "people's home" with full employment and security for all.

---

21  In this sense, more recent accounts have criticized Herbert Tingsten's (1941/1973: esp. 246–335) magisterial account of the ideological development of Swedish social democracy for overstating the contrast between the party's appeal before 1920 and after 1930 (cf. Sainsbury 1980; Tilton 1990).

22  Tilton (1990: 45) claims that the influences of guild socialism were only felt in the 1970s, when the party embraced industrial democracy.

With World War II and the temporary rise of the Soviet Union's reputation in the eyes of some Western intellectuals who were inspired by the global antifascist struggle, both the British Labour Party and the Swedish social democrats witnessed the resurgence of reformist versions of Marxian socialism. In Sweden, the socialist renewal reached its high water mark in 1948 when the SAP ran on an electoral platform that envisioned a dramatic change in ownership rights, more planning, industrial democracy, and greater social equality. In Britain, the new socialism articulated itself in a realigned Left around Aneurin Bevan, many of whose younger followers were later involved in the Labour Party's socialist Left during the 1970s and 1980s (cf. Foote 1986: 267–86; Schneer 1988). The dominant moderate coalitions in both parties, however, were able to contain the socialist demands, when bourgeois parties electorally benefited from the labor parties' internal controversies and began to undermine the socialists' capacity to govern.

In the 1950s and the 1960s, both parties were led by coalitions firmly supporting the Keynesian welfare state. In Britain, Harold Wilson, a former participant in the Bevanite Left, emphasized economic growth through technological change rather than redistribution. In Sweden, the most important innovations promoted by the social democrats concerned a supplementary pension scheme, the accumulated funds of which would be reinvested in the economy, and a variety of labor market and investment policies. The student movement of 1968 and the economic crises of the early 1970s triggered a reideologization of social democracy in both countries, but characteristically the emerging debates did not focus on the new issues and challenges of individual emancipation and participatory democracy surfacing in the late 1960s and early 1970s. Instead, the parties channeled the new radical impulses into the old language of Marxist socialism, with an emphasis on property rights, workers' empowerment on the shop floor, and income distribution.

This tendency is most clear-cut in the case of the Labour Party, where the socialist Left gradually began to strengthen from the closing days of Wilson's administration in 1969–70 through the era of the Conservative Heath government. The Left's influence burgeoned under the renewed Wilson–Callaghan Labour government from 1974 to 1979 and reached its zenith with Michael Foot's election as party leader in 1981. The thrust of the leftist challenge had to do with the nationalization of industry, the preservation of the unions' right to engage in unregulated strike action, workers' control over the shop floor and investment decisions, a more redistributive system of taxation, and a host of other redistributive class issues. The only prominent nonclass issues featured by the Labour Left – rejection of the stationing of new NATO medium-range nuclear missiles and unilateral disarmament – had a long tradition in party debates and did not constitute a breakthrough to a new agenda.

A perusal of programmatic statements by the Labour Left in the mid-1980s reveals no readiness to consider the new themes of left-libertarian politics. Ecology rarely surfaces in such debates, and feminism appears only in the garb of equality-oriented socialist feminism, concerned with questions of distributive justice rather than gender identity.[23] Nonclass social movements, if discussed at all, are considered to be phenomena subordinate to the class struggle. In the second half of the 1980s, when the ideological pendulum in the Labour party began to swing back toward the center after two consecutive electoral defeats with conventional socialist programs, it was also difficult to discern new policy departures beyond a middle-of-the-road neo-Keynesian approach to economic management. This situation has remained true in the early 1990s. Most rank-and-file activists are still firmly entrenched in the Marxist-socialist discourse (Seyd and Whiteley 1992). And even in the 1992 election campaign, the most important promise the party made to voters was that a prospective Labour government would impose a more redistributive income tax to pay for social policy reforms.[24]

The Swedish social democrats also were unable to break the mold of conventional discursive patterns established in the first half of the century and thus could not overcome the polarity between liberalism and socialism. In the early 1970s, the party redefined the new libertarian challenge in terms of the old themes of property, industrial control, and redistribution. The social democrats seized on the idea of co-determination in Swedish corporations, an issue that generated next to no enthusiasm in the electorate (Elvander 1980: 254). Instead, the nonsocialist parties trumped the social democrats with the left-libertarian issues of administrative decentralization and ecology (cf. Therborn 1992: 113–4).

Another important policy idea eventually advocated by the Swedish social democrats, the introduction of wage earners' funds, was initially proposed by the main Swedish blue collar union in 1975 and strictly adhered to a socialist discourse fixated on large, centralized, formal organizations. This interpretation particularly applies to the outline of the so-called Meidner plan, which envisioned a surcharge on corporate profits to be deposited in union-controlled central funds that would gradually acquire Sweden's productive capital. Subsequent, less centralized versions of the plan responding to the outrage not only of bourgeois, but also libertarian forces in Swedish politics about the centralization of power envisioned by the Meidner plan did little to allay popular fears of a new and unaccountable concentration of economic power resulting from the plan's implementation. The plan's concerns seemed out of touch with those voters whose main political worries had not much to do with the ownership and control of productive property. Even when the new social democratic government diluted the original proposal in 1983 by reducing the amount of revenue the funds could collect, decentralizing fund management to the regional level, partially removing them from the control of labor unions, and placing a cap on the proportion of capital the funds could hold

---

23 Good examples of the perseverance of the traditional left agenda are Coates and Johnston (1983) and Curran (1984).
24 In the 1992 campaign platforms of all three parties, left-libertarian issues, especially ecology and women's issues, played a subordinate role and were not prominently featured during their campaigns.

in any single company, the majority of social democratic voters and union members still would not support the proposal.[25]

At the same time, the SAP was slow in responding to the left-libertarian agenda that began to emerge with the struggle against nuclear power in the early 1970s. Not by chance, it was the small (post-)Communist Party and the Center Party that saw a political opening and claimed the left-libertarian themes for themselves. The SAP never regained the intellectual initiative on environmental issues, although it tried to adapt its policy to the exigencies of a continued strong environmental mobilization. This change was too late and too halfhearted to be fully accepted by many voters.[26]

Swedish social democrats have also adopted only those elements of the feminist agenda that easily fit into the conventional socialist discourse on equality and gender solidarity. They shun, however, a feminism that insists on women's self-organization, the right to be different from men, and the expression of a new gender-based communitarian culture (Eduards 1991). Joyce Gelb (1989: 175) quotes a study on Swedish feminism and politics which concludes that " '[q]ualitative' gender issues, unrelated to economic concerns, have been neglected in a system that defines equality almost exclusively in economic terms." And her own study finds that in Sweden equality is still defined in male terms:

An equal-opportunities mentality pervades society and policy-making; the emphasis on sex neutrality coupled with cooperation has produced a system in which women's issues are no longer perceived as a problem and are almost wholly integrated into family and social policy. Nevertheless, thus far equality has been defined exclusively in male terms. As most Swedish women interviewed for this study agreed, gender-neutral policies in a society still highly stratified by gender end up by benefiting the already powerful – that is, males. (Gelb 1989: 176)

Overall, it is fair to conclude that the Swedish social democrats, like their British colleagues, missed the opportunity to seize the new issues and build electoral coalitions around ecology and feminism (Tilton 1990: 246–7). Where the Swedish and British labor parties diverged from strategies of vote or office maximization it was not to embrace left-libertarian issues but to fight losing battles to push thoroughly unpopular policies inspired by traditional socialist ideas such as further nationalization of industry or the Meidner plan aiming at a cold socialization of Swedish business. Such policies failed to rally support not only because even most left voters felt they were too radical, but because citizens perceived such changes as largely irrelevant for their concerns with life chances in a postindustrial society.

I have described the ideological thrust of non–vote- or office-maximizing currents in British and Swedish left parties at some length because they provide the

25 See, among others, Lewin (1988: 291–6).
26 See, e.g., the party's new program (Socialdemokraterna 1989b). One would go too far, however, to claim with Therborn (1992: 118–19) that for a while the party focused on postindustrial issues and that a new alignment of labor and environmentalists came about after the 1988 election. For example, in 1988 the strongest advocate of administrative decentralization and more citizens' choice in the social democratic cabinet was dismissed from office (cf. Premfors 1991).

hardest evidence for the autonomous causal impact of ideas on party strategy. In both cases, intraparty radicals advocated that the parties diverge from rational strategies not simply by being more extreme than electorally necessary on the dominant competitive dimension of their party system, but by fighting against a qualitative reorientation of the competitive dimension from distributive socialist–capitalist to more sociocultural libertarian–authoritarian issues. In the two other groups of social democratic parties I discuss next, the problem of nonrational party strategies is more a quantitative problem of the parties' location on the competitive dimension than a qualitative problem of whether the parties should position themselves on that dimension at all.

### *Group II: Social democratic versus left-libertarian discourse*

In contrast to Britain and Sweden, electorally suboptimal strategies followed by the German and Austrian parties are not attributable to their propensity to gravitate back to conventional socialist positions, but to their oscillation between support of conventional Keynesian welfare state policies and incorporation of the left-libertarian discourse. The German SPD and, to a lesser extent, the Austrian SPÖ have faced an onslaught by new left-libertarian forces that have been intent on disorganizing the parties' conventional social democratic discourse at a time when the parties have undertaken efforts to respond to the challenge of market efficiency with centrist platforms designed to capture the pivot of the party system. The Austrian and German social democrats belong to a group of countries in which the socialist discourse never constituted the sole adversary of a market-liberal Right. Instead, it has had to compete with religious-paternalist visions of the good social order, as well as ethnic, regional, and linguistic particularisms, which have often kept both socialist and market-liberal thinking on the defensive.

The diversity of the ideological universe in these countries where communitarian visions cut across the liberalism-socialism divide is likely to have facilitated the defection of leftist intellectuals from conventional socialist tenets and promoted the emergence of visions of libertarian community within socialist politics that constituted a counterpoint to the established authoritarian and paternalist communitarian appeals encountered in these countries. It is not coincidental that anticlericalism has always been a powerful mobilizing force within socialist politics, although the Austrian and German socialists attempted to tone down their anticlerical rhetoric from the 1960s onward. Moreover, the importance of non-distributive ideological divisions led socialist politicians to search for new issues that would divide the bourgeois parties' electoral appeal. Thus, in the 1961 electoral campaign the SPD's candidate for the office of chancellor, Willy Brandt, somewhat prematurely seized on environmental issues by promising a blue sky over Germany's heavy industrial areas long before environmentalism attracted popular attention.

There is also a more indirect path that reveals a micro-logic linking the pluralism of political discourses in these countries to the susceptibility of social democrats to left-libertarian topics. Activists who express such ideas tend to come from professional and white collar families steeped in nonsocialist beliefs. In the 1950s and 1960s, the dominant nonsocialist creed in Germany and Austria, however, was not market liberalism pure and simple, but a belief in capitalism combined with religious-paternalist communitarianism. While the student and peace movements of the late 1960s discarded the reverence for paternalist authority and capitalism, young radicals kept a spirit of community alive that, within a different ideological context, had been nurtured in their parents' homes. For this reason, on the European continent, and particularly in Catholic countries, the New Left established a discourse that was concerned with community (through participation) at least as much as with equality. Eventually, this spirit entered socialist parties through turnover of activists and inspired radicals to reshape the parties' programmatic debates.[27] The erosion of the authoritarian and communitarian Catholic "pillar" of middle-class political organization through generational change thus contributed to the rise of a libertarian Left.

Studies of German SPD activists show that between the mid-1970s and the mid-1980s the party's conventional socialist Left was transformed and absorbed into a new libertarian Left embracing the new issues of ecology, feminism, and participatory politics (cf. Schmitt 1987). By the early 1980s, the Marxist-socialist Left in the SPD was virtually dead. Nevertheless, given the organizational inertia of the SPD, left-libertarians could not make a decisive breakthrough to strategic dominance and succeeded only in causing the party to oscillate between alternative strategies in the 1980s. The party went through a protracted debate to formulate a new program that was intended to supersede the Bad Godesberger Programm of 1958. The compromise formula agreed upon in 1989 at a special party conference attempts to integrate conventional social democratic concerns with the new participatory, ecological and feminist themes (SPD 1989).[28] As Lösche (1988: 461) has argued, the debate about the new program was probably more important than the final document that eventually emerged from it.

The process of left-libertarian experimentation within socialist parties, of course, has gone much further in another country with a strong, but since 1960 rapidly eroding religious-communitarian tradition, the Netherlands. New party members in the PvDA were able to sweep away much of the conventional social democratic discourse by the early 1970s and blend its remnants into a left-libertarian appeal.[29] In the Netherlands, however, the cues sent by the balance of party system fractionalization and the overall left-libertarian mobilization of the

27 Empirically, to substantiate this micro-logic, it would have to be shown that (1) left-libertarian radicals in socialist parties primarily come from "middle-class" homes where fathers were professionals, civil servants, or small businessmen, and that (2) these homes put great emphasis on religious devotion either within Catholicism or an austere version of Protestant-Lutheran-pietist doctrine.

28 The party's new discourse between the various alternatives is also documented in the various publications by its 1990 chancellor candidate Oskar Lafontaine. See especially Lafontaine (1988).

29 Cf. Wolinetz (1977) and Boivin et al. (1978). Voerman (1991) emphasizes the uneasy linkage between socialist and libertarian ideals in the PvDA's new dominant coalition.

electorate made the PvDA's left-libertarian party strategy vote maximizing. For that reason, it is more difficult to attribute the PvDA's strategic change in the 1970s to a logic of ideas rather than a logic of competition.

While the Dutch PvDA has done more than the German SPD to embrace left-libertarian ideology, the Austrian socialists have certainly done less. The relatively slow development of new left-libertarian conflicts is rooted in the extraordinary organizational and ideological tenacity of both the Catholic and the socialist camps in Austrian society. In the 1950s and the 1960s, the SPÖ met with stiff internal resistance when it tried to distance itself from conventional socialist doctrines. The party that had created its own "Austro-Marxist" ideological tradition, found it difficult to accept the exigencies of modern social democracy (Sully 1982: ch. 6). This was still evidenced in the 1978 party program that generally modernized the party's program under Bruno Kreisky's leadership but still contained remnants of Marxist doctrines as the price of achieving a broad intraparty consensus, such as the call for superseding class divisions (Kriechbauer 1984; Matka 1984: 373). By the mid-1980s, the party's main problem was its tenacious clinging to time-honored social democratic principles rather than a vigorous socialist challenge (Faulhaber 1986; Mayr and Seitlinger 1989: 36). Not until the later 1980s did the party's new program finally begin to respond to new issues raised by both the challenge of market efficiency and that of left-libertarian politics.[30]

The Danish social democratic party is a mixed case lying between the Swedish-British pattern and the Northern continental discourse. The Danish social democrats share with the Swedes and the Britons an immobility vis-à-vis left-libertarian issues throughout much of the 1970s and 1980s, a position that con-tributed to the rapid growth of ideologically more astute new competitors. But in common with the continental social democrats, the Danish party failed to move decisively back toward a Marxist-socialist discourse on property rights and distribution. After some initial vacillation in the 1970s between more socialist and more moderate positions (Elvander 1980: 252), the party decided upon a firmly conventional social democratic stance, which it held until the late 1980s, when it began to compete for the left-libertarian vote under its new leader Sven Auken. Had the party always followed a vote-maximizing strategy, it would have created a voter appeal closer to that of the Dutch PvDA than those of more staid social democratic parties.

*Group III: Socialist versus left-libertarian discourse*

The Italian, French, and Spanish socialist parties were characterized by a polarity between traditional socialist and left-libertarian discourses in the 1970s. All these parties were located in political settings that shared three characteristics. First, the conventional socialist discourse was already cultivated by another party, the

---

30 The new party program was passed at the 1989 party conference (SPÖ 1989). For an analysis of
  the SPÖ's new "technocratic" programmatic approach in the debates about the program, see Ernst
  (1988) and Pleschberger (1988).

Communist. Nevertheless, this fact, taken by itself, does not explain why socialists chose not to compete head-on with communists over control of the conventional socialist turf.

Second, in all three countries the bourgeois Right engaged in a discourse that endorsed state intervention in the marketplace and economic regulatory or planning activities to a considerable extent. Especially in Spain, and to a lesser extent in Italy and in France, right-wing justifications for an antiliberal organization of the economy were derived from a Catholic and state-corporatist system of beliefs. The fight for economic concertation under the tutelage of the state thus was not the unique ideological property of the Left. Under these circumstances, socialist parties were in a weaker position to gain electoral mileage out of economic programs calling for greater state concertation, particularly in countries where public sector industries were inefficient. In this sense, socialist statism was a particularly unlikely objective for the Spanish socialists confronted with a large inefficient sector of state enterprises established by the Franco regime. In contrast, the French socialists faced a rather more efficient state industrial sector and therefore could more easily embrace doctrines of *planification.*

Finally, socialist parties faced not only a statist-communitarian ideological tradition on the Right, but also a leftist, libertarian communitarianism. Since the nineteenth century this tradition has been articulated in anarchist and syndicalist movements and labor unions but remained organizationally submerged after World War II. In the 1970s, it is this discourse on which socialists could draw with some prospect of popular success. It was likely to strike a responsive chord with voters familiar with the anarcho-syndicalist tradition. Moreover, it helped to differentiate the socialist Left from their communist competitors.

The ideological position the Italian, French, and Spanish socialists occupied in the 1970s – socialist and syndicalist economics of "workers' self-management" (autogestion) plus libertarian sociocultural stances – rapidly gave way in the 1980s to a decidedly moderate social democratic view of economics, combined with a moderately libertarian position on sociocultural issues. The strategic reversal rationally responds to the changing competitive configuration in Mediterranean party systems. By the early 1980s, in all three countries, the communist parties had either suffered severe electoral losses (France, Spain) or been compelled to change their political appeal to an extent that it became electorally unnecessary for socialist parties to appeal to conventional socialist objectives (Italy). Once Mediterranean socialists began to replace their economic radicalism by a pragmatic policy of "modernizing" their economies through a mixture of economic liberalization and state incentives to create markets, libertarian policies could be maintained only inasmuch as they did not conflict with the imperatives of capital accumulation. This, for example, constrained the parties' emphasis on environmental protection and their enthusiasm for a new role of women in society. The French, Italian, and Spanish parties, therefore, did not make a transition from socialism to left-libertarianism, but to a "republicanism" that emphasizes civil liberties and tolerance for cultural diversity (Padgett and Paterson 1991: 31). In the

1980s, Mediterranean "Eurosocialism" began to stand for cultural renewal and secularization. It was more a democratic than a socialist project (Boggs 1986: 95–9). As Padgett and Paterson (1991: 61) conclude, "[t]he task of nation building and economic modernization eclipsed the goals of socialist transformation contained in party ideology." Therefore in all Mediterranean socialist governments, the objectives of social, administrative, legal, educational, and cultural reforms took precedence over socialist reforms of property rights and income redistribution.

The most clear-cut case for this strategic trajectory is the Spanish PSOE. Before Franco's authoritarian regime, the PSOE always had to contend with strong anarcho-syndicalist rivals and remained particularly weak in industrial Catalonia (Gillespie 1989: 31–2). During the transition from the post-Franquist authoritarian regime, the PSOE initially took a radical libertarian and socialist position that may have preempted the resurgence of successor organizations to the anarcho-syndicalist tradition. Moreover, the emphasis on participation and citizens' self-governance fit well into the popular mood of the democratic transition period and contrasted to the communists' eagerness to participate in interelite bargaining and strike deals over the heads of the citizens. Finally, a corporatist authoritarian state with a large public enterprise sector made nationalizations of industry unpalatable to many democrats and therefore neutralized significant elements of the traditional socialist discourse.

After 1980, the disarray among the communist Left and the democratic Center facilitated the party's transition to an economically neoliberal position, while preserving some of its republican, democratic, and libertarian features. It is these features that have found their way into PSOE government policy more so than the party's earlier commitment to economic redistribution.

In France, a strong anarcho-syndicalist undercurrent of the working-class movement present in the nineteenth and early twentieth centuries (Perrot 1986: 105–10) was organizationally submerged for several decades after World War II but began to resurface with the left-socialist and left-Catholic PSU and the cohort of far left groups mushrooming after May 1968 (Hauss 1978; Nugent and Lowe 1982: 179–94). Such groups, and particularly the PSU, were to prepare important contingents of future PS activists. After its reorganization in 1970–71, the PS initially incorporated elements of the traditional socialist discourse, particularly the program for industrial nationalization, in order to consolidate its alliance with the PCF. This strategy was possible because French state industry generally enjoyed a better reputation than comparable industries elsewhere.

At the same time, the remodeled socialist party appealed to a libertarian tradition with deep roots in leftist politics.[31] Moreover, in the 1970s the left-libertarian mobilization of the French women's and environmental movements increased and attracted socialist sympathies. At least for a while, the French socialists became the "privileged conduit for 'post-industrial' causes" (Bell and Criddle 1988: 261). The

---

31  The intellectual lineage of various strands of the PS is instructively detailed in Roucaute (1983: ch. 1). For an empirical analysis of socialist party militants' ideologies, see also Lagroye et al. (1976: esp. 93–102).

party's conference resolutions contained many references to the women's movement and enabled it to coopt important elements of the movement into the party (cf. Judt 1986: 276–9; Randall 1987: 236; Gaffney 1989: 169). Moreover, the party promised to reconsider the French nuclear program after a victory of the Left and, above all, it appealed to the magic formula of *autogestion* or industrial democracy, which was meant to build a bridge between the conventional socialist discourse and new left-libertarian ideas, while simultaneously differentiating it from the PCF.[32]

In the mid-1980s, however, the discourse of the French socialists changed dramatically. As Gaffney's (1989) careful textual analysis of intraparty debates and programs in 1974, 1975, and 1984 shows, by 1984 the rhetoric of autogestion had yielded to a vague appeal to modernization and social progress that thinly veiled the overriding concern of the party with a strategy of market efficiency. Just as in Spain, the party program made it clear that socialist government achievements and claims should be sought more in the area of civil rights, justice, and institutional reforms, all areas that belong to the classic themes of the French political Left (Judt 1986: 10).

In the French and Spanish cases, the autonomy of ideas both in the 1970s and in the 1980s is difficult to ascertain because the strategies that were consistent with the plural traditions of socialist discourse in these countries also happened to conform to different variants of vote- or office-maximizing strategic appeals under changing competitive conditions. The situation is different in Italy where a vote- or office-maximizing strategy would have always demanded a policy of moderation, but where the PSI in the 1970s, after exiting from the center-left coalition government, began to cultivate the non-PCI Left with a more left-libertarian strategy (DiScala 1988: 170–1). The PSI's oscillation from "center-left" to "alternative-left" in the 1970s (Pridham 1988: 162), however, was too short-lived to draw any definite conclusions about the long-term ideological underpinnings of the new party strategy. Nevertheless, the incident shows that in another country where communitarian traditions played an important role in the political discourses both on the left as well as on the right, a socialist party was capable of jumping outside the conventional socialist versus liberal polarity and position itself around a very different appeal. The lack of success with this strategy in 1972 and 1976 precipitated the reversal that led to Craxi's domination of the party and a program of economic modernization that decisively committed itself to market efficiency as the overriding political objective.[33]

32 Gaffney (1989: 147) comments on the notion of autogestion or self-management: "Autogestion is a mythical referent through which the participants in the ritual obtain a more fundamental sense of union. Furthermore, autogestion evokes social and cultural, rather than economic, considerations in the search for a solution to socio-economic problems and is therefore a quasi-religious rejection of materialist solutions to the problems posed by capitalism. In this way autogestion, by referring to total solutions, refers to a mythical order."

33 As I discussed in earlier chapters, however, Craxi's strategy was constrained by the exigencies of a patronage-oriented party apparatus and increasing competition with the former communists, the radicals, and the Greens for libertarian voters.

CONCLUSION

The political ideas of the Left have appeared twice in my account of socialist and social democratic party fortunes in the 1970s and 1980s. In the first chapter, I argued that societal change in advanced industrial capitalism, together with the outcomes of the Keynesian welfare state compromise between business and labor, have reshaped popular demands for political alternatives from a politics of (re)distribution to a more complex continuum of preferences ranging from left-libertarian to right-authoritarian programs in many European democracies. Popular political preferences, however, do not entirely depend on societal change, but also on politicians' issue leadership and patterns of party competition. Societal change, by itself, does not determine the strategic stances of political parties. As I discussed in Chapters 4 and 5, the competitive configuration of party systems, and more precisely the balance of party fragmentation encountered by socialist parties, and the processes of intraparty coalition formation play an important role in shaping parties' strategic stances.

Chapter 6 now has added another facet to this picture by examining a second way in which ideas play a role in democratic party politics. It is not just societal change and structures of party competition that affect citizens' and politicians' ideas, but also the *discursive traditions* that are available in different countries and that can be (re)combined in new innovative programs. The extent to which parties are capable of issue leadership and of staking out new appeals thus depends on ideological resources, the stock of arguments and visions that can count on acceptance within a particular political community. This logic of ideas can be identified most clearly where parties diverge from vote- or office-seeking strategies. The *substantive direction* of parties' electorally inefficient strategies can be accounted for by the ideological alternatives present in specific national settings.

The key independent variable I have focused on is the presence or absence of national communitarian ideological traditions that have historically surfaced in more paternalistic-authoritarian versions on the "Right" and in "anarcho-syndicalist" versions on the "Left." Wherever precedents for a communitarian discourse exist, socialist parties have found it easier to recenter their discourse from the conventional socialist agenda of economic property rights and distributive politics to one prominently featuring the sociocultural alternative of libertarianism.

The independent influence of "ideas" on parties' and citizens' preferences can be assessed in a methodologically straightforward way only in cases where electoral vote- or office-seeking rationality yields different predictions about party positions than a logic of ideas. The fact *that* parties diverge from electoral strategic rationality is explicable in terms of organizational mechanisms of interest articulation and aggregation within parties (Chapter 5), yet not the *content* of the political appeals that diverge from a party's electoral rationality.

For this reason, the cases of the British Labour Party and the Swedish social democrats have been particularly instructive. In both instances, Chapters 4 and 5 explained *why* these parties diverge from electorally efficient positions, but only a logic of ideas shows *how* and *in which way* that divergence was accomplished. Both left parties are located in nations whose political traditions strongly emphasize the tension between liberalism and socialism and leave little room for communitarian concerns. In such discursive environments, strategic deviance could lead only to a socialist party appeal in the 1970s and 1980s. In other countries, where communitarian alternatives are prominent, the socialists' direction of strategic deviance has occurred in the direction of left-libertarian programs. The German SPD, and, to a lesser extent, the Austrian SPÖ found themselves in this situation. Each experienced a withering away of traditional socialist intraparty opposition groups and, at least in the German party, the growth of a vocal left-libertarian current.

In another group of parties, it is much harder to disentangle the logic of ideas from the logic of electoral interests. At least in Spain and France, not only communitarian traditions within and outside the historical orbit of the socialist movement, but also the competitive configuration of the party systems that made a strategy of oligopolistic competition against communist parties a promising course of action in the 1970s, predisposed the parties to stake out left-libertarian positions. Still, from a purely rational-electoral point of view, a conventional socialist strategy also might have accomplished the objective of undercutting communist support, and it is the unique tradition of ideas that enabled socialist parties in Spain and France to seize on libertarian appeals. The logic of ideas is again easier to assess in the final Mediterranean party I have examined, the Italian socialists. In this case, the appeal to left-libertarianism in the 1970s before Craxi's ascent to the position of party secretary was clearly inconsistent with the demands of a logic of electoral rationality. Ideas, by themselves, certainly cannot explain party strategies. But I hope to have shown in this chapter that politicians' debates are important at critical junctures in party strategy.

# Social democracy in decline? Analytical and normative extensions of the argument

In this book I have argued that changes in the socioeconomic class structure of advanced capitalism and in the organization of political-economic institutions, such as the welfare state and channels of interest group intermediation, reshape the stage on which social democratic parties compete by influencing the nature of citizens' political demands that are articulated in the political arena. The nature of citizens' political preferences, in turn, delimits the range of social democratic appeals that promise success at the polls as well as participation in governments.

Advanced capitalism tends to transform citizens' preferences as well as their capacity for collective organization and political action. New experiences at intellectually more demanding and versatile workplaces, particularly in the rapidly expanding client-interactive professions of the personal service sector, foster a construction of political demands that places more emphasis on individual self-realization and direct political participation than on questions of economic income distribution and security. Conversely, the losers of the modernization process, primarily young less skilled blue and white collar workers in manufacturing industries and the marginal self-employed, express an authoritarian backlash against the advanced liberal democracies and call for a hierarchical social and political order that undercuts the dynamism and the participatory desires of the new libertarian social strata.

The social democratic Keynesian welfare state, established in the post–World War II era, has contributed to the transformation of citizens' preferences, but now becomes a victim of its own success. Most citizens take for granted the key accomplishments of social democratic policy, such as the rather substantial minimum standard of economic equality and security, but turn against what they perceive to be the excesses and unintended negative consequences of comprehensive welfare states, such as the bureaucratic control of social life and the lack of individualized attention to the clients of educational, health care, and other social services. The centralized management of social democratic policy institutions becomes the target of libertarian, decentralizing political demands.

Sociocultural and political-economic change thus fosters a *recentering of the political space* from purely distributive conflicts between socialist left and capitalist right positions to a more complex division that incorporates a second communitarian division between libertarian and authoritarian demands. In this process, citizens who are more inclined to support left socialist ideas also tend to endorse libertarian perspectives, whereas those who support right wing capitalist positions often also exhibit a penchant for authoritarian institutions. These elective affinities are based on a logic of ideas and a logic of experiences and interests in everyday work and reproductive life. For example, educational sophistication and client-interactive task structures foster libertarian orientations and jobs characterized by such experiences typically tend to be situated in the public sector or in private sectors protected from international competition. Hence, individuals with libertarian orientation are likely to express less concern with international capitalist market competitiveness and therefore favor social democratic redistribution because their jobs do not hinge on international efficiency.

The extent to which the new left-libertarian versus right-authoritarian political division gains prominence depends to a considerable extent on the success of social democracy in the past. Where there have been comprehensive welfare states, corporatist institutions of interest intermediation, and long periods of left party government, such as in Denmark, Germany, the Netherlands, or Sweden, left-libertarian preferences tend to be prominent. Conversely, in countries less affected by social democratic institutions, the political space in the 1980s still centered primarily around distributive capitalist–socialist issues and gave rise to a relatively weak libertarian Left (especially Britain, France, Italy). Social institutions alone, however, do not explain the extent of left-libertarian cleavage mobilization. Over time, parties themselves can actively resist or promote the emergence of new issue agendas. Examples are the British or Swedish social democrats, who were reluctant to embrace libertarian issues. In contrast, the Southern European socialist parties in Italy or Spain emphasized libertarian demands, yet all but abandoned commitments to economic redistribution in the 1980s.

While social and institutional change reshapes the political arena in which social democratic parties compete, such developments, however, are not the primary and direct cause of social democratic political fortunes. Political parties are not prisoners of the external societal environment and the distribution of citizens' political preferences; rather, their electoral trajectory and legislative power depends on internal conditions in the arena of party competition, inside party organization, and in their own political discourse, all of which affect their strategic choices in appealing for popular support. My argument does not suggest a voluntaristic notion of choice according to which political actors can make anything happen. Instead, I am claiming that the causes of social democratic success and failure are situated in the institutions and processes *internal* to the field of political competition and debate rather than in external social and political-economic institutions.

There is, however, a critical voluntarist element in my argument. Since internal causes are situated closer to the level of political action and can be manipulated by politicians more easily than basic social structures and political-economic institutions, such determinants are more malleable and open to fundamental political redefinition by the actors, particularly in times of political crisis. In this sense, in Chapter 5 I have analyzed party organization as an independent determinant of intraparty coalitions that favor certain strategic alternatives, yet also as a dependent variable that is subject to voluntarist change by party leaders, particularly during episodes of political defeat and electoral decline. If political factors internal to the field of party competition are critical for social democratic electoral fortunes, theoretical statements about the conditions governing the parties' electoral success and failure are therefore necessarily less determinist than propositions that tie the fate of social democracy to class structures and political-economic institutions. This is so because political conditions are more accessible to conscious political intervention than socioeconomic conditions. An analysis that features internal political determinants of electoral success thus accents strategic choice, whereas an analysis that emphasizes economic processes and institutions stresses political fate.

According to the "internal" account of left party performance I have developed in Chapters 4 through 6, social democratic strategies and electoral fortunes are explained primarily in terms of how parties respond to the patterns of party competition that they confront in the electoral and legislative arena and how they engage in intraorganizational coalition building that promotes particular strategies. The critical variables in the arena of party competition are the extent of left-libertarian popular mobilization and the socialists' position within the balance of party fractionalization. The more voters express left-libertarian preferences and the more numerous are the rival parties social democrats face in the center of the main competitive space of a party system relative to the number of competitors they face at the extreme left and libertarian end of that space, the more vote-maximizing socialist parties will be drawn away from the center. Conversely, where the center of the competitive space is relatively empty and few voters endorse left-libertarianism, moderate policies will pay off.

I have shown, however, that only in a minority of instances do parties actually follow a strategy of short-term vote maximization. This finding does not imply that most parties are uninterested in the outcomes of electoral competition or do not take the strategies of their competitors into account. But parties may choose more sophisticated preference schedules than short-term vote maximization, particularly the strategic objective of maximizing the party's probability of entering government (office seeking or "pivoting") or the objective of wiping out a more radical competitor in the long term through oligopolistic competition and then to pursue vote-seeking strategies.

Still, even with these further qualifications, socialist parties in a relatively large number of instances have positioned themselves in a systemically nonrational way. Often their appeals do not maximize voter support, nor do they rationally pursue the goals of more sophisticated office-seeking and oligopolistic strategies because circumstances make these two strategies infeasible. Chapter 5 therefore focuses on parties' internal organizational structures and the rationality of intraparty group coalitions to explain systemically irrational choices. While most of the theoretical literature on party organization has postulated simple dichotomies between leaders and activists or between "efficient" and "representative" party organizations, the effects of party structure on strategy and electoral success are better assessed in a triangular relationship matching the challenges of the competitive situation, parties' organizational opportunities for innovation from below through membership recruitment and their opportunities for innovation from "above" through granting organizational autonomy to party leaders.

Within a contingency model of party organization that relies on the triangulation of these three conditions, no single organizational model can be identified that is invariably capable of delivering superior electoral strategies. Where the libertarian Left is highly mobilized, openness to innovation from "below" may boost a socialist party's fortunes (Dutch PvDA). In instances where it is low, the influence of radicalized rank-and-file members may drive the party into strategic dead-end positions (British Labour Party). The advantages or disadvantages of leadership autonomy from rank-and-file demands depend on a party's competitive situation. Where a party has good opportunities to control the pivot of the party system and thus the process of government formation, it is better able to take advantage of such chances where leadership autonomy enhances flexible "innovation from above" (e.g., in France, Spain) than where leadership autonomy is relatively limited (e.g. in Britain, Germany). In countries where pivoting offers few prospects and rewards, party performance and strategic choice may not be negatively affected by a relatively weak party leadership (e.g., Netherlands, Belgium).

Where social democratic parties face both high left-libertarian cleavage mobilization and an intense competitive situation with opportunities for office seeking, they must find a balance between intraorganizational responsiveness to the rank and file and the advantages of leadership autonomy. In order to accomplish this, they are forced to give up traditional mass party organizations that impose inertia both on party members and party leaders in favor of more malleable, stratified framework organizations that reconstitute parties as systems of continuous conflict where leaders are exposed to the constant criticism of the rank and file yet also have considerable autonomy in the daily affairs of party tactics.[1]

Party organization, however, is not simply an independent variable that shapes the fate of social democratic parties within a given competitive context. Party activists and leaders also consciously manipulate party structures in order to bring about what they believe will be beneficial results. Particularly in times of electoral crisis, parties such as the French, Italian, and Spanish socialists, and perhaps the Dutch social democrats and the British Labour Party of the 1990s are able to bring about profound changes in their parties' internal decision-making processes.

Chapter 6, finally, showed that beyond competitive configurations and organizational rules or power relations, semantic traditions ("discourses") within individual parties and party systems shape the ability of parties to respond to new challenges and assimilate new arguments into their appeal. The relative autonomy

---

1 Lewin (1980) has called this model of organizational governance "interactive democracy."

of political ideas, of course, can be demonstrated only where predictions of party strategies based on semantic traditions diverge from predictions based on what might be expected if party appeals rationally act on the competitive position and intraorganizational power relations alone. To explore the role of ideas in political strategy, it is particularly useful to analyze the ideological appeals of each party's radical currents, driven by people not attributing much priority to electoral success as a goal in itself. Even though such currents rarely govern party strategy directly, as did the far Left in the British Labour Party from the late 1970s through the mid-1980s, they shape the programmatic alternatives parties are able to consider. There is considerable variance across the nine socialist parties in the stances each party's left current has supported since the late 1970s. While in some countries leftists have embraced the left-libertarian agenda, in others they have remained faithful to a pure socialist-redistributive perspective. This variance can be explained in terms of the salience communitarian political arguments have had in the history of each party and in its competition with nonsocialist adversaries. Where communitarian arguments have been more salient, also the parties' mainstreams have been more willing to embrace libertarian positions and to reposition social democracy in a new competitive space.

As always, the systematic explanation of political processes, such as party strategies and electoral payoffs, cannot account for all of the variance observed. My emphasis on patterns of party competition, party organization, and ideological legacies by and large leaves out the impact of the charisma of unique political personalities on the success of left parties. Moreover, it represents citizens' preference formation exclusively as a *structural* process induced by socioeconomic change and long-term patterns of party competition, but ignores the *conjunctural* forces that propel certain issues to the top of the political agenda in a particular electoral campaign. While I do not deny the importance of such phenomena, they are too idiosyncratic to be incorporated into a systematic comparative analysis. But since such idiosyncratic factors do play an important role, social democratic political fortunes are characterized by an ineradicable element of historical contingency.

Rival theories of social democratic transformation also suffer from the handicap of leaving certain historical contingencies unexplained. In this sense, chance events, political personality, and historical conjuncture are irrelevant for the comparative assessments of the strength or weakness of rival theories. My analysis of political preference formation, party competition, party organization, and ideological discourses in socialist parties is directed against class accounts of social democratic party fortunes, such as Przeworski and Sprague's (1986), but also against political-economic approaches that predict the irreversible decline of social democracy as a consequence of the contraction of blue collar employment, the demise of industrial mass production, and the erosion of corporatist interest intermediation.

First, I disagree with the proposition that social structure and party fortunes are directly linked. According to a class account of social democracy, left parties are inexorably wedded to their core constituencies and will go down with these clienteles. To the contrary, I have argued that parties can choose their constituencies and modify their appeals, a process that is propelled by politicians' rational calculation of electoral objectives in a competitive situation, by the turnover of activists, the realignment of coalitions, and the change of organizational statutes inside parties, and finally by parties' efforts to modify the discursive universe in which they explain their objectives. The *diversity* in the trajectories of socialist and social democratic parties in the 1970s and 1980s illustrates that there is no inexorable logic of decline at work that is driven by class structure. At the same time, this diversity can be accounted for in terms of party competition, party organization, and ideological appeals in advanced postindustrial democracies.

My second disagreement with class and political economic explanations of social democracy's fate has to do with the way such theories reconstruct external constraints imposed on the parties' strategic choices. The language of "class," "class interests," "class factions," and "class compromise" still suggests that modern politics is a purely distributive game between the haves and the have nots about income and property titles and that socialist parties are agents of class relations. Such approaches do not recognize the complications and substantive shifts of popular preference schedules brought about by the transformation of modern occupational and sectoral structures as well as by the increasing diversity of personal life-styles and subcultures. Because they are blind to such changes, they systematically misinterpret important political conflicts. They view dissatisfaction with existing welfare states as right-wing efforts to "roll back" the state in favor of free market capitalism rather than also as protests against the bureaucratization of social life. They attribute the defeat of the Swedish wage earners' funds solely to the power of capital over the working class, rather than to the disaffection of many wage earners with the creation of a new union-controlled concentration of economic power. Those who attack the centralist-bureaucratic manifestations of past social democratic policies are often *not* inspired by neo-liberal desires to reestablish free markets, but by libertarian concerns with individual self-realization and communitarian participation.

Because class and political economy approaches tend to misconceive citizens' political preferences, they cannot explain why the electoral losses of social democratic parties often do not benefit their conventional bourgeois competitors rallying around a neoliberal free market agenda, but new left-libertarian or right-authoritarian parties. This applies to all countries where social democrats lost a significant share of their voters in the 1980s and early 1990s. In Britain, Germany, Austria, and recently Sweden, the social democrats' electoral decline has boosted the fortunes of new parties rather than those of their established bourgeois competitors.[2]

---

2 The same phenomenon can be observed in the case of the Spanish socialists who lost to a left-libertarian electoral alliance in the 1989 parliamentary elections and of the French socialists who lost heavily to the ecologists in the 1992 regional elections.

Nevertheless, my own explanatory account of social democratic party fortunes agrees with class and political economy approaches on one important proposition. Socialist and social democratic parties can no longer win elections if they primarily represent blue collar workers in manufacturing industries and stick to the agenda of property rights and income distribution. Yet unlike Przeworski and Sprague (1986), I see no evidence that social democratic parties are irreversibly chained to this particular electoral clientele or political agenda. Economic group relations and citizens' political demands have changed over time, but so has the capacity of social democrats to weld together new electoral coalitions. Some of the most basic social democratic objectives – such as citizens' protection from the vagaries of the labor market and the provision of a decent minimum standard of living for everyone – have always been universalist "supraclass" goals around which parties can build a wide variety of electoral coalitions. Such traditional goals are likely to remain attractive to large electoral constituencies, *provided* social democratic parties find an electorally successful mix of economically left and socioculturally libertarian appeals that matches their national competitive situation.

Finally, it should be emphasized again that the theory and the cases detailed in my study do not warrant the prescription of an unconditional "best way" for social democracy to remain a powerful political force in advanced capitalist democracies in the future. In particular, it would be wrong to conclude that the strategies and appeals of the Mediterranean socialist parties set an example to be followed by other socialist and social democratic parties. In various chapters, I have underlined that the success of these parties in the 1980s has been self-limiting. First, their economic austerity policies preempted an early resurgence of their conservative competitors, but, in the long run, were self-destructive because they could not reduce unemployment and eventually alienated elements of the socialists' own constituencies (Chapter 3). Second, Mediterranean socialists were lucky to benefit from the one-time windfall of voters released by strategically rigid and hence declining communist parties, as well as from the failure of their conservative and left-libertarian competitors to choose vote-maximizing strategies (Chapter 4). Third, when left-libertarian competitors did stage more serious challenges, socialist parties so far have been unable to strike back, as is shown especially by the French party and its increasingly vacuous appeal to social modernization in the later 1980s and early 1990s (Chapters 4 and 6). Fourth, all Mediterranean socialist parties in the 1980s lost organizational flexibility and slid back into old patterns of patronage organization that exposed them to the risk of major political scandals and strategic immobility (Chapter 5). Nevertheless, when faced with electoral disaster, the French socialists, at least, have shown an impressive willingness to remake their party and abandon cherished voter appeals. This capacity is clearly a legacy of the fluid cadre organization instituted in the 1970s and it may facilitate a strategic rejuvenation of the party in the post-Mitterrand era. While Northwest European social democratic parties may learn from this organizational flexibility, strategies of vote maximization or office seeking probably compel them to search for a rather different mix of center-left distributive policies and libertarian reform initiatives than that offered by the Mediterranean socialist parties in the 1980s.

In the remainder of this chapter, I wish to extend my argument in analytical and normative respects. First, I will show in brief sketches that the analytical framework I have proposed can also be applied to socialist and social democratic parties I could not discuss in detail in this study. Second, I will consider in greater detail the normative programmatic visions that circumscribe the ideological "feasibility space" of future social democratic party appeals in countries where the main competitive dimension runs more along a sociocultural libertarian–authoritarian divide than along economic socialist–capitalist divisions.

## 7.1 EXTENDING THE THEORETICAL ARGUMENT TO FURTHER SOCIALIST AND SOCIAL DEMOCRATIC PARTIES

The fruitfulness of a theory is reinforced by its capacity to account for new observations. I therefore provide brief outlines of how my theoretical argument might be fleshed out for a further set of social democratic parties in modern democracies not covered in the main body of this book. These abstracts suggest tentative assessments that must be revised through detailed empirical research. I first examine socialist parties in countries that look like the winners in my original sample but have actually experienced rather different fortunes, the Greek and Portuguese socialists. I then explore the career of parties that have considerable affinities to the Northwest European model of relatively immobile social democratic mass organizations in environments characterized by intermediate to high left-libertarian mobilization, the Finnish, Norwegian, and Swiss social democrats. Next, labor parties in two countries, Australia and New Zealand, share a number of features and circumstances familiar from the British case, but they have performed spectacularly well in the 1980s. I also analyze the career of the Japan Socialist Party, a party that shares a few traits with European socialist parties but is otherwise unique both in terms of its competitive setting as well as its internal organization. Finally, I briefly discuss the Canadian New Democratic Party and the Israeli Labor Party. Because of the prominence of ethnic or regional cleavages in both instances, my theoretical model fails to capture the dynamic of these parties.[3]

### *Mediterranean socialists in Greece and Portugal: Strategic flexibility, but mixed results*

The Greek socialists (Pan-Hellenic Movement, or PASOK) and the Portuguese socialists (PSP) share with other Mediterranean left parties an environment of moderate to intermediate left-libertarian mobilization and the existence of fairly

3 I will not address the fortunes of social democrats in the "small" European democracies whose overall population is no greater than that of a midsized or large city in any of the other countries: Ireland, Luxembourg, and Malta.

large communist parties.[4] Both parties also initially faced a moderately crowded party space filled with competitors in the center and on the right of the political spectrum. In France and in Spain, socialists in the 1970s engaged in a policy of oligopolistic competition with left-libertarian appeals to undercut the entrenched communist parties. Then, in the 1980s, they moved back to a centrist position intended to yield control of the pivot of the party system. With some modifications, PASOK followed the same trajectory and established its electoral supremacy in the 1980s, but the Portuguese socialists did not.

PASOK began to mobilize with a radical Third World rhetoric after the collapse of the Greek junta in 1974 that combined antiimperialist, populist, and a few left-libertarian themes, including some demands of the peace and women's movement (Clogg 1987: 122; Lyrintzis 1989). When the party performed very badly in the 1974 election, its leader Andreas Papandreou toned down its rhetoric and ousted several of his radical followers but did little to change the party's basic message (Spourdalakis 1988: 135–9). The more important of the two communist parties, the Greek Communist Party–exterior (KKE-exterior), never represented a serious threat to Papandreou's emerging party because it was incapable of strategic innovation (Kitsikis 1988: 104–7; Spourdalakis 1989: 206–8). In the late 1970s, when PASOK had established itself as the key competitor to the bourgeois governing party, New Democracy, and had wiped out other competitors, Papandreou veered to the center and won a parliamentary majority in 1981. After a period of deficit spending, winning another election, and overcoming resistance from the party's own ranks, PASOK was able to embark on a strict austerity policy. Although financial and patronage scandals weakened the party, it still retained enough popular support to give its bourgeois competitor only the thinnest of winning margins after three consecutive national elections between June 1989 and April 1990.

Just as in other Mediterranean countries, PASOK's strategic flexibility was built on a centralist system of personal leadership, buttressed by a growing patronage system in the public sector, a recipe for decline also in other socialist parties (cf. Spourdalakis 1989: 242–50). Papandreou as party leader could not only appoint and fire members of his central committee (Clogg 1987: 130), but also avoid holding frequent party conventions (Featherstone 1990a: 187), subduing the labor unions when they rebelled against austerity policy (Featherstone 1990a: 194), and subjecting the party organization to the government apparatus (Lyrintzis 1989: 44). By the 1980s, the bulk of PASOK members were public employees and party functionaries (Papadopoulos 1989: 64). Papandreou ran a system of bureaucratic clientelism (Featherstone 1990b: 101) that tolerated no factional divisions but employed the party purely as an electoral machine. The power of PASOK's leader is probably more extreme than in any other Mediterranean socialist party, making it more similar to Latin American populism (Papadopoulos 1989: 67).

4 Calculations on Eurobarometer data extending the analysis I reported in Table 4.3 show that Greece polls in around the lower midrange and Portugal at the low end of left-libertarian cleavage mobilization.

The Portuguese Socialist Party (PSP) could not copy the other Mediterranean socialist parties' sequence of strategic moves with first launching oligopolistic competition against a communist left competitor and then crossing over to centripetal pivoting, *although* the party organization gave a free hand to its leader Mario Soares. The party has a small membership of predominantly professionals and academics estimated at no more than 30,000. As elsewhere in the Mediterranean, the organization is more a patronage machine than a locus of active political debates (cf. Gallagher 1989: 16–18). Moreover, the party has few linkages to interest groups or labor unions (Bruneau and MacLeod 1986: 67).

Nevertheless, because the socialists ascended to government office during the democratic transition of 1975/76 and were constrained to pursue a moderate policy by the international circumstances of the transition and coalition politics, they could *not* engage in tactical maneuvers to marginalize their communist competitor through oligopolistic competition. The coalition government lent support to bourgeois upstart parties, thereby establishing them as competent allies in center-right governments. The Portuguese Communist Party (PCP) initially followed a revolutionary strategy intent on bringing down "bourgeois" parliamentary democracy. It was also complemented by anarchist forces that enjoyed considerable backing among junior army officers.

As a consequence, and in contrast to Spain or France, the socialists were squeezed by the Left as well as the Right in the late 1970s and early 1980s. When the PS entered another centrist coalition in 1983 and pursued a rigorous austerity policy, voters had little reason to continue to favor it over its center-right coalition partner, the Portuguese Social Democrats (PSD). Although the communist PCP finally began to decline in the mid-1980s,[5] not the socialists, but the PSD could establish itself as hegemonic party of government and win absolute majorities in the 1987 and 1991 elections. Due to its inability to become the dominant party of the Left before engaging in a centrist policy, the Portuguese socialists could never equal the electoral achievements of their counterparts in France, Greece, or Spain in the 1980s.

## 7.2 NORTHERN EUROPEAN SOCIAL DEMOCRATS IN FINLAND, NORWAY, AND SWITZERLAND: THE ELECTORAL LIABILITIES OF STRATEGIC INFLEXIBILITY

The situation in these countries is similar to the Northwest European social democracies I discussed in earlier chapters. In all three of them, left-libertarian politics is mobilized with intermediate to high intensity and the balance of party fractionalization would lead a short-term vote-maximizing party to pursue a moderately left-libertarian policy. In at least two instances, Finland and Switzerland, there are so many competitors in the center of the political space that social democrats have no hope of becoming pivotal, yet opportunities for oligopolistic competition are equally weak. Only in Norway, as in Sweden, are the social

5 PCP electoral support in national parliamentary elections fell from 18.2% (1983) to 8.8% (1991).

democrats sufficiently close to the system pivot to be able to capture it with any regularity.

Because of their political environment, the strategic immobility of the Finnish and Swiss social democrats, particularly their inability to adopt left-libertarian appeals, has cut into their electorate. By the late 1980s, the Swiss social democrats were at a historically low level. The Finnish party was unable to benefit from the collapse of communist support, so that the entire Left fell to a historic low there as well.[6] In Norway, the social democratic Labor Party (DNA) declined from an average support of 45.5% in the 1960s to 38.9% in the 1970s and 37.5% in the 1980s. Nevertheless, because of the rise of strong left-libertarian and right-authoritarian parties, which together received 23.1% in the 1989 election, the party remained still close to the pivot of its party system.

In Finland, which has an intermediate level of left-libertarian mobilization compared to other Scandinavian countries (cf. Knutsen 1990a,b), the Greens made inroads at the expense of the left and center, but the social democrats were unable to respond with new issue appeals. As elsewhere, an entrenched party machine and limited leadership autonomy cut down on the party's ability to embrace left-libertarian themes, although the environmental issue clearly dominated the public issue agenda before the 1987 election (cf. Berglund 1987. In the 1970s, about 80% of party members were unionists (Helenius 1977: 279) and the party engaged in few efforts to reach out to young people and students. For this reason, it was unable to benefit from the Communist Party's failure to modernize (Hyvaerinen and Paastela 1988).

The situation in Switzerland is similar, although there was no communist party to be potentially exploited by social democratic predators. In 1987, environmental issues topped the agenda (Sidjanski 1988: 168), but the Swiss social democrats (SDS) did not benefit from it. Instead, the party fell from 24.4% (1979) to 18.4% (1987), while the share of two left-libertarian and Green parties increased from 2.4% to 9.3%. In 1991, the SDS recovered slightly to 20% but the Greens also increased their share of the vote to about 11%. The nature of the Swiss social democrats' strategic problem is traceable to the party's internal organization. In 1983, the party was sharply divided between labor unionists and left intellectuals (Lohneis 1984). Only after the Chernobyl disaster did it reluctantly withdraw its support of nuclear power, an issue that had greatly polarized Swiss politics. Although the party replaced some labor unionists with environmental leaning candidates in the 1987 election, the SDS could not overcome its image of an internally divided party (Sidjanski 1988).

Norway has the lowest level of left-libertarian mobilization of all Scandinavian countries (cf. Aardal 1990: 152–3; Knutsen 1990a,b), yet it is still high enough to

6 In Finland, in the 1966 parliamentary election, social democrats received 27.2% and the Finnish People's Democratic Union 21.2%, amounting to a combined total of 48.4%. Since that time, support has gradually fallen to the historic low of 24.1% for social democrats and 13.9% for the by now split communist parties or a total of only 38.0% in the 1987 parliamentary election. In 1991, the combined total fell further to 32.2% (22.1 + 10.1).

represent a considerable challenge. Moreover, public sector workers, who comprise about 35% of the work force, strongly tend to support left and libertarian positions (Lafferty 1990: 84). As have the parties in Sweden and Britain, the established Norwegian parties, and particularly the DNA, do their best to prevent the political competition from recentering around the left-libertarian versus right-authoritarian axis rather than the dominant distributive economic dimension. Despite these efforts, environmental and immigration issues have moved to the top of voters' concerns.[7] As a consequence, the Socialist People's Party, and initially in the 1960s left-socialist, but since that time an increasingly left-libertarian party, has won votes at the expense of the Labor Party (Modeley 1990: 290).The organizational inertia of Norwegian social democracy has nevertheless not undermined its hegemonic position in the party system. By not competing for left-libertarian votes, it has suffered electoral losses but preserved its pivotal role in coalition formation and policy-making.

*Australian and New Zealand labor parties as contrast to British labor:*
*Success in an Anglo-Saxon competitive democracy*

As in Britain, the electoral and the party system of Australia and New Zealand places a high premium on centripetal competition and pivoting. Labor parties compete against a single conservative bloc and have not been exposed to serious left-libertarian competitors.[8] Unlike their British counterparts, both the Australian and New Zealand labor parties were able to cope with this opportunity structure in a vote-maximizing way and avoided a takeover by a leftist faction.

In both countries, labor governments pursued economic austerity policies throughout the 1980s that robbed their conservative competitors of issues (cf. Altmann 1988; Boston and Jackson 1988: 70; Denmark 1990: 281–83). Moreover, they engaged in social reforms and libertarian initiatives. For example, the Australian government implemented health care reform, vigorous affirmative action for women and a comprehensive environmental policy (Altmann 1988). New Zealand's Labour prime minister David Lange became best known for his campaign against nuclear weapons tests in the South Pacific, heavily exploiting this issue in the 1987 election (Boston and Jackson 1988: 71).

How could the two labor parties engineer such policies? A recent article on Australian party organization by McAllister (1991) offers some insight. The Australian Labour Party evolved in the 1980s into organized factions, dividing itself between left-libertarians and moderates, that could claim formal representa-

7 In addition to the Socialist People's Party, only the centrist liberals tried to seize on libertarian issues. But, predictably, the latter failed to win significant electoral support. The electorate for a party that stakes out a clearly libertarian, but more pro-capitalist position is rather limited and only in a few countries have parties with such an appeal managed to gain a small slice of the electorate, for example, the Danish Radicals, the Dutch Democrats '66, and the Italian Republicans.
8 In New Zealand, a Values Party won some support in 1975 (5.2%), but this success proved ephemeral. In 1984 and 1987, the Australian Labour Party faced some competition from the Nuclear Disarmament Party, but could hold the latter's support at bay.

tion on the party boards. The party absorbed intraparty conflict by channeling it. This approach is similar to the methods of integration prominent in the French Socialist Party in the 1970s and first half of the 1980s.

At the same time, the Australian party maintained sufficient leadership autonomy by imposing corporatist incomes policies on a union structure relatively more centralized than its British counterpart. Australian unions accepted moderate incomes policies in exchange for wage indexation and privileged relations to the government. In the hostile economic environment of the 1980s, unions had few other strategic options for protecting their members.[9]

The extent to which similar mechanisms explain strategy formation in the New Zealand Labour Party is an open question. The fact is that in New Zealand Labour's austerity policy and efforts to liberalize the economy were so severe that not only a more leftist New Labour Party split off after the 1987 election and won 5% of the popular vote in 1990,[10] but also the conservatives could leapfrog Labour in the 1990 campaign and complain about Labour's privatization policy as "selling off the state silver to pay the bills" (*New York Times* 10/28/90: 6). As a consequence, Labour lost the 1990 election, but has since recovered voter support in opinion polls because the new conservative government has yet to offer any dramatic policy alternative.

### Japanese socialists: The logic of self-destruction

An examination of the socioeconomic context and the party system of Japan in the mid-1950s would have led to the promise of a glorious future for the Japan Socialist Party (JSP), comparable to that of the German SPD. Instead, the party's support steadily fell from 32.9% in the 1958 Japanese House of Representatives elections to its low point of 17.2% in 1986. While both the German SPD and the JSP faced hegemonic conservative governments receiving upward of 50% of the vote in the 1950s, the SPD was able to match Christian Democratic support by the early 1970s, whereas the JSP was never able to break the Liberal Democrats' electoral hegemony. In some ways, the JSP had even better preconditions for electoral success in the 1950s than did the SPD. In terms of the occupational profile of the JSP's voters, the party enjoyed much more even electoral support than the German SPD and, unlike the Liberal Democratic Party's (LDP) entrenchment in backward rural areas, it could count on the urban industrial population and white collar supporters, two groups that began to swell in the Japanese economic boom (Curtis 1988: 121). Instead, by the end of the 1970s, the party had been ousted from the big cities and had become a rural and small town pressure group of the public sector labor union confederation *Sohyo*.

---

9  As Scharpf (1987a) argues, when faced with a government intent on austerity policy, the unions' best policy is to reply with cooperation and wage restraint.

10  Already in 1987, Labour suffered its greatest losses in its strongholds and safe seats because workers abstained from voting, while new nonworking class constituencies were attracted (Holland 1990: 33).

In strategic terms, the JSP was never able to maximize its vote share or even to become the electoral pivot because it failed to respond to the very strong incentives that existed for moderating its left-socialist program. Since the governing LDP also lost support from the 1950s to the 1970s, the vacuum opened by the JSP's inflexibility was filled by a surge of the Communist Party (JCP), with a modern "Eurocommunist" appeal, a moderate split-off from the JSP, the Democratic Socialist Party (DSP), and the Buddhist Komeito (Clean Government Party), all parties gathering most of their support in the large urban areas (Hoston 1987: 180). A *formal* structural explanation for the JSP's demise might be sought in the interaction effect between electoral system and party organization. A *substantive* explanation has to refer to the party's discursive universe and its ideological traditions rooted in the 1920s.

The Japanese single nontransferable vote (SNTV) electoral system with small multimember districts (typically three to five seats) creates factions within parties that hope to win more than one seat per constituency and hence field more than one candidate. Because voters cast their ballots for a single candidate and not a party, candidates with the same party affiliation compete with each other for votes and thus create intraparty divisions.[11] Moreover, this dynamic decentralizes party power and leads to personal electoral machines supported by local interests. The logic of SNTV makes it very difficult for parties to expand beyond one representative per constituency. As soon as a party wishes to put up a second candidate, its local incumbent will fight vigorously against the proposed challenger, because she will risk losing her otherwise secure seat by splitting the party's electorate. In fact, the number of constituencies in which the JSP fielded more than one candidate declined from over 80% in the 1950s to less than 20% by the late 1970s (Stockwin 1986: 102).[12]

Personalized campaigns in districts require major funding. For the JSP, the dominant source of funding has remained *Sohyo*. This union became progressively more militant, particularly after the departure, in the 1950s, of its private sector union affiliates, which generally had greater sympathies for business concerns; the union now has a narrow appeal to militant public sector workers (Stockwin 1986: 89–91). Overall, the party has become mired in a mixture of ideological and personnel struggles fueled by the SNTV election system. As a consequence, the majority of JSP activists in the 1960s and 1970s, in conjunction with *Sohyo* opposed not only a social democratic moderation, but also the influx of the libertarian New Left (Curtis 1988: 29–30, 149) and of environmentalists (Curtis 1988: 20).[13] At the same time, the radical rhetoric of the party was divorced from the pragmatic bargaining style of its MPs in the parliamentary committees where

---

11 The emergence of intraparty factionalism produced by personal preference voting systems has been analyzed by Katz (1980).

12 The general logic of fielding candidates in the Japanese SNTV system is discussed in Reed (1990).

13 Not by chance, *Soyho* also opposed a drive to increase party membership in the 1970s (cf. Curtis 1988: 153–4).

they served as public sector lobbyists. The rift between parliamentary pressure group politics and radical strategic posturing increased when the power to select the party leader shifted from the MPs to the annual party conference (Steel and Tsurutani 1986: 246).

The formal rules of Japanese politics explain the factionalization of the JSP, but they do not explain (1) why the factionalism is ideological rather than merely personal as in the LDP and (2) why the factions until recently have represented only varieties of radical Marxist leftism within the party as well as in *Sohyo*. To explain this situation, we have to explore the discursive universe in which the party has been placed. Unlike European labor parties, the JSP started out as a party of intellectuals after the Russian revolution (Curtis 1988: 127). The only ideological contender to orthodox Marxism among intellectuals at the time was anarchism, not in its communitarian version, but its terrorist Russian mode.

Because it never became a mass organization incorporating a cross section of occupations, the JSP remained an intellectuals' party, inspired by different brands of extreme antiparliamentary and anticapitalist radicalism and never made it out of its political ivory tower. At the same time, MPs running uncontested as the party's sole candidates in their districts had little incentive to change the terms of the party discourse. Only in the mid-1980s, when the party reached its electoral nadir and many single seats were threatened as well by further electoral decline, did the party begin to open up and pursue a more moderate appeal that paid off in the 1990 election. Whether the party can escape the trap of fielding single candidates per district, however, remains to be seen.

### Ethnic or regional conflicts and social democracy: Canada and Israel

While the eight cases surveyed appear to fit the logic of my general theoretical argument that the parties' success depends on their strategic response to the competitive situation and on the organizational and ideological forces in the parties' internal life, two remaining social democratic parties in Canada and Israel are situated in a more complex competitive space that includes cross-cutting ethnic or regional conflicts complicating the parties' strategic position. While the Belgian socialists have coped with an ethnolinguistic cleavage through regional segmentation of the party organization, this strategy is less feasible in Canada and not possible in Israel.

As Morley (1988) as well as Bradford and Jenson (1992) explain, the Canadian New Democratic Party (NDP) has had to resort to "contentless populism" in order to overcome its regional divisions, its internal conflicts on constitutional reform, and its weakness in the Francophone province of Quebec. Moreover, its linkage to labor unions has prevented it from venturing into libertarian politics. The party's greatest problem, however, may be the existence of a strong liberal party in the center of the party system. Although formal theory can show that three-party systems have no equilibrium among the parties' strategic stances, the need to maintain continuity and reputation cuts down on the NDP's strategic mobility. The party cannot leapfrog the liberals, but whenever the NDP has appeared to become strong on its own account, the liberals have demonstrated the flexibility to adopt mildly social democratic positions and thus undercut the surge of their leftist competitors. Unlike the British Labour Party, which has had the good fortune that its centrist liberal democratic competitor is a "third party," the NDP faces a centrist party that is really the first or second party while the NDP is better cast in the role of third party. Only an extraordinary weakness of the liberals could open an opportunity for the NDP to trade places.

In Israel, the Labor Party's past electoral successes have a great deal to do with its early role in nation building and only little to do with class politics. Israel's Labor Party became entrenched in the European Jewish (Ashkenazi) community and from the inception of the state built a broad network of organizations around the *Histradut* union and quasi-state industrial companies that were run under union management. Hence, unlike its West European counterparts, the primary appeal of Israel's Labor Party was never based on class or universalist social concerns, but nation building, protection of a state-led economic sector, and ethnicity. The growing electoral weight of Middle Eastern and North African Jews (Sephardim) and the crisis of the state-controlled industrial sector in the 1970s and 1980s weakened the party and it has not been able to recover the economic initiative since that time (cf. Arian and Talmud 1992). The party's electoral success in 1992 was due to the electoral support of new Russian immigrants and the declining capacity of the Likud bloc to satisfy the political demands of Sephardic Jews. Thus, Israel's ethnic dynamic of party politics makes it impossible to equate it with the competitive situation of West European social democratic parties and makes it even difficult to impose the same roster of theoretical concerns on this case.[14]

With the exception of the countries complicated by ethnic subnational divisions, the general explanatory model I have employed in this book appears to hold also in a range of other cases. Parties' vote-maximizing positions depend on the extent of left-libertarian cleavage mobilization and the balance of party system fractionalization. Whether parties choose vote-seeking, office-seeking, or oligopolistic strategies in rational ways or not depends on intraparty coalition building and conflict management.

## 7.3 SOCIAL DEMOCRACY IN A NEW COMPETITIVE ENVIRONMENT: WHAT APPEALS MAY SUCCEED?

How may social democratic parties wish to respond to their environment in the years to come in order to preserve or improve their long-term electoral position? Social democratic parties *can* make choices, although their options are constrained by the distribution of voters over the political space. The appeals of individual

14 Of course, the balance of party fractionalization in Israel makes a strategic difference, but due to the prominence of ethnic, religious, and foreign policy divisions, the nature of the competitive space is quite different than the familiar left-(libertarian) versus right-(authoritarian) space encountered elsewhere.

parties and the overall configuration of competitors in the electoral arena can influence this voter distribution, but only in the long run. Social democratic parties show the greatest capacity to change their strategic appeals in times of electoral decline and organizational crisis. This is evidenced by the Dutch Labor Party and the French socialists in the late 1960s, the Italian socialists in the mid-1970s, the British Labour Party from the late 1970s to the late 1980s, and the Austrian socialists in the second half of the 1980s.

Substantively, the choices before social democratic parties concern the *salience* they wish to give communitarian and distributive dimensions of party competition and the *position* they wish to adopt on each of these two dimensions. On both of them, they are probably confined to the "progressive" half of ideological continuum, i.e., to mildly or more radically socialist positions on distributive dimension and to mildly or more radically libertarian positions on communitarian dimension. I have shown that the position parties adopt depends on their objectives (competition for votes, government office, oligopolistic domination), the balance of fractionalization in a party system, and the prevalent voter distribution. Nevertheless, let me propose several generalizations applicable to all social democratic parties in all advanced capitalist democracies.

First, I do not see *any other dimensions* than the distributive and communitarian dimensions on which social democrats could conceivably compete and stake out new positions. Allocative decisions are the bread and butter of modern politics. The communitarian dimension affects a deeper layer of conflicts in contemporary democracy, namely the nature (hierarchical or participatory?) and scope (broad or narrow?) of collective decision making. This dimension is more fundamental because conflicts over procedures indirectly affect resource allocation as well. A third dimension of political conflict is even more basic and concerns the very *definition of citizenship* in democracy. Are all adults recognized as citizens or only certain groups, characterized by gender, ethnicity, lineage, or place of birth? Decisions on citizenship are fundamental because they have consequences for the process of political decision making as well as resource allocation. These three constituents of democratic politics (citizenship, collective decision-making procedures, resource allocation) may well exhaust the alternatives on which conflictual issues that generate party cleavages can be located.

In my view, social democracy has no option to modify its position on the dimension of citizenship rights where political conflicts concern racism and tolerance for cultural diversity in contemporary democracies. Within rather narrow bounds, social democracy is committed to a clear-cut universalist position accepting cultural diversity and broad citizenship rights for individuals of different ethnic or racial backgrounds. It is true that some of the left parties' working-class constituencies harbor racist and authoritarian resentments and are inclined to support xenophobic parties of the New Radical Right, particularly young workers not organized in unions and left parties, but such constituencies have become too small in advanced industrial societies to risk the loss of the many other occupational and social groups that have supported social democratic parties in recent decades and that subscribe to more libertarian and cosmopolitan orientations.[15]

On the citizenship dimension, the European integration process may create a greater potential for internal divisions in social democratic parties or their contemporary competitors and for the emergence of a new cleavage dimension unrelated to the left-libertarian versus right-authoritarian than racism. On the one hand, left-libertarians have a cosmopolitan orientation that induces them to embrace supranational collaboration. On the other, they fight technocratic governance structures, insist on localized democratic participation, and reject the inegalitarian consequences of open market competition. These preferences lead them to be skeptical of European integration. While this issue may divide social democrats, they cannot turn a vice into a virtue and run on the European agenda as the centerpiece of their voter appeal (cf. Lindström 1992: 116–17).

Second, if social democratic parties continue to compete on the distributive dimension, the new challenges of international market competition and the fragmentation of occupational groups and industrial sectors force the parties to give up far-reaching objectives to change economic property rights and income equalization. What remains of social democratic economic leftism is the defense of basic principles of the welfare state, such as the right to a minimum standard of living for all citizens and equal opportunities in the educational system, together with advocacy of a moderate system of income redistribution through taxes and benefits that serve this purpose. Socialist parties, however, are compelled to abandon demands for the nationalization of enterprises or for workers' control of corporate investment decisions in order to remain electorally viable. Instead, social democratic parties will embrace an agenda of economic policies that offers public investments to enhance the capacity of private market participants to compete internationally. Social democrats thus lose the capacity to contrast their economic and social policy message to that of the mainstream bourgeois conservative parties. At stake between the parties are only slightly different methods to support and to correct private market allocation of scarce goods. In advanced industrial democracies, parties can no longer offer voters stark alternatives on the distributive dimension.

To a large extent, economic policy turns from being a "positional" issue, controversial between parties, to a "valence" issue on which the technocratic "capacity" of parties is all that divides them in the eyes of the voters. This does not mean that social democrats will begin to subscribe to the full credo of free market liberalism. There is a wide range of capitalist governance structures and even bourgeois parties often support nonmarket economic institutions. But social democrats' issue positions will rely less on some kind of generalized ideological

---

15 A closer analysis of racist and New Radical Right potentials that employs the theoretical frame developed in this book can be found in Kitschelt (1991d) and Kitschelt (forthcoming). The commitment of social democratic parties to broad citizenship rights does not, of course, imply that the parties cannot opt for restrictions on new entrants to a country.

disposition than on national, regional, and sectoral policy preferences that are tied to concrete problems of economic growth and employment.[16]

Third, social democrats face more opportunities to distinguish themselves from their bourgeois competitors by staking out alternative positions on the communitarian dimension that call for "regulatory" decisions, instituting participatory decision-making procedures, strengthening the ability of voluntary associations to organize and deliver collective goods, or improving the autonomy of citizens vis-à-vis state supervision. Although conflicts over regulatory policy in the areas of environmental protection, women's rights, health care, education, municipal services, cultural diversity, and moral issues may not always be as salient as economic policy issues, there is more room for alternative visions between competing parties than on the distributive dimension. Political conflict in advanced capitalism will become increasingly a *cultural conflict* about political parameters constraining citizens' choice of life-styles and actual quality of life. Whereas the economy becomes a pure *salience issue* where parties agree in principle on objectives and even on the basic methods of policy-making but compete over the *competence* to realize such objectives, communitarian conflicts constitute *directional issues* on which parties stake out alternative visions of society.

In light of changing citizens' preferences and aspirations, the main problem of social democratic policy is no longer to strike a compromise between individual liberty and social equality within a capitalist market economy tempered by a strong welfare state, but to find a balance among at least three ultimate objectives and their institutional correlates: liberty, equality, and libertarian community. Whereas liberty is served by markets organized around voluntary contracts and equality is instituted by centralized bureaucratic institutions that redistribute resources, libertarian community relies on the capacity of individuals and voluntary groups to organize interest associations and to participate in policy-making processes. In advanced capitalist welfare states, characterized by an increasing disaffection of citizens with large hierarchical agencies and corporations in the private and public sectors, left political visions can no longer be wedded to the extension of state planning and equality at the expense of liberty and community, but must give more weight to individual autonomy and communitarian self-organization.

By triangulating liberty, equality, and community, we may formulate a new conception of what "left" and "right," "progressive," "conservative," or "reactionary" policies mean in advanced industrial societies. The premises of my reasoning are in line with Hirschman's (1981) theory of shifting involvements. Once people build institutions that come close to realizing one of the three objectives, the marginal returns on further improvements in realizing the privileged objective diminish significantly and citizens become aware of the trade-offs with other objectives that realization of the dominant goal entails. "Progressive" or "left" political visions are oriented toward redressing the institutional balance among principles of social order in favor of the realization of those values and their

16  About national and sectoral influences on the variance of capitalist governance structures, see Kitschelt (1991c).

organizational correlates that have been ignored to the greatest extent in the existing social order. Conservative or "right" visions, in contrast, defend the dominant values and organizational correlates of the existing society. Reactionary or "extreme right" visions try to reestablish the hegemony of an organizational principle dominant in the past.

If social democratic parties wish to remain "progressive" in advanced Keynesian welfare states, they cannot confine themselves to the pursuit of equality, the value social democrats have best institutionalized in contemporary capitalism. Instead, they must also consider the liberating potential of market transactions that free citizens from collective dependency relations and allow them to develop a measure of personal accountability and control, provided each market participant is endowed with a minimum of resources. Most important, social democrats must rethink the role of libertarian community that surfaces in citizens' quest for social autonomy from markets and state bureaucracies. If anything, the history of social democratic parties in the 1980s has shown that it is vital for progressive currents to embrace this theme as a guiding principle of policy-making and electoral appeal.

Social democratic programs need to identify a new balance between liberty, equality, and community that may exhibit several striking contrasts to the typical leftist programs of the 1960s and 1970s.[17] The discourse on the redistribution of economic property rights and incomes would assume a lower priority, at least in affluent countries with a relatively generous social safety net. Similarly, the question of corporate governance would not concern workers' participation so much as would general regulatory restraints on private investments that involve consumers, local governments, and residents in political decisions as well. Finally, quasi-market policy instruments that leave individuals more freedom to choose the best form of action, such as vouchers, fees, or taxes, would displace direct bureaucratic regulatory command structures in many areas of policy-making like environmental policy or certain areas of health and educational policy.

The need to redesign social democratic programs in light of demands for individual choice and communitarian self-governance concerns not only general state policies, but also the internal decision making of the parties themselves. A party's methods for organizing its internal life send a message to potential constituents about the kind of society and the kind of political practices the party is likely to advocate for society at large; in many ways a party's political medium becomes its message (Kitschelt 1989a: ch. 2). Up to now, in their internal governance structures most social democratic parties have opted for a restrictive form of representative democracy over decentralized, participatory decision procedures. Bureaucratic centralism had the effect of creating stable internal power relations and made it difficult for small bands of rank-and-file activists or leaders to shape innovative party strategies. Most social democratic parties have rejected a liberal conception of democracy relying on autonomous leaders who compete for office and limit the role of voters and party members to the (dis)approval of the

---

17 I have discussed such principles of social democratic policy in greater detail in Kitschelt (1991a: 206–21).

incumbents. They have also rejected a syndicalist model of participatory democracy with internal plebiscites and revocable representation in favor of a collective, hierarchical, and bureaucratized style of decision making in a mass organization.

The bureaucratic-representative model of party organization, however, is ineffective in light of changing voter aspirations and intensified party competition to capture a growing market of uncommitted voters. Social democrats are confronted with various avenues of reform they can pursue individually or in combination. They may become more responsive to selective issue-related political mobilization from below by abandoning their unwieldy mass organizations in favor of more fluid functionally specific study groups and issue organizations led by rank-and-file members. Social democracy may also consider increasing leadership autonomy in order to gain more strategic flexibility in the competition with its adversaries. This would necessarily involve cutting its ties to labor unions, particularly to unions defending inefficient subsidized private and public industries or advocating centralized bureaucratic welfare state institutions.

If organizational reforms from both above and below are instituted, social democratic parties will become stratified conflict systems with dense interaction between different groups of activists and party leaders, yet with considerable autonomy at the top to manage the party's daily affairs. A model for permitting more input from below and flexible leadership from above is provided by the French PS in the 1970s and early 1980s when the party was organized by ideological currents proportionally represented in the party leadership.[18]

If social democratic parties change their electoral appeal by emphasizing libertarian objectives and market efficiency and replace the parties' mass organization by more flexible stratified conflict systems, they are likely to attract a new electoral coalition. First, in an age of more refined voter tastes, social democratic parties can no longer hope to be traditional catch-all parties, but will appeal to more sophisticated, but limited groups of voters. In a simplified formula, Kirchheimer's "catch-all" parties correspond to a Fordist capitalism in which occupational and sectoral stratification, as well as the differentiation of consumer demands, was relatively limited. Post-Fordism in the political sphere promotes the demise of catch-all parties in favor of parties with more precisely defined target audiences. The electoral stabilization of social democratic parties is therefore likely to proceed from a lower baseline of voter support than many socialists have become accustomed to in the post–World War II era. Some of the electoral losses social democrats sustained in the 1980s were probably "tragic" in the sense that no rational competitive strategy could have avoided them. New competitors, particularly new radical left-libertarian parties, have squeezed the socialists' electoral terrain. Social democrats therefore do well to concentrate on the struggle to control

18 The PS, however, reverted to a localized patronage organization in the 1980s, enmeshed in cliquish struggles among individual politicians jockeying for the best position to succeed Mitterrand as party leader and president. The Spanish PSOE appears to have gone through a similar trajectory of organizational change.

the pivot in the party system, because competitors on the left-libertarian extreme are difficult to displace, as the German social democrats have experienced.

In light of changes in the social structure, the continuing social democratic loyalty of core sectors in the shrinking traditional industrial working class can no longer be an overriding strategic concern of social democratic electoral coalition building. In the short run, social democratic parties who stop appealing to the traditional agenda of Keynesian welfare state capitalism risk losing party stalwarts to the authoritarian Right, once they have been cut loose from the moorings of conventional social democracy. In the long run, however, working class support is no longer important enough for social democratic parties to forsake a strategy that is more libertarian, yet more moderate on distributive economic issues than some working class constituencies would welcome. In order to be electorally successful and remain viable as government coalition partners, social democrats must reach out to an electoral constituency built around sophisticated industrial technicians and engineers, white collar employees and middle managers, and the large sector of professionals in personal services. In particular, the parties will attract younger women whose disposition toward libertarian values and center-left economic policies is stronger than that of any other group.

The extent to which social democratic parties may wish to pursue such strategies and to reorganize their internal structures depends on the particular parameters of a country's electoral marketplace and political competition. The Southern European socialist parties as well as the Australian and New Zealand labor parties have clearly emphasized economic liberalism, with only a modest left-libertarian component. For reasons discussed throughout this study, Mediterranean socialist strategies have offered electoral benefits only under very special and probably transitory circumstances. Social democratic parties in other countries may need to find different solutions to their strategic problems. But no social democratic party can ignore the challenges of market efficiency or of libertarian community and self-governance and continue on with conventional Keynesian welfare state policies. Everywhere, the transformation of social democracy involves substantial changes in the parties' programmatic appeals, organizational structures, and electoral support coalitions.

# References

Aardal, Dennis. 1990. "Green Politics: A Norwegian Experience." *Scandinavian Political Studies* 13, no. 1: 147–64.

Adorno, Theodor W., Else Frenkel-Brunswick, Daniel H. Levinson, and R. Nevitt Sanford. 1950. *The Authoritarian Personality*. New York: Harper.

Ahlen, Kristina. 1989. "Swedish Collective Bargaining under Pressure: Inter-union Rivalry and Incomes Policies." *British Journal of Industrial Relations* 27, no. 3: 330–46.

Alber, Jens. 1988. "Continuities and Changes in the Idea of the Welfare State." *Politics and Society* 16, no. 4: 451–68.

Aldrich, John H. 1983. "A Downsian Spatial Model with Party Activism." *American Political Science Review* 77, no. 4: 974–90.

Aldrich, John H., and Michael D. McGinnis. 1989. "A Model of Party Constraints on Optimal Candidate Position." *Mathematical and Computer Modelling* 12, no. 4/5: 437–50.

Aleman, Ulrich v. 1990. "Parteien und Gesellschaft in der Bundesrepublik. Rekrutierung, Konkurrenz und Reziprozität." In Alf Mintzel and Heinrich Oberreuter, eds., *Parteien in der Bundesrepublik Deutschland*. Bonn: Bundeszentrale für politische Bildung, pp. 84–125.

Alesina, Alberto. 1989. "Politics and Business Cycles in Industrial Democracies." *Economic Policy* no. 8: 57–87.

Allum, Percy, and Renato Mannheimer. 1985. "Italy," In Ivor Crewe and David Denver, eds., *Electoral Change in European Democracies*. New York: St. Martin's Press, pp. 287–318.

Alt, James E. 1985. "Party Strategies, World Demand and Unemployment in Britain and the United States, 1947–1983." In Michael Lewis-Beck and Heinz Eulau, eds., *Economic Conditions and Electoral Outcomes*. New York: Agathon, pp. 32–61.

Alt, James E., and Alec Chrystal. 1983. *Political Economics*. Berkeley: University of California Press.

Altmann, Dennis. 1988. "The Paradox of Australian Labor's Success." *Socialist Review* 18, no. 1: 119–28.

Alvarez, Michael, Geoff Garrett, and Peter Lange. 1991. "Government Partisanship, Labor Organization and Economic Performance, 1967–1984." *American Political Science Review* 85, no. 2: 539–56.

Amodia, Jose. 1990. "Personalities and Slogans: The Spanish Election of October 1989." *West European Politics* 13, no. 2 (April): 293–8.

Andersson, Jan Otto. 1987. "The Economic Policy Strategies of the Nordic Countries." In Hans Keman, Heikki Paloheimo, and Paul F. Whiteley, eds., *Coping with the Economic Crisis*. Beverly Hills, Calif.: Sage, pp. 163–81.

Arian, Asher, and Ilan Talmud. 1992. "Electoral Politics and Economic Control in Israel." In

Frances Fox Piven, ed., *Labor Parties in Postindustrial Politics*. New York: Oxford University Press, pp. 169–89.

Austen-Smith, David, and Jeffrey Banks. 1988. "Elections, Coalitions, and Legislative Outcomes." *American Political Science Review* 82, no. 2: 405–22.

Baker, Kendall L, Russell J. Dalton, and Kai Hildebrandt. 1981. *Germany Transformed. Political Culture and the New Politics*. Cambridge, Mass.: Harvard University Press.

Barnes, Samuel H., and Max Kaase, eds. 1979. *Political Action. Mass Participation in Five Western Democracies*. Beverly Hills, Calif.: Sage.

Barnes, Samuel H., Peter McDonough, and Antonio Lopez Pina. 1985. "The Development of Partisanship in New Democracies: The Case of Spain." *American Journal of Political Science* 29 no. 4: 695–720.

Barry, Brian. 1980. *Sociologists, Economists, and Democracy*. Chicago: University of Chicago Press.

Bartolini, Stefano. 1983a. "The Membership of Mass Parties: The Social Democratic Experience, 1889–1978." In Hans Daalder and Peter Mair, eds., *Western European Party Systems. Stability and Change*. Beverly Hills, Calif.: Sage, pp. 177–220.

1983b. "The European Left since World War I: Size, Composition, and Patterns of Electoral Development." In Hans Daalder and Peter Mair, eds., *Western European Party Systems. Stability and Change*. Beverly Hills, Calif.: Sage, pp. 139–75.

Bartolini, Stefano, and Peter Mair. 1990. *Identity, Competition, and Electoral Availability: The Stability of European Electorates 1885–1985*. Cambridge: Cambridge University Press.

Baudrillard, Jean. 1975. *The Mirror of Production*. St. Louis: Telos Press.

Bayer, Kurt, and Peter Kreisky. 1988. "Die österreichische Gemeinwirtschaft. Der Anfang vom Ende des österreichischen Weges?" In Peter Pelinka and Gerhard Steger, eds., *Auf dem Weg zur Staatspartei. Zur Geschichte und Politik der SPÖ seit 1945*. Vienna: Verlag für Gesellschaftskritik, pp. 95–107.

Beck, Ulrich. 1983. "Jenseits von Stand und Klasse? Soziale Ungleichheiten, gesellschaftliche Individualisierungsprozesse und die Entstehung neuer sozialer Formationen und Identitäten." *Soziale Welt*, 34 no. 1: 35–74.

1986. *Risikogesellschaft*. Frankfurt am Main: Suhrkamp.

Becker, Horst, and Bodo Hombach. 1983. *Die SPD von Innen. Bestandaufnahme an der Basis der Partei*. Bonn: Verlag Neue Gesellschaft.

Bell, Daniel. 1973. *The Coming of Post-Industrial Society. A Venture in Social Forecasting*. New York: Basic Books.

1976. *The Cultural Contradictions of Capitalism*. New York: Basic Books.

Bell, David S., and Byron Criddle. 1987. "The Communist Party: Out of the Frying Pan." In Patrick McCarthy, ed., *The French Socialists in Power, 1981–86*. New York and Westport, Conn.: Greenwood, pp. 155–69.

1988. *The French Socialist Party. The Emergence of a Party of Government*. 2nd ed. Oxford: Clarendon Press.

1989. "Review Article: The Decline of the French Communist Party." *British Journal of Political Science* 19, no. 4: 515–36.

Bennulf, Martin, and Sören Holmberg. 1990. "The Green Breakthrough in Sweden." *Scandinavian Political Studies* 13, no. 2: 165–84.

Berger, Manfred, Wolfgang G. Gibowski, Dieter Roth, and Wolfgang Schulte. 1983. "Regierungswechsel und politische Einstellungen: Eine Analyse der Bundestagswahl 1983." *Zeitschrift für Parlamentsfragen* 14, no. 4: 556–82.

1987. "Die Konsolidierung der Wende. Eine Analyse der Bundestagswahl 1987." *Zeitschrift für Parlamentsfragen* 18, no. 2: 253–84.

Berger, Peter A. 1986. *Entstrukturierte Klassengesellschaft?* Opladen: Westdeutscher Verlag.

Berglund, Steen. 1987. "The Finnish General Election of 1987." *Electoral Studies* 6, no. 3: 271–3.
1991. "The Finnish Parliamentary Election of 1991." *Electoral Studies* 10, no. 3: 256–61.
Berglund, Steen, and Ulf Lindström. 1978. *The Scandinavian Party System(s). A Comparative Study.* Lund: Studentliteratur.
Bergqvist, Christina. 1991. "Corporatism and Gender Equality. A Comparative Study of Two Swedish Labour Market Organizations." *European Journal of Political Research* 20, no. 2: 107–25.
Bergström, Hans. 1991. "Sweden's Politics and Party System at the Crossroads." *West European Politics* 14, no. 3: 8–30.
Bille, Lars. 1989. "Denmark: The Oscillating Party System." *West European Politics* 12, no. 4: 42–58.
Billiet, J., and Luc Huyse. 1984. "Verzorgingsstaat en verzuiling. Een dubbelzinnige relatie." *Tijdschrift voor Sociologie* 5, no. 1/2: 129–51.
Biorcio, Roberto, and Paolo Natale. 1989. "La mobilità elletorale degli anni ottanta." *Rivista Italiana di Scienza Politica* 19, no. 3: 385–430.
Boggs, Carl. 1986. *Social Movements and Political Power. Emerging Forms of Radicalism in the West.* Philadelphia: Temple University Press.
Boivin, Bertus, Herman Hazelhoff, Bert Middle, and Bob Molenaar. 1978. *Een Verjongingskuur voor de Partij van de Arbeid.* Dewenter: Kluwer.
Borre, Ole. 1988. "The Danish General Election of 1987." *Electoral Studies* 7, no. 1: 75–8.
1991. "The Danish General Election of 1990." *Electoral Studies* 10, no. 2: 133–8.
Boston, Jonathan, and Keith Jackson. 1988. "The New Zealand General Election of 1987." *Electoral Studies* 7, no. 1: 70–5.
Boudon, Raymond. 1989. *The Analysis of Ideology.* Chicago: Chicago University Press.
Bourdieu, Pierre. 1977. *Outline of the Theory of Practice.* Cambridge: Cambridge University Press.
Boy, Daniel. 1981. "Le vote écologiste en 1978." *Revue française de science politique* 31, no. 2: 394–416.
Boyer, Robert. 1988. "Formalizing Growth Regimes." In Giovanni Dosi et al., *Technical Change and Economic Theory.* London: Pinter, pp. 608–30.
Bradford, Neil, and Jane Jenson. 1992. "Facing Economic Restructuring and Constitutional Renewal: Social Democracy Adrift in Canada." In Frances Fox Piven, ed., *Labor Parties in Postindustrial Society.* New York: Oxford University Press, pp. 190–211.
Brand, Jack. 1989. "Kavanagh and McKenzie on Power." *West European Politics* 12, no. 2: 112–21.
Brand, Karl-Werner, Detlef Büsser, and Dieter Rucht. 1983. *Aufbruch in eine andere Gesellschaft. Neue soziale Bewegungen in der Bundesrepublik.* Frankfurt am Main: Campus.
Braunthal, Gerard. 1983. *The West German Social Democrats, 1969–1982. Profile of a Party in Power.* Boulder, Colo.: Westview Press.
Brinkmann, Heinz Ulrich. 1988. "Wahlverhalten der 'Neuen Mittelschicht' in der Bundesrepublik Deutschland." *Aus Politik und Zeitgeschichte* 38 (July 22): 19–32.
Brint, Steven. 1984. "'New Class' and Cumulative Trend Explanations of the Liberal Political Attitudes of Professionals." *American Journal of Sociology* 90, no. 1: 30–71.
Bruneau, Thomas C., and Alex MacLeod. 1986. *Politics in Contemporary Portugal. Parties and the Consolidation of Democracy.* Boulder, Colo.: Lynne Rienner.
Budge, Ian. 1987. "The Internal Analysis of Election Programmes." In Ian Budge, David Robertson, and Derek Hearl, *Ideology, Strategy, and Party Change.* Cambridge: Cambridge University Press, pp. 15–38.

Budge, Ian, and Dennis Farlie. 1977. *Voting and Party Competition*. London: Wiley 1977.

1983a. *Explaining and Predicting Elections. Issue Effects and Party Strategies in Twenty-Three Democracies*. London: Allen and Unwin.

1983b. "Party Competition. Selective Emphasis or Direct Confrontation? An Alternative View with Data." In Hans Daalder and Peter Mair, eds., *Western European Party Systems. Continuity and Change*. Beverly Hills, Calif.: Sage, pp. 267–306.

Budge, Ian, and Hans Keman. 1990. *Parties and Democracy. Coalition Formation and Government Functioning in Twenty States*. Oxford: Oxford University Press.

Budge, Ian, and David Robertson. 1987. "Comparative Analyses of Post-War Election Programmes." In Ian Budge, David Robertson, and Derek Hearl, *Ideology, Strategy, and Party Change*. Cambridge: Cambridge University Press, pp. 388–416.

Budge, Ian, David Robertson, and Derek Hearl. 1987. *Ideology, Strategy, and Party Change, Spatial Analysis of Post-War Elections. Programmes in 19 Democracies*. Cambridge: Cambridge University Press.

Bundervoet, Jan. 1983. "Vakbond en politiek in crisistijd." *Res Publica* 25, no. 2–3: pp. 220–36.

Burowoy, Michael. 1989. "Marxism without Micro-Foundations." *Socialist Review* 19, no. 2: 57–86.

Butler, David, and Dennis Kavanagh. 1984. *The British General Election of 1983*. New York: St. Martin's Press.

1988. *The British General Election of 1987*. New York: St. Martin's Press.

Byrd, Peter. 1986. "The Labour Party in Britain." In William E. Paterson and Alastair H. Thomas, eds., *The Future of Social Democracy*. Oxford: Clarendon Press, pp. 59–107.

1987. "Great Britain. Parties in a Changing Party System." In Alan Ware, ed., *Political Parties. Electoral Change and Structural Response*. Oxford: Blackwell, pp. 204–24.

Cameron, David. 1984. "Social Democracy, Corporatism, Labour Quiescence, and the Representation of Economic Interest in Advanced Capitalist Society." In John Goldthorpe, ed., *Order and Change in Advanced Capitalism*. Oxford: Oxford University Press, pp. 143–78.

Capdeville, Jacque, Elisabeth Dupoirier, Gérard Grunberg, Etienne Schweisguth, and Colette Ysmal. 1988. *France de Gauche – Vote à Droite?* 2nd ed. Paris: Presses de la Fondation Nationale de Science Politiques.

Carmines, Edward O., and James A. Stimson. 1989. *Issue Evolution. Race and the Transformation of American Politics*. Princeton, N.J.: Princeton University Press.

Castles, Francis G. 1978. *The Social Democratic Image of Society. A Study of the Achievements and Origins of Scandinavian Social Democracy in Comparative Perspective*. London: Routledge and Kegan Paul.

ed. 1982. *The Impact of Parties. Politics and Policies in Democratic Capitalist States*. Beverly Hills, Calif.: Sage.

Cayrol, Roland. 1988. "The Electoral Campaign and the Decision-Making Process of French Voters." In Howard Penniman, ed., *France at the Polls 1981 and 1986*. Durham, N.C.: Duke University Press, pp. 130–54.

Ceri, Paolo. 1988. "The Nuclear Power Issue. A New Political Cleavage within Italian Society?" In *Italian Politics. A Review*. 2. London: Pinter, pp. 71–89.

Cerny, Carl, ed. 1990. *Germany at the Polls. The Bundestag Elections of the 1980s*. Durham, N.C.: Duke University Press.

Ceulers, Jan. 1977. "De lijstensamenstelling in de Belgische Socialistische Partij." *Res Publica* 19, no. 3: 411–21.

1981. (directing debate) "Evaluatie van de Partiecratie." *Res Publica* 23, no. 2/3: 155–77.

Chappell, Henry W., and William R. Keech. 1986. "Policy Motivation and Party Differences in a Dynamic Spatial Model of Party Competition." *American Political Science Review* 80, no. 3: 881–9.

Christian, Reinhold, and Manfred Welan. 1985. "Umweltpolitik in Österreich." *Österreichisches Jahrbuch für Politik 1984.* Vienna: Verlag für Wissenschaft und Politik.

Clarke, Harold D., and Nitish Dutt. 1991. "Measuring Value Change in Western Industrialized Society. The Impact of Unemployment." *American Political Science Review* 85, no. 3: 905–20.

Clarke, Harold D., Marianne C. Stewart, and Gary Zuk. 1986a. "Politics, Economics and Party Popularity in Britain, 1979–1983." *Electoral Studies* 5, no. 2: 123–41.

1986b. "The Political Economy of Party Support in Canada, 1980–84." *European Journal of Political Economy* 12, no. 1: 25–45.

Clarke, Harold D., and Paul Whiteley. 1990. "Perception of Macroeconomic Performance, Government Support, and Conservative Party Strategy in Britain, 1983–87." *European Journal of Political Research* 18, no. 1: 97–120.

Clogg, Richard. 1987. *Parties and Elections in Greece.* Durham, N.C.: Duke University Press.

Coates, David, and Gordon Johnston, eds. 1983. *Socialist Strategies.* Oxford: Martin Robertson.

Cole, Alistair M. 1988. "La France Unie? François Mitterrand." In John Gaffney, ed., *The French Presidential Elections of 1988. Ideology and Leadership in Contemporary France.* Aldershot: Gower, pp. 81–100.

1989. "Factionalism, the French Socialist Party and the Fifth Republic. An Explanation of Intra-Party Divisions." *European Journal of Political Research* 17, no. 1: 77–94.

Collovald, Annie. 1985. "La république du militant. Recrutement et filières de la carrière politique des deputés." In Pierre Birnbaum, ed., *Les élites socialistes au pouvoir. Les dirigeants socialistes face à l'Etat.* Paris: Presse Universitaires de France, pp. 11–52.

Corbetta, Piergiorgio, Arturo M. L. Parisi, and Hans M. A. Schadee. 1988. *Elezioni in Italia.* Bologna: Il Mulino.

Courtois, Stephane, and Denis Peschanski. 1988. "From Decline to Marginalization. The PCF Breaks with French Society." In Michael Waller and Meindert Fennema, eds., *Communist Parties in Western Europe.* Oxford: Blackwell, pp. 47–68.

Cox, Gary W. 1990a. "Multicandidate Spatial Competition." In James Enelow and Melwin J. Hinich, eds., *Advances in the Spatial Theory of Voting.* Cambridge: Cambridge University Press, pp. 179–98.

1990b. "Centripetal and Centrifugal Incentives in Electoral Systems." *American Journal of Political Science* 34 no. 4: 903–35.

Crepaz, Markus M. L. 1992. "Corporatism in Decline? An Empirical Analysis of the Impact of Corporatism on Macroeconomic Performance and Industrial Disputes in 18 Industrialized Democracies." *Comparative Political Studies* 25, no. 2: 139–68.

Crewe, Ivor. 1985a. "Great Britain." In Ivor Crewe and David Denver, eds., *Electoral Change in Western European Democracies.* New York: St. Martin's Press, pp. 100–50.

1985b. "How to Win a Landslide without Really Trying: Why the Conservatives Won in 1983." In Austin Ranney, ed., *Britain at the Polls 1983. A Study of the General Election.* Durham, N.C.: Duke University Press, pp. 155–96.

1986. "On the Death and Resurrection of Class Voting: Some Comments on *How Britain Votes.*" *Political Studies* 34, no. 4: 620–38.

1990. The Decline of Labour and the Decline of Labour: Social and Electoral Trends in Post-War Britain. Paper Prepared for Delivery at the 1990 American Political Science Association Meeting in San Francisco.

1992 "Labor Force Changes, Working Class Decline and the Labour Vote: Social and Electoral Issues in Postwar Britain." In Frances Fox Piven, ed., *Labor Parties in Post-industrial Societies.* New York: Oxford University Press, pp. 20–46.

Crewe, Ivor, and Martin Harrop. 1989. *Political Communications: The General Election Campaign of 1989.* Cambridge: Cambridge University Press.

Crewe, Ivor, and Anthony King. 1992. *SDP: The Social Democratic Party and British Politics, 1981–1988.*

Curran, James, ed. 1984. *The Future of the Left.* Cambridge: Polity Press.

Curtis, Gerald L. 1988. *The Japanese Way of Politics.* New York: Columbia University Press.

Cusak, Thomas R., Ton Notermans, and Martin Rein. 1989. "Political Economic Aspects of Public Employment." *European Journal of Political Research* 17, no. 4: 471–500.

Daalder, Hans. 1984. "In Search of the Center of European Party Systems." *American Political Science Review* 78, no. 1: 92–109.

1986. "Changing Procedures and Changing Strategies in Coalition Building." *Legislative Studies Quarterly* 11, no. 4: 507–31.

1987. "The Dutch Party System. From Segmentation to Polarization – and Then?" In Hans Daalder, ed., *Party Systems in Denmark, Austria, Switzerland, the Netherlands, and Belgium.* London: Pinter, pp. 193–284.

Daalder, Hans, and Peter Mair, eds. 1983. *Western European Party Systems. Continuity and Change.* Beverly Hills, Calif.: Sage.

Dahl, Robert R. 1971. *Polyarchy.* New Haven, Conn.: Yale University Press.

1989. *Democracy and Its Critics.* New Haven, Conn.: Yale University Press.

Dahrendorf, Ralf. 1959. *Classes and Class Conflict in Industrial Society.* Stanford, Calif.: Stanford University Press.

Dalton, Russell J. 1984. "The West German Party System between Two Ages." In Russell J. Dalton, Scott C. Flanagan, and Paul Allen Beck, eds., *Electoral Change in Advanced Industrial Democracies. Realignment or Dealignment?* Princeton, N.J.: Princeton University Press, pp. 104–35.

1985. "Political Parties and Political Representation. Party Supporters and Party Elites in Nine Nations." *Comparative Political Studies* 18, no. 3: 267–99.

1988. *Citizen Politics in Western Democracies.* Chatham: Chatham House.

1990. The Green Rainbow. manuscript. forthcoming at Yale University Press.

Dalton, Russell J., and Manfred Kuechler, eds. 1990. *Challenging the Political Order.* New York: Oxford University Press.

De Esteban, Jorge, and Luis Lopez Guerra. 1985. "Electoral Rules and Candidate Selection." In Howard R. Penniman and Eusebio M. Juhal-Leon, eds., *Spain at the Polls 1977, 1989, and 1982.* Durham, N.C.: Duke University Press, pp. 48–72.

Della Porta, Donatella, and Dieter Rucht. 1991. Left-libertarian Movements in Context. A Comparison of Italy and West Germany, 1965–1990. Wissenschaftszentrum Berlin. Paper FS III.91–102.

DeNardo, James D. 1985. *Power in Numbers.* Princeton, N.J.: Princeton University Press.

Denmark, David. 1990. "Social Democracy and the Politics of Crisis in New Zealand, Britain, and Sweden." In Martin Holland and Jonathan Boston, eds., *The Fourth Labour Government. Politics and Policy in New Zealand.* 2nd ed. Auckland: Oxford University Press, pp. 270–89.

Denver, David. 1988. "Britain: Centralized Parties with Decentralized Selection." In Michael Gallagher and Michael Marsh, eds., *Candidate Selection in Comparative Perspective.* London: Sage, pp. 47–71.

Deschouwer, Kris. 1989. "Patterns of Participation and Competition in Belgium." *West European Politics* 12, no. 4: 28–41.

De Swaan, Abram. 1982. "The Netherlands: Coalitions in a Segmented Polity." In Eric C. Browne and John Dreijmanis, eds., *Government Coalitions in Western Democracies.* New York: Longman, pp. 217–36.

Dewachter, Wilfried. 1987. "Changes in a Particratie: The Belgian Party System from 1944 to 1986." In Hans Daalder, ed., *Party Systems in Denmark, Austria, Switzerland, the Netherlands, and Belgium.* London: Frances Pinter, pp. 285–364.

Deweerdt, Mark. 1987. "Overzicht van het Belgische politiek gebeuren in 1986." *Res Publica* 29, no. 3: 285–357.

Deweerdt, Mark, and Jozef Smits. 1982. "Belgian Politics in 1981: Continuity and Change in the Crisis." *Res Publica* 24, no. 2: 261–72.

De Winter, Lieven. 1981. "De Parteipolitisering als instrument van particratie." *Res Publica* 23, no. 1: 53–107.

——— 1988. "Belgium: Democracy or Oligarchy?" In Michael Gallagher and Michael Marsh, eds., *Candidate Selection in Comparative Perspective.* London: Sage, pp. 20–46.

Diani, Mario. 1989. "Italy. The 'Liste Verdi'." In Ferdinand Müller-Rommel, ed., *New Politics in Western Europe. The Rise and Success of Green Parties and Alternative Lists.* Boulder, Colo.: Westview Press, pp. 113–22.

DiScala, Spencer. 1988. *Renewing Italian Socialism. Nenni to Craxi.* New York: Oxford University Press.

Dittrich, Karl. 1987. "The Netherlands 1946–1981." In Ian Budge, David Robertson, and Derek Hearl, eds., *Ideology, Strategy, and Party Change.* Cambridge: Cambridge University Press, pp. 202–29.

Dodd, Lawrence C. 1976. *Coalitions in Parliamentary Government.* Princeton, N.J.: Princeton University Press.

Donovan, Mark. 1989. "Party Strategy and Centre Domination in Italy," *West European Politics* 12, no. 4: 114–28.

Douglas, Mary. 1986. *How Institutions Think.* Syracuse: Syracuse University Press.

Douglas, Mary, and Aaron Wildavsky. 1982. *Risk and Culture.* Berkeley: University of California Press.

Downs, Anthony. 1957. *An Economic Theory of Democracy.* New York: Harper and Row.

Dunleavy, Patrick, and Christopher T. Husbands. 1985. *British Democracy at the Crossroads. Voting and Party Competition in the 1980s.* London: George Allen and Unwin.

Dupoirier, Elisabeth. 1986. "Chosses-croises électoraux." In Gérard Grunberg, ed., *Mars 1989: la drôle de la défaite de la gauche.* Paris: Presses Universitaires de France.

Duverger, Maurice. 1954. *Political Parties.* London: Methuen.

Dyson, Kenneth. 1977. *Party, State, and Bureaucracy in Western Germany.* Beverly Hills, Calif.: Sage.

Eduards, Maud L. 1991. "The Swedish Gender Model: Productivity, Pragmatism, and Paternalism," *West European Politics* 14, no. 3: 166–81.

Edwards, Richard. 1979. *Contested Terrain.* New York: Basic Books.

Elder, Neil, Alastair H. Thomas, and David Arter. 1988. *The Consensual Democracies?* 2nd ed. Oxford: Blackwell.

Eldersveld, Samuel J. 1964. *Political Parties. A Behavioral Analysis.* Chicago: Rand McNally.

Eley, Geoff. 1991. "Reviewing the Socialist Tradition." In Christiane Lemke and Gary Marks, eds., *The Crisis of Socialism in Europe.* Durham, N.C.: Duke University Press, pp. 21–60.

Elkins, David J., and Richard E. B. Simeon. 1979. "A Cause in Search of Its Effects, or What Does Political Culture Explain?" *Comparative Politics* 11, no. 2: 127–45.

Elster, Jon. 1983. *Sour Grapes.* Cambridge: Cambridge University Press.

——— 1985. *Making Sense of Marx.* Cambridge: Cambridge University Press.

1986. "Introduction." In Jon Elster, ed., *Rational Choice.* New York: New York University Press, pp. 1–33.

Elvander, Nils. 1980. *Skandinavisk Arbetarrörelse.* Stockholm: Liber Förlag.

1990. "Incomes Policies in the Nordic Countries." *International Labour Review* 129, no. 1: 1–21.

Enelow, James M., and Melvin J. Hinich. 1984. *The Spatial Theory of Voting. An Introduction.* Cambridge: Cambridge University Press.

eds. 1990. *Advances in the Spatial Theory of Voting.* Cambridge: Cambridge University Press.

Epstein, Leon. 1967. *Political Parties in Western Democracies.* New York: Praeger.

Ernst, Werner W. 1988. "Zur Programmatik der SPÖ seit 1985." In Peter Pelinka and Gerhard Steger, eds., *Auf dem Wege zur Staatspartei.* Vienna: Verlag für Gesellschaftskritik, pp. 199–211.

Esping-Andersen, Gösta. 1985. *Politics against Markets. The Social Democratic Road to Power.* Princeton, N.J.: Princeton University Press.

1990. *The Three Worlds of Welfare Capitalism.* Princeton, N.J.: Princeton University Press.

Farneti, Paolo. 1985. *The Italian Party System (1945–1980).* New York: St. Martin's Press.

Faulhaber, Theodor. 1986. " 'doch greulich, Freunde, ist die Praxis . . . ' Anmerkungen zur 'Perspektiven 90' Diskussion der SPÖ." In *Österreichisches Jahrbuch für Politik 1985.* Vienna: Verlag für Wissenschaft und Politik, pp. 187–96.

Fearon, James D. 1991. "Counterfactuals and Hypothesis Testing in Political Science." *World Politics* 43, no. 2: 169–95.

Featherstone, Kevin. 1990a. "Political Parties and Democratic Consolidation in Greece." In Geoffrey Pridham, ed., *Securing Democracy. Political Parties and Democratic Consolidation.* London: Routledge and Kegan Paul, pp. 179–202.

1990b. "The 'Party State' in Greece and the Fall of Papandreou." *West European Politics* 13, no. 1: 101–16.

Fedele, Marcello. 1987. "The Ambiguous Alternative: The Italian Communist Party in the 1983 Election." In Howard Penniman, ed., *Italy at the Polls. A Study of the 1983 National Elections,* Durham, N.C.: Duke University Press, pp. 60–77.

Ferree, Myra Marx. 1987. "Equality and Autonomy. Feminist Politics in the United States and West Germany." In Mary Feinsod Katzenstein and Carol McClurg Mueller, eds., *The Women's Movements of the United States and Western Europe.* Philadelphia: Temple University Press, pp. 172–95.

Fiorina, Morris. 1981. "Short- and Long-term Effects of Economic Conditions on Individual Voting Decisions." In Douglas A. Hibbs and Heino Fassbender, eds., *Contemporary Political Economy.* Amsterdam: North Holland, pp. 73–100.

Fitzmaurice, John, and Guido Van den Berghe. 1986. "The Belgian General Election of 1985." *Electoral Studies* 5, no. 1 (April): 73–6.

Flanagan, Scott. 1987. "Value Change in Industrial Society." *American Political Science Review* 81, no. 4: 1303–19.

Flora, Peter, and Jens Alber. 1981. "Modernization, Democratization, and the Development of Welfare States in Western Europe." In Peter Flora and Arnold Heidenheimer, eds., *The Development of Welfare States in Europe and America.* New Brunswick, N.J.: Transaction Books, pp. 37–80.

Flora, Peter, and Arnold Heidenheimer, eds. 1981. *The Development of Welfare States in Europe and America.* New Brunswick, N.J.: Transaction Books.

Flora, Peter, Franz Kraus, and Winfried Pfennig. 1987. *State, Economy, and Society in Western Europe, 1815–1975.* Vol. II: *The Growth of Industrial Societies and Capitalist Economies.* Frankfurt am Main: Campus Verlag.

Foote, Geoffrey. 1986. *The Labour Party's Political Thought. A History.* London: Croom Helm.

Franklin, Mark N. 1985. *The Decline of Class Voting in Britain. Changes in the Bases of Electoral Choice, 1964–83.* Oxford: Clarendon Press.

Franklin, Mark N., Tom Mackie, Henry Valen, et al. 1992. *Electoral Change. Responses to Evolving Social and Attitudinal Structures in Western Countries.* Cambridge: Cambridge University Press.

Frears, John. 1988. "The 1988 French Presidential Election," *Government and Opposition* 23, no. 3: 276–89.

Frey, Bruno S. 1979. "Politometrics of Government Behavior in a Democracy," *Scandinavian Journal of Economics* 81, no. 2: 308–22.

Frognier, Andre-Paul. 1975. "Vote, classe sociale et religion/pratique religieuse." *Res Publica* 17, no. 4: 479–90.

Gaffney, John. 1989. *The French Left and the Fifth Republic. The Discourses of Communism and Socialism in Contemporary France.* New York: St. Martin's Press.

Gallagher, Michael. 1988. "Conclusion." In Michael Gallagher and Michael Marsh, eds., *Candidate Selection in Comparative Perspective.* London: Sage, pp. 236–84.

1989. "The Portuguese Socialist Party: The Pitfalls of Being First." In Tom Gallagher and Allan M. Williams, eds., *Southern European Socialism.* Manchester: Manchester University Press, pp. 12–33.

Gallagher, Michael, and Michael Marsh, eds. 1988. *Candidate Selection in Comparative Perspective.* London: Sage.

Garrett, Geoffrey, and Peter Lange. 1986. "Performance in a Hostile World: Economic Growth in Capitalist Democracies." *World Politics* 38, no. 4: 517–45.

1989. "Government Partisanship and Economic Performance: When and How Does 'Who Governs' Matter?" *Journal of Politics* 51, no. 3: 675–93.

1991. "Political Responses to Interdependence: What's 'Left' of the Left?" *International Organization* 45, no. 4: 539–64.

Gaxie, Daniel. 1977. "Economie des partis et retributions du militantisme." *Revue française de science politique* 27, no. 1 (February): 123–54.

Gelb, Joyce. 1989. *Feminism and Politics. A Comparative Perspective.* Berkeley: University of California Press.

Gerlich, Peter, Edgar Grande, and Wolfgang C. Müller. 1988. "Corporatism in Crisis. Stability and Change of Social Partnership in Austria." *Political Studies* 36, no. 2: 209–23.

Gerretsen, Rob, and Marcel Van der Linden. 1982. "Die Pazifistisch-Sozialistische Partei der Niederlande (PSP)." In Jürgen Baumgarten, ed., *Linkssozialisten in Europa.* Hamburg: Junius, pp. 85–106.

Gibowski, Wolfgang G., and Max Kaase. 1991. "Auf dem Weg zum politischen Alltag. Eine Analyse der ersten gesamtdeutschen Bundestagswahl vom 2. Dezember 1990." *Aus Politik und Zeitgeschichte* 41, no. B11–12 (March 8): 3–20.

Giddens, Anthony. 1973. *The Class Structure of Advanced Societies.* London: Hutchinson.

Gillespie, Richard. 1988. "Spain: Crisis and Renewal in the PCE." *Journal of Communist Studies* 4, no. 3: 335–9.

1989. *The Spanish Socialist Party. A History of Factionalism.* Oxford: Clarendon Press.

1990. "The Breakup of the 'Socialist Family': Party-Union Relations in Spain, 1982–89." *West European Politics* 13, no. 1: 47–62.

Gillespie, Richard, and Tom Gallagher. 1989. "Democracy and Authority in the Socialist Parties of Southern Europe." In Tom Gallagher and Allan M. Williams, eds., *Southern European Socialism.* Manchester: Manchester University Press, pp. 163–87.

Gilljam, Mikael, and Sören Holmberg. 1990. *Rött blatt grönt.* Stockholm: Bonnier Fakta Förlag.

Gladdish, Ken. 1987. "The Centre Holds. The 1986 Netherlands Election." *West European Politics* 10, no. 1 (January): 115–19.

Glatz, Harald. 1988. "Die Umweltpolitik der SPÖ." In Peter Pelinka and Gerhard Steger, eds., *Auf dem Weg zur Staatspartei*. Vienna: Verlag für Gesellschaftskritik, pp. 403–10.

Gluchowski, Peter. 1987. "Lebensstile und Wandel der Wählerschaft in der Bundesrepublik Deutschland." *Aus Politik und Zeitgeschichte* 37, no. B12 (March 21): 18–32.

Goldthorpe, John. 1987. *Social Mobility and Class Structure in Modern Britain*. 2nd ed. Oxford: Oxford University Press.

Goul-Andersen, Jörgen. 1984. "Decline of Class Voting or Change in Class Voting? Social Classes and Party Choice in Denmark in the 1970s." *European Journal of Political Research* 12, no. 3: 243–59.

1990a. "'Environmentalism,' 'New Politics' and Industrialism: Some Theoretical Perspectives." *Scandinavian Political Studies* 13, no. 2: 101–18.

1990b. "Denmark. Environmental Conflict and the 'Greening' of the Labour Movement." *Scandinavian Political Studies* 13, no. 2: 185–210.

Greenberg, Joseph, and Kenneth A. Shepsle. 1987. "Multiparty Competition with Entry: The Effect of Electoral Rewards on Candidate Behavior and Equilibrium." *American Political Science Review* 81, no. 2: 525–37.

Greenberg, Joseph, and Shlomo Weber. 1985. "Multiparty Equilibria and Proportional Representation." *American Political Science Review* 79, no. 3 (September): 693–703.

Greven, Michael Th. 1987. *Parteimitglieder. Ein politischer Essay*. Opladen: Leske und Buderich.

Günther, Klaus. 1979. *Sozialdemokratie und Demokratie*. Bonn: Verlag Neue Gesellschaft.

Gunther, Richard. 1989. "Electoral Laws, Party Systems, and Elites: The Case of Spain." *American Political Science Review* 83, no. 3: 835–58.

Gunther, Richard, Giacomo Sani, and Goldie Shabad. 1988. *Spain after Franco. The Making of a Competitive Party System*. Berkeley: University of California Press.

Gusenbauer, Alfred. 1988. "SPÖ und Neue Soziale Bewegungen," In Peter Pelinka and Gerhard Steger, eds., *Auf dem Weg zur Staatspartei*. Vienna: Verlag für Gesellschaftskritik, pp. 353–9.

Guyomarch, Alain, and Howard Machin. 1989. "François Mitterrand and the French Presidential and Parliamentary Elections of 1988: Mr. Norris Changes Trains?" *West European Politics* 12, no. 3: 196–210.

Gyford, John. 1985. *The Politics of Local Socialism*. London: George Allen and Unwin.

Habermas, Jürgen. 1975. *Legitimation Crisis*. Boston: Beacon Press.

1985. *Theory of Communicative Action*. Boston: Beacon Press.

Haerpfner, Christian. 1985. "Austria." In Ivor Crewe and David Denver, eds., *Electoral Change in European Democracies*. New York: St. Martin's Press, pp. 264–86.

1989. "Austria: The 'United Greens' and the 'Alternative List/Green Alternative'." In Ferdinand Müller-Rommel, ed., *New Politics in Western Europe*. Boulder, Colo: Westview, pp. 23–38.

Hall, Peter. 1987. "The Evolution of Economic Policy under Mitterrand." In George Ross, Stanley Hoffmann and Sylvia Malzacher, eds., *The Mitterrand Experiment*. New York: Oxford University Press, pp. 54–72.

Hamilton, Malcolm B. 1989. *Democratic Socialism in Britain and Sweden*. New York: St. Martin's Press.

Hanley, David. 1986. *Keeping Left? CERES and the French Socialist Party*. Manchester: Manchester University Press.

Harmel, Robert, and Kenneth Janda. 1982. *Parties and Their Environments. Limits to Reform?* New York: Longman.

Hartl, Rupert. 1986. *Österreich und der schwierige Weg zum Sozialismus.* Vienna: Orac.

Hauss, Charles. 1978. *The New Left in France. The Unified Socialist Party.* Westport, Conn.: Greenwood.

Hayek, August Friedrich A. 1977. *The Political Order of a Free People. Law, Legislation and Liberty.* 3. Chicago: Chicago University Press.

Hearl, Derek. 1987. "Belgum 1946–1981." In Ian Budge, David Robertson, and Derek Hearl, eds., *Ideology, Strategy, and Party Change.* Cambridge: Cambridge University Press, pp. 230–53.

Heath, Anthony, Roger Jowell, and John Curtice. 1985. *How Britain Votes.* Oxford: Pergamon Press.

Heath, Anthony, Roger Jowell, John Curtice, and Geoff Evans. 1990. "The Rise of the New Political Agenda?" *European Sociological Review* 6, no. 1: 31–48.

Helenius, Ralf. 1977. "The Finnish Social Democratic Party." In William E. Paterson and Alastair H. Thomas, eds., *Social Democratic Parties in Western Europe.* New York: St. Martin's Press, pp. 272–91.

Hellemans, Staf. 1990. *Strijd om de Moderniteit. Sociale Bewegingen en Verzuiling in Europa Sinds 1800.* Leuven: Universitaire Pers Leuven.

Hellman, Stephen. 1990. Strategy and Organization in the Crisis of the Italian Communist Party. Paper Prepared for the Panel on "The Decline of Communism in Italy and France" at the 7th International Conference of Europeanists, Washington, D.C., March 23–25.

Hermansson, Jörgen. 1988. "A New Face for Swedish Communism. The *Left Party Communists*" In Michael Waller and Meindert Fennema, eds., *Communist Parties in Western Europe.* Oxford: Blackwell, pp. 134–57.

Hess, Hans-Jürgen. 1984. *Innerparteiliche Gruppenbildung. Macht- und Demokratieverlust einer politischen Partei am Beispiel der Berliner SPD in den Jahren von 1963 bis 1981.* Bonn: Verlag Neue Gesellschaft.

Hibbs, Douglas A. 1977. "Political Parties and Macroeconomic Policy." *American Political Science Review* 71, no. 4: 1467–87.

1981. "Economics and Politics in France. Economic Performance and Mass Political Support for Presidents Pompidou and Giscard D'Estaing." *European Journal of Political Research* 9, no. 2: 133–45.

1982. "On the Demand for Economic Outcomes: Macroeconomic Performance and Mass Political Support in the United States, Great Britain, and Germany." *Journal of Politics* 44, no. 2: 426–62.

1987. *The Political Economy of Industrial Democracies.* Cambridge, Mass.: Harvard University Press.

Hibbs, Douglas, and Henrik Madsen. 1981. "The Impact of Economic Performance on Electoral Support in Sweden, 1967–78. *Scandinavian Political Studies* 4, no. 1: 33–50.

Hicks, Alexander. 1988. "Social Democratic Corporatism and Economic Growth." *Journal of Politics* 50, no. 3: 677–704.

Hicks, Alexander, and William David Patterson. 1989. "On the Robustness of the Left Corporatist Model of Economic Growth." *Journal of Politics* 51, no. 3: 662–75.

Hill, Keith. 1974. "Belgium. Political Change in a Segmented Society." In Richard Rose, ed., *Electoral Behavior. A Comparative Handbook.* New York: Free Press, pp. 29–107.

Himmelstrand, Ulf, Göran Ahrne, Leif Lundberg, and Lars Lundberg. 1981. *Beyond Welfare Capitalism.* London: Heinemann.

Hine, David. 1986. "Leaders and Followers. Democracy and Manageability in the Social Democratic Parties of Western Europe." In William E. Paterson and Alastair H.

Thomas, eds., *The Future of Social Democracy.* Oxford: Clarendon Press, pp. 261–90.

1987. "Italy. Parties and Party Government under Pressure." In Alan Ware, ed., *Political Parties. Electoral Change and Structural Response.* Oxford: Blackwell, pp. 72–95.

1989. "The Italian Socialist Party." In Tom Gallagher and Allan M. Williams, *Southern European Socialism.* Manchester: Manchester University Press, pp. 109–30.

Hinich, Melvin, and Michael C. Munger. 1990. A Spatial Theory of Ideology. Ms. University of Texas at Austin.

Hirsch, Fred. 1976. *Social Limits to Growth.* Cambridge, Mass.: Harvard University Press.

Hirschman, Albert O. 1970. *Exit, Voice and Loyalty.* Cambridge, Mass.: Harvard University Press.

1981. *Shifting Involvement.* Princeton, N.J.: Princeton University Press.

Hochschild, Jennifer. 1981. *What's Fair? American Beliefs about Distributive Justice.* Cambridge, Mass.: Harvard University Press.

Hofrichter, Jürgen, and Karlheinz Reif. 1990. "Evolution of Environmental Attitudes in the European Community." *Scandinavian Political Studies* 13, no.2: 119–46.

Hofstetter, C. Richard. 1971. "The Amateur Politician: A Problem in Construct Validation." *Midwest Journal of Political Science* 15, no. 1: 36–53.

Holland, Martin. 1990. "Engineering Electoral Success. Electoral Reform and Voting Behavior under the Fourth Labour Government." In Martin Holland and Jonathan Boston, eds, *The Fourth Labour Government. Politics and Policy in New Zealand.* 2nd ed. Auckland: Oxford University Press, pp. 41–61.

Holmberg, Sören. 1989. "Political Representation in Sweden." *Scandinavian Political Studies* 12, no. 1: 1–16.

Holmberg, Sören, and Mikael Gilljam. 1987. *Väljare och Val i Sverige.* Stockholm: Bonnier Facta Bokfoerlag.

Holmstedt, Margareta, and Tove-Lise Schou. 1987. "Sweden and Denmark 1945–1982. Election Programmes in the Scandinavian Setting." In Ian Budge, David Robertson and Derek Hearl, eds., *Ideology, Strategy, and Party Change.* Cambridge: Cambridge University Press, pp. 177–206.

Hoston, Germaine A. 1987. "Between Theory and Practice: Marxist Thought and the Politics of the Japanese Socialist Party." *Studies in Contemporary Communism* 20, no. 2: 175–207.

Huber, John D. 1989. "Values and Partisanship in Left–Right Orientations: Measuring Ideology." *European Journal of Political Research* 17, no. 5: 599–621.

Hummel, Ralph. 1982. *The Bureaucratic Phenomenon.* 2nd ed. New York: St. Martin's Press.

Huyse, Luc. 1984. "Pillarization Reconsidered." *Acta Politica* 19, no. 1: 145–58.

Hyvaerinen, Matti, and Jukka Paastela. 1988. "Failed Attempts at Modernization. The Finnish Communist Party." In Michael Waller and Meindert Fennema, eds., *Communist Parties in Western Europe.* Oxford: Blackwell, pp. 114–33.

Inglehart, Ronald. 1977. *The Silent Revolution. Changing Values and Political Styles among Western Publics.* Princeton, N.J.: Princeton University Press.

1984. "The Changing Structure of Political Cleavages in Western Societies." In Russell J. Dalton, Scott C. Flanagan, and Paul Allen Beck, eds., *Electoral Change in Advanced Western Democracies.* Princeton, N.J.: Princeton University Press, pp. 25–69.

1987. "Value Change in Industrial Society." *American Political Science Review* 81, no. 4: 1289–1303.

1990. *Culture Shift.* Princeton, N.J.: Princeton University Press.

Inglehart, Ronald, and Paul R. Abramson. 1992a. Value Change in Advanced Industrial Society. Problems in Conceptualization and Measurement. Prepared for Delivery at the 1992 Annual Meeting of the Western Political Science Association, San Francisco.

1992b. "Generational Replacement and Value Change in Eight West European Societies." *British Journal of Political Science* 22, no. 2: 181–228.

International Labour Office. 1988. *The Cost of Social Security.* Geneva: ILO.

1990a. *Yearbook of Labour Statistics.* Geneva: ILO.

1990b. *Yearbook of Labour Statistics. Retrospective Edition.* Geneva: ILO.

Irwin, Galen, and Karl Dittrich. 1984. "And the Walls Came Tumbling Down. Party Dealignment in the Netherlands." In Russell J. Dalton, Scott C. Flanagan, and Paul Allen Beck, eds., *Electoral Change in Advanced Western Democracies.* Princeton, N.J.: Princeton University Press, pp. 267–97.

Irwin, G. A., and J. J. M. van Holsteyn. 1989. "Towards a More Open Model of Competition." *West European Politics* 12, no. 3: 112–38.

Irwin, G. A., C. van der Eijk, J. M. van Holsteyn, and B. Niemöller. 1987. "Verzuiling, Issues, Kandidaten en Ideologie in de Verkiezingen van 1986." *Acta Politica* 22, no. 2: 129–79.

Irwing, R. E. M., and Walter E. Paterson. 1983. "The *Machtwechsel* of 1982–83: A Significant Landmark in the Political and Constitutional History of West Germany" *Parliamentary Affairs* 36, no. 4: 417–35.

Iversen, Torben. 1991. Political Leadership and Representation in West European Democracies: A Test of Three Models of Voting (to appear in: *American Journal of Political Science*).

1992. The Logics of Electoral Politics: Spatial, Directional and Mobilization Effects (to appear in: *Comparative Political Studies*).

Jackman, Robert W. 1987. "The Politics of Economic Growth in the Industrial Democracies, 1974–80: Leftist Strength or North Sea Oil?" *Journal of Politics* 49, no. 1: 242–56.

1989. "The Politics of Economic Growth, Once Again." *Journal of Politics* 51, no. 3: 646–61.

Jackson, Keith. 1985. "The New Zealand General Election of 1984." *Electoral Studies* 4, no. 1: 75–9.

Jaffe, Jerome. 1980. "The French Electorate in March 1978." In Howard R. Penniman, ed., *The French National Assembly Elections of 1978.* Washington, D.C.: American Enterprise Institute, pp. 38–76.

Jasper, Jim. 1988. "The Political Life Cycle of Technological Controversies." *Social Forces* 67, no. 2: 357–77.

Jenson, Jane. 1990. From Party Formation to Paradigm Shift. The Experience of the French Greens. Paper Prepared for Delivery at the 1990 Annual Conference of the American Political Science Association, San Francisco.

Jenson, Jane, and George Ross. 1984. *The View from Inside. A French Communist Cell in Crisis.* Berkeley: University of California Press.

Jong, Jan De, and Bert Pijnenburg. 1986. "The Dutch Christian Democratic Party and Coalitional Behavior in the Netherlands. A Pivotal Party in the Face of Depillarization." In Geoffrey Pridham, ed., *Coalitional Behavior in Theory and Practice.* Cambridge: Cambridge University Press, pp. 145–70.

Jonung, Lars, and Eskil Wadensjö. 1979. "The Effect of Unemployment, Inflation, and Real Income Growth on Government Popularity in Sweden." *Scandinavian Journal of Economics.* 81, no. 2: 343–53.

Judt, Tony. 1986. *Marxism and the French Left. Studies in Labour and Politics in France, 1830–1981.* Oxford: Clarendon Press.

Kaase, Max, and Alan Marsh. 1979. "Political Action Repertory: Changes over Time and a New Typology." In Samuel Barnes and Max Kaase, eds., *Political Action.* Beverly Hills, Calif.: Sage, pp. 137–66.

Kalma, Paul. 1988. *Het Socialisme op Sterk Water. Veertien Stellingen.* Deventer: Van Lughum Slaterus.

Kanter, Rosabeth. 1972. *Communes and Commitment.* Cambridge, Mass: Harvard University Press.

Katz, Richard S. 1980. *A Theory of Parties and Electoral Systems.* Baltimore: Johns Hopkins University Press.

Katznelson, Ira. 1986. "Working Class Formation: Constructing Cases and Comparisons." In Ira Katznelson and Aristide Zolberg, eds., *Working Class Formation.* Princeton, N.J.: Princeton University Press, pp. 3–41.

Katznelson, Ira, and Aristide Zolberg, eds. 1986. *Working Class Formation.* Princeton, N.J.: Princeton University Press.

Kavanagh, Dennis. 1987. *Thatcherism and British Politics. The End of Consensus?* Oxford: Oxford University Press.

Keane, John. 1988. *Democracy and Civil Society.* London: Verso.

Kedros, André. 1986. *Les socialistes au pouvoir en Europe.* Paris: Plon.

Keller, Fritz. 1988. "Die Organisation der Pimpfe. Die vom Parteitag beaufsichtigte Jugenddorganisation." In Peter Pelinka and Gerhard Steger, eds.,*Auf dem Wege zur Staatspartei.* Vienna: Verlag füer Gesellschaftskritik, pp. 153–63.

Kellmann, Klaus. 1988. *Die kommunistischen Parteien in Westeuropa, Entwicklung zur Sozialdemokratie oder Sekte?* Stuttgart: Klett-Cotta.

Kergoat, Jacques. 1983. *Le Parti Socialiste.* Paris: Le Sycomore.

Kern, Horst, and Michael Schumann. 1984. *Das Ende der Arbeitsteilung?* Munich: Beck.

Kiewiet, D. Roderick. 1983. *Macroeconomics and Micropolitics. The Electoral Effects of Economic Issues.* Chicago: Chicago University Press.

Kiewiet, D. Roderick, and Douglas Rivers. 1985. "A Retrospective on Retrospective Voting." In Michael Lewis-Beck and Heinz Eulau, eds., *Economic Conditions and Electoral Outcomes.* New York: Agathon, pp. 207–31.

King, Desmond, and Mark Wickham-Jones. 1990. "Review Article: Social Democracy and Rational Workers." *British Journal of Political Science* 20, no. 3: 387–413.

Kirchgässner, Gebhard. 1989. "Der Einfluss wirtschaftlicher Variablen auf die Popularität der Parteien. Ein Vergleich der sozialliberalen Koalition von 1970 bis 1982 und der Zeit der Regierung Kohl von 1982 bis 1986." In Jürgen W. Falter, Hans Rattinger, and Klaus G. Troitzsch, eds., *Wahlen und politische Einstellungen in der Bundesrepublik Deutschland.* Frankfurt am Main: Peter Lang, pp. 175–95.

Kirchheimer, Otto. 1966. "The Transformation of the Western European Party Systems." In Joseph LaPalombara and Myron Weiner, eds., *Political Parties and Political Development.* Princeton, N.J.: Princeton University Press, pp. 177–200.

Kirkpatrick, Jeane. 1976. *The New Presidential Elite.* New York: Russell Sage.

Kitschelt, Herbert. 1980. *Kernenergiepolitik. Arena eines gesellschaftlichen Konflikts.* Frankfurt am Main: Campus.

1984. *Der ökologische Diskurs.* Frankfurt am Main: Campus.

1985. "Materiale Politisierung der Produktion. Gesellschaftliche Herausforderungen und institutionelle Innovationen in fortgeschrittenen kapitalistischen Demokratien," *Zeitschrift für Soziologie* 14, no. 3: 188–208.

1986. "Political Opportunity Structures and Political Protest. Anti-Nuclear Movements in Four Countries." *British Journal of Political Science* 16, no. 1: 57–85.

1988. "Left-libertarian Parties: Explaining Innovation in Competitive Party Systems." *World Politics* 40, no. 2: 194–234.

1989a. *The Logics of Party Formation.* Ithaca, N.Y.: Cornell University Press.

1989b. "The Internal Politics of Parties. The Law of Curvilinear Disparity Revisited." *Political Studies* 37, no. 3: 400–21.

1990. "La gauche libertaire et les écologistes français." *Revue Française de Science Politique* 40, no. 3: 339–65.

1991a. "The Socialist Discourse and Party Strategy in West European Democracies." In Christiane Lemke and Gary Marks, eds., *The Crisis of Socialism in Europe*. Durham, N.C.: Duke University Press, pp. 191–227.

1991b. "Industrial Governance Structures, Innovation Strategies, and the Case of Japan: Sectoral or Cross-national Comparative Analysis?" *International Organization* 45, no. 4: 453–94.

1991c. "The 1990 German Federal Election and the National Unification." *West European Politics* 14, no. 4: 121–48.

1991d. The New European Right: A Backlash against the Libertarian Left? Paper Delivered at the Conference on the Radical Right in Western Europe, November 7–9, 1991, University of Minnesota, Western European Area Studies Center.

1993. "Socialist Parties in Western Europe and the Challenge of the Libertarian Left." To appear in: Wolfgang Merkel, ed., *Social Democracia en europa*. Madrid: Espasa-Calpe.

1994. "Austrian and Swedish Social Democrats in Crisis. Party Strategy and Organization in Corporatist Regimes." *Comparative Political Studies* 27.

Forthcoming. The European New Radical Right. A Comparative Analysis. Ms., Duke University, Durham, N.C.

Kitschelt, Herbert, and Staf Hellemans. 1990a. *Beyond the European Left*. Durham, N.C.: Duke University Press.

1990b. "The Left-Right Semantics and the New Politics Cleavage." *Comparative Political Studies* 23, no. 2: 210–38.

Kitschelt, Herbert, and Helmut Wiesenthal. 1979. "Organization and Mass Action in the Political Works of Rosa Luxemburg." *Politics and Society* 9, no. 2: 152–202.

Kitsikis, Dimitri. 1988. "Populism, Eurocommunism and the KKE." In Michael Waller and Meindert Fennema, eds., *Communist Parties in Western Europe*. Oxford: Blackwell, pp. 96–113.

Klandermans, Bert, Hanspeter Kriesi, and Sidney Tarrow, eds. 1988. *From Structure to Action: Comparing Movement Participation across Cultures*. Greenwich, Conn.: JAI Press.

Klingemann, Hans-Dieter. 1987. "Election Programmes in West Germany: 1949–80. Explorations in the Nature of Political Controversy." In Ian Budge, David Robertson, and Derek Hearl, eds., *Ideology, Strategy, and Party Change*. Cambridge: Cambridge University Press, pp. 294–323.

Klöti, Ulrich, and Franz-Xaver Risi. 1988. "Neueste Entwicklungen im Parteiensystem der Schweiz." In Anton Pelinka and Fritz Plasser, eds., *Das österreichische Parteiensystem*. Vienna: Böhlau, pp. 717–37.

Klotzbach, Kurt. 1982. *Der Weg zur Staatspartei. Programmatik, praktische Politik und Organisation der deutschen Sozialdemokratie, 1945–1965*. Berlin: J. H. W. Dietz, Nachfahren.

Knutsen, Oddbjørn. 1988. "The Impact of Structural and Ideological Party Cleavages in West European Democracies: A Comparative Empirical Analysis." *British Journal of Political Science* 18, no. 3: 323–52.

1989. "Cleavage Dimensions in Ten West European Countries. A Comparative Empirical Analysis." *Comparative Political Studies* 22, no. 4: 495–534.

1990a. "The Materialist/Post-Materialist Value Dimension as a Party Cleavage in the Nordic Countries." *West European Politics* 13, no. 2: 258–74.

1990b. "Materialist and Postmaterialist Values and Social Structures in the Nordic Countries. A Comparative Study." *Comparative Politics* 23, no. 1 (October): 85–104.

Koelble, Thomas A. 1987. "Trade Unionists, Party Activists, and Politicians. The Struggle for Power over Party Rules in the British Labour Party and the West German Social Democratic Party." *Comparative Politics* 19, no. 3: 253–66.

1991. *The Left Unravelled. The Impact of the New Left on the British Labour Party and the West German Social Democratic Party, 1968–1988.* Durham, N.C.: Duke University Press.

Kofler, Anton. 1985. *Parteigesellschaft im Umbruch. Partizipationsprobleme von Grossparteien.* Vienna: Böhlau.

1989. "Between Old Symbolic Worlds and New Challenges. A Glance at the Internal Life of the Parties." In Anton Pelinka and Fritz Plasser, eds., *The Austrian Party System.* Boulder, Colo.: Westview, pp. 297–307.

Kogan, David, and Maurice Kogan. 1983. *The Battle for the Labour Party.* 2nd ed. London: Kogan Page.

Kok, Franz, and Christian Schaller. 1986. "Restrukturierung der Energiepolitik durch neue soziale Bewegungen? Die Beispiele Zwentendorf und Hainburg." *Österreichische Zeitschrift für Politikwissenschaft* 15, no. 1: 61–72.

Kolinsky, Eva. 1984. *Parties, Opposition and Society in West Germany.* New York: St. Martin's Press.

Koller, Peter. 1989. Das Konzept der politischen Freiheit. Bielefeld: Zentrum für interdisziplinäre Forschung.

Konecny, Albrecht. 1980. "Innerparteiliche Demokratie in der SPÖ." In *Österreichisches Jahrbuch für Politikwissenschaft.* Vienna: Verlag für Wissenschaft und Politik, pp. 377–90.

Konecny, Albrecht, and Herbert Tieber. 1988. "Bewegung und Organisation. Zur Organisationssoziologie der SPÖ." In Peter Pelinka and Gerhard Steger, eds., *Auf dem Wege zur Staatspartei.* Vienna: Verlag für Gesellschaftskritik, pp. 111–26.

Koole, Ruud and Monique Leijenaar. 1988. "The Netherlands: Th Predominance of Regionalism." In Michael Gallagher and Michael Marsh, eds., *Candidate Selection in Comparative Perspective.* London: Sage, pp. 190–209.

Koole, Ruud, and Philip van Praag. 1990. "Electoral Competition in a Segmented Society. Campaign Strategies and the Importance of Elite Perceptions." *European Journal of Political Research* 18, no. 1: 51–69.

Köpl, Regina. 1984. "SPÖ Frauenpolitik am Beispiel der Entkriminalisierung des Schwangerschaftsabbruchs," *Österreichische Zeitschrift für Politikwissenschaft* 13, no. 3: 451–63.

Korpi, Walter. 1983. *The Democratic Class Struggle.* London: Routledge and Kegan Paul.

Kostelka, Peter. 1988. "Die Kleine Koalition." In Peter Pelinka and Gerhard Steger, eds., *Auf dem Wege zur Staatspartei.* Vienna: Verlag für Gesellschaftskritik, pp. 75–93.

Krauss, Ellis S., and James M. Fendrich. 1980. "Political Socialization of U.S. and Japanese Adults: The Impact of Adult Roles on College Leftism." *Comparative Political Studies* 13, no. 1: 3–37.

Krauss, Ellis S., and Jon Pierre. 1990. "The Decline of Dominant Parties: Parliamentary Politics in Sweden and Japan in the 1970s." In T. J. Pempel, ed., *Uncommon Democracies. The One-Party Dominant Regimes.* Ithaca, N.Y.: Cornell University Press. pp. 226–59.

Kreile, Michael. 1988. "The Crisis of Italian Trade Unionism in the 1980s." *West European Politics* 11, no. 1: 54–67.

Kriechbauer, Robert. 1984. "Die Renaissance des Austromarxismus. Zur Ideologiedebatte der SPÖ 1978–1983." *Österreichisches Jahrbuch für Politik 1983.* Vienna: Verlag für Wissenschaft und Politik.

Kriesi, Hanspeter. 1987. "Neue soziale Bewegungen: Auf der Suche nach ihrem gemeinsamen Nenner," *Politische Vierteljahresschriften* 28, no. 3: 315–34.

1989. "New Social Movements and the New Class in the Netherlands." *American Journal of Sociology* 94, no. 5: 1078–116.

Kriesi, Hanspeter, Ruud Koopmans, Jan Willem Duyvendak, and Marco G. Clugni. 1992. "New Social Movements and Political Opportunities in Western Europe." *European Journal of Political Research* 22, no. 2: 219–44.

Kronawitter, Georg. 1979. *Mit allen Kniffen und Listen. Strategie und Taktik der dogmatischen Linken in der SPD*. Münich: Molden.

Ladrech, Robert. 1989. "Social Movements and Party Systems. The French Socialist Party and New Social Movements." *West European Politics* 12, no. 3: 262–79.

1990. The French Socialist Party as a 'Party of Government.' Paper Prepared for Delivery at the 1990 Annual Meeting of the American Political Science Association in San Francisco.

Lafay, Jean-Dominique. 1985. "Political Change and Stability of the Popularity Function: The French General Election of 1981." In Michael Lewis-Beck and Heinz Eulau, eds., *Economic Conditions and Electoral Outcomes. The United States and Western Europe*. New York: Agathon, pp. 78–97.

Lafferty, William M. 1990. "The Political Transformation of a Social Democratic State: As the World Moves in, Norway Moves Right." *West European Politics* 13, no. 1: 78–100.

Lafontaine, Oskar. 1988. *Die Gesellschaft der Zukunft*. Hamburg: Hoffmann & Campe.

Lagroye, Jacques. 1989. "Change and Permanence in Political Parties." *Political Studies* 37, no. 3: 362–75.

Lagroye, Jacques, Guy Lord, Lise Mounier-Chazel, and Jacques Palard. 1976. *Les militants politiques dans trois partis français*. Paris: Pedone.

Lancaster, Thomas D., and Michael S. Lewis-Beck. 1986. "The Spanish Voter: Tradition, Economics, Ideology." *Journal of Politics* 48, no. 3: 648–74.

Lane, Robert. 1991. *The Market Experience*. Cambridge: Cambridge University Press.

Lange, Peter. 1984. *Liberal Corporatism and Union Responsiveness: Exit, Voice, and Wage Regulation*. Ithaca, N.Y.: Cornell University Press.

Lange, Peter, and Geoffrey Garrett. 1985. "The Politics of Growth." *Journal of Politics* 47, no. 3: 792–827.

1987. "The Politics of Growth Reconsidered." *Journal of Politics* 49, no. 1: 257–74.

Lange, Peter, Cynthia Irwin, and Sidney Tarrow. 1990. "Mobilization, Social Movements, and Party Recruitment: The Italian Communist Party since the 1960s." *British Journal of Political Science* 20, no. 1: 15–42.

Laver, Michael. 1989. "Party Competition and Party System Change. The Interaction of Coalition Bargaining and Electoral Competition." *Journal of Theoretical Politics* 1, no. 3: 301–24.

Laver, Michael, and Kenneth A. Shepsle. 1990a. "Coalitions and Cabinet Government." *American Political Science Review* 84, no. 3: 873–90.

1990b. "Government Coalitions and Intraparty Politics." *British Journal of Political Science* 20, no. 4: 489–507.

Laver, Michael, and W. Ben Hunt. 1992. *Policy and Party Competition*. London: Routledge and Kegan Paul.

Le Gall, Gérard. 1986. "Mars 1986: des élections de transition?" *Revue Politique et Parlementaire* 88, no. 922 (March-April): 6–18.

1988. "Printemps 1988: Retour à une Gauche Majoritaire." *Revue Politique et Parlementaire* 90, no. 936 (July-August): 14–24.

1989. "Un triple avertissement: pour l'Europe, la democratie et les Socialistes." *Revue Politique et Parlementaire* 91, no. 942 (July-August): 11–20.

Leonard, Dick. 1989. "The Belgian General Election of December 13, 1987." *Electoral Studies* 8, no. 2: 157–62.

Leser, Norbert. 1988. *Salz der Gesellschaft. Wesen und Wandel des Österreichischen Sozialismus.* Vienna: Orac.

Levy, David A. L., and Howard Machin. 1986. "How Fabius Lost: The French Elections of 1986." *Government and Opposition* 21, no.3: 269–85.

Lewin, Leif. 1980. *Governing Trade-Unions in Sweden.* Cambridge, Mass.: Harvard University Press.

———. 1988. *Ideology and Strategy. A Century of Swedish Politics.* Cambridge: Cambridge University Press.

———. 1991. *Self-interest and Public Interest in Western Politics.* Oxford: Oxford University Press.

Lewis, Steven C., and Serenella Sferza. 1987. "French Socialists between State and Society." In George Ross, Stanley Hoffmann, and Sylvia Malzacher, eds., *The Mitterrand Experiment.* Oxford: Oxford University Press, pp. 100–15.

Lewis-Beck, Michael. 1980. "Economic Conditions and Executive Popularity. The French Experience." *American Journal of Political Science* 24, no. 2 (May): 306–23.

———. 1984. "France: The Stalled Electorate." In Russell J. Dalton, Scott C. Flanagan, and Paul Allen Beck, eds., *Electoral Change in Advanced Industrial Democracies.* Princeton, N.J.: Princeton University Press, pp. 425–48.

———. 1988. *Economics and Elections. The Major Western Democracies.* Ann Arbor: University of Michigan Press.

Lewis-Beck, Michael, and Heinz Eulau. 1985. "Economic Conditions and Electoral Behavior in Transnational Perspective." In Lewis-Beck and Eulau, eds., *Economic Conditions and Electoral Outcomes. The United States and Western Europe.* New York: Agathon, pp. 1–13.

Lichbach, Mark. 1984. "Optimal Electoral Strategies for Socialist Parties. Does Social Class Matter to Party Fortunes?" *Comparative Political Studies* 16: 419–55.

Lieberman, Sima. 1982. *The Contemporary Spanish Economy.* Boston: Allen and Unwin.

Lijphart, Arend. 1984. *Democracies.* New Haven, Conn.: Yale University Press.

Lijphart, Arend, and Markus M. L. Crepaz. 1991. "Corporatism and Consensus Democracy in Eighteen Countries. Conceptual and Empirical Linkages." *British Journal of Political Science* 21, no. 2: 235–46.

Lindblom, Charles. 1977. *Politics and Markets.* New York: Basic Books.

Lindström, Ulf. 1992. Euro-Consent, Euro-Contract or Euro-Coercion? Scandinavian Social Democracy and the European Impasse. Ms., Department of Comparative Politics. University of Bergen.

Lindström, Ulf, and Lars Svasand. 1990. To Be or Not to Be: Austria, Finland, Norway, Sweden, and the European Community. Paper Prepared for Presentation at the Seventh International Conference of Europeanists, Washington D.C., March 23–25.

Lipset, Seymour Martin. 1961/1981 *Political Man.* Enlarged ed. Baltimore: Johns Hopkins University Press.

Lipset, Seymour Martin, and Stein Rokkan. 1967. "Cleavage Structures, Party Systems, and Voter Alignments. An Introduction." In Lipset and Rokkan, eds., *Party Systems and Voter Alignments. Cross-National Perspectives.* New York: Free Press, pp. 1–64.

Lipset, Seymour Martin, Martin A. Trow, and James S. Coleman. 1956. *Union Democracy.* New York: Free Press.

Listhaug, Ola. 1986. "The Norwegian Parliamentary Election of 1985." *Electoral Studies* 5, no. 1: 79–83.

Listhaug, Ola, Stuart Elaine MacDonald, and George Rabinowitz. 1990a. "A Comparative Spatial Analysis of European Party Systems." *Scandinavian Political Studies* 13, no. 3: 227–54.

———. 1990b. Issue Voting in Multiparty Systems. Paper Prepared for Presentation at the 1990 American Political Science Association Meeting in San Francisco.

Lockwood, David. 1985. "Das schwächste Glied in der Kette? Einige Anmerkungen zur marxistischen Handlungstheorie." *Prokla* 15, no. 1: 5–33.

Logue, John. 1982. *Socialism and Abundance. Radical Socialism in the Danish Welfare State*. Minneapolis: University of Minnesota Press.

Lohneis, Hans. 1984. "The Swiss Election: A Glacier on the Move?" *West European Politics* 7, no. 3: 117–19.

Lopez-Pintor, Rafael. 1985. "The October 1982 General Election and the Evolution of the Spanish Party System." In Howard R. Penniman and Eusebio M. Mujal-Leon, eds., *Spain at the Polls 1977, 1989, and 1982*. Durham, N.C.: Duke University Press.

Lösche, Peter. 1988. "Ende der sozialdemokratischen Arbeiterbewegung?" *Die Neue Gesellschaft/ Frankfurter Hefte* 35, no. 5: 453–63.

Löw, Raimund. 1988. "Von der Kreisky'schen Modernisierung zur Konterreform." In Peter Pelinka and Gerhard Steger, eds., *Auf dem Wege zur Staatspartei*. Vienna: Verlag für Gesellschaftskritik, pp. 65–74.

Lucardie, Paul, Jelle van der Knoop, Wijbrandt van Schuur, and Gerrit Voerman. 1991. Greening the Reds or Reddening the Greens? The Case of the Green Left in the Netherlands. Paper presented at the 1991 Annual Meeting of the American Political Science Association, Washington, D.C.

Luebbert, Gregory M. 1986. *Comparative Democracy. Policymaking and Governing Coalitions in Europe and Israel*. New York: Columbia University Press.

——— 1991. *Liberalism, Fascism, and Social Democracy*. New York: Oxford University Press.

Luker, Kristine. 1984. *The Politics of Abortion*. Berkeley: University of California Press.

Lund, Baastrup. 1982. "Sozialistische Volkspartei (SF) und Linkssozialisten (VS). Dänische Parteien zwischen Sozialpartnerschaft und Klassenkampf." In Jürgen Baumgarten, ed., *Linkssozialisten in Europe. Alternative zu Sozialdemokratie und kommunistischen Parteien*. Hamburg: Junius, pp. 58–84.

Luther, K. R. 1987. "Austria's Future and Waldheim's Past. The Significance of the 1986 Elections," *West European Politics* 10, no. 3: 376–99.

Lyrintzis, Christos. 1989. "PASOK in Power: The Loss of the 'Third Road to Socialism'." In Tom Gallagher and Allan M. Williams, eds., *Southern European Socialism*. Manchester: Manchester University Press pp. 34–56.

Mabille, Xavier, and Val R. Lorwin. 1977. "The Belgian Socialist Party." In William E. Paterson and Alastair H. Thomas, eds., *Social Democratic Parties in Western Europe*. New York: St. Martin's Press, pp. 389–407.

MacDonald, Stuart Elaine, Ola Listhaug, and George Rabinowitz. 1991. "Issues and Party Support in Multi-Party Systems." *American Political Science Review,* 85, no. 4: 1107–31.

Machin, Howard. 1989. "Stages and Dynamics in the Evolution of the French Party System." *West European Politics* 12, no. 4 (October): 59–81.

Maguire, Diarmuid. 1990. Citizen Protest and Military Policy. The INF Crisis in Western Europe, 1979–1989. Paper prepared for delivery at the 1990 Annual Meeting of the American Political Science Association, San Francisco.

Maor, Moshe. 1991. "The 1990 Danish Election: An Unnecessary Contest?" *West European Politics* 14, no. 3: 209–14.

——— 1992. The Institutional Determinants of Coalition Behavior. Paper prepared for delivery at the 1992 Annual Meeting of the American Political Science Association, Chicago.

Maraval, Jose Maria. 1985. "The Socialist Alternative: The Policies and Electorate of the PSOE." In Howard R. Penniman and Eusebio M. Muhal-Leon, eds., *Spain at the Polls 1977, 1979, and 1982*. Durham, N.C.: Duke University Press. pp. 129–59.

March, James G. 1978. "Bounded Rationality, Ambiguity, and the Engineering of Choice." *The Bell Journal of Economics* 9, no. 2: 587–608.

March, James G., and Herbert A. Simon. 1958. *Organizations*. New York: Wiley.

Marklund, Staffan. 1988. "Welfare State Policies in the Tripolar Class Model of Scandinavia." *Politics and Society* 16, no. 4: 469–86.

Marks, Gary. 1989. *Unions in Politics.* Princeton, N.J.: Princeton University Press.

Marshall, T. H. 1977. *Class, Citizenship, and Social Development.* Chicago: University of Chicago University Press.

Marx, Karl. 1867/1967. *Capital. A Critique of Political Economy.* Vol. 1. New York: International Publishers.

Massari, Oreste. 1989. "Changes in the PSI Leadership: The National Executive Committee and Its Membership." *European Journal of Political Research* 17, no. 5: 563–82.

Masters, Marick F., and John D. Robertson. 1988a. "Class Compromise in Industrial Democracies." *American Political Science Review* 82, no. 4: 1183–1201.

1988b. "The Impact of Organized Labor on Public Employment. A Comparative Analysis." *Journal of Labor Research* 9, no. 4: 347–62.

Matka, Manfred. 1984. "Zwischen Austromarxismus und Volkspartei." In *Österreichisches Jahrbuch für Politik 1983.* Vienna: Verlag für Wissenschaft und Politik, pp. 359–78.

Mayer, Nonna. 1986. "Pas de chrysanthèmes pour les variables sociologiques." In Elisabeth Dupoirier and Gérard Grunberg, eds., *Mars 1986. La drôle de defaite de la gauche.* Paris: Presses Universitaires de France, pp. 149–66.

Mayr, Hans, and Karl Seitlinger. 1989. *Neue Modelle für Österreich.* Vienna: Verlag Jugend und Volk.

McAllister, Ian. 1991. "Party Adaptation and Factionalism within the Australian Party System." *American Journal of Political Science* 35, no. 1: 206–27.

McAllister, Ian, and Anthony Mughan. 1987. "Class, Attitudes, and Electoral Politics in Britain, 1974–1983." *Comparative Political Studies* 20, no. 1: 47–71.

McCarthy, Patrick. 1981. "The Parliamentary and Nonparliamentary Parties of the Far Left." In Howard R. Penniman, ed., *Italy at the Polls, 1979* Washington, D.C.: American Enterprise Institute, pp. 193–211.

McDonough, Peter, Samuel H. Barnes, and Antonio Lopez Pina. 1986. "Economic Policy and Public Opinion in Spain." *American Journal of Political Science* 30, no. 2: 446–79.

McKenzie, Robert T. 1955 *British Political Parties.* London: Heinemann.

Meng, Richard. 1985. *Die sozialdemokratische Wende. Aussenbild und innerer Prozess der SPD 1981–1984.* Giessen: Focus.

Merkel, Wolfgang. 1985. *Die Sozialistische Partei Italiens. Zwischen Oppositionssozialismus und Staatspartei.* Bochum: Studienverlag Brockmeyer.

Merli, Franz. 1984. "Die Alternative Liste Graz als Erweiterung des kommunalpolitischen Systems." In *Österreichisches Jahrbuch für Politik 1983.* Vienna: Verlag für Wissenschaft und Politik, pp. 295–319.

Michal, Wolfgang. 1988. *Die SPD – staatstreu und jugendfrei. Wie altmodisch ist die Sozialdemokratie?* Reinbek: Rowohlt.

Micheletti, Michele. 1989. "The Swedish Election of 1988." *Electoral Studies* 8, no. 2: 169–74.

1990. "Toward Interest Articulation. A Major Consequence of Corporatism for Interest Organizations." *Scandinavian Political Studies* 13, no. 3: 255–76.

1991. "Swedish Corporatism at a Crossroads: The Impact of New Politics and New Social Movements." *West European Politics* 14, no. 3: 144–65.

Michels, Ank, and Hans Slomp. 1990. "The Role of Government in Collective Bargaining: Scandinavia and the Low Countries." *Scandinavian Political Studies* 13, no. 1: 21–35.

Michels, Robert. 1911/1962. *Political Parties.* New York: Free Press.

Middel, Bert. 1976. *De Nieuwe Elite van de PvdA.* Groningen: Xeno.

Middentorp, C. P., and P. R. Kolkhuis Tanke. 1990. "Economic Voting in the Netherlands." *European Journal of Political Research* 18, no. 5: 535–55.

Middlemas, Keith. 1980. *Power and the Party. Changing Faces of Communism in Western Europe.* London: Deutsch.

Miller, David. 1990. *Market, State, and Community. Theoretical Foundations of Market Socialism.* Oxford: Clarendon Press.

Minkin, Lewis. 1978. *The Labour Party Conference. A Study in the Politics of Intra-Party Democracy.* London: Allen Lane.

———. 1989. "Mobilization and Distance. The Role of the Trade Unions in the 1987 Election Campaign." In Ivor Crewe and Martin Harrop, eds. *Political Communications. The General Election Campaign of 1987.* Cambridge: Cambridge University Press, pp. 261–74.

Missika, Jean-Louis, and Dorine Bregman. 1988. "La campagne: la selection des controverses politiques." In Elisabeth Dupoirier and Gérard Grunberg, eds., *Mars 1986. La Drôle de Defaite de la Gauche.* Paris: Presses Universitaires de France, pp. 97–116.

Mjøset, Lars. 1987. "Nordic Economic Policies in the 1970s and 1980s." *International Organization* 41, no. 3: 403–56.

Modeley, John. 1990. "Norway's 1989 Election: The Paths to Polarized Pluralism?" *West European Politics* 13, no. 2: 287–92.

Morgan, Kenneth O. 1987. *Labour People. Leaders and Lieutenants, Hardie to Kinnock.* Oxford: Oxford University Press.

Morley, J. Terence. 1988. "Annihilation Avoided: The New Democratic Party in the 1984 Federal General Election." In Howard Penniman, ed., *Canada at the Polls, 1984.* Durham, N.C.: Duke University Press, pp. 120–36.

Morris, Aldon D., and Carol McClurg Mueller, eds. 1992. *Frontiers in Social Movement Theory.* New Haven, Conn.: Yale University Press.

Mujal-Leon, Eusebio. 1983. *Communism and Political Change in Spain.* Bloomington: Indiana University Press.

Müller, Wolfgang C. 1988. "Privatising in a Corporatist Economy. The Politics of Privatization in Austria." *West European Politics* 11, no. 4: 100–16.

———. 1989. "Party Patronage in Austria." In Fritz Plasser and Anton Pelinka, eds., *The Austrian Party System.* Boulder, Colo: Westview Press, pp. 327–56.

Müller, Wolfgang C., and Delia Meth-Cohn. 1991. "The Selection of Party Chairmen in Austria: A Study of Intra-Party Decision-Making." *European Journal of Political Research* 20, no. 1: 39–65.

Müller-Rommel, Ferdinand. ed. 1989. *New Politics in Western Europe. The Rise and Success of Green Parties and Alternative Lists.* Boulder, Colo.: Westview Press.

———. 1990. "The Social Democratic Party. The Campaigns and Election Outcomes of 1980 and 1983." In Karl H. Czerny, ed., *Germany at the Polls. The Bundestag Elections of the 1980s.* Durham, N.C.: Duke University Press, pp. 88–110.

Nassmacher, Karl-Heinz. 1987. "Öffentliche Parteifinanzierung in Westeuropa: Implementationsstrategien und Problembestand in der Bundesrepublik Deutschland, Italien, Österreich und Schweden." *Politische Vierteljahresschriften* 28, no. 1: 101–25.

———. 1989. "Parteifinanzierung als verfassungspolitsches Problem." *Aus Politik und Zeitgeschichte* 39, no. B11: 27–38.

Neuwirth, Erich. 1983. "Analyse der Nationalratswahl 1983 aus statistischer Sicht" *Österreichische Zeitschrift für Politikwissenschaft* 12, no. 3: 261–76.

Newman, Michael. 1987. "Conflict and Cohesion in the British Labour Party and French Communist Party." *West European Politics* 10, no. 2: 176–92.

Nick, Rainer. 1986. "Rahmenbedingungen und Entwicklung der grün-alternativen Szene im Vorarlberg." *Österreichische Zeitschrift für Politikwissenschaft* 15, no. 3: 157–70.

Nicolon, Alexandre, and Marie-Josephe Carrieu. 1979. "Les partis face au nucléaire et la contestation." In Francis Fagnani and Alexandre Nicolon, eds., *Nucléopolis. Materiaux pour l'analyse d'une société nucléaire.* Grenoble: Presses Universitaires de Grenoble, pp. 79–159.

Nielsson, K. Robert. 1987. "The Italian Socialist Party. An Indispensable Hostage." In Howard Penniman, ed., *Italy at the Polls. A Study of the National Elections 1983.* Durham, N.C.: Duke University Press, pp. 78–99.

Noël, Alain. 1987. "Accumulation, Regulation, and Social Change. An Essay on French Political Economy." *International Organization* 41, no. 2: 303–33.

Nordhaus, William. 1975. "The Political Business Cycle," *Review of Economic Studies* 42, no. 2: 162–90.

Norpoth, Helmut. 1987. "Guns and Butter and Government Popularity in Britain." *American Political Science Review* 81, no. 3: 949–59.

Nugent, Neil, and David Lowe. 1982. *The Left in France.* New York: St. Martin's Press.

Obler, Jeffrey. 1974. "Intraparty Democracy and the Selection of Parliamentary Candidates. The Belgian Case." *British Journal of Political Science* 4, no. 2: 163–86.

Offe, Claus. 1984. *Contradictions of the Welfare State.* Cambridge, Mass.: MIT Press.

Offe, Claus, and Helmut Wiesenthal. 1980. "Two Logics of Collective Action." In Maurice Zeitlin, ed., *Political Power and Social Theory.* 1, Greenwich, Conn.: JAI Press, pp. 67–115..

Olsen, Johan P. 1983. *Organized Democracy. Political Institutions in a Welfare State. The Case of Norway.* Bergen: Universitetsforlaget.

Olson, Mancur. 1965. *The Logic of Collective Action.* Cambridge, Mass.: Harvard University Press.

Organization of Economic Cooperation and Development. 1987. *Environmental Data Compendium.* Paris: OECD.

Ouchi, G. William. 1980. "Markets, Hierarchies, and Clans." *Administrative Science Quarterly* 25, no. 1: 129–41.

Padgett, Stephen. 1987. "The West German Social Democrats in Opposition, 1982–86." *West European Politics* 10, no. 3: 333–55.

Padgett, Stephen, and William E. Paterson. 1991. *A History of Social Democracy in Postwar Europe.* London: Longman.

Paldam, Martin. 1981. "A Preliminary Survey of the Theories and Findings on Vote and Popularity Functions." *European Journal of Political Research* 9, no. 2: 181–99.

Panebianco, Angelo. 1988a. *Political Parties: Organization and Power.* Cambridge: Cambridge University Press.

1988b. "The Italian Radicals: New Wine in an Old Bottle." In Kay Lawson and Peter Merkl, eds., *When Parties Fail. Emerging Alternative Organizations.* Princeton, N.J.: Princeton University Press, pp. 111–30.

Panitch, Leo. 1987. "Review of *Paper Stones*, by Adam Przeworski and John Sprague." *American Journal of Sociology* 93, no. 2: 490–3.

Papadopoulos, Yannis. 1989. "Parties, the State and Society in Greece: Continuity within Change." *West European Politics* 12, no. 1: 55–71.

Pappi, Franz Urban. 1973. "Parteiensystem und Sozialstruktur in der Bundesrepublik." *Politische Vierteljahresschriften* 14, no. 2: 191–214.

1977. "Bewegungstendenzen des politisch-sozialen Systems in der Bundesrepublik Deutschland." *Politische Vierteljahresschriften* 18, no. 2–3: 195–229.

1984. "The West German Party System." *West European Politics* 7, no. 4: 7–26.

1990. "Klassenstruktur und Wahlverhalten im sozialen Wandel." In Max Kaase and Hans-Dieter Klingemann, eds., *Wahlen und Wähler. Analysen aus Anlass der Bundestagswahl 1987.* Opladen: Westdeutscher Verlag, pp. 15–30.

1991. "Wahrgenommenes Parteiensystem und Wahlentscheidung in Ost- und West-deutschland. Zur Interpretation der ersten gesamtdeutschen Bundestagswahl." *Aus Politik und Zeitgeschichte* 41, no. B44 (October 25): 15–26.

Parkin, Frank. 1972. *Middle Class Radicalism. The Social Bases of the British Campaign for Nuclear Disarmament.* Manchester: Manchester University Press.

Parodi, Jean-Luc. 1978. "Essai de problematique du movement écologiste. Les écologistes et la tentation politique." *Revue politique et parlementaire* 80, no. 827: 25–43.

Partij van de Arbeid. 1988a. *Bewogen Beweging. Sociaal-Democratie als Program en Methode.* Amsterdam: PvdA-brochures.

1988b. *Schuivende Panelen. Continuiteit en Vernieuwing in de Sociaal-Democratie.* Report of the Commissie Programmatische Vernieuwingen. Amsterdam: PvdA-brochures.

Pasquino, Gianfranco. 1977. "The Italian Socialist Party: An Irreversible Decline?" In Howard R. Penniman, ed., *Italy at the Polls. The Parliamentary Election of 1976.* Washington, D.C.: American Enterprise Institute, pp. 183–227.

1988. "Mid-Stream and under Stress. The Italian Communist Party." In Michael Waller and Meindert Fennema, eds., *Communist Parties in Western Europe.* Oxford: Blackwell, pp. 26–46.

Paterson, William E. 1986. "The German Social Democratic Party." In William E. Paterson and Alastair H. Thomas, eds., *The Future of Social Democracy.* Oxford: Clarendon Press, pp. 127–52.

Peffley, Mark. 1985. "The Voter as Juror. Attributing Responsibility for Economic Conditions." In Michael Lewis-Beck and Heinz Eulau, eds., *Economic Conditions and Electoral Outcomes.* New York: Agathon, pp. 187–206.

Peffley, Mark, Stanley Feldman, and Lee Sigelman. 1987. "Economic Conditions and Party Competence: Process of Belief Revision." *Journal of Politics* 49, no. 1: 100–21.

Pelinka, Anton. 1983. *Social Democratic Parties in Europe.* New York: Praeger.

1987. "Hainburg – mehr als ein Kraftwerk." *Österreichisches Jahrbuch für Politik* Vienna: Verlag für Wissenschaft und Politik, pp. 93–107.

1989. "Zur Entwicklung einer Oppositionskultur in Österreich. Bedingungen politischen Erfolgs in den achtziger Jahren." *Österreichische Zeitschrift für Politikwissenschaft* 18, no. 2: 141–9.

Penniman, Howard R., ed. 1988. *France at the Polls, 1981 and 1986. Three National Elections.* Durham, N.C.: Duke University Press.

Peretz, Paul. 1981. "The Effect of Economic Change on Political Parties in West Germany." In Douglas A. Hibbs and Heinz Fassbender, eds., *Contemporary Political Economy.* Amsterdam: North Holland, pp. 101–17.

Perrot, Michelle. 1986. "On the Formation of the French Working Class." In Ira Katznelson and Aristide Zolberg, eds., *Working Class Formation.* Princeton, N.J.: Princeton University Press, pp. 71–110.

Perrow, Charles. 1986. *Complex Organizations. A Critical Essay.* 3rd ed. New York: Random House.

Petersson, Olof, Anders Westholm, and Göran Blomberg. 1989. *Medborgarnas Makt.* Stockholm: Carlssons.

Petry, François. 1987. "France 1958–81. The Strategy of Joint Government Platforms." In Ian Budge, David Robertson, and Derek Hearl, eds., *Ideology, Strategy, and Party Change.* Cambridge: Cambridge University Press, pp. 324–44.

Pierce, Roy, and Thomas R. Rochon. 1988. "The French Socialist Victories of 1981 and the Theory of Elections" In Howard R. Penniman, *France at the Polls, 1981 and 1986.* Durham, N.C.: Duke University Press, pp. 179–195.

Pierre, Jon. 1986. *Partiekongresser och Regeringspolitik.* Lund: Kommunfakta Förlag.

Pierson, Stanley. 1979. *British Socialists. The Journey from Fantasy to Politics.* Cambridge, Mass.: Harvard University Press.

Pijnenburg, Bert. 1987. "Political Parties and Coalition Behaviour in Belgium. The Perspective of Local Politics." *European Journal of Political Research* 15, no. 1: 53–73.

Piore, Michael J., and Charles F. Sabel. 1984. *The Second International Divide.* New York: Basic Books.

Pircher, Erika. 1984. "Gesetzwerdung und Fraueninteressen am Beispiel des Gleichbehandlungsgesetzes." *Österreichische Zeitschrift für Politikwissenschaft* 13, no. 4: 443–56.

Plasser, Fritz. 1985. "Die Unsichtbare Fraktion. Struktur und Profil der Grün-Alternativen in Österreich." *Österreichisches Jahrbuch für Politik 1984.* Vienna: Verlag für Wissenschaft und Politik.

1989. "The Austrian Party System between Erosion and Innovation." In Anton Pelinka and Fritz Plasser, eds., *The Austrian Party System.* Boulder, Colo.: Westview Press, pp. 41–67.

Plasser, Fritz, and Peter A. Ulram. 1987. "Das Jahr der Wechselwähler. Wahlen und Neustrukturierung des österreichischen Parteiensystems 1986." In *Österreichisches Jahrbuch für Politik 1986.* Vienna: Verlag für Wissenschaft und Politik, pp. 31–80.

1989. "Major Parties on the Defensive. The Austrian Party and Electoral Landscape after the 1986 National Council Election." In Anton Pelinka and Fritz Plasser, eds., *The Austrian Party System.* Boulder, Colo.: Westview Press, pp. 69–90.

Plasser, Fritz, Peter A. Ulram, and Alfred Grausgruber. 1987. "Vom Ende der Lagerparteien. Perspektivenwechsel in der österreichischen Parteien- und Wahlforschung," *Österreichische Zeitschrift für Politikwissenschaft* 16, no. 3: 241–58.

Pleschberger, Werner. 1988. "'Modernisierung' als Perspektive der österreichischen Sozialdemokratie." In Peter Pelinka and Gerhard Steger, eds., *Auf dem Wege zur Staatspartei.* Vienna: Verlag für Gesellschaftskritik, pp. 179–96.

Pontusson, Jonas. 1988a. *Swedish Social Democracy and British Labour. Essays on the Nature and Conditions of Social Democratic Hegemony.* Ithaca, N.Y.: Cornell University Press.

1988b. "The Triumph of Pragmatism. Nationalization and Privatization in Sweden." *West European Politics* 11, no. 4: 129–40.

1990 Austerity, Government Crisis, and Political Realignment in Sweden, 1989–90. Paper delivered at the 1990 Annual Meeting of the American Political Science Association, San Francisco.

Poulantzas, Nicos. 1978. *Classes in Advanced Capitalism.* London: New Left Books.

Premfors, Rune. 1991. "The 'Swedish Model' and Public Sector Reform." *West European Politics* 14, no. 3: 83–95.

Prendiville, Brendan. 1989. "France. 'Les Verts'." In Ferdinand Müller-Rommel, ed., *New Politics in Western Europe. The Rise and Success of Green Parties and Alternative Lists.* Boulder, Colo.: Westview Press, pp. 87–100.

Pridham, Geoffrey. 1988. *Political Parties and Coalition Behavior in Italy.* London: Routledge and Kegan Paul.

1989. "Southern European Socialists and the State: Consolidation of Party Rule or Consolidation of Democracy?" In Tom Gallagher and Allan M. Williams, *Southern European Socialism.* Manchester: Manchester University Press, pp. 132–62.

Przeworski, Adam. 1985. *Capitalism and Social Democracy.* Cambridge: Cambridge University Press.

Przeworski, Adam, and John Sprague. 1986. *Paper Stones. A History of Electoral Socialism.* Chicago: University of Chicago Press.

Przeworski, Adam, and Michael Wallerstein. 1982. "The Structure of Class Conflict in Democratic Capitalist Societies." *American Political Science Review* 76, no. 2: 215–38.

Pumm, Günther. 1977. *Kandidatenauswahl und innerparteiliche Demokratie in der Hamburger SPD.* Frankfurt am Main: Lang.

Putnam, Robert D. 1973. *The Beliefs of Politicians. Ideology, Conflict, and Democracy in Britain and Italy.* New Haven, Conn.: Yale University Press.

Rabinowitz, George, and Stuart Elaine MacDonald. 1989. "A Directional Theory of Issue Voting." *American Political Science Review* 83, no. 1: 93–121.

Rabinowitz, George, Stuart Elaine MacDonald, and Ola Listhaug. 1991. "New Players in an Old Game. Party Strategy in Multiparty Systems." *Comparative Political Studes* 24, no. 2: 147–85.

Radice, Giles, and Lisanne Radice. 1986. *Socialists in the Recession. The Search for Solidarity.* London: Macmillan.

Rae, Douglas, and Michael Taylor. 1970. *The Analysis of Political Cleavages.* New Haven, Conn.: Yale University Press.

Randall, Vicki. 1987. *Women and Politics. An International Perspective.* 2nd ed. Chicago: University of Chicago Press.

Raschke, Joachim. 1974. *Innerparteiliche Opposition. Die Linke in der Berliner SPD.* Hamburg: Hoffman & Campe.

Raymond, Gino. 1988. "His Master's Voice? André Lajoine." In John Gaffney, ed., *The French Presidential Elections of 1988.* Aldershot: Gower, pp. 156–85.

Reed, Steven R. 1990. "Structure and Behaviour: Extending Duverger's Law to the Japanese Case." *British Journal of Political Science* 20, no. 3: 335–56.

Remy, Dominique. 1985. "The Pivotal Party. Definition and Measurement." *European Journal of Political Research* 13, no. 3: 293–301.

Rihoux, Benoît. 1991. "Resultats électoraux d'Ecolo 1981–91." *Courier Hébdomadaire*, no. 1371–2. Brussels: CRISP.

Riker, William H. 1986. *The Art of Political Manipulation.* New Haven, Conn.: Yale University Press.

Roberts, Geoffrey. 1988. "The German Federal Republic: The Two-Lane Route to Bonn." In Michael Gallagher and Michael Marsh, eds., *Candidate Selection in Comparative Perspective.* London: Sage, pp. 94–118.

Robertson, David. 1976. *A Theory of Party Competition.* London: Wiley.

1984. *Class and the British Electorate.* Oxford: Blackwell.

Rochon, Thomas. 1989. *Mobilizing for Peace.* Princeton, N.J.: Princeton University Press.

Roemer, John. 1982. *A General Theory of Exploitation and Class.* Cambridge, Mass.: Harvard University Press.

ed. 1985. *Analytical Marxism.* Cambridge, Mass.: Cambridge University Press.

Rohrschneider, Robert. 1990a. "The Roots of Public Opinion toward New Social Movements: An Empirical Test of Competing Explanations." *American Journal of Political Science* 34, no. 1: 1–30.

1990b. Environmentalism and Political Conflicts in Western Europe. Paper prepared for delivery at the 1990 Council of European Studies Meeting, Washington, D.C., March 23–25.

Roosendahl, Peter Van. 1990. "Centre Parties and Coalition Cabinet Formations. A Game Theoretic Approach." *European Journal of Political Research* 18, no. 3: 325–48.

Rootes, Chris A. 1992. "The New Politics and the New Social Movements. Accounting for British Exceptionalism." *European Journal of Political Research* 22, no. 2: 171–91.

Rose, Richard. 1974. *The Problem of Party Government.* London: Macmillan.

Rose, Richard, and Thomas T. Mackie. 1983. "Incumbency in Government: Asset or Liability?" In Hans Daalder and Peter Mair, eds., *Western European Party Systems. Continuity and Change.* Beverly Hills, Calif.: Sage, pp. 115–37.

Rose, Richard, and Ian McAllister. 1986. *Voters Begin to Choose. From Closed-Class to Open Elections in Britain.* Beverly Hills, Calif.: Sage.

Ross, George. 1992. "Party Decline and Changing Party Systems. France and the French Communist Party." *Comparative Politics* 25, no. 1: 43–61.

Ross, George, Stanley Hoffmann, and Sylvia Malzacher, eds. 1987. *The Mitterrand Experiment.* New York: Oxford University Press.

Rothbard, Murray N. 1973. *For a New Liberty. The Libertarian Manifesto.* London: Macmillan

Roubini, Nouriel, and Jeffrey Sachs. 1989. "Fiscal Policy." *Economic Policy* no. 8 (April): 99–127.

Roucaute, Yves. 1983. *Le parti socialiste.* Paris: Bruno Huisman.

Rowies, Luc. 1977. *Les Partis Politiques en Belgique.* Dossiers du CRISP, no. 7. Brussels: CRISP.

Rudd, Chris. 1986. "Coalition Formation and Maintenance in Belgium." In Geoffrey Pridham, ed., *Coalition Behavior in Theory and Practice.* Cambridge: Cambridge University Press, pp. 117–44.

Rüdig, Wolfgang. 1985. "The Greens in Europe. Ecological Parties and the European Elections of 1984." *Parliamentary Affairs* 38, no. 1: 56–72.

Rüdig, Wolfgang, and Philip D. Lowe. 1986. "The Withered 'Greening' of British Politics. A Study of the Ecology Party." *Political Studies* 34, no. 2: 262–84.

Ruggie, Mary. 1987. "Workers' Movements and Women's Interests: The Impact of Labor-State Relations in Britain and Sweden." In Mary Fainsod Katzenstein and Carol McClurg Mueller, eds., *The Women's Movements of the United States and Western Europe.* Philadelphia: Temple University Press, pp. 247–66.

Sainsbury, Diane. 1980. *Swedish Social Democratic Ideology and Electoral Politics, 1944–1948. A Study of the Functions of Party Ideology.* Stockholm: Almqvist & Wiksell.

1986. "The 1985 Swedish Election. The Conservative Upsurge is Checked," *West European Politics* 9, no. 2: 293–7.

1989. "The 1988 Swedish Election. The Breakthrough of the Greens." *West European Politics* 12, no. 3: 140–2.

1990. "Party Strategies and the Electoral Trade-off of Class-based Parties." *European Journal of Political Research* 18, no. 1: 29–50.

1991. "Swedish Social Democracy in Transition. The Party's Record in the 1980s and the Challenge of the 1990s." *West European Politics* 14, no. 3: 31–51.

1992. "The 1991 Swedish Election. Protest, Fragmentation and a Shift to the Right." *West European Politics* 15, no. 2: 160–6.

Sandel, Michael. 1982. *Liberalism and the Limits of Justice.* Cambridge: Cambridge University Press.

Sanders, David, Hugh Ward, and David Marsh (with Tony Fletcher). 1987. "Government Popularity and the Falklands War: A Reassessment." *British Journal of Political Science* 17, no. 3: 281–313.

Sani, Giacomo. 1987. "The Electorate. An Ambiguous Verdict." In Howard Penniman, ed., *Italy at the Polls. A Study of the 1983 National Election.* Durham, N.C.: Duke University Press, pp. 18–34.

Sani, Giacomo, and Giovanni Sartori. 1983. "Polarization, Fragmentation and Competition in Western Democracies" In Hans Daalder and Peter Mair, eds., *Western European Party Systems* Beverly Hills, Calif.: Sage, pp. 307–41.

Särlvik, Bo, and Ivor Crewe. 1983. *Decade of Dealignment. The Conservative Victory of 1979 and Electoral Trends in the 1970s.* Cambridge: Cambridge University Press.

Sartori, Giovanni. 1966. "European Political Parties. The Case of Polarized Pluralism." In Joseph LaPalombara and Myron Weiner eds., *Political Parties and Political Development*. Princeton, N.J.: Princeton University Press, pp. 137–76.

1976. *Parties and Party Systems. A Framework for Analysis*. Cambridge: Cambridge University Press.

Savage, James. 1985. "Postmaterialism of the Left and Right: Political Conflict in Postindustrial Society." *Comparative Political Studies* 17, no. 4: 431–51.

Scarbrough, Elinor. 1987. "Review Article: The British Electorate Twenty Years on: Electoral Change and Election Surveys." *British Journal of Political Science* 17, no. 2: 219–46.

Scharpf, Fritz W. 1987a. *Sozialdemokratische Krisenpolitik in Europa*. Frankfurt am Main: Campus.

1987b. "A Game-Theoretic Interpretation of Inflation and Unemployment in Western Europe." *Journal of Public Policy* 7, no. 3: 227–57.

Schlesinger, Joseph A. 1965. *Ambition and Politics*. Chicago: Rand McNally.

1984. "On the Theory of Party Organization." *Journal of Politics* 46, no. 2: 369–400.

Schmidt, Manfred. 1982. *Wohlfahrtsstaatliche Politik unter bürgerlichen und sozialdemokratischen Regierungen*. Frankfurt am Main: Campus Verlag.

1983. "Politische Konjunkturzyklen und Wahlen. Ein internationaler Vergleich." In Max Kaase and Hans-Dieter Klingemann, eds., *Wahlen und Politisches System*. Opladen: Westdeutscher Verlag, pp. 174–97.

1988. "The Politics of Labour Market Policy: Structural and Political Determinants of Rates of Unemployment in Industrial Nations." In Francis Castles, Franz Lehner, and Manfred G. Schmidt, eds., *Managing Mixed Economies*. Berlin: De Gruyter, pp. 4–53.

Schmitt, Hermann. 1987. *Neue Politik in alten Parteien. Zum Verhältnis von Gesellschaft und Parteien in der Bundesrepublik*. Opladen: Westdeutscher Verlag.

1990. "Die Sozialdemokratische Partei Deutschalnds." In Alf Mintzel and Heinrich Oberreuter, eds., *Parteien in der Bundesrepublik Deutschland*. Bonn: Bundeszentrale für politische Bildung, pp. 129–57.

Schmitt, Karl. 1989. *Konfession und Wahlverhalten in der Bundesrepublik Deutschland*. Duncker and Humblodt.

Schmitter, Philippe C. 1981. "Interest Intermediation and Regime Governability in Contemporary Western Europe and North America." In Suzanne Berger, ed., *Organizing Interests in Western Europe*. Cambridge, Mass.: Cambridge University Press, pp. 287–330.

Schneer, Jonathan. 1988. *Labour's Conscience. The Labour Left 1945–51*. Boston: Unwin Hyman.

Schneider, Friedrich, and Bruno S. Frey. 1988. "Politico-Economic Models of Macroeconomic Policy: A Review of the Empirical Evidence." In Thomas D. Willett, ed., *Political Business Cycles. The Political Economy of Money, Inflation and Unemployment*. Durham, N.C.: Duke University Press, pp. 239–75.

Schonfield, William R. 1980. "La stabilité des dirigeants de partis politiques: la théorie de l'oligarchie de Robert Michels." *Revue française de science politique* 30, no. 4: 846–66.

1983. "Political Parties. the Functional Approach and the Structural Alternative." *Comparative Politics* 15, no. 4: 477–99.

1985. *Ethnographie du PS et du RPR. Les élephants et l'aveugle*. Paris: Economica.

Schüttemeyer, Suzanne S. 1989. "Denmark. 'De Grønne'." In Ferdinand Müller-Rommel, ed., *New Politics in Western Europe. The Rise and Success of Green Parties and Alternative Lists*. Boulder, Colo.: Westview Press, pp. 55–60.

Schultze, Rainer-Olaf. 1987. "Die Bundestagswahl 1987 – eine Bestätigung des Wandels." *Aus Politik und Zeitgeschichte* 37, no. B12 (March 21): 3–17.

Schumpeter, Joseph A. 1975. *Capitalism, Socialism, and Democracy.* New York: Harper.

Seyd, Patrick. 1987. *The Rise and Fall of the Labour Left.* New York: St. Martin's Press.

Seyd, Patrick, and Paul Whiteley. 1991. Labour's Modernization Strategy – Has It Reached the Grassroots? Paper prepared for delivery at the 1991 Annual Meeting of the American Political Science Association, Washington D.C.

1992. *Labour's Grass Roots. The Politics of Party Membership.* Oxford: Clarendon Press.

Sferza, Serenella. 1991. Organizational Forms and Strategies of Growth. The Case of the French Socialist Party. Paper prepared for delivery at the 1991 Annual Meeting of the American Political Science Association, Washington D.C.

Shaffer, William R. 1992. A Congruence Model of Issue Voting. Revised version of a paper delivered at the 1992 Annual Meeting of the American Political Science Association in Chicago, September 3–6.

Share, Donald. 1988a. "Spain: Socialists as Neoliberals." *Socialist Review* 18, no. 1: 38–67.

1988b. "Dilemmas of Social Democracy in the 1980s. The Spanish Socialist Workers Party in Comparative Perspective." *Comparative Political Studies* 21, no. 3: 408–35.

1989 *Dilemmas of Social Democracy. The Spanish Socialist Workers' Party in the 1980s.* New York: Greenwood.

Shaw, Eric. 1988. *Discipline and Discord in the Labour Party.* Manchester: Manchester University Press.

Shell, Kurt. 1962. *The Transformation of Austrian Socialism.* New York: State University Press of New York.

Shepsle, Kenneth A. 1989. "Studying Institutions. Some Lessons from the Rational Choice Approach." *Journal of Theoretical Politics* 1, no. 2: 131–47.

1991. *Models of Multiparty Electoral Competition.* Chur: Harwood Academic Publishers.

Shepsle, Kenneth A., and Ronald N. Cohen. 1990. "Multiparty Competition, Entry, and Entry Deterrence in Spatial Models of Elections." In James Enelow and Melvin J. Hinich, eds., *Advances in the Spatial Theory of Voting.* Cambridge: Cambridge University Press, pp. 12–45.

Sidjanski, Dusan. 1988. "The Swiss Elections of 1987." *Electoral Studies* 7, no. 2: 167–73.

Sigelman, Lee. 1983. "Mass Political Support in Sweden. Retesting a Political-Economic Model." *Scandinavian Political Studies* 6, no. 4: 309–15.

Simon, Herbert A. 1985. "Human Nature in Politics: The Dialogue of Psychology with Political Science." *American Political Science Review* 79, no. 2: 293–304.

Singer, Daniel. 1988. *Is Socialism Doomed? The Meaning of Mitterrand.* New York: Oxford University Press.

Smith-Jespersen, Mary Paul. 1989. "A Danish Defense Dilemma. The Election of May 1988." *West European Politics* 12, no. 3: 190–5.

Socialdemokraterna. 1989a. *Folk i rörelse. Förslag till organisatorisk program.* Stockholm: SAP.

1989b. *90-tals Programmet. En debattbok om arbetarrörelsens viktigaste fragor under 90-talet.* Stockholm: Tidens Förlag.

Sozialdemokratische Partei Deutschlands. 1989. *Berliner Programm.* Bonn: SPD.

Sozialistische Partei Österreichs. 1989. *Sozialdemokratie 2000. Vorschläge zur Diskussion über die Zukunft Österreichs.* Beschlossen am 31. Ordentlichen Bundesparteitag der SPÖ am 20. October 1989 in Graz. Vienna: SPÖ.

Spourdalakis, Michalis. 1988. *The Rise of the Greek Socialist Party.* London: Routledge.

Statistical Office of the European Community. 1989. *Basic Statistics of the Community.* Luxembourg: Eurostat.

Steel, Brent, and Takatsugu Tsurutani. 1986. "From Consensus to Dissensus. A Note on Postindustrial Political Parties." *Comparative Politics* 18, no. 2: pp. 235–48.

Steinmo, Sven. 1988. "Social Democracy vs. Socialism: Goal Adaptation in Social Democratic Sweden." *Politics and Society* 16, no. 4: 403–6.

1989. "Political Institutions and Tax Policy in the United States, Sweden, and Britain." *World Politics* 41, no. 3: 500–35.

Stirnemann, Alfred. 1989. "Recruitment and Recruitment Strategies." In Anton Pelinka and Fritz Plasser, eds., *The Austrian Party System*. Boulder. Colo.: Westview, pp. 401–27.

Stockwin, J. A. A. 1986. "The Japan Socialist Party. A Politics of Permanent Opposition." In Ronald J. Hrebenar, ed., *The Japanese Party System. From One-Party Rule to Coalition Government*. Boulder, Colo.: Westview, pp. 83–115.

Streeck, Wolfgang. 1987. "Vielfalt und Interdependenz. Überlegungen zur Rolle von inter-mediären Organisationen in sich ändernden Umwelten." *Kölner Zeitschrift für Soziologie und Sozialpsychologie* 39, no. 3: 471–95.

Streeck, Wolfgang, and Philippe Schmitter. 1985. "Private Interest Government. Order beyond or between Community, Market, and State." *European Sociological Review,* 1, no. 2: 119–138.

Strom, Kaare. 1984. "Minority Governments in Parliamentary Democracies." *Comparative Political Studies* 17, no. 2: 199–227.

1990a. *Minority Government and Majority Rule*. Cambridge: Cambridge University Press.

1990b. "A Behavioral Theory of Competitive Political Parties." *American Journal of Political Science* 34, no. 2: 565–98.

Sully, Melanie A. 1982. *Continuity and Change in Austrian Socialism. The Eternal Quest for the Third Way*. New York: Columbia University Press.

Sweezy, Paul. 1942. *The Theory of Capitalist Development. Principles of Marxian Economics*. New York: Monthly Review Press.

Swenson, Peter. 1990. *Fair Shares. Unions, Politics, and Pay in Sweden and West Germany*. Ithaca, N.Y.: Cornell University Press.

1991a. "Labor and the Limits of the Welfare State. The Politics of Intraclass Conflict and Cross-Class Alliance in Sweden and West Germany." *Comparative Politics* 23, no. 4: 379–99.

1991b. "Bringing Capital Back in, or Social Democracy Reconsidered: Employer Power, Cross-Class Alliances, and Centralization of Industrial Relations in Denmark and Sweden." *World Politics* 43, no. 4: 513–44.

Swyngedouw, Marc. 1986. De Veranderingen van het Kiesgedrag in Vlaanderen bij de Parlementskieyingen von 1981 en 1985. Een statistische Analyse. University of Leuven: Vakgroep "Methoden van Sociologisch Onderzoek." Bulletin No. 10.

Swyngedouw, Marc, and Jaak Billiet. 1988. "Stemmen in Vlaanderen op 13 December 1987." *Res Publica* 30, no. 1: 25–50.

Talos, Emmerich. 1988. "Alles erreicht? Sozialdemokratische Sozialpolitik in der zweiten Republik." In Peter Pelinka and Gerhard Steger, eds., *Auf dem Weg zur Staatspartei*. Vienna: Verlag für Gesellschaftskritik, pp. 247–65.

Tarrow, Sidney. 1989. *Democracy and Disorder. Protest and Politics in Italy, 1965–1975*. Oxford: Oxford University Press.

1990a. *Struggle, Politics, and Reform*. Ithaca, N.Y.: Cornell University Press.

1990b. "Communism in Western Europe. Of Roots, Crafts, Growth, and Decline." In Peter Katzenstein, Theodore Lowi, and Sidney Tarrow, eds., *Comparative Theory and Political Experience*. Ithaca, N.Y.: Cornell University Press, pp. 144–66.

Taylor, Andrew. 1987. *The Trade Unions and the Labour Party*. London: Croom Helm.

Taylor, Michael. 1982. *Community, Anarchy, and Liberty*. Cambridge: Cambridge University Press.

Therborn, Göran. 1992. "Swedish Social Democracy and the Transition from Industrial to Postindustrial Politics." In Frances Fox Piven, ed., *Labor Parties in Postindustrial Politics*. New York: Oxford University Press, pp. 101–23.

Thiebault, Jean-Louis. 1988. "France. The Impact of Electoral System Change." In Michael Gallagher and Michael Marsh, eds., *Candidate Selection in Comparative Perspective*. London: Sage, pp. 72–93.

Thomas, Alastair H. 1977. "Social Democracy in Denmark." In William E. Paterson and Alastair H. Thomas, eds., *Social Democratic Parties in Western Europe*. New York: St. Martin's Press, pp. 234–71.

   1986. "Social Democracy in Scandinavia: Can Dominance Be Regained?" In William E. Paterson and Alastair H. Thomas, eds., *The Future of Social Democracy*. Oxford: Clarendon Press, pp. 172–223.

Thomas, John Clayton. 1982. "Ideological Change in Competitive Labor Parties. A Test of Downsian Theory." *Comparative Political Studies* 15, no. 2: 223–40.

Thomassen, Jacques, and Jan van Deth. 1989. "How New Is Dutch Politics?" *West European Politics* 12, no. 3: 61–98.

Thompson, E. P. 1963. *The Making of the English Working Class*. London: Penguin.

Thompson, James D. 1967. *Organizations in Action*. New York: McGraw-Hill.

Thompson, John B. 1990. *Ideology and Modern Culture. Critical Social Theory in the Era of Mass Production*. Stanford, Calif.: Stanford University Press.

Thompson, Michael, Richard Ellis, and Aaron Wildavsky. 1990. *Cultural Theory*. Boulder, Colo.: Westview Press.

Threfall, Monica. 1989. "Social Policy toward Women in Spain, Greece and Portugal." In Tom Gallagher and Allan M. Williams, *Southern European Socialism*. Manchester: Manchester University Press, pp. 217–46.

Tilton, Timothy. 1990. *The Political Theory of Swedish Social Democracy. Through the Welfare State to Socialism*. Oxford: Clarendon Press.

Timmermann, Heinz. 1987. *The Decline of the World Communist Movement*. Boulder, Colo.: Westview Press.

Tingsten, Herbert. 1941/1973. *The Swedish Social Democrats. Their Ideological Development*. Totowa, N.J.: Bedminster Press.

Togeby, Lise. 1990. "Political Radicalism in the Working Class and the Middle Class." *European Journal of Political Research* 18, no. 4: 423–36.

Toinet, Marie-France. 1985. "Economic Determinants and Electoral Outcomes. Some Personal Observations." In Michael Lewis-Beck and Heinz Eulau, eds., *Economic Conditions and Electoral Outcomes*. New York: Agathon, pp. 232–45.

Touraine, Alain. 1971. *The Post-industrial Society*. New York: Random House.

   1977. *Production of Society*. Chicago: University of Chicago Press.

   1981. *The Voice and the Eye*. Cambridge: Cambridge University Press.

Touraine, Alain, François Dubet, Zsusza Hegedus, and Michel Wieviorka. 1980. *L'utopie anti-nucléaire*. Paris: Seuil.

Tovey, Craig A. 1991. The Instability of Instability. Ms. Georgia Institute of Technology, May.

Traar, Kurt, and Franz Birk. 1989. "Factors of Voting Behavior. Why Do Austrian Voters Vote the Way They Do?" In Anton Pelinka and Fritz Plasser, eds., *The Austrian Party System*. Boulder, Colo.: Westview, pp. 117–43.

Tromp, Bart. 1989. "Party Strategies and System Change in the Netherlands." *West European Politics* 12, no. 4: 82–97.

Ulram, Peter A. 1989. "Changing Issues in the Austrian Party System." In Anton Pelinka and Fritz Plasser, eds., *The Austrian Party System*. Boulder, Colo.: Westview, pp. 197–222.

United Nations. 1989. *Bulletin of Housing and Building Statistics for Europe.* New York: United Nations.

Van der Eijk, Cornelius, Galen Irwin, and and Kees Niemöller. 1986. "The Dutch Parliamentary Election of May 1986." *Electoral Studies* 5, no. 3: 289–96.

Van der Eijk, Cornelius, and Kees Niemöller. 1983. *Electoral Change in the Netherlands. Empirical Results and Methods of Measurement.* Amsterdam: CT-Press.

——— 1987. "Electoral Alignments in the Netherlands." *Electoral Studies* 6, no. 1: 17–30.

Van Deth, Jan W., and Peter A. T. M. Geurts. 1989. "Value Orientation, Left-Right Placement and Voting." *European Journal of Political Research* 17, no. 1: 17–34.

Van Haegendorn, Mieke. 1981. "Veranderingen in het Belgische Partijenstelsel van 1945 tot 1980" *Res Publica* 23, no. 1: 29–45.

Vis, Jan. 1983. "Coalition Government in a Constitutional Monarchy. The Dutch Experience." In Vernon Bogdanor, ed., *Coalition Government in Western Europe.* London: Heinemann, pp. 153–68.

Visser, Wessel, and Rien Wijnhoven. 1990. "Politics Do Matter, but Does Unemployment? Party Strategies, Ideological Discourse and Ending Mass Unemployment." *European Journal of Political Research* 18, no. 1: 71–96.

Voerman, Gerrit. 1991. "The State Oppresses . . . Alpha and Omega of Dutch Social Democratic Theory of the State." *Journal of Behavioral and Social Sciences* 35, no. 1: 21–38.

Waller, Michael. 1988. "The Radical Sources of the Crisis in West European Communist Parties." *Political Studies* 37, no. 1: 39–61.

Weber, Max. 1915/1958a. "The Social Psychology of the World Religions." In Günther Roth and C. Wright Mills, eds., *From Max Weber. Essays in Sociology.* New York: Free Press, pp. 267–301.

——— 1915/1958b. "Religious Rejections of the World and Their Directions." In Günther Roth and C. Wright Mills, eds., *From Max Weber. Essays in Sociology.* New York: Free Press, pp. 323–59.

——— 1920/1978. *Economy and Society.* Berkeley: University of California Press.

Wellhofer, E. Spencer. 1979. "Strategies for Party Organization and Voter Mobilization. Britain, Norway, and Argentina" *Comparative Political Studies* 12, no. 2: 169–204.

Wellhofer, E. Spencer, and Timothy Hennessey. 1974. "Models of Political Party Organization and Strategy: Some Analytic Approaches to Oligarchy." In Ivor Crewe, ed., *Elites in Western Democracy. British Political Sociology Yearbook.* London: Croom Helm, pp. 279–316.

Wertman, Douglas A. 1988. "Italy: Local Involvement, Central Control." In Michael Gallagher and Michael Marsh, eds., *Candidate Selection in Comparative Perspective.* London: Sage, pp. 145–68.

Whiteley, Paul. 1983. *The Labour Party in Crisis.* London: Methuen.

——— 1984. "Inflation, Unemployment and Government Popularity. Dynamic Models for the United States, Britain, and West Germany." *Electoral Studies* 3, no. 1: 3–24.

——— 1985. "Perceptions of Economic Performance and Voting Behavior in the 1983 General Election in Britain." In Michael Lewis-Beck and Heinz Eulau, eds., *Economic Conditions and Electoral Outcomes. The United States and Western Europe.* New York: Agathon, pp. 62–77.

——— 1986a. "Macroeconomic Performance and Government Popularity in Britain. The Short Run Dynamics." *European Journal of Political Research* 14, no. 1–2: 45–61.

——— 1986b. "Predicting the Labour Vote in 1983: Social Background versus Subjective Evaluation." *Political Studies* 34, no. 1: 82–98.

Wicha, Barbara. 1989. "Party Funding in Austria." In Anton Pelinka and Fritz Plasser, eds., *The Austrian Party System.* Boulder, Colo.: Westview, pp. 357–86.

Wiesendahl, Elmar. 1990. "Der Marsch aus den Institutionen. Zur Organisationsschwäche politischer Parteien in den achtziger Jahre." *Aus Politik und Zeitgeschichte* 40, no. B21 (May 18): 3–14.

Wildavsky, Aaron. 1987. "Doing More and Using Less: Utilization of Research as a Result of Regime." In Meinolf Dierkes, Hans N. Weiler, and Ariane Berthoin Antal, eds., *Comparative Policy Research. Learning From Experience.* New York: St. Martin's Press, pp. 56–93.

Wilensky, Harold J. 1981. "Leftism, Catholicism, and Democratic Corporatism: The Role of Political Parties in Recent Welfare State Development." In Peter Flora and Arnold J. Heidenheimer, eds., *The Development of Welfare States in Europe and America.* New Brunswick, N.J.: Transaction Books, pp. 345–82.

Williams, Allan M. 1989. "Socialist Economic Policies: Never Off the Drawing Board?" In Tom Gallagher and Allan M. Williams, *Southern European Socialism.* Manchester: Manchester University Press, pp. 188–216.

Williamson, Oliver. 1975. *Markets and Hierarchies.* New York: Free Press.

1985. *The Institutions of Capitalism.* New York: Basic Books.

Williamson, Peter J. 1986. *Varieties of Corporatism. A Conceptual Discussion.* Cambridge: Cambridge University Press.

Wilson, James Q. 1962. *The Amateur Democrat.* Chicago: Chicago University Press.

Witte, Els. 1980. "De Evolutie van de Rol der Partijen in Het Belgische Parlementaire Regeringssysteem." *Res Publica* 22, no. 1: 7–33.

Wolinetz, Steven. 1977. *"The Dutch Labour Party. A Social Democratic Party in Transition."* In William E. Paterson and Alastair H. Thomas, eds., *Social Democratic Parties in Western Europe.* New York: St. Martin's Press, pp. 342–88.

1988. Structure and Strategy of the Dutch Socialist Party in the 1970s and the 1980s. Prepared for delivery at the 1988 Annual Meeting of the APSA. Washington D.C.

1990. "The Dutch Election of 1989: Return to the Center Left." *West European Politics* 13, no. 2: 280–6.

World Bank. 1989. *World Tables.* 3rd ed. Baltimore: Johns Hopkins University Press.

1990. *World Development Report.* New York: Oxford University Press.

Wörlund, Ingemar. 1989. "The Election to the Swedish Riksdag 1988." *Scandinavian Political Studies* 12, no. 1: 77–82.

Wright, Erik Olin. 1985. *Classes.* London: Verso.

ed. 1989. *The Debate on Classes.* London: Verso.

Wright, William E. 1971. "Comparative Party Models. Rational-Efficient and Party Democracy." In Wright, *A Comparative Study of Party Organization.* Columbus: Merrill, pp. 17–54.

# Index